Revolts, Protests, Demonstrations, and Rebellions in American History

Revolts, Protests, Demonstrations, and Rebellions in American History

An Encyclopedia

Volume 1

Steven L. Danver, Editor

Santa Barbara, California • Denver, Colorado • Oxford, England

Copyright 2011 by ABC-CLIO, LLC

All rights reserved. No part of this publication may be reproduced, stored in a retrieval system, or transmitted, in any form or by any means, electronic, mechanical, photocopying, recording, or otherwise, except for the inclusion of brief quotations in a review, without prior permission in writing from the publisher.

Library of Congress Cataloging-in-Publication Data

Revolts, protests, demonstrations, and rebellions in American history : an encyclopedia / Steven L. Danver, editor.
    v. cm.
  Includes bibliographical references and index.
   ISBN 978-1-59884-221-0 (hard copy : alk. paper) — ISBN 978-1-59884-222-7 (ebook)
1. Protest movements—United States—History. 2. Revolutions—United States—History.
3. Protest movements—United States—Encyclopedias. 4. Revolutions—United States—Encyclopedias. I. Danver, Steven Laurence.
   HN57.R48 2011
   303.48'40973—dc22   2010038363

ISBN: 978-1-59884-221-0
EISBN: 978-1-59884-222-7

15 14 13 12 11   1 2 3 4 5

This book is also available on the World Wide Web as an eBook.
Visit www.abc-clio.com for details.

ABC-CLIO, LLC
130 Cremona Drive, P.O. Box 1911
Santa Barbara, California 93116-1911

This book is printed on acid-free paper ∞
Manufactured in the United States of America

Contents

Acknowledgments	xix
Introduction	xxi

Volume 1

BACON'S REBELLION (1675–1676)	1
Bacon, Nathaniel (1647–1676)	9
Berkeley, Sir William (1605–1677)	11
House of Burgesses	13
Indentured Servants	15
Susquehannock Indians	17
Tobacco	19
Nathaniel Bacon's Manifesto (1676)	21
Nathaniel Bacon's "Declaration of the People of Virginia" (1676)	24
PUEBLO REVOLT (1680)	27
Franciscans (1209–Present)	37
Oñate, Juan de (c. 1552–1626)	39
Otermin, Antonio de (dates unknown)	41
Popé (dates unknown)	43
Pueblo Religions	45
Santa Fé	47
Declaration of Pedro Naranjo, December 19, 1681	49
LEISLER'S REBELLION (1689–1691)	53
Calvinism	57
Dominion of New England (1686–1689)	58
Leisler, Jacob (c. 1640–1691)	60
Religious Conflict in 17th-Century New York	61
Jacob Leisler's Letter to the Governor and Committee of Safety at Boston, June 4, 1689	62
Jacob Leisler: "A Modest and Impartial Narrative" (1690)	63

STONO REBELLION (1739) — 69

- Slave Codes — 73
- South Carolina — 75
  - *Description of the Rebellion by Georgia Governor James Oglethorpe (1739)* — 76

NEW YORK SLAVE INSURRECTION (1741) — 79

- Fires — 83
- Manhattan Island — 84
  - *Investigation into a New York Slave Conspiracy (1741)* — 85

PHILADELPHIA ELECTION RIOT (1742) — 91

- Anglicanism — 95
- Quakers — 96

PIMA REVOLT (1751) — 99

- Jesuits — 103
- Oacpicagigua, Luis (d. 1755) — 104
- Parrilla, Diego Ortiz (c. 1715–c. 1775) — 105
- Tohono O'odham — 106

PONTIAC'S REBELLION (1763) — 109

- Amherst, Jeffrey (1717–1797) — 117
- French and Indian War (1754–1763) — 118
- Neolin (dates unknown) — 119
- Ohio River Valley — 121
- Pontiac (d. 1769) — 122
- Smallpox — 124

STAMP ACT PROTESTS (1765) — 127

- Adams, Samuel (1722–1803) — 139
- Declaratory Act (1766) — 140
- Salutary Neglect — 142
- Stamp Act Congress (1765) — 144
- Taxation without Representation — 145
  - *Stamp Act Resolutions of the Virginia House of Burgesses (1765)* — 147
  - *An Account of the Destruction of Lt. Governor Hutchinson's House by the Stamp Act Rioters in Boston (1765)* — 148

BOSTON MASSACRE (1770) — 151

- Adams, John (1735–1826) — 157
- Attucks, Crispus (c. 1723–1770) — 158
- Broadsides — 159
- Preston, Thomas (1722–1798) — 161
- Revere, Paul (1734–1818) — 162
  - George R. T. Hewes's Account of the Boston Massacre (1770) — 164
  - Richard Palmes's Account of the Boston Massacre (1770) — 166

REGULATOR MOVEMENT (1771) — 169

- Battle of Alamance (1771) — 177
- Dobbs, Arthur (1689–1765) — 178
- Husband, Herman (1724–1795) — 179
- Tryon, William (1729–1788) — 181

PINE TREE RIOT (1772) — 183

- Royal Authority — 187
- Shipbuilding — 188

BOSTON TEA PARTY (1773) — 191

- Coercive Acts (1774) — 199
- First Continental Congress (1774) — 200
- Sons of Liberty — 202
- Townshend Acts (1767) — 203
  - George R. T. Hewes's Account of the Boston Tea Party (1773) — 204

SHAYS' REBELLION (1787) — 207

- Bowdoin, James (1726–1790) — 217
- Massachusetts General Court — 218
- Shays, Daniel (1747–1825) — 220
- Taxes — 222
  - An Address to the People of Hampshire County, Massachusetts, Setting Forth the Causes of Shays' Rebellion (1786) — 223
  - A Letter to the Hampshire Herald Listing the Grievances of the Rebels (1786) — 224

WHISKEY REBELLION (1794) — 227

- Federal Supremacy — 237

Hamilton, Alexander (1755–1804)	239
Martial Law	241
Tom the Tinker	243
President George Washington's Proclamation against the Whiskey Rebellion (1794)	245
President George Washington's Second Proclamation against the Whiskey Rebellion (1794)	248

ANTEBELLUM SUPPRESSED SLAVE REVOLTS (1800s–1850s) — 251

Boxley, George (c. 1779–1865)	261
Deslondes, Charles (d. 1811)	262
Gabriel (d. 1800)	263
Vesey, Denmark (c. 1767–1822)	265
Description of Denmark Vesey (1822)	266

NAT TURNER'S REBELLION (1831) — 269

Abolitionists	279
Confessions of Nat Turner	280
Moses Story	282
Slave Preachers	283
Turner, Nat (1800–1831)	285
A Contemporary Account of Nat Turner's Revolt (1831)	286

TEXAS REVOLT (1835–1836) — 289

Battle of the Alamo (1836)	303
Austin, Stephen F. (1793–1836)	305
Houston, Samuel (1793–1863)	307
Santa Anna, Antonio Lopez de (1794–1876)	308

DORR REBELLION (1841–1842) — 311

Charterites	315
Dorr, Thomas Wilson (1805–1854)	316
Universal White Male Suffrage	318
Luther v. Borden: The Judicial Aftermath of Rhode Island's Dorr Rebellion (1849)	319

PHILADELPHIA NATIVIST RIOTS (1844) — 325

- Catholicism — 329
- German Americans — 330
- *Index* — I-1

Volume 2

BEAR FLAG REVOLT (1846) — 333

- Bear Flaggers — 339
- Frémont, John Charles (1813–1890) — 341
- Sonoma — 343
  - *William B. Ide's Proclamation Declaring California an Independent Republic (1846)* — 345

BLEEDING KANSAS (1854–1858) — 347

- Guerilla Warfare in Kansas and Missouri — 353
- Jayhawkers — 354
- Missouri Compromise (1820–1821) — 356
- Popular Sovereignty — 358
- Pottawatomie Massacre (1856) — 359
- Topeka Constitution (1855) — 361

PORTLAND RUM RIOT (1855) — 365

- Immigrants — 369
- Temperance — 370

KNOW-NOTHING RIOTS (1855–1856) — 373

- Bloody Monday (1855) — 377
- Nativism — 378
- Plug Uglies — 379
- Rip Raps — 380
- Vigilance Committees — 381

UTAH WAR (1857–1858) — 383

- Buchanan, James (1791–1868) — 389
- Church of Jesus Christ of Latter-day Saints — 390
- Nauvoo Legion — 391
- Polygamy — 392

State of Deseret	394
Young, Brigham (1801–1877)	395
Major J. H. Carleton's Special Report on the Mountain Meadows Massacre (1859)	396

HARPERS FERRY RAID (1859) — 415

Brown, John (1800–1859)	423
Causes of the Civil War	425
Lee, Robert E. (1807–1870)	427
"Secret Six"	429
John Brown's Last Speech to the Court and Last Statement before Execution (1859)	430
Southern Editorial Responses to John Brown's Raid on Harpers Ferry, Virginia (1859)	432

NEW YORK DRAFT RIOTS (1863) — 435

Civil War (1861–1865)	441
Conscription	442
Copperheads	443
Racism	444
Excerpts from a New York Times *Account of the New York City Draft Riots (1863)*	446
A Rioter's Letter to the New York Times *and the Newspaper's Response (1863)*	447

NEW ORLEANS RIOT (1866) — 449

Carpetbaggers	453
Reconstruction (1863–1877)	454
Voting Rights	456

MOLLY MAGUIRES (1870s) — 459

Irish Americans	463
Pennsylvania	464
Unionism	465
Excerpts from an Article Describing James McPartland's Infiltration of the Molly Maguires in the 1870s (1894)	467

WOMEN'S MOVEMENT (1870s) — 473

- American Woman Suffrage Association (AWSA) — 483
- Anthony, Susan B. (1820–1906) — 484
- Dix, Dorothea (1802–1887) — 486
- National Woman Suffrage Association (NWSA) — 487
- Nineteenth Amendment (1920) — 489
  - *Congressional Debate on Women's Suffrage (1866)* — 491
  - *Sojourner Truth Urges Women to Continue the Fight for Equal Rights for All Women, White and Black (1867)* — 493
  - *Address of Victoria C. Woodhull to the Judiciary Committee of the House of Representatives (1871)* — 494
  - *The Comstock Law, Enacted to End the Circulation of Obscene and Immoral Literature (1873)* — 496
  - U.S. v. Susan B. Anthony: *The Sentencing of Anthony for Voting Illegally (1873)* — 497
  - Bradwell v. Illinois: *The Rights and Privileges of a Citizen (1873)* — 499
  - *Excerpts from Susan B. Anthony's "Social Purity" Speech (1875)* — 501
  - *Declaration of Rights for Women (1876)* — 504
  - *Letter to Susan B. Anthony (1881)* — 508
  - *Elizabeth Cady Stanton's "Solitude of Self" Address (1892)* — 510
  - *Excerpts from Elizabeth Cady Stanton's Introduction to* The Woman's Bible *(1895)* — 512
  - Muller v. Oregon: *The Weakness of Women (1908)* — 515
  - *Excerpts from* History of Women in Industry in the United States *(1910)* — 516
  - *Excerpts from Emma Goldman's* The Traffic in Women *and* Marriage and Love *(1910)* — 522
  - *Excerpts from Anna Garlin Spencer's* Woman's Share in Social Culture *(1912)* — 529
  - *Margaret Sanger on Sex Education and Contraception (1913)* — 533

COLFAX MASSACRE (1873) — 537

- Freedmen — 541
- Klanism — 542

BROOKS-BAXTER WAR (1874) — 545

- Baxter, Elisha (1827–1899) — 549
- Brooks, Joseph (1821–1877) — 550
- Republican Party — 551

FLIGHT OF THE NEZ PERCÉ (1877) — 553

- Indian Reservations — 557
- Joseph, Chief (1840–1904) — 558
- Relocation — 560
  - *Surrender Speech of Chief Joseph of the Nez Percé, October 5, 1877* — 561

GREAT RAILROAD STRIKES (1877) — 563

- Pittsburgh — 569
- Railroad Workers — 570
- Robber Barons — 571
- Workingmen's Party of the United States (WPUS) — 572

HAYMARKET RIOT (1886) — 575

- Anarchism — 585
- Bombings — 586
- Eight-Hour Workday — 587
- May Day — 589
- McCormick Harvesting Machine Company — 590
  - *The Circular of Anarchist August Spies (1886)* — 591
  - *Excerpts from the Merritt Conspiracy Act (1887)* — 592

SEATTLE RIOT (1886) — 593

- Chinese Immigrants — 597
- Knights of Labor — 598

WOUNDED KNEE I (1890) — 601

- Dakota Uprising (1862) — 611
- Sioux — 613
- Sitting Bull (c. 1831–1890) — 614
  - *Excerpts from Philip Wells's Eyewitness Account of the Massacre at Wounded Knee (1890)* — 616

HOMESTEAD STRIKE (1892–1893) — 619

- Amalgamated Association of Iron and Steel Workers (AA) — 629
- Carnegie Steel — 630
- Lockouts — 631
- Pinkerton National Detective Agency — 632
- Yellow-Dog Contracts — 633
  - *Account of Violence between Strikers and Company Security Guards (1892)* — 634
  - *Account of the Course of the Strike (1892)* — 637
  - *Two Examples of Yellow-Dog Contracts (1904 and 1917)* — 640

PULLMAN STRIKE (1894) — 643

- American Railway Union (ARU) — 651
- Debs, Eugene V. (1855–1926) — 652
- Pullman Palace Car Company — 654
- Wage Cuts — 656
  - *Two Excerpts from U.S. Strike Commission Report on the Railway Strikes of 1894* — 657

LATTIMER MASSACRE (1897) — 661

- Eastern European Immigrants — 665
- Miners — 666
  - *Strikers' Resolutions and Editorials Appearing in the* Philadelphia Public Ledger *Following the Deaths of Striking Coal Miners at the Lattimer Mine, Hazleton, Pennsylvania (1897)* — 668

NEW ORLEANS RACE RIOT (1900) — 671

- Charles, Robert (c.1866–1900) — 675
- Jim Crow Laws — 676
- *Plessy v. Ferguson (1896)* — 678

ATLANTA RACE RIOT (1906) — 681

- Economic Competition — 685
- White Supremacy — 686

SPRINGFIELD RACE RIOT (1908) — 689

- Jewish Americans — 693
- National Association for the Advancement of Colored People (NAACP) — 694

BLACK PATCH WAR (1909) — 697

- American Tobacco Company (ATC) — 701
- Dark Tobacco District Planters' Protective Association (DTDPPA) — 702
  - *Statement of Charles H. Fort, President of the Tobacco Growers' Association of the United States, February 4, 1904* — 703

LUDLOW MASSACRE (1914) — 707

- Colorado Fuel and Iron Company (CF&I) — 713
- Industrial Violence — 714
- United Mine Workers of America (UMWA) — 716
  - *Excerpt from Godfrey Irwin's Account of the Killings at the Mining Encampment in Ludlow, Colorado (1914)* — 718
  - *Walter Fink's Depiction of Events at the Ludlow Camp (1914)* — 719

- Index — I-1

Volume 3

PLAN DE SAN DIEGO (1915–1916) — 727

- Mexico — 733
- Tejanos — 735
- Texas Rangers — 736

GREEN CORN REBELLION (1917) — 739

- Conscription Act (World War I, 1917) — 743
- Industrial Workers of the World (IWW) — 744
- Socialism — 746

HOUSTON RIOT (1917) — 749

- Black Soldiers — 753
- Discrimination — 754

BOSTON POLICE STRIKE (1919) — 757

- Coolidge, Calvin (1872–1933) — 761
- Unionization — 762

RED SUMMER (1919) — 765

- Great Migration — 773
- Lynching — 775
- Race Riots — 777

Excerpt from the Cook County Coroner's Report Regarding the 1919 Chicago Race Riots (1920)	778
Excerpts from the "Anti-Lynching" Hearings Held before the House Judiciary Committee (1920)	782
Excerpts of Testimony from Laney v. United States *Describing Events during the Washington, D.C., Riot of July 1919 (1923)*	789

BATTLE OF BLAIR MOUNTAIN (1921)   793

Coal Mining	797
Hatfield, Sid (1893–1921)	798
Matewan Massacre (1920)	799

TULSA RACE RIOT (1921)   801

Ku Klux Klan	805
Segregation	806
Final Report of the Grand Jury on the Tulsa Race Riot (1921)	808
Excerpts from the Preliminary and Final Reports of the Oklahoma Commission to Study the Tulsa Race Riot of 1921 (2000 and 2001)	809

BONUS ARMY (1932)   829

Battle of Anacostia Flats (1932)	835
Great Depression (1930s)	836
Hooverville	837
MacArthur, Douglas (1880–1964)	840
Veterans' Rights	841
Waters, Walter W. (1898–1959)	843
Maintaining Order in the District of Columbia: Excerpts of President Herbert Hoover's Letter to the District Commissioner and from His Press Conference (1932)	844

TOLEDO AUTO-LITE STRIKE (1934)   847

American Federation of Labor (AFL)	851
Battle of Toledo (1934)	852
National Industrial Recovery Act (1933)	854

WEST COAST LONGSHOREMEN'S STRIKE (1934)   857

Bloody Thursday (1934)	861
Bridges, Harry (1901–1990)	862

Communism	864
International Longshoremen's Association (ILA)	865
San Francisco	866

ZOOT SUIT RIOTS (1942) — 869

Mexican Americans	877
Police Brutality	878
Servicemen	880

BATTLE OF ATHENS (1946) — 883

Mansfield, Pat (dates unknown)	887
Political Corruption	888

CIVIL RIGHTS MOVEMENT (1953–1968) — 891

Carmichael, Stokely/Kwame Ture (1941–1998)	903
King, Martin Luther Jr. (1929–1968)	904
Malcolm X (1925–1965)	907
March on Washington (1963)	908
Southern Christian Leadership Conference (SCLC)	910
Student Nonviolent Coordinating Committee (SNCC)	912
President John F. Kennedy's Proclamation and Executive Order against State Resistance to Desegregation in Mississippi (1962)	913
Excerpts from the Civil Rights Act of 1964	915

ANTIWAR MOVEMENT (1960s–1970s) — 925

Counterculture	937
Kent State (1970)	938
The Moratorium (1969)	941
Students for a Democratic Society (SDS)	943
Speech Delivered by Paul Potter, President of Students for a Democratic Society, at the Washington Monument (1965)	945
Students for a Democratic Society Leaflet Distributed at the Antiwar March on Washington (1965)	950
Statements of the Fort Hood Three (1966)	951
Excerpts from United States v. Spock: *Dr. Benjamin Spock, William Sloane Coffin, and Others Accused of Conspiring to Aid and Abet Draft Evasion (1969)*	957
A Father's Disgust with Antiwar Demonstrations (1970)	960

Displaying the Flag on the Seat of His Pants: Excerpts from Smith v. Goguen *(1974)*	961

WATTS RIOT (1965) — 965

Arson	973
Looting	974
Excerpt from the Governor's Commission Report on the Watts Riots in Los Angeles, California (1965)	976

DETROIT RIOTS (1967) — 987

Excessive Force	993
Housing	994
Kerner Commission (1967–1968)	995
Excerpts from Cyrus R. Vance's Report on the Riots in Detroit (1967)	997

CHICAGO RIOTS (1968) — 1009

Chicago Seven	1019
Daley, Richard J. (1902–1976)	1021
Democratic National Convention (1968)	1022
Hayden, Tom (1939–)	1024
Hoffman, Abbie (1936–1989)	1025
National Mobilization Committee to End the War in Vietnam (Mobe)	1027

ALCATRAZ ISLAND OCCUPATION (1969–1971) — 1031

Indians of All Tribes	1035
Oakes, Richard (1942–1972)	1036
Termination	1038
Trudell, John (1946–)	1039
The Alcatraz Proclamation to the Great White Father and His People, November 1969	1040

FEMINIST MOVEMENT (1970s–1980s) — 1043

Equal Rights Amendment (ERA)	1053
Roe v. Wade (1973)	1055
Steinem, Gloria (1934–)	1056

ATTICA PRISON RIOT (1971) — 1059

Cruel and Unusual Punishment	1063
Rockefeller, Nelson A. (1908–1979)	1064

TRAIL OF BROKEN TREATIES (1972) — 1067
- American Indian Movement (AIM) — 1071
- Indian Treaties — 1072
- Red Power — 1073

WOUNDED KNEE II (1973) — 1075
- Bureau of Indian Affairs (BIA) — 1079
- Federal Bureau of Investigation (FBI) — 1080
- Pine Ridge Reservation — 1081
- Wilson, Dick (1934–1990) — 1082

SAGEBRUSH REBELLION (1979–1981) — 1085
- Federal Land Policy and Management Act of 1976 — 1089
- Public Lands — 1090
- Reagan, Ronald (1911–2004) — 1091
- Watt, James G. (1938–) — 1093

LOS ANGELES UPRISING (1992) — 1095
- Denny, Reginald (1953–) — 1101
- King, Rodney (1965–) — 1102
- Los Angeles Police Department — 1103
- Williams, Damian Monroe (1973–) — 1105
  - *Progress Report of the Presidential Task Force on Los Angeles Recovery (1992)* — 1106

WORLD TRADE ORGANIZATION PROTESTS (1999) — 1121
- Direct Action Network — 1125
- Economic Justice — 1126
- Globalization — 1127

DAY WITHOUT AN IMMIGRANT (2006) — 1129
- Undocumented Immigrants — 1133

List of Contributors — 1137
Index — I-1
About the Editor

Acknowledgments

This work represents not only my efforts over the past two years, but those of 44 other scholars with whom I have had the privilege to work. Their investigations of the instances of collective civil unrest in American society have taught me much about what has worked in our nation's history, and which areas we still need to address. The project would not have been possible without their considerable analytical prowess. Additionally, I would like to thank the editorial and production staff at ABC-CLIO, including James Sherman, with whom I conceived this project; Barbara Patterson, who administered the considerable paperwork involved; Alex Mikaberdze and John Wagner, who went through the manuscript submissions with a fine-toothed comb; and Donald Schmidt and his team, who oversaw the production work to turn the manuscript into a book. Finally, I would like to thank and acknowledge the dedication of my life partner and business partner, Lauren Danver, for her constant support in ways related both directly to the outcome of the book and generally to my state of mind!

—Steven L. Danver
San Marcos, California

Introduction

In one of the most misused quotations in American history, Thomas Jefferson famously said that the "tree of liberty must be refreshed from time to time with the blood of patriots and tyrants. It is its natural manure" (Jefferson 1955). This phrase has been used to justify many violent actions throughout the nation's history, many of which would be actions that might cause Jefferson, as president, many nights of troubled thought. Its consistent use, however, reflects a simple truth about people in general and Americans in particular. When a situation is perceived as unacceptable, people take action. Although some pursue change on an individual basis, when it comes to large social issues, Americans have tended to form groups of like-minded people to achieve the desired ends. Americans, throughout their history, have addressed the circumstances of their lives by taking collective action.

It is not the intent of the essays collected in the volumes of *Revolts, Protests, Demonstrations, and Rebellions in American History* to argue whether such actions were justified. Obviously, in any such situation, there are two sides that usually see things quite differently. Sometimes, basic morality dictates that one side is "right" and the other is "wrong." But determining such things is not our task. Rather, it is more instructive for historians to look at the situations that brought about such actions. What were the circumstances that caused people to decide that collective action was necessary? Who was involved? Why did people respond the way they did? What were the events that were the turning points in such actions? By finding the answers to all these questions, we can take some important steps toward understanding how these revolts, protests, and other collective actions function within American society. To do so, it might be instructive to look at the different types of events and movements that qualified for inclusion in this work.

Among the most basic forms of revolt (not to mention the earliest) are the reactions that American Indian peoples had when their rights, their land, or their cultures were being taken from them. The Pueblo Revolt, in 1680, was one of the earliest large-scale uprisings against the encroaching European presence on the continent. It had many elements: land loss, cultural repression, religious suppression, and forced labor. Similarly, the Pima Revolt in 1751, Pontiac's Rebellion in 1763, the Flight of the Nez Percé in 1877, the Sioux resistance that culminated in the Wounded Knee Massacre of 1890, though all different in their expression, shared the common feature of a group or groups of American Indians taking action, sometimes against hopeless odds, to defend different aspects of their way of life. Similarly, a revitalized "Red Power" movement during the 1960s and 1970s saw a revival of resistance in the Alcatraz Island Occupation of 1969–1970, the Trail of Broken Treaties protest in 1972, and the Wounded Knee Occupation in 1973.

Of course, the United States was founded as a result of a collective action that was, at times, called a revolt or a rebellion. Going back as far as Bacon's Rebellion in 1676, those who came over to North America showed a propensity for taking action against the government when they felt that it was not serving their interests. With the onset of the 1760s and the growing debate over taxation in the American colonies, the pace of revolt quickened. In 1765, the Stamp Act Protests gave the colonists a common cause. The Boston Massacre in 1770 galvanized the colonists through the effective use of propaganda. The Regulator Movement in 1771 gave those theoretical movements some meaning, with the addition of violent action. The Pine Tree Riot in 1772 again protested the rising royal authority over the colonies' economic lives. The move toward revolution became almost inevitable after the Boston Tea Party in 1773 led to greater repression by the British government, which led to greater resistance by the colonies. The onset of the American Revolution was, largely, the culmination of this particular set of revolts and protests over the prior 12 years.

But even after the American Revolution ended, the colonists-turned-Americans were not averse to protesting against the government they had just installed if they felt that their needs were not being met. Only three years after the end of the Revolution, Shays' Rebellion demonstrated that the newly elected leaders could not afford to rest on their laurels at the expense of the common farmers. The Whiskey Rebellion in 1794, the Dorr Rebellion in 1841, the actions of the Molly Maguires in the 1870s, the Brooks-Baxter War in 1874, the Black Patch War in 1909, the Bonus Army protests in 1932, the Battle of Athens in 1946, the Sagebrush Rebellion in 1979, and the World Trade Organization protests in 1999 all had to do with the discontent different groups of Americans felt over political and economic conditions, and that the governing authorities were to blame.

But one of the most common ways that Americans collectively protested against economic injustice was through organized labor action. As America's population grew with the arrival of many immigrants during the late 19th century, labor activism began to take over as one of the most common forms of revolt. The Great Railroad Strikes of 1877, the Haymarket Square Riot in 1886, the Homestead Strike in 1892, the Pullman Strike in 1894, the Ludlow Massacre in 1914, the Boston Police Strike in 1919, the Battle of Blair Mountain in 1921, the Toledo Auto-Lite Strike in 1934, and the West Coast Longshoremen's Strike the same year all featured organized labor as one of the moving forces in American life, allowing ordinary people to take an active role in advocating for better treatment in society.

American Indians, of course, were not the only ethnic group to take action to defend their cultural heritage and to fight for the rights they should have been rightfully accorded in American society. Slave rebellions were also among the earliest collective actions against the imposition of racial power. Africans and African Americans naturally found slave life intolerable, and resisted their situations in many ways. Some acted as individuals, slowing their work or breaking the machines used in their labor. Occasionally, armed insurrection was a more attractive, more immediate alternative. Sometimes, it was all the people had left. Many examples can be cited: the Stono Rebellion in 1739, the New York Slave Insurrection in 1741, Gabriel Prosser's Virginia Uprising in 1799, Charles Deslondes's German Coast Uprising in 1811, the abortive effort of white abolitionist George Boxley to spark an insurrection in 1815, and Denmark Vesey's uprising in 1822. All these actions caused Americans, especially southerners, to be extremely vigilant and watchful over their slaves' actions. But none of these incidents had the society-wide impact of Nat Turner's Rebellion in 1831. In its aftermath, vigilance committees roamed the South, looking out for possible insurrections. Largely because of this, John Brown's takeover of the federal armory at Harper's Ferry in 1859 with the goal of sparking a large-scale slave insurrection scared white southerners to such a degree as to make it one of the factors that contributed to the onset of the Civil War two years later.

Even after slavery ended in 1865, African Americans and Americans of many other minority groups had to take action to have their constitutional and other social rights recognized by mainstream American society. Women began to advocate for voting rights in the 1830s, with their movement really gaining momentum by the 1870s. Hispanic Americans included African Americans and members of other marginalized groups in the Plan de San Diego in 1915. The Zoot Suit Riot in 1942 showed that even though Mexican Americans were serving in the military during World War II, they still were not viewed as equal partners in American society. Of course, the African American Civil Rights Movement of the 1950s–1960s is one of the most notable examples of the creation of a large-scale movement to achieve some significant changes. It became the model for many other later movements, such as the Red Power Movement, the Chicano Movement, and the Feminist Movement. But even though the Civil Rights Movement achieved important things in terms of expanding the constitutional rights of all Americans, it did not address all the issues, such as the economic and social aspects of life that many people saw as important. As such, the Civil Rights Movement spawned other protests, such as the Watts Riots in 1965, the Detroit Riots in

1967, the Attica Prison Riot in 1971, the Los Angeles Uprising in 1992, and the "Day without an Immigrant" protests in 2006.

The dark side of protest by ethnic groups in the United States, however, was always present as a counterpoint. Frequently taking the form of race riots, Americans protested and sometimes resorted to violence when they felt their lifestyle was being threatened by minority ethnic groups. The Philadelphia Nativist Riots in 1844 saw many people protest the increasing presence of German Americans, most of whom were Catholic. A decade later, Bleeding Kansas, although technically over states' rights, had a significant racial component, as Jayhawkers did not want slavery in their free-soil territory. The list that follows is almost too long to believe. A selective recounting would include the Portland Rum Riot in 1855, the Know-Nothing Riots in 1855–1856, the New York Draft Riots in 1863, the New Orleans Riot of 1866, the Colfax Massacre in 1873, the Seattle Riot in 1886, the Lattimer Massacre in 1897, the New Orleans Race Riot in 1900, the Atlanta Race Riot in 1906, the Springfield Race Riot in 1908, the Houston Riot in 1917, the Red Summer of 1919, and the Tulsa Race Riot of 1921.

These are but a few of the reasons that groups of Americans, over the course of their histories, have chosen to rise up against what they saw as the powers of repression in their lives. There are many other reasons why revolts have broken out. Religion (Leisler's Rebellion in 1689, the Philadelphia Election Riot in 1742, and the Utah War in 1857), independence movements (the Texas Revolt in 1835, the Bear Flag Revolt in 1846), and antiwar activism (the Green Corn Rebellion in 1917 and the Chicago Riots in 1968) have all been powerful motives causing Americans to turn to collective action. If this history shows us anything, it must be obvious that collective rebellion and revolt is a constant theme in American life. The reasons have changed through the years, but the fact that Americans take action to feed the "tree of liberty" with regularity has not. A look at the news in early 2010 shows that a new movement known as the Tea Party, whose history is still being written, is taking collective action against what they see as troubling signs of leftist leanings in their government. Although violence has not yet broken out, there has been enough violent rhetoric—with gun-owning Tea Partiers congregating on the banks of the Potomac, across from Washington, DC— to cause concern. Whether or not one agrees with the Tea Partiers' agenda, it is obvious that they are more than willing to stage another revolt, rebellion, or even a revolution, if it means a restoration of their vision of America.

Intended for high school and undergraduate students and for the interested general public, *Revolts, Protests, Demonstrations, and Rebellions in American History* is divided into 71 topic sections, which each section containing from three to seven essays. An introductory essay describes the causes, course, and consequences of the particular rebellion, revolt, riot, or uprising, with subsequent essays providing more detailed information on specific persons, organizations, concepts, battles, or groups related to the event. Each essay concludes with a Further Reading bibliography, and many sections conclude with relevant primary documents, which open with brief introductions describing the document and discussing its importance. "See also" cross-references at the ends of the introductory essays in each section direct the reader to related sections. Finally, a detailed subject index provides additional access to the sections and to the essays within them.

—Steven L. Danver
San Marcos, California

Further Reading

Thomas Jefferson, Letter to William Stephens Smith, November 13, 1787. In *The Papers of Thomas Jefferson*, ed. Julian P. Boyd, vol. 12 (1955), 356.

Bacon's Rebellion (1675–1676)

A 1676 uprising in the colony of Virginia, Bacon's Rebellion takes its name from Nathaniel Bacon, the man who served as the primary leader of the movement. Bacon's Rebellion is generally considered a rebellion of nonelite (former indentured servants, some slaves, as well as small and middling planters) western Virginians against the powerful tobacco elite of the eastern portions of the colony. Early historical treatments tended to focus on whether or not it constituted a prequel to the American Revolution 100 years before the fact. Over the past 30 years, that interpretation faded in light of work that focuses on the rebellion's role in hastening race-based African slavery and ending indentured servitude. In addition to the relationship between colonists and their colonial governments and the development of slavery in North America, the rebellion also provides significant insight into colonial attitudes toward Native Americans (see Wertenbaker 1940; Washburn 1957; Morgan 1975).

Bacon's Rebellion began with an attempt by a group of Maryland Indians to obtain redress from a Virginia colonist. In July 1675, a group of Doegs and Susquehannocks crossed the river and took some hogs from one Thomas Mathew, a trader whom they said had defrauded them. Mathew and a group of men then gave chase, caught up with some of the raiding party, and beat several of them to death. The Indians who made it back to the Maryland side of the Potomac soon recrossed the river and killed two men in Mathew's service as well as his son. This incident, combined with the general Indian fear spawned by the outbreak of King Philip's War in New England, provided an opportunity for those Virginians already predisposed toward violence against Indians to continue that animosity.

Despite an earlier conviction for a plot to frame one of the leaders of the Patawomeck Indians for murder, George Mason was dispatched with a force of 30 men to punish the Indians for the killings at Mathew's plantation. When the fleeing Indians crossed to what they thought was the inviolable safety of Maryland soil, the Virginians refused to stop and instead crossed the Potomac themselves. When they caught up to the Indians at their village, Mason and Brent killed the group's leader and 10 other Indians. According to one account, the killing occurred after the Indians emerged from their meetinghouse in response to Brent's

2 | Bacon's Rebellion (1675–1676)

Frustrated by the colonial government's moderate stance in the face of Indian raids on settlers and the settlers' demand for Indian land, Nathaniel Bacon leads Virginians in an attack on Native Americans in 1676. Known as Bacon's Rebellion, the civil revolt was the first serious test of British authority in the New World. (Library of Congress)

request for a parley. Additionally, the group reportedly killed nearly 15 peaceful Susquehannocks from nearby houses who had come out to investigate the noise caused by Brent's attack on the meetinghouse (Washburn 1957, 21; Andrews 1915, 105–106; Morgan 1975, 251).

Brent and Mason's actions then touched off many acts of revenge on the part of Indians and whites. Sir William Berkeley, the royal governor of Virginia, then ordered out 1,000 militia to deal with the escalating conflict on the Virginia-Maryland border. On September 26, the militia under the command of Colonel John Washington and Major Isaac Allerton besieged a party of approximately 100 Susquehannocks on their way back from retaliatory raids into Virginia in response to Mason and Brent's actions the previous summer. When the Susquehannocks sent a party of men to parley, the Virginians killed them all. Eventually, the remaining Susquehannocks escaped and began to raid the frontier settlements of the upper Rappahannock in Virginia. In combination with the news of King Philip's War in New England, the attacks by these Maryland Indians caused landowning westerners like Nathaniel Bacon to consider all Indians as dangerous, and fit for destruction (Andrews 1915, 18–19; Morgan 1975, 250–253).

Governor Berkeley at first appeared to accede to these demands. In January 1676, he ordered a punitive expedition against the Susquehannocks. As the expedition was about to set out, Berkeley abruptly recalled the troops and cancelled the entire expedition, preferring instead to take a defensive rather than an offensive approach to the crisis. This caused the residents of the western counties that bordered the tributary remnants of the Powhatan chiefdom to take matters into their own hands with Bacon as their leader (Washburn 1957, 24–25).

Many of them interpreted Berkeley's plan as nothing more than an attempt to profit from the crisis on the part of Virginia's wealthy leadership. They focused their ire on provisions of Berkeley's plan that called for the building of a string of defensive forts. These westerners, Bacon among them, objected to the plan for several reasons. First, Berkeley planned to build the forts on lands held by members of his inner circle. He then proposed to pay the outsiders with whom he planned to man the forts more than the typical westerner earned in a year. He planned to raise the funds to pay for the forts by taxing those very same western landowners. Frontier residents resented this fact considerably. Secondly, recent explorations beyond the Blue Ridge Mountains had revealed to many enterprising westerners the potential profits to be gained from trade with the native groups of that region. The tributary (peaceful) Indian groups of Virginia, located as they were between these colonists and the groups on the other side of the Blue Ridge, constituted a significant barrier to the development of this trade. Therefore, many western planters were eager to use the incursions of the Maryland Susquehannocks as a pretext for eliminating the tributary Indian barrier to the western trade. Therefore, Berkeley's announced intentions to head off further Indian conflict by forbidding the general public from engaging in trade with all Indians angered these western Virginians even further (Morgan 1975, 253; Andrews 1915, 51; see also Briceland, 1987).

For the landless poor who made up the majority of the rebellion's foot soldiers, the inequitable tax structure, the abrogation of their political and legal rights, and the government's refusal to acknowledge their perceived right to take native land at will combined with their perception of Berkeley's unwillingness to protect them from Indian attack to push them violence in 1676.

In many ways, the true nature of Nathaniel Bacon remains somewhat of an enigma. He had not been in Virginia long by the time of the rebellion, and he was still somewhat young, just 29 years old, even by the standards of a death trap like 17th-century Virginia. A relative to a prominent Virginia official of the same name, he quickly exploited that connection as well as his wife's friendship with Lady Berkeley to gain for himself a seat on the Governor's Council. By the fall of 1675, he had fallen out of favor with the governor for arresting a group of Indians whom he accused of theft. The fact that Berkeley dared to criticize his actions seems to have ingrained in Bacon both a recalcitrant attitude toward the governor and a deep hatred of Indians. In addition, Bacon expressed a marked disdain for Patrician Virginians in general. He also suffered the loss of the overseer of one of his two Henrico County plantations at the hands of the Susquehannocks who had escaped Washington and Allerton's forces, and therefore Bacon had a personal score to settle in pushing for punitive raids against the Indians. Finally, his closest associates among the county's planters, most of them newcomers like Bacon, all shared his attitudes toward both Indians and the Patricians who dominated the east (Washburn 1957, 18, 181; *Virginia Magazine of History and Biography* 1907–1908).

In April 1676, after much drinking, Bacon and several of his like-minded fellow western planters decided to cross the James River and meet with the landless freemen and small planters who had been encouraged to gather there by a man named Giles Bland in preparation for a campaign against the Indians. Bland recently had been punished by Governor Berkeley for his insubordinate attitude toward Virginia's Patrician leadership. Bland also shared Bacon's attitude toward Indians. When Bacon and his neighbors arrived at Bland's encampment (with a plentiful supply of liquor to dole out to the small planters and freemen gathered there), they were received as heroes of people who would lead them to victory. After several speeches, the group began to beg Bacon to lead them in a campaign to destroy all Indians in Virginia. For his part, Bacon accepted and immediately dispatched a message to Berkeley asking for such a commission. Twice he proposed that Governor Berkeley authorize a punitive expedition against all Indians to diffuse the potential for an outright western mutiny of the landless against the landed. In other words, Bacon suggested that Berkeley allow the frontiersmen to satiate their anger with the blood of various indigenous peoples. Fearful of a general Indian war like the one occurring in New England at the time, Berkeley chose instead to honor his promises of friendship to the tribes with whom he had previously made peace. In addition, he came to distrust Bacon as nothing more than an upstart, intent on stirring up a rabble to serve his own ambitions. When Berkeley twice refused his pleas, Bacon enacted his desire to annihilate all Indians regardless of their relationship to the Virginia government (Washburn 1957, 35–39; Morgan 1975, 255–259).

After first threatening the nearby Pamunkeys into fleeing their village, Bacon and his 300-man "army" marched to an Indian fort near the border with Carolina held by the Siouan-speaking Occoneechees. After convincing them to capture and kill several Susquehannocks in the area, Bacon demanded that they provide him and his men with food. When he determined that the Occoneechees had not complied with his request with enough alacrity, Bacon and his men attacked and killed 150 of them (Morgan 1975, 259).

For his part, Sir William Berkeley attempted to destabilize Bacon's movement. In particular, the governor promised that those Virginians who joined him against Bacon would be exempt from taxes, and he called for the election of a new assembly for the express purpose of allowing the representatives of the people to present their grievances against him. He then invited Bacon to submit himself and intimated his willingness to pardon the rebel or allow him to go to England to plead his case. Berkeley also took the step of classifying all Indians as enemies of Virginia in an effort to placate the intense Indian hatred that Bacon had aroused. However, he strongly insisted that only those given express permission by the Crown via himself as the Crown's direct representative in the colony could enforce that decree. Since he had denied Bacon's calls for a commission to lead an expedition against Virginia Indians and they had proceeded anyway, Bacon and his followers were now rebels against the king (Morgan 1975, 259; Washburn 1957, 40–42).

In the May elections, New Kent County voters sent Nathaniel Bacon himself to the assembly. After he returned from the campaign on the Roanoke River, Bacon left for Jamestown. Still believing that he could convince the governor to see the wisdom of his position, Bacon anchored a few miles from Jamestown and sent word asking for permission to enter the town. Berkeley responded by instructing one of his lieutenants to apprehend the rebel leader. A few days after he left for the assembly, Nathaniel Bacon entered Jamestown as a prisoner (Washburn 1957, 48–51; Morgan 1975, 261–262).

In a dramatic scene described in several sources, Berkeley confronted Bacon face to face. Seemingly forced into submission, Bacon appeared before the assembly in chains and begged Berkeley for his pardon. Berkeley, realizing that killing Bacon would only create a martyr, set him free and restored him to full membership in his Council. In a further effort to pacify Bacon's supporters, Berkeley promised Bacon a proper commission to proceed against the Indians (Washburn 1957, 48–51; Morgan 1975, 261–262).

Over the next several days, the new assembly passed several significant pieces of legislation designed to remake Virginia society in a more egalitarian mold. The assembly granted suffrage to all landless freemen, curtailed the powers of appointed magistrates, and rewrote the tax code to end all the tax exemptions previously granted to Berkeley and his elite brethren. Berkeley assented to all of these measures, but continued to resist efforts to sanction genocide campaigns against Indians. On one occasion, the governor vented his frustration over the killing of the surrendering Susquehannocks by the Washington and Allerton expedition, vehemently admonishing the assembly that the Indians who had sought to parley and peace with the expeditions sent to Maryland were murdered. His resistance to measures calling for the indiscriminate destruction of all Indians succeeded in forcing the assembly to admit the possibility that not all Indians harbored murderous intentions toward the colony. In the end, it did little to check the genocidal aims of Bacon and his followers. While the preamble to an act regarding the Indian conflict differentiated between those friendly and those unfriendly to Virginia, the provisions of the act made very little distinction. The act defined any Indian who left their village without express permission from the Virginians as an enemy. Additionally, the assembly discarded Berkeley's previous defensive policy toward Indians and created a force of 1,000 men with which to attack Indian villages. The legislation also ordered that the members of the expedition would be paid with both Indian possessions and individual Indian prisoners as slaves (Andrews 1915, 25–27; Hening 1810–1823, 341–365; Washburn 1957, 54–55; Morgan 1975, 263–264).

Bacon, who had left Jamestown after his pardon to return to his wife and plantations, returned and issued his "Declaration of the People" on July 30, in which he portrayed himself as the true representative of the king in Virginia. The declaration also spelled out Bacon's intent to eradicate all the Indians of Virginia. Bacon then attacked the Pamunkey Indians who had taken refuge in the Great Dragon Swamp (Andrews 1915, 116–118; Washburn 1957, 56–58, 71).

Berkeley then fled to the countryside to recruit a volunteer force to pursue the rebel leader. At first, Berkeley succeeded in recruiting nearly 1,200 men, but when these men discovered that he intended to use them against Nathaniel Bacon and not Indians, his force disintegrated. Upon discovering Berkeley's plans to march against him, Bacon turned to take the fight back to the governor. Lacking enough troops to match Bacon's numbers, Berkeley once again officially declared Bacon an outlaw and retreated to Virginia's Eastern Shore (Andrews 1915, 34, 56–57).

Berkeley's decision to seek refuge on the Eastern Shore actually aided his fortunes. The colonists there were much more willing to aid him. When Bacon sent two men to sail to the Eastern Shore and apprehend the governor, Berkeley, with the help of Eastern Shore colonists, managed to capture the two assailants instead. This success allowed him to recruit a force of nearly 600 men and with which he retook Jamestown on September 8, 1676 (Andrews 1915, 36–37, 64–67).

When Bacon learned of Berkeley's successes as well as the fall of Jamestown, he once again moved against the capital. On his way, Bacon abducted the wives of Berkeley's most loyal supporters. He besieged Jamestown in mid-September and prominently displayed both the Indian captives he had taken and the female loyalists, many of whose husbands now opposed him inside Jamestown. In the face of this and Bacon's superior numbers, the governor once again retreated via the water to the Eastern Shore. Not long after, Bacon burned Jamestown, England's oldest settlement in North America, to the ground (Morgan 1975, 268–269; Andrews 1915, 68–69).

After the recapturing of Jamestown, Bacon's men went wild in an orgiastic frenzy of heavy drinking as well as looting. The sources disagree as to whether or not Nathaniel Bacon was troubled by this turn of events. If he was, his death from dysentery in late October 1676 prevented him from acting upon those concerns. The loss of the rebellion's leader opened up yet another opportunity for Sir William Berkeley to reestablish control. By early November, having returned from his exile on the Eastern Shore, he defeated several rebel bands. On November 13, Berkeley condemned the leader of one of the defeated bands, Thomas Hansford, to death by hanging. From the scaffold, Hansford proclaimed himself a true and loyal subject of King Charles and refused to repent of his participation in the rebellion (Andrews 1915, 79–81).

In January 1677, Berkeley executed five of the rebellion's leaders and would have surely hanged more had he not been prevented from doing so by the arrival from England of a commission sent by King Charles II to investigate the causes of the unrest. Their report signaled their agreement with many of the rebels that Berkeley and other elites had dealt with them unfairly, but the commissioners also agreed with Berkeley's contention that the actions of Bacon and his associates constituted an illegal rebellion against the authority of the Crown as manifested in the personage of the royal governor. As a result of Bacon's Rebellion, elite Virginians placed fewer restrictions on nonelite attempts to acquire Indian land in the west, and the entire colony began to switch from indentured servitude to lifetime African chattel slavery as the colony's preferred labor system. This switch would help to control the tremendous growth in the landless free population that had occurred in the latter half of the 17th century due to the significant increase in the number of servants who survived their period of indenture (Morgan 1975, 257–272; Andrews 1915, 65).

—*Ethan Schmidt*

See also all entries under Leisler's Rebellion (1689–1691); Regulator Movement (1771); Pine Tree Riot (1772); Shays' Rebellion (1787); Whiskey Rebellion (1794).

Further Reading

Andrews, Charles McLean. *Narratives of the Insurrections, 1675–1690*. New York: Charles Scribner's Sons, 1915.

Bacon, Nathaniel. "Manifesto Concerning the Present Troubles in Virginia." *Virginia Magazine of History and Biography* 1 (1894).

Briceland, Alan Vance. *Westward from Virginia: The Exploration of the Virginia-Carolina Frontier*. Charlottesville: University Press of Virginia, 1987.

"The Family of Nathaniel Bacon, the Rebel." *Virginia Magazine of History and Biography* 14 (1907) and 15 (1907–1908).

Hening, William Waller. *The Statutes at Large: Being a Collection of All the Laws of Virginia, from the First Session of the Legislature, in the Year 1619*. Vol. 2. Richmond, VA: Samuel Pleasants, 1810–1823.

Morgan, Edmund. *American Slavery, American Freedom: The Ordeal of Colonial Virginia*. New York: W. W. Norton, 1975.

Washburn, Wilcomb. *The Governor and the Rebel: A History of Bacon's Rebellion in Virginia*. Chapel Hill: University of North Carolina Press, 1957.

Webb, Stephen Saunders. *1676: The End of American Independence*. New York: Alfred A. Knopf, 1984.

Wertenbaker, Thomas Jefferson. *Torchbearer of the Revolution: The Story of Bacon's Rebellion and Its Leader*. Princeton, NJ: Princeton University Press, 1940.

Bacon, Nathaniel (1647–1676)

Nathaniel Bacon is best known for his leadership of the 1676 rebellion that bears his name. Two years after he arrived in Virginia, Bacon led an uprising against Sir William Berkeley, the royal governor of the colony. He and his rebels even succeeded in burning Jamestown, the colony's capital, to the ground. The rebellion fizzled in October 1676 when Bacon died suddenly of dysentery (Morgan 1975, 250–270).

In many ways, the details of Bacon's personality remain somewhat obscure. At 29 years of age, he was still somewhat young even by the standards of 17th-century Virginia, which was a death trap. Born to an ambitious family in Suffolk, England, Bacon consistently failed to live up to his father's expectations. His father enrolled him at Cambridge only to withdraw him after two years, citing his son's propensity toward "extravagancies (*Virginia Magazine of History and Biography* 1907–1908)."

After his forced departure from Cambridge, Bacon continued his ne'er-do-well ways. He entered into a forbidden marriage to the daughter of a local aristocrat and became involved in a plot to swindle a neighboring youth's inheritance. Bacon's frustrated father then put young Nathaniel and his wife on a ship bound for

In 1676, English colonist Nathaniel Bacon led a popular revolt of colonial Virginia's frontier settlers, known as Bacon's Rebellion, against Virginia governor William Berkeley and his allies. (Library of Congress)

Virginia where his kinsmen, also named Nathaniel Bacon, served as the colony's treasurer (*Virginia Magazine of History and Biography* 1907–1908).

Upon his arrival in Virginia, Bacon quickly exploited his family connections as well as his wife's friendship with Governor Berkeley's wife to gain for himself a seat on the Governor's Council. Like many of his neighbors, Bacon had recently obtained a commission from Berkeley and constructed a trading post for the purpose of setting himself up in the increasingly lucrative western Indian trade. Upon learning of Berkeley's decision to assert greater control over the trade, Bacon reacted furiously. Furthermore, Bacon and his family experienced personally the effects of the increased raiding by Susquehannock Indians from Maryland when a 1675 attack claimed the life of one of his overseers. By the fall of 1675, he had fallen out of favor with Berkeley for arresting a group of Indians whom he accused of stealing corn. His subsequent rebuke by Berkeley seems to have ingrained in him both an antagonistic stance toward the governor and a deep hatred of Indians (Morgan 1975, 254–255).

One day after drinking with several of his neighbors, Bacon decided to assume command of a group of landless frontiersmen gathering near his plantation for the purpose of leading them in a campaign to rid Virginia of all Indians. Upon learning of Bacon's actions, Berkeley, who favored a more diplomatic approach with the colony's Indians, declared Bacon in rebellion against the government and set out to apprehend him (Morgan 1975, 255–259).

From that point, the rebellion quickly descended into a personal battle for supremacy between Berkeley and Bacon, and an opportunity for landless Virginians to redistribute the wealth and possessions of Virginia patricians. After gaining the upper hand militarily, Bacon quickly moved to head off a general rebellion among the landless by forcing Berkeley to commission him as the leader of a campaign (manned by landless frontiersmen) aimed at exterminating all of Virginia's Indigenous Peoples regardless of their previous relationship to the colony's government. However, once Bacon set off on the expedition, Berkeley again declared him a rebel and called out the militia against him. To defend himself from Berkeley's forces, Bacon had to call off the campaign against the Indians and subsequently burned Jamestown to the ground. Shortly thereafter, he became violently ill and died in October 1676. The rebellion subsided not long after his death, but many of the grievances that Bacon and his followers demanded were eventually adopted (Morgan 1975, 259–270).

—Ethan Schmidt

Further Reading

Andrews, Charles McLean. *Narratives of the Insurrections, 1675–1690*. New York: Charles Scribner's Sons, 1915.

"The Family of Nathaniel Bacon, the Rebel." *Virginia Magazine of History and Biography* 14 (1907) and 15 (1907–1908).

Morgan, Edmund. American *Slavery, American Freedom: The Ordeal of Colonial Virginia*. New York: W. W. Norton, 1975.

Washburn, Wilcomb. *The Governor and the Rebel: A History of Bacon's Rebellion in Virginia*. Chapel Hill: University of North Carolina Press, 1957.

Webb, Stephen Saunders. *1676: The End of American Independence*. New York: Alfred A. Knopf, 1984.

Wertenbaker, Thomas Jefferson. *Torchbearer of the Revolution: The Story of Bacon's Rebellion and Its Leader*. Princeton, NJ: Princeton University Press, 1940.

Berkeley, Sir William (1605–1677)

Sir William Berkeley served, with one interruption, as governor of Virginia from the middle of the 17th century until the events of Bacon's Rebellion ended his tenure. He died in July 1677, shortly after he returned to England to answer for his conduct during the events of the rebellion.

Born in Middlesex in 1605, Berkeley spent much of his early adult life as a favorite courtier of Charles I and even dabbled in playwriting. In 1642, he accepted an appointment as governor and captain general of the Virginia Colony. A staunch defender of royal prerogative and patrician privilege, Berkeley actively supported the efforts of the Virginia assembly to enforce deference and submission on the part of the lower orders. During his first year as governor, the assembly passed laws punishing runaway and disobedient servants, forbade servants from marrying during their time of service, granted serving burgesses immunity from arrests, and exempted members of the Governor's Council from tax levies (Billings 2004, 1; Morgan 1975, 146–147).

The other significant achievement of his early tenure was his role in vanquishing the Powhatan Chiefdom, with whom the Virginians had been engaged in intermittent warfare since the earliest years of the colony. On April 18, 1644, Opechancanough, now the titular and de facto leader of the remnants of the paramount chiefdom created by his older brother Powhatan, launched a surprise attack against the English. In the summer of 1644, Berkeley led his troops on what the Virginians referred to as the "Pamunkey and Chickahominy march." His actions forced the abandonment of the Chickahominy village of Oraniock, and destroyed Opechancanough's capital village of Menmend. Later that summer, the English attacked the remaining Powhatan groups. In 1645, Berkeley ordered the construction of forts along their border with the Algonquians to aid in the reduction of the

Sir William Berkeley ruled colonial Virginia almost continuously between 1642 and 1677. He suppressed a popular revolt, known as Bacon's Rebellion, although the ordeal ended his career as governor. (Maurice du Pont Lee)

chiefdom. Finally, in March 1646, Berkeley himself marched against the Algonquians ostensibly to negotiate peace with Opechancanough. When the Indian leader refused his offers of negotiation, Berkeley took "that bloody monster, upon 100 years old," to Jamestown as his prisoner. By October of that year, the Third Anglo-Powhatan War was over, and the paramount chiefdom of Powhatan had been destroyed. A treaty signed by Berkeley and representatives of the remaining chiefdom groups placed the Indians in a subordinate position to the Virginians (Billings 2004, 96–98; Morgan 1975, 149; Rountree 1996, 84–88).

The fall of Charles II's government to Parliamentary forces and his subsequent beheading forced Berkeley, ever loyal to his executed sovereign, to resign his post. However, he did not return to England. Instead, he retired to his plantation, Green Spring, and awaited his next opportunity to further his political career. That opportunity arrived in early 1660, with end of the Cromwellian Protectorate in England. Within weeks of Richard Cromwell's abdication, Sir William Berkeley officially began his second tenure as governor and captain general of the colony of Virginia (Billings 2004, 105–112).

In 1676, Berkeley responded to Nathaniel Bacon's extermination campaign against Virginia's Indians by declaring him a rebel and attempting to arrest him. Eventually, Bacon's death diffused the rebellion and in an effort to restore his authority and exact vengeance on Bacon's followers, Berkeley hanged twelve of Bacon's followers before a royal commission sent from England stopped him and ordered him back to England to answer for his role in driving Virginia's nonelites to rebellion (Morgan 1975, 250–270).

—Ethan Schmidt

Further Reading

Billings, Warren. *Sir William Berkeley and the Forging of Colonial Virginia*. Baton Rouge: Louisiana State University Press, 2004.

Morgan, Edmund. *American Slavery, American Freedom: The Ordeal of Colonial Virginia*. New York: W. W. Norton, 1975.

Rountree, Helen. *Pocahontas's People: The Powhatan Indians of Virginia through Four Centuries*. Norman: University of Oklahoma Press, 1996.

Washburn, Wilcomb. *The Governor and the Rebel: A History of Bacon's Rebellion in Virginia*. Chapel Hill: University of North Carolina Press, 1957.

Webb, Stephen Saunders. *1676: The End of American Independence*. New York: Alfred A. Knopf, 1984.

House of Burgesses

The House of Burgesses represents the first elected assembly in the New World. However, at the time, its establishment represented the failure of the colony both to attract enough settlers and to establish a profitable staple crop economy.

The establishment of a representative assembly was one in a series of reforms begun in 1617 by the governing Virginia Company of London in an attempt to revive the sagging fortunes of the 10-year-old colony. Originally, participation in the election of burgesses was limited to landowning males over the age of 20.

Despite limitations to the House of Burgesses' authority in 1624 when the Crown revoked the Virginia Company's charter and placed the colony under direct royal control, membership in the House continued to represent a significant status symbol for Virginia planters hoping to establish themselves among Virginia's political and economic elite.

Eventually, elite Virginians, wary of challenges to their position by those below them on the social scale, began to restrict membership in the House of Burgesses only to those of their own station. In 1646, the burgesses outlawed secret ballot elections, therefore making it much harder for nonelite Virginians to challenge their social betters for election to the House (Hening 1810–1823, Vol. 1, 334).

14 | Bacon's Rebellion (1675–1676)

Patrick Henry addresses the Virginia House of Burgesses in opposition to the Stamp Act on May 29, 1765. Henry advocated that only colonial legislatures could require colonists to pay taxes. It was during a decisive speech on this issue that he associated King George III of England with Julius Caesar and Charles I. Interrupted by cries of treason, Henry replied, "If this be treason, make the most of it!" (National Archives)

During the mid-1650s, the assembly also attempted to further curtail the political and legal rights of Virginia's populace. In the 1655 session, the burgesses attempted to ensure the election of only "persons of known integrity and of good conversation," by limiting suffrage to housekeepers. This act, in effect, disfranchised landless freemen, who heretofore had participated in the election of burgesses (Hening 1810–1823, Vol. 1, 412, 403; Morgan 1975, 238).

In addition to these attempts to curtail the political rights of nonelites, the House of Burgesses in the latter half of the 17th century also attempted to restrict lower-class Virginians access to Indian land and trade. By the mid-1670s, small planters and artisans found themselves subject to a heavier tax burden, denied recourse to the ancient traditions of custom and usage, and forced to watch as the wealthy few who dominated Virginia society engrossed more land, trade, and tobacco to themselves. It is, therefore, not surprising that they revolted against both Sir William Berkeley and the House of Burgesses in 1676.

For a brief time during Bacon's Rebellion, men who sympathized with Bacon dominated the House of Burgesses. The enactments of that assembly of 1676 demonstrate the extent to which the previous Houses had alienated nonelite and middling Virginians. Among them were bills that curtailed the powers of the governor and restored voting rights to landless Virginians (Washburn, 1957, 49–67).

Eventually, the House of Burgesses came back under the control of the Virginia gentry, and it was there in 1775 that another rebel, Patrick Henry, delivered his famous "give me liberty or give me death" speech. The House of Burgesses also launched the careers of such influential American Revolutionary figures as Thomas Jefferson, George Mason, and George Washington.

—*Ethan Schmidt*

Further Reading

Hatch, Charles E., Jr. *America's Oldest Legislative Assembly & Its Jamestown Statehouses*. Appendix II. Washington, DC: U.S. Department of the Interior, National Park Service, 1956.

Hening, William Waller. *The Statutes at Large: Being a Collection of All the Laws of Virginia, from the First Session of the Legislature, in the Year 1619*. Vol. 2. Richmond, VA: Samuel Pleasants, 1810–1823.

Morgan, Edmund. *American Slavery, American Freedom: The Ordeal of Colonial Virginia*. New York: W. W. Norton, 1975.

Washburn, Wilcomb. *The Governor and the Rebel: A History of Bacon's Rebellion in Virginia*. Chapel Hill: University of North Carolina Press, 1957.

Indentured Servants

Indentured servants represented the best possible solution to meet the intense labor demands of plantation agriculture in England's colonies. It also created a situation ripe for the outbreak of rebellion. In the colonies, the system was first employed in Virginia. The tobacco boom of the 1620s and 1630s, combined with the high mortality rate, produced a situation in which Virginia's labor needs far outpaced the available pool of laborers. Colonial planners therefore decided to address this problem while at the same time acting to decrease the idle population back in England. Under the system of indentured servitude, an individual could sign a contract whereby, in return for transportation to Virginia, they agreed to work for the holder of the contract for a specified amount of time. Seven years constituted the most common length of service (Morgan 1975, 84–85, 106–107).

During the length of the indenture, the owner of the contract held almost complete power over the servant. Masters in this system restricted the freedom of movement and association of their indentured servants and had to give them permission to marry. Masters could also beat their indentured servants. When a servant lived to the end of his/her period of indenture, the contract often required that their masters provide them with land, money, tools, clothing, and food to help them establish themselves as Virginia tobacco planters. However, due to the very active disease environment, the poor nourishment and treatment given them by most masters, and the arduous nature of tobacco work, most servants during the first half of the 17th century died before serving out their full period of indenture (Morgan 1975, 106–107).

During the second half of the 17th century, conditions in Virginia improved to the point that many more indentured servants began to outlive their contracted time of servitude. This created a situation in which many masters (whose own profit margins were often incredibly thin) were unable or refused to provide their newly free servants the items for which they had previously contracted. Additionally, even for those servants fortunate to receive their goods and payments from their former masters, the overwhelming majority of the land in the eastern portion of Virginia was already held by a small minority of very large and very powerful tobacco planters. This left landless freeman, as they came to be known, no choice but to head to less settled western reaches of the colony and squat on any land they could find. This brought them into conflict with the Indians who lived in that region under the auspices of treaties negotiated with the Virginia government as well as many wealthy eastern planters who had already established legal claim to the lands themselves, but had not yet developed it. Therefore, during the mid-1670s, when Nathaniel Bacon began to call for a general campaign to rid Virginia of all Indians and eventually to revolt against the wealthy planters who dominated Virginia's government, he found a fertile ground for recruits to his "people's army" among landless freeman. There is considerable evidence to support the claim that because of this, in the years after Bacon's Rebellion, the Virginia government took steps to eliminate the practice of indentured servitude and replace it with lifetime African chattel slavery (Morgan 1975, 184–270).

—*Ethan Schmidt*

Further Reading

Brown, Kathleen. *Good Wives, Nasty Wenches and Anxious Patriarchs: Gender, Race and Power in Colonial Virginia.* Chapel Hill: University of North Carolina Press, 1996.

Carr, Lois Green. *Colonial Chesapeake Society*. Chapel Hill: University of North Carolina Press, 1991.

Hening, William Waller. *The Statutes at Large: Being a Collection of All the Laws of Virginia, from the First Session of the Legislature, in the Year 1619*. Vol. 2. Richmond, VA: Samuel Pleasants, 1810–1823.

Jernegan, Marcus Wilson. *Laboring and Dependent Classes in Colonial America, 1607–1783*. Westport, CT: Greenwood Press, 1980.

Kulikoff, Allan. *Tobacco and Slaves: The Development of Southern Cultures in the Chesapeake, 1680–1800*. Chapel Hill: University of North Carolina Press, 1986.

Morgan, Edmund. *American Slavery, American Freedom: The Ordeal of Colonial Virginia*. New York: W. W. Norton, 1975.

Salinger, Sharon V. *To Serve Well and Faithfully: Labor and Indentured Servants in Pennsylvania, 1682–1800*. Westminster, MD: Heritage Books, 2000.

Susquehannock Indians

The Susquehannock Indians (later referred to as the Susquehannas or Conestogas) played a crucial role in initiating the 1676 Virginia revolt known as Bacon's Rebellion. At the time of the initial English settlement of Virginia, the Susquehannocks, an Iroquoian-speaking group, lived north of the territory inhabited by the Algonquian-speaking Powhatan Chiefdom. According to early colonial sources, particularly the writings of Captain John Smith, the Susquehannocks often raided south into Powhatan's domain and he was quite interested in establishing an alliance with the English to protect his people from them (Rountree, 1989, 120; Washburn 1957, 43; Andrews 1915, 112).

Throughout the first half of the 17th century, the Susquehannocks engaged in multiple struggles over access to beaver-hunting grounds with the Algonquians of Virginia and Maryland as well as their fellow Iroquoians of the Five Nations. By the 1640s, they had extended Susquehannock control from their original villages along the Susquehanna River in present-day Pennsylvania, east to the Delaware River, south to the Potomac River in Virginia, and as far north as New York. Additionally, they established lucrative trading and military alliances with the Huron in Canada as well as the Erie and Shawnee to their west in the Ohio and Great Lakes regions. This large geographic sphere of Susquehannock influence placed them in an extremely advantageous position for trade with European powers in two ways. First, their location allowed them access to the very productive beaver-hunting grounds of western Pennsylvania, New York, and the Ohio

River Valley. Secondly, this location allowed them to demand a high price from three competing European powers, each of which were intent on keeping the others out of the fur trade. Through their Huron allies in Canada, they could access French fur traders. In the east, just across the Delaware River, the Dutch eagerly pursued Susquehannock commodities. If neither of those competitors could meet their price (usually large quantities of firearms), the Susquehannocks could take their furs to the English in Virginia. Their success at exploiting this geopolitical advantage made the Susquehannocks one of the most heavily armed native groups in the 1640s. Reportedly, one of their villages in western Pennsylvania even possessed a cannon (Kent 1984, 25–28; Sultzman, "Susquehannock History").

By the time of Bacon's Rebellion, many Susquehannocks lived in villages just across the Potomac River in Maryland. In July 1675, a group of Susquehannocks became entangled in a trading dispute with a Virginian named Thomas Mathew. In response to his refusal to pay them for some hogs, a group of Susqehannocks crossed the Potomac River and stole the hogs back. This set off a series of reprisals between Mathew and the Susquehannocks, which resulted in the deaths of several Indians as well as two of Mathew's servants and his son. Over the course of the next few weeks, the Virginia government dispatched retaliatory expeditions against the Susquehannocks that crossed into Maryland and destroyed entire Susquehannock villages. In response to these expeditions, the remaining Susquehannock groups crossed into Virginia in late 1675 and began raiding the outlying settlements indiscriminately. These raids prompted western Virginians under the leadership of Nathaniel Bacon to demand authorization for a genocide campaign against all Indians. When the royal governor of Virginia refused, Bacon and the westerners rose up in rebellion during the spring of 1676 (Andrews 1915, 15–16; Washburn 1957, 20–21).

—*Ethan Schmidt*

Further Reading

Andrews, Charles McLean. *Narratives of the Insurrections, 1675–1690*. New York: Charles Scribner's Sons, 1915.

Kent, Barry. *Susquehanna's Indians*. Harrisburg: Pennsylvania History and Museum Commission, 1984.

Morgan, Edmund. *American Slavery, American Freedom: The Ordeal of Colonial Virginia*. New York: W. W. Norton, 1975.

Rountree, Helen. *The Powhatan Indians of Virginia: Their Traditional Culture*. Norman: University of Oklahoma Press, 1989.

Sultzman, Lee. "The Susquehannock." *The Susquehannock Fire Ring*. http://susquehannock.brokenclaw.net/susquehannock (accessed August 20, 2010).

Washburn, Wilcomb. *The Governor and the Rebel: A History of Bacon's Rebellion in Virginia*. Chapel Hill: University of North Carolina Press, 1957.

Webb, Stephen Saunders. *1676: The End of American Independence*. New York: Alfred A. Knopf, 1984.

Wertenbaker, Thomas Jefferson. *Torchbearer of the Revolution: The Story of Bacon's Rebellion and Its Leader.* Princeton, NJ: Princeton University Press, 1940.

Tobacco

The introduction of West Indian tobacco to Virginia by John Rolfe in 1612 created the economic boom that ensured Virginia's survival. It also instigated a need for land and labor that spawned over 30 years of warfare against the Powhatan Chiefdom, eventually led to the institution of African slavery in North America, and placed the colony's social classes on the path toward a cataclysmic rebellion in the latter half of the century (Morgan 1975, 90–91).

Initially, James I of England resisted the widespread cultivation and exportation of what he termed a "vile stinking weed" from one of his colonies. However, after he realized the extent to which the exportation of tobacco was rapidly filling his coffers, he relented in his opposition, and Virginia's entire social and economic life came to revolve around the production of it to the point that they began to grow it in the streets of Jamestown and use tobacco as their currency (Morgan 1975, 196–197).

Already on shaky ground with the Powhatan Indians in the midst of whose land they had founded Jamestown, the need for more land on which to produce tobacco

Workers harvest tobacco in colonial Virginia, c. 1650. (Library of Congress)

led to a series of wars against the Powhatan for control of the area. Since tobacco rapidly depletes the soil in which it grows, and the tobacco economy was so hot during the 1620s and 1630s, the voracious Virginia appetite for land during this period knew no limits. By 1646, the Virginians had completely vanquished the once-powerful chiefdom and converted almost the entire eastern half of the colony to tobacco-producing plantations (Morgan 1975, 92–101, 149).

The reliance on tobacco as a staple crop created another problem in that since tobacco was such a labor-intensive crop, the only way to maximize profit was to utilize some sort of mass labor system. Indentured servitude constituted the first attempt by the Virginians to solve their labor shortage. This system, by which poor Englishmen would agree to provide a set number of years' labor in return for passage to the colony, worked well enough during the heyday of the tobacco boom years. However, it very quickly created an extremely exploitative society in which wealthy planters often utilized unscrupulous methods to extend the service time of their indentured servants, defraud other colonists of their land and servants, and generally avoid living up to their responsibilities under the agreement (Morgan 1975, 115–130).

By the 1670s, the inequalities created by the exploitative nature of the tobacco economy in Virginia combined with the fact that indentured servants were increasingly living out their period of indentures to produce a volatile situation in which a large population of landless former indentured servants now demanded land and rights. When the planter elite who dominated the assembly refused them political rights, increased their tax burden, and forbade them from taking the Indian land in western Virginia by force, thus dealing a death blow to their hopes of establishing themselves as a planter, they joined Nathaniel Bacon and rose up against the government. In aftermath of the rebellion, the Virginia government deemphasized indentured servant labor in favor of African slaves who could never attain the status of a landless free man (Morgan 1975, 235–249).

—Ethan Schmidt

Further Reading

Brown, Kathleen. *Good Wives, Nasty Wenches and Anxious Patriarchs: Gender, Race and Power in Colonial Virginia*. Chapel Hill: University of North Carolina Press, 1996.

Carr, Lois Green. *Colonial Chesapeake Society*. Chapel Hill: University of North Carolina Press, 1991.

Hening, William Waller. *The Statutes at Large: Being a Collection of All the Laws of Virginia, from the First Session of the Legislature, in the Year 1619*. Vol. 2. Richmond, VA: Samuel Pleasants, 1810–1823.

Kulikoff, Allan. *Tobacco and Slaves: The Development of Southern Cultures in the Chesapeake, 1680–1800*. Chapel Hill: University of North Carolina Press, 1986.

Morgan, Edmund. *American Slavery, American Freedom: The Ordeal of Colonial Virginia*. New York: W. W. Norton, 1975.

Nathaniel Bacon's Manifesto (1676)

This document articulates both the reasons and the justifications for Bacon's Rebellion, a revolt against the planter class by the lower-class farmers of inland areas of the colony. In it, the rebellion's leader, Nathaniel Bacon, argues that the royal governor, William Berkeley, is to blame because he places greater importance on assuaging the demands of the region's Native American populations rather than the demands of English landowners.

If virtue be a sin, if piety be guilt, all the principles of morality, goodness and justice be perverted, we must confess that those who are now called rebels may be in danger of those high imputations. Those loud and several bulls would affright innocents and render the defence of our brethren and the inquiry into our sad and heavy oppressions, treason. But if there be, as sure there is, a just God to appeal to; if religion and justice be a sanctuary here; if to plead the cause of the oppressed; if sincerely to aim at his Majesty's honour and the public good without any reservation or by interest; if to stand in the gap after so much blood of our dear brethren bought and sold; if after the loss of a great part of his Majesty's colony deserted and dispeopled, freely with our lives and estates to endeavour to save the remainders be treason; God Almighty judge and let guilty die. But since we cannot in our hearts find one single spot of rebellion or treason, or that we have in any manner aimed at subverting the settled government or attempting of the person of any either magistrate or private man, notwithstanding the several reproaches and threats of some who for sinister ends were disaffected to us and censured our innocent and honest designs, and since all people in all places where we have yet been can attest our civil, quiet, peaceable behaviour far different from that of rebellion and tumultuous persons, let truth be bold and all the world know the real foundations of pretended guilt.

We appeal to the country itself what of what nature their oppressions have been, or by what cabal and mystery the designs of many of those whom we call great men have been transacted and carried on; but let us trace these men in authority and favour to whose hands the dispensation of the country's wealth has been committed. Let us observe the sudden rise of their estates composed with the quality in which they first entered this country, or the reputation they have held here amongst wise and discerning men. And let us see whether their extractions and education have not been vile, and by what pretence of learning and virtue they could so soon [come] into employments of so great trust and consequence. Let us consider their sudden advancement and let us also consider whether any public work for our safety and defence or for the advancement and propagation of trade, liberal arts, or sciences is here extant in any way adequate to our vast charge. Now let us compare these things together and see what sponges have sucked up the public treasure, and whether it has not been privately contrived away by unworthy favourites and juggling parasites whose tottering fortunes have been repaired and supported at the public charge. Now if it be so, judge what greater guilt can be than to offer to pry into these and to unriddle the mysterious wiles of a powerful cabal; let all people judge what can be of more dangerous import than to suspect the so long safe proceedings of some of our grandees, and whether people may with safety open their eyes in so nice a concern.

Another main article of our guilt is our open and manifest aversion of all, not only the foreign but the protected and darling Indians. This, we are informed, is rebellion of a deep dye for that both the governor and council are by Colonel Cole's assertion bound to defend the queen and the Appamatocks with their blood. Now, whereas we do declare and can prove that they have been for these many years enemies to the king and country, robbers and thieves and invaders of his Majesty's right and our interest and estates, but yet have by persons in authority been defended and protected even against his Majesty's loyal subjects, and that in so high a nature that even the complaints and oaths of his Majesty's most loyal subjects in a lawful manner proffered by them against those barbarous outlaws, have been by the right honourable governor rejected and the delinquents from his presence dismissed, not only with pardon and indemnity, but with all encouragement and favour; their firearms so destructful to us and by our laws prohibited, commanded to be restored them, and open declaration before witness made that they must have ammunition, although directly contrary to our law. Now what greater guilt can be than to oppose and endeavour the destruction of these honest, quiet neighbours of ours? . . .

The Declaration of the People

> For having upon specious pretences of public works, raised unjust taxes upon the commonalty for the advancement of private favourites and other sinister ends, but no visible effects in any measure adequate.
>
> For not having during the long time of his government in any measure advanced his hopeful colony, either by fortification, towns or trade.
>
> For having abused and rendered contemptible the majesty of justice, of advancing to places of judicature scandalous and ignorant favourites.
>
> For having wronged his Majesty's prerogative and interest by assuming the monopoly of the beaver trade.
>
> By having in that unjust gain bartered and sold his Majesty's country and the lives of his loyal subjects to the barbarous heathen.
>
> For having protected, favoured and emboldened the Indians against his Majesty's most loyal subjects, never contriving, requiring, or appointing any due or proper means of satisfaction for their many invasions, murders, and robberies committed upon us.
>
> For having, when the army of the English was just upon the track of the Indians, which now in all places burn, spoil, and murder, and when we might with ease have destroyed them who then were in open hostility, for having expressly countermanded

and sent back our army by passing his word for the peaceable demeanour of the said Indians, who immediately prosecuted their evil intentions, committing horrid murders and robberies in all places, being protected by the said engagement and word passed of him, the said Sir William Berkeley, having ruined and made desolate a great part of his Majesty's country, have now drawn themselves into such obscure and remote places nad are by their successes so emboldened and confirmed, and by their confederacy so strengthened that the cries of blood are in all places, and the terror and consternation of the people so great, that they are now become not only a difficult, but a very formidable enemy who might with ease have been destroyed, etc. When upon the loud outcries of blood, the Assembly had with all care raised and framed an army for the prevention of future mischiefs and safeguard of his Majesty's colony.

For having with only the privacy of some few favourites, without acquainting the people, only by the alteration of a figure, forged a commission by we know not what hand, not only without but against the consent of the people, for raising and effecting of civil wars and distractions, which being happily and without bloodshed prevented.

For having the second time attempted the same thereby calling down our forces from the defence of the frontiers, and most weak exposed places, for the prevention of civil mischief and ruin amongst ourselves, whilst the barbarous enemy in all places did invade, murder, and spoil us, his Majesty's most faithful subjects.

Of these, the aforesaid articles, we accuse Sir William Berkeley, as guilty of each and every one of the same, and as one who has traitorously attempted, violated and injured his Majesty's interest here, by the loss of a great part of his colony, and many of his faithful and loyal subjects by him betrayed, and in a barbarous and shameful manner exposed to the incursions and murders of the heathen.

And we further declare these, the ensuing persons in this list, to have been wicked, and pernicious counselors, aiders and assisters against the commonalty in these our cruel commotions: . . . [a list of 19 names follows] . . .

And we do further demand, that the said Sir William Berkeley, with all the persons in this list, be forthwith delivered up, or surrender themselves, within four days after the notice hereof, or otherwise we declare as followeth: that in whatsoever house, place, or ship any of the said persons shall reside, be hid, or protected, we do declare that the owners, masters, or inhabitants of the said places, to be confederates and traitors to the people, and the estates of them, as also of all the aforesaid persons, to be confiscated. This we, the commons of Virginia, do declare desiring a prime union amongst ourselves against the common enemy. And let not the faults of the guilty be the reproach of the innocent, or the faults of crimes of the oppressors divide and separate us, who have suffered by their oppressions.

These are therefore in his Majesty's name, to command you forthwith to seize the persons above mentioned as traitors to the king and country, and them to bring to Middle Plantation, and there to secure them, till further order, and in case of opposition, if you want any other assistance, you are forthwith to demand it in the name of the people of all the counties of Virginia.

[signed]   Nath Bacon, Gen'l.

By the Consent of the People.

Source: Nathaniel Bacon, "Manifesto Concerning the Troubles in Virginia," *Virginia Magazine of History and Biography* 1 (1894): 56–61.

Nathaniel Bacon's "Declaration of the People of Virginia" (1676)

In July 1676, rebel planter Nathaniel Bacon and his supporters issued the following declaration criticizing the administration of Virginia's royal governor, Sir William Berkeley. In the document, Bacon accuses Berkeley of governing on behalf of a privileged minority whose members control political office and economic power in the colony. Depicting himself as acting with the will and consent of the people, Bacon denounces the governor for levying unjust taxes, promoting unworthy favorites, and failing to defend the people from Indian raids. After issuing this Declaration, Bacon and his rebels attacked the heretofore friendly Pamunkey Indians and, in September, seized and burned Jamestown. Bacon's sudden death in October led to the rapid collapse of the rebellion.

1. For having, upon specious pretenses of public works, raised great unjust taxes upon the commonalty for the advancement of private favorites and other sinister ends, but no visible effects in any measure adequate; for not having, during this long time of his government, in any measure advanced this hopeful colony either by fortifications, towns, or trade.

2. For having abused and rendered contemptible the magistrates of justice by advancing to places of judicature scandalous and ignorant favorites.

3. For having wronged his Majesty's prerogative and interest by assuming monopoly of the beaver trade and for having in it unjust gain betrayed and sold his Majesty's country and the lives of his loyal subjects to the barbarous heathen.

4. For having protected, favored, and emboldened the Indians against his Majesty's loyal subjects, never contriving, requiring, or appointing any due or proper

means of satisfaction for their many invasions, robberies, and murders committed upon us.

5. For having, when the army of English was just upon the track of those Indians, who now in all places burn, spoil, murder and when we might with ease have destroyed them who then were in open hostility, for then having expressly countermanded and sent back our army by passing his word for the peaceable demeanor of the said Indians, who immediately prosecuted their evil intentions, committing horrid murders and robberies in all places, being protected by the said engagement and word past of him the said Sir William Berkeley, having ruined and laid desolate a great part of his Majesty's country, and have now drawn themselves into such obscure and remote places and are by their success so emboldened and confirmed by their confederacy so strengthened that the cries of blood are in all places, and the terror and consternation of the people so great, are now become not only difficult but a very formidable enemy who might at first with ease have been destroyed.

6. And lately, when, upon the loud outcries of blood, the assembly had, with all care, raised and framed an army for the preventing of further mischief and safeguard of this his Majesty's colony.

7. For having, with only the privacy of some few favorites without acquainting the people, only by the alteration of a figure, forged a commission, by we know not what hand, not only without but even against the consent of the people, for the raising and effecting civil war and destruction, which being happily and without bloodshed prevented; for having the second time attempted the same, thereby calling down our forces from the defense of the frontiers and most weakly exposed places.

8. For the prevention of civil mischief and ruin amongst ourselves while the barbarous enemy in all places did invade, murder, and spoil us, his Majesty's most faithful subjects.

Of this and the aforesaid articles we accuse Sir William Berkeley as guilty of each and every one of the same, and as one who has traitorously attempted, violated, and injured his Majesty's interest here by a loss of a great part of this his colony and many of his faithful loyal subjects by him betrayed and in a barbarous and shameful manner exposed to the incursions and murder of the heathen. And we do further declare these the ensuing persons in this list to have been his wicked and pernicious councilors, confederates, aiders, and assisters against the commonalty in these our civil commotions.

Sir Henry Chichley

Lieut. Coll. Christopher Wormeley

William Sherwood

William Claiburne Junior

Thomas Hawkins

Phillip Ludwell

John Page Clerke	Robert Beverley
John Cluffe Clerke	Richard Lee
John West	Thomas Ballard
Hubert Farrell	William Cole
Thomas Reade	Richard Whitacre
Matthew Kempe	Nicholas Spencer
Joseph Bridger	

John West, Hubert Farrell, Thomas Reade, Math. Kempe

And we do further demand that the said Sir William Berkeley with all the persons in this list be forthwith delivered up or surrender themselves within four days after the notice hereof, or otherwise we declare as follows.

That in whatsoever place, house, or ship, any of the said persons shall reside, be hid, or protected, we declare the owners, masters, or inhabitants of the said places to be confederates and traitors to the people and the estates of them is also of all the aforesaid persons to be confiscated. And this we, the commons of Virginia, do declare, desiring a firm union amongst ourselves that we may jointly and with one accord defend ourselves against the common enemy. And let not the faults of the guilty be the reproach of the innocent, or the faults or crimes of the oppressors divide and separate us who have suffered by their oppressions.

These are, therefore, in his Majesty's name, to command you forthwith to seize the persons above mentioned as traitors to the King and country and them to bring to Middle Plantation and there to secure them until further order, and, in case of opposition, if you want any further assistance you are forthwith to demand it in the name of the people in all the counties of Virginia.

Nathaniel Bacon
General by Consent of the people.
William Sherwood

Source: "Declaration of Nathaniel Bacon in the Name of the People of Virginia, July 30, 1676." *Massachusetts Historical Society Collections,* 4th series, vol. 9 (1871): 184–87.

Pueblo Revolt (1680)

> After eighty years of submissive resentment, the Pueblos had finally gone for the jugular.
>
> —Kessell, *Kiva, Cross, and Crown*, 1987, 228

Pueblo Indians of New Mexico had lived under Spanish rule since 1598 when Governor Juan de Oñate won the contract to settle New Mexico for the Spanish crown, to expand political and religious control beyond the confines of Mexico City and the Zacatecas mine. La Bufa, the Zacatecas silver mine, had effectively stopped the northward progression of Spanish interest in the late 1540s. But renewed interest to the far north resurfaced after a few illegal expeditions had meandered into New Mexico over 40 years after Francisco Vasquez de Coronado's exploratory expedition in 1540–1542 failed to find immediate wealth in the desert and mountainous regions of New Mexico. So in 1598, Governor Oñate led 129 soldier-colonists and their families, hired by him to join him on a settlement expedition to expand Spanish control and religion into what was called La Nueva México (short for La Nueva Ciudad de México, as they hoped to find the same wealth of Mexico City to the north). With them they brought 10,000 head of livestock, including horses, cattle, sheep, pigs, goats, and fowl, all with the intention of supporting the new colony amidst a Pueblo Indian population topping 50,000 (and untold numbers of nomadic peoples). Located some 1,500 miles north of Mexico City, through hostile Chichimeca Indian territory, and through a 90-mile stretch of desert referred to as *La Jornada del Muerto* ("Journey of the Dead Man," not journey of death as is so oftentimes incorrectly reported). The Spanish colonists, their Indian allies, and their livestock separated into several groups, miles between them, spreading out for days along what would later be known as El Camino Real de Tierra Adentro (the Royal Road to the Interior). They learned that through the jornada, which held precious little water, for their animals to get enough water, they would have to allow time for the springs to regenerate. This in turn made their band vulnerable to nomadic Indian attacks (which resulted from early illegal slave raiding expeditions by Nuño de Guzmán in the early 1500s near Arizona).

As they entered the Rio Grande Valley north of the jornada, they noticed the absence of Indians living in the villages that they encountered. They confiscated corn from one village, renaming it *Socorro* (meaning assistance or help in

Spanish), for they needed the sustenance. Pueblo Indians witnessed this theft, and word spread to the north that the invaders would take at will what they wanted. Pueblo Indians fled their villages to the hillsides to watch the Spanish trudge north. According to oral history, the people of Ohkay Owingeh (renamed San Juan Pueblo by the Spanish) took pity on the Spanish settlers, even to the point of giving up one of their villages for the families who had brought their children with them. The Spanish renamed the village San Gabriel de Yungue, and this interaction would be the beginning of an over-200-year, nearly constant association between the Pueblo Indians and the Spanish, who would continue to dominate their homelands until 1821.

Once at Ohkay Owingeh, the Spanish built an altar and thanked their Christian God, then immediately began enlisting Pueblo Indians to help them build an irrigation ditch so they could prepare fields to plant crops for the upcoming year. No doubt these fields, laying near the Río Chama and the Río Grande's confluence, lay on Pueblo Indian lands, but they could do little to convince the Spanish to leave. Perhaps they thought they were merely traveling through, without the intention of remaining; or perhaps they believed that they would stay for a short while. Pueblo Indians had a tradition of sharing resources with their neighbors in times of need, understanding that reciprocal sharing would occur if necessary. But the Spanish did not seem to be leaving; in fact, they became more entrenched as the years passed. Equally as frustrating involved demands made by one group of men who wore long dresses, referred to as friars, or fathers, by the Spanish people.

Oñate had a contract with the king and queen of Spain, required of all Spaniards interested with expanding into territories. His contract explicitly stated that he would finance the settlement expedition with private funds in the name of the Spanish Crown. He would pay the salaries and bring supplies for his settlers, as well as bring Franciscan missionaries to Christianize the Indians that they encountered. In repayment, he would become chief executive (governor), adjudicate cases that might arise, protect both Spanish and Pueblo Indian populations from potential enemies, and reap the financial rewards of the kingdom, among other things. He could also grant *encomiendas* (grants of Indian tribute, oftentimes incorrectly identified as grants of Indian labor—those were *repartimientos*—or Indian land). In other words, if he chose to reward his soldiers, they could get a written document that granted him (or her) permission to go to a particular pueblo and collect tribute biennially from a specified number of heads of households. Oftentimes, this involved a bushel of corn and a blanket per home twice a year; sometimes the grant included only half a pueblo, sometimes two pueblos. In return, the *encomendero* (grant holder) had to protect the pueblo from enemies and provide for their Christianization. It was colonial control divvied out among soldier-colonists, and the encomienda would lay at the heart of much Pueblo Indian anger.

Pueblo Indians already had their own religion, a very extensive and all-inclusive spiritualism that encompassed far more than just going to mass once a week (see the entry "Pueblo Religion"). Therefore, when the friars began to show up and demand Indian labor in building the missions, they balked. Unfortunately, they had little choice but to build the friar's missions, tend to his fields (if he happened to live among them in the cloister), and kiss his ring in submission. Luckily for the pueblo people, Oñate only brought a dozen friars, and far more Indian villages existed throughout New Mexico (which included everything north of El Paso del Norte until other borders became more defined). They likely appreciated Spanish protection against the Apache (Lipan Apache to the southeast and Western Apache groups to their south and west), but grew frustrated at the new body of Spanish laws to which they had to acquiesce, including prohibitions on Pueblo Indians putting together military responses, owning and using weaponry and horses, or even leaving their villages without permission. The Spanish had confined them to their villages, making traditional trips to the salt lakes, to the Plains for trading, and to the west along the Zuñi Trail, in essence, illegal.

Oñate failed in his attempt to, as John L. Kessell put it, "[m]ake New Mexico pay." In 1607, he resigned, declaring New Mexico a loss. While he and the majority of colonists suggested abandoning New Mexico, the Franciscans argued that they had converted 7,000 souls (likely an inflated number and based on baptisms, not actual conversions). So the crown decided to make New Mexico a royal colony, for they could not turn their backs on neophytes. Oñate remained in New Mexico until his replacement Pedro de Peralta arrived, but Peralta arrived with new problems. Friars believed that they had saved New Mexico from abandonment and wielded authority as if they had acquired the governorship of the region. Throughout the "Missionary Era" (1610–1680), a continuous clash occurred between civil and religious authorities in New Mexico, forcing Pueblo Indians and Spaniards to chose sides, and suffering the consequences of their choice (excommunication or lack of governmental support in terms of jobs, land grants, assistance with subsistence, and more).

But most frustrating to the Pueblo Indians was not just the increased pressure on them to convert to Christianity, but a new pressure to give up traditional ways. In the past, friars had their hands full, attempting to convert Indians to Christianity who had never before been exposed to these odd, nonnative belief systems. Indian pueblos far outnumbered friars, so some freedom to continue traditional spiritualism occurred due to the friar's absences as they visited other pueblos. By mid-century, the number of friars grew and their resolve became stronger; as a result, they began to clamp down on Pueblo Indian religions and moved throughout New Mexico, destroying kivas and ceremonial accouterments, and outlawing Pueblo Indian ceremonials. The mixed messages they received from the governor in 1661, who rather enjoyed Indian ceremonial dances, frustrated the Pueblo Indians even further.

By the 1660s, a drought intensified, causing Spanish and Pueblo Indian crops to fail. Raiding by nomadic tribes seemed to intensify, for they felt the impact of the drought on their ability to hunt and gather enough to sustain their families, too. The nomadic tribes also had acquired horses through raiding, becoming far more capable of running off with more booty, not just in grains, but in sheep and even human captives as well. The Spanish redoubled their efforts to control the Rio Grande corridor as the *encomenderos* traveled throughout their designated pueblo villages collecting more than their share of tribute. In fact, by the 1670s, stories circulated of Spanish *encomenderos* coming into Pueblo Indian villages and taking the last of the seed corn that the Indians had saved for the upcoming four or five years. The Pueblo women followed the Spanish wagons for miles, picking up and saving individual pieces of corn that had fallen through the slats of the wagons.

A few Pueblo Indians hatched plots to overthrow the Spanish authorities, most of which were discovered before the plan came to fruition, including Esteban Clemente, a much trusted governor of the Salinas Pueblos (Abó, Quarai, and Tavibo), villages located in the Manzano Mountains. He had served as a military lieutenant (atypical for an Indian), spoke Spanish, dressed as a Spaniard, and even professed to have converted to Christianity. In the 1660s, however, the Spanish uncovered his plot to drive all of the Spanish horses into the hills, then kill off all of the Spaniards until the last was dead. Apparently, he held wide authority across New Mexico among his fellow oppressed pueblo peoples. Summarily executed, Clemente's message would not die. The drought intensified and Pueblo Indians once began to realize that the Spanish god could not save them from the drought, nor the ensuing food shortages and illnesses that followed the drought. In some pueblos, over 450 died of hunger and disease, for epidemics circulated among New Mexico's residents who were more prone to succumb to illnesses due to stress, malnutrition, and increased demands on them for labor. Apache raids stepped up as well. By 1672, the Salinas pueblos were abandoned due to increased nomadic Indian attacks. Shortly thereafter, Governor Juan Francisco Treviño outlawed Pueblo congregations at kivas and ordered the remainder of kivas destroyed. Pueblo Indian identity centered on their spiritualism, however, so their reaction is not surprising. A growing movement rejected Christianity and joined their fellow tribal members who had always remained true to their traditional spiritualism. Their gods had never allowed them to suffer as the Christian god had. So secretly, they retreated to their kivas that had not been destroyed, continued with their ceremonial dances, and returned to beating their drums, singing their songs, and trying to restore the balance that had been lost.

But the Spanish had lived in their world for more than 80 years and established relationships with Hispanized Indians among them, and soon the Treviño learned that Fray Andrés Durán and several of his relatives believed that Indian sorcerers had bewitched him. Treviño, angered that Pueblo religious leaders had refused to turn their back on traditionalism, in 1675 rounded up 47 people that the friars and their allies identified as "sorcerers." Brought to Santa Fé, these Pueblo Indians found themselves belittled, ridiculed, and charged with sorcery. Treviño sentenced four to death by hanging (one committed suicide before the sentence could be carried out), which incensed the pueblo community. Seventy warriors forced their way into his abode and threatened to kill him and his dependents and incite a broad rebellion if the rest were not set free. The rest had been publicly beaten and whipped, but in the end Treviño acquiesced and sent them home as an example that the Spanish government would not tolerate sorcery. He had unwittingly averted a major rebellion, for Pueblo Indian warriors had scattered about the hills above Santa Fé, awaiting orders.

One of those "sorcerers," an Ohkay Owingeh (San Juan) spiritual elder, returned home to his village to plot revenge. The Spanish minister of government and war under Treviño and the new governor, Antonio de Otermín, however, found out about his brooding and plotting. Pohé-yemo astutely moved north to Taos, far from the tentacles of Spanish authority. He retreated into a kiva and, according to oral history, word spread among the pueblos that while in the kiva, he encountered and was counseled by three key deities of pueblo cosmology. They told him that he needed to lead a rebellion that would eliminate the Spanish from their homelands, but that they must return to traditional ways—destroying all that the Spanish had brought with them: buildings, livestock, missions, and even seeds. For the "God of the Spaniards was worth nothing and theirs was very strong, the Spaniard's God being rotten wood." (Knaut 1995, 168). With the assistance of numerous other tribal war and religious leaders from San Ildefonso, Picurís, San Lorenzo, Taos, Jemez, Pecos, Tesuque, Santa Clara, and Santo Domingo, Pohé-yemo (more commonly known as Popé), began orchestrating a plan to remove the Spanish and destroy all that they had brought. The revolt would begin on August 12, 1680. To keep the Spanish from finding out, Popé and the others observed the strictest secrecy. When it came time to notify other pueblos of the plot, he sent runners out under the pain of death to keep the secret if they were apprehended by Spanish authorities. Moreover, the *quipo*, or knotted cord that indicated which day the revolt should occur (by untying a knot every day), and instructions were to be accepted and the rebellion agreed to by each village on pain of death. When he held meetings, he held them only during feast days at pueblo villages that he believed to be sympathetic, that no one would question a gathering of so many Pueblo men. At one point, Pohé-yemo learned that his own son-in-law, governor of Ohkay Owingeh Pueblo, had found out about the plot, and Pohé-yemo had him assassinated.

When two of the runners were apprehended and told all they knew, confirmed by the governors of la Ciénega, San Marcos, and San Cristobál (who refused to participate in the rebellion), the Spanish recognized immediately that a rebellion could occur at any moment. When Pohé-yemo learned of the leak, he moved the rebellion up to August 10, 1680. With the killing of Padre Juan Pío at Tesuque village, the Pueblo Revolt began. Pueblos rose up all over the Río Grande corridor, cutting down individual Spaniards where they found them. Whole families were slaughtered out of anger and frustration and travelers were cut down, but the friars suffered the most humiliating and excruciatingly painful deaths. Not all pueblos supported the killing of their friars, however. At San Felipe Pueblo, downriver from Cochití, Pueblos encountered a padre fleeing downriver from the violence. They took him in, and hid him. Realizing that he was not safe in their village, they took him to a mesatop, where they sequestered him from the violence in the valley below. Going without water for days, oral history reports that he performed a miracle by causing water to gush forth from a rock. Therefore, examples of Indians protecting the lives of friars do exist.

As news began to spread of the atrocities committed against the Spanish settlers, those who could gathered up what they could and rushed to Santa Fé in the north or Isleta Pueblo in the south. For jurisdictional purposes, the governor had divided New Mexico into two districts, the Río Arriba (the upper river, above Cochití Pueblo) and the Río Abajo (lower river, including all south to El Paso del Norte) which had a headquarters in Isleta Pueblo. They hoped that their sheer numbers would protect them against the brutality and wrath of the pueblo people. On their journeys, they encountered horrific scenes of death (animals and humans) and destruction of homes, orchards, and fields. Upon arriving in Santa Fé, they began to understand the extent of the revolt. The governor quickly realized the gravity of the situation and attempted to get word to Isleta Pueblo and the other Spaniards to the south. The Pueblo Indians quickly surrounded Santa Fé and began hollering threats, taunting the Spanish by shouting that God and Santa María were dead, and that their god whom they had always obeyed had never died. They had clearly turned their backs on the Christian god who let them down, and they quickly diverted the water to Santa Fé.

Pueblo Indians continued arriving at Santa Fé, setting fire to buildings and infiltrating the outskirts of town. On August 20, confronted by his colonists who were in mourning for the friends and family they had lost and the desperate situation in which they found themselves without food and water, and under constant threat of attack, Governor Otermín broke out of the city walls and broke the siege. He received wounds on his face and chest from arrows and gunshots, but when the

Spanish had once again retreated behind the gates, they had captured 47 Pueblo men. Interrogating them at length, the governor fully understood that he had lost New Mexico. He began to plan for retreat to El Paso del Norte, to recuperate, request more troops, and rebuild his forces to return and take New Mexico militarily. In the meantime, his charges suffered, and they began to plan for the long and difficult journey south—not knowing if the Pueblos would harass them the entire way or if they would be allowed to leave unencumbered. They had lost most of their horses and oxen, they had few wagons, and those who had made it to Santa Fé barely had enough clothing for the cold desert nights, but they had no other choice. Two days later, Otermín led his people from Santa Fé, hoping to gather themselves up with the rest of the survivors in Isleta Pueblo in the Río Abajo.

In Isleta, however, the southern survivors had also heard rumors of the brutality throughout the province, especially in the north, and within just over a week, heard that all of the Spaniards to the north had been killed. Realizing the futility of remaining, they gathered up what they could and began the long trek south along the Camino Real de la Tierra Adentro that had brought Juan de Oñate and the first settlers north nearly 100 years before. Little did they know that a motley crew of ragged survivors were slowly making their way south, along the northern reaches of the Camino Real. Along the way, they witnessed the carnage: whole families lay dead, naked, and beaten, some at the doorways to their homes.

Four hundred of their fellow Spaniards had perished in the first few days of the revolt, including 21 of the 32 friars in the province. It was a devastating blow to a far-flung province of New Spain. At Sandía Pueblo, just north of what would become la Villa Real de Alburquerque (1706), the mission had been destroyed and the vestments scattered about. Piles of excrement lay on the altar, defiling the sanctity of the mission. Spaniards saw bodies strewn about at ranches, men and women beaten and stripped naked, homes and barns and fields on fire. Relatives they had to leave behind, hoping that the Pueblo Indians watching them from the mesa tops as they left chose to remain in waiting, and not swoop down on them for one final blow. But the Pueblo Indians were not interested in killing more Spaniards; instead, they wanted them gone from their province so they could return to their traditional ways.

When the Spanish arrived at Isleta Pueblo, they were dismayed to learn that the survivors had already left for El Paso del Norte, the southernmost outpost of New Mexico. Otermín sent messengers ahead to ask the other survivors to await them before entering into the Jornada del Muerto. Gathering together, they headed south for El Paso, where they would establish camp until such time as they could reconquer the apostate province. As they arrived, they encountered Father Ayeta, who had come too late with reinforcements (mostly convicts) to assist the colony. Disheartened by the prospects of reporting to the viceroy, Otermín quickly reconstituted his rabble into a community and began reorganizing for a mission to reconquer New Mexico the following year.

Meanwhile in New Mexico, the Pueblo people celebrated their victory and began the long process of destroying all remnants of Spanish authority and dominance. They first went after the churches, and the enormous mission at Pecos served as an example of the wrath of the pueblos against the demands of the friars. First, they set the wood on fire, the altar, doors, and roof. The fire raged with such intensity that the front doors blew outwards, but because the building was made of adobe, the fire died and the bricks still stood. So they scaled the walls and, one by one, began knocking the bricks off the tops of the walls until they tired of the task. Throughout New Mexico, they destroyed and defiled churches, burned homes, ran off livestock, burned fields, cut down orchards, and destroyed documents in Santa Fé. Their rage, acquired over the past few generations, culminated in the attempted destruction of all things Spanish. To encourage them, Pohé-yemo circulated among the Pueblo villages, reminding them what the gods had told him. He demanded that they destroy all tools, seeds, livestock, and buildings, everything they had gained from Spanish trade. He demanded that they go down to the river and wash off their baptisms with yucca and water from their sacred rivers. But he began to meet resistance. He even started to make demands upon the villages he encountered, as if they owed him for his leadership. According to Spanish sources based on interviews during Otermín's attempted reconquest in 1681, Pohé-yemo demanded tribute and carried an arrogance of authority. Very shortly, Luis Tupatú, war captain of Picurís Pueblo, renounced and removed him from power.

For the next several years, the Pueblo Indians attempted to survive in a world without Spanish influence. But with the Spanish, they took their guns and horses, and their military power. Very quickly, the Apache and Navajo saw the confusion that resulted from the removal of the colonial authority and the deteriorating condition of the pueblo coalition. They were joined by the newly arrived Comanche and Ute, who arrived in the region in the late 1600s and early 1700s from the northern Plains and the Plateau region (respectively). The drought did not let up immediately, and the pueblos continued to suffer.

South in El Paso, Otermín's attempted reconquest failed, and he was quickly replaced by a new governor, Domingo Jironza Petris de Cruzate in 1683 (1683–1686, 1689–1691). Jironza rallied forces and attempted to reconquer New Mexico in 1688, making it as far north as Zía Pueblo, sacking and destroying it. From Zía, he took captives that he brought to El Paso for questioning. Perhaps the most information about the post-revolt confusion comes from Bartolomé de Ojeda, a Zía man who shared what he knew about the revolt with his captors. Fluent in Spanish, Ojeda informed the Spanish about post-revolt New Mexico, the disarray that had developed, the continued Apache and Navajo raids, and the disillusionment of the people with Pohé-yemo and Tupatú's authority.

Shortly after Jironza's attempted reconquest, New Mexico once again broke into disarray. Several Pueblos rejected Tupatú's authority, and Pohé-yemo once again rose to authority, only to be deposed again and likely killed before 1692. Jironza attempted to gain yet another appointment as governor, but he lost out to Don Diego de Vargas (1691–1701, 1703–1704), who arrived just in time to lead an expedition into New Mexico in 1692. He successfully marched all the way to Santa Fé, where he confronted the apostates and demanded a meeting. He entered the gates of Santa Fé without weapons and only a friar at his side. He negotiated a settlement whereby the Spanish would return the following year. During his expedition, he visited numerous pueblos and gained their assurances that they would welcome the Spanish. Standing in as godfather to many whose parents requested baptisms for their children, Vargas secured his position as a "member" of the community with reciprocal responsibilities.

In El Paso, he mustered his forces, colonists, and supplies, and in 1693, he headed north for the last time. Upon arriving in Santa Fé, however, the Pueblo Indians refused to vacate the capital, and Vargas set up camp outside the walls, hoping to negotiate their removal. As winter set in and the colonists began to shiver in the cold Santa Fé winds, he laid siege to Santa Fé—much as had the inhabitants 13 years before—and forced them out. They reoccupied the capital and reestablished Spanish authority in New Mexico once and for all. While they faced intermittent violence among some of the pueblos, by 1696, the Pueblo Revolt had officially ended. Vargas had successfully reconquered a willing New Mexico population. Instead of subservience, encomiendas, demands of tribute, the inability of pueblos to defend themselves or leave at will, and forced conversion to Catholicism, new rules applied. Accommodation would be the goals of the new administration.

—*Sandra K. Mathews*

See also all entries under Pima Revolt (1751); Pontiac's Rebellion (1763); Flight of the Nez Percé (1877); Wounded Knee I (1890); Alcatraz Island Occupation (1969–1971); Trail of Broken Treaties (1972); Wounded Knee II (1973).

Further Reading

Chávez, Frey Angélico. "Pohé-yemo's Representative and the Pueblo Revolt of 1680." *New Mexico Historical Review* 42, no. 2 (1967): 85–126.

Espinosa, José Manuel. *Crusaders of the Río Grande: The Story of Don Diego de Vargas and the Reconquest and Refounding of New Mexico*. Chicago: Institute of Jesuit History, 1942.

Hackett, Charles Wilson, and Charmion C. Shelby, eds. and trans. *Revolt of the Pueblo Indians of New Mexico and Otermín's Attempted Reconquest, 1680–1682*. 2 vols. Albuquerque: University of New Mexico Press, 1942.

Kessell, John L. *Spain in the Southwest: A Narrative History of Colonial New Mexico, Arizona, Texas, and California*. Norman: University of Oklahoma Press, 2002.

Kessell, John L., ed. *Remote beyond Compare: Letters of Don Diego de Vargas to His Family from New Spain and New Mexico, 1675–1706*. Albuquerque: University of New Mexico Press, 1989.

Kessell, John L. *Kiva, Cross, and Crown: The Pecos Indians and New Mexico, 1540–1840*. Albuquerque: University of New Mexico Press, 1987.

Kessell, John L., and Rick Hendricks, eds. *By Force of Arms: The Journals of Don Diego de Vargas, 1691–1693*. Albuquerque: University of New Mexico Press, 1992.

Knaut, Andrew L. *The Pueblo Revolt of 1680: Conquest and Resistance in Seventeenth-Century New Mexico*. Norman: University of Oklahoma Press, 1995.

Ortiz, Alfonso. *The Pueblo*. New York: Chelsea House Publishers, 1994.

Sánchez, Jane C. "Spanish-Indian Relations during the Otermín Administration, 1677–1683." *New Mexico Historical Review* 58, no. 2 (April 1983): 133–152.

Sando, Joe. *Pueblo Nations: Eight Centuries of Pueblo Indian History*. Santa Fé, NM: Clear Light Publishers, 1992.

Simmons, Marc. *New Mexico: An Interpretive History*. New York: Norton, 1977.

Twitchell, Ralph Emerson. *The Leading Facts of New Mexico History*. Volume 1. Albuquerque, NM: Horn & Wallace Publishers, 1963.

Weber, David J. *The Spanish Frontier in North America*. New Haven, CT: Yale University Press, 1992.

Weber, David J., ed. *What Caused the Pueblo Revolt of 1680: Readings*. Selected and Introduced by David J. Weber. Historians at Work Series. Boston: Bedford/St. Martins, 1999.

Franciscans (1209–Present)

A Catholic religious order based on the life of St. Francis de Assisi (1181–1226), the Franciscans are best known for their obligation to "poverty of disposition." In other words, they could not own property as individuals or as a community (although variations do occur within the various divisions of Franciscans). The first Franciscans arrived in the New World in 1523, and many became avid spokespersons for the Indian people.

A primary historical focus for Franciscans involved missionary work and preaching, yet they also have served as confessors, ambassadors, mediators, and inquisitors. Dressed in a habit of brown, tied by a distinctive white cord, they traveled throughout colonial landscapes wearing sandals or barefoot. Rarely did they ride beasts of burden. Their method of travel, in fact, frustrated numerous Spanish explorers as they traveled into New Spain's northern interior.

The first Franciscan to venture into the American West, Fray Marcos de Niza, traveled in 1539 on foot in sandals, much to the consternation of his guide, Esteban. After much haranguing, Fray Marcos allowed his guide to hurry ahead, but to send back signs of his discoveries. Before being killed by the Zuni Indians, Esteban had sent a sign indicating a great find. Fray Marcos hurried to peak over a ridge as the setting sun shined on Hawikuh in western New Mexico, and returned to Mexico City to report on the city of great wealth. The following year, he guided the first expedition into New Mexico under Francisco Vasquez de Coronado. Finding no wealthy city, Coronado sent the first Franciscan back to Mexico City to explain his lies.

When Juan de Oñate came to New Mexico in 1598, the Franciscans joined his colonization effort—salaries paid by the Spanish Crown. Since the Pope had granted Spain a *Patronato Real*, the king had almost complete control over the Catholic Church in the New World. By 1607 when New Mexico failed to produce any immediate wealth, the Franciscans convinced the king that they had Christianized over 7,000 Pueblo Indians. For the next 80 years, New Mexico became a missionary colony. Franciscans would engage in missionary efforts in Texas after 1700, Arizona in 1767 (after the Jesuits were removed), and California in 1769.

They served the Spanish populations as priests, the Indians as missionaries, and some served the Holy Office of the Inquisition. Often living among Indians, they brought new seeds and livestock for the Indians to master. They made the tribes build their missions, monasteries, and granaries, and attempted to convert them to the Catholic faith.

Some regions had a checkered past. In California, Spanish authorities forced *Ranchería* Indians to live in consolidated missions. Disease spread rapidly exacerbated by a different diet, dissention broke out, and some authorities forced them to work in *obrajes* (sweatshops). Mortality rates soared.

While the experience in Texas was devastating to Indians in other ways, the friars spread the faith through missions by enticing poorly defended tribal groups into missions stretching outward from San Antonio. The Indians there purportedly appreciated the protection that the Spanish offered; moreover, they learned key elements of farming, irrigation, and dam building, and instituted new crops. Some of those tribes melded into the local populations and, in essence, seemed to disappear as individually recognizable tribes.

In New Mexico leading up to the Pueblo Revolt of 1680, the Franciscans began destroying all Pueblo Indian religious sites (kivas in particular) and ceremonial accouterments, and outlawing Indian ceremonies (see Pueblo Revolt). The Pueblo Indians rose up against the Franciscans in New Mexico and succeeded in forcing the Spanish out of their homeland—even if for only 12 years. Of the 32 Franciscans in New Mexico, 21 were killed—many of them in the most humiliating and violent ways. Pueblo Indians defiled the missions that the Franciscans had forced them to build.

Upon returning in 1692, the Franciscans allowed syncretization of Catholicism with native beliefs. The Franciscans never had enough missionaries to succeed in their task, and by the early 1800s, missionaries were not replaced and at times, only one Franciscan tended the entire population of New Mexico—leading to the rise of the *Hermanos Penitentes*. By the 1820s, Mexico called for the secularization of missions. In the end, the Franciscans succeeded in converting thousands of Indians who today still practice Catholicism (and some, also their traditional beliefs).

—Sandra K. Mathews

Further Reading

Bandelier, Adolph F. *The Discovery of New Mexico by the Franciscan Monk Friar Marcos de Niza in 1539*. Translated, edited, and with an introduction by Madeleine Turrell Rodack. Tucson: University of Arizona Press, 1981.

Chipman, Donald. *Spanish Texas: 1519–1821*. Austin: University of Texas Press, 1992.

Jackson, Robert H., and Edward Castillo. *Indians, Franciscans, and Spanish Colonization: The Impact of the Mission System on California Indians*. Albuquerque: University of New Mexico Press, 1996.

Kessell, John L. *Spain in the Southwest: A Narrative History of Colonial New Mexico, Arizona, Texas, and California*. Norman: University of Oklahoma Press, 2002.

Weber, David J. *The Spanish Frontier in North America*. New Haven, CT: Yale University Press, 1994.

Oñate, Juan de (c. 1552–1626)

Born the son of a wealthy silver miner from Zacatecas, New Spain, Juan de Oñate became the first European to establish a permanent colonial settlement in what would become the United States of America in 1598. He won the contract to settle northern New Spain from the Spanish king, who forbade any exploration or settlement without a contract and culpability. Funded mostly out of his own pocket and by investors, Oñate hoped to find great wealth as Mexico City had yielded.

For his contract, he was to recruit then arm and equip 200 soldier-colonists—all of whom had to abide by the Colonization Laws of 1573 that demanded peaceful and charitable expansion and to avoid any conflict with Indian people unless in self-defense. Oñate supplied 10,000 head of livestock, food, gear, clothing, farming equipment and seed, trade goods, medicines, and other supplies for their arduous 1,500-mile trek north from Mexico City. His contract stipulated he would receive the titles of governor (including civil and criminal jurisdiction), captain-general, and *adelantado* (economic power). He could give out land grants and *encomiendas* (grants of Indian tribute with responsibilities to Christianize and protect), and he drew a small salary from the royal coffers. The crown furnished five friars and a lay priest to accompany him and convert the Indian people.

While many of the Rio Grande Indian villages had been abandoned since Francisco Vasquez de Coronado's visit in 1540–1542, New Mexico's Indian population perhaps topped 60,000. Arriving along the *Camino Real de la Tierra Adentro* (royal road to the interior), they traveled through mountains, a 90-mile stretch of desert, and along the Rio Grande again until they reached Okey-Owinge village. Here they immediately set up an altar, thanked God, and began digging an *acequia* (ditch) with the assistance of the Indians so they would have crops the following year.

Within months, Oñate and several dozen men headed west to find the Sea of Cortez, potentially a less dangerous and shorter resupply route from Mexico City. Along the way, Acoma Pueblo enticed some of the soldiers to ascend their mesa for supplies, then killed 8 of the 13. Oñate realized that he could not let the act go unpunished with so many tribes surrounding them. After consulting with the colonists, Oñate called for a brutal campaign, *guerra de sangre y fuego* (war by blood and fire), against the Acoma people. His nephew and 70 men laid siege to Acoma, and in the ensuing battle killed more than 600 Acoma Indians. They marched the surviving Indians to Santo Domingo Pueblo to stand trial for killing Spaniards. Found guilty, Oñate intended his sentence to scare the other pueblos. The 24 men over age 25 would have a foot cut off and serve 20 years of personal servitude. The rest of the people over 12 years of age were condemned to 20 years

Statue of the Spanish conqueror Juan de Oñate (1550–1630), who established the colony of New Mexico for Spain. (Advanced Source Productions)

of personal servitude. Children would be distributed to friars for Christian upbringing. Within a year, most Acomas had escaped servitude and returned home (except for the 60 girls sent to monasteries in Mexico City).

Oñate immediately continued searching for mines, but the raids from Apache and Navajo Indians, continued unease between Pueblo and Spanish settler, frustration and attempted abandonment by settlers, and lack of financial rewards caused Oñate to give up in 1607. He left New Mexico to the Franciscans, who claimed to have baptized 7,000 Indians, and headed to Mexico City to defend himself at his *residencia* ("trial" held at the terminus of a term to determine whether he had broken any laws). Oñate was found guilty of 12 charges, among them using excessive force against Acoma, being a poor example by committing adultery, and execution of two of his men (for desertion). He was exiled from New Mexico forever, forced to live in Mexico City for four years, fined, and forced to pay court costs. His honor destroyed, he spent the next nearly 20 years seeking exoneration—even to the Council of the Indies and two kings. Finally, by 1623, he was exonerated, and two years later, the king appointed him to the most-sought-after and prestigious Military Order of Santiago, proving that he had transcended above his disgrace from the New Mexico venture. The following year, he died.

—Sandra K. Mathews

Further Reading

Ayer, Mrs. Edward E. *The Memorial of Fray Alonzo de Benavides*. Albuquerque, NM: Horn and Wallace, 1965.

Hammond, George P. *Don Juan de Oñate and the Founding of New Mexico: A New Investigation into the Early History of New Mexico*. Santa Fé, NM: Quivira Society, 1927.

Kessell, John L. *Spain in the Southwest: A Narrative History of Colonial New Mexico, Arizona, Texas, and California*. Norman: University of Oklahoma Press, 2002.

Simmons, Marc. *The Last Conquistador: Juan de Oñate and the Settling of the Far Southwest*. Norman: University of Oklahoma Press, 1991.

Weber, David J. *The Spanish Frontier in North America*. New Haven, CT: Yale University Press, 1994.

Otermin, Antonio de (dates unknown)

Governor of New Mexico from 1678 until 1682, Antonio de Otermin oversaw the worst loss that the Spanish ever experienced in the colonial world: New Mexico following the Pueblo Revolt of 1680. But the New Mexico that Otermin inherited was already on the verge of collapse. Uprisings had occurred in the 1670s, as well as a serious drought that led to famine and diseases rampaging through communities. To make things worse, the Franciscan friars had lost their tolerance for Pueblo Indian ceremonies and begun destroying ceremonial accoutrements and sacred sites. Serious disagreements between the religious and civil authorities grew, and colonists and Pueblo Indians were caught in the midst.

For months, New Mexico's governor and town council had pleaded with Mexico City to resupply the colony and send reinforcements. Finally, in February 1677, they acquiesced, sending a new governor, Antonio de Otermin, as well. The governor quickly established two defensive outposts at key points along the trail.

When Otermin first heard of the Pueblo Indian uprising that began on August 10, 1680, he sent Lieutenant Governor and Maestro de campo Francisco Gomez Robledo and a well-armed contingent to investigate the rumors. The reports could not have been worse. They found that angry Pueblo Indians had brutally killed Spaniards all over New Mexico, defiled churches, and burned homes.

Scared colonists heard the chants of the enraged Pueblo Indians shouting that "now God and Santa Maria were dead . . . and that their own God whom they obeyed never died" (Kessell 2002, 121). The revolt had moved quickly throughout the Rio Grande Valley, and Otermin had to make a decision. There was no turning back.

Barricaded inside the defensive walls of Santa Fé, Otermin held out hope that he could muster enough survivors and retake New Mexico. Nearly a thousand arrived, but as the days wore on, the pueblos laid siege to Santa Fé, cutting the ditch carrying water into Santa Fé. The Indians overran what they could, set fire to the church, and ridiculed Catholicism.

On August 20, 10 days after the revolt had begun, Otermin broke the siege. Despite serious injuries sustained (flesh wounds on his face and a gunshot to his chest), he evacuated Santa Fé and headed south where he hoped to reunite with Lt. Gov. Robledo, who was to wait for him in Isleta Pueblo. But when he arrived, the southern contingent was already gone—having heard the pueblos had killed all the Spaniards in the north. Picking up the pace, Otermin reunited the survivors and continued their march south. The Pueblo Indians watched them go.

Upon his arrival in La Salineta (across from El Paso del Norte) on September 18, they encountered two dozen wagons filled with supplies, thanks to Father Ayeta—too late. La Salineta would be their home for the next 12 years. Immediately, he began to investigate what had happened. The survivors numbered fewer than 2,000; 21 of the 32 friars had been executed; and over 380 Spaniards lay dead, some stripped naked and left for the coyotes.

Popé, the revolt's instigator, demanded that the Indians destroy all things Spanish (homes, churches, livestock, seeds, papers, etc.), but not all pueblos agreed and, in fact, hid religious items from destruction. Otermin hoped to bank on that sentiment, and in 1681, he led his men into New Mexico. He failed to bring New Mexico back under the fold of the Spanish Crown and, in a desperate request sent via Father Ayeta to Mexico City, he begged, "Do everything you possibly can to get me out of here" (Kessell 2002, 152). As he waited, his health began to fail, and in August 1683, his replacement Don Domingo Jironza Petriz de Cruzate relieved him of New Mexico's governorship.

—*Sandra K. Mathews*

Further Reading

Bancroft, Hubert Howe. *History of the North Mexican States and Texas*. 2 vols. San Francisco: History Company, 1886, 1889.

Hackett, Charles Wilson. *Revolt of the Pueblo Indians of New Mexico and Otermin's Attempted Reconquest 1680–1682*. Albuquerque: University of New Mexico Press, 1942.

Kessell, John L. *Spain in the Southwest: A Narrative History of Colonial New Mexico, Arizona, Texas, and California*. Norman: University of Oklahoma Press, 2002.

Knaut, Andrew L. *The Pueblo Revolt of 1680: Conquest and Resistance in Seventeenth-Century New Mexico.* Norman: University of Oklahoma Press, 1995.

Weber, David J. *The Spanish Frontier in North America.* New Haven, CT: Yale University Press, 1994.

Weber, David J., ed. *What Caused the Pueblo Revolt of 1680?* New York: Bedford/St. Martins, 1999.

Popé (dates unknown)

Popé is one of the least-known leaders of a major revolt, certainly in what became the United States, and more broadly, in the Americas. After the Spanish retook New Mexico in 1692 under the leadership of Don Diego de Vargas, a native of Spain, Popé had already died. Therefore, the only information that survived about Popé came from interviews with participants of the Pueblo Revolt, which began officially on August 10, 1680, in Tesuque when Pueblo Indians killed Padre Juan Pio.

Often known as Pohé-yemo, sources explain that Popé lived in San Juan Pueblo, in northern New Mexico. He served his community as a respected and unyielding religious leader, but found himself rounded up by the Spanish authorities in 1675 in response to the Franciscan friars' desire to squelch Pueblo Indian religions once and for all. They believed they had reason not to trust even those Pueblos who had most closely affiliated with Spaniards—for in the Tompiro Pueblos to the south in the Rio Abajo (lower river, or the southern two-thirds of New Mexico), a well-trusted and Christianized Pueblo Indian governor of the Salinas Pueblos, who had also served as a lieutenant in the Pueblo Indian auxiliaries, had attempted to lead a general rebellion against the Spanish colonists in the 1660s. Authorities uncovered the plot and summarily executed Clemente, only to find in his home a stash of traditional spiritual accoutrements, and learned of his intention to leave not a Spaniard alive in the province. Tensions and fear continued to mount, as friars redoubled their efforts to eliminate all traces of Pueblo Indian spiritualism from the province. In 1675, Pohé-yemo, along with 46 other Pueblo Indians, were brought to Santa Fé and put on trial for being sorcerers. Found guilty, the Spanish authorities sentenced four of them to death by hanging (one purportedly committed suicide before the hangings could proceed) and publicly whipped and humiliated the rest. Allowed to return home, they bore physical and psychological scars that helped lead to the revolt of 1680.

Pohé-yemo retreated first to his home in San Juan, but then after threats from authorities, he sequestered himself in the farthermost pueblo of Taos, hoping to

44 | Pueblo Revolt (1680)

Statue of Popé, Tewa spiritual leader and organizer of the Pueblo Revolt in 1680. No image or written description of Popé is known to exist. This depiction, by New Mexico artist Cliff Fragua, shows him holding the knotted cord that was used to determine when the revolt would begin. (Architect of the Capitol)

get as far from the tentacles of Spanish authority as possible. For the next five years, Pohé-yemo plotted revenge. Overcautious in his deliberations, fearful that the Spanish would uncover this plot too, Pohé-yemo kept his deliberations secret in one of the Taos kivas—purportedly meeting with three key dieties from Pueblo cosmology who helped him plot revenge. Other Pueblo leaders joined him, including men from the pueblos of San Ildefonso, Picurís, San Lorenzo, Taos, Jemez, Pecos, Tesuque, Santa Clara, and Santo Domingo. Popé feared the discovery of his plot so much that he called for the assassination of his own son-in-law, who had learned about the plans for a region-wide rebellion.

According to reports, after the Spanish left and before 1682, Luis Tupatú deposed Popé. Popé disappeared from the record until 1688, when he deposed Tupatú. Many of the pueblos rejected his authority, and a general uprising occurred during which Popé was likely killed. Pohé-yemo, or Popé, led the Pueblo Indians on the greatest rebellion in the Americas, and the only successful rebellion by indigenous peoples that ended in the complete eviction of their colonial oppressors.

—*Sandra K. Mathews*

Further Reading

Chávez, Frey Angélico. "Pohé-yemo's Representative and the Pueblo Revolt of 1680." New *Mexico Historical Review* 42, no. 2 (1967): 85–126.

Hackett, Charles Wilson, and Charmion C. Shelby, eds. and trans. *Revolt of the Pueblo Indians of New Mexico and Otermín's Attempted Reconquest, 1680–1682*. 2 vols. Albuquerque: University of New Mexico Press, 1942.

Kessell, John L. *Spain in the Southwest: A Narrative History of Colonial New Mexico, Arizona, Texas, and California*. Norman: University of Oklahoma Press, 2002.

Knaut, Andrew L. *The Pueblo Revolt of 1680: Conquest and Resistance in Seventeenth-Century New Mexico*. Norman: University of Oklahoma Press, 1995.

Weber, David J. *The Spanish Frontier in North America*. New Haven, CT: Yale University Press, 1992.

Weber, David J., ed. *What Caused the Pueblo Revolt of 1680: Readings*. Selected and Introduced by David J. Weber. Historians at Work Series. Boston: Bedford/St. Martins, 1999.

Pueblo Religions

Pueblo Indian spiritualism is very different than the Western notion of "religion"; rather, it is all inclusive that requires observance 24 hours a day and seven days a week. There is no single "Pueblo Religion" that encompasses all of the 19 New Mexico Pueblos, or the Hopi Pueblo in Arizona, yet several key similarities can be gleaned. Primarily, Pueblo Indians have a universal belief that all things created by the creator, or as Joe Sando (Jemez Pueblo) writes, "the Great One," have a spirit. This Great One is omnipresent, yet this omnipresence does not carry the same connotation as the Christian god. In fact, Sando writes that in no pueblo tongue is there a word for "religion."

A general belief among pueblos, indeed among many native tribes, involves the belief in the spiritualism that emanates throughout the earth, sky, water, all plants and animals, and all things. They do not believe they have dominion over the Great One's creations, but rather that they are merely a part of a balance that exists as a result of the respect and deference that they show the earth and all creation. This included periods in which Indian people needed to utilize the resources of the land.

Therefore, when a Pueblo Indian needed to hunt, he would first ask permission from the animal to offer up its life for the sustenance of the human. That animal would be treated with the utmost respect according to long-standing spiritual traditions before, during, and in its preparations after the kill. Every time a hunt, or illnesses, drought, battle, or other abnormal event occurred, balance had to be restored. Prayer, ceremony, song, or offering helped provide this balance. They also believed that plants had spiritual components as well. Tree branches, in particular fir trees, played a key role in ceremonial dances, held at various intervals throughout the year. Any part of the natural world taken and not used would be returned to the land in some fashion (branches burned, placed in fields, or given to the river, all of which allowed the branch to return to the earth from whence it came). In fact, traditionalist native peoples maintain a rather rigorous spiritual and ceremonial schedule, to preserve their spiritual connection to Mother Earth and Father Sky (for ceremonies that outsiders may attend, see the Indian Pueblo Cultural Center at http://www.indianpueblo.org).

Songs (in particular drumming and singing), stories, and dances played an integral role in the ceremonial dances ritualized in the numerous pueblo communities. These had been passed down for innumerable generations, sometimes by gender, family, or clan. Social and spiritual organization therefore also played a key role in their spiritualism. Traditionally a matrilineal people, Pueblo Indians passed their clan "totem" (corn, turkey, cloud, gopher, to name a few) through the mother's family, and with clan came a host of stories and obligations that were shared orally from mother to child. Because one could not marry within their own clan, obligations crossed family lines and bonded the community together. Furthermore, clans served important functions within the spiritual system of obligation within a community, and provided the basis for the moiety (a grouping of specific clans). In some pueblos, moieties were divided celestially by the solstices: the winter or northern moiety took over leadership of the tribe and ceremonial functions during the winter months, and the summer or southern moiety took their turn during the summer period.

Pueblo spiritualism was confronted by the Spanish, Mexicans, and Americans, and, up until the 1970s, continued to survive despite these outsiders' best efforts to destroy it. For a complete understanding of the Pueblo spiritualism, the importance of clans, spacial organization of spiritualism and ceremony, and more, the best source is Elsie Clews Parsons's two-volume *Pueblo Religion*.

—*Sandra K. Mathews*

Further Reading
Hodge, Frederick Webb. "Pueblo Indian Clans." *The American Anthropologist* 9 (October 1896): 345–353.

Ortiz, Alfonso. *The Tewa World: Space, Time, Being, and Becoming in a Pueblo Society.* Chicago: University of Chicago Press, 1969.

Parson, Elsie Clews. *Pueblo Religion.* 2 vols. Lincoln: University of Nebraska Press, 1996.

Sando, Joe S. *Pueblo Nations: Eight Centuries of Pueblo Indian History.* Santa Fé, NM: Clear Light Publishers, 1992.

Santa Fé

Established in 1609 officially, Santa Fé saw its first permanent Spanish inhabitants perhaps as early as 1608, when Juan de Oñate began moving some of his colonists south from San Gabriel del Yungue, in an attempt to find a more defensible and certainly less crowded community. When colonial proprietor and son of a silver miner Juan de Oñate won the contract to settle this northern province of New Spain in 1598, he brought with him 129 soldier-colonists and their families as well as Indian allies as auxiliaries, over 10,000 head of livestock, and seed provisions to start farming immediately. He found relatively receptive Pueblo Indians at Okay Owinge (San Juan Pueblo), where they established the first Spanish community in New Mexico. By 1607, New Mexico had failed to yield profitable resources, so Oñate gave up his term as governor and began reshifting the remaining colonists further south to what would become the first formal villa under the Spanish legal system.

Governor Oñate's replacement, Pedro de Peralta, declared the community La Villa Real de Santa Fé de San Francisco de Asisi by viceregal orders in 1610. Moving the capital officially from San Gabriel to Santa Fé, Peralta hoped to provide his constituencies with the same that Oñate hoped to provide, a more defensible position, but also a more central one to the numerous pueblos that surrounded the Spanish settlers. Santa Fé's location, along the river and at the base of the beautiful Sangre de Cristos, was an excellent location for a community. The valleys provided farmland that had not already been claimed by Pueblo Indian people, and also had enough space for the Indian auxiliaries, the Tlaxcalans, to also have homes and farm sites. Therefore, at Santa Fé, the longest-established U.S. capital continued to operate into the 21st century from very humble beginnings.

Built around a center square or plaza, Santa Fé emanated out from its official buildings on the plaza to neighborhoods divided by narrow streets. On the plaza, one would typically find the governor's mansion (now part of the Museum of New Mexico), a mission or cathedral, a military installation, and perhaps other official homes or headquarters. Santa Fé, however, is the "city different," and instead located San Miguel Mission off the main plaza. The Spanish military did eventually have a presidio at Santa Fé, but it did not occur in 1610. The plaza provided the focal point for the community, and the stream became its lifeblood. Because of the constant raids and counterraids by Apache and Navajo, who had historically raided Pueblo Indian communities for stores of grain but now found that the Spanish had even better selections of goods (horses, sheep, crops, and even human captives for the taking), the Spanish turned Santa Fé into a walled city.

The walls could not keep out the Pueblo Revolt of 1680, however, and many of the Spanish outside those walls suffered death at the hands of angry Pueblo Indians, incensed at demands made by their colonial oppressors (see the entry "Pueblo Revolt"). When the Pueblo Indians arrived at Santa Fé, inside was huddled just over half of the remaining 2,500 Spanish colonists and their allies. When the Spanish refused to leave the city, the rebels diverted the river of life and forced the Spanish to vacate Santa Fé and flee south to El Paso del Norte, where they waited more than a dozen years to retake their capital. In the meantime, Pueblo Indians occupied the buildings of Santa Fé, turning the governor's mansion into a multistoried, pueblo-styled building. When the Spanish returned in 1692 under the leadership of Governor Diego de Vargas, he walked boldly inside the walls of Santa Fé to parlay with the Pueblo Indians at the plaza—with no weapons and only a friar at his side. His show of bravado and promises of protection against the nomadic raiders caused the pueblos, one by one, to acquiesce to the return of Spanish control.

When the Spanish returned to Santa Fé the following year, however, the Pueblo occupiers refused to give up the homes they had occupied for over half a generation. The Spanish laid siege and took back the capital, which served as the capital of Spanish New Mexico until 1821. That year, Mexico declared its independence from Spain, and Santa Fé became a Mexican capital. Within 25 years, Santa Fé would fall under U.S. authority when General Stephen Watts Kearney and the Army of the West conquered New Mexico without encountering any resistance. Santa Fé, "The City Different," has since become a mecca for tourists from all over the world. Its downtown plaza retains its charm as a quiet small town, but just outside of the old Spanish district, Santa Fé bustles like any town of the 21st-century American West.

—*Sandra K. Mathews*

Further Reading

Kessell, John L. *Spain in the Southwest: A Narrative History of Colonial New Mexico, Arizona, Texas, and California*. Norman: University of Oklahoma Press, 2002.

Knaut, Andrew L. *The Pueblo Revolt of 1680: Conquest and Resistance in Seventeenth-Century New Mexico*. Norman: University of Oklahoma Press, 1995.

Simmons, Marc. *New Mexico: An Interpretive History*. New York: Norton, 1977.

Weber, David J. *The Spanish Frontier in North America*. New Haven, CT: Yale University Press, 1992.

Weber, David J., ed. *What Caused the Pueblo Revolt of 1680: Readings*. Selected and Introduced by David J. Weber. Historians at Work Series. Boston: Bedford/St. Martins, 1999.

Declaration of Pedro Naranjo, December 19, 1681

Taking the form of testimony given, this document presents the views of Pedro Naranjo, of San Felipe Pueblo, as to the course of events that led to the Pueblo Revolt of 1680. In it, Naranjo explains the role that religion played in the revolt, although the transcription of the testimony is clearly from the Spanish point of view.

Declaration of Pedro Naranjo of the Queres Nation
[Place of the Rio del Norte, December 19, 1681.]

In the said plaza de armas on the said day, month, and year, for the prosecution of the judicial proceedings of this case his lordship caused to appear before him an Indian prisoner named Pedro Naranjo, a native of the pueblo of San Felipe, of the Queres nation, who was captured in the advance and attack upon the pueblo of La Isleta. He makes himself understood very well in the Castilian language and speaks his mother tongue and the Tegua. He took the oath in due legal form in the name of God, our Lord, and a sign of the cross, under charge of which he promised to tell the truth concerning what he knows and as he might be questioned, and having understood the seriousness of the oath and so signified through the interpreters, he spoke as indicated by the contents of the autos.

Asked whether he knows the reason or motives which the Indians of this kingdom had for rebelling, forsaking the law of God and obedience to his Majesty, and committing such grave and atrocious crimes, and who were the leaders and principal movers, and by whom and how it was ordered; and why they burned the images, temples, crosses, rosaries, and things of divine worship, committing such atrocities as killing priests, Spaniards, women, and children, and the rest that he might know touching the question, he said that since the government of Señor General Hernando Ugarte y la Concha they have planned to rebel on various occasions through conspiracies of the Indian sorcerers, and that although in some pueblos the messages were accepted, in other parts they would not agree to it; and that it is true that during the government of the said senor general seven or eight Indians were hanged for this same cause, whereupon the unrest subsided. Some time thereafter they [the conspirators] sent from the pueblo of Los Taos through the pueblos of the custodia two deerskins with some pictures on them signifying conspiracy after their manner, in order to convoke the people to a new rebellion, and the said deerskins passed to the province of Moqui, where they refused to accept them. The pact which they had been forming ceased for the time being, but they always kept in their hearts the desire to carry it out, so as to live as they are living today. Finally, in the past years, at the summons of an Indian named Popé who is said to have communication with the devil, it happened that in an estufa of the pueblo of Los Taos there appeared to the said Popé three figures of Indians who never came out of the estufa. They gave the said Popé to understand that they were going underground to the lake of Copala. He saw these figures emit fire from all the extremities of their bodies, and that one of them was called Caudi, another Tilini, and the other Tleume; and these three beings spoke to the said Popé, who was in hiding from the secretary, Francisco Xavier, who wished to punish him as a sorcerer. They told him to make a cord of maguey fiber and tie some knots in it which would signify the number of days that they must wait before the rebellion. He said that the cord was passed through all the pueblos of the kingdom so that the ones which agreed to it [the rebellion] might untie one knot in sign of obedience, and by the other knots they would know the days which were lacking; and this was to be done on pain of death to those who refused to agree to it. As a sign of agreement and notice of having concurred in the treason and perfidy they were to send up smoke signals to that effect in each one of the pueblos singly. The said cord was taken from pueblo to pueblo by the swiftest youths under the penalty of death if they revealed the secret. Everything being thus arranged, two days before the time set for its execution, because his lordship had learned of it and had imprisoned two Indian accomplices from the pueblo of Tesuque, it was carried out prematurely that night, because it seemed to them that they were now discovered; and they killed religious, Spaniards, women, and children. This being done, it was proclaimed in all the pueblos that everyone in common should obey the commands of their father whom they did not know, which would be given through El Caydi or El Popé. This was heard by Alonso Catití, who came to the pueblo of this declarant to say that everyone must unite to go to the villa to kill the governor and the Spaniards who had remained with him, and that he who did not obey would, on their return, be beheaded; and in fear of this they agreed to it. Finally the senor governor and those who were with him escaped from the siege, and later this declarant saw that as soon as the Spaniards had left the kingdom an order came from the said Indian, Popé, in which he commanded all the Indians to break the lands and enlarge their cultivated fields, saying that now they were as they had been in ancient times, free from the labor they had performed for the religious and the Spaniards, who could not now be alive. He said that this is the legitimate cause and the reason they had for rebelling, because they had always desired to live as they had when they came out of the lake of Copala. Thus he replies to the question.

    Asked for what reason they so blindly burned the images, temples, crosses, and other things of divine worship, he stated that the said Indian, Popé, came down in person, and with him El Saca and El Chato from the pueblo of Los Taos, and other captains and leaders and many people who were in his train, and he ordered in all the pueblos through which he passed that they instantly break up and burn the images of the holy Christ, the Virgin Mary and the other saints, the crosses, and everything pertaining to Christianity, and that they burn the temples, break up the bells, and separate from the wives whom God had given them in marriage and take those whom they desired. In order to take away their baptismal names, the water, and the holy oils, they were to plunge into the rivers and wash themselves with amole, which is a root native to the country, washing even their clothing, with the understanding that there would thus be taken from them the character of the holy sacraments. They did this, and also many other things which he does not recall, given to understand that this mandate had come from the Caydi and the other two who emitted fire from their extremities in the said estufa of Taos, and that they thereby returned to the state of their antiquity, as when they came from the lake of Copala; that this was the better life and the one they desired, because the God of the Spaniards was worth nothing and theirs was very strong, the Spaniard's God being rotten wood. These things were observed and obeyed by all except some who, moved by the zeal of Christians, opposed it, and such persons the said Popé caused to be killed immediately. He saw to it that they at once erected and rebuilt their houses of idolatry which they call estufas, and made very ugly masks in imitation of the devil in order to dance the dance of the cacina; and he said likewise that the devil had given them to understand that living thus in accordance with the law of their ancestors, they would harvest a great deal of maize, many beans, a great abundance of cotton, calabashes, and very large watermelons and cantaloupes; and that they could erect their houses and enjoy abundant health and leisure. As he has said, the people were very much pleased, living at their ease in this life of their antiquity, which was the chief cause of their falling into such laxity. Following what has already been stated, in order to terrorize them further and cause them to observe the diabolical commands, there came to them a pronouncement from the three demons already described, and from El Popé, to the effect that he who might still keep in his heart a regard for the priests, the governor, and the Spaniards would be known from his unclean face and clothes, and would be punished. And he stated that the said four persons stopped at nothing to have their commands obeyed. Thus he replies to the question.

Asked what arrangements and plans they had made for the contingency of the Spaniards' return, he said that what he knows concerning the question is that they were always saying they would have to fight to the death, for they do not wish to live in any other way than they are living at present; and the demons in the estufa of Taos had given them to understand that as soon as the Spaniards began to move toward this kingdom they would warn them so that they might unite, and none of them would be caught. He having been questioned further and repeatedly touching the case, he said that he has nothing more to say except that they should be always on the alert, because the said Indians were continually planning to follow the Spaniards and fight with them by night, in order to drive off the horses and catch them afoot, although they might have to follow them for many leagues. What he has said is the truth, and what happened, on the word of a Christian who confesses his guilt. He said that he has come to the pueblos through fear to lead in idolatrous dances, in which he greatly fears in his heart that he may have offended God, and that now having been absolved and returned to the fold of the church, he has spoken the truth in everything he has been asked. His declaration being read to him, he affirmed and ratified all of it. He declared himself to be eighty years of age, and he signed it with his lordship and the interpreters and assisting witnesses, before me, the secretary. ANTONIO DE OTERMÍN (rubric); PEDRO NARANJO; NICOLÁS RODRIGUEZ REY (rubric); JUAN LUCERO DE GODOY (rubric); JUAN Ruiz DE CASARES (rubric); PEDRO DE LEIVA (rubric);

SEBASTÍAN DE HERRERA (rubric); JUAN DE NORIEGA GARCÍA (rubric); Luis DE GRANILLO (rubric); JUAN DE LUNA Y PADILLA (rubric). Before me, FRANCISCO XAVIER, secretary of government and war (rubric).

Source: Charles Wilson Hackett, *Revolt of the Pueblo Indians of New Mexico and Otermin's Attempted Reconquest, 1680–1682*, vol. 2 (Albuquerque: University of New Mexico, 1942), 245–249.

Leisler's Rebellion (1689–1691)

Leisler's Rebellion was a New York–based uprising against the Dominion of New England that lasted from May 31, 1689, to March 20, 1691. Jacob Leisler's brief regime was characterized by virulent anti-Catholicism and suppression of dissent, but it also made important strides toward intercolonial cooperation and representative government.

In the 1680s, New York witnessed the clash of conflicting impulses toward absolutism and representative government. In the autumn of 1683, New York's first legislature drafted the Charter of Liberties and Privileges, a liberal constitution that provided for individual liberties and triennial meetings of the colonial assembly. The colonists' timing was poor: Charles II was considering a massive reorganization of imperial administration to strengthen the Crown's authority over the British dominions in North America. After Charles's death in 1685, his brother James II disallowed New York's charter and, in 1688, ordered that the colony be incorporated into the highly centralized Dominion of New England. James's administrative reforms were widely unpopular. They fanned his subjects' fears that James, a Catholic, might have a penchant for absolutism. Anxiety escalated when James's young wife gave birth to a son on June 10, 1688. The new baby, by virtue of his sex, would displace his older, Protestant sisters in the line of succession. His very existence raised the specter of an enduring Catholic dynasty in England.

In the spring of 1689, word reached America that James II's Dutch son-in-law, William of Orange, had invaded England at the behest of Parliament and established a Protestant monarchy. On April 18, 2,000 militiamen staged a coup d'état in Boston, arresting the Dominion's governor, Sir Edmund Andros. The four New England colonies then reinstated elected governments under their old charters. In New York, the Dominion's lieutenant governor, Francis Nicholson, nervously expanded his council in an attempt to ward off a similar uprising or a foreign invasion.

He did so in vain. On May 31, the New York militia seized Fort James. Nicholson fled to England. His absence created a vacuum of power in the colony, especially as Nicholson's councilors hesitated to swear loyalty to William III. On June 8, a provincial committee of safety declared a prominent militia officer, Jacob Leisler, captain of Fort James, and on June 22, Leisler's government proclaimed William and Mary's reign. On August 16, the committee of safety appointed Leisler commander in chief of the province and dispatched two agents to England to seek validation for the new government. Meanwhile, two of the Dominion councilors, Nicholas Bayard and Stephanus Van Cortlandt, fled to Albany, where they organized opposition to Leisler's government. Leisler dispatched troops to take the city by force, but the expedition failed when Mohawks who were loyal to the opposition threatened to attack them on the outskirts of Albany.

Leisler's agents, particularly the uneducated publican Joost Stoll, made a poor impression at court, and Leisler grew impatient waiting for their return. In December 1689, Leisler received an Order in Council addressed to Francis Nicholson or whomever was administering New York in Nicholson's absence. Leisler interpreted these instructions as legitimizing his government. He claimed the title of lieutenant governor, dissolved the committee of safety, formed a new council, and called for elections to a provincial assembly. This regularization of the rebels' de facto government was accompanied by a purge of Leisler's opposition and the imprisonment of Nicholas Bayard.

By now, anti-Catholicism was fast becoming one of the distinguishing traits of Leisler's regime. In February 1690, an allied French and Iroquois force attacked the frontier settlement of Schenectady, killing 60, taking 27 prisoners, and burning the settlement to the ground. Leisler responded by imprisoning Catholics and Catholic sympathizers. He also seized this opportunity to recover his authority over the cowed residents of Albany by promising to protect them from French aggression. To do so, he solicited other colonies' military assistance. On May 1, 1690, delegates from Massachusetts, Plymouth, Connecticut, and New York met to plan a military expedition to Quebec; Maryland and Barbados participated by letter. This convention marked the colonies' first attempt to plan coordinated military interaction on their own initiative, rather than under the auspices of the Crown.

Leisler's regime grew steadily more unpopular over time. In June 1690, New Yorkers learned that William had appointed Nicholson lieutenant governor of Virginia. Dissidents rioted and attacked Leisler, who soon had to face the failure of his military campaign to Quebec as well. Leisler responded by briefly imprisoning the commander, Fitz-John Winthrop, thereby alienating the English Puritan settlers on Long Island. The anti-Leislerians were a diverse group, including James II's protégés ("the Duke's men"), affluent Dutch merchants who had assimilated to English rule, and commercially oriented English immigrants. All of these men valued broad toleration and individual civil liberties, as outlined in the 1683 charter, and feared Leisler's authoritarian tendencies. Although Leisler aimed to establish legislative government in New York, he never made a coherent statement of his constitutional philosophy and seemed to believe that military authority trumped individual freedoms.

Meanwhile, William III, unimpressed by Leisler's agents' presentation of his case, had appointed Henry Sloughter governor of New York and reinstated Nicholson's council. The first detachment of troops representing Sloughter's government arrived in January 1691, under Captain Richard Ingoldesby. Leisler held Ingoldesby's troops at bay for two months, refusing to surrender to anyone other than the duly appointed governor. When he did at last surrender to the newly arrived Sloughter on March 20, Sloughter—responding in part to the persuasions of Leisler's old rival Nicholas Bayard—had him arrested and tried for treason. Leisler refused to plead; nevertheless, he was convicted, hanged, and beheaded on May 16, 1691. Jacob Milborne, Leisler's secretary, lieutenant, and son-in-law, was also executed. Several other Leislerians suffered imprisonment and confiscation of property.

The hasty executions of Leisler and Milborne garnered criticism for Sloughter's regime. The Dutch initiated an inquiry into the executions, and Dutch pressure on the English government led Parliament, in 1695, to reverse both men's convictions and posthumously legitimize Leisler's administration. In 1702, the New York Assembly followed suit by voting an indemnity of £2,700 to Leisler's heirs. In the same year, Leisler's old nemesis, Nicholas Bayard, was tried for treason by a government sympathetic to Leisler's rule. Though Bayard was acquitted, Leislerian and anti-Leislerian factions remained discernible forces in provincial politics until at least 1710.

Leisler's Rebellion defies easy interpretation. Clearly, it was one manifestation of the Glorious Revolution in America, a counterpart to similar uprisings in Massachusetts and Maryland. Some historians have envisioned Leisler's Rebellion as an expression of ethnic conflict, a last-ditch effort by Dutch nationalists to reestablish Dutch hegemony in New York. Yet the Leislerians and the anti-Leislerians were both Anglo-Dutch coalitions; Leisler's bitterest enemies, Bayard and Van Cortlandt, were themselves members of the Anglicizing Dutch merchant class. A class model, pitting New York's liberal Anglo-Dutch mercantile elite against the more traditional middling Dutch colonists whom Leisler mobilized, fits the facts somewhat better. What can be said with some certainty is that Leisler's Rebellion was the last hurrah of Dutch power in New York; after 1691, Dutch colonists, Leislerians and anti-Leislerians alike, rapidly assimilated to a British colonial identity.

In the aftermath of Leisler's Rebellion, New York's political scene stabilized along lines that, though fractious and corrupt, were decidedly more liberal than those that prevailed in the 17th century. From its founding until 1689, New York was ruled by a series of regimes that privileged royal or proprietary prerogative. Leisler, though an uncertain republican, set an important precedent by summoning a provincial legislature to legitimate his rule. When anti-Leislerians returned to power in 1691, they swiftly established a colonial assembly that would meet annually and pass laws that would be effective unless and until they were disallowed by the Crown. Ironically, Leisler's coup d'état helped his colony attain its longed-for representative government.

—*Darcy R. Fryer*

See also all entries under Bacon's Rebellion (1675–1676); Regulator Movement (1771); Pine Tree Riot (1772); Shays' Rebellion (1787); Whiskey Rebellion (1794).

Further Reading

Archdeacon, Thomas J. *New York City, 1664–1710: Conquest and Change*. Ithaca, NY: Cornell University Press, 1976.

Kammen, Michael. *Colonial New York: A History*. New York: Oxford University Press, 1996.

Lovejoy, David S. *The Glorious Revolution in America*. Middletown, CT: Wesleyan University Press, 1987.

Murrin, John. "The Menacing Shadow of Louis XIV and the Rage of Jacob Leisler: The Constitutional Ordeal of Seventeenth-Century New York." In *Colonial America: Essays in Politics and Social Development*, ed. Stanley N. Katz, John M. Murrin, and Douglas Greenberg. 5th ed., 380–418. Boston: McGraw-Hill, 2001.

Ritchie, Robert C. *The Duke's Province: A Study of New York Politics and Society, 1664–1691*. Chapel Hill: University of North Carolina Press, 1977.

Calvinism

Calvinism, also known as the Reformed theological tradition, was a form of Protestantism that sprang from the teachings of the Swiss pastor John Calvin (1509–1564). It took root in New England as "Puritanism" and in New Netherland under the aegis of the Dutch Reformed Church.

Calvin's numerous writings, especially *The Institutes of the Christian Religion* (1536–1560), laid the groundwork for Calvinist theology. The Synod of Dort (1618–1619) identified five core tenets of Calvinism, including the total depravity of human beings; God's unconditional election of a few human beings for eternal life; Christ's limited atonement for the sins of the elect, but not for the sins of others; and irresistible grace, which those elected for salvation achieved not by works but solely by overwhelming awe before the incomprehensible majesty of God and corresponding disgust for the loathsome insignificance of human beings. The role of the Calvinist church was to gather those who were predestined for salvation—the "visible saints"—and unite them in a quest to reform society along godly lines. The Synod of Dort's final tenet, the perseverance of the saints, assured the elect that God would preserve them in a state of grace and prevent them from falling permanently into a state of sin.

In practice, Calvinists emphasized an austere lifestyle and rigid community discipline. In Calvin's model city, Geneva, the consistory strictly regulated residents' behavior and excommunicated those who failed to abide by community standards.

During the 16th century, John Calvin developed a strict moral brand of Protestantism that would become known as Calvinism, which would become the primary religious influence of the Puritans in New England. (Library of Congress)

Most European Calvinists adopted a ÿresbyterian organizational model, in which individual congregations sent representatives to regional presbyteries and synods. Most New Englanders preferred Congregationalism, a form of Calvinism in which individual congregations exercised complete autonomy. In either case, Christ was considered the sole head of the Church; ministers and elders were called by their congregations and answered to them, not to an ecclesiastical bureaucracy.

Swiss in origin, Calvinism took root in many parts of Europe, including France, the Netherlands, Scotland, and England, by the end of the 16th century. French Calvinists were known as Huguenots, while the most influential group of English Calvinists—those who sought to "purify" the established Church of England by purging it of latitudinarian practices—were called Puritans. In 17th-century North America, Calvinists dominated the religious scene north of the Hudson River; the Puritans of New England and the Dutch Reformed of New Netherland shared the same tenets of faith. Louis XIV's revocation of the Edict of Nantes in 1685 brought a third wave of Calvinists, approximately 2,000 Huguenot refugees, to British North America, where their arrival roused popular indignation at Catholic persecution of Protestants.

Calvinism was a religious movement with political implications. By the late 17th century, Protestants on both sides of the Atlantic associated Calvinism with representative government and opposition to tyrants and Catholicism with the centralizing tendencies of such absolutists as Louis XIV of France. Calvinists were prominent among those who opposed James II's scheme of centralization, and Jacob Leisler's ardent Calvinist faith was a major factor that propelled him to assume leadership of the rebellion that bears his name.

—*Darcy R. Fryer*

Further Reading

Benedict, Philip. *Christ's Churches Purely Reformed: A Social History of Calvinism*. New Haven, CT: Yale University Press, 2002.

McNeill, John T. *The History and Character of Calvinism*. New York: Oxford University Press, 1954.

Dominion of New England (1686–1689)

The Dominion of New England was a short-lived conglomerate colony created by James II in 1686 to streamline colonial administration and strengthen the monarch's authority over the American colonies. Unpopular from the start, the Dominion was overthrown by Leisler's Rebellion in 1689.

When the Duke of York—the patron for whom New York was named—came to the throne as James II in 1685, one of his priorities was to exert greater royal control over England's diverse and individualistic American colonies. James II had spent several of his formative years in France following the execution of his father, Charles I, in 1649. As the son of a deposed king, and as a Catholic, he admired the French absolutist model of monarchy. James II also believed that wringing more revenue from the colonies would diminish the monarch's financial dependence on Parliament—one of the chief sources of his father's political struggles—and thus enhance his authority at home.

In 1686, James II consolidated five colonies—Massachusetts, Plymouth, New Hampshire, Rhode Island, and Connecticut—into a single super-colony called the Dominion of New England. In 1688, he added New York and East and West Jersey as well. James II dissolved the existing colonial assemblies and concentrated power in the hands of a governor-general, Sir Edmund Andros, a deputy governor, Francis Nicholson, and an appointed council. Andros ruled from Boston, while Nicholson was stationed in New York.

As governor of the Dominion, Andros introduced numerous innovations, all of them unpopular. Many of his measures were specifically designed to yield revenue: he rejected existing land titles to reap fees from the reissuance of land grants, required landholders to pay annual quitrents, substantially increased taxes, and strictly enforced the Navigation Acts. Andros also infringed on colonists' political rights, limiting New England town meetings to one per year and suspending the colonial legislatures. He sought to undermine New England's Puritan churches by forbidding ministers to draw their salaries from public funds. Andros raised the specter of absolutism by articulating a radical new political theory that inhabitants of the British Empire, unlike Englishmen at home, were subject solely to the arbitrary power of the monarch and were not entitled to representative government or other English civil rights.

The Dominion of New England was unpopular from the start. American colonists resented the loss of elected assemblies, rising taxes, and the Crown's interference with local religious, social, and legal traditions. When rumors of the Glorious Revolution reached New England in the spring of 1689, the residents of Boston promptly arrested Andros and reinstated the old, separate colonial governments throughout New England. New York's uprising, which began in late May of the same year, was complicated by the colonists' tangled ethnic and religious loyalties, but at root, it too was a popular effort to restore the colony's government to a form that better reflected the needs and values of the people who lived there.

—*Darcy R. Fryer*

Further Reading

Lovejoy, David S. *The Glorious Revolution in America*. Middletown, CT: Wesleyan University Press, 1987.

Taylor, Alan. *American Colonies*. New York: Viking, 2001.

Leisler, Jacob (c. 1640–1691)

Jacob Leisler served as New York's de facto lieutenant governor from June 1689 until March 1691. He governed the colony with a mixture of pragmatism, militant Calvinism, and tendentious autocracy.

Leisler was born in Frankfurt-am-Main, Germany, in a region roiled by the vicissitudes of the Thirty Years' War (1618–1648). His family was both highly educated—his grandfather was a prominent jurist who championed subjects' rights to oppose monarchs—and devoutly Calvinist—Leisler's father, a Huguenot minister, had fled the Inquisition in Spanish-occupied Frankenthal just a few years before Jacob's birth. After studying at a Protestant military academy, Leisler immigrated to New Netherland in 1660 as second-in-command of the Dutch West India Company's troops.

Leisler prospered in America, trading in furs, tobacco, and slaves and investing extensively in real estate. His marriage to Elsie Tymens van der Veen linked him to the port's emerging mercantile elite. By the 1680s, Leisler was one of the richest men in New York and one of the city's leading civic activists. At various times, he served as a juror, court-appointed arbitrator, justice of the peace, tax assessor, militia captain, and colonial agent. A founding member of New York's French Reformed Church, he became an activist on behalf of Huguenot refugees. Aside from his championship of the Calvinist faith, Leisler had few discernible political convictions; he cooperated with both the Dutch and English regimes.

Soon after the Dominion of New England crumbled in the spring of 1689, Leisler emerged as the leader of the dissident faction in New York. The exact sequence of events that brought him to power remains obscure, but on August 16, 1689, Leisler became the province's commander in chief, and in December, he seized the title of lieutenant governor.

Leisler's leadership of New York was pragmatic and vigorous. He strengthened the fortifications at Fort James and, after an initial defeat, succeeded in quelling a rival regime based in Albany. He called for new elections to a provincial assembly, symbolically restoring legislative government. Following a French and Indian attack on Schenectady on February 9, 1690, Leisler lashed out against Catholics and, in May, convened a meeting of delegates from four colonies (two others participated by letter) to plan a military response to the perceived Catholic menace. This meeting marked the American colonies' first attempt at coordinated military action independent of the British government.

Leisler's fall came swiftly. Henry Sloughter, whom William III had appointed to govern New York, finally arrived in the province in March 1691. Leisler, who had been holding Sloughter's deputy at bay, promptly surrendered to the new governor. Nevertheless, Sloughter, influenced by Leisler's political opponents, had his predecessor arrested. He was convicted of treason, hanged, and beheaded on May 16, 1691. This was not, however, the final verdict on Leisler's role in the Glorious Revolution. In 1695, Parliament, under diplomatic pressure from the Dutch, posthumously legitimized Leisler's administration and reversed his conviction for treason. The New York Assembly subsequently granted an indemnity of £2,700 to Leisler's heirs.

—Darcy R. Fryer

Further Reading

Archdeacon, Thomas J. *New York City, 1664–1710: Conquest and Change*. Ithaca, NY: Cornell University Press, 1976.

Voorhees, David William. "The 'Fervent Zeale' of Jacob Leisler." *William and Mary Quarterly*, 3rd ser., 51 (1994): 447–472.

Religious Conflict in 17th-Century New York

Religious conflict between Catholics and Protestants, among different types of Protestants, and within the Dutch Reformed Church played a prominent role in Leisler's Rebellion. The intermingling of religious and political conflict in Leisler's New York echoed the situation in early modern Europe, where the fusion of religious and political agendas had sparked the French Wars of Religion (1562–1598), the Thirty Years' War (1618–1648), and the English Civil War (1642–1649).

Late-17th-century New York was characterized by exceptional ethnic and religious diversity. The Netherlands was an oasis of religious freedom, and the Dutch settlements in America attracted every sort of Protestant, as well as some Catholics and Jews. These immigrants were chagrined to find that New Netherland granted them less latitude than Holland did; Peter Stuyvesant, in particular, vigorously suppressed the worship of Lutherans, Quakers, Mennonites, Catholics, and Jews. Some religious minorities welcomed the English conquest in 1664 because the English, unlike the Dutch, permitted them to worship publicly.

Dutch Calvinists felt threatened by the English government's welcoming attitude toward other Protestants, but they reserved their greatest animus for Catholics. The Duke of York (later James II) appointed several Catholic administrators, including Thomas Dongan, who served as governor from 1683 to 1688. The establishment of a Jesuit school in New York City also attracted Catholics to the province. Anti-Catholic prejudice was particularly strong among poor and middling Dutch colonists, and Jacob Leisler—a devout Calvinist—effectively mobilized this prejudice to secure popular support for his government.

Ironically, some of the bitterest religious conflict associated with Leisler's Rebellion took place within the Dutch Reformed Church. Churches were one of the principal settings in which 17th-century colonists participated in civic life, and conflicts evoked by Leisler's Rebellion often played themselves out, at the local level, as disputes over church affairs. The intermingling of political and religious conflict cut both ways: sometimes attitudes toward Leisler determined parties within the local church; sometimes, as in the scandal over the behavior of Reverend Laurentius van den Bosch of Kingston, local issues took precedence over provincial affairs, forging unlikely coalitions between Leislerians and anti-Leislerians.

The principal fault line within the Dutch Reformed Church lay between the clergy and the laity, especially laymen of modest means. By the 1680s, the Dutch Calvinist clergy had discovered that a quiet acquiescence to English rule was the most effective means of securing doctrinal autonomy. Some found Leisler's rabid anti-Catholicism repugnant, and many feared that the collapse of English authority would make it difficult to collect the taxes that supported the church. For all of these reasons, the Dutch clergy hesitated to support Leisler's regime. Many less affluent congregants resented the clergy's failure to embrace Leisler. This resentment played itself out in diminished attendance at services, disputes over church finance, and ultimately, a shift in popular allegiance. In the early 18th century, middling Dutch colonists drifted away from the established Dutch Reformed Church to join congregations led by less learned, more pietistic preachers.

—*Darcy R. Fryer*

Further Reading

Balmer, Randall. *A Perfect Babel of Confusion: Dutch Religion and English Culture in the Middle Colonies*. New York: Oxford University Press, 1989.

Balmer, Randall. "Traitors and Papists: The Religious Dimensions of Leisler's Rebellion." *New York History* 70 (1989): 341–372.

Haefeli, Evan. "A Scandalous Minister in a Divided Community: Ulster County in Leisler's Rebellion, 1689–1691." *New York History* 88 (2007): 357–389.

Jacob Leisler's Letter to the Governor and Committee of Safety at Boston, June 4, 1689

This letter, written by Jacob Leisler near the beginning of the rebellion he led against the government of the Dominion of New England, reflects the religious and political strife taking place at the time, both in the colonies and in England. In it, he asks for the help of the Committee of Safety in Boston and newly installed governor Simon Bradstreet, against those supporters of James II (England's new, Catholic king).

Honored Sirs—I make bold to acquaint you of the securing of the fort by the traine bonds of New york. Here enclosed is the declaratione N: 1: In two dayes after the Governor & his Counsell w th severall of their creatures had gained so much upon the people that they were afraied & halfe of myne company were they worked most upon had left me, but the second of this instant being my watch in the fort I came with 49 men & entered in the fort, without the word, nor to be questioned whereupon I resolved not to leave till I had brought all the traine bound fully to joine with me, The 3d wee had newes of three ships in sight upon which I tooke occasione to allarume the towne & gott five Captanes besides me & 400 men to signe the enclosed paper N: 2: which discouraged the adverse party, and since they have been indifferent still, The Lievt Governor Nicholls is departed last night without taking leave, It is beleeved he intends to goe with Collo" dongane who has layen in the bay this sixteen dayes. N: 3: is a copie of an evidence whereof we have three of the same tenor, N: 4 is a copie of an address to his ma'ies sent to four merchants with Capt Selock & one with Capt wathland who has faithfullie promised to deliver for to be presented to the King, and depose what they know more, then wee declare, I have made one full Inventory of the fort with guns and ammunitione, and found of 33 great gunes but fifteen fitt to use of 50 barrells pouder was but one that could goe 7 degrees the rest &ct. 3. 4: & 5 some non at all, the most part of the country have invited the rest to appeare as a counsell of safty two men out of one County, the 26th of this instant In the mean tyme the fort is guarded by five companies two watches 1^ company per night, and the Capt whose watch it is is for that tyme Capt of the fort, the Collector in the Custome house is a rank papist, I cannot gett the other Captanes to resolve to turne him out but acts still as before The Mayer medles with no civil I affaires & discourages constables to keep the peace expecting some seditione for to make the Inhabitants odious, there is non acts others then in quality of a single Capt, sir Edmond Andross & his wicked crew have carried all the Records out of this country to Boston, I hope by the prudent care in the late expeditione at Boston have taken care to preserve it, and I request you to take a speciall care for it, till our Committee of safety may take some prudent care about it, the time will not permitt me to enlarge onely I desire your advice in approbatione in our actione, If wee deserve it and after myne respects I remain & c.

Jacob Leisler.

Source: E. B. O'Callaghan, *Documentary History of the State of New York*, vol. 2 (Albany, NY: Weed, Parsons & Co., 1849), 3–4.

Jacob Leisler: "A Modest and Impartial Narrative" (1690)

Leisler's Rebellion was a popular uprising that erupted in the colony of New York in May 1689. Led by Jacob Leisler, the rebellion was a Protestant reaction to the colonial administration appointed by the Catholic king, James II. The following description of the start of the insurrection comes from an account of the rebellion entitled "A Modest and Impartial Narrative," which is attributed to Nicholas Bayard, one of Leisler's most vocal opponents. As such, the account is neither "modest" nor "impartial," but a virulent attack on Leisler and his supporters, who governed the colony between 1689 and 1691. Opposed by the landed and merchant interests, who lost control of the colonial economy during his administration, Leisler was subsequently arrested and executed for treason.

A Modest and Impartial Narrative Of several Grievances and Great Oppressions That the Peaceable and most Considerable Inhabitants of Their Majesties Province of New-York in America Lye Under, By the Extravagant and Arbitrary Proceedings of Jacob Leysler and his Accomplices.

Printed at New-York, and Re-printed at London 1690.

The Reader is hereby advertised, That the Matters contained in the following Declaration and Narration, were intended to have been presented to the Mayor's Court in New York, the 25th of January last past, but that the Fury and Rage of this Insolent Man Leysler, was grown to that height, that the day before, by his order, several Persons of Note were violently seized and divers Houses broken open, so as it was not thought safe to proceed in such Method. For which reason it's thought well to publish the same, for information of all into whose hands it may come, but more especially for the benefit of our fellow Inhabitants, who are abused by the Pretentious of this common Violator of our Laws and Liberties, as by the following Narrative will plainly appear: Wherein the Courteous Peruser is desired to take notice, it hath been our great Care to relate nothing but Matters of Fact, of which we have substantial Credible Evidences.

The Narrative, etc.

Out of the deep sense we have of the good providence of Almighty God, in their Majesties happy accession to the Imperial Crown of England, etc., In the first place we, in a most Christian manner, with hearts and hands lifted up to Heaven, give Glory to Almighty God, for this so happy a Revolution, whereof it hath pleased the most High to appear the Principal Author. In the next place, we cannot but declare and publish to the world our hearty and thankful resentments of the Noble, though hazardous Enterprise of the late Prince of Orange, our most dread Sovereign King of England, Scotland, France and Ireland, Defender of the Faith etc., the Noble Hero of this Age, for the Protestant Religion, and the preservation of the Laws and Liberties of the English Nation inviolated, manifesting hereby that as in duty bound, so in point of Gratitude, we can do no less than dedicate our Lives and fortunes to their Majesties services, with our most serious and continued prayers for their Majesties long and happy Reign over us, being well satisfied in our own selves, that what our native Land so plentifully enjoys under their Reign, to wit, the Laws and Liberties of the English Nation, we (though inhabiting a remote part of their Dominions) shall share with them in the common Propriety.

In consideration whereof, in all humble and obedient manner as Dutiful subjects to their Majesties, and well wishers to this their Province of New York, we can do no less than in the presence of God, and to the world, declare our abhorrence and dislike of the unreasonable, Illegal and Arbitrary proceedings of some Men inhabiting with us in this their Majestys Province who have usurped Authority over us.

Against all such proceedings of theirs hereafter faithfully and impartially set down and against them, as the Actors thereof, we do hereby publickly declare and protest.

Now to the end that the Reasonableness of this our Protestation may appear unto all to whose hands it may come, we count ourselves obliged to give a brief recital of the case of our Late Lieutenant Governour Francis Nicholson, for the more peaceable quiet and satisfactory governing this their Majestys Province.

To obviate all suspicion of Jealousies that might arise in ill affected turbulent spirits, our said Lieutenant Governour by and with the consent of so many of the Council as here resided (upon the whispering of the late happy change) did convene together, I with the Mayor, Aldermen and Common Council men of the City of New York, with all the Commission Officers of the Militia of this City and Country; at which convention our said Lieutenant Governour proposed to admit of part of the Train-bands of this City and County to take their turns of watching and warding within their Majesties Fort under their own Officers; And further offered, with the advice and consent of his Council, Civil and Military Officers, there met and assembled, that the Customs formerly paid by the Inhabitants of this Province should still continue, only with this alteration, that whereas formerly it was expended and laid out in defraying of the charges of the Government and Soldiers in pay in the Garrison, it should thence forward be imployed in the fortifying and putting this City in a posture of defence against a foreign Enemy, on which the welfare and safety of this Province so much depends.

In pursuance of the same an order issued forth from the said convention, signed by the Lieutenant Governour, his Council, the Mayor and Aldermen of this City, and most of the Commission Officers of the Militia, none shewing so great a dislike to it as Jacob Leysler, one of the Captains of the Train bands of this City, who at that time had a Ship loaden with wines, the customs whereof amounted to upwards of one hundred pounds; the payment of this he utterly refused, alledging, The Collector, being a Papist, was not qualified to receive it, denying the then power to be legal; but whether for that or his own private interest let the impartial judge.

The turbulent mind of this person not being satisfied in denying the payment of the usual Customs, though appointed for the use aforesaid, he sets himself upon inventing ways how he might overturn the Gov't which was then peaceable and quiet. The first thing he falls upon was to stir up and animate the people of the East end of Long Island to advance with sufficient force to take possession of the Fort, lest it should be in danger of being delivered up to a Foreign Power; this readily took with them whose minds were already heated by the example of Boston in clapping up of our Governour Sir Edmund Andros, and after some consultations amongst themselves, they put forward in a Hostile manner increasing as they came along the Island, until they were so far advanced as the Town of Jamaica, being then about eighty in number, whence they halted, and sent up three1 of their principal leaders to discourse the Lieutenant Governour, who upon their coming convened his council, the Mayor and Aldermen of this City, and the Commission Officers of the Militia of City and County, into which Convention the Persons sent were admitted, where after some long debates they seemingly went away satisfied, at least so far as that they and the men accompanying them returned home to their own Townes and habitations, without doing the least hurt or damage to any.

This stratagem failing . . . Leysler, in a short time after a Rumour was spread amongst the quiet Inhabitants of this City, of a horrible design there was of murdering them, their wives and children, as they were worshipping of God in the Dutch Church within the Fort, and the Sunday prefixed, when this cruel act was to be accomplished; Captain Leysler in the mean time instigating and stirring up the Inhabitants to self preservation against this imaginary design, which so far prevailed with part of the Inhabitants as that the Friday before the Sunday markt out by this report for the pretended massacre, they rose in a hostile manner; the first who appeared in arms were some under Leyslers Command who (as a plot was laid) went to the House of their Captain, and threatened to shoot him if he did not head them. This no ways surprised the courageous Captain; a substantial reason why, himself being the sole contriver of it: Yet whether prevailed most, the want of valour, or the apprehensions, if he should miscarry in this bold attempt, the Country would be destitute of one so fit as himself to command, we leave the judicious to determine.

However it was it seemed not good unto this Champion to venture himself, but commits the conduct of his Men unto one Stoll, famous for nothing, unless his not being worth a groat; up marches Stoll with his brisk followers, and to the Fort gates they draw near, where they met with a very civil Gentleman, one Hendrick Cuyler, left under Captain Abraham Depeyster, who commanded that part of the Train bands, who by turn had the Guard in the Fort that day; this Persons civility was such that it's hard to determine whether Stoll and his party without were more desirous to enter, than he within was ready to open the Gates to them. In fine, entrance they had with great acclamations and joy on both sides, that so meritorious a design was not prevented.

How far this valiant Lieutenant Cuyler, in this base act of his, hath answered the Law of Arms or the trust reposed in him, we will not now determine; but sure we are, the season they took for accomplishing this their unmanlike contrivance, doth not a little add to their crime, it being of that juncture of time when our Lieutenant Governour and conventment (whereof we have before made mention) were consulting for the more orderly and peaceable Governing this their Majesties Province, who at this sudden change were startled, and acted what was left in their power, publickly protesting against this rude Action, and the Actors thereof. By this time their great Champion Leysler being well assured all danger and hazard was over, he most courageously Girds on his Sword, Marches stoutly up to the Fort, in order to his carrying the Game he had so fairly begun, where he is joyfully received, and a consultation immediately held, how they should obtain the Keys of the Fort, which the Lieutenant Governour had in Custody, being in the City Hall, where he was in consultation as is already hinted.

The evening approaching, Captain Lodwick and his Company advances to the Fort to mount the Guard, as his turn was; some time after his being in the Fort, nothing would satisfy the Tumultuous Multitude, but that three or four files of men must be sent under the Command of William Churchill, Sergeant to Captain Lodwick, to fetch the keys from the Lieutenant Governour (a fitter person for such a Message could not be sent than this Churchill, infamous for v/his mutinous and turbulent spirit). With much Insolence this impertinent impudent fellow rushed into the room where the Lieutenant Governour was, and demanded the keys; the Lieutenant Governour commanded him to call his Captain, who was prevailed with to come, hoping thereby to appease the people, unto whom the Lieutenant Governour delivered the keys, and Captain Lodwick returning to the Fort, the expectations of the multitude being answered, after publishing Ja. Leysler Colonel, all leave the Fort to Captain Lodwick and his Company, who stayed their usual time and it was then agreed upon amongst the Captains, that each should take his turn to reside in the Fort as Chief, till their Majestys pleasure should be further known.

The Lieutenant Governour, his Council and Convention aforesaid, taking into their serious considerations, what danger the Moneys was in, paid by the Inhabitants of this their Majestys Province as well for Customs as Publick Taxes, which at that time was secured in the Fort, The said convention agreed upon and ordered the Moneys should be removed to the House of Frederick Phillips1 one of the Council, a man of known credit and the most considerable for Estate in their Majesties Province.

This was concluded on the day our Usurper Leysler, by his Instruments, seized the Fort, being the 31st day of May last past. But to no purpose was this agreement of the convention; for those who had made themselves masters of their majesties Fort were resolved to command the Money too, being the sum of seven hundred seventy three pounds, which they peremptorily denied the removal of, when demanded by the Lieutenant Governour, in pursuance of the order aforesaid. How they have disposed of this Money, is not our present business to enquire; we leave that until the happy arrival of a Governour Legally commissionated from the King.

The Fort being thus in possession of the Captains of this City, by turns, all the violence used for severall days was that upon the arrival of any Vessel, great or small, a file of Musqueteers were sent on board, the Masters and Passengers carried to the Fort, and the Letters taken from them, some whereof were open'd, and publickly read amongst the People. Never the like known in this place, under any former English Governor.

Source: Charles M. Andrews, ed., *Narratives of the Insurrections 1675–1690*, Original Narratives of Early American History (New York: Charles Scribner's Sons, 1915), 320–326.

Stono Rebellion (1739)

In 1739, approximately 20 slaves in South Carolina developed a plan for escaping to freedom in Spanish-held Florida. This event, known as the Stono Rebellion, is the largest and bloodiest slave rebellion of colonial British North America.

South Carolina emerged in the early 18th century as an agricultural colony based on a plantation economy that centered on rice and later indigo. Both crops were labor intensive and grown on large plantations along the coast. Demands for labor were met by the initial enslavement of Native Americans and then the importation of individuals from Africa. In particular, South Carolinians favored slaves from the west coast of Africa. Slaves exceeded the number of free individuals in South Carolina as early as 1708. By 1740, there were approximately 39,000 slaves in South Carolina representing 66.1 percent of the total population in the colony (Edgar 1998, 78).

The resistance of slaves to their condition assumed many forms. At times, a slave would strike a white overseer or other individual mistreating him. However, such actions led to severe punishments, including death. Slaves learned to hold their anger and frustration or to resist through other means. Slaves practiced many alternative forms of resistance to their plight, with sabotage or work slowdowns the most common choices. Barns mysteriously burned and animals disappeared from their pens. Many slaves yearned to escape and head south toward Spanish Florida, where freedom awaited them.

In 1726, South Carolina dispatched an official delegation to St. Augustine, Florida, to secure Spanish acknowledgement to abide by a 1713 agreement to return fugitive slaves from the English colonies. The delegation returned without receiving a firm assurance from the Spanish. Slaves continued to escape and make their way to Florida, where some were armed and returned to raid farms in English-held territory. Despite the hope of freedom, many fugitive slaves or those on captured English vessels were sold rather than freed by the Spanish. In 1733, the king of Spain issued a decree that officially granted freedom to all fugitive slaves from English territory. Although the Spanish in Florida did not immediately abide by the decree, by 1738 they began freeing many fugitives who had escaped from English colonies to the north.

The Spanish Decree of 1733 and increasing rumors of slave unrest were issues addressed by the South Carolina Assembly when it met in early 1739. The members also discussed the problem of increasing numbers of slaves escaping and heading south toward Spanish Florida, where apparent freedom awaited. In July 1739, a Spanish vessel arrived in Charleston (spelled Charlestown at that time) reportedly carrying a message from James Oglethorpe of Georgia. Rumors later emerged that the vessel carried a man of African origin who spoke English and stopped at several small inlets along the coast as it approached Charleston. Whether these rumors are true and the Spanish helped instigate the Stono Rebellion have never been proven.

On September 9, 1739, approximately 20 slaves met near the Stono River in St. Paul's Parish. Many of these slaves were recent arrivals from Angola and were led by a man whose name has been definitively lost to history but reported as "Jemmy" or "Jonny." The group crossed the Stono Bridge, approximately 20 miles south of Charleston, and entered Hutchinson's Store where they stole weapons and gunpowder and murdered Robert Bathurst and Mr. Gibbes, who operated the establishment. The fugitives left the heads of both men on the front steps. They then entered the home of Mr. Godfrey and murdered him, his son, and daughter. Continuing southward, the fugitives arrived at Wallace's Tavern. The innkeeper, known to be benevolent to slaves, survived the encounter. However, the group murdered Mr. Lemy along with his wife and child before moving on and burning the home of Colonel Hext, whose overseer and his wife did not survive the incident. The fugitives burned the homes of three more families and killed the inhabitants as they continued south toward the Georgia border at the Savannah River. They approached the home of Thomas Rose, another man well known for this benevolence toward slaves. Rose's slaves hid him and his family to ensure their safety.

As the fugitives marched, they gathered those who willingly joined them and forced many others to accompany the group to prevent any from warning the white population. Reportedly, the fugitives raised a standard and acquired two drums to mark their advance. Many other white individuals who encountered the band were murdered. Lieutenant Governor William Bull and four other men were riding north toward Charleston when they encountered the fugitive group, which numbered approximately 50 individuals at this point. Bull and his companions managed to escape and rode to the south, warning the countryside. The fugitives continued their progress toward the Georgia border while increasing their numbers. By the afternoon, they halted near the Jacksonboro (Jacksonborough) ferry at the Edisto River.

Armed white citizens organized and rode to intercept the fugitives marching toward them. They found the group resting where they had stopped along the Edisto River. At least two of the fugitives fired upon their opposition, while others loaded weapons or turned to run. The armed white planters fired a volley killing or wounding approximately 14 individuals. Others surrendered, only to be shot after brief questioning. Some who persuaded the planters that they had been forced to join the fugitives were spared. Escaping fugitives were hunted and killed before the planters placed their heads on the mileposts along the road as a warning to other slaves

The Stono Rebellion resulted in the deaths of approximately 75 black and white individuals. Fear and shock resulted in rumors of other supposed plots over the next few months. Many white planters moved their families to Charleston for safety while militia members increased patrols. Six months later, a slave tipped white settlers to another plot that resulted in trials for 67 slaves and the execution of 10. In the spring of 1740, the South Carolina Assembly passed a piece of legislation known as the Slave Codes. The document modified earlier codes that set rules of behavior for slaves and slave owners. Viewing Spanish Florida as an instigator of slave agitation in the colony, South Carolina authorized public funds, vessels, and men to accompany James Oglethorpe of Georgia for a punitive expedition against the Spanish. The operation failed and proved to be a waste of money. The legislature also placed a new importation tax on slaves, doubling their cost. Recent slaves arriving from Angola were seen as organizers of the Stono Rebellion and South Carolina wanted to reduce the numbers of these individuals who were seen as troublemakers. This plan succeeded and reduced the number of imported slaves during the 1740s to 1,562 from 12,589 brought into the colony between 1735 and 1740 (Edgar 1998, 76). In turn, the colony encouraged increased immigration from white settlers to ease the high percentage of slaves in South Carolina. This action failed to make a significant reduction in the percentage of slaves in the colony.

Historical questions about the Stono Rebellion still linger. First, the Stono Rebellion is sometimes known as "Cato's Rebellion"; however, it is not accurately known whether the slave named "Cato" was associated with the Stono Rebellion or the suppressed insurrection of 1740. Second, despite the existence of Spain's 1773 decree and the arrival of the Spanish vessel in Charleston, there is little historical evidence for direct Spanish involvement in the Stono Rebellion. However, the knowledge that possible freedom awaited in Florida did prompt those in the Stono Rebellion, as well as many other individuals before 1739, to escape south toward the Spanish colony.

—*Terry M. Mays*

See also all entries under New York Slave Insurrection (1741); Antebellum Suppressed Slave Revolts (1800s–1850s); Nat Turner's Rebellion (1831); New Orleans Riot (1866); New Orleans Race Riot (1900); Atlanta Race Riot (1906); Springfield Race Riot (1908); Houston Riot (1917); Red Summer (1919); Tulsa Race Riot (1921); Civil Rights Movement (1953–1963); Watts Riot (1965); Detroit Riots (1967); Los Angeles Uprising (1992).

Further Reading

Edgar, Walter. *South Carolina: A History.* Columbia: University of South Carolina Press, 1998.

Smith, Mark M. "Remembering Mary, Shaping Revolt: Reconsidering the Stono Rebellion." *Journal of Southern History* 67, no. 3 (August 2001): 513–534.

Thornton, John K. "African Dimensions of the Stono Rebellion." *American Historical Review* 96, no. 4 (October 1991): 1101–1113.

Wax, Darold D. " 'The Great Risque We Run': The Aftermath of Slave Rebellion at Stono, South Carolina, 1739–1745." *Journal of Negro History* 67, no. 2 (Summer 1982): 136–147.

Wood, Peter H. *Black Majority: Negroes in Colonial South Carolina from 1670 through the Stono Rebellion.* New York: Alfred A. Knopf, 1974.

Slave Codes

Many states enacted slave codes as early as the 17th century and maintained them until the end of the Civil War. The codes were state regulations governing the movement and activities of slaves and, in some cases, the conduct of plantation owners. The purposes for developing these codes included the suppression of slaves to prevent escape attempts from servitude as well as possibly reduce the chances of any slaves gathering in large numbers for the purpose of revolts. South Carolina passed its first slave code in 1686 and the state's Slave Code of 1740, written as a result of the Stono Rebellion of 1739, proved to be the most comprehensive in colonial America and the pre–Civil War United States. Georgia based its 1755 slave code on South Carolina's 1740 document.

The Slave Code of 1740, known by its official title as *An Act for the Better Ordering and Governing Negroes and Other Slaves in This Province*, restated many of the regulations in South Carolina's earlier slave codes as well as added new provisions specifically developed as a result of the 1739 Stono Rebellion. The Code consisted of 17 handwritten pages directed at all individuals who could be classified as slaves,

The plantation police, or home guard, examine African American passes on the levee road in the South. Black codes were used during Reconstruction to control and regulate the movement of former slaves. (Bettmann/Corbis)

including "Negroes" (those individuals transported directly from Africa or other locations and sold in South Carolina as well as their children), "Indians," "mulattoes" (individuals of ethnically black/white mixed parentage), and "mustizoes" (individuals of ethnically Native American/white mixed parentage). The document's official purpose can be seen in two separate categories. First, the Slave Code established rules to ensure slaves remained in obedience and subjugation. Second, it outlined regulations to govern the conduct of slaveholders to ensure they did not prompt slaves to run away or rebel through excessive mistreatment.

After listing those categories of people who could be held as slaves, the 1740 document defined the institution of slavery and outlined the position of individual slaves and their offspring as personal property to be held in perpetuity unless changed in accordance with existing laws such as those permitting the granting or purchasing of personal freedom. Regulations governing the conduct of slaves included restrictions on movement. A slave could not cross the boundary of a plantation or town, if living in the latter, without being accompanied by a white person unless carrying written permission of the slaveholder. The 1740 Act even included an example of a permission note. Punishment for this violation could be the receipt of up to 20 lashes on the bare back. Any white individual who provided written permission for the movement of a slave without consent of the slaveholder had to pay 20 pounds to the latter.

Other restrictions placed on slaves included details on the trial and punishment of slaves who violated the 1740 Act, punishments for striking free individuals, and the banning of personal business transactions conducted by slaves in Charleston. The 1740 Act outlined guidance for slaveholders and included the punishment for beating a slave without "sufficient cause" as a 40-shilling fine. Slaveholders who did not provide slaves with a labor-free Sunday without justification were subject to fines. The document provided the laws associated with the pursuit and capture of escaping slaves. The General Assembly of South Carolina agreed in the document to compensate any individual injured while pursuing or apprehending a runaway slave or a slave conducting an act deemed unlawful by the Slave Act of 1740. Despite the existence of the rigid slave code, both slaves and slaveholders tended to ignore the regulations whenever possible. A scanned copy and a transcription of the actual Slave Code of 1740 from South Carolina can be found at the website of the *Teaching American History in South Carolina* project funded by the U.S. Department of Education.

—*Terry M. Mays*

Further Reading

"1740 South Carolina Slave Code." Acts of the South Carolina General Assembly, 1740 # 670. South Carolina Department of Archives and History, Columbia, South Carolina.

Teaching American History in South Carolina. "Transcript of the 1740 Slave Code." http://www.teachingushistory.org/tTrove/1740slvcodetranscrip.html (accessed August 30, 2008).

Wax, Darold D. " 'The Great Risque We Run': The Aftermath of Slave Rebellion at Stono, South Carolina, 1739–1745." *Journal of Negro History* 67, no. 2 (Summer 1982): 136–147.

Wood, Peter H. *Black Majority: Negroes in Colonial South Carolina from 1670 through the Stono Rebellion*. New York: Alfred A. Knopf, 1974.

South Carolina

Colonial South Carolina developed an early plantation-based economy requiring a large work force. Landowners solved the labor issue by importing slaves from Africa and the Caribbean when Native Americans did not work out well as plantation labor. The pre-American Revolution economy of South Carolina depended heavily on the production of rice and later indigo for export. Rice in particular was a very labor-intensive and challenging crop to produce on a large scale. As a result, South Carolinians favored the importation of slaves from what is referred to as the Senegambia region of West Africa, where slaves were often experienced in rice production. In fact, many of these individuals had been slaves in West Africa before being sent to South Carolina. As the plantation economy grew, so did the number of slaves imported to Charleston. Slaves exceeded the number of free individuals in South Carolina as early as 1708. By 1740, the approximately 39,000 slaves in the colony made up 66.1 percent of the colony's total population (Edgar 1998, 78). Charleston served as a major importation and transit center for slaves bound for the American colonies. Approximately 40 percent of all slaves brought directly from Africa to the 13 colonies transited through the city. The large number of West African slaves retained in the South Carolina lowcountry surrounding Charleston led to the development of a unique coastal culture and the Gullah language, which was still spoken by some individuals in the early 21st century.

Although South Carolina developed slave regulations beginning in the late 17th century and, in 1740, passed the strictest slave code in the colonies as well as independent America, slaves in the colony often lived in better conditions than those in other areas, including North Carolina and Virginia. The sheer numbers of slaves in South Carolina and their critical importance to a successful plantation economy prompted many slaveholders to ignore some provisions of the slave codes and not interfere in various aspects associated with the personal lives of slaves, although such benevolence could not substitute for freedom (Littlefield 1991, 62–64; Edgar 1998, 78–79). Other slaveholders could be quite repressive. Slaves not only worked the plantations and performed household tasks, but also served in the early-18th-century militia fighting against both the Spanish and Native Americans.

Many slaves practiced passive resistance against the institution of slavery, while others offered a more active form by running away alone or in larger numbers. Rebellions involving mass runaways and violence were not common but stirred fear among the white population and prompted the development of slave regulations, known as slave codes, as early as 1686. The first slave rebellion in South Carolina dates from 1720 and is known as the Primus Plot. A slave reported the scheme before it could fully develop, forcing the escape of those involved. Many associated with the plot were later captured and executed. The largest and most famous slave revolt in the 13 American colonies is known as the Stono Rebellion. The 1739 South Carolina incident resulted in the deaths of approximately 75 people (black and white) and the passage of the Slave Code of 1740. South Carolina resisted attempts to end slavery throughout the latter half of the 18th century and played a significant role in ensuring its protection was added to the fledging U.S. Constitution in 1787.

—Terry M. Mays

Further Reading

Edgar, Walter. *South Carolina: A History*. Columbia: University of South Carolina Press, 1998.

Littlefield, Daniel C. *Rice and Slaves: Ethnicity and the Slave Trade in Colonial South Carolina*. Urbana: University of Illinois Press, 1991.

Wax, Darold D. " 'The Great Risque We Run': The Aftermath of Slave Rebellion at Stono, South Carolina, 1739–1745." *Journal of Negro History* 67, no. 2 (Summer 1982): 136–147.

Wood, Peter H. *Black Majority: Negroes in Colonial South Carolina from 1670 through the Stono Rebellion*. New York: Alfred A. Knopf, 1974.

Description of the Rebellion by Georgia Governor James Oglethorpe (1739)

On September 9, 1739, a literate slave named Jemmy (or, in some sources, Cato) led about 20 other slaves in an armed uprising that eventually resulted in the deaths of about 25 whites. After recruiting another 50 to 60 slaves, Jemmy tried to lead his followers into Spanish Florida, but the slaves were caught by the South Carolina militia, and more than 40 died in the ensuing battle. Below is a description of the uprising and its aftermath by James Oglethorpe, the governor of the colony of Georgia. The Stono Rebellion was the largest African slave insurrection of the colonial period.

Sometime since there was a Proclamation published at Augustine, in which the King of Spain (ther at Peace with Great Britain) promised Protection and Freedom to all Negroes Slaves that would resort thither. Certain Negroes belonging to Captain Davis escaped to Augustine, and were received there. They were demanded by General Oglethorpe who sent Lieutenant Demere to Augustine, and the Governour assured the General of his sincere Friendship, but at the same time showed his Orders from the Court of Spain, by which he was to receive all Run away Negroes. Of this other Negroes having notice, as it is believed, from the Spanish Emissaries, four or five who were Catte-Hunters, and knew the Woods, some of whom belonged to Captain Macpherson, ran away with His Horses, wounded his Son and killed another Man. These marched f [sic] for Georgia, and were pursued, but the Rangers being then newly reduced [sic] the Countrey people could not overtake them, though they were discovered by the Saltzburghers, as they passed by Ebenezer. They reached Augustine, one only being killed and another wounded by the Indians in their flight. They were received there with great honours, one of them had a Commission given to him, and a Coat faced with Velvet. Amongst the Negroe Salves there are a people brought from the Kingdom of Angola in Africa, many of these speak Portugueze [which Language is as near Spanish as Scotch is to English,] by reason that the Portugueze have considerable Settlement, and the Jesuits have a Mission and School in that Kingdom and many Thousands of the Negroes there profess the Roman Catholic Religion. Several Spaniards upon diverse Pretences have for some time past been strolling about Carolina, two of them, who will give no account of themselves have been taken up and committed to Jayl in Georgia. The good reception of the Negroes at Augustine was spread about. Several attempted to escape to the Spaniards, & were taken, one of them was hanged at Charles Town. In the latter end of July last Don Pedro, Colonel of the Spanish Horse, went in a Launch to Charles Town under pretence of a message to General Oglethorpe and the Lieutenant Governour.

On the 9th day of September last being Sunday which is the day the Planters allow them to work for themselves, Some Angola Negroes assembled, to the number of Twenty; and one who was called Jemmy was their Captain, they suprized a Warehouse belonging to Mr. Hutchenson at a place called Stonehow [Stono]; they there killed Mr. Robert Bathurst, and Mr. Gibbs, plundered the House and took a pretty many small Arms and Powder, which were there for Sale. Next they plundered and burnt Mr. Godfrey's house and killed him, his Daughter and Son. They then turned back and marched Southward along Pons Pons, which is the Road through Georgia to Augustine, they passed Mr. Wallace's Tavern towards day break, and said they would not hurt him, for he was a good Man and kind to his Slaves, but they broke open and plundered Mr. Lemy's House, and killed him, his wife and Child. They marched on towards Mr. Rose's resolving to kill him; but he was saved by a Negroe, who having hid him went out and pacified the others. Several Negroes joyned them, they calling out Liberty, marched on with Colours displayed, and two Drums beating, pursuing all the white people they met with, and killing Man Woman and Child when they could come up to them. Collonel Bull Lieutenant Governour of South Carolina, who was then riding along the Road, discovered them, was pursued, and with much difficulty escaped & raised the Countrey. They burnt Colonel

Hext's house and killed his Overseer and his Wife. They then burnt Mr. Sprye's house, then Mr. Sacheverell's, and then Mr. Nash's house, all lying upon the Pons Pons Road, and killed all the white People they found in them. Mr. Bullock got off, but they burnt his House, by this time many of them were drunk with the Rum they had take in the Houses. They increased every minute by new Negroes coming to them, so that they were above Sixty, some say a hundred, on which they halted in a field, and set to dancing, Singing and beating Drums, to draw more Negroes to them, thinking they were now victorious over the whole Province, having marched ten miles & burnt all before them without Opposition, but the Militia being raised, the Planters with great briskness pursued them and when they came up, dismounting; charged them on foot. The Negroes were soon routed, though they behaved boldly several being killed on the Spot, many ran back to their Plantations thinking they had not been missed, but they were there taken and [sic] Shot, Such as were taken in the field also, were after being examined, shot on the Spot, And this is to be said to the honour of the Carolina Planters, that notwithstanding the Provocation they had received from so many Murders, they did not torture one Negroe, but only put them to an easy death. All that proved to be forced & were not concerned in the Murders & Burnings were pardoned, And this sudden Courage in the field, & the Humanity afterwards hath had so good an Effect that there hath been no farther Attempt, and the very Spirit of Revolt seems over. About 30 escaped from the fight, of which ten marched about 30 miles Southward, and being overtaken by the Planters on horseback, fought stoutly for some time and were all killed on the Spot. The rest are yet untaken. In the whole action about 40 Negroes and 20 whites were killed. The Lieutenant Governour sent an account of this to General Oglethorpe, who met the advices on his return form the Indian Nation He immediately ordered a Troop of Rangers to be ranged, to patrole through Georgia, placed some Men in the Garrison at Palichocolas, which was before abandoned, and near which the Negroes formerly passed, being the only place where Horses can come to swim over the River Savannah for near 100 miles, ordered out the Indians in pursuit, and a Detachment of the Garrison at Port Royal to assist the Planters on any Occasion, and published a Proclamation ordering all the Constables &c. of Georgia to pursue and seize all Negroes, with a Reward for any that should be taken. It is hoped these measures will prevent any Negroes from getting down to the Spaniards.

Source: Allen Chandler, ed., *The Colonial Records of the State of Georgia*, vol. 22 (Atlanta: Chas. P. Byrd Press, 1913), 232–236.

New York Slave Insurrection (1741)

The New York Slave Insurrection of 1741, also known as the New York Conspiracy of 1741, involved some slaves and also poor white settlers planning to burn down New York City in a series of fires, and then take over. The ill treatment of slaves in New York had led to plots and conspiracies hatched by slaves either to escape or to take revenge on their masters as well as ordinary people whose attitude to slavery was seen to be, at best, apathetic. These seem to have taken place every two or three years from the 1690s, and in 1737, George Clarke, the acting governor of New York, told the state legislature that slaves should not be hired out to businesses where they could undercut the rates of pay charged by white craftsmen and artisans because this was forcing some of the latter out of business, and some of these had been forced to leave the state.

The War of Jenkins' Ear, between Britain and Spain, broke out in 1739, and in the following year, it became part of the bigger War of Austrian Succession. The Spanish, to stir up trouble in the British colonies, had offered freedom to any slave who supported them, and this had led to a small slave revolt in South Carolina known as the Stono Rebellion, which had broken out in September 1739. With many of the state troops in New York helping with the British attack on Cuba, there were also fewer soldiers in the state than normal.

In the winter of 1740–1741, there was an economic depression in New York City, which at that time had a population of 11,000, of whom 2,000 were slaves. It was a cold winter, and some of the people were living in miserable conditions, unable to afford enough fuel to keep warm. There was also great tension between the poor whites and the slaves. Although the economic situation improved slightly, by the early spring of 1741, many people were still in hardship. On March 18, 1741, the residence of the governor caught fire, and the flames spread to the church adjoining it. Worried that the city archives might be destroyed if another nearby building, where they were kept, also caught fire, the governor ordered all the records thrown out the windows, and they were then taken to the City Hall. A soldier, Griffith Evans, was burned to death in the fire.

Another fire broke out on March 25, after the one at the governor's house, and this time it was at the Battery, which burned down quickly. There was another fire a week later, on April 1, and more fires followed this on a weekly basis. There were often fires in the city, but the number of them and their locations did make some people suspicious. On April 6, 1741, a series of four fires broke out, and a white passerby saw a black man running away. He tried to catch him, and although he was unsuccessful, with the help of other people, the suspect was identified as a slave called Cuffee who was owned by Adolph Philipse. In theory, the slaves were supposed to be watched and prevented from wandering the street at night, but this was found to be impractical and hence not enforced.

The Council of the City of New York then began an investigation into the fires, and this task was entrusted to Daniel Horsmanden, who established a grand jury to investigate "whites who sold liquor to blacks." The first man in his sights was John Hughson, a poor shoemaker who had grown up in the town of Yonkers and then moved to New York City about five years earlier along with his wife, daughter, and mother-in-law. Unable to find work as a cobbler, he opened a tavern near Trinity Churchyard on the Hudson River, quickly gaining a reputation as a place for slaves, free African Americans, and soldiers. Stolen goods were regularly sold there but the police were unable to pin the thefts on Hughson. The investigations by Horsmanden centered on a group of convicted thieves—Cuffee, and two others called Caesar (a slave owned by John Vaarck, a baker) and Prince (a slave owned by John Auboyneau)—who became known as the Geneva Club. Caesar and Prince had already come to the notice of the authorities in 1736 when they led slaves to steal gin from Baker's Tavern in New York—both being publicly whipped as punishment.

Horsmanden had to get evidence on Hughson, which was finally provided by Mary Burton, an indentured servant of Hughson. She told him that there was a conspiracy by which poor whites and African Americans were intent on burning down New York. Gradually, Horsmanden managed to get more information from Burton, especially after he threatened to jail her. She told him that Hughson was working with Caesar, Prince, and Cuffee, and the four of them were hiring other people to light a number of the fires. Horsmanden then offered a reward of £100 for a white person, £45 for a free black or Indian, and £20 and freedom for any slave, for information.

On May 2, 1741, Caesar and Prince were found guilty of burglary and sentenced to death. On the following day, a fire engulfed seven barns, and the two slaves who were caught were then burned at a stake. On May 6, Hughson and an Irish woman called Peggy or Margaret Sorubiero, who worked as a prostitute at Hughson's tavern, were also arrested. Caesar and Prince were hanged on May 11, and enough evidence was collected to start trials of other conspirators. Those arrested named other people, and those investigated named more. It was not long before the hysteria had seen the naming of about half the adult male population of New York. Some of the slaves captured were Spanish sailors, or at any rate claimed to be such, and this meant that they had to be sold to slave dealers who took them to the Caribbean.

However, in his investigations, Horsmanden was convinced that the arson attacks were too well organized for somebody such as John Hughson to organize. This led him to investigate the background of John Ury, a teacher who had recently arrived in New York. He spoke Latin and was arrested on suspicions that he was actually a Roman Catholic priest, and then Horsmanden came to the view that he was a Spanish agent who came to New York to stir up trouble. He was tried, named by Burton as a conspirator, and executed. The result of the trials was that 17 African Americans and 4 whites were hanged, 13 African Americans were burned to death, and 70 were banished from New York City. As the hysteria died down, many of the remaining prisoners were released. There is doubt that the Spanish were actually involved, with many historians believing that it was actually a conspiracy of slaves rather than inspired by the Spanish.

—Justin Corfield

See also all entries under Stono Rebellion (1739); Antebellum Suppressed Slave Revolts (1800s–1850s); Nat Turner's Rebellion (1831); New Orleans Riot (1866); New Orleans Race Riot (1900); Atlanta Race Riot (1906); Springfield Race Riot (1908); Houston Riot (1917); Red Summer (1919); Tulsa Race Riot (1921); Civil Rights Movement (1953–1968); Watts Riot (1965); Detroit Riots (1967); Los Angeles Uprising (1992).

Further Reading

Davis, Thomas J. *A Rumor of Revolt: The Great Negro Plot in Colonial New York.* New York: Free Press, 1985.

Hoffer, Peter Charles. *The Great New York Conspiracy of 1741: Slavery, Crime and Colonial Law.* Lawrence: University of Kansas Press, 2003.

Johnson, Mat. *The Great Negro Plot: A Tale of Conspiracy and Murder in Eighteenth-Century New York.* New York: Bloomsbury, 2007.

Lepore, Jill. *New York Burning: Liberty, Slavery, and Conspiracy in Eighteenth-Century Manhattan.* New York: Alfred A. Knopf, 2005.

Fires

With most homes in New York in 1741 having a large number of open fireplaces, and with candles being used throughout the city, which boasted many wooden houses, the likelihood of a fire was high. It was made worse by many places having quantities of hay for horses and other livestock. As a result, as early as 1648, the Dutch in New Amsterdam introduced the first Fire Ordinance, a "bucket law" by which people needed to have a bucket ready in case of fires. Because many thought that these precautions were wholly inadequate, in 1731, "A Law for the Better Preventing of Fire" was passed, and a New York Fire Brigade was established, with two water-pumping machines—'two Compleat fire Engines,'" which cost $200—being bought from a Mr. Newshams, from England. These needed trained operators, and there was also sufficient worry about arson that in 1736 the first fire brigade office was established in front of City Hall, and on December 16, 1737, the New York Volunteer Fire Department was established, with a staff of 30. In addition, the firemen would always be helped by members of the public, who would form a line passing buckets of water to any conflagration.

The problem with the arson attack on March 18, 1741, was that as the fire spread from the residence of the governor, people thought that it might set ablaze the gunpowder store at the fort, in spite of the store being sealed underground. It was at times such as these that many people who were helping the firemen pulled out. Moreover, during times of arson attacks such as that on March 18, 1741, the city authorities feared that looting might also take place and quickly put soldiers onto the street. Certainly instances like this led some slaves to feel that a series of arson attacks might destroy the city and allow them to escape.

Because the crime of arson could be so indiscriminate—fires easily spreading from one place to another, especially in cities where most buildings were made of wood—the penalties for arson were very severe. In British America, arson was a common law offense, with first-degree felony arson being when people were harmed or killed in the fire. Second-degree felony arson involved significant loss of property. There were also severe penalties for setting fire to uninhabited buildings such as sheds. Executions for arson often involved the culprits being burned to death, with 13 slaves being executed by this manner between May and August 1741. During the period of British rule at the start of the American Revolutionary War, there were two large fires of suspicious origins in New York City.

—*Justin Corfield*

Further Reading

Costello, A. E. *Birth of the Bravest: A History of the New York Fire Department from 1609 to 1887*. New York: Forge Books, 2003.

Davis, Thomas J. *A Rumor of Revolt: The Great Negro Plot in Colonial New York*. New York: Free Press, 1985.

Lepore, Jill. *New York Burning: Liberty, Slavery, and Conspiracy in Eighteenth-Century Manhattan*. New York: Alfred A. Knopf, 2005.

Manhattan Island

Covering nearly 23 square miles, Manhattan Island is the location of New York City, which, in 1741, covered only five square miles of the island, although that still made it one of the largest cities in British North America, and certainly one of the major ports on the East Coast, along with Boston and Charleston. There has been debate about the origin of the word Manhattan, which is thought to have meant "Island of many hills" in the language of the Lenape people. It is certainly mentioned (as "Manna-hata") in the logbook of Robert Juet in 1609 and on a map of the following year. Legally, the Walloon trader Peter Minuit had bought the island from the local Native Americans for goods then worthy 60 guilders. In 1736, the city had expanded to incorporate the nearby town of Harlem, the area between the two being farmland, and early maps of New York during this period show that the vast majority of Manhattan Island was devoted to farming.

As one of the major commercial centers at the time, the city had long expanded from the fort that the Dutch had built there, and the palisade wall from which Wall Street partially gets its name had been removed in 1699 and Walloons from Belgian (the other origin of the street name) moved there soon afterwards.

Manhattan Island, in 1741, was part of the Province of New York, and at that time was one of the main urban centers of slavery in British North America. Indeed, only Charleston in South Carolina had more slaves per capita. On Manhattan Island, some 20 percent of the 11,000 living on the island were African Americans, the vast majority of whom were slaves. This was in spite of widespread migration from Europe to Manhattan during the late 17th and early 18th centuries. Living in Manhattan, numbers of Dutch families traced their time there back to before August 27, 1664, when the island was captured by the British from the Dutch; and also British families who had moved to New York from other parts of North America. From 1710, there were also large numbers of German migrants from the Palatine.

—*Justin Corfield*

Further Reading

Davis, Thomas J. *A Rumor of Revolt: The Great Negro Plot in Colonial New York.* New York: Free Press, 1985.

Lepore, Jill. *New York Burning: Liberty, Slavery, and Conspiracy in Eighteenth-Century Manhattan.* New York: Alfred A. Knopf, 2005.

Smith, William, Jr. *The History of the Province of New York.* Cambridge, MA: Harvard University Press, 1972.

Investigation into a New York Slave Conspiracy (1741)

In the spring of 1741, a series of mysterious fires led many New York residents to suspect arson. When a black slave was arrested fleeing one of the fires, rumors of a slave conspiracy to burn the whole town quickly sprang up. Within days, over 100 slaves and some poor whites who were suspected of being party to the conspiracy were in custody. Reproduced here are records of the initial investigation into the supposed slave plot.

At a Supreme Court of Judicature held for the province of New York, at the city-hall of the city of New York, on Tuesday, April 21, 1741-Present, Frederick Philipse, esq. Second justice; Daniel Horsmanden, esq. third justice.

The grand jury were called. The following persons appeared, and were sworn-viz.: Mr. Robert Watts, merchant, foreman; Messrs. Jeremiah Latouche, Joseph Read, Anthony Rutgers, John M'Evers, John Cruger, jun. John Merritt, Adoniah Schuyler, Isaac De Peyster, Abraham Keteltass, David Provoost, Rene Hett, Henry Beekman, jun. David Van Horne, George Spencer, Thomas Duncan, Winant Van Zant, merchants. Mr. Justice Philipse gave the charge to the grand jury, as followeth:

Gentlemen of the grand jury,

It is not without some concern, that I am obliged at this time to be more particular in your charge, than for many preceding terms there hath been occasion. The many frights and terrors which the good people of this city have of late been put into, by repeated and unusual fires, and burning of houses, give us too much room to suspect, that some of them at least did not proceed from mere chance, or common accidents; but on the contrary, from the premeditated malice and wicked pursuits of evil and designing persons; and therefore, it greatly behoves us to use our utmost diligence, by all lawful ways and means to discover the contrivers and perpetrators of such daring and flagitious undertakings: that, upon conviction, they may receive condign punishment; for although we have the happiness of living under a government which exceeds all others in the excellency of its constitution and laws, yet if those to whom the execution of them (which my lord Coke calls the life and soul of the law) is committed, do not exert themselves in a conscientious discharge of their respective duties, such laws which were intended for a terror to the evil-doer, and a protection to the good, will become a dead letter, and our most excellent constitution turned into anarchy and confusion; every one practising what he listeth, and doing what shall seem good in his own eyes: to prevent which, it is the duty of all grand juries to inquire into the conduct and behaviour of the people in their respective counties; and if, upon examination, they find any to have transgressed the laws of the land, to present them, that so they may by the court be put upon their trial, and then either to be discharged or punished according to their demerits.

I am told there are several prisoners now in jail, who have been committed by the city magistrates, upon suspicion of having been concerned in some of the late fires; and others, who under pretence of assisting the unhappy sufferers, by saving their goods from the flames, for stealing, or receiving them. This indeed, is adding affliction to the afflicted, and is a very great aggravation of such crime, and therefore deserves a narrow inquiry: that so the exemplary punishment of the guilty (if any such should be so found) may deter others from committing the like villainies; for this kind of stealing, I think, has not been often practised among us.

Gentlemen,

Arson, or the malicious and voluntary burning, not only a mansion house, but also any other house, and the out buildings, or barns, and stables adjoining thereto, by night or by day, is felony at common law; and if any part of the house be burned, the offender is guilty of felony, notwithstanding the fire afterwards be put out, or go out of itself.

This crime is of so shocking a nature, that if we have any in this city, who, having been guilty thereof, should escape, who can say he is safe, or tell where it will end?

Gentlemen,

Another Thing which I cannot omit recommending to your serious and diligent inquiry, is to find out and present all such persons who sell rum, and other strong liquor to negroes. It must be obvious to every one, that there are too many of them in this city; who, under pretence of selling what they call a penny dram to a negro, will sell to him as many quarts or gallons of rum, as he can steal money or goods to pay for.

How this notion of its being lawful to sell a penny dram, or a pennyworth of rum to a slave, without the consent or direction of his master, has prevailed, I know not; but this I am sure of, that there is not only no such law, but that the doing of it is directly contrary to an act of the assembly now in force, for the better regulating of slaves. The many fatal consequences flowing from this prevailing and wicked practice, are so notorious, and so nearly concern us all, that one would be almost surprised, to think there should be a necessity for a court to recommend a suppression of such pernicious houses: thus much in particular; now in general.

My charge, gentlemen, further is, to present all conspiracies, combinations, and other offences, from treasons down to trespasses; and in your inquiries, the oath you, and each of you have just now taken will, I am persuaded, be your guide, and I pray God to direct and assist you in the discharge of your duty.

Court adjourned until to-morrow morning ten o'clock.

The grand jury having been informed, that Mary Burton could give them some account concerning the good stolen from Mr. Hogg's, sent for her this morning, and ordered she should be sworn; the constable returned and acquainted them, that she said she would not be sworn, nor give evidence; whereupon they ordered the constable to get a warrant from a magistrate, to bring her before them. The constable was some time gone, but at length returned, and brought her with him; and being asked why she would not be sworn, and give her evidence? she told the grand jury she would not be sworn; and seemed to be under some great uneasiness, or terrible apprehensions; which gave suspicion that she know something concerning the fires that had lately happened: and being asked a question to that purpose, she gave no answer; which increased the jealousy that she was privy to them; and as it was thought a matter of the utmost concern, the grand jury was very importunate, and used many arguments with her, in public and private, to persuade her to speak the truth, and tell all she knew about it. To this end, the lieutenant governor's proclamation was read to her, promising indemnity, and the reward of one hundred pounds to any person, confederate or not, who should make discovery, etc. She seemed to despise it, nor could the grand jury by any means, either threats or promises, prevail upon her, though they assured her withal, that she should have the protection of the magistrates, and her person be safe and secure from harm; but hitherto all was in vain: therefore, the grand jury desired alderman Bancker to commit her; and the constable was charged with her accordingly; but before he had got her to jail, she considered better of it, and resolved to be sworn, and give her evidence in the afternoon.

Accordingly, she being sworn, came before the grand jury; but as they were proceeding to her examination, and before they asked her any questions, she told them she would acquaint them with what she knew relating to the goods stolen from Mr. Hogg's, but would say nothing about the fires.

This expression thus, as it were providentially, slipping from the evidence, much alarmed the grand jury; for, as they naturally concluded, it did by construction amount to an affirmative, that she could give an account of the occasion of the several fires; and therefore, as it highly became those gentlemen in the discharge of their trust, they determined to use their utmost diligence to sift out the discovery, but still she remained inflexible, till at length, having recourse to religious topics, representing to her the heinousness of the crime which she would be guilty of, if she was privy to, and could discover so wicked a design, as the firing houses about our ears; whereby not only people's estates would be destroyed, but many person might lose their lives in the flames: this she would have to answer for at the day of judgment, as much as any person immediately concerned, because she might have prevented this destruction, and would not; so that a most damnable sin would lie at her door; and what need she fear from her divulging it; she was sure of the protection of the magistrates? or the grand jury expressed themselves in words to the same purpose; which arguments at last prevailed, and she gave the following evidence, which however, notwithstanding what had been said, came from her, as if still under some terrible apprehensions or restraints.

Deposition, No. 1.-Mary Burton, being sworn, deposeth,

1. "That Frince (a) and Caesar (b) brought the things of which they had robbed Mr. Hogg, to her master, John Hughson's house, and that they were handed in through

the window, Hughson, his wife, and Peggy receiving them, about two or three o'clock on a Sunday morning. (c)

2. "That Caesar, prince, and Mr. Philipse's negro man (Cuffee) used to meet frequently at her master's house, and that she had heard them (the negroes) talk frequently of burning the fort; and that they would go down to the Fly (d) and burn the whole town; and that her master and mistress said, they would aid and assist them as much as they could.

3. "That in their common conversation they used to say, that when all this was done, Caesar should be governor, and Hughson, her master, should be king.

4. "That Cuffee used to say, that a great many people had too much, and others too little; that his old master had a great deal of money, but that, in a short time, he should have less, and that he (Cuffee) should have more.

5. "That at the same time when the things of which Mr. Hogg was robbed, were brought to her master's house, they brought some indigo and bees wax, which was likewise received by her master and mistress.

6. "That at the meetings of the three aforesaid negroes, Caesar, Prince and Cuffee, at her master's house, they used to say, in their conversations, that when they set fire to the town, they would do it in the night, and as the white people came to extinguish it, they would kill and destroy them.

7. "That she has known at times, seven or eight guns in her master's house, and some swords, and that she has seen twenty or thirty negroes at one time in her master's house; and that at such large meetings, the three aforesaid negroes, Cuffee, Prince and Caesar, were generally present, and most active, and that they used to say, that the other negroes durst not refuse to do what they commanded them, and they were sure that they had a number sufficient to stand by them.

8. "That Hughson (her master) and her mistress used to threaten, that if she, the deponent, ever made mention of the goods stolen from Mr. Hogg, they would poison her; and the negroes swore, if ever she published, or discovered the design of burning the town, they would burn her whenever they met her.

9. "That she never saw any white person in company when they talked of burning the town, but her master, her mistress, and Peggy."

This evidence of a conspiracy, not only to burn the city, but also destroy and murder the people, was most astonishing to the grand jury, and that any white people should become so abandoned as to confederate with slaves in such an execrable and detestable purpose, could not but be very amazing to every one that heard it; what could scarce be credited; but that the several fires had been occasioned by some combination of villains, was, at the time of them, naturally to be collected from the manner and circumstances attending them.

The grand jury therefore, as it was a matter of the utmost consequence, thought it necessary to inform the judges concerning it, in order that the most effectual measures might be concerted, for discovering the confederates; and the judges were acquainted with it accordingly.

SUPREME COURT
Friday, May 1.
Present, the second and third justices.
The king against Caesar and prince, negroes. On trial.

The jury called, and the prisoners making no challenge, the following persons were sworn, viz.:
Roger French, John Groesbeek, John Richard, Abraham Kipp, George Witts, John Thurman, Patrick Jackson, Benjamin Moore, William Hamersley, John Lashier, Joshua Sleydall, John Shurm Jr.

These two negroes were arraigned on two indictments, the twenty fourth of April last; the one for their entering the dwelling house of Robert Hogg, of this city, merchant, on the first day of March then last past, with intent then and there to commit some felony; and for feloniously stealing and carrying away then and there the goods and chattels of the said Robert Hogg, of the value of four pounds five shillings sterling, against the form of the statutes in such case made and provided, and against the peace of our sovereign lord the king, his crown and dignity.

The other for their entering the dwelling house of Abraham Meyers Cohen in this city, merchant, on the first day of March with the intent then and there to commit some felony; and for feloniously stealing and carrying away then and there the goods and chattels of the said Abraham Meyers Cohen of the value of five pounds sterling, against the form of the statutes, etc. And against the king's peace, etc.

To each of which indictments they pleaded, not guilty.

The Attorney General having opened both the indictments, he with Joseph Murray, Esq. of council for the king, proceeded to examine the witnesses, viz.,

For the king. Mrs. Hogg, Mrs. Boswell, Christopher Wilson, Rachina Guerin, Mr. Robert
 Hogg, Mr. Robert Watts, Margaret Sorubiero, alias Kerry, Abraham Meyers Cohen,
James Mills, Thomas Wenman, John Moore, Esq. Cornelius Brower, Anthony Ham, Mary
 Burton.
For the prisoners, Alderman Bancker, Alderman Johnson, John Auboyneau.
The prisoners upon their defence denied the charge against them. And,
The evidence being summed up, which was very strong and full, and the jury charged, they
 withdrew, and being returned, found them guilty of the indictments.
Ordered, that the trials of the Hughsons and Margaret Kerry, be put off until Wednesday of
 the 6th inst.
Court adjourned until Monday morning, 4th May, at ten o'clock. (a) Caesar.

SUPREME COURT Friday, May 8
Present, the second and third justices.
The king against Caesar and Prince, negroes.

The prisoners having been capitally convicted on two several indictments for felony, and being brought to the bar the court proceeded to give sentence; which was passed by the second justice as followeth:

You, Caesar and Prince, the grand jury having found two indictments against each of you, for feloniously stealing and taking away from Mr. Hogg, and Mr. Meyers Cohen, sundry goods of considerable value. To these indictments you severally pleaded not guilty; and for your trials put yourselves upon God and the country; which country having found you guilty, it now only remains for the court to pronounce that judgment which the law requires, and the nature of your crimes deserve.

But before I proceed to sentence, I must tell you, that you have been proceeded against in the same manner as any white man, guilty of your crimes, would have been. You had not only the liberty of sending for your witnesses; asking them such questions as you thought proper; but likewise making the best defence you could; and as you have been convicted by twelve honest men upon their oaths, so the just judgement of God has at length overtaken you.

I have great reason to believe, that the crimes you now stand convicted of, are not the least of those you have been concerned in; for by your general characters you have been very wicked fellows, hardened sinners, and ripe, as well as ready, for the most enormous and daring enterprizes, especially you, Caesar: and as the time you have yet to live is to be but very short, I earnestly advise and exhort both of you to employ it in the most diligent and best manner you can, by confessing your sins, repenting sincerely of them, and praying God of his infinite goodness to have mercy on your souls: and as God knows the secrets of your hearts, and cannot be cheated or imposed upon, so you must shortly give an account to him, and answer for all your actions; and depend upon it, if you do not truly repent before you die, there is a hell to punish the wicked eternally.

And as it is not in your powers to make full restitution for the many injuries you have done the public; so I advise both of you to do all that in you is, to prevent further mischiefs, by discovering such persons as have been concerned with you, in designing or endeavouring to burn this city, and to destroy its inhabitants. This I am fully persuaded is in your power to do if you will; if so, and you do not make such discovery, be assured God almighty will punish you for it, though we do not: therefore I advise you to consider this well, and I hope both of you will tell the truth.

And now, nothing further remains for me to say, but that you Caesar, and you Prince, are to be taken hence to the place whence you came, and from thence to the place of execution, and there you, and each of you, are to be hanged by the neck until you be dead. And I pray the Lord to have mercy on your souls.

Ordered, that their execution be on Monday next, the eleventh day of this instant, between the hours of nine and one of the same day. And further ordered that after the execution of the said sentence, the body of Caesar be hung in chains.

Court adjourned till Monday morning next ten o'clock.

Source: Supreme Court of Judicature, New York City, "New York Conspiracy," *Journal of the Proceedings against the Conspirators, at New York in 1741.*

Philadelphia Election Riot (1742)

The election riots that took place in Philadelphia, the state capital of Pennsylvania, on October 1, 1742, came from an attempt by the Anglicans to break the political dominance of the Quakers in the city. It was during the War of Jenkins' Ear, which had broken out in 1739, but Pennsylvania was to be largely unaffected by the war, which was mainly fought in the Americas at sea, although in Europe it became subsumed by the War of Austrian Succession.

Pennsylvania itself had owed its origins as a British colony to the Quaker thinker and activist William Penn (1644–1718), who was granted the land on March 4, 168_, by King Charles II of England. Penn had the aims of establishing a region that would allow religious freedom for Quakers who were, at that stage, often persecuted and discriminated against elsewhere, especially in England. They had been granted freedom of worship during the rule of Oliver Cromwell, but his death in 1658 led to the Restoration of the Monarchy in England two years later. With this, the Anglicans of the Church of England were keen to enact laws to reverse the liberal religious laws of Cromwell.

The freedom of worship in Pennsylvania became known around the world and attracted not only Quakers, but also substantial numbers of German settlers and some Quakers from Scotland and Ireland. By 1742, about a third of the population of Pennsylvania were Germans, but this community tended to vote for the Quakers because of their support for pacifism and also their belief in less influence of government and hence low taxes. With the War of Austrian Succession, some of the Germans were from states in modern-day Germany that sided with the Austrians (against the British and the Prussians), and they were also supporters of the Quakers, again as a way of keeping out of the conflicts of Europe.

Gradually, however, migrants from Britain from the Church of England—the Anglican faith—started coming to Philadelphia, and one of these, William Allen (1704–1780), established the Proprietary Party, which relied heavily on Anglican voters. His father, William Allen Sr., who had migrated from Dungannon, County Tyrone, Ireland, had been a close colleague of William Penn, but his son, emerging as wealthy and powerful, was keen to demonstrate his support for the British Crown. He had been mayor of the city of Philadelphia in 1735, and had bought, five years earlier, the site on which the Pennsylvania State House (now Independence Hall) was later built. Allen wanted to take control of the city and had started trying to gain support from the Germans. This led to heightened tensions as the Anglicans and the Germans could certainly control the political process. These came to a head on October 1, 1742, the election day, when Allen himself was nominated to be inspector for the elections. It was a significant victory and was based on Anglicans turning out in large numbers after rumors spread that the Quakers were bringing in Germans from nearby to boost their support. This caused Anglican vigilantes to start taking to the streets to prevent what they thought might be Germans arriving to vote out Allen and his supporters.

For many people in Philadelphia, there was much concern about whether Allen would be impartial, and with disputes arising as to how the election should be properly supervised; some 70 sailors who supported Allen declared their support for him. They produced clubs, and shouting anti-Quaker slogans, they attacked a number of Quakers and Germans in the city's courthouse—the Quakers and the Germans having objected to the choice of Allen. The Germans, and also the Quakers, fought back, the latter claiming self-defense as Quakers were against fighting. They managed to drive the sailors out, and bolted the doors of the courthouse to continue their debate. Rumors quickly spread that the Quakers and Germans were holding one of the Anglican sailors in the courthouse, and Anglican supporters marched on the building.

It was soon established that the Quakers were not holding any hostages, and a Quaker was able to explain this to the Anglican vigilantes. Certainly, this stopped some of the overzealous Anglican demonstrators who held back, and this allowed the sheriff to arm the Germans and the Quakers, who were able to drive out the Anglicans. The election then proceeded with the Quakers and Germans in control of the voting area, and many Anglicans worried about approaching. The result was that the Quakers won the poll, with the Proprietary Party being convincingly defeated. There was evidence that some of the voters had changed their original vote, and many of those who had voted for the Proprietary Party altered their votes to support the Quakers and their candidates. Either way, it was a clear vote in favor of the Quakers and against Allen.

The rioting led to some 54 sailors and people connected with the Proprietary Party being jailed on charges or rioting and other related charges. However, the main legal repercussion was that Allen sued one of the leaders of the Quakers, who had declared that Allen had prepared for an attack. The court heard from 49 witnesses, most of whom were Quakers. At the end of these proceedings, the court ruled that Allen; a business partner of Allen; Clement Plumsted, the Mayor of Philadelphia; and two other Anglicans were all to be investigated for negligence in their work, and also for the subversion of the Pennsylvania Charter of 1682.

The matter was finally referred to the Pennsylvania Supreme Court, which was controlled by the Quakers. Eventually, George Thomas, the state governor, intervened, and he decided that the Mayor's Court had jurisdiction, and that the recorder, the alderman, and the mayor, all of whom were Anglicans, would hear the case, with the unusual legal quirk of the mayor hearing the case against himself.

Finally the two sides compromised, and with Allen dropping the court case, and his adversary their slander, the rules for voting were changed to prevent similar disturbances from happening again. Allen was to be the eponym of Allentown, Pennsylvania, which he founded in 1762, being chief justice of the Supreme Court of Pennsylvania from 1750 until 1774. He was a prominent loyalist in the American War of Independence 24 years later, and died on September 6, 1780.

—*Justin Corfield*

See also all entries under Pueblo Revolt (1680); Pima Revolt (1751); Philadelphia Nativist Riots (1844); Know-Nothing Riots (1855–1856).

Further Reading

Cohen, Norman S. "The Philadelphia Election Riot of 1742." *Pennsylvania Magazine of History and Biography* 92, no. 3 (July 1968): 306–319.

Nash, Gary B. *The Urban Crucible: The Northern Seaports and the Origins of the American Revolution.* Cambridge, MA: Harvard University Press, 1986.

Anglicanism

The Church of England was created in 1534, breaking from the Roman Catholic Church during the reign of King Henry VIII (r. 1509–1547) of England. It created a church for which the king or queen of England was the head of the Church of England and its sister churches, the Church of Scotland, the Church of Ireland, and the Church of Wales. The group together, later joined with other churches, became known as the Anglican Communion—after the American War of Independence, the followers of the Church of England became known as the Episcopalians, as the Church of England upholds that the king (or queen) of England is the supreme head of the Church of England.

Because of the close connections between church and state, most of the members of the British establishment were Anglicans, as were a majority of people in England and a sizeable proportion of people in Wales and Scotland. Certainly during the reign of Queen Elizabeth I (r. 1558–1603), although most of the people had probably grown up as Roman Catholics, they attended Church of England services in parish churches, and many came to prefer the more independent thought allowed by the Anglicans. With the introduction of the Authorized Bible, or King James Bible, in 1611, the majesty of the new translation of the Bible, combined with the Book of Common Prayer introduced in 1549 during the reign of King Edward VI (r. 1547–1553), many people had access to the Biblical texts in English, allowing for greater knowledge of the Biblical events, which led to "free thinkers," which in turn led to the emergence of nonconformists and later Puritans.

In 17th- and 18th-century England, Anglicanism was not just a religious belief as it now is. The country was divided into counties, but the church dioceses were also important in terms of the church courts, which prove wills and the like. These dioceses were divided into parishes, and much of the local administration of England took place on a parish basis with the local vicar recording the dates of baptism, marriage, and burial in parish registers and also in rural areas, helping with the administration of the Poor Law, which was done on a parish basis. As municipal cemeteries had not yet come into being, the vast majority of people were also buried in the grounds of parish churches, or nearby areas. This system had been translated to parts of British North America, but unlike England, the parish administration did not control the Poor Law—indeed, there was no such institution—and there were some municipal cemeteries. This helped separate church and state from an early period, and as a result, the Anglicans were never as powerful as a single political unit in the Americas as they were in England.

—*Justin Corfield*

Further Reading

Edel, Wilbur. *Defenders of the Faith: Religion and Politics from the Pilgrim Fathers to Ronald Reagan*. New York: Praeger, 1987.

Rhoden, Nancy L. *Revolutionary Anglicanism: The Colonial Church of England Clergy during the American Revolution*. New York: New York University Press, 1999.

Quakers

On March 4, 1681, William Penn managed to get a grant of a land tract by King Charles II of England. This colony was for religious freedom, with William Penn being a Quaker and anxious for a place for Quakers to settle. This was unlike many of the other settlements in North America, where the majority of the population were Anglican (Episcopalian).

The Quaker movement started in 1648 as the Religious Society of Friends as a breakaway movement from Puritanism. This coincided with the period after the English Civil War when there was the formation of many Nonconformist movements with the spread of the Quaker movement. They refused to fight in wars or

Quakers became known for their quiet worship, waiting to be moved by the Spirit. (Special Collections, Davidson Library, University of California—Santa Barbara)

kill people, and they also refused to bow or doff their hats to social superiors, which led to problems in the societies in which they lived.

The Quakers were persecuted in England with one of the movement's most famous members, William Penn—a friend of George Fox, the founder of the Quakers—being accused of "preaching Quakerism to an unlawful assembly." The jury, much to the anger of the Lord Mayor of London, who was judging the case, found Penn not guilty, whereupon he moved to North America, where many other Quakers had settled.

Penn, after he managed to get the grant of land in 1680, was soon joined by Quaker settlers from Wales, and also others from England, Germany, and the Netherlands, with complete freedom of religion for anybody who believed in God being guaranteed in Pennsylvania. This drew not only Quakers, but also Huguenots (French protestants), and Amish, Catholics, Jews, Lutherans from southern Germany, and Mennonites. The Quakers enjoyed this, and these groups generally had more in common with the Quakers than they did with the Anglicans in the other states. This allowed the Quakers to effectively control the early politics of Pennsylvania. Gradually, many migrants from Germany, and also Scotland of Ireland, led to the Quakers becoming a minority, but with clear political control.

The Quakers and their connections dominated politics in Pennsylvania for many years. The first governor, William Markham (c.1635–1704), governor from 1681 to 1682 and 1693 to 1699, was a cousin of William Penn; and he was followed by Penn who served as governor from 1682 to 1684, and from 1699 to 1701. The third governor, Thomas Lloyd (1640–1694), governor from 1684 to 1688 and 1690 to 1693, had been jailed for a period because of his Quaker beliefs. The sixth man to be governor, Edward Shippen (1639–1712; governor, 1703–1704), joined the Quakers after arriving in America; his successor from 1709 until 1717, Charles Gookin, was from a Puritan family; and James Logan (1674–1751), governor from 1736 to 1738, had been a secretary of William Penn. Many of other early officials, including some mayors of Philadelphia, were also Quakers.

—*Justin Corfield*

Further Reading

Baltzell, E. Digby. *Puritan Boston and Quaker Philadelphia*. New York: Free Press, 1979.

Dobrie, Bonamy. *William Penn*. London: Constable, 1932.

Dunn, Richard S., and Mary Maples Dunn. *The World of William Penn*. Philadelphia: University of Pennsylvania Press, 1986.

Geiter, Mary K. *William Penn*. New York: Longman, 2000.

Pima Revolt (1751)

The Pima Revolt occurred in 1751, when the Pima Indians attacked the Spanish settlers in Arizona in what became one of the largest conflicts on the northern frontier of New Spain. It came after attacks by Native Americans on Spanish settlers going back to 1684, when the Spanish started impacting on the lives of the Pima Indians through mining and the enclosing of lands. At the time of the revolt, the Spanish settlers had come to equal the population of Native Americans, and as a result, the Native Americans feared that the Spanish would quickly try to take over the entire region.

Most of the Spanish did try to have positive interactions with the Native Americans, and vice-versa, but many of the tribes were worried about the increase in Spanish settlements and the expansion of their areas of control. Cattle were easy to raise in the frontier areas, and these rapidly became the cause of many disputes. The Spanish were angered when the Native Americans hunted them—they had become important sources of food, and also leather for clothing—and they were also often after horses, which had become important in their societies. Some Spanish had not been too concerned about the loss of some cattle, but with the theft of horses, and the ability for the Native Americans to use the horses to round up cattle, problems arose more and more frequently. Introduced diseases also proved a problem for many Native Americans.

By the early 1700s, some of the Native Americans also had access to firearms, which they bought from the French. They started raiding outlying Spanish settlements, and in return the Spanish started providing guards for these and also mining camps and other larger establishments. The Spanish were also involved in punitive raids, which were similar in some ways to those by some Native Americans. Raiding parties would attack any opposition, and use the attack as a way of seizing cattle, horses, and slaves. Counter-reprisals started a series of border conflicts that came to a head in 1751 when the Pima Indians decided to act. The increasing numbers of Spanish meant that they were soon becoming a minority in what had been their lands, and they were worried about the continual colonization of the most fertile areas of the region. The harshness of the terrain in Arizona had meant that there was going to become fierce competition for the resources, but had also meant that for the early part of the 18th century, the Spanish and Native American communities had lived in relative harmony, and this had led to a large mixed

Spanish–Native American population. There were also many Native Americans who had grown up influenced by Spanish missions.

The first revolt in the region was in 1737 when the Seris and the Western Apache, and the Lower Pimas were involved in attacks on the Spanish. In 1740, the rebellion was joined by the Yaquis and the Mayos, but the Spanish troops were able to prevail. In 1749, the great Seri Revolt led to a prolonged series of attacks on the Spanish, and as a result, the colonial authorities had to transfer many of their troops from Sonora to fight the Seris and the Apaches. This left the Spanish population in Arizona without much military support, and this was one of the reasons why the Pima undoubtedly decided to attack in 1751.

There had been a rising level of discontent among the Pima Indians, and as a result, Luis Oacpicagigua (Luis "of Sáric") started trying to unite the Native Americans, a difficult task as the tribes had no central authority. It had been achieved in the Seri Revolt, and with that as an inspiration, gradually Luis Oacpicagigua had managed to get about 15,000 people together and then decided to launch his attack. It has been suggested by historians that there was no single "spark" that caused the Pima Revolt, but rather long, simmering discontent, along with resentment about the missionaries taking a larger role in the educating of children, and the whippings they administered to men. Before the attack came, however, Oacpicagigua recognized that the Spanish would lead a punitive raid against the Pima women and children, and thus he managed to get most of the civilians to move their families to the mountains of Baboquivari, taking with them enough food to sustain themselves there.

The attack on the Spanish began when Oacpicagigua lured some 18 settlers to his home in Sáric. There, the settlers were all killed, and Luis Oacpicagigua then led his supporters in attacks on a number of other isolated settlements including the mission at Tubutama. However a missionary, Father Jacobo Sedelmayr, had alerted another priest, Father Juan Nentvig, and the two had time to rally some loyal Native Americans and barricade the mission as Oacpicagigua and some 125 men attacked it. They set fire to some of the mission but were unable to take it. Two missionaries were killed in the fighting, and attacks broke out elsewhere in the region. Most of these were scattered, and about 100 settlers were killed in total. Captain José Diaz del Carpio was sent to deal with the problem, and Luis Oacpicagigua was forced to surrender on March 18, 1752, in a negotiated agreement. The leaders of the revolt blamed the disturbances on the Jesuit missionaries—and Oacpicagigua was able to provide details on the actions of Jesuits there who had been involved in using land to produce revenue for their order. This went down well with the Spanish authorities as they were looking to expelling the Jesuits from Spain and the Spanish Empire, which took place in 1767. It also allowed the Spanish military commander, Captain José Díaz del Carpio, to be more accommodating toward the Native Americans who surrendered.

Fighting continued on a small scale, and Luis Oacpicagigua himself died in 1755 in a Spanish jail. This followed the arrest of two other Pima chiefs who had continued the fighting against the Spanish and had been captured and tortured. Both had attempted to commit suicide in prison, and some people suspected that Oacpicagigua's death was from suicide. To prevent any further outbreaks of revolt from the Pima, the Spanish then split the region into three presidios: San Ignacio de Tubac (now Tubac County, Arizona), Santa Gertrudis de Altar (now Altar, Sonora, Mexico) and San Carlos de Buenavista (now Buenavista, Sonora, Mexico). Gradually, the tribes were assimilated with many more Native Americans were converted to Christianity.

—*Justin Corfield*

See also all entries under Pueblo Revolt (1680); Pontiac's Rebellion (1763); Flight of the Nez Percé (1877); Wounded Knee I (1890); Trail of Broken Treaties (1972); Wounded Knee II (1973).

Further Reading

Bannon, John Francis. *The Spanish Borderlands Frontier 1513–1821*. Albuquerque: University of New Mexico Press, 1974.

Dobyns, Henry F. *Tubac through Four Centuries: An Historical Resume and Analysis*. Phoenix: Arizona State Parks Board, 1999.

Ewing, Russell C. "The Pima Uprising 1751–1752: A Study in Spain's Indian Policy." PhD thesis. University of California, Berkeley, 1934.

Ewing, Russell C. "Investigations into the Causes of the Pima Uprisings of 1751." *Mid-America* 23 (April 1941): 138–151.

Ewing, Russell C. "The Pima Outbreak in November 1751." *New Mexico Historical Review* 8 (1938): 337–346.

Ewing, Russell C. "The Pima Uprising of 1751." In *Greater America: Essays in Honor of Herbert E. Bolton*, ed. Adele Ogden. Berkeley: University of California, 1945.

Salmón, Roberto Mario. "A Marginal Man: Luis of Saric and the Pima Revolt of 1751." *The Americas* 45, no. 1 (July 1988): 61–77.

Jesuits

The Jesuits were members of the Roman Catholic religious order called the Society of Jesus, which was formed following a meeting in 1534 in Paris of Ignatius of Loyola and other ardent Catholic students who wanted to form a group to work against the ideas of the Protestant Reformation. They received papal approval for their work three years later, and they were soon heavily involved in the Counter-Reformation

Over time, the Jesuits became feared in Protestant countries where persecution was common. In Roman Catholic countries they became a powerful religious force which was heavily involved in gaining support from some of the wealthiest and most powerful Catholic rulers in Europe. As the Catholic powers, in particular Portugal and Spain, started taking land in Asia, parts of Africa, and the Americas, the Jesuits soon became associated with missionary work. To help pay for this, many were involved in establishing what were, effectively, communes. Native American tribesmen were encouraged to operate farms, which provided the Jesuits with funds to keep their missions going. The most famous of these communes were the reductions in Paraguay, shown in Robert Bolt's film *The Mission* (1986). In North America, the Jesuits operated in New Spain, where they worked with the Pima and other peoples. Initially some of these were successful, but the way in which the Jesuits administered the ones in modern-day Arizona was clearly a cause of the Pima Revolt.

The Pima saw the produce from these Jesuits' "plantations" going to enrich the Jesuits, and not necessarily for the benefit of the people. They also resented the Jesuits building whipping posts and being involved in publically flogging Pima. The Pima saw this as unnecessarily humiliating, as were the use of canes by missionaries who treated Native American warriors as children. However the Jesuits do seem genuinely to have converted so many people to Christianity that the number involved in the revolt was far lower than otherwise would have been the case.

As a result, when the leader of the revolt, Luis Oacpicagigua, came to an accommodation with the Spanish with his surrender in March 18, 1752, the Spanish colonial authorities (in particular the governor Diego Ortiz Parilla) saw that the dislike of the Jesuits provided an easy scapegoat for the revolt. They were able to catalog the grievances of the Pima against the Jesuits, and this in turn was to help encourage—in time—members of the Spanish government bring together their plans for ejecting the Jesuits from the lands they controlled. However because of the Seven Years' War, this did not happen until the end of that conflict, when, in

1767, the rulers of Portugal, Spain, France, Parma, and the Two Sicilies (Naples) decided to suppress the order and banish all Jesuits from lands they controlled.

—*Justin Corfield*

Further Reading

Ewing, Russell C. "Investigations into the Causes of the Pima Uprisings of 1751." *Mid-America* 23 (April 1941): 138–151.

Salmón, Roberto Mario. "A Marginal Man: Luis of Saric and the Pima Revolt of 1751." *The Americas* 45, no. 1 (July 1988): 61–77.

Oacpicagigua, Luis (d. 1755)

Luis Oacpicagigua was the leader of the Pima Revolt; little is known about his life before 1751. He had been appointed by the Spanish as the "Indian governor" of the province of Sáric, and this obviously meant that they trusted him. Undoubtedly, Oacpicagigua must have spoken Spanish and been able to study some of their military tactics. He also had contact with the Seri, which helped him coordinate his attack on the Spanish. It is also recorded that he spoke many of the dialects of the Pima Indians, and this gave him an advantage in getting people from other tribes together to attack the Spanish.

The outbreak of the revolt was the meeting Oacpicagigua held on November 20, 1751, where he outlined his plans to attack the Spanish. This shows that he clearly expected Spanish reprisals, and taken the precautions of moving the women and children into the mountains of Baboquivari so that they would not be able to be attacked when the revolt started. Certainly the first attack on the Spanish—the massacring of the 18 settlers when they came to visit Oacpicagigua at his house in Sáric, showed that he recognized the need to have an incident to show that the revolt had started. However, the very lackluster nature of the subsequent attack on the nearby mission, and then the rapid collapse of any really organized attack on the Spanish, points to another possible interpretation into the cause of the revolt.

Oacpicagigua certainly knew about the war between the Spanish and the Seri, and he was well known to Diego Ortiz Parilla, who may have even encouraged him in his resentment of the Jesuits. Luis may also have known that the Spanish were planning to expand their settlements on the Gila and Colorado rivers, and felt he had to strike before this took place. In spite of this, Luis would have needed to persuade many people uncertain about attacking the Spanish to take part in the revolt, and it might also have been that the killing of the first settlers in

Oacpicagigua's own house was to show to them his commitment to the cause. Nevertheless, in spite of this, the revolt petered out fairly quickly. It failed to draw many of the Native Americans from Spanish settlements into it, and Luis Oacpicagigua seemed to have recognized quickly the futility of any other major attacks, although isolated ones continuing for months.

It seems that his former friendship with Diego Ortiz Parilla had caused Luis Oacpicagigua to finally turn himself in. In May 1753, Oacpicagigua and another Pima Indian leader, Luis of Pitic, were asked to meet with the Spanish authorities. They were immediately arrested and brutally interrogated by the Spanish. Both tried to commit suicide in prison, but remained alive—Oacpicagigua remaining a prisoner until his death at Horcasitas Jail in early 1755.

—*Justin Corfield*

Further Reading

Salmón, Roberto Mario. "A Marginal Man: Luis of Saric and the Pima Revolt of 1751." *The Americas* 45, no. 1 (July 1988): 61–77.

Waldman, Carl. *Who Was Who in Native American History. Indians and Non-Indians from Early Contacts through 1900*. New York: Facts on File, 1990.

Parrilla, Diego Ortiz (c. 1715–c. 1775)

Diego Ortiz Farilla was a Spanish governor of Nuevo Reyno de Andalucia (Sinaloa and Sonora) at the time of the Pima Revolt of 1751. Little is known about his early life except that he was born in about 1715, at Villa de Lúcar, near Almeria, in the south of Spain, and was the son of Tomás Ortiz Parrilla y Montoya and Doña Andrea Parrilla y Montana, both of whom were from the Spanish nobility. In 1734, he was commissioned as an alferez (second lieutenant) in the Almanza Dragoons, and sent to Cuba where he served under Juan Francisco de Guemes, Conde de Revillagigedo. When the count was appointed as Viceroy of New Spain, Parilla moved with him to Mexico, and was captain of the dragoons at Veacruz. In 1747 he was involved in putting down a revolt by the local people at Puebla de los Angeles, and in June 1748 he was promoted to lieutenant colonel.

The next appointment was on March 27, 1749, when Parilla was appointed as governor and captain-general of Nuevo Reyno de Andalucia (Sinaloa and Sonora), and also captain of Presidio del Pitic. He took his oath of office on September 12, and his first task was to take part in the crushing of the Seri revolt, his earlier involvement in putting down another revolt being why he was promoted at this difficult juncture. Parilla led the Spanish on an attack on Isla de Tiburón, and was also involved in mapping the region—his maps providing some of the earliest surviving charts of the region.

There is some controversy about Diego Ortiz Parilla's friendship with Luis Oacpicagigua, the leader of the Pima Revolt, and it now seems certain that he did encourage Luis and other Pima in their opposition to the increasing influence in the region of the Jesuits. It was perhaps because of that friendship that Parilla did not leave sufficient garrisons when he took the Spanish troops off to fight the Seri, and this provided the opportunity for Oacpicagigua to attack. However it was this friendship with the Native Americans which seems to have prevented many more taking part in the revolt, and also the subsequent surrender of Luis himself.

Subsequently, Diego Ortiz Parilla was involved in other actions against the Native Americans, and from June 1764 until December 1765, he was interim governor of Coahuila (now a part of Mexico). After this, he was sent to start mapping some of the Texas Gulf Coast. In 1766, the Spanish were worried about a possible British invasion, and he organized engineers to map the region up to Galveston Bay. However, in 1774, Parilla finally agreed to requests that he return to Spain, and he was appointed as a brigadier in Valencia by November of that year. He died between then and November of the following year.

—*Justin Corfield*

Further Reading

Bannon, John Francis. *The Spanish Borderlands Frontier 1513–1821*. Albuquerque: University of New Mexico Press, 1974.

Weddle, Robert S. "Diego Ortiz Parrilla," The Handbook of Texas Online, www.tshaonline.org/handbook/online/articles/OO/for12.html (accessed November 10, 2008).

Weddle, Robert S. *The San Sabá Mission*. Austin: University of Texas Press, 1964.

Tohono O'odham

The Tohono O'odham, or "People of the Desert," are aboriginal American people who live in the Sonoran Desert in northwestern Mexico and the southwestern United States. The name was first applied to them by the Spanish, and the people were forced north by the Apaches from the early 17th century. However it was not long before, by the early 18th century, the Apache started to make common cause with the other Native American peoples to prevent the Spanish from establishing settlements in their region.

During the Pima Revolt of 1751, the Pima also sought an alliance with the Tohono O'odham, who had been heavily subject to missionary influences of the Jesuits, which some of them had tried to reject. Eusebio Kino (d. 1711), born in Italy and trained in Germany, had arrived in Mexico in 1681, hoping to work with other Jesuits in China. However, he remained in Mexico, and in the northern parts, he was involved in establishing the Mission San Xavier del Bac, near the present-day city of Tucson. Although some of the Pima and other people were converted to Catholicism, many of the Tohono O'odham resisted fiercely. This was partly because they resented the Spanish settlements, preferring their own isolated villages. In the 1660s, they had staged a major rebellion against the Spanish who had ruthlessly crushed them, and it was not until the 1750s that they were able to stage another large revolt coinciding with the Pima Revolt. This was called the Papago Revolt, the Tohono O'odham being known at the time by the Spanish as the Papago.

The advantage that the Tohono O'odham had was that they were able to launch isolated attacks against the Spanish. However, the Spanish were initially able to tolerate these, prior to embarking on their own counteroffensive by sending large numbers of soldiers against the Tohono O'odham. The sheer inhospitableness of the terrain initially hampered the Spanish, but also meant that once the Tohono O'odham villages were destroyed, the people were unable to easily reestablish themselves.

Following the defeat of the Tohono O'odham, the Spanish worked more heavily on establishing missions run by the Franciscans, and these helped extend the level of integration of the people into European frontier culture. During the 1770s, the Tohono O'odham were also involved in winning a series of battles against the Apache.

—*Justin Corfield*

Further Reading

Erickson, Winston P. *Shaping the Desert: The Tohono O'odham in History.* Tucson: University of Arizona Press, 1994.

McIntyre, Allan J. *The Tohono O'odham and Pimeria Alta.* Charleston, SC: Arcadia Publishing, 2008.

Pontiac's Rebellion (1763)

The fall of Montreal in 1760 marked the effective end of the Seven Years' War in the Upper Ohio Valley and the Great Lakes regions. The defeat of their French allies left many of the natives forced to negotiate peace agreements with the British. General Amherst, commander in chief of British forces in North America, set the stage for the parlays in 1761 by forbidding the customary practice of gift giving to native leaders. Amherst also raised the prices for most trade goods, making it difficult for native peoples to get needed supplies. Trade for certain items, most notably gunpowder, was severely restricted. Amherst's actions angered and offended native leaders and their followers. The Seneca in New York attempted to seize upon native disillusionment by calling in 1761 for the creation of a confederacy, but their call for war did not elicit the desired response. Despite advice from people experienced in native affairs, such as Sir William Johnson and George Croghan, Amherst continued to sow seeds of discontent. He ordered the construction of a number of forts and then encouraged British colonists to build communities around the structures.

The growing presence of British colonists and soldiers and an outbreak of famine and disease during the early 1760s were used as evidence by Neolin, the Delaware Prophet, that native peoples needed to rid themselves of European influences and return to traditional ways. Neolin's religious message resonated among native peoples of many groups because it helped explain their continued suffering and gave them hope for a brighter future. At a meeting convened on the Ecorse River during April 1763, attended by the Wyandot, Ottawa, Potawatomi, and Ojibwas, Pontiac embraced Neolin's doctrines with the condition that the French be the exception to the rejection of European influences. He then called on the respective native groups to join him in expelling the British from their homelands. With Neolin's assistance, Pontiac subsequently utilized the Delaware Prophet's existing intertribal religious revitalization movement to help craft a loosely organized Native American military confederacy.

On May 7, 1763, Pontiac and a force made up of Ottawa, Potawatomi, and Huron warriors initiated the conflict known as Pontiac's Rebellion when they attempted to take Fort Detroit through subterfuge. They had made arrangements with Major Henry Gladwin to stage a ceremonial dance within the fort with the intent of attacking its unsuspecting defenders with concealed weapons. Someone

Pontiac's men release captives taken during Pontiac's Rebellion, an outgroth of the French and Indian War. (Library of Congress)

forewarned Gladwin of the plot, thus he and his men were fully armed and prepared. Upon seeing the readiness of the fort's defenders when he entered the fort, Pontiac called off the planned attack. Pontiac's decision infuriated the warriors. To placate his critics, he then attempted to lure Gladwin outside the fort under the pretense of negotiations to force his surrender, but that ploy also failed. Since native warriors were leery of sustaining heavy casualties in a direct assault on Fort Detroit, Pontiac opted to besiege the fortified post.

Trickery proved an effective tactic for other Native American leaders early in the conflict because intercultural relationships were everyday occurrences at British posts. Native American warriors utilized this familiarity and feigned friendships to further their military aims. Fort Sandusky fell on May 16 after its defenders agreed to a council with war leaders of a force comprised of Ottawas and Hurons. At the onset of negotiations, the warriors overpowered the small garrison and claimed an easy victory. Fort Miamis was taken on May 27 with the aid of the native mistress of ensign Robert Holmes, the fort's commander. She enticed her lover to leave the fort to help bleed a native woman who had fallen ill. Holmes was slain as he exited the fort, and his garrison was quickly overwhelmed.

The final fort to fall as a result of deception was Fort Michilimackinac. On June 2, Ottawa, Ojibwa, and Sauk warriors engaged in a game akin to lacrosse outside of the fort. The spectators included the fort's defenders, who felt so secure that they did not even close the fort's entrance during the event. During the game, which had already lasted several hours, someone slung the ball into the fort. As they entered the fort to ostensibly retrieve the ball, the warriors were handed weapons that had been concealed by native women under blankets. Fifteen of the garrison's 35 defenders were quickly killed, as was a trader. The remaining colonists in the fort were taken prisoner. The loss of Fort Michilimackinac was particularly damaging because it had not only been strategically located at the confluence of Lake Michigan and Lake Huron, but its storehouse of supplies contained firearms and a significant amount of gunpowder.

Following so many examples of native creativity in attacking British forts, word was sent to the remaining British garrison to be on their guard. The warning to Fort Venango was ignored by its commanding officer, Lieutenant Francis Gordon. When the Seneca chief Kayashuta approached the fort with a force that included Shawnee and Delaware warriors on June 13, they were welcomed into the fort. The native warriors quickly killed the fort's defenders, leaving only Gordon alive. Gordon was then forced to document Kayashuta's grievances, which included the presence of British forts on native lands and the deliberate effort of British officials to deny native peoples access to gunpowder. Once his task was completed, Gordon was tortured until he died.

Kayashuta's force was then joined by another war party comprised of Ojibwa, Ottawa, Huron, and Mississauga warriors for an assault a week later at Fort Presque Isle. The fort's defenders were forced to surrender the post on June 23 after two days of fighting. The Senecas then turned their attention to Fort Le Boeuf. The attack was launched on June 18. During the fighting, the fort's blockhouse caught on fire. The smoke helped cover the retreat of the British soldiers as they fled into the night to Fort Pitt.

Mid-June 1763 marked the height of the Native American offensive. Native warriors had taken eight forts, including Fort St. Joseph and Fort Ouiatenon. Their military successes had forced the abandonment of Forts Burd and Edward Augustus. Active sieges were underway at Forts Pitt, Ligonier, Bedford, and Detroit. The ease of so many of the victories had obscured the problems that were beginning to affect the war effort. Epidemic diseases, most notably smallpox, had begun to ravage Native American communities. Also, the long-desired support from the French had failed to materialize. While limited supplies were flowing to native forces from French outposts in Illinois, virtually no support was coming from Canada. The French in Canada justifiably feared that any assistance to the native cause would result in severe retribution by Great Britain. Pontiac's confederates were also unable to gain the support of the majority of the six nations of the Iroquois. Although the Seneca took part in the conflict, the Oneida, Mohawk, Onondaga, Cayuga, and Tuscarora followed the advice of Sir William Johnson and used their demonstrated friendship to forge closer economic and military ties with Great Britain.

Although it was obvious by mid-July 1763 that General Amherst had grossly underestimated the capabilities of his native opposition, he placed the blame for the fall of so many forts on the commanders and soldiers at the respective posts. He was incredulous that so many of his subordinates had been so gullible as to fall for the number of incidences of subterfuge that occurred, considering that he himself had constantly warned them of what he believed to be the duplicitous nature of Native Americans in general. Amherst believed that the forts reflected the military might of Great Britain and thus their loss served to give the native warriors the mistaken impression that the British were militarily impotent on the frontier. Regardless of Amherst's views, the British were incapable of protecting their interests in both the Ohio Valley and the Great Lakes region. The common thread in all of the forts that were either taken or abandoned in the early weeks of Pontiac's Rebellion was that they were all defended by 35 men or fewer. The forts that were well manned, such as Forts Pitt and Detroit, were able to repel repeated assaults by native warriors. Given the state of affairs, Amherst determined that the only solution was to annihilate the opposition by any means necessary. The depths of the British resolve toward that end became evident at Fort Pitt on June 24, 1763.

Fort Pitt had been forewarned of a native attack on May 30, when the survivors from another fort began straggling in with tales of butchery. Believing that they would receive no quarter from native warriors, the fort's defenders determined to fight to the finish once they were finally attacked. They then began destroying the outbuildings in the vicinity of the fort so that they could not be used by attackers. The soldiers also commenced hoarding supplies and food in preparation for a siege. Delaware warriors assailed the fort on June 22 with little success. On June 24, Delaware negotiators Turtle's Heart and Mamaltee were received outside of the fort under the pretense to discuss possible resolutions to the conflict. In truth, Fort Pitt's commander, Captain Simeon Ecuyer, wanted to negotiate with the Delaware so that he could present them with blankets and handkerchiefs that had been intentionally retrieved from smallpox patients who were being treated in the fort's hospital. It was hoped that the vestiges of smallpox on the linens would spark an outbreak of smallpox among the warriors. Whether coincidental or a result of Ecuyer's gift, a smallpox outbreak did erupt among the native peoples in the vicinity of Fort Pitt by the end of the month. Curiously, the native victims of the epidemic did not include Turtle's Heart. Amherst was subsequently blamed for the stratagem of using smallpox for germ warfare, but evidence suggests that he approved of the action after it had actually occurred.

Following the initial Native American victories, the second phase of the conflict turned to British efforts to reinforce and resupply their besieged garrisons at Forts Detroit and Pitt. Pontiac's warriors were able to prevent access to Fort Detroit by land, thus the British resorted to moving personnel and supplies through Lake Erie and the Detroit River. The British used two ships, the *Huron* and the *Michigan*, during the siege. Both ships carried enough cannons and guns to prevent assaults on Fort Detroit by water. The warriors under Pontiac's command attempted to catch the ships on fire by floating burning rafts towards them, but the effort went for naught. During the month of July, the British were able to expand their dominance on the water with the addition of four gunboats. As the siege of Fort Detroit wore on, it was Pontiac who began having supply troubles. Native warriors who had begun to question Pontiac's leadership from the time he had aborted the initial attack on Fort Detroit saw his inability to acquire needed supplies from the French as further evidence of his ineffectiveness in the field. Disillusioned, they quit the fight and began returning to their home communities. By November 1763, the siege had been abandoned, and Pontiac had retreated to a village on the Maumee River.

On July 7, Amherst ordered Colonel Henry Bouquet to gather troops to relieve the garrison at Fort Pitt. While en route, Bouquet's soldiers helped break the sieges at Forts Ligonier and Bedford. The relief column was attacked by Delaware, Huron, Mingo, Shawnee, and Wyandot warriors on August 5 at Bushy Run. During the two-day Battle of Bushy Run, Bouquet sustained heavy casualties but ultimately succeeded in driving off his attackers. Bouquet's force arrived on August 10 at Fort Pitt with much needed supplies and reinforcements. The ability of the British to break the native siege led to the abandonment of the native effort to seize Fort Pitt.

Pontiac's Rebellion was ultimately brought to a conclusion using the traditional diplomatic methods that Amherst had eschewed from the time he had first arrived in North America. Sir William Johnson took the lead in using diplomacy to break the Native American confederacy. Through his experiences with native peoples, especially the Iroquois, Johnson knew that individual native leaders had joined the conflict to fulfill their personal agendas. Johnson had counseled Amherst on how to use diplomacy to mollify individual native groups, but Amherst had stubbornly insisted on bringing them to submission militarily. Belatedly realizing that Amherst himself was largely responsible for the outbreak of the conflict, British officials recalled him to London during November 1763. Sir William Johnson was subsequently empowered by General Thomas Gage, Amherst's successor, to address the grievances of the respective native groups in the traditional fashion. Being an astute diplomat, Johnson had anticipated that he would eventually be given that power and had acted accordingly.

In meetings held with Iroquois delegations during the months of June and September 1763, Johnson managed to convince them to aid the British effort to end the conflict. Amherst had disapproved of the negotiations because the Seneca were included in the discussions. Johnson's efforts resulted in the Seneca joining the other members of the Iroquois Confederacy in calling for the other native groups to lay down their arms and make peace with the British. The Iroquois did not act out of loyalty to the British, but rather felt that being allied to the British would strengthen their claims to sovereignty over the Ohio Valley.

The support of General Thomas Gage and the backing of the Iroquois enabled Sir William Johnson to host a peace conference at Fort Niagara in January 1764 that was attended by the leaders of most of the native groups that had participated in Pontiac's Rebellion. During the monthlong meeting, Johnson proved a gracious host who fed his guests well and who plied them with an abundance of gifts. The goodwill that was generated resulted in a number of native nations allying themselves with the British and pledging to fight against their former native allies.

Although the sieges had been broken at Fort Pitt and at Fort Detroit and many of the warriors, such as Pontiac, had retreated westward, that did not mean that the British considered the war to be over. Two British armies invaded the Ohio Valley during the summer of 1764. Colonel John Bradstreet led a force that was nearly 2,000 men strong, including Iroquois warriors, from Fort Niagara. Colonel Henry Bouquet launched his expedition from Fort Pitt. The British assault towards their home communities convinced those native leaders who had wanted to continue fighting the British that further resistance was futile, thus they too eventually came to terms. Pontiac held out until he was forced to capitulate at Fort Oswego in 1766.

—*John R. Burch Jr.*

See also all entries under Pueblo Revolt (1680); Pima Revolt (1751); Flight of the Nez Percé (1877); Wounded Knee I (1890); Trail of Broken Treaties (1972); Wounded Knee II (1973).

Further Reading

Anderson, Fred. *Crucible of War: The Seven Years' War and the Fate of Empire in British North America, 1754–1766*. New York: Alfred A. Knopf, 2000.

Barr, Daniel P., ed. *The Boundaries between Us: Natives and Newcomers along the Frontiers of the Old Northwest Territory, 1750–1850*. Kent, OH: Kent State University Press, 2006.

Calloway, Colin. *The Scratch of a Pen: 1763 and the Transformation of North America*. New York: Oxford University Press, 2006.

Cave, Alfred A. *Prophets of the Great Spirit: Native American Revitalization Movements in Eastern North America*. Lincoln: University of Nebraska Press, 2006.

Dixon, David. *Never Come to Peace Again: Pontiac's Uprising and the Fate of the British Empire in North America*. Norman: University of Oklahoma Press, 2005.

Dowd, Gregory Evans. *A Spirited Resistance: The North American Struggle for Unity, 1745–1815*. Baltimore: Johns Hopkins University Press, 1992.

Dowd, Gregory Evans. *War under Heaven: Pontiac, the Indian Nations & the British Empire*. Baltimore: Johns Hopkins University Press, 2002.

Hinderaker, Eric, and Peter C. Mancall. *At the Edge of Empire: The Backcountry in British North America*. Baltimore: Johns Hopkins University Press, 2003.

McConnell, Michael N. *A Country Between: The Upper Ohio Valley and Its Peoples, 1724–1774*. Lincoln: University of Nebraska Press, 1992.

Middleton, Richard. *Pontiac's War: Its Causes, Course and Consequences*. New York: Routledge, 2007.

Nelson, Larry L. *A Man of Distinction among Them: Alexander McKee and British-Indian Affairs Along the Ohio Country Frontier, 1754–1799*. Kent, OH: Kent State University Press, 1999.

O'Toole, Fintan. *White Savage: William Johnson and the Invention of America*. New York: Farrar, Straus and Giroux, 2005.

Ward, Matthew C. *Breaking the Backcountry: The Seven Years' War in Virginia and Pennsylvania, 1754–1765*. Pittsburgh, PA: University of Pittsburgh Press, 2003.

White, Richard. *The Middle Ground: Indian, Empires, and Republics in the Great Lakes Region, 1650–1815*. New York: Cambridge University Press, 1991.

Amherst, Jeffrey (1717–1797)

Amherst, born on January 29, 1717, began his military career in 1731 under the command of Sir John Ligonier. He served under Ligonier during the War of the Austrian Succession as an aide-de-camp. During the French and Indian War, Ligonier used his influence with William Pitt the elder to advance his protégé's military career. Amherst was a relatively obscure officer who was tapped by Pitt to lead an expedition against the French fort of Louisbourg, which was located on Cape Breton Island. The expedition was launched in March 1758, and the French surrendered the fort on July 26, 1758. Amherst's victory resulted in his appointment as commander in chief of Great Britain's forces in North America by late 1758. His greatest military accomplishment was his three-pronged invasion of Canada that was launched in August 1760. The campaign proved so successful that Pierre de Rigaud de Vaudreuil de Cavagnial surrendered New France on September 8, 1760.

Following the conclusion of the French and Indian War, Amherst turned his attention to Native American affairs. He generally detested Native Americans and saw little value in them as allies. Thus, he stopped the customary practice of giving gifts to tribes that were friendly to the British in 1761. This stance deprived Native American groups of the gunpowder they required for both hunting and warfare. Amherst also actively began encouraging settlers to build communities around British forts. The discontent among native peoples that resulted from Amherst's actions erupted into open warfare in 1763 when British forts throughout the Great Lakes region and the Ohio River Valley were attacked by a number of different native groups in a conflict that has become popularly known as Pontiac's Rebellion.

During the initial stages of the conflict, Amherst appeared to have underestimated the military capabilities of his opponents. Once he realized his error, he ordered British troops to reinforce the posts that did not fall during the initial assaults. His reputation has been besmirched by an act that may not have been committed under his orders. Amherst is credited with having ordered the British garrison at Fort Pitt to intentionally distribute as gifts to the Native Americans besieging the fort blankets that were contaminated with smallpox, in the hopes that an epidemic would eradicate their numbers. General dissatisfaction with Amherst's handling of relations with Native American groups and the subsequent war led British officials to relieve him of command and recall him to England prior to the conclusion of Pontiac's Rebellion.

Amherst's military career prospered upon his return to England. His military honors included being named Baron Amherst of Holmesdale in 1776. He received a second peerage in 1782 as first Baron Amherst of Montreal. He was twice named commander in chief, first in 1778 and again in 1793. He died on August 3, 1797.

—*John R. Burch Jr.*

Further Reading

Anderson, Fred. *Crucible of War: The Seven Years' War and the Fate of Empire in British North America, 1754–1766.* New York: Alfred A. Knopf, 2000.

Dowd, Gregory Evans. *War under Heaven: Pontiac, the Indian Nations & the British Empire.* Baltimore: Johns Hopkins University Press, 2002.

Johnston, A. J. B. *Endgame 1758: The Promise, the Glory, and the Despair of Louisbourg's Last Decade.* Lincoln: University of Nebraska Press, 2007.

Nester, William R. *"Haughty Conquerors": Amherst and the Great Indian Uprising of 1763.* Westport, CT: Praeger Publishers, 2000.

French and Indian War (1754–1763)

The French and Indian War was the North American theater of the Seven Years' War between Great Britain and France, which was fought from 1754 to 1763. The conflict was ignited in 1754 when Virginia governor Robert Dinwiddie ordered Lieutenant Colonel George Washington to construct a fort at the confluence of the Ohio River. Washington's expedition ended with his surrender at Fort Necessity. Sporadic warfare then followed in 1755, which included the displacement of the Acadians in Nova Scotia by the British and the French defeat of General Edward Braddock's expedition against Fort Duquesne.

The escalation of hostilities led the European powers to formally declare war on May 17, 1756. France selected the marquis de Montcalm to command its forces in North America. British authorities named Lord Loudoun to serve as its commander in chief. Loudon proved ineffectual in that capacity against the French and their Native American allies and was replaced in late 1758 by General Jeffrey Amherst.

Great Britain's military fortunes had begun to change in 1758 with the success of Amherst's capture of Louisbourg and the successes of General John Forbes in the Ohio country. The British achieved a decisive victory on September 13, 1759, when they took the city of Quebec. Both the marquis de Montcalm and British general James Wolfe were killed during the battle. Amherst completed the conquest of Canada the following year with a three-pronged invasion that culminated with the capture of Montreal on September 7, 1760. Pierre de Rigaud de Vaudreuil de Cavagnial surrendered New France the following day.

Although the surrender of New France resulted in the general end of warfare within North America between France and Great Britain, it did not end warfare between Great Britain and France's former Native American allies. The sovereign native peoples continued to fight to preserve their autonomy. Rather than trying to negotiate a peaceful end to hostilities with the Native Americans, Amherst opted to inflame their enmity. He banned ceremonial-gift giving to all Native Americans during negotiations in 1761 and began encouraging British settlers to begin building permanent communities around British forts. The resentment over these actions would live long after the French and Indian War technically ended.

The war ended with the signing of the Treaty of Paris on February 10, 1763. The terms of the agreement ceded all of France's claims to North America to the British, with the exception of New Orleans, which was ceded to Spain. Spain, who had belatedly entered the conflict as a French ally, yielded its claim to Florida to Great Britain.

—*John R. Burch Jr.*

Further Reading

Anderson, Fred. *Crucible of War: The Seven Years' War and the Fate of Empire in British North America, 1754–1766*. New York: Alfred A. Knopf, 2000.

Jennings, Francis. *Empire of Fortune: Crowns, Colonies & Tribes in the Seven Years War in America*. New York: W. W. Norton & Company, 1988.

Johnston, A. J. B. *Endgame 1758: The Promise, the Glory, and the Despair of Louisbourg's Last Decade*. Lincoln: University of Nebraska Press, 2007.

Schwartz, Seymour I. *The French and Indian War 1754–1763: The Imperial Struggle for North America*. New York: Simon & Schuster, 1994.

Neolin (dates unknown)

Neolin, also known as "The Delaware Prophet," was a Lenni Lenape who rose to prominence after experiencing a religious vision sometime during the early 1760s. His subsequent religious prophecies helped inspire Pontiac's Rebellion in 1763.

In his religious vision, the Master of Life taught Neolin that the reason why the path to Heaven for Native Americans had become more difficult to traverse was that they had become too dependent on Europeans and their trade goods. To avoid going to Hell, Native Americans were required to abstain from drunkenness, hunt in the traditional fashion with bow and arrow, cease their dependence on European trade goods, set aside intertribal warfare, and drive the British from their homelands. Ironically, the presence of Heaven and Hell in his nativist vision indicated the influence of European Christianity. Neolin reinforced his teachings to his adherents through a prayer they were required to recite twice a day, in the morning and the evening, and a map to Heaven that included the Master of Life's requirements.

Neolin's religious movement spread quickly with the aid of other prophets because it placed the blame for all of the ills that native peoples were experiencing on Europeans. For Native Americans who had suffered through displacement from their homelands, constant warfare, starvation, and epidemic disease, Neolin promised a brighter future once they repudiated and repelled the British interlopers that had brought them so much misery. Although Neolin's religious movement was but one of many factors that led to the eruption of warfare in 1763, it provided a means for Native American military leaders, such as Pontiac, to set aside intertribal rivalries and fight together against a common enemy. Although Pontiac was influenced by Neolin's religious teachings, he selectively utilized the prophet's doctrines. Pontiac did not advocate the abandonment of European technologies. He also was not anti-European, as he hoped that a Native American victory would herald the reestablishment of New France. Pontiac endeavored to direct the ire of his followers against the British.

During the spring of 1763, a series of attacks by native groups such as the Delaware, Ojibwa, Ottawa, Potawatomie, Shawnee, and Wyandots were launched against British installations throughout the Great Lakes region and the Ohio River Valley. Neolin, who was with Pontiac during the siege of the British fort at Detroit, had promised the warriors that the Master of Life assured them of victory. Despite some initial success, victory proved elusive. Following Pontiac's failure to capture the British fort at Detroit in 1764, Neolin faded into obscurity. Although his personal influence had waned, his nativist rhetoric and teachings continued to influence other Native American religious leaders, most notably Tenskwatawa, "The Shawnee Prophet."

—*John R. Burch Jr.*

Further Reading

Cave, Alfred A. *Prophets of the Great Spirit: Native American Revitalization Movements in Eastern North America*. Lincoln: University of Nebraska Press, 2006.

Dowd, Gregory Evans. *A Spirited Resistance: The North American Indian Struggle for Unity, 1745–1815*. Baltimore: Johns Hopkins University Press, 1992.

Dowd, Gregory Evans. *War under Heaven: Pontiac, the Indian Nations & the British Empire*. Baltimore: Johns Hopkins University Press, 2002.

Ohio River Valley

The Ohio River Valley was vaguely defined during the colonial era as the area west of the Allegheny River in present-day Pennsylvania to the Muskingum River in present-day Ohio. The Ohio River marked the southern border of the area, which extended northward into portions of the Great Lakes region.

As a result of a series of conflicts with a number of native groups, most notably the Erie and the Shawnee during the 1600s, the Iroquois Confederacy claimed dominion over the sparsely populated Ohio River Valley. Beginning in the early 1700s, the population of the region began growing rapidly as native groups, such as the Delaware, Shawnee, and Iroquois, began establishing communities within the region. Many of these new immigrants had been displaced from their homelands in the east due to the growth of the British colonies. Other native groups from the west also migrated to the region in hopes of exploiting the abundance of available game for the purpose of trade. These migrants, especially the Shawnee and Delaware, showed little deference to the Iroquois Confederacy. The Iroquois, also known as Mingoes, proved unable to impose their will on these native groups, which helped destabilize the region as native leaders competed against each other both economically and militarily.

Representatives of France and Great Britain sought alliances with the various native groups within the Ohio River Valley. Native American leaders actively played the two European powers against each other to benefit their interests. The desire of the European powers to curry favor with the native groups led to a constant influx of European goods into their communities. Native Americans became dependent on access to trade goods, which led them to choose sides when the Seven Years' War erupted in North America.

The conclusion of the Seven Years' War in 1763 was disastrous for all native peoples in the valley, even those who had fought in the war as British allies. They had lost the ability to play New France against the British, which weakened their negotiating power. The natives soon discovered that Great Britain was not interested in negotiations of any sort with them. Great Britain's commander in chief, General Amherst, went so far as to even cut off traditional gift giving that helped native leaders maintain their authority within their home communities. Great Britain had come to consider the Ohio River Valley theirs by right of conquest and began encouraging settlement of the region by their colonists. Faced with a heavy-handed foe that had no interests in peaceable coexistence, native peoples within the Ohio River Valley were left only with the option of fighting against Great Britain or fleeing the area entirely.

—John R. Burch Jr.

Further Reading

Hinderaker, Eric. *Elusive Empires: Constructing Colonialism in the Ohio Valley, 1673–1800*. New York: Cambridge University Press, 1997.

Hinderaker, Eric, and Peter C. Mancall. *At the Edge of Empire: The Backcountry in British North America*. Baltimore: Johns Hopkins University Press, 2003.

Hurt, R. Douglas. *The Ohio Frontier: Crucible of the Old Northwest, 1720–1830*. Bloomington: Indiana University Press, 1998.

McConnell, Michael N. *A Country Between: The Upper Ohio Valley and Its Peoples, 1724–1774*. Lincoln: University of Nebraska Press, 1992.

White, Richard. *The Middle Ground: Indians, Empires, and Republics in the Great Lakes Region, 1650–1815*. New York: Cambridge University Press, 1991.

Pontiac (d. 1769)

Very little is known about Pontiac's early years. Approximations of his birth year range from 1714 to 1720. By the late 1740s, he had become a respected war leader among the Ottawa who was valued as an ally by New France. During the Seven Years' War, it is believed that he fought alongside the French at both Fort Duquesne and Fort William Henry in 1757.

Pontiac, an excellent military strategist, instigated and led the greatest Native American uprising ever faced by the British in colonial North America. His call for a pan-tribal alliance nearly succeeded in stopping white encroachment onto Native American lands, and served as a model for later resistance efforts led by Little Turtle, Tecumseh, and Black Hawk. (North Wind Picture Archives)

Sometime in the early 1760s, Pontiac came under the sway of Neolin, the Delaware Prophet. Although Pontiac echoed Neolin's call to reject European culture and goods, there is evidence that suggests that Pontiac's interpretation of Neolin's teachings excluded the French. It is believed that Pontiac's Rebellion was launched, at least partially, in the hopes that Native American success would be followed by the return of the French into the region. While France, through its settlements in Illinois, did supply Pontiac and his confederates with some supplies and weapons, it rebuffed his efforts to gain active military assistance in the field.

While Pontiac has been immortalized as the primary leader of Pontiac's Rebellion, he was but one of many influential Native American leaders in a loosely organized confederation. He did provide the conflict's opening salvo when he led a multitribal force against Fort Detroit on May 9, 1763. During the early stages of the conflict, more than eight forts fell or were abandoned by the British. While other native leaders were finding military success, Pontiac unsuccessfully besieged Fort Detroit until October 1763. The combination of a British counterattack that had reversed the initial successes, a smallpox epidemic, and the realization that the French were not going to intervene on their behalf led to a collapse of the Native American confederacy that had launched the conflict. While the war had effectively been over for several years, Pontiac finally came to a peace agreement with the British at Fort Oswego in 1766.

Following the signing of the peace treaty, the British mistakenly believed that Pontiac was a valuable ally who would help allay Native American militancy within the region. While Pontiac did his part by ignoring calls from native groups in the west to continue warring with the British, his own people came to question his loyalty and motives. It is believed that he was severely beaten on multiple occasions before being exiled by the Ottawa from his home community. With his reputation in tatters, Pontiac moved to southern Illinois. While visiting the town of Cahokia on April 20, 1769, he was clubbed and then stabbed to death by a Peoria, whose people were part of the Illinois Confederacy. The attack was probably in retaliation for Pontiac's stabbing of an Illinois chief in 1766.

—*John R. Burch Jr.*

Further Reading

Dowd, Gregory Evans. *War under Heaven: Pontiac, the Indian Nations & the British Empire*. Baltimore: Johns Hopkins University Press, 2002.

Middleton, Richard. *Pontiac's War: Its Causes, Course and Consequences*. New York: Routledge, 2007.

White, Richard. *The Middle Ground: Indian, Empires, and Republics in the Great Lakes Region, 1650–1815*. New York: Cambridge University Press, 1991.

Smallpox

Smallpox is an extremely contagious disease caused by the variola virus. Its symptoms include a high fever, headache, backache, nausea, vomiting, convulsions, and pus-filled corpuscles all over the body. Due to the incubation period of the disease, which on average exceeds 10 days, a person unknowingly exposes others to smallpox before the obvious symptoms appear. The disease either kills the afflicted individuals or leaves them horribly scarred. From the time smallpox was first introduced to the Americas by European colonizers, it proved particularly deadly among Native American populations because they had not had previous exposure to the variola virus in any form.

During Pontiac's Rebellion, the defenders of Fort Pitt famously engaged in biological warfare through the use of smallpox. On June 24, 1763, Delaware negotiators Turtle's Heart and Mamaltee were given two blankets and two silk handkerchiefs as gifts by British dignitaries at Fort Pitt. Since gift giving was an established tradition during negotiations, the Delawares accepted the items graciously from their hosts. The British had intentionally obtained the four items from their hospital, which was treating quarantined smallpox patients, with the hope that a smallpox epidemic would erupt among the many Native American groups that were besieging the fort. Within the month, a smallpox epidemic had erupted among native peoples throughout the Ohio Valley and the Great Lakes region.

General Jeffrey Amherst, Great Britain's commander in chief in North America, has historically been credited with devising the plan to use smallpox as a biological agent against the Native Americans at Fort Pitt. In truth, there are no known records that definitively identify who originated the idea. The most likely culprit was Captain Simeon Ecuyer, who commanded the garrison at Fort Pitt. Undoubtedly, both Amherst and his subordinate Colonel Henry Bouquet approved of the course of action, because both were openly advocating spreading smallpox as a military strategy by July 1763. The very fact that high-level British officers advocated the use of smallpox to attack their enemies was illustrative of the initial successes of the Native Americans besieging the British forts because, under the European conventions of war of the day, such an act was considered an atrocity. It may be too simplistic to credit the outbreak of smallpox among Native Americans in 1763 solely to the defenders of Fort Pitt when one considers that the presence of afflicted individuals in the fort's hospital suggests that there were probably others afflicted with the disease in the region that were not showing symptoms due to the virus's incubation period. Irrespective of the number of potential sources for the smallpox epidemic of 1763, its toll on the native warriors and their home communities helped Great Britain to quell Pontiac's Rebellion.

—*John R. Burch Jr.*

Further Reading

Fenn, Elizabeth A. "Biological Warfare in Eighteenth-Century North America: Beyond Jeffery Amherst." *Journal of American History* 86 (2000): 1552–1580.

Kelton, Paul. *Epidemics and Enslavement: Biological Catastrophe in the Native Southeast 1492–1715*. Lincoln: University of Nebraska Press, 2007.

Kiple, Kenneth F., ed. *The Cambridge World History of Human Disease*. New York: Cambridge University Press, 1993.

Stamp Act Protests (1765)

Nonviolent Stamp Act protests began in 1607 when the first English settlers came ashore in New England. They understood their relationship with London. Having being nurtured by the Crown, these pioneers concerned themselves with survival under the protection of England. Fortunately, London through its largess adopted a policy of "salutary neglect," permitting the growing number of colonies and their populations to develop a newly unique culture. Parliament's colonial expansion initiated the dawn of a new age.

As time passed, these colonists began to identify themselves with their colony and gave less thought and consideration to their traditional rights as Englishmen. They legislated new and more rigid laws, some of which contradicted the English and nascent American common law. In many cases, such as the witchcraft trials, the defendant's guilt was assumed, and she had to prove her innocence in an environment less than just.

These rights, not challenged, became an increasingly important issue after British successes in the French and Indian War in sparsely settled areas west of the colonies. A British achievement in clearing the region of the French "menace" in 1763 was viewed favorably by London. Settlers moved west of the mountains, with or without Crown permission, further removing themselves from English culture.

Having bankrupted the Exchequer because of the colonial wars, having had to muster sufficient forces to protect the colonies, and maintaining a fleet to prevent the French from dominating trade and the seas, the Crown changed its conduct toward the colonies. Financial needs required Parliament to remold its attitudes toward her English subjects. Since the colonials generally paid few taxes, the Stamp Act provided a means of returning the Empire to fiscal solvency. First attempts included the American Revenue Act, also known as the Sugar Act, and the extension of the Molasses Act of 1733 were quite comprehensive but did not resolve the problem. In 1764, George Grenville strengthened the Imperial Custom Service, allowing for tighter enforcement regulations against smuggling. Grenville also modified the Currency Act.

This change of circumstances is illustrated by Parliament's passage of the Stamp Act by 245–49 on February 6 (29), 1765, when Grenville presented his Stamp Act Bill. The House of Lords approval the Act on March 8 and the king

128 | Stamp Act Protests (1765)

Stamp Act rioters hang a stamp distributor in effigy in 1765. (North Wind Picture Archives)

on March 22. It was ordered into effect two weeks later. The debt had grown from 72-plus million pounds to 129-plus million shortly before the act went into effect. The restiveness of the English population because of the high taxes it paid was causing the Crown concern with a possible revolution.

The Stamp Act, the first direct parliamentary tax, numbed colonials who lived in "splendid Isolation." In one moment, the 63 pages of the Stamp Act Orders changed the landscape for the colonies; the colonials were informed that the tax would be used for colonial administration. Direct means of collection were imposed because London realized prior relations could make application of the new laws a controversial matter. Legal documents of all sorts, newspapers, and apprenticeship status were taxed. Merchants and others who would trade in promissory or other forms of financial notes, such as transportation documents, were most vulnerable.

At the same time that the Stamp Act became law, the Crown also passed the Quartering Act. Fearful of civil disobedience, the Crown sent large detachments to Boston and other commercial and mercantile centers. The colonials had to provide lodging and supplies for soldiers garrisoning in colonial homes. A second Quartering Act required the billeting of soldiers in inns, almshouses, and unoccupied dwellings.

Such legislation ignited the events that led to a family separation. The colonies never had voting representations in Parliament, which passed laws for the benefit of the Empire. The colonials had experienced the effect of legislation prior to the Stamp Act, but the harshness of the act encompassed all avenues of income producing taxation.

When colonial leaders opposed the act as illegitimate, the members of the colonial community mostly affected resorted to "no taxation without representation." Calls arose to protect the traditional rights of Englishmen as evidenced by the Magna Carta of 1215 and the Bill of Rights of 1689 that had forbidden the imposing of taxes without the consent of parliament. When protests rose from civil disobedience to physical action, London answered with Blackstone's theory of "virtual representation." The concept was clear: Parliament in London made laws governing the Empire, and since the colonials were British subjects, they were bound by its legislation.

The theory of "virtual representation" affirmed the legality of control over colonial affairs. But, Parliament was not representative of all classes of society as land requirements and other restrictions limited membership in the House of Commons such that approximately only 3 percent of the men could vote: only Anglicans, and wealthier elements in land and commerce of society. The Crown and Parliament justified their actions by reminding the colonies of the aid and protection they had received on land and sea. Since the English taxpayer bore the burden of supporting the colonies, Parliament had to act. Prime Minister Lord George Grenville advocated the tax by arguing that geography did not matter, but the Empire as a whole supported all English subjects, whether in London or the colonies. The colonies argued that true representation occurred only when one was present and allowed to vote for or against any particular legislation, a view contrary to this parliamentary decision.

This ideological loggerhead frustrated the Crown and associated it with the civil disobedience of the colonies. Parliament passed the Stamp Act in 1765. The comprehensive act addressed every possible source of income for the Crown. Unfortunately, many of its provisions affected the educated and politically astute colonials, many of whom had studied history and geography. This small minority of the population had the capacity to arouse the general public with arguments challenging the Crown's demands. For example, having to pay higher duties as a result of the legislation meant every legal document had to carry a tax stamp to be legal.

One of many, Isaac Barre, a veteran of the French and Indian War, responded negatively to Parliament. He offered the colonial viewpoint to Parliament. He reminded the august body of the colonial contributions in fighting the French and Indians. His minority views failed to alter the situation, and instead, the colonies were called upon to support the Empire and not selfishly concern themselves. Parliament reinforced its new attitude toward the colonies by its conduct.

Benjamin Franklin, colonial American representative then living in London, met with Prime Minister Lord Grenville prior to the Stamp Act's approval. Franklin and others asked the British to reconsider their plan. Lord Grenville offered an alternative. He proposed that the colonial assemblies tax themselves to pay the costs involved for keeping the British in North America. The problem with this potential solution was that none of the colonials in London had authority to negotiate. The offer was declined without submission to the various colonial assemblies.

Samuel Adams referred to a spontaneous reaction, and through his influence, the Massachusetts Assembly approved his instructions, and copies were sent to all the colonies. Colonial governor Francis Bernard opposed the efforts to unite all the colonies in an effort to protest the Stamp Act. The governor understood the consequences of the call for colonial unity, stating that "demagoguery" was the aim of this conduct. He also alleged that joint action in opposition to the act was against the rights of the people. He didn't explain the reasons for his allegations. But, the governor saw the economic class of the protesters was not "meddling," but members of aristocratic and wealthy commercial interests.

James Otis appeared more of a legalist and writer than other revolutionary leaders and wrote *A Vindication of the British Colonies in 1765*. His early views were not generally accepted, but he served in the Stamp Act Congress, advocating colonial representation in Parliament and conceding its supremacy. As an attorney, he opposed the issuance of a Writ of Assistance—a general warrant issued before the crime—to assist in the enforcement of the Sugar Act.

Thomas Paine, writing anonymously, sent a large number of copies of his *Common Sense* throughout the colonies. He advocated an immediate declaration of independence on practical, ideological, and legal grounds. Later, he joined the Revolutionary army and took part in the retreat across New Jersey.

Patrick Henry, in the Virginia House of Burgess, on May 30, 1765, carried the legal issues to the fore. He made his famous, or infamous, "Caesar had his Brutus, Charles I his Cromwell" speech. As a result, the Burgesses resolved "it had the sole and exclusive right to lay taxes ... upon the inhabitants of this colony ... who were not bound to yield obedience to any law of parliament attempting to tax them."

The act's preamble stated its purpose: defraying Crown cost and expenses for defending the western frontiers against the French and Indians and British commerce against the French. Foreign trade was a particular concern. The establishment of Admiralty Courts in 1763 and then Vice-Admiralty Courts represented Crown concern over revenue. The first Admiralty Act gave the Crown wide jurisdiction over laws affecting the colonies that were expanded by the Stamp Act of 1765. Since these courts were not common-law courts, Admiralty trials were not considered within the scope of the "rights of Englishmen." Therefore, the Magna Carta did not protect them with the right to a trial by jury. The acts' provisions agitated the colonies. Jurisdiction could be anywhere in the Empire. Judges received a percentage of the fines levied, and naval officials were compensated for successful prosecutions. Defendants had no right to trial by jury, and the evidence requirements were slack.

This effort to improve the collection of revenue and taxes was highly resented and became a *cause célèbre* to those opposing the Stamp Act. Smugglers had avoided paying taxes and, like the Peter Zenger Case, the jury would probably vote against the Crown. Vice-Admiralty Courts had concurrent jurisdiction; these courts heard conflicts between merchants and seamen. Its judges were appointed by the Crown and came from England. Its jurisdiction covered the entire east coast of the American colonies. Contrary to existing law, the defendant was presumed guilty. One's failure to appear resulted in an automatic guilty verdict, even if the defendant could not travel to the court for the hearing.

With such threats to commerce, the Massachusetts Colonial Assembly sent a circular letter to all of the colonies in June 1765. All those invited had previously served in colonial assemblies and understood parliamentary procedures. Nine colonies responded to this first American call to the Stamp Act Congress. The various attendees realized their attitudes were all similar. A proposal was made that colonials be appointed members of parliament. The concept of the colonial assemblies' managing their own financial matters and concern over the number of Loyalists who could be sent to London dissuaded its proponents. The suggestion went nowhere, but what would have happened if London had agreed?

Colonials had supported King George III, but the provisions of the Stamp Act proved burdensome. As the cry of "no taxation without representation" spread, and no revenues were collected, Lord Pitt in Parliament opposed the act, and the Crown eventually repealed it. Having evidenced its weakness to colonial resistance, London passed the Declaratory Acts asserting her dominion over the American colonies, but to what effect? The issue now moved from a solely economic matter to a legal, constitutional issue defining the rights of British subjects.

On August 14, 1765, the first manifestations against the Stamp Act occurred when tax collectors were hung in effigy in the Boston Commons. A crowd of merchants, skilled craftsmen, and other directly interested parties—financially and politically—led the crowd in a protest against the Crown's interference in colonial affairs. Within a short time, colonials—women, skilled and unskilled workers, and (freed) slaves—gathered at the Liberty Tree to express their anger over the British imposition. Liberty trees became symbols of resistance and appeared throughout the colony. November 11, Pope's Day, was selected for the protest. This enabled the populace to gather gleefully; the anti-Catholic Protestants used this day to hang the pope in effigy, set fires, and have brawls throughout the city. The lower, and poorer, classes used this day not as a response to the Stamp Act but as a vehicle for augmenting their age-old prejudice against Rome.

Two effigies appeared; one represented Andrew Oliver, the Boston Stamp Act Commissioner and the brother-in-law of the colony's second-highest official, Lieutenant Governor Thomas Hutchinson. The other, a boot, represented a parliamentarian, the Earl of Bute, the innovator of the Stamp Act. When the crowd gathered, the public response initially was mockery, which quickly adopted a political overtone. The crowd went through the city "stamping" everything; it was large and composed of artisans, male and female laborers, children, a few merchants, and a few gentlemen. The effigies were hung to shouts of "liberty, property, and no stamps." The crowd went to the stamp office and tore the building down. Crown officials became concerned at the disorder and all marched to the Liberty Tree.

Zachariah Hood, the Boston tax collector, had to flee. The mob had burned his stamps, and he rode to New York for the protection of the English garrison. Riding his horse to death en route, Hood entered a colony that opted for the nonimportation of goods from England.

The mob's mood changed. Its organizers had lost control of the crowd, and the public officials now became concerned. When a bonfire was lit, an unruly crowd assembled. The object of the anger was Thomas Hutchinson, who was one of the most unpopular figures in Boston and the symbol for all that the mob opposed. His home was ravaged while a large gathering stood by and did nothing. Samuel Adams, an ardent revolutionary, understood the importance of the rioting, and he publicly disavowed knowledge or participation.

In every seaport, groups formed were composed of the "middle class." The Sons of Liberty dressed as workmen and sailors, probably to conceal their middle-class status. They forced Stamp Act distributors to destroy their materials and resign under threat of harm. They also attacked those deemed conspirators of the act's acceptance. When the act came into effect on November 1, 1765, the apparatus existed to forcibly resist. Colonial Governor Colden had to flee the city; his home was destroyed and carriage burned. He sought refuge on a British vessel. The protesters then marched across the city and attacked the garrison commander's home, destroying everything in sight.

The insurrection continued to spread. In North Carolina, for example, Royal Governor William Tryon, famous for the Regulator revolt, promised the leading merchants and planters special privileges should they obey the Stamp Act. He promised to write London for special privileges for these 50 individuals and promised to reimburse them for their expenses caused by the stamp tax. Tryon refused to allow the colonial assembly to convene. Despite his objections, most North Carolinians refused to pay the tax, so royal officials closed Cape Fear River port and others. One thousand Carolinians traveled to Wilmington to confront the tax collector, William Dry, who refused to let vessels pass since they had unstamped clearance papers.

North Carolinians forced the *North Carolina Gazette* editor to issue unstamped editions. The editor made "inflammatory expressions" about the Stamp Act, and the governor hired another newspaper as its official printer. The royal governor tried to enforce the act, and his efforts to quell resistance increased the popularity of the Sons of Liberty. In the February 26, 1766, edition, after declaring its loyalty to the Crown, it related historical freedoms granted the colonies and ended by stating its intent to "prefer death to slavery." The *Gazette* called for peaceful protests, if possible. All freeholders entered into a compact to resist by unity of the colonies.

Charleston, South Carolina, another notable port city, did not escape the mayhem. Henry Laurens, a leading member of the community who was wealthy in land and commerce, received the crowd's venom. His residence was searched for Stamp Act stamps. In Newport, Rhode Island, the Sons of Liberty paid someone to terrify the stamp distributors and local customs collectors.

Street violence burst forth in Newport in August. Gallows were built, and effigies were hung of Augustus Johnson, the stamp distributor, and two other leading conservative figures in the colony. The mob then attacked homes and destroyed property. The Sons of Liberty opposed violence, but were threatened if they interfered. There were other protests: Maryland, Georgia, and Pennsylvania leaders all argued for a rescission of the Stamp Act.

The Sons of Liberty was established in 1765; local groups of protesters assembled in all the colonies, a unifying action not witnessed before in British-American colonial history. This intercolonial organization existed in various forms before 1765. It was instrumental in developing a pattern for resistance to the Crown that led to American independence. The organization communicated with all the colonies. On November 6, a committee in New York began intercolonial correspondence with the various colonies and they all expressed an interest in joint action to protect their "legal and legitimate rights."

The Sons of Liberty's membership, an engine in the struggle to rebalance the relationship of the mother country with her North American children, was composed of financially comfortable subjects whose personal interests were greatly affected. The declared intention to enlarge the base of colonial participation may have been ingenious; most colonials, being uneducated, reacted and accepted the verbiage of the aforementioned. Symbolic of the effort, the Sons of Liberty strove to control the streets and crowds against violence. The Sons reiterated their loyalty to the Crown and confidence in the belief that Parliament would repeal the act, which violated their historic and legal rights.

The Stamp Act, the first direct parliamentary tax, numbed colonials who lived in "splendid Isolation." In one moment, the 63 pages of the Stamp Act orders would change the landscape for the colonies; the colonials were informed that the tax would be used for colonial administration. Direct means of collection were imposed because London realized prior relations could make the application of the new taxes a controversial matter. Legal documents of all sorts, newspapers, and apprenticeship status were taxed. Merchants and other would trade in promissory or financial notes, such as transportation documents were most vulnerable.

In the effort to remove the Stamp Act tax, the first Stamp Act Congress was held in New York in October 1765. The participants included the wealthiest and most influential people in the colonies. The delegates were attorneys (10), merchants (10), and planters and land-owning farms (7). All of the participants had served in elective office, and all but three were born in the colonies. Four would be signatories to the Declaration of Independence; nine would attend the First and Second Continental congresses. Three would remain Loyalists.

No delegate appeared from New Hampshire at the Congress; North Carolina, Georgia, and Virginia were not represented since their respective colonial governors did not call their legislatures into session for the purpose of selecting representatives to the Stamp Act Congress. Six of the nine colonies agreed to sign a petition to the Crown and Parliament. New York, Connecticut, and South Carolina were not authorized to sign any documents.

Robert Livingston's New York led the assault, questioning Parliament's legal authority to regulate internal and external trade. Not considering independence, many hoped a resolution to the Stamp Act controversy would strengthen the bond between family members. When Congress met, it was in secret, and no information was released about all its deliberations. A document, "The Declaration of Rights and Grievances" was prepared by Pennsylvanian John Dickinson. It raised 14 points of contention between the two sides. Congress's members also asserted their traditional and historic rights as Englishmen. They affirmed the conviction that Parliament did not represent the colonies; only colonial assemblies had the authority to tax. They were especially angered by the use of Admiralty Courts, non-common-law courts that did not require trial by jury. Lord Dartmouth, colonial governor, rejected their petition as an "inappropriate" document.

While William Beard argued the revolution was solely economic, it may not have been the complete case, but there is some merit to his argument. Many of the delegates discussed their natural rights as Englishmen. Massachusetts and Pennsylvania proposed a resolution referring to the "natural rights of mankind" and "common rights of mankind." Christopher Gadsden of South Carolina raised a point of legal contention. He averred that the law originated with the Crown and not Parliament. Therefore, the petition should be sent to the king. Still unsure, the declaration was sent to the king and the petition to both houses of Parliament. The signatories feared being viewed as traitors, and none signed the document other than the clerk of court.

Just prior to the news of the colonial reaction to the Stamp Act, Grenville was relived of the prime minister's post and replaced by Lord Rockingham, the first lord of the Treasury. At the same time, public attitudes in Great Britain were shifting; some wished to resist application of the Stamp Act, completely oblivious to the precedent's effect. Others, realizing that colonial resistance did not promise the anticipated finances, urged rescission of the act. Resistance to importation and other commercial issues caused the trading and financial interests to view the situation differently. It became obvious when 200 New York merchants agreed not to import from England until the act's repeal.

Parliament, meeting in December 1765, refused a resolution offered by Grenville. He suggested Parliament condemn colonial resistance to the Stamp Act and take remedial steps. A faction outside of Parliament led by Rockingham, Burke, and others organized London's merchants, who formed a committee of correspondence to support the act's repeal. They adopted a "grass roots" approach to the problem by calling on all members to communicate with merchants throughout the country to contact their parliamentary representatives and call for repeal, an action taken by Rockingham on January 14, 1766. A palliative was sought; the colonies would be allowed to pay the tax in their own script to reduce the financial impact on them. However, these efforts to ameliorate the situation failed.

William Pitt, no longer silent, declared that Grenville's colonial program had been wrong, and he remonstrated that Parliament lacked authority to tax the colonies. He did not deny the Crown's control over the colonies, which was to remain supreme in all matters of government and legislation. His nonplus statement evidenced a desire not to break with the colonies. In a confusing statement, Pitt said taxes were voluntary gifts and grants of the Commons. He did support his claim by averring that "virtual representation" reflected the English common law.

Lord Grenville, still in Parliament, made a telling response to Rockingham. He spoke of control, reciprocity, protection, the long historic relationship, and mutual benefits gained by this union. Denial of these terms constituted ingratitude and treason. Pitt's response spoke of three million people submitting to slavery. In rebuttal, Rockingham continued his attacks about economic repercussions, and the House passed a resolution showing support for the Crown. England's secretary of state, Henry Conway, introduced what became known as the Declaratory Acts. These acts affirmed the right of Parliament to tax the colonies in all cases and admitted the difficulty in enforcing the Stamp Act. Parliament also passed resolutions condemning rioting and granting compensation to those injured by the riots.

But the damage had already affected relations between the mother country and her children across the Atlantic. Parliament reaffirmed its right to tax colonials by the Declaratory Taxes by stating it was the sovereign legislature of the British Empire. The Crown agreed to the repeal of the Stamp Act on March 17, 1766. William Pitt and John Burke, ardent supporters of liberty, made speeches attacking the legality of the act, whose effects greatly contributed to colonial unification and opposition to the Crown.

Sometime in May 1766, the colonies found out about the repeal, and the masses that John Adams feared rejoiced and proclaimed their loyalty to George. The environment was especially charged because on the day of the repeal, all celebrated the king's birthday. The happy mob celebrated and the Assembly voted the construction of statutes to William Pitt and George III.

—Arthur K. Steinberg

See also all entries under Boston Massacre (1770); Boston Tea Party (1773).

Further Reading

Alexander, John K. *Samuel Adams: America's Revolutionary Politician*. Lanham, MD: Rowman & Littlefield, 2002.

Ammerman, David. *In the Common Cause: American Response to the Coercive Acts of 1774*. Charlottesville: University Press of Virginia, 1974.

Hoerder, Dirk. *Crowd Action in Revolutionary Massachusetts 1765–1780*. New York: Academic Press, 1977.

Knollenberg, Bernhard. *Origin of the American Revolution, 1759–1766*. New York: Macmillan, 1960.

Labaree, Benjamin Woods. *The Boston Tea Party*. New York: Oxford University Press, 1964.

Maier, Pauline. *From Resistance to Revolution: Colonial Radicals and the Development of American Opposition to Britain, 1765–1776*. New York: Knopf, 1972.

Martin, James Kirby. *Men in Rebellion: Higher Governmental Leaders and the Coming of the American Revolution*. New Brunswick, NJ: Rutgers University Press, 1973.

Middlekauff, Robert. *The Glorious Cause: The American Revolution, 1763–1789*. New York: Oxford University Press, 2005.

Morgan, Edmund S., and Helen M. Morgan. *The Stamp Act Crisis: Prologue to Revolution*. Chapel Hill: University of North Carolina Press, 1995.

Nash, Gary B. *The Unknown American Revolution: The Unruly Birth of Democracy and the Struggle to Create America*. New York: Viking, 2005.

Reid, John Phillip. *Constitutional History of the American Revolution: The Authority to Tax*. Madison: University of Wisconsin Press, 1987.

Roche, John F. *The Colonial Colloquies in the War for American Independence*. Millwood, NY: Associated Faculty Press, Inc., 1986.

Ryerson, Richard Alan. *The Revolution Is Now Begun: The Radical Committees of Philadelphia, 1765–1776*. Philadelphia: University of Pennsylvania Press, 1978.

Schlesinger, Arthur Meier. *The Colonial Merchants and the American Revolution, 1763–1776*. New York: Columbia University Press, 1918.

Shaw, Peter. *American Patriots and the Rituals of Revolution*. Cambridge, MA: Harvard University Press, 1981.

Thomas, Peter D. G. *British Politics and the Stamp Act Crisis: The First Phase of the American Revolution, 1763–1767*. Oxford, UK: Clarendon Press, 1975.

Tucker, Robert W., and David C. Hendrickson. *The Fall of the First British Empire: Origins of the War of American Independence*. Baltimore: Johns Hopkins University Press, 1982

Webking, Robert H. *The American Revolution and Politics of Liberty*. Baton Rouge: Louisiana State University Press, 1988.

Weslager, C. A. *The Stamp Act Congress*. Newark: University of Delaware Press, 1976.

Adams, Samuel (1722–1803)

Samuel Adams was born on September 27, 1722, in Boston, Massachusetts. He was educated at the Boston Latin School and Harvard University. At Harvard, John Locke's *Two Treatises of Government* influenced him when he wrote of the rights of man and governmental responsibility to care for its people. In his MA thesis, he raised the perennial question of one's duty to obey government and recognized that revolution might be necessary to secure individual rights. He believed that British colonial control was illegal. Adams, a zealot for American independence, used any tools at his disposal to gain that freedom.

Adams's abilities as a speaker and political theorist gained him notoriety. In 1746, he became a clerk of the Boston market. His views found expression in his publication. *The Public Advertiser*'s intention was to be "open to whatever may be adapted to the state and defined the rights and liberties of mankind." He suggested Parliament had overstepped its bounds by restricting the rights of American colonists. Another admonition was a mirror reflection of John Adams; people should not be mesmerized by the wealthy and/or permit themselves to be controlled by government. The constitution is the authoritative rule of law.

Adams was active at Boston town meetings, and a member of the "Whipping Post Club." He opposed British taxation instituted as a result of the debt caused by the French and Indian War because London hoped to balance the budget by passing the Sugar Act (April 5, 1764). Adams recognized the result of no public reaction would allow for continued violations by Parliament concerning taxation without representation, attacking freedom and liberty. His opposition was the first public effort to unite the colonies. Massachusetts's legislature joined Adams in opposing the act, but the colonial governor closed the legislature. Adams convinced local merchants to boycott importations of British goods.

All the colonies were urged to assemble; the Stamp Act Congress passed motions to the king. Adams, in the assembly, referred to the traditional rights of Englishmen. Adams's effort contributed to London's repeal of the Stamp Act. The relationship between colonies and parliament did not improve. After the imposition of the Townshend Act, Adams sought to obtain the passage of a circular letter describing British policy to all colonies, citing the problem as a "national" problem. Britain sent troops to Boston to enforce the new acts. Adams then published the *Journal of Occurrences*, describing events on a daily basis in Boston. The atmosphere deteriorated after the Boston Massacre. Massachusetts resolved to remove British troops and refuse to pay for their housing. Adams responded with proclamations referring to "the inherent and unalienable rights of the people."

Samuel Adams contributed to the atmosphere that led to the Boston Tea Party. His latest circular cautioned that the new act would have a detrimental effect on colonial commerce. He urged a united front. The Sons of Liberty became more active. Adams traveled throughout the colony, receiving support for opposition to the act from other communities. Unity came with the convening of the Continental Congress. In September 1774, Adams was selected as a member of the First Continental Congress and was among the most vocal. He signed the Declaration of Independence, debated for check on a strong central government, and opposed a standing army. He died on October 2, 1803, at the age of 81.

—*Arthur K. Steinberg*

Further Reading

Alexander, John K. *Samuel Adams: America's Revolutionary Politician*. Lanham, MD: Rowman & Littlefield, 2002.

Ammerman, David. *In the Common Cause: American Response to the Coercive Acts of 1774*. Charlottesville: University Press of Virginia, 1974.

Hoerder, Dirk. *Crowd Action in Revolutionary Massachusetts 1765–1780*. New York: Academic Press, 1977.

Labaree, Benjamin Woods. *The Boston Tea Party*. New York: Oxford University Press, 1964.

Maier, Pauline. *From Resistance to Revolution: Colonial Radicals and the Development of American Opposition to Britain, 1765–1776*. New York: Knopf, 1972.

Morgan, Edmund S., and Helen M. Morgan. *The Stamp Act Crisis: Prologue to Revolution*. Chapel Hill: University of North Carolina Press, 1995.

Nash, Gary B. *The Unknown American Revolution: The Unruly Birth of Democracy and the Struggle to Create America*. New York: Viking, 2005.

Shaw, Peter. *American Patriots and the Rituals of Revolution*. Cambridge, MA: Harvard University Press, 1981.

Weslager, C. A. *The Stamp Act Congress*. Newark: University of Delaware Press, 1976.

Declaratory Act (1766)

The French and Indian War (1754–1763) ended colonial reliance on the British Empire for protection against the French and Indians on the colonial frontier. British successes were absolute, and the colonies went from adolescents to adults. The colonies now resented the presence of British authority when they realized that there was no need for a large contingent of British forces on colonial soil. To London, the most outrageous aspect of the growing conflict was colonial determination to enact legislation to regulate colonial society without British consent. Despite Blackstone's theory of virtual representation, a legalism manufactured in the hope of quelling colonial restiveness, no colonials represented their colonies in London in either house of Parliament.

In response to growing disrespect for the Crown, Parliament passed the Declaratory Act, "an act passed for the better securing the dependency of his Majesty's dominions in America upon the Crown and parliament of Great Britain," 6 George III, c.12., on March 18, 1766. The act gave the Crown the exclusive right to impose all duties and taxes and finding any attempt to do so illegal.

Despite the repeal of the Stamp Act, colonials attacked parliamentary actions viewed as contradictory to the Magna Carta. Colonial businessmen, merchants, and attorneys ranted that the traditional rights of Englishmen were under assault. They argued that the traditional rights their forefathers fought for had been killed by London. The passage of this all-encompassing act could be used to justify passage of other legislation against the interest of the colonies.

Notable Americans like John Otis, "No Taxation without Representation"; Samuel Adams of Boston and the Sons of Liberty, who published materials and held meetings for the common people; and Patrick Henry of Virginia were instrumental in guiding the responses. Thomas Paine's *American Crisis* represented the growing belief that independence was necessary.

Colonial business was negatively affected; mercantile trade would be controlled as smuggling fell under the control of the Admiralty Courts that were not common-law bodies. Attorneys had to deal with the abundance of legalistic paperwork, all restricting and making it more difficult for the average colonial to make a living as British control tightened and affected colonial moneyed interests. The Massachusetts Assembly refused to obey the new act and circulated a letter to all colonies calling all to not obey the internal and external actions demanded under the acts, such as the Quartering and Mutiny Acts.

The circulation of grievances to other colonies made all consciously aware of their common causes. The colonies and their various business and political leaders realized some sort of action was necessary if they were to prosper, whether as part of the British Empire or not. But as the atmosphere became increasingly charged, the more rationalized the forces for independence grew. From intercolonial correspondence committees to Stamp Congresses, from committees of grievance to the Constitutional Convention, the flame had been ignited. By the time George III offered to ameliorate the relationship, colonials no longer viewed themselves as subjects, but rather as representative citizens of a new nation. The clash of interests and the controversy arising from two opposed self-interests led to a parting of the ways.

—*Arthur K. Steinberg*

Further Reading

Knollenberg, Bernhard. *Origin of the American Revolution, 1759–1766*. New York: Macmillan, 1960.

Morgan, Edmund S., and Helen M. Morgan. *The Stamp Act Crisis: Prologue to Revolution*. Chapel Hill: University of North Carolina Press, 1995.

Nash, Gary B. *The Unknown American Revolution: The Unruly Birth of Democracy and the Struggle to Create America*. New York: Viking, 2005.

Reid, John Phillip. *Constitutional History of the American Revolution: The Authority to Tax*. Madison: University of Wisconsin Press, 1987.

Thomas, Peter D. G. *British Politics and the Stamp Act Crisis: The First Phase of the American Revolution, 1763–1767*. Oxford: Clarendon Press, 1975.

Tucker, Robert W., and David C. Hendrickson. *The Fall of the First British Empire: Origins of the War of American Independence*. Baltimore: Johns Hopkins University Press, 1982.

Webking, Robert H. *The American Revolution and Politics of Liberty*. Baton Rouge: Louisiana State University Press, 1988.

Salutary Neglect

Salutary neglect represented intelligent British efforts to develop a viable colonial system within the bounds of the mercantile and legal traditions exemplified by the Magna Carta. This policy, beginning with colonization until the French and Indian War (Seven Years' War), allowed growth and expansion void of interference from London or Parliament. Whig prime minister Robert Walpole, a founder and supporter of the policy of salutary neglect, believed less governmental interference was best for growth.

Colonial growth from total dependence to independence was evidence of the success of this benign policy, but politicians did not foresee the political consequences in London. Colonials, due to a lack of governmental interest from London, functioned independently. Neither party enforced the Navigation Acts—acts compelling the colonies to trade only with Britain—legislated by Cromwell and Charles II but intentionally neglected by Walpole.

The Crown's successes in the French and Indian War caused unexpected responses and attitudes; colonials settling the west contrary to the Proclamation of 1763 no longer feared the French or Indians, and London now believed that the colonies should contribute to satisfying the national debt. Colonials had little regard for Crown subjects in the British Isles, whose taxes were higher than colonial taxes, but the same subjects did care about the financial cost for the new security given colonials. Few colonials knew or spoke of the Jumonville Affair, in which George Washington led colonial forces into the west and killed 50 French soldiers, a cause for the international conflict. At the time that the British were losing, William Pitt the Elder, the secretary of state, directed London's response. He confiscated colonial supplies, drafted colonials into the British army, and took charge of the course of the war. Angered by Pitt's action, the colonials began expressing their resentment to sudden British interference in their lives.

Demands that the colonies contribute to the economic welfare of the Empire clashed with the traditional rights of Englishmen; local control of colonial matters had been accepted as a fait accompli. Colonial resistance to Britain's attempt to address her financial needs worldwide caused Britain to exert a heavy hand in colonial affairs; the abandonment of salutary neglect resulted when London could refer to Blackstone's "virtual representation" and the colonies to the traditional rights of Englishmen.

Lord George Grenville resigned the chancellorship in July 1765 as the relationship further deteriorated with British attempts to circumvent common law by the imposition of Admiralty Courts to try "smugglers," the increased efforts to tax without representation, the Stamp Act, the Intolerable Acts, opposition from such vocal groups as the Sons of Liberty, the Boston Tea Party, and London's continual policy of denying the colonies to print their own coin for business and trade. Colonies relied on their legislatures, commercial conduct, and even various religious creeds to stress their independence.

King George III's "Olive Branch" was met by American, not colonial responses; by citizens, not subjects; by adults, and not children. From Thomas Paine to John Adams, colonials had turned from those seeking an arrangement to those calling for independence. The die was cast because Britain had been too successful in decisively winning the French and Indian War and the commercial and merchant classes were the hardest hit by Parliament's taxing system.

—Arthur K. Steinberg

Further Reading

Knollenberg, Bernhard. *Origin of the American Revolution, 1759–1766.* New York: Macmillan, 1960.

Maier, Pauline. *From Resistance to Revolution: Colonial Radicals and the Development of American Opposition to Britain, 1765–1776.* New York: Knopf, 1972.

Middlekauff, Robert. *The Glorious Cause: The American Revolution, 1763–1789.* New York: Oxford University Press, 2005.

Morgan, Edmund S., and Helen M. Morgan. *The Stamp Act Crisis: Prologue to Revolution.* Chapel Hill: University of North Carolina Press, 1995.

Nash, Gary B. *The Unknown American Revolution: The Unruly Birth of Democracy and the Struggle to Create America.* New York: Viking, 2005.

Tucker, Robert W., and David C. Hendrickson. *The Fall of the First British Empire: Origins of the War of American Independence*. Baltimore: Johns Hopkins University Press, 1982.

Webking, Robert H. *The American Revolution and Politics of Liberty*. Baton Rouge: Louisiana State University Press, 1988.

Stamp Act Congress (1765)

As a result of the passage of the Stamp Act by Parliament, representatives from nine of the colonies assembled in Federal Hall, New York, in October 1765. Only Georgia, Virginia, and New Hampshire were absent from a successful meeting of the various colonies in their call for unity. The subject for discussion was to "consult together on the present circumstances of the colonies." Most of the vocal opponents were educated and influential members of colonial society. This congress provided the first opportunity for passionate individuals to express their views colony-wide. This action scorched the political atmosphere after a period of political neglect by London caused by the French and Indian War.

The Massachusetts colonial assembly, operating under the auspices of he royal governor, sent a circular letter to all the colonies in June 1765. All the invited delegates had served in colonial legislatures; they were aware of parliamentary procedures, and all supported King George III. But the provisions of the Stamp Act were onerous to the colonials but a necessity for the financial maintenance of the Empire.

The assembled met in secret. The major issues reflected their "traditional rights of Englishmen": lack of self-representation, lack of a jury trial and opposition to the Admiralty Court, not a common-law court, whose jurisdiction covered smuggling. Robert Livingston led the attack by questioning the right of Parliament to regulate, and the issue of internal and/or external trade arose. The lack of representation, gleaming back to the Magna Carta, only irritated those averring the legislation was a violation of their traditional rights of Englishmen. Assertions of "virtual representation" did not mollify the assemblage.

When the delegates gathered on October 19, the delegates adopted a Declaration of Rights and Grievances. Fearing being identified as traitors and subject to execution, they did not sign the document. Only the clerk of the court affixed his signature. The document was redacted several times, but the number willing to sign the petitions was small.

Lord Dartmouth, who alleged the document was inappropriate, rejected the final petition by the New York House under grounds that an unapproved body submitted it. However, the threat of a united front compelled the Crown to revoke the act because of the broad level of opposition realizing that it was unenforceable. In March 1766 while revoking it, the Crown and parliament reasserted its right to complete legislative authority over the colonies. Despite the repeal, the damage had been done. Both the colonies and London recognized the power of colonial America to assert itself. British withdrawal of the act convinced many that pressure would force England to reconsider its conduct.

Those who eventually aspired to independence could take heart and look to the future. From passage of the Stamp Act to a call for independence was not a long trip. Replicating the organizational efforts of the colonies and their reaction to London provided a form for Americans such as Patrick Henry, James, Jonathan Mayhew, and Samuel Adams a forum from which to preach independence.

—Arthur K. Steinberg

Further Reading

Ammerman, David. *In the Common Cause: American Response to the Coercive Acts of 1774.* Charlottesville: University Press of Virginia, 1974.

Knollenberg, Bernhard. *Origin of the American Revolution, 1759–1766.* New York: Macmillan, 1960.

Maier, Pauline. *From Resistance to Revolution: Colonial Radicals and the Development of American Opposition to Britain, 1765–1776.* New York: Knopf, 1972.

Middlekauff, Robert. *The Glorious Cause: The American Revolution, 1763–1789.* New York: Oxford University Press, 2005.

Morgan, Edmund S., and Helen M. Morgan. *The Stamp Act Crisis: Prologue to Revolution.* Chapel Hill: University of North Carolina Press, 1995.

Nash, Gary B. *The Unknown American Revolution: The Unruly Birth of Democracy and the Struggle to Create America.* New York: Viking, 2005.

Reid, John Philip. *Constitutional History of the American Revolution: The Authority to Tax.* Madison: University of Wisconsin Press, 1987.

Thomas, Peter D. G. *British Politics and the Stamp Act Crisis: The First Phase of the American Revolution, 1763–1767.* Oxford, UK: Clarendon Press, 1975.

Weslager, C. A. *The Stamp Act Congress.* Newark: University of Delaware Press, 1976.

Taxation without Representation

"No taxation without representation" originated in English history long before the British Crown settled the colonies. When pre-feudal and feudal societies merged with monarchy and finally democracy, the means of supporting the governmental functions were established. Originally, tax collection to support society evolved without concern for representative government.

The first "statutory" espousal of the "traditional rights of Englishmen" occurred in 1215 with the signing of the Magna Carta. Nobility and king agreed to contractual obligations governing their relationship, and with time, one of the provisions mutated into no taxation without representation. King John conceded much of his fiscal control to representatives of the people, a term loosely used at this time.

Fiscal obligations governed colonial development. Because their establishment aided trade and immigration, the Crown made few efforts to establish a viable tax system. While British competition with Spain waned, French rivalry remained intense, requiring the stationing and use of British troops to protect colonial frontiers against the French and their Indian allies. When the French and Indian War (1754–1763) in the colonies ended, England was victorious. Her success was not pyrrhic, only the results of the war. Secure western borders with the removal of French and Indian hostility no longer required large numbers of British garrisons, but the issue of recovering her financial equilibrium remained.

London resolved to restore fiscal solvency and chose to tax the colonies for its efforts in North America. British leaders ignored the "traditional rights of Englishmen" as interpreted by the colonials. Parliament defined this as having its parliamentary members legislate colonial tax issues for the benefit of Great Britain. When American colonials objected, the Crown relied upon Blackstone's concept of "virtual representation," whereby he argued that Parliament represented the colonials. Unfortunately, his argument did not satisfy the colonials. Parliament could have mollified her position with the colonies. Neither English nor colonial statesmen suggested colonial representation in Parliament.

When London passed the Stamp Act in 1765, she instituted what Jonathan Mayhew and others called the Intolerable or Declaratory Acts. Mayhew was a powerful and popular clergyman. His *Discourse Concerning Unlimited Submission* spoke of traditional rights and he assumed the Crown and not Parliament was the culprit; he referred to tyrannical powers exercised by the Crown and initially sought the aid of Parliament to ameliorate the situation.

His works were widely published; John Adams and John Otis mirrored his views. Boston, a major center of trade and commerce, witnessed the first organized resistance to the Stamp Act requiring fees for notarization of official documents, meaning an increased cost of all sorts of legal documents. The Stamp Act Congress met in protest, and London, facing violence, withdrew the tax. This did not resolve the impasse, for London instituted new tax legislation. The English response passed a surfeit of legislation covering all aspects of British-American relations, and their intercourse worsened.

London passed the Admiralty Act, a non-common-law court not requiring trial by jury. The quick succession of acts only irritated their relationship; London's actions were perceived as hostile to the colonies. In 1773, Parliament granted a monopoly for the importation of tea to the East India Company accompanied by a tax, causing the Boston Tea Party. With the evolving relationship from parent and child to adolescence and parent, the interests of the two parties continued to separate until the child declared his independence and begin its life as an adult.

—Arthur K. Steinberg

Further Reading

Maier, Pauline. *From Resistance to Revolution: Colonial Radicals and the Development of American Opposition to Britain, 1765–1776*. New York: Knopf, 1972.

Middlekauff, Robert. *The Glorious Cause: The American Revolution, 1763–1789*. New York: Oxford University Press, 2005.

Nash, Gary B. *The Unknown American Revolution: The Unruly Birth of Democracy and the Struggle to Create America*. New York: Viking, 2005.

Reid, John Philip. *Constitutional History of the American Revolution: The Authority to Tax*. Madison: University of Wisconsin Press, 1987.

Tucker, Robert W., and David C. Hendrickson. *The Fall of the First British Empire: Origins of the War of American Independence*. Baltimore: Johns Hopkins University Press, 1982.

Webking, Robert H. *The American Revolution and Politics of Liberty*. Baton Rouge: Louisiana State University Press, 1988.

Stamp Act Resolutions of the Virginia House of Burgesses (1765)

After his ally, George Johnston, moved that the House resolve itself into a committee of the whole, Patrick Henry introduced the following provocative resolutions into a thinly attended session of Virginia's House of Burgesses in May 1765. Because many of the conservative plantation owners and gentlemen who comprised the membership of the House were not present, Henry's resolutions were adopted after some debate. A fifth resolution was also passed, but on the following day, when Henry was not present, the House leadership succeeded in having it rescinded, thought attempts to also rescind the only four resolutions failed. The fifth resolution, the text of which was later found among Henry's papers, stated that only the House of Burgesses had the right to impose taxes on the people of Virginia, and that attempts by anyone else to do so had "a manifest Tendency to destroy British as well as American Freedom."

Attorney, from the Committee of the whole House, reported, according to Order, that the Committee had considered of the Steps necessary to be taken in Consequence of the Resolutions of the House of Commons of *Great Britain* relative to the charging Stamp Duties in the Colonies and Plantations in *America*, and that they had come to several Resolutions thereon; which he read in his Place, and then delivered in at the Table, where they were again twice read, and agreed to by the House, with some Amendments, and are as follow:

Resolved, That the first Adventurers and Settlers of this his Majesty's Colony and Dominion of *Virginia* brought with them, and transmitted to their Posterity, and all other his Majesty's Subjects since inhabiting in this his Majesty's said Colony, all the Liberties, Privileges, Franchises, and Immunities, that have at any Time been held, enjoyed, and possessed, by the people of *Great Britain*.

Resolved, That by two royal Charters, granted by King *James* the First, the Colonists aforesaid are declared entitled to all Liberties, Privileges, and Immunities of Denizens and natural Subjects, to all Intents and Purposes, as if they had been abiding and born within the Realm of *England*.

Resolved, That the Taxation of the People by themselves, or by Persons chosen by themselves to represent them, who can only know what Taxes the People are able to bear, or the easiest Method of raising them, and must themselves be affected by every Tax laid on the People, is the only Security against a burdensome Taxation, and the distinguishing Characteristick of *British* Freedom, without which the ancient Constitution cannot exist.

Resolved, That his Majesty's liege People of this his most ancient and loyal Colony have without Interruption enjoyed the inestimable Right of being governed by such Laws, respecting their internal Polity and Taxation, as are derived from their own Consent, with the Approbation of their Sovereign, or his Substitute; and that the same hath never been forfeited or yielded up, but hath been constantly recognized by the Kings and People of *Great Britain*.

Source: Kennedy, John Pendleton, ed., *Journals of the House of Burgesses of Virginia 1761– 1765* (Richmond, VA: The Colonial Press, E. Waddey Co., 1907), 359–360.

An Account of the Destruction of Lt. Governor Hutchinson's House by the Stamp Act Rioters in Boston (1765)

The following selection from the diary of Boston resident John Tudor describes the violence that erupted in Boston in August 1765 as a result of American anger over the Stamp Act. Tudor, who was an eyewitness but not a participant, describes the destruction by a mob of the home of Lieutenant Governor Thomas Hutchinson, who was held by the citizens to be partly responsible for the Stamp Act. Tudor, like many Bostonians, later felt ashamed of his failure to act in preventing the destruction, once it became known that Hutchinson had nothing to do with the passage of the act, and had even apparently protested against it.

August 14

This morning was discovered hanging on the great Trees at the South end of Boston the Effigies of . . . Oliver Esqr as Stamp Master & a Large Boot with the Devil coming out of the top &c. The Boot to represent Lord Bute &c. The effigies hung all Day and towards evening a number of people assembled, took down the effigies carried them through the Town as far as the Townhouse, then March'd down King Street, and then proceeded to Oliver's dock, pulled down a New Brick Building called the Stamp Office, belonging to said Oliver & carried the Wooden part of it up to Fort Hill and with Shouting made a Bonfire of it with said Oliver's Fence which stood near said Hill; and then surrounded Mr. Oliver's House, Broke his Windows & entered the House & destroyed great part of the Furniture &c. The next Day a Proclamation was Issued out by Governor Bernard and the Council offering £100... Reward for the discovery of any person concerned as aforesaid &c. Things remained something quiet till the 26th when toward evening a number of people assembled in King Street & Attack'd the House and office of WTM Story, Esqr Deputy Register of the Court of Admiralty (which stood near the Town House) Broke the Windows of the House and Office, destroy'd & burnt part of the Goods scattered & burnt most of the papers in a Bonfire they made in King Street near the House. Then proceeded to the House of Benj. Hallowell, Esqr Comptroller of the Custom House; Broke down the Fence & Windows of his Dwelling house, & then entered the House, Broke the Wainscot and great part of the Furniture &c. and carried off £30 Sterling in money &c. This brought it to the dusk of the evening, though it was a moonlight Night near the full Moon. Then the Monsters being enflam'd with Rum & Wine which they got in said Hallowell's Celler proceeded with Shouts to the Dwelling House of the Hon. Thos. Hutchinson Esqr Lieutenant Governor & enter'd in a Voyalant manner, broke the Wainscot, partitions, Glasses &c.; broke & distroy'd every Window, Broke, tore or carried off all the Family"s Apparel Jewels, Books &c. and Carried off about £900 Sterling in Cash, they worked hard from 8 O'clock on the House, Fences &c. till about 12 or one O'Clock; when they got on the top of the House and cut down a large Cupola, or Lanthron which took up their Time till near Daylight, leaving the House a mere Shell. So great a piece of Cruelty (I believe) on so good, so innocent a Gentleman was never committed since the Creation The next Day the Governor & Council Issued out a proclamation of £300 Lawful money to anyone who should discover the Leader, or Leaders of the Mob and £100 reward for the discovery of any Actors in the affair. T'was supposed that several Country Fellows & sailors was concerned in this Mob, as there was but few of them known. There was a number of Boys from 14 to sixteen years of age, some mere Children which did a great deal of damage in breaking the Windows & destroying the Furniture Apparel &c. But what is surprising there was some hundreds of people looking on as spectators, I was one, that had they known each other's minds they might have prevented the Mischief done at the Lieutenant Governor's; But there was such a Universal abhorrence of the Stamp Act which [had] past in England & was soon to be put in execution in America and which was the cause of the Mob's rising and committing such cruelty on the Governor; thinking he had some hand in the Stamp Act, but it was soon known that he was not only innocent, but had protested against it.

Aug. 26

The next Day there was a full town Meeting, when they Voted unanimously their utter detestation of the violent proceedings of the Mob &c. and had the minds of the people and the Innocence of Governor Hutchinson been known before, as it was at this meeting, the mischief at his house might easily have been prevented, as the next day there was a Universal Lamentation for the Destruction done.

Source: Tudor, William, ed. *Deacon Tudor's Diary* (Boston: Press of Wallace Spooner, 1896), 17–20.

Boston Massacre (1770)

The Boston Massacre was the term given to the event that involved a small group of British soldiers shooting on American civilians who were taunting them in Boston on March 5, 1770. It led to tensions which, in turn, proved to be a cause of the general distrust among the Whigs who opposed elements of British rule, which resulted in the outbreak of the War of American Independence five years later. The shooting in Boston itself resulted in the death of three civilians at the scene, and two afterwards. Although the incident was important, and led to a trial of some of the soldiers, it is best known by the engraving by Paul Revere, and became one of the causes of rise in tensions that was to lead to the War of American Independence, which broke out in 1775.

There had been tension in North America since the end of the Seven Years' War (1754–1763). The British victory in the war had removed the French as a threat to the British settlements in the region, but the costs incurred in winning the war had meant that the British government had to raise the level of taxation. The Townshend Revenue Act and other laws, collectively known as the Townshend Acts, were passed by the British Parliament in 1767, taking their name from the proposer, the politician Charles Townshend, who wanted a tax placed on common products imported into the British colonies in North America—Townshend himself died just before the Act became law. This included taxes placed in tea, lead, painters' colors, glass, and paper. It was expected that this would help the government raise about £40,000.

The taxes led to much opposition from many of the residents in North America. Some objected to paying the taxes, but others were angry because the taxes were paid to the British governor and other British-appointed officials in each of the colonies, whereas most other taxes were paid to town assemblies. This would therefore mean that the British authorities were able to fund their rule directly, rather than having to rely on the will of the local assemblies. For the British, however, they saw the taxes as fair owing to the large expense incurred in defending British North America in the wars against the French and the Indians. The latter argument was supported by the Tories—Americans who supported the British—who were, in the American War of Independence, to become the Loyalists.

The British foresaw that many people in the city of Boston might resist the new taxes—it was a hotbed of radicalism—so, as a result, the British general Thomas

Boston Massacre (1770)

Paul Revere's sensational illustration of the Boston Massacre, a skirmish on March 5, 1770, in which British soldiers fired on and killed five townspeople. Revere's historic print, released within a month, publicized the event and was hugely influential in stoking anti-British sentiment in the years before the American Revolution. An interesting example of Revere's emphasis on impact over accuracy is the depiction of one of the victims, Crispus Attucks, who was of mixed African-American and Native American heritage, as a white man. (National Archives and Records Administration)

Gage sent over the 29th Regiment of Foot and the 14th West Yorkshire Fusiliers to Boston. The former, after 1881 the 1st Bn, Worcestershire Regiment, was largely raised in Worcestershire in the west Midlands of England. The latter, largely drawn from men from Yorkshire and Kent, had previously been based in Dublin, Ireland, and then in the south of England. As the ships brought the soldiers to Boston, there were problems over accommodating the soldiers, and only after these problems had been surmounted, the reinforcements on disembarked on October 1, 1768, and marched into Boston.

There were many tensions between the British troops and the local colonists, but the first time they came to a head with fatal results was on February 22, 1770, when a mob of people started causing a nuisance outside the house of Ebenezer Richardson, a local man who supported the British and was involved in informing on anti-British activists. When the crowd started throwing stones, and one of these hit the wife of Richardson, the Loyalist confronted the crowd with an unloaded shotgun. When they stormed his house, he loaded the gun and opened fire at the people breaking down his front door. Several people were injured, and an 11-year-old local boy, Christopher Seider, died later from his wounds. With a radical doctor performing the autopsy, Richardson found himself charged with murder, but the trial did not take place until after the Boston Massacre itself.

The tensions started again in the late afternoon of March 5, 1770. A group of Bostonians, including some radicals, were heading home with Private Hugh White, on sentry duty outside the Custom House (now the Old State House). During this time, Edward Garrick (or Gerrish), an apprentice to a wigmaker, spotted Captain-Lieutenant John Goldfinch and called out, "There goes the fellow that won't pay my master for dressing his hair." Goldfinch had actually paid the bill from Garrick's master, but this did not stop Garrick from continuing with his abuse. Garrick then taunted Private White, who left his sentry box and put Garrick with his (White's) musket.

It did not take long for a crowd to form, and they all started taunting White. Captain Thomas Preston, the Officer of the Day, was unsure exactly what to do. Initially, he had hoped that the situation would die down of its own accord. However, White had been forced by the crowd up the stairs to the Custom House and had his back to a locked door. It was now clear that events were escalating, so Preston sent for a noncommissioned officer, Corporal William Wemms, and several soldiers from the 29th Regiment of Foot, which included John Carroll, James Hartigan, Matthew Kilroy, William McCaulay, Hugh Montgomery, and William Warren. The men—with bayonets fixed—went out, followed by Preston and James Basset. They were able to rescue White at the stairs and drove back some of the crowd. By this time, there were about 300 to 400 people in the crowd, forming a semicircle around the soldiers. The soldiers all had their guns raised with Captain Preston in front of them as people in the crowd shouted "fire" inciting the soldiers to open fire.

During this, Private Hugh Montgomery was hit with a club and hit heavily. When he had recovered his balance, he fired his gun and then shouted "Damm you, fire," a phrase he later admitted to one of his lawyers. After a pause, the soldiers started firing into the large crowd. Some remarked that the firing was a little haphazard, and certainly the soldiers did not let off a volley in unison. Three people were killed instantly. These were an African American sailor (possibly with Native American ancestry) called Crispus Attucks; a rope maker called Samuel Gray; and a mariner called James Caldwell. Samuel Maverick, aged 17, was hit by a ricocheting bullet, and he died several hours later, early on the morning of March 6; and Patrick Carr, aged 30 from Ireland, who made leather breeches, died two weeks later from wounds incurred in the shooting. He made a deathbed testimony to his doctor in which he said that he felt that the soldiers probably acted out of fear for themselves.

The funerals for the first of those killed took place on March 8, with the coffins containing the bodies of Attucks, Gray, Caldwell, and Maverick being taken on a procession around the Liberty Tree and then to the cemetery—following the route of that of Seider—with possibly 10,000 people turning up. Shocked by the mock sincerity of some of the people leading the funeral, the Reverend Mather Byles turned to a friend and remarked, "They call me a brainless Tory, but tell me, my young friend, which is better—to be ruled by one tyrant three thousand miles away, or by three thousand tyrants not one mile away."

The size of the funeral procession was so large that authorities were worried about further repercussions, and they withdrew soldiers from the Custom House to Castle Island in Boston Harbor. They had arrested Preston at 3:00 a.m. on March 5, the morning after the shooting, and the eight soldiers involved turned themselves in later that morning. On March 27, Preston and four of the men who were thought to have been involved in the shooting were formally charged with murder. By this time, the incident had become well known throughout the city and further afield. Some anonymous pamphlets circulated, and Henry Pelham, a local artist and the half-brother of John Singleton Copley, the famous local portrait painter (who also painted many of the Bostonian political figures of the period involved in the subsequent trials), produced a picture of the incident, and Paul Revere, a Bostonian silversmith and engraver than produced his famous carton of the "Boston Massacre" as it had become called. Revere's drawing became famous, and Christian Remick, a local painter, hand-colored some pictures, some of which show Attucks as an African American. They also have Preston standing behind his soldiers and ordering them to open fire. The bright blue sky was also an artistic license as it was dusk at the time. Revere also added a sniper shooting from out of the Custom House (which was labeled in the engraving as "Butcher's Hall"). However, the most inaccurate part of the drawing was that the soldiers fired at intervals, possibly reloading, and they never fired a volley at the crowd, which would probably have resulted in much higher casualties.

At the Suffolk County Court, Captain Preston and the soldiers were put on trial. The government wanted the trial to be fair so that moderates would continue to support them, and to show that justice would be upheld. However, there were not many local attorneys who would represent the soldiers. Eventually John Adams, a leading patriot, agreed to defend them to ensure fairness, and he was assisted by Josiah Quincy II and Robert Auchmuty. The prosecution was led by the solicitor general for Massachusetts, Samuel Quincy, and Robert Treat Paine, an attorney hired by the town of Boston. All the jurors were drawn from outside Boston, and the trial itself was not held until later in the year.

The first trial was that of Thomas Preston, who, some claimed, gave the order to shoot. While in custody, Preston had written a number of letters, some of which were published in the local press. Preston's trial lasted from October 24 to October 30, 1770. Fifteen people testified at the trial, and there were depositions from another 91 people. Some included information of what they actually saw, or believed they had seen, with others citing hearsay and other evidence that was clearly inadmissible. Garrick was the first to give evidence, and Thomas Marshal, a tailor who served in the militia, was the second to speak for the prosecution. It was a witness called William Wyat, who claimed that he had actually heard Preston give the order—but had said that Preston was wearing a neutral-colored overcoat, later conceding that the man wearing the overcoat was not Preston. The jury acquitted Preston because they clearly did not believe that he had ordered the soldiers to open fire. The most convincing evidence was that Preston was standing in front of the soldiers, and hence any call by him to open fire would have endangered himself.

The trial of the eight soldiers started a month later, on November 27. Their defense, argued by John Adams, was that the soldiers were acting to defend themselves from possible harm. Even if they were provoked, Adams stated that there was no aim to shoot anybody, and they could only be found guilty of manslaughter. A plan of the area of the Boston Massacre, attributed to Paul Revere, is held at the Boston Public Library, and it has been claimed that the diagram was used in the court, although there are some doubts. The claim of self-defense was sustained by the jury in the case of six of the soldiers. However, two of the soldiers—Kilroy and Montgomery—were found guilty of murder as there were statements from many people that they had shot into the crowd. Some of the jurymen were later quoted as saying that they felt that the solders should have held their fire for longer. However, for the two convicted of manslaughter, Adams managed to get the crime reduced to manslaughter by using a part of the British Common Law whereby they could read from the Bible to prove that they could read and therefore had "prayed clergy" protesting their innocence and holding out their right thumbs. This meant that the two privates were punished by being branded on their thumbs by Sheriff Stephen Greenleaf.

The Boston Massacre was one of the events that were to engender great anger in the American public against the British authorities. Much of this came from Paul Revere's engraving which is still used in many school textbooks, although now the problematic nature of the image is highlighted. There remain some disputes—based on the conflicting evidence given at the trials—over whether some of the soldiers reloaded their guns before firing again. The site where the Boston Massacre took place is now marked by a cobblestone circle in the square around what is now the Old State House—and indeed it was from a balcony of the same building that the Declaration of Independence was read to crowds on July 18, 1776.

—*Justin Corfield*

See also all entries under Stamp Act Protests (1765); Boston Tea Party (1773).

Further Reading

Bourne, Russell. *Cradle of Violence: How Boston's Waterfront Mobs Ignited the American Revolution.* Hoboken, NJ: John Wiley & Sons, 2006.

Burgan, Michael. *Boston Massacre*. Minneapolis: Compass Point Books, 2005.

Langguth, A. J. *Patriots: The Men Who Started the American Revolution*. New York: Simon and Schuster, 1988.

Phelan, Mary Kay. *The Story of the Boston Massacre*. New York: Thomas Y. Crowell, 1976.

Reid, John Phillip. "A Lawyer Acquitted: John Adams and the Boston Massacre." *American Journal of Legal History* 18, no. 3 (1974): 189–207.

Zobel, Hiller B. *The Boston Massacre*. New York: W. W. Norton & Company, 1970.

Adams, John (1735–1826)

Already a leading patriot in Boston, Massachusetts, John Adams, later the second president of the United States, was a prominent lawyer involved in defending Captain Thomas Preston, who was being charged with ordering soldiers to open fire on civilians in the Boston Massacre of March 5, 1770, and also some of the soldiers charged with opening fire.

Adams was born on October 30, 1735, at Braintree, Massachusetts, his father, John Adams, being descended from a Welsh migrant, Ap Adam, who migrated to the Americas in 1636. He was educated at Harvard College, and his father, a Puritan deacon, wanted him to become a minister. However, he taught for a while and then decided to study law. With the emergence of the Patriot movement, Samuel Adams, a second cousin of John, became a leading activist. The two were prominent opponents of the Stamp Act of 1765, and John Adams himself wrote criticisms that appeared in the *Boston Gazette* and were then republished in the *London Chronicle*.

A well-known attorney in Boston by the time of the Boston Massacre, John Adams was hired to present a defense for Captain Preston and the eight soldiers. Initially, all the British soldiers were unable to find a lawyer, and Preston asked Adams to help. Adams was concerned that defending them might lose friends locally, and he would certainly not be well remunerated for his efforts. As it was, defending Preston earned him 18 guineas (£18, 18 shillings), for what Adams was to describe as "the most exhausting and fatiguing" case he had worked on. However, Adams was keen that the soldiers should have a fair trial, and his work on their behalf certainly showed him a fair person anxious that the legal process should triumph over mob rule of any sort.

During the trial, Adams ably defended Preston. Assisted by Josiah Quincy II and Robert Auchmuty, he was able to find discrepancies in some of the arguments raised by the witnesses. Preston's case was relatively easy as it was quickly proven that he did not give the order to open fire, and as he did not personally fire into the crowd, Adams was able to persuade the jury to acquit him. For the soldiers, the trial was harder as they did fire into the crowd. Two of the eight soldiers—Matthew Kilroy and Hugh Montgomery—were found guilty of the lesser charge of manslaughter (the others being entirely acquitted), and Adams was able to make a plea for them by which they had their right thumbs branded.

John Adams went on to be a leading political activist, taking part in the Declaration of Independence, and becoming the U.S. ambassador to the Netherlands from 1782 to 1788, and to Great Britain from 1785 to 1788. He was the first vice president of the United States, serving under George Washington, from 1789 until

1797, and was president of the United States from March 4, 1797, until March 4, 1801. He died on July 4, 1826. His son John Quincy Adams became the sixth president of the United States in 1825.

—*Justin Corfield*

Further Reading

Ferling, John. *John Adams: A Life*. Knoxville: University of Tennessee Press, 1992.

McCullough, David. *John Adams*. New York: Simon & Schuster, 2001.

Smith, Page. *John Adams*. Garden City, NY: Doubleday, 1962.

Attucks, Crispus (c. 1723–1770)

Crispus Attucks was the first person killed in what became known as the Boston Massacre. Born of an African father and Native American mother, Attucks was a slave for one William Brown of Framingham, Massachusetts, until he escaped in 1750. Although little is known about Attucks's life, a runaway advertisement in the *Boston Gazette* (October 2, 1750) described him as "a mulatto Fellow, about 27 years of age ... 6 feet 2 inches high, short curl'd Hair, his Knees near together than common." The advertisement offered a reward of "10 pounds" and "cautioned against" seamen who would help him escape. The caution was not heeded. For the next 20 years, Attucks labored on a whaling ship out of Boston Harbor. At other times, he served as a rope maker on Boston's North End. It was here where Attucks led a mob against British soldiers.

On the North End, Attucks and others like him clashed with British soldiers, who were stationed in Boston after the French and Indian War. As a sailor, Attucks felt especially vulnerable to British impressment, which was a standard practice in the 18th century. As a common laborer, he came to resent the competition from British troops who worked during their off hours to supplement their meager wages in the military. On Friday, March 2, 1770, tensions heated up when Attucks and a group of rope makers fought with a British soldier, after which a rope maker insulted a Redcoat. Tensions culminated on the evening of Monday, March 5, 1770, when a group of 30 angry seamen, whom John Adams described as "a motely rabble of saucy boys, negroes and molattoes, Irish teagues, and jack tarrs," pelted a British guard at the customs house with snowballs and sticks. Seven soldiers came to his aid, immediately opening fire on the angry crowd. Attucks was struck first. Two balls tore through his chest, puncturing his chest and liver. Four others were also killed.

Newspapers on that fateful day noted that the five men were "barbarously murdered" (*New Hampshire Gazette*, March 13, 1772), but the trial did not bare that out. The soldiers were acquitted when John Adams, one of the finest legal minds in Boston, won an acquittal for the soldiers, setting off a public uproar throughout the city. Pamphleteers and propagandists called the affair the "Boston Massacre," and the victims, Attucks included, became immediate heroes.

Attucks was buried at Granary Burying Ground in Boston, the same yard that bears the remains of Samuel Adams, John Hancock, and other notable patriots of the American Revolution. Today he is remembered as a martyr and a symbol of American freedom. In 1998, the U.S. Treasury honored him by putting his image on a silver dollar.

—*Matthew L. Harris*

Further Reading

Allison, Robert J. *The Boston Massacre*. Beverly, MA: Commonwealth Editions, 2006.

Zobel, Hiller B. *The Boston Massacre*. New York: W. W. Norton, 1970; reissued, 1996.

Broadsides

One-sheet documents printed on one side only, broadsides date back to the 15th century as a popular format for quick distribution of official public announcements, commercial advertisements, news, and commentary. Broadsides generally fall in the category of ephemera, since most were considered disposable and tended to address issues of immediate but short-lived relevance. However, historians value broadsides for insights they offer into popular discourse—literally, the views on the street—as opposed to more formal written histories.

Broadsides competed for attention in public spaces using graphics, distinctive typography, and provocative language. Broadside ballads, poems intended to be sung to a familiar tune, further helped communicate a message memorably. Often sold at low cost or distributed for free, broadsides have a long history as tools of revolutionary action. In Boston, articles, verse, and cartoons rallying anti-British sentiments were posted on the Liberty Tree, from which an effigy of stampmaster Andrew Oliver was hanged in November 1765. Boston's literate middle class, including merchants and craftsmen, was a prime audience for propaganda decrying burdensome taxes and encroachments on liberty.

Printers of dissenting materials, such as Isaiah Thomas and Alexander McDougall, risked a charge of seditious libel, imprisonment, and destruction of their presses if publications were traced back to them. Authors often signed their work with pseudonyms if at all. But Stamp Act duties on newspapers and advertisements severely antagonized colonial publishers, motivating disobedience.

In Boston, where Sons of Liberty activities could be violent and vindictive, printers complying with British laws ran risks as well. A broadside published under the banner "No Stamped Paper to Be Had" described Stamp Act protests noting, "We have certain information from Boston that printers there intend to continue their papers, and to risk the penalties . . . and that if any of them were to stop on account of the stamp act, their offices would be in danger from the enraged people."

In the 18th century, graphic elements were typically printed from woodblocks, often generic designs that could be reused. In the Revolutionary era, a boot motif frequently appeared in reference to John Stuart, Lord Bute, First Lord of the Treasury and a favorite counselor of George III, and the devil denoted misdeeds and malign influence of various public figures.

The Boston Massacre became the subject of numerous broadsides in the months following the shooting of several belligerent colonists in a confrontation with British soldiers. "In Memory of the (Never to be Forgotten) Fifth of March, 1770" featured coffins and death's-head graphics common to funeral announcements, as well as an elegiac poem appealing to divine justice for vengeance. A large broadside published by the *Boston Gazette* included Paul Revere's famed copperplate print "The Bloody Massacre perpetrated in King Street Boston on March 5th 1770 by a party of the 29th Reg't." Revere's depiction of the fatal incident as a wanton act of violence perpetrated against innocent colonists was copied by several printers. Thomas, who printed a woodblock version in 1771, particularly helped keep the Boston Massacre fresh in the public mind, printing annual memorials to the men killed.

—*Tess Mann*

Further Reading

Barker, Hannah, and Simon Burrows, eds. *Press Politics and the Public Sphere in Europe and North America*. Cambridge: Cambridge University Press, 2002.

Brigham, Clarence S. *Paul Revere's Engravings*. New York: Atheneum, 1969.

Lowance, Mason I., and Georgia B. Bumgardner, eds. *Massachusetts Broadsides of the American Revolution*. Amherst: University of Massachusetts Press, 1976.

"No Stamped Paper to Be Had." Philadelphia: Printed by Hall & Franklin, 1765. Library of Congress Printed Ephemera Collection; Portfolio 346, Folder 45.

Plakas, Rosemary Fry. "Introduction to Printed Ephemera Collection." American Memory: American Time Capsule, Three Centuries of Broadsides and Other Printed Ephemera, Rare Book and Special Collections Division, Library of Congress. August 3,

2008: http://memory.loc.gov/ammem/rbpehtml/pessay.html (accessed August 28, 2008).

"A Poem, In Memory of the (Never to be Forgotten) Fifth of March, 1770." Boston: Printed and sold next to the Writing-School, in Queen-Street, 1770. Massachusetts Historical Society.

Schlesinger, Arthur M. "The Colonial Newspapers and the Stamp Act." *New England Quarterly* (March 1935): 63–83.

Preston, Thomas (1722–1798)

Captain Thomas Preston was the Officer of the Day from the 29th Regiment of Foot in the British army, and was responsible for ordering the soldiers to open fire leading to the Boston Massacre of 1770. Little is known of his origins. There have been some suggestions that he might have been from Ireland, although there seems to be no real evidence for this except for records of a number of men called Thomas Preston living there, and the 29th Regiment having been based at Kilkenny, Ireland, before it moved to North America.

It was in 1768 that the 29th Regiment was sent to Boston, Massachusetts, along with the 14th Regiment. On the night of March 5, 1770, he ordered the British soldiers to form a semicircle to keep back the crowd that was gathering, and told them not to fire, although a soldier, Private Hugh Montgomery, did shout out "fire." After the Boston Massacre, Preston was arrested at about midnight and taken to the Town Hall, where he was charged before two justices with the shooting. At 3:00 a.m., he was taken to the jail and was held there for seven months until he was put on trial for the shootings, which had lead to the deaths of five people, three at the site, and two afterwards.

While in jail, Preston wrote a number of letters that appeared in the *Boston Gazette* in which he thanked the local people. However, he also wrote letters to people elsewhere, and one of his letters sent to London was published in Boston, in which he complained about Bostonians. Preston hired a local lawyer, John Adams, later U.S. president, as his attorney. In the trial that took place on October 24–30, Preston stated that he felt that some of the crowd were intent on looting the Customs House. After his acquittal, he wrote to General Thomas Gage, "I take the liberty of wishing you joy at the complete victory obtained over the knaves and foolish villains of Boston."

Preston waited until the trial of the soldiers ended and he then left America on the HMS *Glasgow*. He retired from the army and moved to England, where he received a pension of £200, and he is said to have either settled in London or in Ireland, although John Adams did report that he saw him in London in the 1780s.

A number of stories have emerged around Thomas Preston who appears in the Revere print of the Boston Massacre. It has variously been stated that Preston was aged 40, or elsewhere that he was born in the same year as Adams, making him 48. A history of the massacre by Michael Burgan states that Preston died in 1798.

—*Justin Corfield*

Further Reading

Bourne, Russell. *Cradle of Violence: How Boston's Waterfront Mobs Ignited the American Revolution*. Hoboken, NJ: John Wiley & Sons, 2006.

Zobel, Hiller B. *The Boston Massacre*. New York: W. W. Norton & Company, 1970.

Revere, Paul (1734–1818)

Boston artisan, printmaker, businessman, and patriot mythologized in Henry Wadsworth Longfellow's romantic poem *Paul Revere's Ride*, whose print of the Boston Massacre depicted the confrontation between colonists and soldiers as an act of unwarranted aggression.

Paul Revere was a silversmith who became a folk hero of the American Revolution, though his real importance was in publicizing the cause in the years leading up to independence. (Library of Congress)

A silversmith by profession, Revere learned his craft from his father, French-born Apollos De Revoire (1702–1754). Taking over his father's silver shop in 1757, Revere struggled to compete in a limited market for fine silverwork. He supplemented his income making and mending common items like buckles and buttons and took up copperplate engraving, printing advertisements, trade cards, and bookplates. Seeing his business further threatened by the 1765 Stamp Act, Revere became increasingly engaged in revolutionary politics. In addition to his involvement with the North End Caucus and the Sons of Liberty, and later service as a courier for the Continental Congress, Revere printed patriotic cartoons.

In March 1770, after seven British soldiers fired on an angry mob leaving five dead and six wounded, Revere produced a print titled "The Bloody Massacre perpetrated in King Street Boston on March 5th 1770 by a party of the 29th Reg't." Below an illustration of the incident liberally skewing the facts, Revere included the names of the dead and a poem claiming the soldiers, "Like fierce barbarians grinning o'er their prey, Approve the carnage and enjoy the day." First published and sold individually, the picture also appeared on a broadside with a *Boston Gazette* article describing "the Consequences of Quartering Troops in a populous well-regulated town."

A talented silversmith but an awkward draftsman, Revere generally based his cartoons on pictures by other artists, not an unusual practice in a time before copyright law. For "The Bloody Massacre," he closely copied a print by artist Henry Pelham, prompting a letter from Pelham protesting Revere's failure to share credit and profits. The swiftness with which Revere copied and circulated the picture suggests he recognized a potent appeal to moral outrage for the shooting specifically and the state of affairs between Britain and America generally.

As in Pelham's original, Revere depicts a line of eight smiling soldiers in red coats firing into a group of distressed colonists chiefly in blue. Both versions indentify a building behind the soldiers as the Custom House and feature a small dog (a symbol of loyalty) facing the soldiers but siding with the colonists. Unlike Pelham, Revere chose not to show any colonists fleeing and changed the direction of the moon in the corner above the colonists so that it waxes rather than wanes. He also added a building called "Butcher's Hall" (a pun reading as "Butchers All") and a gun firing from one of its windows.

Though "The Bloody Massacre" was extensively distributed in 1770 and copied in turn by other artists, it did not necessarily inflame the hearts of all colonial Americans, particularly those beyond Boston, or those within Boston who tired of civil unrest. However, through frequent reproduction over ensuing centuries and association with Revere's folk hero status, the print became the iconic image of the Boston massacre for later generations.

—Tess Mann

Further Reading

Agresto, John. " 'Art and Historical Truth': The Boston Massacre." *Journal of Communication* (Autumn 1979): 170–174.

Brigham, Clarence S. *Paul Revere's Engravings*. New York: Atheneum, 1969.

Ford, Paul Leicester. "Some Pelham Copley Letters." *Atlantic Monthly*, April 1893, 499–510.

Korsmeyer, Carolyn. "Pictorial Assertion." *Journal of Aesthetics and Art Criticism* 43, no. 3 (Spring 1985): 257–265.

Paul Revere—Artisan, Businessman, and Patriot: The Man behind the Myth. Boston: Paul Revere Memorial Association, 1988.

Triber, Jayne E. *A True Republican: The Life of Paul Revere*. Amherst: University of Massachusetts Press, 1998.

George R. T. Hewes's Account of the Boston Massacre (1770)

In 1833, writer James Hawkes discovered one of the last surviving participants of the American Revolution in Richland Springs, New York. He was 91-year-old George R. T. Hewes, who had witnessed the Boston Massacre, participated in the Boston Tea Party, and served in the American militia during the Revolutionary War. Hawkes wrote a biography of Hewes and published his memoir, in which Hewes describes the events he witnessed. These publications made Hewes famous. Reproduced here is Hewes's account of the Boston Massacre of March 1770.

On my inquiring of Hewes what knowledge he had of that event, he replied, that he knew nothing from history, as he had never read anything relating to it from any publication whatever, and can therefore only give the information which I derived from the event of the day upon which the catastrophe happened. On that day, one of the British officers applied to a barber, to be shaved and dressed; the master of the shop, whose name was Pemont, told his apprentice boy he might serve him, and receive the pay to himself, while Pemont left the shop. The boy accordingly served him, but the officer, for some reason unknown to me, went away from the shop without paying him for his service.

After the officer had been gone some time, the boy went to the house where he was, with his account, to demand payment of his bill, but the sentinel, who was before the door, would not give him admittance, nor permit him to see the officer; and as some angry words were interchanged between the sentinel and the boy, a considerable number of the people from the vicinity, soon gathered at the place where they were, which was in King street, and I was soon on the ground among them. The violent agitation of the citizens, not only on account of the abuse offered to the boy, but other causes of excitement, then fresh in the recollection, was such that the sentinel began to be apprehensive of danger, and knocked at the door of the house, where the officers were, and told the servant who came to the door, that he was afraid of his life, and would quit his post unless he was protected. The officers in the house then sent a messenger to the guard-house, to require Captain Preston to come with a sufficient number of his soldiers to defend them from the threatened violence of the people. On receiving the message, he came immediately with a small guard of grenadiers, and paraded them before the custom-house, where the British officers were shut up. Captain Preston then ordered the people to disperse, but they said they would not, they were in the king's highway, and had as good a right to be there as he had. The captain of the guard then said to them, if you do not disperse, I will fire upon you, and then gave orders to his men to make ready, and immediately after gave them orders to fire. Three of our citizens fell dead on the spot, and two, who were wounded, died the next day; and nine others were also wounded. The persons who were killed I well recollect, said Hewes; they were, Gray, a rope maker, Marverick, a young man, Colwell, who was the mate of Captain Colton; Attuck, a mulatto, and Carr, who was an Irishman. Captain Preston then immediately fled with his grenadiers back to the guard-house. The people who were assembled on that occasion, then immediately chose a committee to report to the governor the result of Captain Preston's conduct, and to demand of him satisfaction. The governor told the committee, that if the people would be quiet that night h» would give them satisfaction, so far as was in his power; the next morning Captain Preston, and those of his guard who were concerned in the massacre, were, accordingly, by order of the governor, given up, and taken into custody the next morning, and committed to prison.

    It is not recollected that the offence given to the barber's boy is mentioned by the historians of the revolution ; yet there can be no doubt of its correctness. The account of this single one of the exciting causes of the massacre, related by Hewes, at this time, was in answer to the question of his personal knowledge of that event.

    A knowledge of the spirit of those times will easily lead us to conceive, that the manner of the British officers application to the barber, was a little too strongly tinctured with the dictatorial hauteur, to conciliate the views of equality, which at that period were supremely predominant in the minds of those of the Whig party, even in his humble occupation; and that the disrespectful notice of his loyal customer, in consigning him to the attention of his apprentice boy, and abruptly leaving his shop, was intended to be treated by the officer with contempt, by so underrating the services of his apprentice, as to deem any reward for them beneath his attention. The boy too, may be supposed to have imbibed so much of the spirit which distinguished that period of our history, that he was willing to improve any occasion to contribute his share to the public excitement; to add an additional spark to the fire of political dissention which was enkindling.

    When Hewes arrived at the spot where the Massacre happened, it appears his attention was principally engaged by the clamours of those who were disposed to aid the boy in avenging the insult offered to him by the British officer, and probably heard nothing, at that time, of any other of the many exciting causes which lead to that disastrous event, though it appeared from his general conversation, his knowledge of them was extensive and accurate.

But to pursue the destiny of Captain Preston, and the guard who fired on the citizens; in about a fortnight after, said Hewes, they were brought to trial and indicted for the crime of murder.

The soldiers were tried first, and acquitted, on the ground, that in firing upon the citizens of Boston, they only acted in proper obedience to the captain's orders. When Preston, their captain, was tried, I was called as one of the witnesses, on the part of the government, and testified, that I believed it was the same man, Captain Preston, that ordered his soldiers to make ready, who also ordered them to fire. Mr. John Adams, former president of the United States, was advocate for the prisoners, and denied the fact, that Captain Preston gave orders to his men to fire; and on his cross examination of me. asked whether my position was such, that I could see the captain's lips in motion when the order to fire was given; to which I answered, that I could not. Although the evidence of Preston's having given orders to the soldiers to fire, was thought by the jury sufficient to acquit them, it was not thought to be of weight enough to convict him of a capital offence; he also was acquitted.

Source: James Hawkes, *A Retrospect of the Boston Tea-Party, with a Memoir of George R. T. Hewes* (New York: S. S. Bliss, Printer, 1834), 28–32.

Richard Palmes's Account of the Boston Massacre (1770)

Boston resident Richard Palmes, who was an eyewitness to the incident, later gave the following account of the Boston Massacre of March 1770. Palmes claimed to be next to Captain Preston, who had just assured him the soldiers had no intention of firing into the crowd when the solders opened fire into reaction to a piece of ice or ball of snow that was thrown at them.

I, Richard Palmes, of Boston, of lawful age, testify and say, that between the hours of nine and ten o'clock of the fifth instant, I heard one of the bells ring, which I supposed was occasioned by fire, and enquiring where the fire was, was answered that the soldiers were abusing the inhabitants; I asked where, was first answered at Murray's barracks. I went there and spoke to some officers that were standing at the door, I told them I was surprised they suffered the soldiers to go out of the barracks after eight o'clock; I was answered by one . . . pray do you mean to teach us our duty; I answered I did not, only to remind them of it. One of them then said, you see that the soldiers are all in their barracks, and why do you not go to your homes. Mr. James Lamb and I said, Gentlemen, let us go home. . . . I then saw Mr. Pool Spear going towards the townhouse, he asked me if I was going home, I told him I was. . . . But when I got to the town-pump, we were told there was a rumpus at the Custom-house door; Mr. Spear said to me you had better not go, I told him I would go and try to make peace. I immediately went there and saw Capt. Preston at the head of six or eight soldiers in a circular form, with guns breast high and bayonets fixed. . . . I went immediately to Capt. Preston . . . and asked him if their guns were loaded, his answer was they are loaded with powder and ball; I then said to him,

I hope you do not intend they shall fire upon the inhabitants, his reply was, by no means. . . . [T]hen . . . I saw a piece of snow or ice fall among the soldiers on which the soldier at the officer's right hand stepped back and discharged his gun at the space of some seconds the soldier at his left fired next, and the others one after the other. After the first gun was fired, I heard the word "fire," but who said it I know not. After the first gun was fired the said officer had full time to forbid the other soldiers not to fire, but I did not hear him speak to them at all; then turning myself to the left I saw one man dead, distant about six feet; I having a stick in my hand made a stroke at the soldier who fired, and struck the gun out of his hand. I then made a stroke at the officer, my right foot slipped, that brought me on my knee, the blow falling short; he says I hit his arm; when I was recovering myself from the fall, I saw the soldier that fired the first gun endeavoring to push me through with his bayonet, on which I threw my stick at his head, the soldier starting back, gave me an opportunity to jump from him into Exchange lane, or I must have been inevitably run through the body. I looked back and saw three persons laying on the ground, and perceiving a soldier stepping round the corner as I thought to shoot me, I ran down Exchange lane, and . . . into King Street, and followed Mr. Gridley with several other persons with the body of Capt. Morton's apprentice, up to the prison house, and saw he had a ball shot through his breast; at my return I found that the officers and soldiers were gone to the main guard. To my best observation there were not seventy people in King Street at the time of the firing, and them very scattering, but in a few minutes after the firing there were upwards of a thousand.

Source: Richard Palmes, "A Short Narrative of the Horrid Massacre in Boston" (Boston, 1770).

Regulator Movement (1771)

The Regulator Movement—actually two distinct movements, centered in North and South Carolina, respectively—was a vigilante protest movement launched by backcountry farmers shortly before the American Revolution. In South Carolina, the Regulators sought to impose law and order and gain fuller access to the colonial legislature and colonial courts. In North Carolina, a more radical and militant group of Regulators protested political corruption, taxation, and the imprisonment of debtors. Though they differed in many respects, the two movements shared an emphasis on making colonial governments more responsive to the colonists' immediate needs. The Regulator Movement was the largest-scale political uprising in British North America between Bacon's Rebellion and the American Revolution.

North and South Carolina were chartered in 1670, but white settlers did not begin to populate the Carolina backcountry until the middle third of the 18th century. Backcountry residents, many of whom were recent immigrants from Scotland, Ireland, and Germany, lived isolated, hardscrabble lives. Many were religious dissenters, which set them apart from the predominantly Anglican residents of the coastal regions. To some extent, backcountry and coastal settlements enjoyed a symbiotic relationship. Coastal planters relied on backcountry settlers to protect them by creating a buffer zone that would keep slaves within the colony and Indians out; backcountry settlers often aspired to emulate coastal leaders by breaking free of subsistence farming, becoming slaveholding planters, and participating in the trans-Atlantic market economy. But in spite of their common aspirations, backcountry farmers and coastal planters differed greatly in lifestyle, wealth, and political power, and their interests often diverged. In fact, the coastal-backcountry axis of conflict was pervasive in 18th-century America; it shaped colonial politics in New England and Pennsylvania as well as the South. In the late 1760s, disaffected Carolina frontiersmen began to organize a protest movement they called "the Regulation." In South Carolina, the term "Regulation" referred to the protesters' wish to "regulate" the disordered affairs of the backcountry. In North Carolina, it denoted the protesters' wish to "regulate" and reform the unfair policies and corrupt administration of the colonial government.

The North Carolina Regulator Movement, which was the more radical of the two, originated with the formation of the Sandy Creek Association in Orange

County in August 1766. The Sandy Creek Association was succeeded in April 1768 by the Regulator Association, from which the Regulator Movement took its name. Though centered in Orange County, the protest also encompassed Anson and Rowan counties and sporadically infected other backcountry districts. The men who joined the North Carolina Regulation reflected the full range of the backcountry's truncated social hierarchy, from impoverished farmers to moderately affluent planters. Some Regulators owned slaves, sawmills, gristmills, and substantial acreage that was reputed to be among the most fertile farmland in North America. The affluence and upward mobility of many Regulators undercuts any notion that the Regulation was a simple class conflict between rich and poor. Altogether, perhaps three-quarters of the adult men who resided in the North Carolina backcountry participated in the Regulator Movement.

The Regulators' principal grievance was the corruption of North Carolina's royal provincial government. They protested exorbitant taxes and court fees, the seizure of farmers' property and livestock to pay taxes, and the widespread practice of imprisonment for debt. They particularly resented the taxes imposed to pay for the construction of a sumptuous governor's palace in New Bern. The Regulators' protests sometimes assumed a hysterical tone; in their most radical phase, in the winter of 1770–1771, the Regulators threatened to slay all judges and lawyers in the colony. But the Regulators also advanced several pragmatic and farsighted proposals for improving provincial government. They advocated the implementation of a more equitable tax system, in which each man would pay in proportion to his income. They sought to diminish corruption by limiting attorneys' fees and providing for clerks to be paid salaries so that they would not have to rely on court fees for income. The Regulators also advocated the use of the secret ballot and sought to make the government more responsive to the people by publishing roll-call votes of the Assembly and allowing voters to instruct their representatives.

For many Regulators, these political proposals were infused with a radical Protestant vision of social reform. Although the established Anglican Church had scarcely made inroads in the North Carolina backcountry, both Quakerism and the evangelical preaching of the First Great Awakening transformed the region in the mid-18th century. These movements emphasized individual freedom of conscience and diminished traditional esteem for social and political hierarchies. Herman Husband, one of the intellectual leaders of the Regulator Movement, published two pamphlets in which he argued that Christians were obliged to ensure that the governments under which they lived were just; a man who neglected to defend his civil rights, Husband argued, was flouting the will of God. Husband's reasoning incorporated elements of Whig country thought, which would later play a pivotal role in the American Revolution.

It is difficult to construct a coherent account of the Regulators' actions because the Regulator Movement was truly a popular movement, with an informal leadership structure and fluid tactics and goals. While a few prominent leaders emerged—Herman Husband as theorist and scribe, James Hunter as "general" of physical resistance—these leaders preferred to influence, rather than command, their followers. The Regulators did create a modicum of organizational structure. They bound themselves to a common cause by creating "associations," drafting resolutions, and, in some cases, swearing oaths (Quaker Regulators, as well as some who were Baptist, abstained from taking oaths). But the Regulation was fundamentally a grassroots movement, characterized by localism, voluntarism, minimal hierarchy, and constant recourse to the dictates of the individual conscience.

Violent clashes between the Regulators and the North Carolina government first erupted in 1768. On April 8, a group of 70 to 100 Regulators rioted to protest the seizure of a fellow Regulator's horse as a tax payment. They fired on the home of Edmund Fanning, a prominent Orange County official, and broke his windowpanes. Fanning attempted to muster the Orange County militia to arrest the ringleaders but found that many militiamen sympathized with the Regulators and refused to turn out. When Fanning arrested Herman Husband and William Butler in May, 700 Regulators gathered to press for the men's release. On June 20, James Hunter and Rednap Howell presented a Regulator petition to Governor Tryon; in this document, the Regulators repeated their long-standing concerns about political corruption and singled out Fanning as an official who had stymied their efforts to secure redress. Tryon, though long sympathetic to backcountry settlers' concerns about political corruption, warned the Regulators not to resort to extralegal means. He promised to tour the backcountry, which he did in the summer of 1768. This visit culminated in a narrowly averted clash between nearly 1,500 militiamen, commanded by Tryon, and 800 Regulators, who apparently planned to disrupt the sessions of the Hillsborough Superior Court. The Regulators opted to disperse rather than confront Tryon's army.

The Regulators continued to petition Tryon throughout 1769, but they gradually lost the governor's goodwill. By early 1770, the Regulators were once again disrupting court sessions and interfering with sheriffs' efforts to collect taxes. On September 24, Regulators disrupted the Hillsborough Superior Court and severely beat Edmund Fanning. In November, they torched the home and barns of Judge Richard Henderson. Soon afterwards, Tryon heard rumors that the Regulators planned to disrupt the meeting of the North Carolina Assembly in December. The Assembly convened in an atmosphere of mounting anxiety, even hysteria. Governor Tryon denounced the popular protest and asked the Assembly to authorize him to suppress it by military force. The Assembly responded by passing the Johnston Riot Act of January 15, 1771. This law made riotous behavior a felony and, in some cases, treason; it also permitted the government to prosecute accused rebels in any of North Carolina's six superior courts, regardless of where the alleged offense had occurred. Finally, it empowered Tryon to suppress the Regulators by force. Meanwhile, the Assembly expelled Herman Husband on charges of seditious libel.

Ironically but predictably, the so-called "Bloody Act" heightened rather than quelled backcountry protest. Angry frontiersmen flocked to join the Regulator cause. They drew up counter-resolutions, forbade courts to meet, and pledged not to pay taxes. In the spring, Tryon, who knew that he would soon be moving on to the provincial governorship of New York, resolved to put down the Regulator Movement briskly and decisively. He marshaled approximately 1,200 to 1,500 militiamen (some under the command of General Hugh Waddell) and marched them west, where they eventually encamped at Great Alamance Creek near Hillsborough. On the evening of May 15, a party of approximately 2,000–3,000 Regulators petitioned Tryon for an audience. Tryon declined, and around noon on May 16, he ordered the militia to open fire on the assembled Regulators. The poorly armed Regulators, their movements uncoordinated by any commanding officer, were easily defeated in a two-hour battle. Tryon subsequently hanged seven Regulators and required approximately 6,400 others to swear allegiance to the province of North Carolina. The Battle of Alamance marked the collapse of the Regulator Movement. Although disaffection lingered in the backcountry, and many families chose to move westward to distance themselves from the provincial government, the Regulators' formal protest was at an end.

Meanwhile, a more moderate movement, also known as "the Regulation," took shape in the South Carolina backcountry. Affluent farmers and planters joined forces to suppress the numerous outlaws, squatters, and drifters who had populated the South Carolina backcountry in the aftermath of the Seven Years' War. They retaliated against suspected criminals by whipping them, burning their homes, or apprehending them and delivering them directly to the Charleston jail. They also harassed impoverished frontier settlers who lived primarily by hunting and foraging. The sedentary, land-owning Regulators denigrated these hunters as shiftless "white Indians"; they loathed them because the hunters subverted conventional norms of respectability, inconvenienced their neighbors by practices such as fire-hunting, and stirred up conflicts with local Native Americans by trespassing on their hunting grounds. The South Carolina Regulator Movement may thus be interpreted as a concerted effort by upwardly mobile settlers to push the backcountry out of a rough-and-ready frontier stage of development and bring it within the orbit of commercial plantation agriculture.

In spite of their propensity for vigilante justice, the South Carolina Regulators evinced a relatively conservative, law-and-order mind-set. Most were substantial landowners who sought to protect private property and make the backcountry safe for agrarian capitalism. In 1767, they presented the South Carolina Assembly with a remonstrance in which they detailed the backcountry's crime problem and urged quick action. They requested local courts, local jails, a more convenient system for processing land warrants, and fuller backcountry representation in the South Carolina Assembly. (Until 1768, the vast backcountry was treated as a single electoral district.) In 1768 and again in 1769, armed Regulators marched from the backcountry to lowcountry polling places, where they demanded the right to vote. Although election officials did not always comply, the Regulators succeeded in electing several candidates in this fashion.

The assemblymen recognized the establishment tone of the Regulators' remonstrance and promptly acceded to several of the Regulators' demands. In November 1767, the Assembly established two ranger companies, composed largely of Regulators, and empowered them to suppress banditry and other crimes. In 1768, two new backcountry parishes were created, permitting greater backcountry representation in the colonial legislature. Finally, the Circuit Court Act of 1769 created a much-needed network of courts, jails, and sheriffs to maintain order in the backcountry. Intermittent Regulator violence continued throughout these years, alienating some coastal residents and spawning counterattacks by a rival backcountry group called the Moderators. Nevertheless, the movement dissipated by 1771, when the governor of South Carolina issued a general pardon to all of the colony's Regulators. The moderate tone of the South Carolina Regulation, the Assembly's prompt and sympathetic response, and the colony's strong tradition of consensus government combined to prevent the sort of open warfare between Regulators and colonial officials that occurred in North Carolina.

Historians continue to debate the Regulator Movement's relationship to the American Revolution. In the 19th century, the Regulator Movement was often interpreted as an overt protest against British rule, and thus as a precursor to the American Revolution. This approach, which fell into disfavor in the early 20th century, was succeeded by an interpretation of the Regulator Movement as a class conflict that anticipated the more extensive post-Revolutionary conflict over "who should rule at home." More recently, historians have noted the recurring pattern of east-west tension in colonial politics, the specific backcountry social and religious context that informed the Regulator Movement, and the complexity and variety of the Regulators' political aims. In South Carolina, the Regulators clearly sought to participate in, not overthrow, the colonial government. Most joined the coastal elite in supporting American independence, even as they continued to contest the coastal parishes' domination of South Carolina politics. The North Carolina Regulators, on the other hand, expressed dissatisfaction with both British imperial rule and the political leadership of North Carolina's resident coastal elite. This dual resentment placed them in an awkward position when the Revolutionary War began.

Recent scholarship by A. Roger Ekirch and Marjoleine Kars, among others, emphasizes that many North Carolina Regulators supported neither the British nor the patriot cause with any enthusiasm during the Revolutionary War. The former Regulators' decision to sit out the war was fueled not only by disaffection with both sets of political leaders, but also by evangelical preaching that advocated neutrality and pacifism. In 1775, the Continental Congress, anxious to overcome Piedmont farmers' disaffection with the patriot cause, hired two Presbyterian ministers to tour the North Carolina backcountry for four months and persuade the region's residents that opposition to British rule was morally justifiable. Some former Regulators, notably Herman Husband, did espouse the patriot cause. But most seem to have recognized that neither major party to the Revolutionary War was likely to bring about the changes the Regulators had sought. Although the Revolutionary War brought prolonged and violent conflict to the North Carolina backcountry, it did not address the backcountry settlers' fundamental grievances about the government's responsiveness to their needs.

In the wake of the Revolution, former Regulators sympathized with other backcountry "regulations" such as Shays' Rebellion in Massachusetts and the Whiskey Rebellion in Pennsylvania. Lingering backcountry distrust of central government made North Carolina one of the last states to ratify the U.S. Constitution, which heightened the powers of a distant federal government. Nevertheless, state leaders in both North and South Carolina slowly came to terms with the need to secure the loyalty of backcountry residents and improve their access to state institutions. Between 1786 and 1801, the North and South Carolina legislatures sited their new state capitals in Raleigh and Columbia, respectively, and their new state universities in Chapel Hill and Columbia—locations in the very heart of the backcountry.

—*Darcy R. Fryer*

See also all entries under Shays' Rebellion (1787); Whiskey Rebellion (1794).

Further Reading

Adams, George R. "The Carolina Regulators: A Note on Changing Interpretations." *North Carolina Historical Review* 49 (1972): 345–352.

Brown, Richard Maxwell. *The South Carolina Regulators*. Cambridge, MA: Belknap Press, 1963.

Denson, Andrew C. "Diversity, Religion, and the North Carolina Regulators." *North Carolina Historical Review* 72 (1995): 30–53.

Ekirch, A. Roger. *"Poor Carolina": Politics and Society in Colonial North Carolina, 1729–1776*. Chapel Hill: University of North Carolina Press, 1981.

Kars, Marjoleine. *Breaking Loose Together: The Regulator Rebellion in Pre-Revolutionary North Carolina*. Chapel Hill: University of North Carolina Press, 2002.

Klein, Rachel. *Unification of a Slave State: The Rise of the Planter Class in the South Carolina Backcountry, 1760–1808*. Chapel Hill: University of North Carolina Press, 1990.

Lee, Wayne E. *Crowds and Soldiers in Revolutionary North Carolina: The Culture of Violence in Riot and War*. Gainesville: University Press of Florida, 2001.

Nelson, Paul David. *William Tryon and the Course of Empire: A Life in British Imperial Service*. Chapel Hill: University of North Carolina Press, 1990.

Battle of Alamance (1771)

The Battle of Alamance, which occurred on May 16, 1771, at Great Alamance Creek near Hillsborough, was a clash between North Carolina Regulators and the North Carolina militia, led by Governor William Tryon. The Regulators' defeat in this conflict effectively ended the Regulator Movement.

On January 15, 1771, in an atmosphere of mounting tension, the North Carolina Assembly passed the Johnston Riot Act, which authorized Tryon to suppress the Regulator Movement by military force. In the spring, Tryon duly summoned the North Carolina militia to the colonial capital, New Bern. He failed to raise as many troops as he hoped, but he nevertheless marched to Hillsborough, the seat of Orange County and a site of past Regulator violence, with an estimated 1,100 men. On May 9, approximately 2,000 Regulators surrounded General Hugh Waddell's encampment of 250 militiamen in Rowan County. Tryon rushed to join Waddell, and for several days, the two armies eyed each other warily. Many militiamen were reluctant to engage the Regulators, and a few went over to the Regulator side.

On May 13, Tryon marched his troops further westward to Great Alamance Creek. There, on the evening of May 15, the Regulators petitioned Tryon for an audience. Tryon refused their request and, on the morning of May 16, positioned his troops to do battle with approximately 2,000 to 3,000 assembled Regulators. A group of Regulators led by Presbyterian minister David Caldwell attempted to negotiate with Tryon to avert an armed confrontation; Tryon responded by issuing an ultimatum that the Regulators lay down their arms within an hour. He also ordered the execution of Regulator Robert Thompson, a member of Caldwell's party.

The Regulators refused to capitulate, although some who were religious pacifists left before Tryon's one-hour ultimatum expired. Just before noon, Tryon order the militia to open fire. The battle was brief; within two hours, Tryon's troops had routed their unprepared opponents. Many of the Regulators, not expecting that their confrontation with Tryon would erupt into an open battle, had arrived at Great Alamance Creek unarmed or without adequate ammunition. Nor did the Regulators have a single commanding officer; James Hunter, the obvious choice, declined to assume the command on the grounds that each individual should command himself. The militia suffered 9 dead and 61 wounded. The Regulator losses, never precisely determined, included 10 to 20 dead and approximately 100 wounded.

After the battle, the royal government of North Carolina executed seven Regulators. One, James Few, was executed without trial; the others were accorded brief and inadequate trials under the terms of the Johnston Riot Act. Tryon pardoned most of the Regulators on the condition that they lay down their arms and swear allegiance to the royal government of North Carolina. More than 6,400 did so. The Regulator Movement collapsed in the aftermath of the Battle of Alamance, although backcountry settlers' disaffection with the North Carolina government remained. Many former Regulators moved west, settling in Tennessee; others sought solace in pacifism and radical Protestantism.

—Darcy R. Fryer

Further Reading

Kars, Marjoleine. *Breaking Loose Together: The Regulator Rebellion in Pre-Revolutionary North Carolina*. Chapel Hill: University of North Carolina Press, 2002.

Lefler, Hugh T., and William S. Powell. *Colonial North Carolina: A History*. New York: Charles Scribner's Sons, 1973.

Dobbs, Arthur (1689–1765)

Arthur Dobbs, a Scots-Irish landowner and politician, served as royal governor of North Carolina from 1753 until his death in 1765. He aimed to unite North Carolina settlers against external threats and bring North Carolina within the British cultural mainstream. In practice, his policies antagonized backcountry settlers and failed to resolve North Carolina's internal conflicts.

A scion of Northern Ireland's affluent Protestant Ascendancy, Dobbs began his career as a British army officer in Scotland. He subsequently returned to Ireland to manage the family estate near Carrickfergus. He was elected to the Irish Parliament in 1727 and was appointed engineer and surveyor general of Ireland in 1733. Dobbs's involvement in Irish politics led him to reflect deeply on the state of the British Empire. He advocated administrative reform and vigorous policies to promote economic development throughout the empire, particularly in North America. Dobbs believed that these policies would assist Britain in its geopolitical struggle with France. Dobbs invested heavily in private ventures to promote North American development. In the mid-1740s, he purchased 200,000 acres of frontier land in North Carolina and sponsored the immigration of 500 Irish Protestants to settle it. In 1749, he was a founding member of the Ohio Company. He also helped fund two unsuccessful expeditions to find the Northwest Passage.

Dobbs's idealistic interest in imperial reform, combined with his financial investments in North Carolina, inspired to him to seek the colonial governorship through his connections at court. Arriving in North Carolina in October 1753, Dobbs initially sought to root out corruption and resolve regional disputes within the colony. He encouraged North Carolinians to present a united front in the face of the French and Native American threat posed by the Seven Years' War. He also sought to strengthen the Anglican Church within the colony. Wealthy, well-established coastal residents recognized the potential benefits of the stabilization Dobbs promoted, but Dobbs's policies antagonized some frontier settlers. His opposition to the printing of paper money caused considerable hardship on North Carolina's cash-poor frontier. On his vast land claims in Anson County (later Mecklenburg County), Dobbs skirmished with settlers who exploited a North Carolina–South Carolina border dispute to avoid paying for their plots and intimidated court officials who attempted to serve them papers.

Ultimately, Dobbs's authority floundered among both frontiersmen and North Carolina's nascent gentry. As early as 1760, Dobbs complained that North Carolina assemblymen equated themselves with members of the British House of Commons and evinced a similar reluctance to submit to the authority of the Crown. The colony's leadership had grown more united under Dobbs's tenure, but in opposition to him rather than in cooperation with him. Meanwhile, frontier settlers exploited social disorder and weak government for their own ends, anticipating the Regulator Movement. In 1764, Dobbs requested permission to return home for health reasons. He ceded authority to the newly appointed lieutenant governor, William Tryon, and died while packing for the trip home.

—*Darcy R. Fryer*

Further Reading

Clarke, Desmond. *Arthur Dobbs, Esquire, 1689–1765: Surveyor-General of Ireland, Prospector and Governor of North America*. London: Bodley Head, 1958.

Ekirch, A. Roger. *"Poor Carolina": Politics and Society in Colonial North Carolina, 1729–1776*. Chapel Hill: University of North Carolina Press, 1981.

Kars, Marjoleine. *Breaking Loose Together: The Regulator Rebellion in Pre-Revolutionary North Carolina*. Chapel Hill: University of North Carolina Press, 2002.

Husband, Herman (1724–1795)

Herman Husband, an ex-Quaker millennialist and North Carolina planter, was one of the intellectual and political leaders of the Regulator Movement. An eccentric visionary, Husband exemplified the crucial role that radical Protestantism played in the Regulators' critique of North Carolina politics.

Born into an Anglican planter family in Maryland, Husband experienced a religious conversion after hearing George Whitefield preach in 1739. He left the

Receipt given to Thomas Sitgreaves for assisting in Herman Husbands' 1771 incarceration. (Courtesy of the North Carolina Office of Archives and History, Raleigh, North Carolina)

Anglican Church to join the Presbyterians, then the New Side (evangelical) Presbyterians, and finally, in about 1743, the Quakers. As a young man, Husband managed his family's properties in Maryland, operated a pig ironworks, and held leadership roles in the local Quaker meeting. He married three times and fathered eight children. Husband first visited North Carolina in 1751, and from the mid-1750s on he purchased 10,000 acres of land in Orange and Rowan Counties, where he installed a grist mill and ironworks. In 1762, he settled in Sandy Creek, North Carolina. Soon afterwards, Husband left the Quakers as a result of a dispute about individuals' freedom to buck the rulings of higher meetings.

Husband aimed to redeem society by means of religiously inspired political activism. In 1766, Husband and his neighbors formed the Sandy Creek Association to promote public officials' accountability to voters. It quickly collapsed. When the Regulator Movement emerged a few years later, Husband assumed the role of intellectual advisor and scribe, drafting resolutions and petitions and incorporating ideas from his extensive reading. In 1770, he wrote two political pamphlets, *An Impartial Relation of the First Rise and Cause of the Recent Differences in Publick Affairs* and *A Continuation of the Impartial Relation*. These pamphlets fused radical Protestant theology with Whig country thought to argue that Christians were obliged to defend their civil rights and ensure that the government under which they lived was virtuous and just. Meanwhile, Regulators and other backcountry voters elected Husband to the North Carolina Assembly in 1769. The North Carolina government, convinced that Husband was the ringleader of the rebellion, jailed him on libel charges in December 1770; he was released in February. Husband was present at the confrontation that preceded the Battle of Alamance but, as a pacifist, slipped away before the shooting started. Soon afterwards, Husband fled the province with a price on his head. His property was confiscated by the government.

Husband settled in Bedford County, Pennsylvania, where he became a large landowner, assemblyman (1777–1778), and supporter of American independence. In 1779, Husband experienced a vision of a New Jerusalem rising west of the Allegheny Mountains; he also experienced a revelation that constitutional reform was necessary to pave the way for the millennium. In his later years, Husband wrote extensively on millenarianism. He criticized the U.S. Constitution as too moderate and welcomed the more radical French Revolution. When western Pennsylvania farmers protested the federal excise tax on whiskey in 1794, Husband once again assumed the role of spokesman and scribe for the protesters. He was charged with treason and spent the winter of 1794–1795 in jail, but a grand jury failed to indict him. Husband died soon after his release from prison, a dissident and freethinker to the end.

—Darcy R. Fryer

Further Reading

Jones, Mark H. "Herman Husband: Millennarian, Carolina Regulator, and Whiskey Rebel." PhD diss., Northern Illinois University, 1983.

Kars, Marjoleine. *Breaking Loose Together: The Regulator Rebellion in Pre-Revolutionary North Carolina*. Chapel Hill: University of North Carolina Press, 2002.

Tryon, William (1729–1788)

William Tryon, who served as royal governor of North Carolina from 1765 to 1771, was the Regulators' principal adversary. His decision to build a sumptuous governor's palace in New Bern became a popular symbol of oppressive and expensive government. Although Tryon sympathized with the Regulators' complaints about fiscal corruption in North Carolina, he quashed their resistance harshly at the Battle of Alamance.

An army officer and son of the English landed gentry, Tryon became a career colonial administrator. In 1764, he secured the lieutenant governorship of North Carolina through the patronage of Lord Hillsborough. He succeeded to the governorship after Arthur Dobbs's death in March 1765. As governor, Tryon sought to integrate the colony more fully into the British imperial mainstream. He secured the full establishment of the Anglican Church in North Carolina, promoted Anglican education and missionary activities, and established a postal service linking North Carolina to other colonies. Tryon also persuaded the North Carolina

Assembly to appropriate £15,000 in provincial currency for the construction of an elegant capitol and governor's palace in New Bern. Tryon believed this project would dignify the colony's royal government and signal the maturation of the British settlement in North Carolina. An effective though somewhat authoritarian administrator, Tryon was initially popular with the residents of North Carolina.

In the early years of his governorship, Tryon was sympathetic to many of the backcountry settlers' grievances. He attempted to increase the supply of paper money, ameliorate abuses in tax collection, and prevent the embezzlement of public funds. Tryon's efforts met with limited success and, in some cases, merely fanned public anxiety about political corruption. When the Regulator Movement erupted in physical violence, Tryon took a harsh line. In the spring of 1768, he called up the militia of eight backcountry counties to suppress the rebellion. Tryon himself led the militia in clashes with Regulators at Hillsborough in September 1768 and at the Battle of Alamance in May 1771. Just before and after the Battle of Alamance, Tryon summarily executed two Regulators. Six others were hanged after being convicted of treason. Tryon ultimately pardoned some 6,400 former Regulators who agreed to swear allegiance to North Carolina. Tryon's response to the Regulator Movement was authoritarian but scarcely vindictive; his paramount goal was to uphold the authority of the royal government of North Carolina.

Tryon transferred to the governorship of New York soon after the Battle of Alamance. There, as in North Carolina, he vigorously promoted social stratification and the Anglican Church, both of which he envisioned as anchors of political stability. In the opening salvos of the American Revolution, Tryon took a moderate stance, just as he had done in the Stamp Act Crisis in North Carolina. He favored the repeal of parliamentary taxes on the American colonies, arguing that only massive military force could subdue the protests. Not until 1775 did Tryon reluctantly accede to British efforts to impose parliamentary authority on the colonies. During the Revolutionary War, he organized Loyalist troops and led several raids on Connecticut towns and arsenals. He retired to England in 1780.

—*Darcy R. Fryer*

Further Reading

Nelson, Paul David. *William Tryon and the Course of Empire: A Life in British Imperial Service*. Chapel Hill: University of North Carolina Press, 1990.

Tryon, William. *The Correspondence of William Tryon and Other Selected Papers*. Edited by William S. Powell. 2 vols. Raleigh, NC: Division of Archives and History, Department of Cultural Resources, 1980–1981.

Pine Tree Riot (1772)

The Pine Tree Riot was one of the first acts of rebellion against the authority of Great Britain that would lead to the American War of Independence three years later. Essentially, it had its origins in the use of pine trees in North America to make masts for ships for the (British) Royal Navy, and was an event that in some ways resembled the Boston Tea Party, which took place 20 months later.

The War of Jenkins' Ear (1739–1748) and the Seven Years' War (1756–1763) had been won by the British, in large part because of their control of the seas through a massive navy. However, the making of so many warships, as well as merchant vessels, resulted in much demand for white pine trees, which could be used to make masts. In the British Isles, the sheer number of ships being built and repaired had meant that there were few large white pines left—this species was regarded as the best for a single-stick mast. With Britain anxious to keep its naval (and also its trading) advantage, laws had been passed in North America whereby white pine trees were ordered to be preserved until the tree was fully grown.

The New Hampshire General Court passed an act in 1722 making it illegal to cut down any white pine that was more than 12 inches in diameter. Cutting down any of them would result in a fine of £5. Any timber found in violation of this was marked with white arrows painted on the wood, signifying that these trees were property of the British Crown.

By this time, in the British North America, there had been growing resentment of the British, and some people started to cut down the trees and use them for floorboards. This led to a fashion among anti-British activists to display proudly the width of the boards used in their property, often as much as 12 inches wide. These laws were not heavily enforced until 1766, when John Wentworth was appointed as governor of New Hampshire. Wentworth had originally been born in New Hampshire and educated at Harvard, his uncle, Benning Wentworth, having been his predecessor as governor (and the person who had introduced the 1722 Act). He was generally thought to be sympathetic to some of the grievances of the colonists, but on the issue of the white pine trees, he held firm.

Finally the British decided to crack down on this use of timber, and in the winter of 1771–1772, John Sherburn, the deputy surveyor in New Hampshire, ordered a search of sawmills. At six sawmills in Goffstown and Weare, Sherburn's men found logs from large white pine trees that had been marked with the broad arrow. Altogether, there were many logs at the sawmills owned by Richards, Asa Pettee and Dow, and 270 logs, which were between 17 and 36 inches in diameter, were at Clement's Mill and at the Old Mill Village in South Weare. In the *New Hampshire Gazette* of February 7, 1772, some of the offenders were named, and the government asked them to show cause why their logs should not be seized by the Crown.

Criminal proceedings began against the owners of the mills, and they were arraigned at the Court of Vice Admiralty at Portsmouth. The mill owners engaged a lawyer called Samuel Blodgett from Goffstown, and he started interceding with Governor John Wentworth in the hope that he would spare the loggers. However, Wentworth appointed Blodgett as the Surveyor of the King's Woods largely so that he would appreciate the nature of the problem. Blodgett urged the sawmill owners to pay for the logs they had cut down, and 3 men from Bedford and 14 from Goffstown did so. However, money was owed from Weare.

To enforce the law, Benjamin Whiting, the county sheriff, and his deputy John Quigly, arrived in South Weare on April 13, 1772, with a warrant for the arrest of Ebenezer Mudgett, the leader of the sawmill owners in Weare. They arrested Mudgett, but released him on his own undertaking, agreeing to him bringing suitable bail in the morning. The two officials then decided to spend the night at the appropriately named Pine Tree Tavern of Aaron Quimby.

It was not long before news about Mudgett spread around Weare, and many supporters flocked to his house. There, some of them offered to provide the bail for him, but others decided that they could attack the British officials and chase them out of town. At dawn the following day, they struck.

Very early in the morning of April 14, 1772, Mudgett went over to the Pine Tree Tavern and woke up Whiting, telling him that he had brought the bail. Whiting was angry that Mudgett had come so early and started to dress. At that point, some 20 men—all with their faces covered in soot—burst into Whiting's room and attacked the two government officials with canes they had made from nearby trees. They seized the guns of the officials and hit Whiting once for every tree that the sawmill owners were to be fined over, and they left him battered and bruised. The attackers then dragged the two men down to their horses. They cut off the manes and tails—and also the ears—of the horses that Whiting and Quigly had used and forced both men to mount their horses. A jeering mob hissed as the men left town.

Whiting then sought help from Colonel Moore in Bedford, and also Edward Goldstone Lutwyche of Merrimack. They assembled a posse, and armed, they rode back to Weare, where they found that the local population had fled. Eventually hunting around, they found one of the culprits involved in the attack on

Whiting, and the others were all named and ordered to post bail and appear in court in due course.

In total, eight men were charged with rioting and disturbing the peace, as well as "making an assault upon the body of Benjamin Whiting," and Timothy Worthley, Jonathan Worthley, Caleb Atwood, William Dustin, Abraham Johnson, Jotham Tuttle, William Quimby (brother of the tavern owner Abraham Quimby) and Ebenezer Mudgett were arraigned before four judges, Chief Justice Honorable Theodore Atkinson, Meshech Weare, Leverett Hubbard, and William Parker. The hearing finally took place in September 1772 at the Superior Court in Amherst, and there the defendants pleaded guilty and were fined 20 shillings each, plus the cost of the hearing. It is believed that this incident might have been the inspiration for the use of disguises at the Boston Tea Party in December 1773.

Of the men charged, Timothy Worthley, his brother Jonathan, and William Dustin all fought the British in the American War of Independence, Timothy Worthley and Dustin both holding commissions in the Continental Army. The lawyer Samuel Blodgett also served in the Continental Army for the first year of the war, returning to Goffstown where he worked on the construction of the Amoskeag Canal. Benjamin Whiting supported the British in the war, had his land confiscated, and probably died in Canada. Of the justices, Meshech Weare was one of the people who framed the New Hampshire Constitution, which was adopted in 1776.

—Justin Corfield

See also all entries under Stamp Act Protests (1765); Boston Massacre (1770); Boston Tea Party (1773).

Further Reading

Brown, Janice (descendant of Jotham Tuttle). "Weare, NH 1772: Rebellion before the Revolution." http://cowhampshire.blogharbor.com/blog/_archives/2006/3/20/1831687.html (accessed November 11, 2008).

Daniell, Jere R. *Experiment in Republicanism: New Hampshire Politics and the American Revolution 1741–1794*. Cambridge, MA: Harvard University Press, 1970.

Pine Tree Riot, April 14, 1772. South Weare, NH: Weare Junior Historical Society, 1972.

Wood, James Playsted. *Colonial New Hampshire*. New York: T. Nelson, 1973.

Royal Authority

The Pine Tree Riot of 1772 was a test of royal authority in New Hampshire whereby local people in a relatively isolated settlement—in this case, the village of Weare—rejected the authority of the Crown. Although the riot produced only a short-lived victory, the evident support of the local judiciary in fining the culprits such small amounts, showed that there were many who might challenge royal authority, undoubtedly providing inspiration for the more famous Boston Tea Party in the following year.

In Great Britain, King George III was the unquestioned ruler of the country—although the elderly and portly Jacobite claimant Charles Edward Stuart ("Bonnie Prince Charlie") maintained a court in Rome—but the British constitution was unwritten, and it gradually changed and adapted to new circumstances. Disputes and other matters that arose were decided by precedent and usage. The king ruled through the houses of Parliament, and laws were passed by the House of Commons and the House of Lords, with the king giving royal assent. As such, the king operated to uphold the law of the country, and the dispute over whether the Crown had any right to arbitrary powers had been resolved by the English Civil War of the 1640s, which had resulted in the execution of King Charles I. The accession of King George III's great-grandfather as George I showed the acceptance of the country for a constitutional monarch who would rule—as he did—through ministers, with Robert Walpole being acknowledged as the first prime minister in the modern sense of the word (although Walpole himself never assumed that title).

However, in the colonies, the British government exercised its authority through governors appointed by the prime minister, in consultation with the king, but who acted in the name of the king. These were often British officials and friends or courtiers of the king, and exclusively drawn from the British ruling class. However, many had close connections with the Americas. Indeed, John Wentworth, the governor of New Hampshire during the Pine Tree Riot, was born in New Hampshire, as had his uncle and predecessor Benning Wentworth. Wentworth was a popular governor and did much to reduce possible tension between the government and the people in New Hampshire, but others were not so accommodating. Thomas Hutchinson, the governor of Massachusetts Bay from 1769 until 1774, had been born in Boston, and was thoroughly immersed in Massachusetts politics. However, he wanted the British to enforce more control over his colony, helping lead to the confrontation with the Boston Tea Party. His successor, Thomas Gage, was born in England, although he had served extensively in North America.

—*Justin Corfield*

Further Reading

Harris, R. W. *Political Ideas 1760–1792*. London: Victor Gollancz, 1963.

Namier, Sir Lewis. *England in the Age of the American Revolution*. London: Macmillan, 1961.

Shipbuilding

When William of Normandy (later William the Conqueror) prepared his invasion fleet for England in 1066, it is known that tens of thousands of trees were cut down for him to build his invasion fleet, many of the boats being burned after his landing. Subsequent to that, many trees throughout England were cut down for building ships during the Hundred Years' War, and in the reigns of Henry VIII and Elizabeth I. The continual building of ships in Britain—both for the Royal Navy and the merchant navy—resulted in the loss of so many large trees in the British Isles that there were not enough long straight logs to make masts for ships. The strength of the mast became increasingly important with the improvement in naval artillery, with cannonballs, linked with chains, being fired at an enemy's rigging and masts.

During the 17th century, the British had mainly used fir trees for the masts, with each mast being cut from a single tree. However, by the early 18th century, there were not enough large fir trees for main masts, and because of the weight of sails, it soon became necessary to make a mast out of a number of pieces of timber, often causing masts to break under strain. As Britain, France, and Spain quickly used up all suitable trees, mast ships brought wood from the Baltic, satisfying the demand for a while. However the British were keen on their own supply of trees for masts. With the increasing trans-Atlantic trade, and the availability of strong pine trees from New England, it was not long before the establishment of a number of shipbuilding facilities in North America, most notably at Newburyport in New Hampshire. This led to timber being sourced in New Hampshire and then floated down the Amoskeag River to Newburyport, where a shipbuilding industry flourished as it also did in Massachusetts and Maine.

The industry involved not only large numbers of carpenters, but also sail makers, rope makers, and people to provision the ships. As much of the food on board ships was kept in barrels and casks, coopers were always needed. The shipbuilding industry resulted in an insatiable demand for wood, and naval architects kept hundreds of carpenters busy sizing and sorting wood, sawing it into planks, and then nailing these into place. Although the workforce could move to a new site, it was the availability of nearby forests and woodland with large numbers of sizeable trees that was most essential for any shipbuilding industry. This indeed explains the location of so many shipbuilding settlements including in Australia, which was able to source Norfolk Island pine trees from Norfolk Island, in the Pacific. Certainly the overall design of ships and the nature of making them changed little from the late 16th to the early 19th centuries, with the major changes being the ships becoming larger, and having to be fashioned out of smaller and smaller planks of wood.

—*Justin Corfield*

Further Reading

Morrison, John S. *Aspects of the History of Wooden Shipbuilding*. London: National Maritime Museum, 1970.

Pollock, David. *The Shipbuilding Industry: Its History, Practice, Science and Finance*. London: Methuen & Co., 1905.

Boston Tea Party (1773)

Few incidents in American history are as well known as the Boston Tea Party. It brings to mind images of colonists dressed as Indians, carrying tomahawks and calling war whoops while traipsing though the cold December air to Griffin's Wharf. However, there is a reason why the Boston Tea Party is a staple in every American history textbook. It marks the turning point between the American colonists and the British government. It helped to deepen the divide among the patriots and the loyalists. And it brought the colonies one step closer to independence.

To understand how the Boston Tea Party came about, one must look back to the Seven Years' War between the British and the French over the territory of Quebec. For as long as the British had been settled in the "New World" of what is now New England, they had to worry about French forces to their north and west in what is now Quebec, Canada. From 1754 until 1763, the British and French fought over the territory, with Britain finally declaring victory and driving the French out once and for all. Despite a victory and a great deal of new territory gained following the Seven Years' War, Great Britain found itself mired in debt. Plus, they needed to maintain 10,000 soldiers in the colonies, in case the French tried to take Quebec back by force.

In an effort toward fiscal improvement, Parliament looked for new ways to tax its colonies. During the Seven Years' War, British officials saw closely just how prosperous many American colonists were. There were tidy farms, and neat villages with bustling shops and tradesmen. Compared to the intolerable living conditions back in Great Britain, the American colonists were doing remarkably well for themselves. British authorities also saw how many colonists ignored laws concerning trade and taxes. Many merchants openly flaunted the laws, not paying taxes or duties on goods. Because there was a high turnover rate of British officials in the colonies, it was hard to maintain an effective policy, making it easy for colonists to do as they pleased.

To this end, the British Parliament reasoned that since so much bloodshed and money had been spent securing the American continent from the French, the colonists should pay their fair share. In comparison to the average British citizen, who paid 26 shillings a year in taxes, colonists paid an average of one shilling per year in taxes. Plus, living conditions in Great Britain were squalid with little hope of improvement, while in the American colonies, there was always the hope

Boston Tea Party (1773)

Bostonians, dressed as Mohawk Indians, throwing East India Company tea into the harbor in December 1773. (National Archives and Records Administration)

to own your own land and work your own farm. So it seemed completely reasonable to Great Britain that the American colonists pay their share in taxes. After all, they the colonists were doing remarkably well, carving prosperous farms out of the vast wilderness. However, the colonists did not agree. With the French removed from Quebec, the American colonists and British no longer had a common enemy to unite them. The colonists did not feel the need for British soldiers to be stationed in the colonies to protect them. They could take care of themselves, they declared.

In an effort to raise much-needed revenue, Parliament passed the Townshend Act in 1767. The act placed new taxes on goods imported from Great Britain, such as tea, paper, lead, and glass. The Townshend Act also used taxes to pay the salaries of certain royal officials in the colonies, removing a considerable amount of leverage from the colonial assemblies, which could withhold official's salaries if they did not like their actions. The Townshend Act was almost immediately repealed, as colonists boycotted English goods. However, the tax on tea remained.

Tea had been imported into the American colonies with regularity, starting in the 1720s. By the passage of the Townshend Act, colonists consumed roughly 1.2 million pounds of tea a year. Tea was not just a beverage; it was an important thread of colonial society. While it was most associated with the women of the upper class, tea parties were social occasions for both men and women, when people took a break from the handwork of everyday life to visit with neighbors and friends. Families displayed their precious china or silver tea services, which was a distinct sign of wealth and prestige. The remaining tax on tea, left over from the Townshend Act, made English tea expensive, and soon colonists began drinking smuggled tea from the Netherlands instead. Because there were not enough customs officials to effectively patrol the American coastline, it was easy to smuggle in tea (and other goods) in the many inlets that were hidden along the rocky shores. Although the boycott stemming from the Townshend Act was strong in 1770, by 1773 it had begun to wane. Many people resumed drinking tea, some in private, others in the open. But the boycott had its intended result. Sales of British tea, especially from the East India Company, dropped drastically.

By May 1773, the market for colonial tea had collapsed, and the East India Company was on the verge of collapse. There was a great deal of vested interest in the East India Company. Many members of the British Parliament held shares in the shipping company. More importantly, the East India Company was the sole British agent in India. Parliament could not afford for the company to go bankrupt. So they passed the Tea Act, which placed special duties on tea. In Boston, East India tea could be sold only by seven designated tea agents, called consignees. It was no coincidence that all seven consignees were Loyalists. Many of them were related to the royal governor of Massachusetts, Thomas Hutchinson. The Tea Act allowed the East India Company to skirt any middlemen and undersell their competitors, even cheaper smuggled Dutch tea. Parliament reasoned that American colonists would gladly pay a small three-pence tax, to buy such cheap tea. It would be a win-win situation for everyone: the colonists would have their tea, the East India Company would stay in business, and the Crown would have some money in the treasury. However, many American colonists did carry this same view.

Many patriots who had helped repeal the Townshend Act, the Stamp Act, and other unwanted taxes saw the new tax on tea as Parliament's way of exercising their right to tax the colonists without representation. Others saw the Tea Act as the first step toward domination of the marketplace by the East India Company. All in all, the Tea Act was a violation of colonists' freedom and liberty. It was okay to pay the taxes levied by local assemblies, but Parliament, an alien body far removed from the colonists, had no right to tell them what to do. The Sons of Liberty, who had remained quiet for the past several years, sprang into action to protest the Tea Act. This time, they were joined by the normally conservative merchant class, whose profits were endangered by the act.

American-British relations were not helped when secret letters from the royal governor of Massachusetts, Thomas Hutchinson to British undersecretary Thomas Whatley, were published in the colonies. In his letters, Hutchinson called for sterner measures of discipline for the colonists. He specifically called for "an abridgement of what are called English liberties." He declared that if "nothing more than declatory acts or resolves, it is all over with us. The friends ... of anarchy will be afraid of nothing be it ever so extravagant." In other words, if all the British government did was repeal acts that were unpopular with colonists and never punished them for offensive acts, they were all in for a lot of trouble in the future. These letters found their way into the hands of American diplomat Benjamin Franklin, who sent them to Boston to be read only by a few "Men of Worth." Franklin was an idealist when it came to international diplomacy. He truly felt that a few reasonable men could solve all the problems of the nation by common sense and logic. He thought if his "Men of Worth" read the letters, they would blame Hutchinson for the unpopular policies and taxes rather than the British government. Franklin could not have been more wrong. Instead of being read by a discretionary few, the letters were reprinted into a pamphlet, and by June 1773, they had circulated around the entire colony. Instead of reason and logic, heated anger and simmering suspicions dictated the colonist's reactions. For many patriots in Massachusetts, their earlier suspicions were confirmed. The British government was looking for ways to suppress their freedoms and their personal liberties. They would do this at first by taxation without representation.

The Tea Act gave radical patriots the perfect excuse to protest the government. The act was boycotted not only in Boston, but also in cities such as New York, Philadelphia, and Charleston, where tea agents either resigned or shipments were refused by local merchants. In Charleston, the tea was unloaded and destroyed on the docks. In New York, the shipment did not arrive on time or at all. In Philadelphia, the captain of the ship was persuaded to turn around and head back to England. However, in Boston, Governor Hutchinson was determined that the tea would be unloaded and taxed accordingly. On November 20, 1773, the ship *Dartmouth* arrived in Boston Harbor with a load of Darjeeling tea. The Sons of Liberty made every effort to make sure the tea was not unloaded onto the docks. Mobs roamed the streets of Boston, intimidating local Crown authorities and tea consignees. They tried unsuccessfully, through coercion and intimidation, to make the consignees refuse the tea. But the agents ignored the patriots, clinging steadfastly to their loyalty to the Crown. The Boston Sons of Liberty was led by patriot Samuel Adams, whom the British thought of as a "cunning professional politician" who exploited mob rule for his own benefit.

On November 29, 1773, thousands of people gathered at Faneuil Hall, but soon the numbers grew even more, and the meeting was moved to the Old South Meeting House. Old South was the largest building in Boston at the time and was a regular meeting place for patriots. The crowd that gathered on that night was a mix of men who could vote (21-year-old landowners) and those who could not. It was called a "body of the people," and no one was excluded from the meeting.

Samuel Adams organized the meeting. He declared that "Whether it is the firm resolution of this body that tea shall not only be sent back but that no duty shall be paid thereon?" Twenty-five men were assigned to guard the *Dartmouth*, making sure that the tea would not be unloaded and taxed, while the consignees considered the situation.

The following day, at 9:00 in the morning, groups of Bostonians converged once more at Old South. Portrait painter John Singleton Copley was assigned as moderator of the meeting between the consignees and the patriots. Copley, who was married to a daughter of one of the tea consignees, tried to help the two groups reach an agreement about what should be done with the tea on the three ships idling in Boston Harbor. The consignees offered to store the tea on land, until they received other instructions from London. However, if the tea was removed from the ships, it would be taxed, even if was to be returned, which was unacceptable to the patriots. The assembly at Old South agreed that the tea should never be landed. Future first lady Abigail Adams attended the meeting. She wrote to her friend Mercy Otis Warren that "The tea that bainfull weed is arrived. Great and effectual opposition has been made to landing of it . . . the proceedings of our citizens have been united, spirited and firm. The flame is kindled and like lightening it catches from soul to soul." The people were united in their resolve to have their voices heard, and they did not want that tea to be unloaded.

In the meantime, two more East India ships arrived in Boston, bearing more tea. The *Eleanor* arrived on December 2 and was followed by the *Beaver* on December 7. On December 8, Governor Hutchinson ordered Admiral Mountagu not to let any ships leave Boston Harbor without a special pass. Because the law stated that the tea tax was to be collected within 20 days of a ship's arrival, the deadline for the *Dartmouth* was midnight on December 16. If the tax on the tea had not been paid by then, the ship could be confiscated by royal authorities. During the interim, the Sons of Liberty kept the public fervor high with public meetings, some as large as 5,000 people filling the streets around the Old South Meeting House, denouncing the Tea Act. This is especially impressive given that only about 15,000 people lived in Boston at the time. A third of the city's population turned out to protest the Tea Act. The Sons of Liberty petitioned the captains of the ships to return their cargo to England. While local tea agents flatly refused to return the tea, the owner of the *Dartmouth*, a Quaker from Nantucket by the name of Francis Rotch, agreed to sail back to England with the tea. However, he needed special permission by the governor, or he risked having his ship fired on by the armed fort that overlooked Boston Harbor, something he could not afford.

On the morning of December 16, the day of the deadline for the tea tax to be paid on the *Dartmouth*, Old South once more filled with thousands of people for the last meeting on how to deal with the unwanted tea. The patriot leaders asked

Francis Rotch to make a personal request of the governor to allow him to sail his ship back to England safely. This would be the last legal means of preventing the tea from being unloaded. Rotch left the meeting house and traveled to nearby Milton, where Governor Hutchinson was staying. Rotch was gone a good part of the day. Yet the crowd waited, lighting lanterns in the meeting hall as the day turned to night. When he returned to Old South later that evening, he announced that the governor had refused his request to sail safely out of Boston Harbor.

At the news that Governor Hutchinson refused to budge on his position, Samuel Adams gave a prearranged signal at Old South, declaring "This meeting can do nothing more to save the country." With that, 50 to 60 men of all walks of life abruptly left the meeting house. Among the group of men, dressed as Mohawk Indians with blankets and headdress, were masons, carpenters, barbers, a silversmith, farmers, doctors, and a teacher. Contrary to popular belief, not everyone was dressed as an Indian. Some simply smeared soot on their faces. Along with Adams, other Sons of Liberty joining the group included Paul Revere and John Hancock, whom the English regarded as a rich and vain businessman. They headed to Griffin's Wharf, where the three ships were anchored. Upon boarding the ships, the men used tomahawks (or hatchets if they were not dressed as Indians) to force open 342 chests of tea (estimated to be around 18.5 million cups of tea) worth £18,000 (about $1 million today) and threw it into the harbor waters below. A crowd on the docks cheered their actions, calling for more "saltwater tea." "Boston's a tea pot tonight!" it was declared. The next morning, men rowed out to the harbor to beat what tea remained with oars and paddles, to make sure none of it could be retrieved. The waters of Boston Harbor turned brown and remained so for several days. Patriot John Adams declared that "so bold, so daring, so firm, intrepid and inflexible, that I can't but consider it as an epoch in history." Only one man was arrested for the Boston Tea Party, Francis Akeley (Ekley). The Boston Tea Party, as it became known, was quickly replicated throughout the other colonies. In Annapolis, New York, and New Jersey, there were incidents of destruction of East India tea.

At first, the Boston Tea Party was hardly noticed across the pond in Great Britain. When the news arrived in Parliament on January 20, 1764, the members of the house were more concerned with dealing with Benjamin Franklin, who by that time had confessed to sending the Hutchinson letters to Massachusetts, rather than dealing with the governor himself. In an effort to save face, Franklin even offered to pay for the tea out of his own pocket. However, it was too late, both for his career as a diplomat and for the easygoing relationship between the colonies and the mother country. The Boston Tea Party was soon magnified into an unforgivable insult to Britain herself. Parliament and the king, which had more or less neglected the American colonies up until the Seven Years' War, saw the Boston Tea Party as a deliberate destruction of private property. They viewed the American colonists' actions as blatant disregard for the law or royal authority, and they would no longer treat the colonists with such leniency. When it was suggested in Parliament that the tea act be repealed, Prime Minister Lord North pointed out that the "Americans have tarred and feathered your subjects [local government agents], plundered your merchants, burnt your ships, denied all obedience to your laws and authority; yet so clement and so long forbearing has our conduct been that it is incumbent on us now to take a different course." Parliament intended to make an example out of Boston. The people could not act like a petulant child and expect to get away with bad behavior any longer.

In retaliation for the Boston Tea Party, the British Parliament passed the first of four laws that would be known as the Coercive (or Intolerable) Acts. The first act, known as the Boston Port Act, closed the port of Boston until the East India Company and the custom service had been paid in full for the tea that had been thrown overboard during the Boston Tea Party. The total sum was estimated to be around £10,000 in silver. The only exceptions were food and firewood. Then the Massachusetts Government Act was passed, which altered the province's charter. It appointed a new council to replace the elected one, increasing the power of the royal governor. Special town meetings were forbidden, discouraging political opponents from speaking up publicly, like the meetings that had been held at the Old South Meeting House. The third act was the Justice Act, allowing the royal governor of a colony to move trials to other colonies or even to England, if he thought that the jury would not be impartial. And the last act, the Quartering Act, allowed military commanders to use private houses and empty buildings to quarter soldiers, at the public's expense. These acts did not just impact Boston, but also all of Massachusetts and the rest of the 13 colonies. They helped unite the colonists against what they viewed as the tyranny of British rule. The rest of the colonies rallied to Boston's aid during the Coercive Acts. The people of Charleston sent money and rice to Boston citizens, while Connecticut and Long Island sent sheep and New York promised 10 years of food. The Sons of Liberty, which had chapters throughout the 13 colonies, rallied more public support in defiance of the British authority. On April 1, 1774, four new regiments arrived in Massachusetts, and Thomas Hutchinson was replaced by General Thomas Gage. A scant 10 months after the Boston Tea Party, the First Continental Congress met in Philadelphia, to decide how best to deal with unjust taxation and the unfair treatment they felt the colonies were receiving from Great Britain.

What started as a simple act of dumping tea overboard had united the colonies under one cause, igniting their passions for liberty and freedom from oppression. The colonists saw the coercive acts as "unjust, illegal and oppressive, and that we and every American are sharers in the insults offered to the town of Boston."

All the colonists of the era had grown up with relatively little supervision from the mother country. They were used to freedoms not found anywhere in Europe. At the end of the Seven Years' War, when Britain finally began to pay closer attention to its American holdings, the colonists chafed under the new restraints. Rather than except their lowered station in life, they rose up and challenged the mother country, claiming their right to representation in Parliament, their right to voice opposition to the Crown, and their right to live as free men. While the official start of the American Revolution was still more than two years away, the Boston Tea Party was a turning point in the resistance of the colonists to British rule. It helped to further polarize sides between Loyalists and patriots, deepening the divide and helping to escalate the oncoming revolution.

The Boston Tea Party has become a symbol of the American spirit. Few students leave school without reading an account of the Tea Party, and for good reason. It showcases a moment in history when the American people took a stand for what they believed in. It helped to stir a revolutionary spirit, not only in Boston, but far beyond to the rest of the 13 colonies. The Boston Tea Party was crucial in setting the stage for the fight for American independence. It is a symbol that still endures today.

—*Lorri Brown*

See also all entries under Stamp Act Protests (1765); Boston Massacre (1770); Pine Tree Riot (1772).

Further Reading

Commanger, Henry Steele, and Richard B. Morris. *The Spirit of Seventy-six: The Story of the American Revolution as Told by Its Participants*. New York: Castle Books, 2002.

Lancaster, Bruce. *The American Revolution*. New York: Mariner Books, 2001.

Taylor, Alan. *American Colonies*. New York: Penguin Books, 2001.

Wood, Gordon S. *The Americanization of Benjamin Franklin*. New York: Penguin, 2004.

Coercive Acts (1774)

Following the rebellion of the Boston Tea Party, the British government decided it was time to put American colonists back in their place. Beginning in March 1774, the British government, under Prime Minister Lord North, passed the first of four laws that would be known as the Coercive (or Intolerable) Acts. These acts impacted not just Boston, but all of Massachusetts and the rest of the 13 colonies.

The first act, known as the Boston Port Act, closed the port of Boston until the East India Company and the custom service had been paid in full for tea that had been thrown overboard during the Boston Tea Party. While firewood and food could still be delivered to the Boston port, the official port of entry was moved to Marblehead, and the capital of Massachusetts was moved to Salem. Later on that same spring, Parliament passed the Massachusetts Government Act, which altered the province's charter. It increased the royal governor's power by replacing the elected council with an appointed one. It also forbade special town meetings in order to discourage public speaking by political opponents.

The third act was the Justice Act. It allowed the royal governor of a colony to move trials to other colonies or even to England, if he thought that the jury would not be impartial. This act protected British officials, who were then encouraged to enforce the new, harsher laws with vigor. For example, any officials who were accused of capital crimes during the suppression of riots or during tax revenue collections could be tried across the Atlantic, in England. The fourth act, the Quartering Act, gave broad authority to military commanders and allowed soldiers to be quartered in private houses and empty buildings, at the public's expense.

The Quebec Act, although not part of the four Coercive Acts, is often grouped with them because it brought the American colonists one step closer to their bid for independence. Quebec was a newly acquired territory by the British. Parliament granted greater religious freedom to the Catholics in Quebec. This alarmed American Protestants, who linked Catholicism with despotism. If Catholics were given favored status in Quebec, who was to say they would not get favored status in Massachusetts, New York, or Pennsylvania? The Quebec Act gave civil government and religious freedom to the people of Quebec that had been denied to the colonists. It also extended the territory of Quebec to the Ohio River, voiding the sea-to-sea boundaries of charters in Connecticut, Pennsylvania, and Virginia.

The Coercive Acts and the Quebec Act reached far beyond Massachusetts. Together, all these acts confirmed fears of many colonists that Parliament would oppress all their rights. After all, if Parliament could close a port in Boston, what was to stop them from closing a port in New York, South Carolina, or Virginia?

If they could change the charter of Massachusetts, what would prevent them from changing the charters of the other 12 colonies? In the quest to keep colonists in their place, the British government inadvertently stirred up revolutionary spirit and set them on the road to independence.

—*Lorri Brown*

Further Reading

Faragher, John Mack, Mari Jo Buhle, Daniel Czitrom, and Susan H. Armitage. *Out of Many: A History of the American People.* Upper Saddle River, NJ: Prentice Hall, 1995.

Norton, Mary Beth, David M. Katzman, Paul D. Scott, Howard P. Chudacoff, and Thomas G. Patterson. *A People and a Nation: A History of the United States.* Boston: Houghton Mifflin Company, 1994.

USHistory.org. "The Intolerable Acts." http://www.ushistory.org/declaration/related/intolerable.htm (accessed August 23, 2008).

First Continental Congress (1774)

Following the Boston Tea Party and the Coercive Acts, American colonists began to realize that their interests differed from those of Great Britain, both culturally and economically. By the summer of 1774, concerns and unrest grew so much among the colonists that they decided hold a meeting to figure out the best way to deal with the unjust laws and taxation imposed upon them by King George III and Parliament. Fifty-five delegates from 12 colonies (Georgia did not send anyone) convened on September 5, 1774, at Carpenter's Hall in Philadelphia, to discuss the needs and concerns of their respective colonies.

The delegates who gathered in Philadelphia were mainly merchants, lawyers, or planters. Among them were some of the future leaders of the American cause, including Boston cousins John and Samuel Adams, and Virginia planters George Washington and Thomas Jefferson. These men represented a wide spectrum of political attitudes, from conservatives such as John Jay of New York, to revolutionaries such as Patrick Henry of Virginia. Most of the delegates fell somewhere in between. They were looking for greater political independence, but not ready to make a final break with Great Britain through war.

The delegates had three main points that they needed to address during their meeting. First, they needed to define American grievances with Great Britain. Second, they had to develop a plan of resistance. Third, they needed to outline their future relationship with Great Britain. The first point was easy to define. The delegates declared that all colonists sprang from a common tradition, and that they all enjoyed the same rights guaranteed by the English constitution as well as by their individual colony charters. For the second point, the delegates decided that the best course of action was to continue an unofficial boycott of British goods and therefore silently resist the unfair taxation placed upon them. The Continental Congress set about placing sanctions against the British. There would be no importation of British goods, and no colonial exports to Britain. While this boycott against Great Britain continued, the colonists would petition King George directly, for relief.

The last point was the hardest to define. Some men, such as Patrick Henry denounced any loyalty to the British Parliament, instead claiming they only needed to show allegiance to King George. Conservatives like Joseph Galloway of Pennsylvania wanted to establish a new legislative branch, which could decide American laws together with Parliament. In the end, the delegates settled on a compromise drafted by Thomas Jefferson, entitled the Declaration of Rights and Grievances. In the document, the delegates deemed the 13 acts that the British Parliament had passed since the end of the French and Indian War void, since they violated the basic rights of the colonists.

Out of the Continental Congress several committees were formed, including one for observation and safety, which took over the role of local government throughout the 13 colonies. This committee helped organize a militia, extralegal of course, and combined to form a colony-wide congress. The committee was also responsible for suppressing Loyalist views in newspapers as well as in general society, when the need arose. These committees helped bridge the gap between old ways and new and marked the beginning of the term "state" rather than colony. American independence was already being won at local levels, without formal acknowledgement and without bloodshed, six months before the first battles of the American Revolution at Lexington and Concord.

—*Lorri Brown*

Further Reading

Faragher, John Mack, Mari Jo Buhle, Daniel Czitrom, and Susan H. Armitage. *Out of Many: A History of the American People*. Upper Saddle River, NJ: Prentice Hall, 1995.

Norton, Mary Beth, David M. Katzman, Paul D. Scott, Howard P. Chudacoff, and Thomas G. Patterson. *A People and a Nation: A History of the United States*. Boston: Houghton Mifflin Company, 1994.

USHistory.org. "Proceedings of the First Continental Congress." http://www.ushistory.org/declaration/related/congress.htm (accessed August 28, 2008).

Sons of Liberty

In 1765, the British Parliament passed the Stamp Act, which called for a special tax stamp on all printed paper, such as newspapers. Though it affected nearly every American colonist, merchants and printers were the most heavily affected. The Stamp Act ignited protests throughout the 13 colonies, as well as in Nova Scotia and the Caribbean. On August 14, 1765, an effigy of the Massachusetts stamp distributor, Andrew Oliver, was hung in a tree in Newbury Street in Boston. The effigy was burned and Oliver's house on Kilby Street was stoned and looted of any valuable contents. The British militia did not dare interfere with the rioting. The gentry class, while glad of the protests, was afraid of mob action and sought a way to keep control of resistance acts. As a way to control the rebellions brewing over the Stamp Act, these men formed an intercolonial association called the Sons of Liberty. At first it was made up of merchants, lawyers, and craftsmen. Branches spread quickly through the rest of the colonies and soon included many working-class men. By early 1766, these groups formed a common bond throughout the colonies, from New Hampshire to South Carolina.

The main goal of the Sons of Liberty was a repeal of the Stamp Act, viewing it as a violation of the people's liberties by corrupt and self-serving rulers. They published pamphlets and circulated petitions that stressed passive means of resistance, such as boycotting English goods. The Sons of Liberty helped spread their messages through local newspapers as well. Many members of the Sons of Liberty were in the printing trade, and even those printers who were not part of the group sympathized with the cause. After all, the Stamp Act affected printers more than anyone. Crowd action, such as riots and other violence, was used only a last resort. While some imposters used the Sons of Liberty for personal revenge and gain, the group policed itself to keep corruption to a minimum.

It did not take long before the Stamp Act was repealed in March 1766. The Sons of Liberty helped to organize joyful celebrations at what they perceived as a victory. Following the repeal of the Stamp Act, the Sons of Liberty chapters dissolved. However, just two years later, chapters took up arms once again, in the face of more unfair taxes passed by the British Parliament.

In 1768, the Townshend Revenue Act was passed, placing special taxes on common goods such as lead, paint, glass, paper, and tea. The Townshend Act garnered an even quicker response from colonists than the Stamp Act. The newly revived Sons of Liberty embarked on a two-year campaign against the Townshend Acts, playing a vital role in spreading rebellion throughout the colonies. In Boston, the Sons of Liberty invited hundreds of citizens to dine with them each August 14 to commemorate the first Stamp Act uprising. In Charleston, the Sons of Liberty held their meetings in public, so that all could attend and listen. This helped spread the word of resistance to ordinary folks, including the illiterate who could not read pamphlets, newspapers, or petitions. Even as they advocated passive resistance to the British Parliament through boycotts and petitions, the Sons of Liberty unwittingly helped bring the colonies one step closer to a bid for independence.

—*Lorri Brown*

Further Reading

Faragher, John Mack, Mari Jo Buhle, Daniel Czitrom, and Susan H. Armitage. *Out of Many: A History of the American People*. Upper Saddle River, NJ: Prentice Hall, 1995.

Norton, Mary Beth, David M. Katzman, Paul D. Scott, Howard P. Chudacoff, and Thomas G. Patterson. *A People and a Nation: A History of the United States*. Boston: Houghton Mifflin Company, 1994.

USHistory.org. "Sons of Liberty." http://www.ushistory.org/Declaration/related/sons.htm (accessed September 23, 2008).

Townshend Acts (1767)

During the 1760s British government officials in the American colonies came and went with regularity. This made it very difficult for Britain to form, let alone enforce, a consistent American policy. In 1766, a new prime minister replaced William Pitt, who had been very popular with colonists. Charles Townshend had been the chancellor of the exchequer and was a great believer in colonial taxation. With a high national debt and soaring unemployment, Townshend decided that it was better to please the people of Britain than to worry about colonists, thousands of miles away. While the largest landowners in Britain had forced a 25 percent tax cut for themselves, Townshend levied a series of taxes on the colonies, which would ultimately bring them one step closer to revolution and independence.

The Townshend Acts placed a new tax on goods such as tea, paper, lead, and glass. However, it was placed only on items imported from Great Britain, which directly contradicted mercantile theory. The Townshend Act also used taxes to pay the salaries of certain royal officials in the colonies. This took a great deal of power away from the colonial assemblies, which could withhold officials' salaries if they did not like their actions. The Townshend Act also created an American board of customs commissioners and vice-admiralty courts at Boston, Philadelphia, and Charleston. This angered merchants further, because rigorous enforcement of taxes, which had been loosely followed, would cut into their profits. As part of the new laws, Townshend also suspended the New York legislature for refusing to comply with the

Quartering Act of 1765, in which firewood and candles, as well as housing, should be given to British soldiers who were stationed permanently in the colonies.

The Townshend Acts revived colonial hostility that had died down following the repeal of the Stamp Act. This time, the new laws drew a much quicker and angrier response by the people. Protest and rebellion sprang up throughout the colonies. One of the most influential pieces of rebellion propaganda was written by John Dickinson, a lawyer from Pennsylvania. He posed as a humble farmer when he penned "Letters from a Farmer in Pennsylvania." His basic argument was that Parliament could regulate colonial trade, but it could not exercise that power just to raise revenue. In other words, Parliament did not have the authority to impose new taxes on the colonies just to make more money for Britain.

The Massachusetts Assembly circulated a letter to other colonial legislatures calling for unity and a joint petition of protest of the Townshend Acts. Parliament acted swiftly to dissolve the Massachusetts legislature. This gave the other colonies a reason to unite in protest. After all, if Parliament could disband the governing body of Massachusetts and New York, what was to stop them from doing so in the rest of the colonies? The Sons of Liberty helped to establish and enforce a boycott of British goods, causing trade to dry up. It was not long before the British merchants stepped in on behalf of the colonies and the Townshend Acts were repealed in 1770, except for the tax on tea. This would lead to one of the most infamous chapters of American history, the Boston Tea Party.

—*Lorri Brown*

Further Reading

Faragher, John Mack, Mari Jo Buhle, Daniel Czitrom, and Susan H. Armitage. *Out of Many: A History of the American People*. Upper Saddle River, NJ: Prentice Hall, 1995.

Norton, Mary Beth, David M. Katzman, Paul D. Scott, Howard P. Chudacoff, and Thomas G. Patterson. *A People and a Nation: A History of the United States*. Boston: Houghton Mifflin Company, 1994.

USHistory.org. "Townshend Acts." http://www.ushistory.org/Declaration/related/townshend.htm (accessed September 23, 2008).

George R. T. Hewes's Account of the Boston Tea Party (1773)

In December 1773, when the British Parliament attempted to confer a monopoly on the importation of tea into America on the East India Company, angry colonists in Boston dressed as Indians, boarded the tea ships, and threw over 300 chests of tea into the harbor. This incident became famous in American history as the Boston Tea Party. Sixty years later, in 1833, 91-year-old George R. T. Hewes, the last surviving member of the group of colonists who boarded the tea ships in 1773, gave the following account of the Boston Tea Party.

The tea destroyed was contained in three ships, laying near each other, at what was called at that time Griffin's wharf, and were surrounded by armed ships of war; the commanders of which had publicly declared, that if the rebels, as they were pleased to style the Bostonians, should not withdraw their opposition to the landing of the tea before a certain day, the 17th day of December, 1773, they should on that day force it on shore, under the cover of their cannon's mouth. On the day preceding the seventeenth, there was a meeting of the citizens of the county of Suffolk, convened at one of the churches in Boston, for the purpose of consulting on what measures might be considered expedient to prevent the landing of the tea, or secure the people from the collection of the duty. At that meeting a committee was appointed to wait on Governor Hutchinson, and request him to inform them whether he would take any measures to satisfy the people on the object of the meeting. To the first application of this committee, the governor told them he would give them a definite answer by five o'clock in the afternoon. At the hour appointed, the committee again repaired to the governor's house, and on inquiry found he had gone to his country seat at Milton, a distance of about six miles. When the committee returned and informed the meeting of the absence of the governor, there was a confused murmur among the members, and the meeting was immediately dissolved, many of them crying out, Let every man do his duty, and be true to his country; and there was a general huzza for Griffin's wharf. It was now evening, and I immediately dressed myself in the costume of an Indian, equipped with a small hatchet, which I and my associates denominated the tomahawk, with which, and a club, after having painted my face and hands with coal dust in the shop of a blacksmith, I repaired to Griffin's wharf, where the ships lay that contained the tea. When I first appeared in the street, after being thus disguised, I fell in with many who were dressed, equipped and painted as I was, and who fell in with me, and marched in order to the place of our destination. When we arrived at the wharf, there were three of our number who assumed an authority to direct our operations, to which we readily submitted. They divided us into three parties, for the purpose of boarding the three ships which contained the tea at the same time. The name of him who commanded the division to which I was assigned, was Leonard Pitt. The names of the other commanders I never knew. We were immediately ordered by the respective commanders to board all the ships at the same time, which we promptly obeyed. The commander of the division to which I belonged, as soon as we were on board the ship, appointed me boatswain, and ordered me to go to the captain and demand of him the keys to the hatches and a dozen candles. I made the demand accordingly, and the captain promptly replied, and delivered the articles; but requested me at the same time to do no damage to the ship or rigging. We then were ordered by our commander to open the hatches, and take out all the chests of tea and throw them overboard, and we immediately proceeded to execute his orders; first cutting and splitting the chests with our tomahawks, so as thoroughly to expose them to the effects of the water. In about three hours from the time we went on board, we had thus broken and thrown overboard every tea chest to be found in the ship; while those in the other ships were disposing of the tea in the same way, at the same time. We were surrounded by British armed ships, but no attempt was made to resist us. We then quietly retired to our several places of residence, without having any conversation with each other.

or taking any measures to discover who were our associates; nor do I recollect of our having had the knowledge of the name of a single individual concerned in that affair, except that of Leonard Pitt, the commander of my division, who I have mentioned. There appeared to be an understanding that each individual should volunteer his services, keep his own secret, and risk the consequences for himself. No disorder took place during that transaction, and it was observed at that time, that the stillest night ensued that Boston had enjoyed for many months.

During the time we were throwing the tea overboard, there were several attempts made by some of the citizens of Boston and its vicinity, to carry off small quantities of it for their family use. To effect that object, they would watch their opportunity to snatch up a handful from the deck, where it became plentifully scattered, and put it into their pockets. One Captain O'Conner, whom I well knew, came on board for that purpose, and when he supposed he was not noticed, filled his pockets, and also the lining of his coat. But I had detected him, and gave information to the captain of what he was doing. We were ordered to take him into custody, and just as he was stepping from the vessel, I seized him by the skirt of his coat, and in attempting to pull him back, I tore it off; but springing forward, by a rapid effort, he made his escape. He had however to run a gauntlet through the crowd upon the wharf; each one, as he passed, giving him a kick or a stroke.

The next day we nailed the skin of his coat, which I had pulled off, to the whipping post in Charlestown, the place of his residence, with a label upon it, commemorative of the occasion which had thus subjected the proprietor to the popular indignation.

Another attempt was made to save a little tea from, the ruins of the cargo, by a tall aged man, who wore a large cocked hat and white wig, which was fashionable at that time. He had slightly slipped a little into his pocket, but being detected, they seized him, and taking his hat and wig from his head, threw them, together with the tea, of which they had emptied his pockets, into the water. In consideration of his advanced age, he was permitted to escape, with now and then a slight kick.

The next morning, after we had cleared the ships of the tea, it was discovered that very considerable quantities of it was floating upon the surface of the water; and to prevent the possibility of any of its being saved for use, a number of small boats were manned by sailors and citizens, who rowed them into those parts of the harbour wherever the tea was visible, and by beating it with oars and paddles, so thoroughly drenched it, as to render its entire destruction inevitable.

Source: James Hawkes, *A Retrospect of the Boston Tea-Party, with a Memoir of George R. T. Hewes* (New York: S. S. Bliss, Printer, 1834), 38–41.

Shays' Rebellion (1787)

On a blustery cold day in January 1787, a force of 1,500 men descended on the armory in Springfield, Massachusetts, in hopes of procuring muskets and gunpowder. These men came from all over central and western Massachusetts, a majority of them farmers. Led by Revolutionary War veteran Daniel Shays, these men gathered in protest of high taxes and unfair debt collection. Hidden within the armory was General William Shepard, who commanded 1,000 militiamen. Shepard, not wanting bloodshed over the armory, sent two aides to warn the rebels of the impending attack. Undeterred, the farmers, who called themselves the New England Regulation, advanced on the armory, urged on by one of their leaders, Daniel Shays. Shepard fired two cannons above the farmer's heads as a warning, and still they advanced. Reluctantly, Shepard ordered his men to fire directly at the rebels. Four men died, 20 were wounded, and the farmers scattered to the surrounding fields, woods, and hills. Just six years earlier, these two opposing groups had been comrades during the American Revolution. What caused this rift in Massachusetts? The incident, which would go down in history as Shays' Rebellion, was brought on by social divisions and economic hardships that followed the end of the American Revolution. High taxes and debt-ridden farmers in the west clashed with wealthy eastern merchants. Though it was only a small event and virtually bloodless, this backcountry rebellion proved a pivotal turning point for the fledging American republic. The rebellion highlighted the many weaknesses the central government suffered when faced with a crisis. In response to Shays' Rebellion, the newly established democracy of the former colonies was put to the test and brought about many changes that helped establish the Constitution of the United States of America.

To understand the causes of Shays' Rebellion, one must first look back to the American Revolution. During the Revolution, there was a great business boom for East Coast merchants. Goods were scarce, since a majority of imports into America came from Great Britain, who maintained a blockade on American seaports. Therefore, all goods were in high demand and fetched high prices. Anyone with something to sell, from equipment to textiles to livestock, was sure to make a tidy profit. The economy flourished, with people buying goods with paper money or through bartering goods. Like all boom-and-bust cycles, the war profits came to an abrupt end following the peace at Yorktown. The stark changes to the American

Shays' Rebellion (1787)

A creditor is attacked while a mob cheers during Shays' Rebellion, an insurgent movement led by Daniel Shays during 1786–1787. During the financial depression following the American Revolution, farmers in western Massachusetts rose up to force the government to decrease taxes and issue paper money. (Hulton Archive/Getty Images)

economy would play a vital role in Shays' Rebellion and the effects it had on government policies, both at the state and federal levels.

Even before the end of the Revolution, the new federation suffered its first growing pains in the form of massive inflation. During the war with Great Britain, Congress and the 13 states (formerly colonies) flooded paper currency into the economy, in an effort to meet the needs for supplies for the army and militia. In addition, each state issued its own paper currency. There was no way to determine the value of all this different paper money. What was the value of a New York dollar versus a Rhode Island dollar or a Pennsylvania dollar? No one had a definitive answer. By 1779, this paper currency was worth a fraction of its face value. For example, a Continental dollar compared to a Spanish dollar was 146 to 1. After the end of the Revolution in 1783, an economic depression settled in over the economy. Causes included inflation during the war and the United States' role as primary producer of raw materials. Until the United States could produce finished goods, it would still import a majority of finished goods from Europe, especially from Great Britain, who was still its most vital trading partner. Due to a lack of exports and too many imports, from 1784 to 1786, the trade deficit with Great Britain increased to £5 million. This deficit drew hard currency (gold and silver) out of the American economy. This in turn caused commercial banks to insist on immediate repayment of old loans and refusal to issue any new loans. By 1786, prices for goods fell to their lowest level, dropping 25 percent. With hard money disappearing from the economy and paper money viewed as worthless, consumers stopped spending on goods and land. At the same time Congress, who lacked the power to raise taxes, petitioned each of the states to do so instead. Many citizens, especially farmers already burdened with debts and low prices for crops, could not pay higher taxes. The depression would last until 1788, at which time the central government would be called upon to act in new ways.

The depression hit those already in debt the hardest, particularly the New England states. With no gold or silver available, many families could not repay debts or their taxes. This was especially true for rural farmers throughout New England, as well as other states. During the prosperous war years, many farmers took out loans to improve their farms, purchasing equipment, livestock, and land. When the depression brought about sharply low prices for crops and other goods, farmers found themselves struggling to feed and house their families. There was no money left for repayments of debt or taxes. In western Massachusetts, the depression was keenly felt by many farmers. According to state records, in 1784 in Worcester County, 2,000 lawsuits were brought about by debt alone. If a man could not pay his debt, he could be thrown into debtors' prison, until it was paid off or he could even sold into servitude to work off his debt. Debtors' prisons were often small, cramped cells, filled with mold and mildew. Those incarcerated for a long period of time suffered health problems, ranging from malnutrition to boils and putrid sores. Once in prison, there was no way to work off one's debt. Throughout Massachusetts, men, many of whom had fought for American independence, were being thrown into debtors' prison over the smallest of debts. In 1785, in Worcester County, 94 of the 104 people jailed were jailed for debt.

Massachusetts was considerably harsher on residents than other New England states. Rhode Island, for example, passed a law making it illegal for creditors to refuse the state's paper money. In 1785, Massachusetts levied the heaviest poll tax of the period—£1 per poll, versus £1.4 in other states. A poll tax was a flat tax levied on any male, age 16 or over. Since it was not based on income, the poll tax was much more difficult for those already in debt to pay. Governor James Bowdoin and the local legislature refused to shape taxes to realistically mirror the economy. Other states were far more lenient than Massachusetts. In Connecticut, for example, tax collection was abated over time, as needed. In Virginia, sheriffs either did not or could not follow through with foreclosure sales. But Massachusetts remained firm about its taxation policies. The hopelessness of the situation in western Massachusetts, as well as the rest of New England, caused a flood of immigration to the newly opened-up Northwest Territory. People from Portland and Salem in New England left their families and friends behind to travel thousands of miles to set up new homes and farms in outlying areas. The result of emigration caused land prices to plummet, further worsening the economic situation in New England.

Farmers in Massachusetts petitioned against what they saw as unfair debt collection practices and high lawyer and court fees. Many of them had fought valiantly in the American Revolution, without pay, only to return home to be hauled into court for debts. The men appealed to Governor Bowdoin and the council of Massachusetts, proclaiming their loyalty to the nation, but opposing the state's policies around debt and taxes. The governor and the council, which was made up in large part of eastern merchants, rejected the farmers' pleas. Bowdoin did not think it fair to punish those who lent the money (mainly merchants) just because those who borrowed could not repay their debts. In the case of Massachusetts, a bulk of the debt was owned by merchants and creditor groups who had a firm grasp on local government. It was these groups who put in place high poll taxes, which affected farmers more than any other group, shifting the debt burden onto those who could least afford it. It is estimated that one-third of a farmer's income went to taxes after 1780. Bowdoin and the rest of the government ignored the political discontent and opted to ride out the storm, believing it would soon subside.

The state's indifference to the plight of rural residents angered farmers throughout central and western Massachusetts. They began meeting in places such as Conkey's Tavern in Pelham, where fiery speakers like Daniel Shays, Samuel Ely, and Luke Days preached for more paper money, tax relief, relief for debtors, and the end of debtors' prisons. Shays, a former captain in the Revolutionary War, admitted to crowds gathered at the tavern that even though he had not lost his farm to foreclosure, he doubted he would be able to hold onto it much longer. He railed against lawyers and their high fees and how to the courts worked only for the wealthy. Shays further emphasized the line between eastern and western Massachusetts. The division between farmers and merchants within the state had existed since its earliest colonial days. The farmers formed the New England Regulation, though they would go down in history as Shaysites, as their opponents called them. At first, they modeled their tactics after those used during the American Revolution. They used liberty poles and liberty trees and believed they were acting in the spirit of the Revolution.

For his part, Daniel Shays always denied being the chief leader of the group. He pointed out that decisions were made collectively by the regulators. Shays, the poor son of Irish immigrants, was reluctant to lead any of his fellow farmers into battle. He believed, however, that he could help maintain peace, while still convincing the government to revise its policies on debt collection and taxation. One farmer described Shays as "a firm leader and a man that is capable of keeping his head in case of emergency." Other men who helped lead Shays' Rebellion included Luke Days, Moses Sash, Job Shattuck, Henry Gale, and William Whiting, who was a judge from Berkshire County. These men all fought in the Revolutionary War, some achieving heroic honors. Shays himself was commended for his bravery at Stony Point in New York by General Lafayette. But in the eyes of the Massachusetts government, they would all be branded traitors and charged with treason and other crimes.

The earliest actions taken by the New England Regulation took place in the summer of 1786. In August, the regulators stormed the Northampton courthouse, where they successfully stopped the trial and imprisonment of many debtors. Even though Shays refused to head up the Pelham contingent of Regulators for the Northampton courthouse, he reluctantly agreed to head up the group one month later, as they marched on the Springfield courthouse. He hoped to keep the men's tempers at bay and keep the situation from getting out of hand. Shays negotiated with General William Shepard, who commanded the militia troops stationed in front of the courthouse. In the end, Shepard agreed that the judges and militia would peaceably abandon the courthouse and that the Regulators would march and demonstrate outside of it, rather than by taking it by force. The New England Regulators traveled to Berkshire, Hampshire, Middlesex, and Worcester counties, where they met little to no resistance. All over central and western Massachusetts, legal proceedings were halted. Through the summer and fall of 1786, Shaysites traveled around Massachusetts preventing foreclosures on farms and keeping courts from opening, thereby spurning the collection debts. They fought to keep honest men from going to jail and opened debtors' prisons to free those incarcerated.

Encouraged by their easy early victories, in which no blood was shed nor a bullet fired, the Shaysites continued their own brand of justice, throwing caution to the wind. However, as winter approached, confrontations grew angrier. Governor Bowdoin and the merchants and creditors of Boston, grew frustrated with the central government's apparent lack of ability to deal with the rabble-rousers. So they funded a special private militia of 4,400 men, led by General Benjamin Lincoln. Shaysites heard rumors of brutal conduct by militia, particularly to innocent bystanders including women and children. They decided that stronger measures were needed, and to do that, they needed weapons.

Despite early victories, the Shaysites were badly organized, poorly armed, and not up to fight a real militia. They had yet to encounter armed forces of any real size, and when they set off for the Springfield armory, they did not expect to be fired upon. In an effort to reason with Shays, whom they perceived as the head of the insurrection, the government sent General Rufus Putnam, Shays' former commander during the Revolution, to speak with Shays about surrender. After a series of talks with Putnam, Shays, still confident with his early victories, refused to submit, proving to be just as stubborn as Bowdoin and his Boston merchants. On January 25, 1787, Shays led a group of 1,500 farmers and other citizens to Springfield Armory, which housed 7,000 muskets and 1,300 barrels of gunpowder. Fellow New England Regulator Luke Days was to lead a force of men from West Springfield to the armory to meet up with Shays' men. However a message that Days would be delayed by one day was intercepted by Shepard, who stationed a group of 1,000 men within the armory. Even after they learned that the armory was filled with militia, Shays and his men continued to advance. From inside the armory, Shepard warned Shays and his men, "come any nearer at your peril" and fired two warming shots, still wanting to avoid bloodshed. However, as the Regulators continued to advance, Shepard ordered his men to fire into the crowd. Four Regulators were killed, and 20 were wounded. The shocked Regulators could not believe Shepard and his men had actually fired on them. There were cries of "Murder!" before Shays' men dispersed, and the rebellions leaders scattered to other states. General Benjamin Lincoln and his forces captured Luke Day in West Springfield. Shays retreated to Pelham, Massachusetts, and then on to Vermont, which was not part of the Union. Lincoln marched through subzero temperatures and a snowstorm to Petersham, where many insurgents fled. He and his men covered an impressive 30 miles in 13 hours on foot. The surprised rebels were captured. After a monthlong pursuit, many Shaysites were captured and sentenced to death, though they would eventually be granted general amnesty in 1788.

Following the uprising at the Springfield Armory, Bowdoin offered amnesty for those involved in the New England Regulation. He passed the Disqualifying Act on February 16, 1787, which set forth conditions for granting pardons to the participants of Shays' Rebellion. Rebels were required to turn in their guns and pledge an oath of allegiance to the government. Their names would then be sent to their town clerks, and they would then be prevented from holding public office or voting. Even positions such as schoolmaster or tavern keeper were forbidden. Attorney General Robert Treat Paine was put in charge of prosecuting offenders, and he started a blacklist of those he believed to be in cahoots with Shays and his ilk. This harsh measure did not please the public, who saw the Disqualifying

Act as a smokescreen for Bowdoin and his supporters to keep power. Even Benjamin Lincoln, who was a foe of Shays right from the start, believed the governor and his advisors were going too far.

Popular support for the Shaysites was apparent immediately following their capture, not just in Massachusetts, but in all of the New England states as well as New York. During the hunt for Shaysites, the government tried to intimidate the women of many of the men involved. These women, hardened already from the Revolution, did not give in to the harassment. In fact, the women of central and western Massachusetts were instrumental in organizing a campaign for leniency once their husbands, sons, fathers, or brothers were captured, traveling many miles to Boston to plead for their release. Bowdoin, always a friend of eastern merchants, remained firm that the rebels be dealt with in the harshest of terms, and he offered up warrants and rewards for the Shaysites. Two rebels were executed before Bowdoin lost the 1787 gubernatorial election to federalist John Hancock.

In fact, political unhappiness with the administration in Massachusetts was painfully clear in the 1787 election. Voter turnout was three times larger that year than the previous year, despite hundreds of men not being able to vote because of the Disqualifying Act. Not only was James Bowdoin ousted from office as governor, half of the state's legislature was replaced as well. New Governor Hancock proved to be much more sympathetic to the plights of poor prisoners. Lincoln was put in charge of a commission to pardon the Shaysites, extending pardons to 790 men who did take the oath of the Disqualifying Act. He pardoned all but one of the condemned men, including Daniel Shays. The one man who did hang had been found guilty of theft, and so went to the gallows for criminal activities rather than for debt or unpaid taxes.

The effects of Shays' Rebellion were felt both immediately and in the long term. It revealed the ineffectuality of the new government in dealing with political stress, such as economic unrest, and it brought to many people's attention how well—or in this case, poorly—the central government was operating. The rebellion convinced a powerful group of Americans that the national government needed more power so that it could strengthen economic policies and protect property owners from attacks by local majorities, like merchant creditors. It came down to private liberty versus public liberty, or keeping unrestrained power in the hands of all citizens, not just the wealthy, landed ones. James Madison pointed out that "Liberty may be endangered by the abuses of liberty as well as the abuses of power."

While the wealthy classes saw Shays' Rebellion as an attack on them, believing paper currency to be as bad as taxation without representation, many others, like the Federalists, saw a need for reforms. Shays' Rebellion reached across all 13 states, evoking similar movements in New York, Connecticut, and New Hampshire. After all, the men who participated in Shays' Rebellion were, just a few years prior, ardent patriots, fighting the British for American independence. These were not rabble-rousers or layabouts, as their opponents would have everyone believe. Many of the men who fought in the New England Regulation were decorated war heroes and gentlemen in their own right. In response to the public outcry for Shays' Rebellion, new laws were put in place to allow the debtor freedom if he pledged a pauper's oath, stating he had no means of repayment. This early form of bankruptcy allowed hundreds of Massachusetts citizens to start over financially and freed them from the fear of debtors' prisons or forced servitude. Other laws passed in Massachusetts included a new fee bill, which reduced court charges. Clothing, household goods, and tools of trade were all exempt from the debt process. Taxes were also considerably lighter under John Hancock, who voluntarily cut his own salary by 300 pounds.

Outside of New England, Shays' Rebellion inspired other rural communities to stand up against urban aggression. In Virginia, farmers boycotted sales of property. The King William County Courthouse in Virginia was burned to the ground in May 1787, destroying all legal records. In Maryland, the Charles County courthouse was closed, and in South Carolina, the Camden County Courthouse was closed, preventing any legal proceedings from taking place. Shays also brought the country one giant step closer to revising the Articles of Confederation and the establishment of the constitution. Before Shays' Rebellion, Congress lacked the power to intervene in state problems "to ensure domestic tranquility." Article IV, Section Four, which gave protection to the states, was inspired by the combined threats of civil unrest and fears of splitting the new Union. The article required the government to protect each state against the invasion of domestic abuse, and establishing a stronger central government would provide more power to intervene in domestic affairs.

The Shays movement and its repression had mobilized both Anti-Federalists and Federalists. In the end, Federalists won the debate about the role of the central government in state affairs, garnering Massachusetts support for the newly drafted Constitution at the Philadelphia Convention in September 1787. The preamble of the Constitution very clearly alludes to Shays' Rebellion and the concern lawmakers felt over the insurgency. It is a result of the uprising in Massachusetts, when social classes collided and the nation's newly established government was put through its first stress test. Even Massachusetts, which had staunchly avoided softening debt laws or taxation policies, gave its approval to the constitution. This is important to note, because if Massachusetts had withheld its approval, it is very likely that New York, Virginia, or any of the other states would have followed suit, thus reducing the Constitution to a well-crafted dead letter, soon forgotten.

There is no question that Shays' Rebellion was a class dispute. Unlike the Revolution, in which all the classes joined together in one cause against the British, Shays represented the first crack in the ideology of democracy on which American independence was based. Political leaders knew they had to act swiftly to end the rebellion before general anarchy became the rule rather than the exception. Thanks to Shays' Rebellion, attendance at the Philadelphia Convention was high. George Washington cited Shays' Rebellion as the very reason he made the trip from Virginia to the Convention. People in western and central Massachusetts were divided in their feelings about the rebellion. On one hand, they had great sympathy for the men who fought in Shays' Rebellion. After all, these men were neighbors who were being unfairly treated by the government. However, high taxes and debt collection did not justify taking up arms against the government. What would become of the country if every person who was discontented decided to take matters into his own hands? Many of the most influential men of the American Revolution sneered at Shays' Rebellion. Samuel Adams, Revolutionary War leader and president of the Massachusetts Senate, and the new Secretary of War Henry Knox both saw the rebellion as one step closer to total anarchy. Adams declared that "Rebellion against a king may be pardoned, or lightly punished, but the man who dares rebel against the laws of a republic ought to suffer death." Other lawmakers, such as Thomas Jefferson and James Madison, viewed the insurrection as a growth opportunity for the new republic. A young Jefferson calmly wrote from his post in France that those who governed were "[i]nattentive to public affairs." He went on to say that "Congress and assemblies, judges and conventions, shall all become wolves.... For I can apply no milder term ... to the general prey of the rich on the poor." James Madison believed that "a little rebellion, now and then, is a good thing.... It is a medicine necessary for the sound health of government."

As for Daniel Shays, whose name has been committed to history for the rebellion, following his pardon by Governor Hancock, he moved to upstate New York, where he farmed until his death at the age of 84 in 1825. Today tourists can visit the Springfield Amory in Springfield, Massachusetts, and see where the last battle of the American Revolution was fought, and where the basis of the United States Constitution was inspired.

—*Lorri Brown*

See also all entries under Whiskey Rebellion (1794).

Further Reading

Aptheker, Herbert. *Early Years of the Republic*. New York: International Publishers, 1976.

Beeman, Richard, Stephen Botein, and Edward C. Carter III. *Beyond Confederation: Origins of the Constitution and American National Identity*. Chapel Hill: University of North Carolina Press, 1987.

Jensen, Merrill. *The New Nation: A History of the United States during the Confederation 1781–1789.* New York: Alfred A. Knopf, 1958.

Morris, Richard B. *The Forging of the Union.* New York: Harper & Row, 1987.

Morris, Richard B. *Witness at the Creation.* New York: Holt, Rinehart and Winston, 1985.

St. John, Jeffery. *Forge of Union, Anvil of Liberty.* Ottawa: Jameson Books, Inc., 1992.

Taylor, Alan. *Liberty Men and Great Proprietors.* Chapel Hill: University of North Carolina Press, 1990.

Bowdoin, James (1726–1790)

The second governor of Massachusetts, James Bowdoin was born into a privileged life as the son of a wealthy merchant. A political and intellectual leader before, during, and after the Revolution, James Bowdoin helped shaped the fledging nation's politics and played an integral part of ratifying the U.S. Constitution. His term as governor coincided with the first economic crisis for the new republic.

James Bowdoin II was born on August 7, 1726, to James and Hannah (Portage) Bowdoin. His grandfather, Pierre Boudouin, was a French Huguenot in exile following the revocation of the Edict of Nantes. Pierre Boudouin fled to Dublin, Ireland, then on to Portland, Maine, and finally settling in Boston in 1690. Pierre accumulated a small estate as a merchant and ship's captain. James Bowdoin's father built on his father's modest success and was one of the wealthiest merchants in Boston. James Bowdoin attended the Boston Latin School and graduated from Harvard in 1745. When his father died in 1747, James inherited a large fortune. He had political aspirations early in his career, being elected to the Massachusetts House of Representatives in 1753 and serving until 1756.

In 1785, James Bowdoin was elected governor of Massachusetts. His term was marred by a deepening economic depression and unhappy citizens throughout the state, due to high taxes and debt collections. When disgruntled farmers petitioned Bowdoin and the rest of the legislature for some debt relief and a change in the tax laws, Bowdoin remained unsympathetic. When the farmers banded together, under the direction of Revolutionary veterans like Daniel Shays, and began shutting down courthouses throughout western and central Massachusetts, Bowdoin took action. He was, after all, a grandson and son of a merchant, and a merchant himself. He viewed the uprising by farmers as a direct threat to the newly established government. Even when popular opinion called for compromise with the disgruntled farmers, Bowdoin refused to budge in his position. Bowdoin believed that any tampering with the courts would "frustrate the great end of government, the security of life, liberty and property."

Following the closing of the Springfield courthouse in September 1786, Bowdoin helped form a special militia of 4,000 men, paid for by himself and his merchant friends in Boston, since the state treasury could not afford it. In an effort to end the rebellion peaceably, he enacted the Disqualifying Act, in which rebels could take an oath of allegiance to the government and prevent them from holding any type of public office or voting in elections for three years. When this failed, Bowdoin persecuted the rebels, sentencing 11 of them to death, despite public cries for leniency. Undoubtedly, the harshness with which he handled Shaysites was a main cause for his losing the 1787 gubernatorial election to John Hancock.

James Bowdoin's reaction to Shays' Rebellion was not so much out of disdain for the poor or farmers, but more about the preservation of liberty and the sanctity of government. Despite his short term as governor, James Bowdoin remained active in politics and Boston society for the rest of his life. He helped ratify the U.S. Constitution. He was a founder and the first president of the American Academy of Arts and Sciences, even leaving his library to the foundation. He also helped found the Massachusetts Humane Society. Bowdoin College in Maine was named in his honor, by his son, James Bowdoin III.

—*Lorri Brown*

Further Reading

Aptheker, Herbert. *Early Years of the Republic.* New York: International Publishers, 1976.

Taylor, Alan. *Liberty Men and Great Proprietors.* Chapel Hill: University of North Carolina Press, 1990.

Massachusetts General Court

During the post–Revolutionary War period, an uprising in western Massachusetts known as Shays' Rebellion brought national attention to the weaknesses of the federal government. The rebellion also brought about big changes in the political landscape of Massachusetts. The governing body of the state, the Massachusetts General Court, had existed long before the United States won its independence from Great Britain. Known as the Great and General Court in colonial days, during the Revolution and the years immediately following, the Massachusetts General Court played a crucial role in the shaping of the nations government and the ratification of the U.S. Constitution.

Immediately following the end of the American Revolution, an economic depression settled over the country. Massachusetts farmers in particular felt the pinch of the depression. As more and more farmers, many of whom had fought in the Revolution without any kind of compensation, lost their farms to unpaid debts and soaring taxes, they petitioned Governor James Bowdoin and the Massachusetts General Court for some kind of assistance or debt relief. The Massachusetts General Court was made up largely of wealthy merchants and traders from the coastal areas. They were completely unsympathetic to the plight of poor farmers and saw no reason why those who loaned the money (merchants, like themselves) should have to take a loss because those who borrowed could not repay their loans.

Farmers in the western and central portions of the state decided to take action against the government and what they viewed as unfair laws. They formed a group known as the New England Regulation and marched peaceably on a courthouse in Northampton, stopping foreclosure sales and preventing people from going to debtors' prison. The men who served on the Massachusetts General Court, along with Governor Bowdoin, were outraged by these actions. A month later, at the Springfield courthouse, war veteran Daniel Shays led a force of 700 farmers to stop the trials of 11 farmers who helped close the Northampton courthouse. Shays negotiated with the militia to let them have the courthouse peacefully. Despite the fact that the Shaysites, as the court called them, protested with little to no force and had a great deal of popular support, the court's attitude could not be swayed. Shays, the perceived ringleader of the group, became public enemy number one, and those who supported him were branded traitors to the Union and charged with treason.

Through the fall and winter of 1786–1787, Shaysites shut down courthouse after courthouse, preventing any legal action from being taken against fellow farmers. Bowdoin and the Massachusetts General Court offered amnesty to those who were willing to take an oath of allegiance to the state. Those who did use the Disqualify Act, as it was called, were unable to vote or hold any type of public office (including tavern keeper or schoolmaster) for three years. People in Massachusetts saw the act as a way for Bowdoin and the rest of the court to keep power out of the hands of dissenters. This attitude was reflected in the 1787 election, when a third of the court was replaced by more moderate politicians.

Following Shays' Rebellion, the Massachusetts General Court, under the guidance of the new governor, John Hancock, reduced taxes and court fees and allowed taxes to be paid in goods other than hard cash. They also helped push through the newly drafted U.S. Constitution, ratifying it by a narrow margin of 187 to 168 votes. With the support of the state of Massachusetts, other states followed suit, ratifying the Constitution and laying the foundation for the modern day government.

—*Lorri Brown*

Further Reading

Aptheker, Herbert. *Early Years of the Republic*. New York: International Publishers, 1976.

Jensen, Merrill. *The New Nation: A History of the United States during the Confederation 1781–1789*. New York: Alfred A. Knopf, 1958.

Morris, Richard B. *The Forging of the Union*. New York: Harper & Row, 1987.

Morris, Richard B. *Witness at the Creation*. New York: Holt, Rinehart and Winston, 1985.

St. John, Jeffery. *Forge of Union, Anvil of Liberty*. Ottawa: Jameson Books, Inc., 1992.

Shays, Daniel (1747–1825)

A pivotal turning point in the early history of the United States was a small revolt known as Shays' Rebellion. Though the rebellion was short and virtually bloodless, it brought attention to the weaknesses of the confederation and promoted lawmakers to draft a new constitution, strengthening the power of the federal government. The man credited with leading the rebellion, Daniel Shays, was a reluctant leader. A Revolutionary War veteran, his role in the "last battle of the American Revolution" earned him a place in history.

Daniel Shays was born to Irish immigrants Patrick and Margaret (Dempsey) Shays in 1747 in Hopkinton, Massachusetts. He was the second of six children. As a young man without land of his own, Shays spent his early adult years hired out as a farmhand. Shays married Abigail Gilbert in 1772. The couple settled in Brookfield, Massachusetts, moving to Shutesbury between 1774 and 1775. When the American Revolution broke out, Shays was an ardent patriot. Thanks to previous drilling instruction with the Brookfield militia, he entered the militia at Shutesbury as a sergeant, soon being promoted to lieutenant. By 1777, he was promoted to captain in the Fifth Massachusetts Regiment of the Continental Army. Shays had a reputation as a strong, competent, and courageous officer. He fought in several notable battles, including the battles of Lexington, Bunker Hill, and Saratoga. At Stony Point in New York, Shays was commanded for heroics by General Lafayette and awarded a special sword for his services. He was promoted to

Daniel Shays was one of the leaders of an uprising of farmers in western Massachusetts in 1786–1787. Shays' Rebellion, as it was called, added momentum to the drive for a stronger central government that led to the adoption of the U.S. Constitution. (North Wind Picture Archives)

the rank of captain before being wounded in battle and retiring from the military in 1780. Upon returning to civilian life, he went back to his main occupation of farming in western Massachusetts, where he lived with his wife and children.

At the age of 39, following the Revolutionary War, Shays found himself in debt and facing high taxes. Having received no compensation for his military service, he was brought before a court for unpaid debts. He was not alone; thousands of farmers across central and western Massachusetts were in similar situations. The disgruntled farmers gathered in places such as Conkey's Tavern in Pelham, Massachusetts, where they shared their unhappy situations. They petitioned the government for help, but their pleas went unanswered. As more and more farmers were thrown into debtors' jail, veterans such as Shays saw the need for more decisive action.

In the autumn of 1786, Shays and his fellow veteran-farmers organized into militia-like squads, known as the New England Regulation. The Regulators, as they called themselves, began shutting down courthouses throughout western and central Massachusetts, preventing foreclosure sales and imprisonment of debts. Even though he always denied being the chief leader of the group, Shays' name became a battle cry for 9,000 men. Opponents of Shays and his men referred to the rebels as Shaysites. Through the fall and early winter of 1786–1787, Shays led his men into peaceable protests at courthouses throughout the state. However, when they decided to take over the Springfield Armory, to gather ammunition and other provisions, they were fired upon by a special militia, waiting inside the armory, killing four Shaysites. Shocked that they were actually fired on, Shays and the other men broke rank and fled to surrounding towns. Shays headed to Pelham before going on to Vermont. The Shaysites were charged with treason, and rewards were offered for their capture by Governor James Bowdoin.

Following a pardon by new Governor John Hancock in 1787, Shays was cleared of any wrongdoing, though his name would always be linked with the rebellion. He moved to upstate New York, where he died at the age of 78 in 1825. Before his death, Shays was granted a petition from the government for a pension for the five years of war service he gave without pay.

—*Lorri Brown*

Further Reading

Aptheker, Herbert. *Early Years of the Republic*. New York: International Publishers, 1976.

Beeman, Richard, Stephen Botein, and Edward C. Carter III. *Beyond Confederation: Origins of the Constitution and American National Identity*. Chapel Hill: University of North Carolina Press, 1987.

Jensen, Merrill. *The New Nation: A History of the United States during the Confederation 1781–1789*. New York: Alfred A. Knopf, 1958.

Morris, Richard B. *The Forging of the Union*. New York: Harper & Row, 1987.

Morris, Richard B. *Witness at the Creation*. New York: Holt, Rinehart and Winston, 1985.

St. John, Jeffery. *Forge of Union, Anvil of Liberty.* Ottawa: Jameson Books, Inc., 1992.

Taylor, Alan. *Liberty Men and Great Proprietors.* Chapel Hill: University of North Carolina Press, 1990.

Taxes

The United States was still in its infancy when its first real economic crisis hit, following the end of the Revolutionary War. Brought on by a combination of high taxes, inflation, and aggressive debt collection, the depression of the 1780s instigated an uprising in western Massachusetts known as Shays' Rebellion. This rebellion became the United States' first call at tax reform.

Politicians serving on the Massachusetts General Court consisted in large part of the wealthy merchant and trading classes surrounding Boston. Many of these men had lent money to the government during the Revolution. When the government could not pay back its debt, Congress petitioned the states to raise taxes. These same men worked hard following the end of the war to resume trade with Europe, particularly Great Britain, who was their most important trading partner.

Congress lacked the power to tax directly, so when it needed money to pay back war loans, it turned to the states to raise the needed revenue. The Massachusetts General Court was overly enthusiastic about raising taxes, since many of the legislators had a direct interest in government repayment of loans. They levied the heaviest tax in New England in 1785 of approximately one pound per poll, while other states' taxes were about a quarter of that amount. While other states modified or abated tax collection altogether, the government of Massachusetts never shaped their taxes to the economic reality of the time.

The taxes that the legislature passed hit farmers the hardest and coincided with the depression brought on by lack of hard currency. Throughout western and central Massachusetts, farmers were losing lands and property or being thrown into debtors' prison by the hundreds. Roughly a third of a farmer's income in 1785 went to pay taxes. That left precious little to feed, house, and maintain a family and farm. Despite pleas for debt relief from farmers, the government continued to push high taxes and support confiscation of property for failure to pay. They also adamantly refused to issue paper money, which the farmers requested, believing that paper money would lead to massive inflation and further economic problems.

During the autumn and winter of 1786–1787, the government began to pass some token tax reforms. In November 1786, they allowed all back taxes to be paid with goods such as beef, pork, leather, iron, or whale oil, rather than with hard currency of gold or silver. But the act came too late to save many farmers from destitution. When John Hancock was elected governor in June 1787, ousting merchant-friendly James Bowdoin, he reduced taxes and also reduced court fees, which were a hinder to debt-ridden farmers.

The tax policies of Massachusetts at the time of Shays' Rebellion helped bring about a shift in both local and federal government policies. At the local level, a powerful group of creditors lost government control to moderates. At the federal level, there was a movement to strengthen the power of the central government, allowing it to raise taxes, rather than delegating the task to states, which, in the case of Massachusetts, provoked rebellion.

—*Lorri Brown*

Further Reading

Aptheker, Herbert. *Early Years of the Republic*. New York: International Publishers, 1976.
Jensen, Merrill. *The New Nation: A History of the United States during the Confederation 1781–1789*. New York: Alfred A. Knopf, 1958.
Morris, Richard B. *The Forging of the Union*. New York: Harper & Row, 1987.
Morris, Richard B. *Witness at the Creation*. New York: Holt, Rinehart and Winston, 1985.
St. John, Jeffery. *Forge of Union, Anvil of Liberty*. Ottawa: Jameson Books, Inc., 1992.

An Address to the People of Hampshire County, Massachusetts, Setting Forth the Causes of Shays' Rebellion (1786)

In 1786, the newly independent United States fell into an economic depression as businesses failed, prices fell, and currency became scarce and unstable. With no power to levy or collect taxes, the central government under the Articles of Confederation could do little to bring the situation under control. In the autumn of 1786, Captain Daniel Shays, a Revolutionary War veteran, became one of the leaders of an insurrection of impoverished former solders and farmers that erupted in western Massachusetts. Later known as Shays' Rebellion, the uprising sought to end court foreclosures on farms and properties whose owners could not afford to pay their taxes. Declared traitors by the state, the rebels attacked the government arsenal in Springfield, Massachusetts, but were defeated and dispersed by state militia forces. In 1788, all participants in Shays' Rebellion were pardoned. The following document describes some of the rebels' grievances, many of which were later remedied by the Massachusetts legislature, and protests against rumors that the insurrection had been instigated by the British.

Gentlemen,

We have thought proper to inform you of some of the principal causes of the late risings of the people, and also of their present movement, viz.

1st. The present expensive mode of collecting debts, which by reason of the great scarcity of cash, will of necessity fill our gaols with unhappy debtors; and thereby a reputable body of people rendered incapable of being serviceable either to themselves or the community.

2nd. The monies raised by impost and excise being appropriated to discharge the interest of governmental securities, and not the foreign debt, when these securities are not subject to taxation.

3rd. A suspension of the writ of Habeas Corpus, by which those persons who have stepped forth to assert and maintain the rights of the people, are liable to be taken and conveyed even to the most distant part of the Commonwealth, and thereby subjected to an unjust punishment.

4th. The unlimited power granted to Justices of the Peace and Sheriffs, Deputy Sheriffs, and Constables, by the Riot Act, indemnifying them to the prosecution thereof; when perhaps, wholly actuated from a principle of revenge, hatred, and envy.

Furthermore, be assured, that this body, now at arms, despise the idea of being instigated by British emissaries, which is so strenuously propagated by the enemies of our liberties: And also wish the most proper and speedy measures may be taken, to discharge both our foreign and domestic debt.

Per Order,
Daniel Gray, Chairman of the Committee

Source: G. R. Minot, *History of the Insurrection in Massachusetts* (Boston: James W. Burditt, 1810), 82.

A Letter to the *Hampshire Herald* Listing the Grievances of the Rebels (1786)

In the following letter sent to the Hampshire Herald *in December 1786, Thomas Grover, after referring to the list of grievances in the previous document, further elaborates on the reforms that the Shays' rebels wished to see implemented. Among those changes are removal of the Massachusetts state capital from Boston, the sale of state lands to pay the foreign debt, and the revision of the state constitution. Many of these measures were passed by the Massachusetts General Court in the years after Shays' Rebellion.*

Sir,

It has some how or other fallen to my lot to be employed in a more conspicuous manner than some others of my fellow citizens, in stepping forth on defense of the rights and privileges of the people, more especially of the county of Hampshire.

Therefore, upon the desire of the people now at arms, I take this method to publish to the world of mankind in general, particularly the people of this Commonwealth, some of the principal grievances we complain of. . . .

In this first place, I must refer you to a draught of grievances drawn up by a committee of the people, now at arms, under the signature of Daniel Gray, chairman, which is heartily approved of; some others also are here added, viz.

1st. The General court, for certain obvious reasons, must be removed out of the town of Boston.

2nd. A revision of the constitution is absolutely necessary.

3rd. All kinds of governmental securities, now on interest, that have been bought of the original owners for two shillings, and the highest for six shillings and eight pence on the pound, and have received more interest than the principal cost the speculator who purchased them—that if justice be done, we verily believe, nay positively know, it would save this Commonwealth thousands of pounds.

4th. Let the lands belonging to this Commonwealth, at the eastward, be sold at the best advantage to pay the remainder of our domestic debt.

5th. Lest the monies arising from impost and excise be appropriated to discharge the foreign debt.

6th. Let the act, passed by the General Court last June by a small majority of only seven, called the Supplementary Act, for twenty-five years to come, be repealed.

7th. The total abolition of the Inferior Court of Common Pleas and General Sessions of the Peace.

8th. Deputy Sheriffs totally set aside, as a useless set of officers in the community; and Constables who are really necessary, be empowered to do the duty, by which means a large swarm of lawyers will be banished from their wonted haunts, who have been more damage to the people at large, especially the common farmers, than the savage beasts of prey.

To this I boldly sign my proper name, as a hearty well-wisher to the real rights of the people.

Thomas Grover
Worcester, December 7, 1786

Source: G. R. Minot, *History of the Insurrection in Massachusetts* (Boston: James W. Burditt, 1810), 82.

Whiskey Rebellion (1794)

The Whiskey Rebellion of 1791–1794 in western Pennsylvania was an organized resistance to a tax on whiskey imposed by the new federal government. In many ways, it was a replay of the Stamp Act crisis of 1765, Shays' Rebellion of 1786, and the American Revolution itself. Ideologically, internal taxes created by a distant central government were seen as fundamental violations of the rights of individuals to tax themselves. The Stamp Act had united the colonists against the common enemy, King-in-Parliament. The Whiskey Tax, enacted in March 1791, united westerners against the new federal government they had distrusted from the beginning.

Opposition to the excise tax, which had deep roots in the ideology of English "Country" radicals and their predecessors, had less to do with the tax than in the means that might be employed to collect it. "Country" radicals like Algernon Sidney, John Trenchard, and Thomas Gordon had warned that this was one of the most egregious uses of a "standing army"—the intrusion on one's personal property of a permanent military force created to enforce unpopular measures, like the excise tax. Local control of affairs was seen by many in this school of thought to be essential to liberty. Power overly concentrated in a distant and centralized national government could be expected to use a standing army for tyrannical purposes. West of the Appalachian Mountains, settlers who had come to the region hoping for some measure of autonomy suddenly found themselves subjected to the kind of thing they had sought to defeat in the war.

The country around "the Forks," shorthand for the headwaters of the Ohio at Pittsburgh, had long suffered from the resistance of Indian peoples to Euro-American expansion as well as what they perceived as indifference from the state legislature in Philadelphia. At the front lines of empire, Indian war was their chief concern, and neither the state government nor the new federal government in New York had given them much help. Indeed, help with the conquest of the Indians and acquiring navigation rights on the Mississippi River—at that point prohibited by the Spanish—were the only reasons for having a federal government at all that they could see. Since they did not have access to the port of New Orleans and the Atlantic market economy, western farmers found that distilling their corn into whiskey and transporting it over the mountains to Philadelphia or other port towns was the most cost-effective way to market their crop. Now, that was in jeopardy

Whiskey Rebellion (1794)

President George Washington and his advisers send Confederation Army troops to pacify western counties of Pennsylvania during the Whiskey Rebellion, October 1794. (National Guard)

from a federal government that threatened to take what little profit they made from their year's labor.

As bad as that seemed to these western subsistence farmers, it was their more wealthy neighbors and economic competitors who not only gained an advantage from the whiskey tax, but who also volunteered to collect it. Moreover, the tax was created, in part, to pay debts-plus-interest incurred to wealthy Americans during the war—individuals like the wealthy Philadelphia banker and land speculator Robert Morris. It was no secret that Morris was a friend of Alexander Hamilton, the author of the hated excise that would pay dividends on the war debt held by Morris and other wealthy Americans. These financiers had welcomed the young Hamilton into their circle as the drive for a federal government gelled in the late 1780s. With the Federalist victory in the battle over the ratification of a new constitution, President George Washington had appointed Hamilton to be the first secretary of the treasury. It appeared that Morris and company would be paid a handsome profit on their investment in the American Revolution and its aftermath.

When the war was going badly for the Continentals in 1776, Congress had offered bonds to investors at 4 percent interest payable in paper money. Morris and company were not interested; continental paper would depreciate rapidly, and indeed, when Congress stopped printing it in 1780, the value ratio between paper and coin was 125 to 1. But Morris was a member of the Continental Congress, and as a successful merchant with a far-flung commercial empire of his own, he was able to coax the French into loaning Congress the cash to cover interest on the bonds in so-called bills of exchange. These bills were exchangeable on the European market for hard currency—silver and gold. This arrangement made the bonds an attractive investment, and Morris and his associates soon bought them up—and they bought them up with Continental paper money. Much of this paper money had been bought up at pennies on the dollar, yet the bondholders would be paid back with interest in hard money.

Robert Morris wielded great power in the Continental Congress. He and his cronies headed the committees of Finance, Foreign Affairs, and War. He routinely used congressional money for his own investments, and the fact that they were often profitable kept him in power instead of getting him imprisoned. But now that the Morris faction held these bonds, issued at 6 percent interest and backed by the bills of exchange, meant that real wealth was needed to pay for them. This real wealth would be provided through taxation. State governments in the 1780s had been hesitant to impose an unpopular excise tax and whether a state militia would even enforce its collection was open to question. With the advent of the new Constitution, which concentrated power in the federal government, an army ostensibly led by President Washington could enforce the payment of an excise tax. The new secretary of the treasury Hamilton, following a long British tradition of taxing "vices" to minimize popular opposition, proposed a tax on whiskey. It was passed by the new Congress on March 3, 1791. One-third of the whiskey distillers in the United States lived at the Forks. Many of these individuals had fought the British and their Indian allies on the battlefield without receiving the pay that was still owed them. Some were paid in the lands west of the mountains, where Indians clung tenaciously to their land base and had no intention of being driven away. Now these people were being ordered to pay a crippling tax so that, as they saw it, Bob Morris and friends could reap a windfall. The majority had no intention of paying it or of countenancing the presence of its collectors.

As with the rationalization of excise taxes in England, there was a long history of resistance to such taxes in folk culture. The majority of westerners were Scots-Irish, a group that had long struggled against the encroachment of imperial Britain. Peasant and artisan communities in the pre-modern, English-speaking world had enforced their standards traditionally through the folk methods of "skimmington" or "rough music." When someone repeatedly violated the norms of the community, a "committee" of self-appointed enforcers, often with faces blackened and dressed in bizarre clothing, perhaps in drag, would arrive at the offender's home, shave his head, strip him naked, ride him around town on a rail while beating on pots and pans and chanting the party's offenses, finally depositing him on the outskirts of the community where he was likely beaten and/or tarred and feathered. This "home remedy" was applied to tax collectors at the Forks as well.

In September 1791, such a committee accosted a recently appointed federal tax collector named Robert Johnson on a lonely road near Pigeon Creek, southwest of Pittsburgh. Johnson had either ignored or failed to see the notice in the *Pittsburgh Gazette* announcing a resolution adopted at a meeting in the nearby town of Washington to treat tax collectors as public enemies. This group of men, about 15 to 20 in number, faces blacked, many wearing dresses, stripped Johnson naked and tarred and feathered him. This occurred the same week that many of the perpetrators were attending a conference in Pittsburgh at the Sign of the Green Tree, a tavern on the Monongahela River side of town. The conference was the culmination of efforts begun that summer to resist the whiskey excise. The first meeting was at Redstone–Old Fort (present-day Brownsville) on July 27, 1791. Two factions were emerging in the resistance that overlapped at the Green Tree conference, those bent on tarring and feathering, and those who insisted on following the rule of law and democratic-republican principles.

The moderates were led by three notable individuals who were involved in state and national politics. William Findlay was one, a future governor of the state. Hugh Henry Brackenridge, who had teamed with Philip Freneau to provide some of the more radical war propaganda during the revolution, had come to Pittsburgh after the war to find elbow room and seek his fortune. Also living in the area was Albert Gallatin, a Swiss immigrant pursuing a land speculation scheme aimed at French émigrés from that revolution. In 1795, he was elected to the House of Representatives, where he expanded his reputation as a formidable opponent of the Hamilton wing of the Federalist Party. Gallatin would go on to serve as secretary of the treasury in the Jefferson administration. Although Findlay, Brackenridge, and Gallatin had a moderating effect on the Whiskey Rebellion, at its height, opposing the outbreak of violence while protesting the excise was not for the feint of heart.

In Kentucky, North Carolina, and northwestern Virginia, the federal government could find no one to collect the tax. News of this phenomenon was somewhat suppressed by the Federalist-dominated newspapers to prevent further rebellion. After all, this was the same kind of protest that Britain had felt in 1765 and 1776. Untaxed spirits from southwestern Pennsylvania flowed southward to markets in that region, frustrating those desiring to collect revenue on it. Hamilton was anxious to deploy troops to enforce the excise, but President Washington and Attorney General Edmund Randolph opposed the move.

As the boycott of the excise stretched into its second year, the question became less whether or not to deploy troops, but where to deploy them. Washington and

Hamilton knew that they did not have the manpower to enforce the excise at all points in the West. While the treasury secretary pondered troop deployments, Washington wrote to the governor of North Carolina, and Randolph stated that he could find no hard evidence to warrant the prosecution of the frontiersmen. Supreme Court chief justice John Jay aptly summarized the predicament: the worst thing that could happen would be for a federal military force to be humiliated on the frontier. Frontiersmen were veteran warriors, having served in the Revolution and often having fought the formidable Native Americans to take and keep the homesteads they now possessed.

By late 1792, Hamilton began to strategize that putting down this "rebellion" might be accomplished by focusing on one area rather than the entire western frontier. Western Pennsylvania was the closest and most easily reached by a military force. Hamilton had allies in the region, most notably John Neville, who had accepted an appointment as the regional inspector of the excise tax. Neville was among the wealthiest men in the Forks region. While most of his neighbors were losing their land, he was buying it. Neville owned a compound known as Bower Hill that included 1,000 acres of land, 18 slaves, 16 head of cattle, 23 sheep, and 10 horses—an extensive holding in southwestern Pennsylvania. His son-in-law supplied the local militia with needed goods through government contracts. Hamilton's information about the area largely came from Neville, who did not bother to distinguish the peaceful resistance movement from the violent one. Neville, with a still that produced up to 600 gallons of whiskey a year, was the kind of man who benefited from the whiskey tax. Being more acclimated to the realm of business, people like Neville were favored by Hamilton and taken more seriously than their lower-class counterparts. Small distillers were at a distinct disadvantage, operating more on a traditional folk culture level than on that of international business and empire that to Hamiltonians was the coin of the realm. Unlike pre-modern society, where the affairs of the common folk were largely left alone, market economics dictated that they be competitive or fall by the wayside. Small-time operators who were not interested in obtaining large sums of material wealth represented unwanted competition that needed to be squelched and, in the Forks region, Neville was happy to oblige.

By 1793, violent opposition to the excise in Pennsylvania had coalesced with the formation of the Mingo Creek Association. Originating southwest of Pittsburgh near the village of Washington, their plan was to use the democratic process to infiltrate the local militia and deprive the Federalists of the use of that entity to enforce the tax. The more radical among them even considered independence, designing their own flag and entertaining the notion of aid from Britain or Spain. Other individuals were accosted and tarred and feathered. William Faulkner, a newcomer to the Forks, rented office space to Neville and had his building vandalized for his trouble. The Whiskey Rebels forced Faulkner to eject Neville and publish a notice saying the tax would not be collected on his property. During a meeting of the Washington County militia in June, an effigy of "General Neville the excise man" was displayed and burned. Benjamin Wells, a tax collector residing in Fayette County, had his life threatened on a couple of occasions and was forced to turn over his account books and commission to a blackfaced, handkerchiefed "committee" of anti-excise men. He was also compelled to publish his resignation as collector in the *Pittsburgh Gazette*. This resistance brought the attention of Hamilton and Washington to the Forks, but the difference between Pennsylvania and other regions of the West was not the resistance, but the presence of Neville and his allies—willing collectors of the excise.

As the seeming headquarters of the tax collector, the compound at Bower Hill was a symbol of oppression. This view intensified as the events of 1794 unfolded in southwestern Pennsylvania. In June, U.S. marshal David Lenox was sent to the area to begin distributing summonses to over 60 distillers who had refused to comply with the excise law. Lenox distributed a large number of these in three of the western counties, remaining unmolested apparently because of his position as a lawman. Hugh Henry Brackenridge, a moderate tax protester who had and would continue to reign in the violent faction to the best of his ability, entertained Lenox at his home in Pittsburgh. He told Lenox that it was likely because of his non-association with Neville and other pro-excise residents that he had escaped attack. Nevertheless, when John Neville offered to guide Lenox to serve one last summons in July, Lenox accepted. This proved to be one of the decisive moments in the Whiskey Rebellion.

Lenox and Neville made their way to the home of William Miller to serve a summons. Miller was outraged that he should have to interrupt his seasonal schedule to go to Philadelphia and likely pay a ruinous $250 fine. The presence of Neville "made my blood boil" he reported, and Miller refused to accept the summons. As this was transpiring, men working in the summer hayfields nearby heard that individuals were being arrested, with the help of the hated Neville, and taken to Philadelphia. While this was hyperbole, the 30 to 40 men who subsequently confronted Lenox and Neville were frustrated and outraged. The presence of a U.S. marshal and the obvious misinformation confused the group, facilitating the exit of the two excise enforcers. Lenox returned to Pittsburgh and Neville to his lair at Bower Hill.

Meanwhile, the Mingo Creek militia had gathered that same day to answer President Washington's call for volunteers to supplement General "Mad Anthony" Wayne's army engaging the Indians in the Ohio country. When the rumors of enforcement action reached these men, it was decided to confront the enforcers, both thought to have gone to Bower Hill. The militia's plan was to capture Marshal Lenox. When they arrived, with "37 guns," they surrounded the house. Neville heard them around daybreak and stepped outside to confront them. He warned them off and fired a shot into the crowd, killing militiaman Oliver Miller. In the ensuing exchange of gunfire, Neville blew a horn, and his slaves opened fire from their quarters behind the militia, wounding several of them. The militia retreated to a place known as Couche's Fort, where they met with reinforcements and considered their alternatives.

With the ante upped by Neville's fatal shot at Miller, the militia felt they had new rationale for their resistance. For his part, Neville applied for protection from the local judges but received none, although Major James Kirkpatrick and 10 volunteers from Fort Fayette came to help Neville defend Bower Hill. On July 17, two days after the original confrontation near William Miller's farm, about 600 men accompanied by drums and riding in formation arrived at Neville's residence. The leader of the militia, James McFarlane, a Revolutionary War veteran, sent a notice demanding that Neville surrender, resign his commission, and decline all further offices related to the excise. Unbeknownst to the militia, Kirkpatrick had smuggled Neville into a thicketed ravine where he lay in hiding. The major refused to leave, arguing that if he did, the militia would burn the property. The militia responded by surrounding the compound, lighting fire to a slave cabin and a barn. The military managed to get the Neville family out of the house, and a pitched battle ensued. At one point, McFarlane thought someone had called out from the house and ordered a cease-fire, thinking the soldiers wanted to negotiate. When he stepped into the open, a shot fired from the house struck him down, killing him instantly. The militia continued to set fire to the buildings at Bower Hill, with the exception of a few that the slaves talked them into sparing. Soon the heat became too intense for the soldiers inside, and they surrendered. The prisoners, along with Lenox, who had been retrieved from Pittsburgh, were brought to Couche's Fort and threatened extensively, although no serious harm was done. The soldiers were released and Lenox escaped, taking his leave from the area by floating on a barge down the Ohio River. In the end, the number of casualties was not clear; several were seriously wounded, and there were reportedly a few deaths on each side. This was the bloodiest day of the Whiskey Rebellion, and the blame for it falls at the feet of John Neville, whose patrician attitude and killing of Oliver Miller caused the escalation of events in July 1794.

The Whiskey Rebellion threatened to expand southward and even eastward after these events. Liberty poles were raised, and rumors of militias forming as far east as Carlisle, Pennsylvania, and Hagerstown, Maryland, were rampant. If the West was to rise up against federalism, now was the time to do it while even rural people east of the mountains were supportive of their cause. The response of people in central and eastern Pennsylvania was the catalyst that spurred the federal government into action.

By September, a federal army composed of nearly 13,000 troops was on its way to the far side of the mountains. Known as the "Watermelon Army" because of its inexperience, the president lent his enormous credibility to the enterprise, rendezvousing with them at Carlisle. As it traveled through increasingly hostile territory, circumstances were exacerbated by the behavior of the army. They had few or no provisions and were authorized by Hamilton to confiscate food and fodder from often impoverished farmers just before the onset of winter.

By November, the army was ensconced at Fort Fayette and the roundup of noncompliers in the Forks region was underway. Their punishment began with their treatment by the soldiers and officers. Many were marched in their nightclothes through rain and sleet, forced to spend the night in the open, and prodded with bayonets if they got too close to the fire. If they were fed at all, it was uncooked dough and raw meat tossed to them on the ground. Discipline at Fort Fayette was lax as the army's stay stretched into the winter. Even officers got into brawls with the local population. Property was looted and destroyed, and the soldiers gained a reputation as an army of occupation having their way with the locals. Fear of the standing army utilized to collect the excise tax proved well founded.

The legacy of the Whiskey Rebellion, above all, was to further instill into a populace already phobic about taxes the distrust of arbitrary rule from a distant center of power. To many, there was now little difference between King-in-Parliament and the federal government in Philadelphia. The democratic-republican societies that the dissenting Jeffersonians had formed, and which President Washington condemned, swelled in number. The Jacobin radicals of the French Revolution were viewed sympathetically by many in America, and Edmund Genet had been welcomed by the Jeffersonians with open arms. The polarizing effects of Hamilton's economic policies were heightened, and an open political struggle for power between the Federalists and the Jeffersonian Republicans would characterize the remainder of the decade. While the Jeffersonians won out in the short term, winning the election of 1800, Hamiltonian policies favoring the wealthy at the expense of the middle and lower classes returned with a vengeance. Some argue that they never really left, given the favoritism shown first to land speculators and bankers, and later railroad men, industrialists, and bankers. The Whiskey Rebellion was both a last gasp of the American Revolution and a defining moment in setting the parameters of American politics to the present day.

—Douglas S. Harvey

See also all entries under Shays' Rebellion (1787).

Further Reading

Baldwin, Leland B. *Whiskey Rebels: A Story of a Frontier Uprising*. Pittsburgh: University of Pittsburgh Press, 1939.

Bouton, Terry. *Taming Democracy: "The People," the Founders, and the Troubled Ending of the American Revolution*. Oxford, UK: Oxford University Press, 2007.

Boyd, Steven R., ed. *The Whiskey Rebellion: Past and Present Perspectives*. Westport, CT: Greenwood Press, 1985.

Cooke, Jacob E. "The Whiskey Insurrection: A Re-evaluation." *Pennsylvania History* 30 (July 1963).

DeMay, John A. *The Settlers' Forts of Western Pennsylvania*. Apollo, PA: Clossen Press, 1997.

Eckert, Allan W. *That Dark and Bloody River: Chronicles of the Ohio River Valley*. New York: Bantam, 1995.

Hogeland, William. *The Whiskey Rebellion: George Washington, Alexander Hamilton, and the Frontier Rebels Who Challenged America's Newfound Sovereignty*. New York: Scribner, 2006.

Kohn, Richard H. "The Washington Administration's Decision to Crush the Whiskey Rebellion." *Journal of American History* 59 (December 1972).

Mainwaring, W. Thomas, ed. "The Whiskey Rebellion and the Trans-Appalachian Frontier." *Topic: A Journal of the Liberal Arts* 45 (Fall 1994).

Slaughter, Thomas P. *The Whiskey Rebellion: Frontier Epilogue to the American Revolution*. Oxford, UK: Oxford University Press, 1986.

Federal Supremacy

Federal supremacy was the concept enshrined in the U.S. Constitution, ratified in June 1788, in which the individual states, hoping for increased security, sacrificed much of their sovereignty to a newly created federal government. The effort to establish federalism had begun with a nationalist movement in 1781 as the Continental forces were scoring a key victory against Lord Cornwallis at Yorktown. The finances of the Continental Congress as well as those of most states were in dismal shape and, beginning among economic elites, the movement for a strong central government with the power of taxation was increasingly seen as a solution to the new republic's economic woes.

To some, federal supremacy was a betrayal of the Revolution. The bottom-up nature of the rebellion of the 1760s and 1770s ran into serious financial trouble as the fighting wore on. Profiteering by some members of Congress and their appointees led some to wonder what the point of the war was if British "placemen" were to simply be replaced by their American equivalents. Issuance of paper money and various certificates of loan created state and national debts that were astronomic for the period. Typically, in the colonial period, such loans and paper issuances would be reabsorbed into the economy as raw materials were traded for finished goods. But that arrangement was dependent on the reputation of British financiers and the power of the British Empire. The struggling new republic had no such reputation or unbridled trade with an economic powerhouse like the Empire. Financial elites in Boston, New York, Philadelphia, and Virginia—people like Robert Morris, Alexander Hamilton, and James Madison—argued for a stronger central government and, in some cases, forced punitive state taxes through state legislatures to pay interest on debts. Often, these debts were owed to the very people who were pushing this legislation through at the state level.

Even before federal supremacy was hatched in Philadelphia in 1787, Daniel Shays and others led a revolt against such punitive taxes in Massachusetts. These reflected similar discontent that had occurred in the western lands of Carolina and Virginia in the 1760s. When Madison and Hamilton called for a convention to "rework" the Articles of Confederation, supporters of state sovereignty—people like Patrick Henry of Virginia—said they "smelled a rat." But by the late 1780s, the economic situation of the United States had reached a point where many people of middling economic status supported the concept of a stronger central power that could tax the citizenry and encourage foreign investment. However, westerners, like their predecessors the Regulators of the 1760s in Carolina, the Sons of Liberty after the Stamp Act, and Shays' Rebellion in Massachusetts in the 1780s, saw this as an attempt by the rich to usurp power and enslave the citizenry.

Indeed, it is unlikely that the new Constitution would have been ratified had its supporters not promised a Bill of Rights guaranteeing that the new federal government would not usurp certain individual rights.

Federal supremacy was enshrined in Article VI, Paragraph 2 of the new Constitution. Almost immediately, the new secretary of the treasury, Alexander Hamilton, began implementing a plan to tax westerners to pay interest and principal on the United States' war debt. This tax, placed on whiskey, created a great hue and cry in places like western Pennsylvania, where whiskey was the lifeblood of the economy. This led to the "Whiskey Rebellion," which was considered the greatest rebellion against federal policy until the Civil War.

Federalism continued to be a bone of contention even after the whiskey rebels gave up their struggle. Fries' Rebellion among ethnic Germans in eastern Pennsylvania in the late 1790s was a protest against the property taxes instituted by the federal government. The election of Thomas Jefferson as president in 1800 quieted some of this protest, but the proponents of centralized power and rule by an economic elite persisted. The rise of the issue of slavery impacted the federalism–states' rights dilemma in the mid-19th century. Southerners feared that a northern-controlled federal government might, like the British and French, abolish slavery. As emancipation gained steam in the Atlantic world, proslavery forces in the American South dug in their heels. When a northern president was elected in 1860—Abraham Lincoln—the deep South seceded from the Union, ostensibly to prevent a federal intrusion into their states' economies. After the Civil War, violent repercussions manifested in southern "Redeemers" who set out to terrorize freed blacks into "keeping their place" in a white-supremacist society. Redeemers were successful in curbing efforts by the federal government to "reconstruct" southern society. Other localist movements have expressed disdain for federalism, from separatist movements in such disparate locations as western Kansas and Vermont. Often, resistance to federal supremacy has found expression in rural southern and western groups who feel controlled from afar by those who do not have their interests at heart. It is an old dichotomy that shows no signs of permanently dissipating.

—*Douglas S. Harvey*

Further Reading

Boyd, Steven R., ed. *The Whiskey Rebellion: Past and Present Perspectives*. Westport, CT: Greenwood Press, 1985.

Hogeland, William. *The Whiskey Rebellion: George Washington, Alexander Hamilton, and the Frontier Rebels Who Challenged America's Newfound Sovereignty*. New York: Scribner, 2006.

Kohn, Richard H. "The Washington Administration's Decision to Crush the Whiskey Rebellion." *Journal of American History* 59 (December 1972).

Slaughter, Thomas P. *The Whiskey Rebellion: Frontier Epilogue to the American Revolution.* Oxford, UK: Oxford University Press, 1986.

Hamilton, Alexander (1755–1804)

Alexander Hamilton was something of a lightning rod in the opening years of the American republic. His policies regarding debt assumption and taxation incited the so-called "Whiskey Rebellion," one of the most serious insurgencies in the United States before the secession of the South in 1860. Hamilton sought to tie the welfare of the federal government to the interests of the financier class—bankers, merchants, and manufacturers—much as Sir Robert Walpole had done with the British Parliament earlier in the 18th century.

Alexander Hamilton was born on January 11, 1755, on the British sugar island of Nevis, to a French Huguenot mother and a Scottish merchant father. When Hamilton's parents moved to the Danish island of St. Croix, they learned that their marriage was invalid because Danish law did not permit a divorcée to remarry. This is the source of the well-known "illegitimacy" of Hamilton's birth, something that haunted his adult life. The elder Hamilton's business ultimately failed, and he returned to England. Shortly after, Alexander's mother died of a fever at the age of 32 in 1768. Young Alexander was entrusted to his employers at the counting house of Nicholas Cruger and David Beekman.

Alexander showed great aptitude in business finance, and at age 17, with the support of his employer Cruger and Hugh Knox, he immigrated to New York. Friends of his St. Croix benefactors, William Livingston and Elias Boudinot, as well as his cousin Ann Lytton Mitchell, aided him once he was on the continent. Hamilton rose through the ranks of the Continental army, and married Elizabeth Schuyler, daughter of the well-connected General Philip Schuyler. He was soon invited into the inner circle of the revolutionary power structure with his appointment as an aide-de-camp to General George Washington.

After the war, moneyed and propertied interests in the new United States felt increasingly threatened by rural soldier-farmers who were shouldered with state tax burdens they often found unreasonable. James Bowdoin of Massachusetts and Robert Morris of Pennsylvania were among those whom Hamilton joined in an effort to create a strong central government with the power to tax. These men supported a system of taxation that would make payments on the debts incurred during the course of the war and afterward. Some of this debt was owed to people like Bowdoin and Morris, and the taxes that working people and farmers would pay included interest payments on these debts. Hamilton and his allies also hoped that some of these taxes would go toward subsidizing manufactures that would bring handsome profits for the owners. His "Economic Plan," proposed as soon as the new federal Constitution allowed him to be sworn in as the secretary of the treasury, included creating a bank that would be controlled by the wealthy and would serve to collect taxes and pay down debt.

Protests such as the Whiskey Rebellion, Fries' Rebellion, and others were responses to Hamilton's economic proposals. In the case of the Whiskey Rebellion, Hamilton pushed a tax through the new federal Congress on the production of whiskey, most of which was produced in the country in and over the Appalachian Mountains. Westerners resented the tax because it was intentionally designed to be more punitive to small distillers. These were typically farmers who could not afford to bring their corn to eastern markets in its raw form, so they turned it into whiskey to make it more valuable and easier to transport. The larger producers were better funded, had access to capital, and could afford to pay the yearly assessment as opposed to the more laborious and expensive per-gallon rate the smaller distillers paid. The only options many of the smaller distillers had, in their minds, was to quit and go to work for the bigger distillers, or protest and work toward either a repeal of the tax or secession from the federal government. To many of them, this was the same reason why they had just fought a long and costly war against the British. On top of this, Hamilton and Morris countenanced the collection of tax by those who both benefited from the tax as large distillers, and received a commission on taxes collected. All in all, Hamilton's heavy-handed policies followed the model of the British Empire and the Bank of London, both of which had been on the opposing side in the Revolution. Since the advent of federalism, supporters of rule by a wealthy few have looked back to Hamilton as their progenitor and inspiration. Alexander Hamilton was a champion of big finance and centralized power in the United States, which is why he was a lightning rod for those whose power is restricted to protest, riot, and rebellion.

—*Douglas S. Harvey*

Further Reading

Bouton, Terry. *Taming Democracy: "The People," the Founders, and the Troubled Ending of the American Revolution*. Oxford, UK: Oxford University Press, 2007.

Boyd, Steven R., ed. *The Whiskey Rebellion: Past and Present Perspectives*. Westport, CT: Greenwood Press, 1985.

Chernow, Ron. *Alexander Hamilton*. New York: Penguin, 2004.

Hogeland, William. *The Whiskey Rebellion: George Washington, Alexander Hamilton, and the Frontier Rebels Who Challenged America's Newfound Sovereignty*. New York: Scribner, 2006.

Kohn, Richard H. "The Washington Administration's Decision to Crush the Whiskey Rebellion." *Journal of American History* 59 (December 1972).

Slaughter, Thomas P. *The Whiskey Rebellion: Frontier Epilogue to the American Revolution.* Oxford, UK: Oxford University Press, 1986.

Martial Law

Martial law is, by most definitions, the suspension of civil law and its replacement by military law. The origins of martial law, like most American legal doctrines, are found in the English tradition. One thread in the history is that martial law comes from the medieval Court of the Marshall and Constable of England. This court system dealt with offenses occurring within the military, and began to be suppressed by common-law courts during the 17th century. Another thread argues for its origins in the early modern period with jurisdiction over British soldiers and alien enemies. Known as "military law" and eventually as "martial law," it came to be accepted as legitimate by parliamentary common law barristers. Thus, whether "Marshall" or "martial" law, both of these pedigrees seem to be applicable.

In the North American colonies, colonial governors were warned against using it. During the period of colonial unrest prior to full-blown revolution, Lord Dunmore of Virginia was instructed, "You shall not upon any occasion whatever establish or put into execution any articles of War or other Law Martial upon any of Our Subjects, Inhabitants of Our said Colony of Virginia, without advice and consent of Our Council there." By the end of 1775 however, both Dunmore and General Thomas Gage in Boston had declared martial law.

In the early republic, New Orleans was the scene of two martial-law declarations. One was a largely trumped-up affair initiated by General James Wilkinson seeking to distance himself from Aaron Burr. The two men had conspired with numerous others to launch a filibustering trip to Spanish territory in Mexico and perhaps Florida after the acquisition by the United States of the Louisiana Purchase. The political enemies of Burr, who were many, set out to discredit this expedition and have the instigators arrested. In 1806, Wilkinson declared martial law in New Orleans, allegedly to protect it from the very militia force he had recently hoped to organize—a force that he in fact invented to separate himself from Burr. Writs of habeas corpus were issued by New Orleans judge James Workman, but Wilkinson ignored them and arrested the judge. Territorial governor William C. C. Claiborne protested that only the legislature could declare martial law, but Wilkinson ignored Clairborne as well, arresting others thought to be associated with Burr's filibustering plans. This episode culminated in the U.S. Supreme Court's decision *Ex parte Bollman and Swartwout*, which pointed to the second paragraph of Article I, Section 9, of the U.S. Constitution in declaring that only the federal legislature could declare martial law.

New Orleans was also the scene of the next instance of martial law in the United States, this time during the War of 1812. Colonel Andrew Jackson had brought an army to the city to defend against British invasion. New Orleans was a multinational, multiethnic city, and was thought to be rife with British spies. To secure control, Jackson issued a proclamation of martial law on December 16, 1814. Anyone entering or exiting the city had to check in at the adjutant general's office or face arrest and interrogation. A passport was required for all watercraft leaving the city, obtainable only from Jackson, his staff, or Commodore Daniel T. Patterson. Street lamps were ordered extinguished at 9:00 p.m., and anyone aboard after that time was arrested and held as a spy.

The conflict culminated in the British defeat on January 8, 1815. But Jackson maintained martial law for weeks after the battle, and the French population became increasingly restless with the situation. A letter written anonymously by state senator Louis Louiaillier calling for an end to martial law brought out Jackson's well-known vindictive side. Louiaillier was arrested and subsequently applied for and received a writ of habeas corpus from Judge Dominick Hall. Jackson responded by arresting Hall. Both men were released when martial law was suspended, when Jackson was fined $1,000 by Judge Hall, a fine that Jackson paid. However, near the end of his life, the now-former president Jackson appealed to Congress to pay him back his $1,000 fine, generating a debate over the constitutionality of his declaration of martial law. Because of the effect on the popular sentiment of the subsequent Battle of New Orleans, in which the nation felt a restored sense of dignity after a thrashing by the British in the Chesapeake, the legality of Jackson's declaration of martial law was largely overlooked by the Madison administration. In 1841, a Democratic-dominated Congress, Jackson's party, granted the reimbursement, but the process left a cloud over the legality of Jackson's martial law proclamation of 1814.

The most widely known example of a martial law case is that of Lambdin P. Milligan and the declaration of martial law by President Lincoln in Indiana during the Civil War. Milligan was a southern sympathizer living in Indiana and reportedly involved with a secret society called "The Order of American Knights." The group was reportedly working toward the overthrow of the federal government. Milligan was arrested by the general of the military district of Indiana, tried, and sentenced to death by a military commission. Milligan applied for a writ of habeas corpus from the Circuit Court of Indiana. The Circuit Court judges were in disagreement over the legality of the request and certified the case, now known as

Ex parte Milligan, to the U.S. Supreme Court. The Supreme Court ruled that the military trial of Milligan was unconstitutional. But it was split on the question of whether the president or Congress can institute military courts.

Other examples of martial law exist, but they are mainly occurrences at the state level and are typically of the "qualified" or limited variety. Curiously, these examples consist mainly of the use of troops in labor disputes almost universally against striking and protesting workers. Legal scholars differ on the legitimacy of martial law as a tool of the executive branch; but the Constitution clearly allows the suspension of habeas corpus rights in Article I, Section 9, paragraph 2, in the event of "Rebellion or Invasion." Whether this means only in the event of a dysfunctional civil law, or whether the power can be used by the executive, are still legal bones of contention.

—Douglas S. Harvey

Further Reading

Baldwin, Leland B. *Whiskey Rebels: A Story of a Frontier Uprising*. Pittsburgh: University of Pittsburgh Press, 1939.

Bouton, Terry. *Taming Democracy: "The People," the Founders, and the Troubled Ending of the American Revolution*. Oxford, UK: Oxford University Press, 2007.

Higham, Robin, ed., *Bayonets in the Streets: The Use of Troops in Civil Disturbances*, Manhattan, KS: Sunflower University Press, 1969.

Hogeland, William. *The Whiskey Rebellion: George Washington, Alexander Hamilton, and the Frontier Rebels Who Challenged America's Newfound Sovereignty*. New York: Scribner, 2006.

Kohn, Richard H. "The Washington Administration's Decision to Crush the Whiskey Rebellion." *Journal of American History* 59 (December 1972).

Slaughter, Thomas P. *The Whiskey Rebellion: Frontier Epilogue to the American Revolution*. Oxford, UK: Oxford University Press, 1986.

Tom the Tinker

The early years of the American republic saw numerous protests against the tax policies of the new federal government. Many citizens saw the excise tax on whiskey as a repeat of King-in-Parliament's Stamp Act they had rebelled against in 1765. The whiskey tax, instituted by the Federalists led by Alexander Hamilton in 1791, led to outright rebellion in western Pennsylvania. During the height of this "Whiskey Rebellion," opponents of the tax used the threat of physical violence against tax collectors and tax abettors. The written warnings they sent to individuals and the public were often signed, "Tom the Tinker."

The use of this appellation grew out of the early resistance movements against the whiskey tax, especially those seen in the activities of the Mingo Creek Association. This was a loose collection of small farmers and landless workers who were struggling with Indian conflicts and the harsh Allegheny climate, as well as the whiskey tax. Hugh Henry Brackenridge was a Pittsburgh resident who witnessed and, to a degree, participated as a moderate in the Whiskey Rebellion. He remembered the name "Tom the Tinker" first being used by John Holcroft after a masked attack on William Cochran. Cochran had registered his still as per the new excise law, an act considered a violation of the rebels' solidarity against the tax and therefore punishable. "Tom the Tinker's men" cut Cochran's still to pieces, saying they had "repaired" it as good tinkers were expected to do. This became a kind of standard operating procedure for them. Advertisements were posted in the *Pittsburgh Gazette* and on trees in the roadways of southwestern Pennsylvania warning residents and potential tax collectors of the consequences of enforcing and collaborating in the hated excise. Such postings warned that Tom the Tinker would not suffer any "class or set of men . . . of this my district" from obstructing any actions that would hasten the repeal of the whiskey tax. Anyone assisting the collection of the tax in any way was deemed an enemy of republican liberty and punished in accordance with the offense. This was a strong sentiment that carried over from the revolutionary rhetoric of the recent war. Tom, so the postings went, was sorry to have been driven to destruction of property and tar-and-featherings by the wayward, but no one could be exempted from the republican cause of whiskey tax repeal.

In short, Tom the Tinker was a western Pennsylvania version of the Sons of Liberty. Opposition was not tolerated as Tom the Tinker's men attempted to enforce solidarity. At their peak, Tom the Tinker's men could be said to have numbered upwards of 6,000 strong when they gathered at Braddock's Field near Pittsburgh at the height of the Whiskey Rebellion. Liberty poles were erected, "Don't Tread on Me" flags were hoisted displaying the unity of western Pennsylvania townships. Tom the Tinker possessed the same spirit as the American revolutionaries in 1776 or, for that matter, 1765. As with the enforcement of the Stamp Act boycotts by the Sons of Liberty in the 1760s, Tom the Tinker's men were radicals bent on keeping the machinations of distant power centers at bay.

—*Douglas S. Harvey*

Further Reading

Baldwin, Leland B. *Whiskey Rebels: A Story of a Frontier Uprising*. Pittsburgh: University of Pittsburgh Press, 1939.

Bouton, Terry. *Taming Democracy: "The People," the Founders, and the Troubled Ending of the American Revolution*. Oxford, UK: Oxford University Press, 2007.

Boyd, Steven R., ed. *The Whiskey Rebellion: Past and Present Perspectives*. Westport, CT: Greenwood Press, 1985.

Cooke, Jacob E. "The Whiskey Insurrection: A Re-evaluation." *Pennsylvania History* 30 (July 1963).

Hogeland, William. *The Whiskey Rebellion: George Washington, Alexander Hamilton, and the Frontier Rebels Who Challenged America's Newfound Sovereignty*. New York: Scribner, 2006.

Mainwaring, W. Thomas, ed. "The Whiskey Rebellion and the Trans-Appalachian Frontier." *Topic: A Journal of the Liberal Arts* 45 (Fall 1994).

Slaughter, Thomas P. *The Whiskey Rebellion: Frontier Epilogue to the American Revolution*. Oxford, UK: Oxford University Press, 1986.

President George Washington's Proclamation against the Whiskey Rebellion (1794)

In 1791, the federal government imposed an excise tax on whiskey. In western Pennsylvania, whiskey was a medium of barter and an important source of income. The tax, by virtually eliminating any profit to be derived from the sale or trade of whiskey, threatened the very livelihood of many western farmers, who quickly showed their displeasure by rioting, assaulting tax collectors, and destroying the homes and property of federal officials. When a federal marshal was attacked in Allegheny County, Pennsylvania, in July 1794, President George Washington responded to the growing disorder on August 7 by issuing the following proclamation, which imposed martial law, ordered all rioters to return to their homes, and called out the militia to suppress the insurrection. The Whiskey Rebellion was the first real test of the power of the new federal government to maintain law and order within the states.

BY AUTHORITY

By the president of the United States of America
    A Proclamation

Whereas, combinations to defeat the execution of the laws laying duties upon spirits distilled within the United States and upon stills have from the time of the commencement of those laws existed in some of the western parts of Pennsylvania.

And whereas, the said combinations, proceeding in a manner subversive equally of the just authority of government and of the rights of individuals, have hitherto effected their dangerous and criminal purpose by the influence of certain irregular meetings whose proceedings have tended to encourage and uphold the spirit of opposition by misrepresentations of the laws calculated to render them odious; by endeavors to deter those who might be so disposed from accepting offices under them through fear of public resentment and of injury to person and property, and to compel those who had accepted such offices by actual violence to surrender or forbear the execution of them; by circulation vindictive menaces against all those who should otherwise, directly or indirectly, aid in the execution of the said laws, or who, yielding to the dictates of conscience and to a sense of obligation, should themselves comply therewith; by actually injuring and destroying the property of persons who were understood to have so complied; by inflicting cruel and humiliating punishments upon private citizens for no other cause than that of appearing to be the friends of the laws; by intercepting the public officers on the highways, abusing, assaulting, and otherwise ill treating them; by going into their houses in the night, gaining admittance by force, taking away their papers, and committing other outrages, employing for these unwarrantable purposes the agency of armed banditti disguised in such manner as for the most part to escape discovery;

And whereas, the endeavors of the legislature to obviate objections to the said laws by lowering the duties and by other alterations conducive to the convenience of those whom they immediately affect (though they have given satisfaction in other quarters), and the endeavors of the executive officers to conciliate a compliance with the laws by explanations, by forbearance, and even by particular accommodations founded on the suggestion of local considerations, have been disappointed of their effect by the machinations of persons whose industry to excite resistance has increased with every appearance of a disposition among the people to relax in their opposition and to acquiesce in the laws, insomuch that many persons in the said western parts of Pennsylvania have at length been hardy enough to perpetrate acts, which I am advised amount to treason, being overt acts of levying war against the United States, the said persons having on the 16th and 17th of July last past proceeded in arms (on the second day amounting to several hundreds) to the house of John Neville, inspector of the revenue for the fourth survey of the district of Pennsylvania; having repeatedly attacked the said house with the persons therein, wounding some of them; having seized David Lenox, marshal of the district of Pennsylvania, who previous thereto had been fired upon while in the execution of his duty by a party of armed men, detaining him for some time prisoner, till, for the preservation of his life and the obtaining of his liberty, he found it necessary to enter into stipulations to forbear the execution of certain official duties touching processes issuing out of a court of the United States; and having finally obliged the said inspector of the revenue and the said marshal from considerations of personal safety to fly from that part of the country, in order, by a circuitous route, to proceed to the seat of government, avowing as the motives of these outrageous proceedings an intention to prevent by force of arms the execution of the said laws, to oblige the said inspector of the revenue to renounce his said office, to withstand by open violence the lawful authority of the government of the United States, and to compel thereby an alteration in the measures of the legislature and a repeal of the laws aforesaid;

And whereas, by a law of the United States entitled "An act to provide for calling forth the militia to execute the laws of the Union, suppress insurrections, and repel invasions," it is enacted that whenever the laws of the United States shall be opposed or the execution thereof obstructed in any state by combinations too powerful to be suppressed by the ordinary course of judicial proceedings or by the powers vested in the marshals by that act, the same being notified by an associate justice or the district judge, it shall be lawful for the President of the United States to call forth the militia of such state to suppress such combinations and to cause the laws to be duly executed. And if the militia of a state, when such combinations may happen, shall refuse or be insufficient to suppress the same, it shall be lawful for the President, if the legislature of the United States shall not be in session, to call forth and employ such numbers of the militia of any other state or states most convenient thereto as may be necessary; and the use of the militia so to be called forth may be continued, if necessary, until the expiration of thirty days after the commencement of the of the ensuing session; Provided always, that, whenever it may be necessary in the judgment of the President to use the military force hereby directed to be called forth, the President shall forthwith, and previous thereto, by proclamation, command such insurgents to disperse and retire peaceably to their respective abodes within a limited time;

And whereas, James Wilson, an associate justice, on the 4th instant, by writing under his hand, did from evidence which had been laid before him notify to me that "in the counties of Washington and Allegany, in Pennsylvania, laws of the United States are opposed and the execution thereof obstructed by combinations too powerful to be suppressed by the ordinary course of judicial proceedings or by the powers vested in the marshal of that district";

And whereas, it is in my judgment necessary under the circumstances of the case to take measures for calling forth the militia in order to suppress the combinations aforesaid, and to cause the laws to be duly executed; and I have accordingly determined so to do, feeling the deepest regret for the occasion, but withal the most solemn conviction that the essential interests of the Union demand it, that the very existence of government and the fundamental principles of social order are materially involved in the issue, and that the patriotism and firmness of all good citizens are seriously called upon, as occasions may require, to aid in the effectual suppression of so fatal a spirit;

Therefore, and in pursuance of the proviso above recited, I, George Washington, President of the United States, do hereby command all persons, being insurgents, as aforesaid, and all others whom it may concern, on or before the 1st day of September next to disperse and retire peaceably to their respective abodes. And I do moreover warn all persons whomsoever against aiding, abetting, or comforting the perpetrators of the aforesaid treasonable acts; and do require all officers and other citizens, according to their respective duties and the laws of the land, to exert their utmost endeavors to prevent and suppress such dangerous proceedings.

In testimony whereof I have caused the seal of the United States of America to be affixed to these presents, and signed the same with my hand. Done at the city of Philadelphia the seventh day of August, one thousand seven hundred and ninety-four, and of the independence of the United States of America the nineteenth.

G. WASHINGTON,
By the President, Edm. Randolph

Source: *Claypoole's Daily Advertiser*, August 11, 1794. Reprinted in J. Richardson, ed., *A Compilation of the Messages and Papers of the Presidents* (New York: Bureau of National Literature, 1897), 150–152.

President George Washington's Second Proclamation against the Whiskey Rebellion (1794)

Issued on September 25, 1794, President Washington's second proclamation against the Whiskey rebels of western Pennsylvania is reproduced here. In this proclamation, the president deplores the failure of the rebels to fully comply with the first proclamation and confirms that the military force of the United States will be used to suppress those who do not immediately cease their rebellion and return quietly to their homes.

Whereas from the hope that the combinations against the Constitution and the laws of the United States in certain of the western counties of Pennsylvania would yield to time and reflection I thought it sufficient in the first instance rather to take measures for calling forth the militia than immediately to embody them, but the moment is now come when the overtures of forgiveness, with no other condition than a submission to law, have been only partially accepted; when every form of conciliation not inconsistent with the being of Government has been adopted without effect; . . . when the opportunity of examining the serious consequences of a treasonable opposition has been employed in propagating principles of anarchy, . . . and inviting similar acts of insurrection; when it is manifest that violence would at defiance, the contest being whether a small portion of the United States shall dictate to the whole Union, and, at the expense of those who desire peace, indulge a desperate ambition:

Now, therefore, I, George Washington, President of the United States, in obedience to that high and irresistible duty consigned to me by the Constitution "to take care that the laws be faithfully executed," deploring that the American name should be sullied by the outrages of citizens on their own Government, . . . resolved to reduce the refractory to a due subordination to the law, do hereby declare and make known that, . . . a force which, according to every reasonable expectation, is adequate to the exigency is already in motion to the scene of disaffection; that those who have confided or shall confide in the protection of Government shall meet full succor under the standard and from the arms of the United States; that those who, having offended against the laws, have since entitled themselves to indemnity will be treated with the most liberal good faith if they shall not have forfeited their claim by any subsequent conduct, and that the instructions are given accordingly.

And I do moreover exhort all individuals, officers, and bodies of men to contemplate with abhorrence the measures leading directly or indirectly to those crimes which produce this resort to military coercion; to check in their respective spheres the efforts of misguided or designing men to substitute their misrepresentation in the place of truth and their discontents in the place of stable government, and to call to mind that, as the people of the United States have been permitted, under Divine favor, in perfect freedom, after solemn deliberation, and in an enlightened age, to elect their own government, so will their gratitude for this inestimable blessing be best distinguished by firm exertions to maintain the Constitution and the laws.

And, lastly, I again warn all persons whomsoever and wheresoever not to abet, aid, or comfort the insurgents aforesaid, as they will answer the contrary at their peril, and I do also require all the officers and other citizens, according to their several duties, as far as may be in their power, to bring under the cognizance of the laws all offenders.

G. Washington

Source: J. Richardson, ed., *A Compilation of the Messages and Papers of the Presidents* (New York: Bureau of National Literature, 1897), 153–154.

Antebellum Suppressed Slave Revolts (1800s–1850s)

There is a popular fiction in American history that slaves who lived on plantations in the years before the outbreak of the Civil War were somehow better off than their counterparts working in factories up north—and that many slaves, in fact, were quite content to live on plantations under the watchful and caring eyes of their masters. To be sure, this is not a fiction supported by the historical record. Although it may be fair to say that some slaveholding elites treated their slaves with better care than others, and while it may be true that workers in northern cities suffered many of the same indignities faced by slaves in the South, little else connects the "wage slaves" of the North to those held in bondage in the South. Those subjected to slavery were systematically dehumanized in ways that not even the poor denizens of northern cities could have imagined.

That this fiction was given any credence whatsoever either before the Civil War or after is a testament to the enduring power of words to shape peoples' perceptions of the experiences of others, especially when it is not possible to witness those experiences firsthand. It was perpetuated by southern intellectuals like George Fitzhugh, who attempted to justify slavery as a more humane system of labor division than the system devised in the industrialized North in an effort to derail attempts to abolish the "peculiar institution." Lost in this rationalization of slavery, however, was the reality that neither system was especially humane. Whether suffering the indignity of working for a pittance in the North to build an industrialized economy, or toiling for no compensation whatsoever in the South to enrich the planter elite and build an entire economy on uncompensated labor, workers in the 18th and 19th centuries shared a common experience of alienation and despair that engendered various forms of resistance against the status quo.

Occasionally, this resistance resulted in violence against white slave owners and their families, which then resulted in state-sanctioned revenge against anyone deemed to have participated in that violence. As a result, both whites and blacks in the South lived in constant fear of violent revolt against the system of slavery. Plantation owners cringed at the thought of slaves murdering them in their sleep, while slaves were well aware of the carnage that would inevitably follow even the threat of an uprising. Nevertheless, from the 17th century through the 19th century, slavery became more firmly ensconced in the cultural and political institutions of the South, and as it did, the system gradually pushed various people to undertake desperate measures to undermine it. Not all of these rebels were slaves, nor were all of them men: some were white abolitionists, some were free blacks, some were women, and some were former slave owners themselves. The most successful slave revolts had as their masterminds men of remarkable intelligence and resolve: men such as Charles Deslondes, Nat Turner, Gabriel Prosser, and Denmark Vesey. These revolts were also suppressed with ruthlessness by the planter class.

For their part, slave owners found themselves increasingly caught between their own boundless greed and an overwhelming desire for security. As slave populations increased (slaves outnumbered whites in many places around the South, sometimes by margins as large as two-to-one or more), whites tried ever harder to prevent revolts from occurring. Well aware that they were outnumbered, but also aware of how reliant their own wealth and lifestyles were on maintaining the system of slavery, whites in the South reacted with increasing paranoia to even the whispered possibility of rebellion, placing ever-tighter restriction on what little freedom their slaves may have had. On the other hand, slaves also paid the price for rebellion—not only were conspirators often caught, but anyone accused of consorting with the conspirators (many of whom were no doubt wrongfully accused and denied due process in kangaroo courts) faced almost certain death in the aftermath of failed attempts at rebellion. The circle of paranoid behavior left a legacy of mutual distrust and fear on the relationship between white and black southerners, a legacy that continues to mar relationships between people today.

Patterns of Slave Resistance

Despite the overwhelming odds working against them, slaves did attempt to undermine the system of slavery in various ways. Some slave uprisings in the years before the Civil War were the result of careful planning on the part of conspirators with grand designs to burn down or capture entire cities, but often the uprisings were extemporaneous affairs that involved large numbers of slaves joining others as they marched from plantation to plantation. Much more common were ongoing and more subtle forms of resistance that slaves employed to undermine the system as much as they could. Slaves resisted the institution of slavery by stealing from their masters, attacking and even killing overseers, and destroying property. Some simply refused to work as hard as they possibly could for their masters, reducing productivity and bravely enduring inhuman punishment to maintain what little dignity the slave system afforded them. Many slaves attempted to escape their captivity by running away, hoping to make it to the "promised land" of the North. Such desperation was uncommon but not altogether rare; historian

Eugene Genovese has argued that patterns of hostility toward slavery, whether they took the form of accommodation of the system or outright resistance to it, were as common as slavery itself in the years before the Civil War. Thus, another common misconception of slaves as docile and content with their lives—a misconception given voice by planters intent on defending the entrenched system—has been rendered largely untrue by historical scholars.

Nevertheless, the planter class tried desperately to keep slaves in their place as slaveholding became more common and more prosperous. Estimates suggest that the number of slaves held in the United States ballooned from 500,000 in 1790 to nearly four million by 1860, and the owners of slaves worked hard to establish a system that would not only make slaves productive, but would also exercise control over every aspect of their lives. Julius Lester, author of *To Be a Slave*, a book that combines analysis of slavery with the words of slaves themselves, made this point well when he asserted that a man can be enslaved in one of two ways: either through violence and force, or by teaching him that he can achieve "freedom" only by doing what his master tells him to do. As Lester points out, slave owners in the antebellum period attempted to do both—but with each additional crack of the whip, slaves were pushed closer to rebellion against the system. Many slaves may well have internalized their masters' efforts to make them feel inferior, but others used their own intelligence and cunning to concoct schemes that would undermine the authority of slave owners.

One technique used by planters to control slaves involved hiring poor white men to act as overseers of the slave population. These overseers, who were paid to "keep the slaves in line," employed all manner of cruel and brutal behavior to do their jobs. Historian Howard Zinn, citing evidence collected by Robert Fogel and Stanley Engerman, concludes that at least one slave endured a whipping every four or five days on the Barrow plantation in Louisiana between 1840 and 1842. Such behavior was common on plantations around the South, and the violence only increased the likelihood of slave rebellion. In the case of a slave named Gabriel, who attempted to lead an insurrection in Virginia in 1800 ("Gabriel's Rebellion"), such violence may have been critical in turning him toward open rebellion. After being apprehended by an overseer named Absalom Johnson for stealing a pig with his brother Solomon and another slave named Jupiter, Gabriel managed to avoid execution by invoking the "benefit of clergy"; after reciting a verse from the Bible, his life was spared, and he was instead branded on his left hand. The branding may well have been the last straw for Gabriel, who soon began to organize an insurrection that would require the attention of Governor James Monroe and the state militia.

In addition to outright resistance, slaves had other ways of opposing the system as well. Slaves built an entire culture around the experience of living in bondage and adapted in ingenious ways to the indignity and pain wrought by the slaveholding system. For instance, slave families were often disrupted by auctions that split family units apart, separating parents from their children and from one another. Slaves in many places adapted to this cruelty by establishing a form of communal family life wherein children became the responsibility of all the adult slaves on a plantation, not just the responsibility of their own parents (if, indeed, those parents even still lived on the plantation). This, in turn, strengthened the bonds between and among slaves across the South and provided a sense of solidarity that would become an integral part of slave resistance, whether it was organized or not.

Slaves also found comfort in religion and took advantage of their owners' attempts to "Christianize" them by forming churches of their own and carefully securing time and space for worship beyond the watchful eyes of overseers and plantation owners. Religion could also be used as a powerful antidote to the cruelty of slave owners and overseers. Slave preachers walked a fine line between inspiring their flocks with uplifting language about freedom and liberation, while at the same time encouraging passive resistance to slavery that would undermine the system but not place too many slaves in danger. Often, slaves themselves were their own worst enemies once insurrection plots were revealed. In Gabriel's case, his own brother Solomon testified against him in a vain effort to have his own life spared. In the case of George Boxley's alleged attempt to incite a revolt in Spotsylvania County, Virginia, around 1815, a slave named Lucy notified her master that something was afoot and thus helped thwart the plot before it could gather steam. Sometimes, such slaves were motivated by specious offers of cash reward to anyone who would inform authorities about potential armed rebellions, but other times, they were motivated simply by fear. Thus, even as preachers stirred the passions of some slaves, they may have stirred the fears of others. Above all, many preachers counseled patience in the face of the inhumanity of slavery and encouraged the men and women to whom they preached to look forward to an afterlife of freedom and justice.

Attempts to carve a sense of community out of life in slavery demonstrated the remarkable resilience of the human spirit in the face of despair. Yet, nearly every form of resistance employed by slaves was made in response to an equally strong effort to control slaves on the part of their owners. When slave owners attempted to control their slaves through religion, slaves took advantage of the opportunity provided to gather together and provide inspirational visions of life outside of the shackles of bondage. Some, like Nat Turner in Virginia, took advantage of their masters' attempts to teach them the Bible to become literate themselves—an idea that frightened some slave owners to the core. When owners attempted to control their slaves through violence, some slaves bravely accepted that violence and permitted it to steel their determination to seek freedom for themselves and their families. Slaves took advantage of their proximity to one another on plantations to develop an entire culture than expressed itself in music, art, religion, and storytelling. In this way, they managed to pass stories of their plight from one generation to another, even despite being denied the opportunity to become literate themselves.

Armed Rebellion and Its Suppression

Still, these efforts were sometimes not enough. Although historian James Oakes observes that armed slave rebellion was a relatively uncommon phenomenon, occasionally such insurrections did occur. Certainly the hyper-militarization of white societies around the South in the antebellum period, coupled with the clear willingness of slave owners to use violence in extraordinarily vicious ways against anyone accused of leading a rebellion, prevented many insurrections from happening. Oakes has argued that one reason slave rebellions in the South were uncommon was because slaves simply had nowhere to go—even if they secured their freedom, slaves could hardly expect to be welcomed with open arms into a society that had previously accepted them, since American society in the 18th and 19th centuries had never really accepted African slaves at all. Nevertheless, as slave culture developed, some slaves began to envision the possibility of constructing a "society within society" consisting of those formerly held in bondage. Gabriel, for instance (he is sometimes known as "Gabriel Prosser" but was known in his time simply as Gabriel, without his master's surname added), envisioned installing himself as "king" of Virginia after burning Richmond to the ground. George Boxley, though a white former slave owner himself, was the alleged mastermind of a plot involving several slaves that would also entail destroying Richmond as well as the city of Fredericksburg and, thus, creating space for former slaves to live in. Denmark Vesey, on the other hand, planned in 1822 to seize the city of Charleston, South Carolina, then escape to Haiti to avoid retaliation by whites. In each case, the conspirators envisioned movement out of slavery into a more sympathetic social and cultural environment where former slaves could live and even prosper

The slaves who led the most prominent rebellions of the antebellum period—Gabriel, Charles Deslondes, Denmark Vesey, Nat Turner—were also inspired by external events that galvanized them. Oakes describes the rebellion in Saint Domingue (now known as Haiti) led by Toussaint L'Ouverture as the only successful slave rebellion in all of human history, but it had a profound effect on Gabriel, Deslondes, Vesey, and even Turner (though Turner attributed his inspiration to visions he saw encouraging him to lead a revolt). Deslondes was himself a native of Saint Domingue, and Gabriel had extensive contact with people who hailed from various places by virtue of the fact that he was a skilled blacksmith and was loaned by his owner, Thomas Prosser, to work in various industrial capacities in Richmond. These contacts enabled Gabriel to hear of the events in Saint Domingue and almost certainly influenced his actions later. Thus, a web of interpersonal relationships enabled slaves to hear inspiring tales of rebellion occurring in other places and provided an impetus for the insurrections led by these men.

Slave owners were also aware of another potential instigator of slave insurrection: the very liberal ideology upon which the American system had presumably been founded. Although, as Oakes notes, slaves had no ability to exercise any political influence through such sanctioned means as voting or petitioning the government for a redress of grievances, slaves did exercise an enormous amount of influence on the political system by imposing themselves on it through their status as runaways and as witnesses in courts of law. In the first place, runaway slaves imposed a certain burden on the communities to which they fled—psychological, moral, economic, and otherwise. As more slaves fled to areas in the North where slavery was outlawed, their presence resulted in growing awareness of the inhumanity of slavery that would eventually contribute to its demise. Likewise, even as slaves were systematically denied the right to fair trials in the antebellum period (and beyond), the basic principles upon which such trials were based—the idea, for instance, that a man could not be convicted of a crime if no witnesses came forward to testify that he had actually committed it—became ingrained in the collective consciousness of slaves. Ironically, then, even as slave owners spread their own culture to their slaves, they helped sow the seeds of the institution's ultimate demise. As Oakes has put it, the political institutions of government did not depend on slavery for their existence—but slavery itself did depend on those institutions to survive. Once slave owners lost control of those structures and institutions—control they fought violently to maintain through the regular admission of additional slave states to the Union in the first half of the 19th century—the existence of slavery as a legally sanctioned system would become significantly more precarious.

So while the slave insurrections led by Gabriel, Denmark Vesey, Charles Deslondes, and Nat Turner may have been suppressed with overwhelming force by slave owners, they still served an important purpose in helping to hasten the demise of the system of slavery. By ratcheting up the level of force used to suppress slave rebellions, slave owners unwittingly insisted on thrusting the "slave problem" into the collective awareness of a wider range of Americans—and into the institutions that formed the legal fabric of American society in the 19th century. Many in the political class were well aware of the contradictions implicit in the slave system and the impending difficulty of extricating the country from it. (These sentiments were expressed by Thomas Jefferson when he famously wrote, discussing the question of whether to admit Missouri into the Union as a slave state, that "we have a wolf by the ear and we can neither hold him nor safely let him go." He added, "Justice is in one scale, and self-preservation in the other.") Nat Turner's rebellion in Virginia occasioned an extraordinary discussion among white elites in 1831–1832 about the system of slavery in which multiple options were considered for finding a way out of that system. In the end, Virginia's political leaders chose to endorse and justify the use of violence against slave insurgents, turning their backs on any possibility that slavery could be peaceably dismantled there. Historian Susan Dunn asserts that 1832 marks the point at which Virginia transitioned from a state where the slave system was widely viewed as a "necessary evil" that should eventually be destroyed, to a radicalized state where approximately 10 percent of its whole population—including men, women, children, and even slaves—was active in the state militia.

Such overwhelming shows of force were complemented by inhuman responses to slave rebellion that included gibbeting, public hanging, and decapitation of conspirators so their heads could be displayed publicly to warn against future agitation. If slave owning itself had not dehumanized slave masters, their collective response to attempts by slaves to extricate themselves from the system almost certainly did. The Southampton Rebellion led by Nat Turner was by far the bloodiest of the antebellum period, and Turner's ruthlessness can almost certainly be traced to his and his fellow insurgents' awareness of earlier responses to similar insurrections. In the end, the increasing paranoia of slave owners—manifested in shocking brutality against anyone accused of fomenting rebellion—did as much as anything to hasten the demise of the slave system. Gabriel, Deslondes, Vesey, and Turner all were executed for their opposition to slavery, but their efforts were not undertaken in vain.

The Legacy of Slave Rebellion in the Antebellum Period

If anything had become clear by the 1850s, it was that neither slave owners nor abolitionists were willing to give ground to one another in the fight over slavery. As security tightened across the South in the wake of Nat Turner's Southampton Rebellion, slave-led uprisings became virtually nonexistent. In 1859, a final antebellum revolt was suppressed when John Brown attempted to rally slaves to seize a federal armory located at Harper's Ferry in what is now West Virginia. Brown's plan was to encourage slaves in Virginia to join him and cause a ripple effect throughout the South that would result in an end to the slave system. Brown was hanged for his actions and the raid was a failure, but it represented an inexorable step toward the Civil War: as a white abolitionist, Brown was the very personification of the things the slave-owning class feared the most. Portrayed as a martyr by abolitionists in the North, Brown was reviled just as passionately in the South as a religious fanatic and murderer. Frederick Douglass paid tribute to Brown after Brown's death, crediting him with beginning the war that ended American slavery. "I could live for the slave," Douglass famously said of Brown; "but he could die for him."

In the final analysis, the constant friction slaves and abolitionist sympathizers brought to bear on the slave system in the South helped contribute immeasurably to its collapse. Over the course of several generations, slaves built a culture that wreaked havoc on their owners' ability to keep them in line, occasionally lashing out in violence against the oppression they endured. Though it took a civil war to finally end legally sanctioned slavery in the United States, it seems unlikely that the war could even have taken place without the efforts of thousands of unnamed slaves who rebelled against the system. Their efforts laid the groundwork for the bloodiest conflict in American history to that point, but also helped end the most persistent, and philosophically inconsistent, system of slavery in the world.

—Dave Powell

See also all entries under Stono Rebellion (1739); New York Slave Insurrection (1741); Nat Turner's Rebellion (1831); New Orleans Riot (1866); New Orleans Race Riot (1900); Atlanta Race Riot (1906); Springfield Race Riot (1908); Houston Riot (1917); Red Summer (1919); Tulsa Race Riot (1921); Civil Rights Movement (1953–1968); Watts Riot (1965); Detroit Riots (1967); Los Angeles Uprising (1992).

Further Reading

Aptheker, Herbert. *American Negro Slave Revolts*. New York: Columbia University Press, 1943.

Dunn, Susan. *Dominion of Memories: Jefferson, Madison, and the Decline of Virginia*. New York: Basic Books, 2007.

Egerton, Douglas R. *Gabriel's Rebellion: The Virginia Slave Conspiracies of 1800 and 1802*. Chapel Hill: University of North Carolina Press, 1993.

Franklin, John Hope. *From Slavery to Freedom: A History of Negro Americans*. New York: Vintage, 1947.

Genovese, Eugene D. *Roll, Jordan, Roll: The World the Slaves Made*. New York: Pantheon Books, 1974.

Genovese, Eugene D. *The World the Slaveholders Made*. Hanover, NH: Wesleyan University Press, 1969.

Higginson, Thomas W. *Black Rebellion: A Selection from Travellers and Outlaws*. New York: Arno Press, 1969.

Jacobs, Harriet A. *Incidents in the Life of a Slave Girl, Written by Herself*. Cambridge, MA: Harvard University Press, 1987.

Lester, Julius. *To Be a Slave*. New York: Scholastic, 1968.

Oakes, James. *Slavery and Freedom: An Interpretation of the Old South.* New York: Vintage Books, 1990.

Raboteau, Albert J. *Slave Religion.* New York: Oxford University Press, 1978.

WGBH Educational Foundation and the Public Broadcasting System, "Africans in America: America's Journey through Slavery." http://www.pbs.org/wgbh/aia/home.html (accessed October 1, 2008).

Zinn, Howard. *A People's History of the United States: 1492 to Present.* New York: HarperCollins, 2003.

Boxley, George (c. 1779–1865)

George Boxley was born around 1779 or 1780 in Spotsylvania County, Virginia. By the time of his death in 1865, Boxley had led a colorful life on the frontier—and on the run. He was, at turns, a Methodist preacher, a social agitator, a fugitive from the law, and a pioneer. Boxley is remembered for allegedly attempting to incite a slave rebellion in Virginia in 1815–1816. He was accused of encouraging slaves from Spotsylvania, Orange, and Louisa counties to collect ammunition and proceed to seize the town of Fredericksburg before assaulting the state capital in Richmond. Boxley was arrested, along with 27 slaves, and charged with conspiracy and insurrection. Five slaves were executed, and six more were transported out of Virginia. Boxley escaped capture when his wife, Hannah, smuggled a saw into his jail cell, and he freed himself and headed for Ohio and, later, Indiana. Despite numerous attempts to return him to Virginia, Boxley lived the remainder of his life on the Indiana frontier.

"Boxley's Plot," as it came to be known, is shrouded in mystery, and Boxley's own role in it is difficult to know. What is known is that Boxley was not popular among the local elites in Spotsylvania County in the first decades of the 19th century, nor were they popular with him. Boxley was described by local magistrates as "a man of restless and aspiring mind; wild and visionary in his theories, and ardent in the pursuit of his designs," and seen as the very personification of the slaveholding class's greatest fear: a white man willing to subordinate his own self-interest to the cause of freedom. Yet Boxley's motives may have been less selfless than they appeared. His own history as the slave-owning son of a slave-owner and as a slave patroller himself suggests that Boxley saw his attempted rebellion as much as a fight against local elites as one to be undertaken on behalf of slaves. He was vilified in Virginia as a man desperate to raise his own profile, as a religious fanatic, and as a dangerous rebel intent on upending the status quo. But, ironically, Boxley ended his life as the head of a reasonably well-respected pioneer family on the American frontier.

Boxley's curious life raises a number of interesting questions about the role slavery played in the lives of lower-class whites in the 19th century. When he discovered that he could not attain the status he sought in Virginia's slave society, Boxley took advantage of the frontier safety valve (an idea popularized by the historian Frederick Jackson Turner) to find a place where he could be among the local elite. Along the way, he became accused of stirring up social tension in various places and appears to have actually befriended many of the slaves and former slaves he met in his travels. Boxley was, like many of his fellow citizens in the

19th century, a complicated figure: equal parts firebrand and pragmatist, apparently driven most of all by a desire to improve his own lot in life.

—*Dave Powell*

Further Reading

Aptheker, Herbert. *American Negro Slave Revolts*. New York: Columbia University Press, 1943.

Schwarz, Philip J. *Migrants against Slavery: Virginians and the Nation*. Charlottesville: University of Virginia Press, 2001.

Turner, Frederick Jackson. *The Frontier in American History*. New York: Holt and Company, 1962.

Deslondes, Charles (d. 1811)

Charles Deslondes was the leader of one of the largest slave revolts in U.S. history. A native of Saint Domingue (known today as Haiti), Deslondes organized a group of about fellow slaves in St. Charles Parish, south of New Orleans, on January 8, 1811. Deslondes and his fellow insurgents wounded his master, Manuel Andry, and killed Andry's son, then began marching toward New Orleans, gathering additional insurgents from plantations along the way. Deslondes may have recruited as many as 500 slaves to join his march to New Orleans. Along the way, the army of slaves burned and pillaged several plantations and killed two white people. As they approached New Orleans, the slaves were met by General Wade Hampton and a detachment of U.S. regular troops, along with two companies of the Louisiana militia. The strong show of force stopped the insurgency abruptly; 66 slaves were killed, and 17 were counted missing and presumed dead. Several others were captured. In the ensuing days, a local judge appointed a jury of plantation owners (some of whom had been directly affected by the uprising) to determine the guilt or innocence of approximately 30 slaves involved in the uprising. Twenty-one slaves, including Deslondes, were convicted between January 12 and January 18 and sent to the plantations from whence they had come to be executed by their masters; another was executed on February 20. The murdered slaves were decapitated and had their heads placed on poles to discourage future uprisings.

Once the insurrection had been successfully halted, recriminations began to fly among the planter elite. Governor William C. C. Claiborne and many native New Orleanians argued that the slaves who had led the uprising were "foreign slaves," not from Louisiana; as such, they said, the solution to the problem of preventing future uprisings was to stop the importation of slaves from other places. Affronted by the governor's suggestion that the uprising was their fault, planters responded by blaming Claiborne himself and demanded that a full regiment of federal troops be placed in New Orleans immediately. They also moved to reform existing laws that had permitted some slaves to provide commercial services in New Orleans, and even to rent quarters and earn income there, out of view of their masters. Others believed that the revolt had been planned by Spanish or French agitators intent on reclaiming Louisiana for themselves.

Overlooked by the white elite was another possibility: that Deslondes and his fellow insurgents had been inspired by a recent battle in Saint Domingue won by Henri Petion, a former black slave and heir to the political legacy of Toussaint L'Ouverture To acknowledge the inspiration of L'Ouverture or Christophe would have been tantamount to acknowledging that the slaves had the sense and capability to desire and demand their own freedom. This was an idea that whites in Louisiana simply were not capable of entertaining.

The immediate impact of the 1811 insurrection was that slave laws were strengthened, and the paranoia of slave owners increased. The insurrection also nearly derailed attempts to bring Louisiana into the Union as many in Congress worried about admitting a state with such a large slave population. In response to the rebellion, slave owners in Louisiana did what slave owners did elsewhere: they doubled-down on their attempts to prevent revolts and made conditions even more inhumane for slaves. For his part, Deslondes lives on as one of the most courageous—and, in some ways, successful—slave insurgents in American history.

—Dave Powell

Further Reading

Ingersoll, Thomas N. *Mammon and Manon in Early New Orleans: The First Slave Society in the Deep South, 1718–1819.* Knoxville: University of Tennessee Press, 1999.

"The Louisiana Purchase: A Heritage Explored." Online Educational Resource from the LSU Libraries' Special Collections. http://www.lib.lsu.edu/special/purchase/history.html (accessed September 4, 2008).

Smith, Jessie Carney. *Black Firsts: 2,000 Years of Extraordinary Achievement.* Detroit, MI: Visible Ink Press, 1994.

Thompson, Thomas Marshall. "National Newspaper and Legislative Reactions to Louisiana's Deslondes Slave Revolt of 1811." *Louisiana History* 33 (1992): 5–29.

Gabriel (d. 1800)

The revolt planned and nearly consummated by a blacksmith named Gabriel, in 1800 in Virginia, was very different from the stereotypical image of slave revolts. By the laws of Virginia, Gabriel was the property of Thomas Prosser.

Commonly referred to as "Prosser's Gabriel," he himself never took Prosser's name. Gabriel organized a predominantly urban insurrection, planning to conclude it by "drinking and dining with the merchants of the city when our freedom has been agreed to." The plan was to seize the state capital, Richmond, secure the person of Governor James Monroe, then bargain for abolition of slavery. At least two other leaders of the conspiracy were blacksmiths, like Gabriel; most of those convicted in court for their participation were also skilled artisans. Many were literate, and Gabriel was well acquainted with published news and political events in the United States and the Atlantic world. In rural areas, support was recruited not only among agricultural laborers, but enslaved workers in nearby coal mines, and the river boatmen who were essential to Virginia's transportation and trade. It is probable that a number of people classified as "white" were at least sympathetic to, if not actively assisting the rebellion. Whatever records that may have shed light on that question were forwarded to Governor James Monroe, never produced in court, and never found again. Gabriel ordered that Quakers, Methodists, and Frenchmen were not to be killed, the first two because both churches had taken strong antislavery positions at the time, the latter because revolutionary France had abolished slavery in all its colonies in 1794.

Slaves comprised 48 percent of Virginia's population, as recorded in the 1800 census, the highest proportion in the state's history. With a substantial free African American population, residents of African descent may have been a majority. In the state capital itself, one-half of the population was African American, and one-fifth of those were free. Virginia agriculture was in a difficult transition, with tobacco production sharply declining and cotton not yet a large-scale cash crop. Farmland was being planted in wheat and corn, which did not require intensive field labor, leaving plantations with little work to assign to large numbers of slaves. A common practice was to instruct slaves to hire their time—which meant, go find a job, and bring your master the money when you get paid. It appears that the enslaved and free African American communities held skilled crafts and literacy in high regard. Organizers for the army Gabriel planned to assemble made a point of displaying such skills to potential recruits. Hiring out was also considered a desirable status, if only because it permitted more freedom of movement, without obtaining a written pass for each trip off an owner's property. The ability to write, of course, meant the ability to forge a pass for oneself, or for others. Planned for the night of August 30, 1800, the insurrection was delayed by torrential rains, which blocked roads into Richmond. On either the day of or the day after the storm, at least four enslaved persons betrayed the plan. Forty-four men were convicted of participation, 26 or 27 were hanged, and the rest either pardoned or sold outside of the United States.

—*Charles Rosenberg*

Further Reading

Egerton, Douglas. *Gabriel's Rebellion: The Virginia Slave Conspiracies of 1800 and 1802.* Chapel Hill: University of North Carolina Press, 1993.

Sidbury, James. *Plowshares into Swords: Race, Rebellion, and Identity in Gabriel's Virginia.* New York: Cambridge University Press, 1997.

Vesey, Denmark (c. 1767–1822)

Denmark Vesey, leader of the largest and perhaps the most tightly organized slave conspiracy in American history, was a free carpenter in Charleston, South Carolina, when he began the work that has made his name so well known. The first record of his existence was in 1781, when he was purchased, at the port of Charlotte Amalie on St. Thomas Island, by Captain Joseph Vesey, at the age of approximately 14. Resold among a cargo of 390 enslaved persons in the French colony of Saint Domingue (now Haiti), the young man either suffered, or contrived, fits of epilepsy, so that on a return voyage, the purchaser demanded that Captain Vesey buy him back as unfit for work. Vesey named him Telemaque, assigning him as a cabin boy during subsequent voyages. At the end of 1782, Captain Vesey sailed into Charles Town (later Charleston), South Carolina, newly evacuated by a British fleet, and Telemaque became a chandler's man—helping to receive and catalog imported merchandise in the captain's business office. By 1800, his given name had evolved to Denmark, when he won a lottery prize of $1,500. He purchased his liberty for $600, and opened his own carpentry shop, at some point adopting the surname of his former owner. Greatly admired in both the free colored community and the enslaved African community—which were quite separate from each other—Denmark Vesey was also respected for the quality of his work by customers designated as "white" who were the city's elite.

Roughly seven years before 1822, when his plans were discovered, Vesey decided to "see what I could do for my fellow creatures." He recruited Peter Poyas, Rolla Bennett, Ned Bennett, Monday Gell, and Gullah Jack, who helped him assemble some 9,000 prepared to rise at his command. Vesey took careful notice of the cultural identities within the enslaved communities of South Carolina at the time, including a substantial number of Ibo, about 10 percent Muslim, as well as the Gullah community, which had blended African and British cultures. Vesey intended to kill every "white" person in Charles Town, at that time no more than one-fifth of the population; load all enslaved persons onto ships in the harbor, with every valuable they could take from the city; and sail to Haiti, the only nation in the world forged in a successful uprising by enslaved people. Vesey scheduled

Sunday, July 22, 1822, as the day to mobilize. Many Africans from surrounding plantations would be in Charleston on a Sunday, and many of the city's elite would be escaping from the summer heat at northern resorts. Like most conspiracies, the plan was betrayed not once, but twice. The first informant knew only a little, so that Poyas, Harth, and Bennett were able to boldly deny that anything was amiss. Vesey moved up the date to strike to Sunday, June 16, but a second betrayal was taken more seriously. A lower-level recruiter spoke to Peter Prioleau, who promptly informed his owner, Colonel J. C. Prioleau. With militia mobilized to secure the previously unguarded armory—a key point Vesey planned to seize—and patrols in the street, there was no hope of success. The leadership was swiftly arrested, 35 hanged, and 37 banished from the state.

—*Charles Rosenberg*

Further Reading

Egerton, Douglas R. *He Shall Go Out Free: The Lives of Denmark Vesey.* Lanham, MD: Rowman & Littlefield, 2004.

Robertson, David. *Denmark Vesey: The Buried Story of America's Largest Slave Rebellion and the Man Who Led It.* New York: Vintage Books, 1999.

Description of Denmark Vesey (1822)

Denmark Vesey (c. 1767–1822) was an African American slave who was brought to Charleston, South Carolina, from the Caribbean island of St. Thomas in the early 1780s. In 1799, he purchased his freedom from his master, Captain Joseph Vesey, and worked in Charleston as a carpenter. Angered by the forced closing of an African Methodist Episcopal Church he had helped found, Vesey began planning a slave insurrection that soon encompassed many slaves in Charleston and along the Carolina coast. Betrayed to the authorities by two slaves who opposed his plan, Vesey and many of his supporters were arrested and convicted of conspiracy. Thirty-five men, including Vesey, were hanged. The following is a 19th-century description of Vesey.

As Denmark Vesey has occupied so large a place in the conspiracy, a brief notice of him will, perhaps, be not devoid of interest. The following anecdote will show how near he was to the chance of being distinguished in the bloody events of San Domingo. During the revolutionary war, Captain Vesey, now an old resident of this city, commanded a ship that traded between St. Thomas and Cape Francais (San Domingo). He was engaged in supplying the French of that Island with Slaves. In the year 1781, he took on board at St. Thomas 390 slaves and sailed for the Cape; on the passage, he and his officers were struck with the beauty, alertness and intelligence of a boy about 14 years of age, whom they made a pet of, by taking him into the cabin, changing his apparel, and calling him by way of distinction Telemaque, (which appellation has since, by gradual corruption, among the negroes, been changed to Denmark, or sometimes Tebaak). On the arrival, however, of the ship at the Cape, Captain Vesey, having no use for the boy, sold him among his other slaves, and returned to St. Thomas. On his next voyage to the Cape, he was surprised to learn from his consignee that Telemaque would be returned on his hands, as the planter, who had purchased him, represented him unsound, and subject to epileptic fits. According to the custom of trade in that place, the boy was placed in the hands of the king's physician, who decided that he was unsound, and Captain Vesey was compelled to take him back, of which he had no occasion to repent, as Denmark proved, for 20 years, a most faithful slave. In 1800, Denmark drew a prize of $1500 in the East-Bay-Street Lottery, with which he purchased his freedom from his master, at six hundred dollars, much less than his real value. From that period to day of his apprehension he has been working as a carpenter in this city, distinguished for great strength and activity. Among his colour he was always looked up to with awe and respect. His temper was impetuous and domineering in the extreme, qualifying him for the despotic rule, of which he was ambitious. All his passions were ungovernable and, savage; and to his numerous wives and children, he displayed the haughty and capricious cruelty of Eastern Bashaw. He had nearly effected his escape, after information had been lodged against him. For three days the town was searched for him without success. As early as Monday, the 17th, he had concealed himself. It was not until the night of the 22d of June, during a perfect tempest, that he was found secreted in the house of one of his wives. It is to the uncommon efforts and vigilance of Mr. Wesner, and Capt. Dove, of the City Guard, (the latter of whom seized him) that public justice received its necessary tribute, in the execution of this man. If the party had been one moment later, he would, in all probability, have effected his escape the next day in some outward bound vessel.

Source: Joshua Coffin, *An Account of Some of the Principal Slave Insurrections, and Others, which Have Occurred, or Been Attempted, in the United States and Elsewhere, during the Last Two Centuries, with Various Remarks* (New York: American Anti-Slavery Society, 1860).

Nat Turner's Rebellion (1831)

Nat Turner's Rebellion, also known as the Southampton County rebellion, began on August 21, 1831, in Virginia, about 70 miles southeast of Richmond. It is remembered as one of a handful of antebellum slave revolts that profoundly changed the attitudes of white Americans toward slavery, and may, in fact, have had the most significant lasting impact on the politics of slavery and on the way slavery is remembered as an institution in American cultural memory. The insurrection's apparent mastermind, Nat Turner, is a man with multiple identities in the historical record, his personality and motives endlessly shaped by the legions of historians who have attempted to place the rebellion in the wider context of American history and, for that matter, in the context of human social relationships in the 19th and 20th centuries. Turner is remembered as a hero, a villain, a remorseless monster, a brave and bold visionary, a crazed madman, and a liberator—all depending on the perspective of the person remembering Turner and his exploits. He has been lionized as a hero of the abolitionist movement and condemned as a mass murderer of innocent women and children. His personality, and the insurrection he led, suffuses American popular culture, at once representing both the tragic consequences of humans holding other humans in bondage while at the same time symbolizing principled resistance to inhuman suffering through cunning, ingenuity, and guile. While certain incontrovertible facts of the rebellion remain, little is actually known of Nat Turner and the motives that caused him to undertake his mission, leaving historians to piece together incomplete accounts of what Turner did and why he did it.

Who Was Nat Turner?

Nat Turner was born on October 2, 1800, in Southampton County, Virginia. He soon found himself identified as a person with unusual gifts of intelligence when, at the age of three or four, he allegedly was overheard by his mother telling some other children about events that had occurred before he was born. Since almost no record exists either of Nat Turner's personal life or events that occurred within it, let alone any record written in his own hand, it is difficult to say if such stories reflect the legend of the plot Turner eventually consummated as an adult, or are

A newspaper cartoon depicts the violent slave uprising led by Nat Turner that began on August 22, 1831, when Turner killed his master and his master's family. The revolt only lasted about a week but Turner eluded capture until October of that year. He was later tried and hanged for the crime. (Library of Congress)

accurate representations of things that happened in his life. Indeed, the predominant caricature of Nat Turner as an astutely intelligent and deeply religious slave has served cross-purposes for historians and cultural commentators since even before Turner was hanged for his role in the Southampton rebellion. On the one hand, his intelligence was used in the immediate aftermath of the insurrection to justify the imposition of even harsher regulations on the education of slaves in Virginia and across the South. On the other hand, Turner's remarkable intelligence is also often cited as evidence of the enormous fissures in the proslavery worldview, much of which was based on the idea that Africans were inherently inferior to white people. What little historians do know about Turner and his life comes largely from a conversation Turner had with a white lawyer named Thomas Ruffin Gray while Turner was awaiting execution. This conversation was, of course, recorded and recounted by Gray, who, for better or worse, filtered Turner's words to publish them in the newspaper.

Whatever Nat Turner's experiences were as a boy, he was encouraged to become a preacher by both his master and his grandmother, who noted in Turner "uncommon intelligence for a child" and, according to Gray's report of Turner's confession, believed that his intelligence would result in him never being "of any service to anyone as a slave." As a young man, Turner began to see visions. He ran away from slavery in 1821, only to return—"to the astonishment of the Negroes on the plantation," he later said—30 days later when he said he was told in a vision to return to the service of his "earthly master." Turner also described seeing, in the same vision, "white and black spirits engaged in battle" as "blood flowed in the streams," while a voice warned him: "Such is your luck, such you are called to see; and let it come rough or smooth, you must surely bear it."

In 1825, after Turner had been sold following the death of his previous owner, he experienced another vision. This time, he said he saw "lights in the sky" that were "the lights of the Saviour's hands" and said that he "wondered greatly" about the visions he saw "and prayed to be informed of a certainty of the meaning thereof." Later, while working in a cornfield, Turner claimed to have seen "drops of blood dripping on the corn, as though it were dew from heaven." Turner shared his strange experience with others, along with an interpretation of them. In his view, "the blood of Christ had been shed on this earth, and had ascended for the salvation of sinners, and was now returning to earth again in the form of dew." Turner took this to mean that "the Saviour was about to lay down the yoke he had borne for the sins of men," signaling that "the great day of judgment was at hand." Turner also reported sharing his visions with a white man named Etheldred T. Brantley, who, upon hearing them, was attacked with a "cutaneous eruption" that could only be healed by nine days of fasting and prayer. This apparently only strengthened Turner's conviction that he had become a messenger of God and had been called to undertake a revolution.

Nearly three years after that, on May 12, 1828, Turner had a third vision. On this occasion, Turner claimed that he was visited by a spirit from heaven that instructed him to "fight against the Serpent, for the time was fast approaching when the first should be last and the last should be first." When he was asked, in his jail cell after the rebellion (where Turner recounted these events to Thomas Ruffin Gray), if he found himself mistaken about what he had seen, Turner replied curtly: "Was not Christ crucified?" Turner expected to receive a sign indicating when he should "commence the great work," and when it did, he would know the time had come: "I should arise and prepare myself and slay my enemies with their own weapons," as he put it.

In February 1831, an eclipse of the sun occurred, and Turner took it to be a sign that he should begin his insurrection. He began to share his plans with four other slaves whom he identified as Henry, Hark, Nelson, and Sam, and together they planned to carry out their attack on July 4. When Turner fell ill at the appointed time, the insurrection was abruptly postponed, but not canceled. A little over a month later, on August 13, another atmospheric disturbance occurred. This time, Turner and his men were ready. They went into the woods a week later, on August 21, to eat and drink and make their plans. At the rendezvous point, the men were joined by two other slaves named Will and Jack. Suspicious of their motives for being there, Turner asked Will what had made him want to join the group of rebels. "He answered," Turner said, that "his life was worth no more than others, and his liberty as dear to him." When Turner asked Will if he hoped to obtain his freedom, Turner said that Will replied "he would, or lose his life."

The Rebellion

The group emerged from the woods at two o'clock the following morning to make their way to the home of Joseph Travis, whom Turner described as "a kind master" who had "placed the greatest confidence" in him. In fact, at the time, Turner was technically owned by Travis's stepson, a child named Putnam Moore, whose mother was the widow of Turner's previous owner, Thomas Moore. It was at the Travis home that the insurrection began.

The plan was set: "until we had armed and equipped ourselves and gathered sufficient force," Turner later said, "neither age nor sex was to be spared"—in other words, not even women and children would be spared by the insurrectionists. Turner reported that he "placed fifteen or twenty of the best armed and most to be relied on in front" after the first attacks to strike terror into the inhabitants of the homes the slaves attacked and to prevent the escape of any of their victims. Turner positioned himself at the rear of the phalanx of attacking slaves, where, as he put it, he sometimes "got in sight in time to see the work of death completed," and to have "viewed the mangled bodies as they lay, in silent satisfaction."

Turner described the murders committed by the slaves in gruesome detail. He described the murder of men and women who were still in their beds, said many times that victims barely had time to utter a word before being clubbed to death, and even described how two members of the group returned to the Travis home to complete their grisly work there after realizing that they had left a sleeping baby untouched. Turner described murdering a woman named Mrs. Waller and 10 children, then proceeding to the home of William Williams, where Williams and two young boys were killed while their mother fled. According to Turner, she was returned to the home and instructed to lay beside her dead husband, "where she was shot dead." He described being unable to kill one woman because his sword blade was too dull; she was finally killed by Will. At the home of a Mrs. Whitehead, Turner found the woman's daughter, Margaret, hiding near the cellar outside. "On my approach, she fled," Turner reported, "but was soon overtaken, and after repeated blows with a sword I killed her by a blow on the head with a fence rail."

Before it was all over, nearly 60 white men, women, and children had been murdered by Turner and the slaves who had joined him. " 'Twas my object to carry terror and devastation wherever we went," Turner allegedly told Thomas Gray, and in this respect, the rebellion was a very successful one indeed.

Retribution

Response to word of the insurrection was swift and extensive: the state of Virginia dispatched local militia, three companies of artillery, and even detachments of men who were stationed aboard naval vessels at Norfolk to suppress the rebellion. Whites from neighboring North Carolina also joined the assembling force. In the immediate aftermath of the killings perpetrated by Turner and the slaves who had joined him, information was limited, and rumors spread quickly. Needless to say, rural Virginia in the 1830s lacked such modern amenities as telephones and other modes of communication. The discoveries made by whites investigating and hoping to suppress the rebellion were undoubtedly augmented and embellished by those who recounted them to others, only adding to the panic that had engulfed white Virginians. One Richmond newspaper reported that the Southampton insurrection was part of a larger group of rebellions carried out as far away as Alabama.

As a result, the paper's editor reported, hundreds of slaves and perhaps even some free blacks were slaughtered without trial and with a level of malice and barbarity that rivaled the murders committed by Turner and his cohorts. The murders continued for several days, even weeks, after the rebellion had been put down. A Lynchburg newspaper reported that a regiment of troops had been commanded to carry out the murders of more than 90 blacks. They had also killed the slaves' presumed leader, then cut off his limbs and hung them separately to inspire terror in the remaining slaves in the area. A minister writing in the *New York Post* reported correctly that the number of blacks killed in the aftermath of the rebellion would never be known.

Meanwhile, Nat Turner evaded capture for over two months while his coconspirators were rounded up, one by one. This, as historian Scot French has noted, only raised Turner's stature. He was finally captured on October 30, when a dog found him hiding in a cave near the Travis plantation where he had been held as a slave. While he was in jail awaiting his trial and eventual execution, Turner was visited by Thomas Ruffin Gray, a white lawyer determined to capture Turner's story and have it published so that white people in Virginia and elsewhere could begin to understand what had happened. Describing Turner, Gray wrote: "The calm, deliberate composure with which he spoke of his late deeds and intentions, the expression of his fiend-like face when excited by enthusiasm; still bearing the stains of the blood of helpless innocence about him; clothed with rags and covered with chains, yet daring to raise his manacled hands to heaven; with a spirit soaring above the attributes of man, I looked on him and my blood curdled in my veins."

Turner was convicted of leading the uprising and sentenced to death, He was hanged in Jerusalem, Virginia, on November 11, 1831. After his death, Turner's body was dismembered and actually distributed as souvenirs to white people desperate for some form of revenge; as recently as 2003, his skull was reported to have been found in Indiana, where it was to be the centerpiece of a new museum located there. All told, the Commonwealth of Virginia executed 56 blacks accused of participating in the insurrection.

Nat Turner's Rebellion in History and Memory

The instant celebrity of Nat Turner, who came to be known as the mastermind of the Southampton rebellion, led the Virginia General Assembly to begin discussing long-term plans for addressing the problem of slavery. The fact that the insurrection is commonly known as Nat Turner's Rebellion, and was even then, indicates that the myth of Nat Turner continues to drive interpretations of what caused it and what it means in the larger context of American history and the history of slavery. Horrified by the symbolism of Turner's rebellion—the fact that the original plan had been to execute the insurrection on July 4, and the overtly religious and militaristic tone used by Turner to explain the event in his "confession"—and aware of Gray's depiction of Turner as a literate and highly intelligent slave, the General Assembly passed a series of laws that forbade the education of slaves and restricted their ability to hold religious meetings without white people present.

The Virginia General Assembly's session of 1831–1832 was a remarkable one, for it helped cement the response of white southerners to the issue of slavery and slave rebellion. Thomas Jefferson had warned in 1820, during the crisis brought about by Missouri's application for admission to the Union, that the slavery issue would eventually explode into something terrifying politically. "We have a wolf by the ear, and we can neither hold him nor safely let him go," he wrote to his friend John Holmes. "Justice is in one scale, and self-preservation in the other." Jefferson's prescient words did little to advance the arguments of the small cadre of abolitionists and moderates in Virginia in the 1820s. Even Virginia's governor, John Floyd, had supported resettlement of slaves outside of Virginia (a position also favored by former president James Monroe, for whom the capital of Liberia, a country on the west coast of Africa established as a potential landing place for exported slaves, was named), but these plans were abruptly halted in the aftermath of the Southampton insurrection. It is unclear whether the insurrection put the southern states on an inexorable collision course with the federal government over the issue of slavery—the issue itself was much larger than a single uprising in Virginia, no matter how significant that uprising was—but the Southampton revolt almost certainly hardened the views of slave owners across the South and likewise changed the positions of white moderates in the region. It also resulted in yet more harsh restrictions being placed on the black populations of southern states. In the end, faced with a decision on how to handle the future of slavery in Virginia, the General Assembly decided to up the ante rather than search for a viable long-term solution. The state's elite would tighten its hold on the slave population.

The tightening grip of the state on slaves did not just represent the growing paranoia of whites about the nature of the slave population, however. Just as other states and cities had responded to slave uprisings by cracking down on the movements of free blacks and limiting the educational and cultural opportunities afforded to slaves, Virginia chose to make slavery even less defensible and tolerable as an institution, if such a thing was possible. Ironically, the "positive good" arguments made to justify slavery during the Missouri crisis and later given new voice by the social theorist George Fitzhugh in his books *Sociology for the South* (1854) and *Cannibals All!* (1857) were crippled immensely by the responses of various government entities to slave uprisings. In a simple sense, it was reasonable for abolitionists in the North to ask why slaves had to be treated so poorly if the institution itself was good for them.

Despite careful attempts to classify slave insurrections as isolated events engineered by charismatic madmen like Nat Turner, it became increasingly clear to many in both the North and South after 1830 that the moral concerns expressed about slavery by abolitionists should be taken very seriously. Social commentators began to wonder how the denial of basic rights to slaves by their owners could result in anything but violence and resentment.

Moreover, decisions to tighten black codes in the South after the Southampton rebellion paved the way for the harsh Fugitive Slave Law that was passed as part of the controversial Compromise of 1850, which was necessitated by the acquisition of new territory following the U.S. war with Mexico. Southern congressmen demanded such a law be included in the Compromise, perhaps only delaying the inevitable: a full-scale war between the states to settle the question of whether slavery should be legal once and for all. To say that Nat Turner's decisions set in motion this extraordinary series of events is not entirely correct—it is not difficult to imagine the Civil War happening even without Turner's rebellion having ever taken place, after all—but certainly the insurrection itself and its aftermath helped sharpen the lines that separated those who supported slavery from those who opposed it.

Regardless, Turner continues to live on in American history and cultural memory as something of an enigma, if not a completely unknowable individual. Because Turner was a slave, and therefore considered property and not fully a person in a legal sense, the only real record of his life comes from the "confessions" he allegedly made to Gray at the Southampton County jail in November 1831. Thus, while the historical record of Turner's insurrection and the its consequences reflects the actions of such parties as the Virginia General Assembly, the U.S. Congress, and countless individuals, the *memory* of Nat Turner in American life is somewhat more difficult to pin down. Whereas history depends on the written record, almost no record exists of Turner's life with the exception of Gray's pamphlet.

As a result, historians and cultural observers continue to be vexed by the confessions, since there is no way of knowing whether the words attributed to Turner by Gray were actually his own. On the one hand, Gray clearly may have been motivated by the same thing that motivated many prominent whites at the time he met Turner: namely, a desire to attach some kind of explanation to the insurrection so that the fears of white people could be assuaged. On the other hand, it is entirely possible that Gray lacked either the creativity or the initiative to create a profile of Turner entirely on his own. To have done so would have been remarkable, given the short time between Gray's interview with Turner and the subsequent publication of *The Confessions of Nat Turner.* Moreover, Gray claimed on the cover of the pamphlet that the entire transcript of the "confessions" had been read in court in Southampton County on November 5, 1831, where Turner allegedly acknowledged the veracity of the account.

Nevertheless, the confessions raise more questions about Nat Turner than answers. The pamphlet has allowed Turner to be portrayed differently by people with disparate motives for remembering him. Gray's insistence that the confessions were accurate provide cover to historians and others intent on portraying Turner as something of a hero, as a person who responded to horrors of slavery with a terrifying rampage of his own, and who spoke of his exploits calmly and with conviction and intelligence. To many, Turner's actions are made understandable, if not necessarily justifiable, by the dehumanization and violence engendered by the institution of slavery; and to these observers, Turner's confessions offer a glimpse into the deep sense of frustration and religious evangelism that must have driven him to do what he did. Others demonize Turner not only for recounting the deaths of so many people to Gray, but for doing so in such grisly detail. In their view, Turner is nothing but a monster, a fanatic bent on exacting revenge blindly from any white person who had the misfortune of crossing his path on the morning of August 22, 1831.

At the same time, doubts about the role Gray may have played in recording Turner's alleged confessions make it possible to discount the more gruesome aspects of Turner's account and focus on the fact that Turner was bold enough to take up arms to fight against slavery. This point is easy for observers to overlook today, but to generations of historians who believed that slaves were irrevocably damaged psychologically and emotionally by slavery, the idea that a slave could have the wherewithal and the desire to foment such an insurrection was a profound one indeed.

The many competing visions of Turner came to a head with the 1967 publication of a novel, *The Confessions of Nat Turner*, written by William Styron. Styron has said that he was encouraged to write the novel from the perspective of Nat Turner by his friend and fellow writer James Baldwin, who praised Styron, after the novel was published, for beginning "to write the common history—ours." The book was awarded the Pulitzer Prize for fiction in 1968 but did not receive universal acclaim. Styron's book was the subject of especially biting criticism from a group of African American writers who were offended by Styron's suggestion in the novel that Turner had harbored amorous feelings for Margaret Whitehead, the young white woman he said he had killed with a fence post during the insurrection. In 1968, a rebuttal to the novel titled *William Styron's Nat Turner: Ten Black Writers Respond* was published, detailing a litany of complaints about the liberties Styron had taken in his portrayal of Turner and the rebellion. The resulting furor made the book more popular than ever and raised serious questions about issues of race, violence, slavery, and reconciliation simmering below the surface of American culture in the 1960s. The controversy was revealing in many ways, not least of all because it exposed the simple reality that Styron's novel could be considered no more or less reliable as an authentic account of the event than was Thomas Ruffin Gray's own report of Turner's "confessions" from 1831.

Today, nearly 200 years after the Southampton rebellion occurred, historians and other cultural commentators continue to investigate the character at its very epicenter: Nat Turner. Many historians, and certainly many teachers, are simply unsure of what to do with Turner, and for many American students, the rebellion he led remains an uninvestigated mystery. Nevertheless Nat Turner's rebellion is remembered by nearly everyone who studies it as a tragic consequence of the United States' long and calamitous association with the "peculiar institution" of legalized slavery.

—*Dave Powell*

See also all entries under Stono Rebellion (1739); New York Slave Insurrection (1741); Antebellum Suppressed Slave Revolts (1800s–1850s); New Orleans Riot (1866); New Orleans Race Riot (1900); Atlanta Race Riot (1906); Springfield Race Riot (1908); Houston Riot (1917); Red Summer (1919); Tulsa Race Riot (1921); Civil Rights Movement (1953–1968); Watts Riot (1965); Detroit Riots (1967); Los Angeles Uprising (1992).

Further Reading

Aptheker, Herbert. *Nat Turner's Slave Rebellion, Together with the Full-Text of the So-called "Confessions" of Nat Turner Made in Prison in 1831.* New York: Humanities Press, 1966.

Drewry, William Sidney. *The Southampton Insurrection.* Washington, DC: The Neale Co., 1900.

French, Scot. *The Rebellious Slave: Nat Turner in American Memory.* Boston and New York: Houghton Mifflin Company, 2004.

Gray, Thomas Ruffin. *The Confession, Trial, and Execution of Nat Turner, the Negro Insurrectionist; Also a List of Persons Murdered in the Insurrection in Southampton County, Virginia, August 21st and 22nd, 1831, with Introductory Remarks.* Petersburg, VA: J. B. Edge, Printer, 1881.

Greenberg, Kenneth S., ed. *Nat Turner: A Slave Rebellion in History and Memory.* New York: Oxford University Press, 2003.

Oates, Stephen B. *The Fires of Jubilee: Nat Turner's Fierce Rebellion.* New York: Harper & Row, 1990.

Styron, William. *The Confessions of Nat Turner.* New York: Random House, 1967.

Tragle, Henry Irving. *The Southampton Slave Revolt of 1831: A Compilation of Source Material.* Amherst: University of Massachusetts Press, 1971.

Wolf, Eva Sheppard. *Race and Liberty in the New Nation: Emancipation in Virginia from the Revolution to Nat Turner's Rebellion.* Baton Rouge: Louisiana State University Press, 2006.

Abolitionists

Abolitionists advocated the immediate and unconditional end of slavery in the United States, primarily in the 18th and 19th centuries. Typically, references to abolitionists relate to American writers, intellectuals, former slaves, freedmen, and social activists who labored to end slavery in the United States beginning in the 1830s.

Although some abolitionists worked tirelessly through well-organized antislavery societies to abolish the institution, abolitionism more broadly describes efforts to end slavery that held adherents together through a shared sense of moral and intellectual purpose. Their work was undertaken with awareness of the fact that the United States had been founded on the premise that "all men are created equal" even though the institution of slavery was very much present at the nation's moment of creation. Although neither the word "slave" nor the word "slavery" are explicitly mentioned in the U.S. Constitution, discussion of the future of slavery was prominent at the Constitutional Convention.

The idea that all men are, in fact, created equal helped galvanize the abolitionist movement. Spurred by Enlightenment philosophy (as the architects of the nation's government had been) and by no small measure of religious fervor, abolitionists formed societies and founded newspapers devoted to the proposition that slavery should be immediately abolished. Abolitionists were not merely antislavery advocates; they saw themselves as participants in a zero-sum game where the complete dismantling of the slave system could be the only acceptable outcome.

Of course slavery was very deeply entrenched in the society of 19th-century America. Abolitionists in the United States—most of whom lived and worked in the North—labored tirelessly to turn the tide of public opinion against slavery. Perhaps the most prominent abolitionist was a newspaper editor named William Lloyd Garrison. He edited a radical abolitionist newspaper known as *The Liberator*, which argued for the "immediate and complete emancipation of all slaves" held in the United States. Garrison, along with Arthur Tappan, founded the American Anti-Slavery Society in 1833, and saw its membership ranks swell in the years that followed. Former slaves, including Frederick Douglass, were frequently featured speakers at meetings of the society, and many prominent white writers, such as John Greenleaf Whittier and Harriet Beecher Stowe (author of *Uncle Tom's Cabin*), were also widely recognized as abolitionists.

Although earlier attempts to end slavery had focused on such schemes as repatriating slaves to Africa either wholesale or by creating colonies there (such as Liberia, which took its capital city's name from a well-known proponent of colonization, President James Monroe), abolitionism was recognized after the 1830s as a movement not only to end slavery, but to see to the integration of former slaves into American society as well. Even after the Emancipation Proclamation was issued by President Lincoln in 1863, abolitionists continued to fight for the total destruction of slavery in all parts of the United States. The Thirteenth Amendment to the Constitution finally put a legal end to slavery in 1865, but the cause of abolishing social, economic, and other forms of discrimination based on race has continued unabated. Abolitionists left a legacy of literary and political discourse on human freedom that distinguishes their efforts and provides inspiration to millions who believe in social justice even today.

—Dave Powell

Further Reading

Alonso, Harriet Hyman. *Growing up Abolitionist: The Story of the Garrison Children.* Amherst: University of Massachusetts Press, 2002.

Harrold, Stanley. *American Abolitionists.* New York: Longman, 2001.

Lowance, Mason, ed. *Against Slavery: An Abolitionist Reader.* New York: Penguin Books, 2000.

Confessions of Nat Turner

The *Confessions of Nat Turner* refers simultaneously to a fictional literary sensation published in 1967, an extant document published in the form of a pamphlet in early 1832, and an actual historical event that occurred in the fall of 1831. That event was a meeting that took place in the Southampton County jail in Virginia following the largest slave insurrection in the history of the United States. The insurrection's mastermind was a slave named Nat (he has since been known by the surname Turner, after his master), one of the more controversial figures in the history of the antebellum United States. Remembered as an intelligent and religious man, Nat Turner conceived and led a rebellion in the Virginia Tidewater in August 1831 that resulted in the murder of 60 white men, women, and children on various plantations in Southampton County.

By October of that year, Nat Turner had been captured and was brought to trial. While awaiting his eventual execution, Turner was interviewed by Thomas Ruffin Gray, a local white lawyer and scion of a wealthy Virginia family. Gray took it upon himself to record Turner's "confession" of the crimes he had committed so that posterity may note both the causes of the insurrection and the singular character of Nat Turner, its mastermind. Gray reported that Turner took sole responsibility for plotting the insurrection and claimed to not have shared his plans with anyone other than a few close confidants. Furthermore, Gray said that Turner claimed to have no knowledge of any wider plot to rebel against slavery in other parts of Virginia or the south. Historians have since suggested that Gray made these claims, with Turner as their mouthpiece, to help quell the fears of whites deeply shaken by Turner's insurrection. Significantly, Gray's motives have also been ascribed to demonstrating to northern abolitionists and evangelist preachers that Turner's intelligence was their fault: by sharing with him the possibility of freedom, Gray argued, abolitionists had turned Turner into a fanatical killing machine.

Gray's report of Turner's "confession" has since ignited controversies that reveal the limitations of historical research even as they shed light on the character of the man who led the largest (and, by some measures, most successful) slave uprising in the history of the United States. Gray's description of his interactions with Turner cemented the view of Nat Turner as a larger-than-life figure who was literate, passionate, and eminently capable of narrating his own story. This image of the intelligent slave did much to humanize Turner and rendered him at once both a seemingly knowable and unknowable historical figure. At the same time, Gray's account disarmed a key component of the proslavery worldview, namely that slaves were practically inhuman and thus incapable of intelligent thought and feeling.

Nat Turner's rebellion and confession also inspired novelist William Styron, a Virginia native born in 1925, to write an eponymous fictional account of Turner's "confession" that won the Pulitzer Prize for fiction in 1968. Despite the acclaim, Styron received heavy criticism from African American historians and writers for repeating many of the stereotypes of slaves given credence by Thomas Gray. The controversy over Styron's novel revealed with great intensity the fine line that runs between "truth" and fiction and illustrated that "historians," such as Thomas Gray, often act with particular motives in mind. Whereas Gray presented himself to the public as a chronicler of Turner's confession, historians now largely agree that Gray's own motives played a significant part in shaping whatever Turner may have said to suit Gray's own aspirations as a lawyer and pamphleteer. In the end, the conversations between Gray and Turner are lost to history, but the legend of Nat Turner lives on, largely because of the confessions he made to Thomas Gray.

—*Dave Powell*

Further Reading

French, Scot. *The Rebellious Slave: Nat Turner in American Memory*. Boston and New York: Houghton Mifflin Company, 2004.

Gray, Thomas Ruffin. *The Confession, Trial, and Execution of Nat Turner, the Negro Insurrectionist; Also a List of Persons Murdered in the Insurrection in Southampton*

County, Virginia, August 21st and 22nd, 1831, with Introductory Remarks. Petersburg, VA: J. B. Edge, Printer, 1881.

Greenberg, Kenneth S., ed. *Nat Turner: A Slave Rebellion in History and Memory.* New York: Oxford University Press, 2003.

Styron, William. *The Confessions of Nat Turner.* New York: Random House, 1967.

Wolf, Eva Sheppard. *Race and Liberty in the New Nation: Emancipation in Virginia from the Revolution to Nat Turner's Rebellion.* Baton Rouge: Louisiana State University Press, 2006.

Moses Story

The Moses story refers to biblical passages that provided inspiration to African Americans who sought freedom from the bonds of slavery in the years before the Civil War. Moses was a figure in the Old Testament who led the Israelites out of slavery and into the Promised Land. The story of Moses served as a powerful allegory for slaves hopeful that they could one day be delivered from their captivity through religious faith and perseverance. It also reflected the influence of Western biblical traditions on slaves who integrated the teachings of Western Christianity with African rhythms and religious customs to forge a distinct culture of their own.

The story of Moses is one of pain, suffering, and deliverance. In the Bible, Moses, the child of a Hebrew slave, is sentenced to death along with other slave children but saved when his mother places him on a makeshift raft and sends him floating down the Nile River. Moses was eventually raised by an Egyptian princess and educated in the advanced Egyptian society. His religious visions began when, at about age 40, he was instructed by a burning bush to lead the Hebrews out of slavery and into the so-called "Promised Land." Moses persuaded the Israelites to follow him, but the Pharaoh would not let them go; this passage became the inspiration for the spiritual hymn "Go Down Moses (Let My People Go)":

> Go down, Moses,
> Way down in Egypt land,
> Tell ole Pharaoh
> Let my people go!

The Pharaoh's refusal to allow the Israelites to follow Moses resulted in the visitation of 10 plagues upon the people of Egypt, and eventually Moses parted the seas to permit the exodus of the Israelites out of captivity.

The story of Moses provided powerful inspiration for slaves who feared that they may never taste the fruit of freedom. Like the Israelites, many slaves believed they would eventually reach the Promised Land despite their many years of debasement, pain, and turmoil. Also like the Israelites, slaves believed that their connection to one another, and their faith in a higher power that believed in justice, would end their misery. The story of Moses and the Israelites inspired countless slaves to resist the institution of slavery and helped sow the seeds of rebellion against it.

The story of the Israelites' exodus from Egypt also had a very real contemporary corollary for many slaves: the Underground Railroad. "Conductors" on the "railroad" led slaves out of the South and into freedom in the North. None was more daring than Harriet Tubman, a slave born in Dorchester County, Maryland, around 1820. During a 10-year period prior to 1860, Tubman made no fewer than 19 trips into the South to escort more than 300 slaves to freedom, including her own parents who had aged into their seventies at the time. For her efforts, Tubman was later anointed "The Moses of Her People"—a fitting moniker for someone who led so many from the darkness of captivity to the light of freedom.

—Dave Powell

Further Reading

Clinton, Catherine. *Harriet Tubman: The Road to Freedom*. Boston: Back Bay Books, 2005.

Johnson, James Weldon, and J. Rosamond Johnson. *The Books of the American Negro Spirituals*. New York: Viking Press, 1925.

Weatherford, Carole Boston, and Kadir Nelson. *Moses: When Harriet Tubman Led Her People to Freedom*. New York: Hyperion Books, 2006.

WGBH Educational Foundation and the Public Broadcasting System. "Africans in America: America's Journey through Slavery." http://www.pbs.org/wgbh/aia/home.html (accessed November 10, 2008).

Slave Preachers

Slave preachers played an extraordinarily important role in shaping the cultural institutions and personal relationships of slaves in the years prior to emancipation. As new scholarship on the nature of slavery has proliferated in the past three decades, slave preachers have received increased attention from historians interested in understanding the dynamics of life among slaves and how slaves expressed themselves through the institutions of family and church. Much of this scholarship turns the previously dominant interpretation of the nature of the slave experience on its head. Whereas earlier generations of historians tended to depict slaves as helpless cogs in an institutional machine, recent scholarship reveals that slaves were far from an "inferior race" in need of civilization, as many historians suggested until the 1960s, and were instead remarkably resilient, creative, and determined to access freedom while they were still alive.

Much of the credit for the development of such attitudes toward freedom may be ascribed to the preachers who brought religion to slaves on plantations and elsewhere. The religion these ministers preached was an amalgamation of Western Christianity enforced by slaveholders and African traditions that lived in the cultural values and relationships forged by slaves amongst themselves. Generally speaking, most slave preachers were itinerant and illiterate, and many were given to sharing vivid images and subversive ideas in their powerful sermons. The most subversive ideas, of course, were those that challenged the conditions of slavery and suggested to slaves that there might be opportunities for freedom within their lifetimes. Significantly, many slave preachers turned the theology of white Protestantism upside down. Whereas slaveholders preferred that their slaves be imbued with the sense that their toil on earth might be rewarded in heaven—a view that doubled as a psychological mechanism protecting some slaveholders from guilt and as a convenient social control device at the same time—many slave preachers encouraged slaves to see themselves as a people chosen by God to bring the light of freedom to themselves and future generations. Rejecting the idea that they should be humble, obedient, and patient, these slave preachers instead presented the biblical tales of Moses and the Israelites, Daniel in the lion's den, and the story of David and Goliath to show their brethren that the interpretation of God's will promoted by their masters was not necessarily the only one.

Of course, many slave preachers had to cloak their sermons in secrecy to avoid being persecuted by the slaveholders for whom they presumably worked (though it should be noted that in many instances, slaves chose their own preachers in a culturally organic way). Because they walked on such a tightrope, a lingering question, as noted by religious historian Albert J. Raboteau, has been whether slave preachers were instruments of the status quo or purveyors of revolutionary thought amongst the slaves to whom they preached. Like many historians of his generation, Raboteau concludes that the weight of historical evidence suggests that slaves recognized the limits under which their preachers worked, lending credence to the argument among many historians that slaves were very much aware of their condition and eager to resist it as much as possible. In this sense, the role of slave preachers in helping to bring about emancipation and in shaping African American culture cannot be overstated.

—Dave Powell

Further Reading

Genovese, Eugene D. *Roll, Jordan, Roll: The World the Slaves Made*. New York: Pantheon Books, 1974.

Raboteau, Albert J. *Canaan Land: A Religious History of African Americans*. New York: Oxford University Press, 2001.

Raboteau, Albert J. *Slave Religion: The "Invisible Institution" in the Antebellum South*. New York: Oxford University Press, 1978.

Wilmore, Gayraud S. *Black Religion and Black Radicalism*. New York: Doubleday, 1972.

Turner, Nat (1800–1831)

Nat Turner led the most infamous slave uprising in the history of the United States in Southampton County, Virginia, in 1831. The story of Turner's life is cloaked in mystery, clouded by a multitude of competing accounts written by historians and contemporaries, and—in one famous and, to some, notorious case—a white author of a fictional account of his life published over a hundred years after Turner's death. The particulars of Turner's life have been sensationalized by some and downplayed by others as he has become for many a larger-than-life representation of the battle to end slavery in the United States prior to the Civil War.

Born on October 2, 1800, Turner was seen by those who knew him as an exceptional child and as someone marked for greatness. He surprised even his masters with his precocious ability to read and write. Turner was also heavily influenced by his maternal grandmother, who was a member of a Methodist church called Turner's Meeting House. The church was a place of worship for slaves on the Turner plantation and was the birthplace of much of Nat Turner's knowledge of biblical passages and his abiding faith in religion as a source of inspiration and emancipation. Indeed, as historian Gayraud Wilmore has argued, Turner's deep understanding of his master's religion led him to discover something that white Christians had attempted to conceal from their slaves: the idea that the God described in the Bible (particularly in the Old Testament) was a God who demanded justice and had the power to liberate people from captivity. Turner also realized that this God acted through prophets sent to earth to help subjugated peoples escape the bonds of their captivity.

Armed with this faith, and galvanized by visions that he later described seeing over a period of several years, Turner traveled throughout southern Virginia and perhaps even North Carolina, sharing his vision with the fellow slaves he came into contact with. Finally, a series of unexplained events culminated in

August 1831 in an unusual atmospheric phenomenon known as the "Three Blue Days," leading Turner to believe that the time had come for him to execute a planned insurrection against slavery. Turner's rebellion was suppressed within 48 hours, but not until as many as 60 white men, women, and children had been killed. A subsequent interview at the Southampton County Jail established Turner's reputation as a wild-eyed religious radical, a depiction that suited the developing narrative of the rebellion as an aberration masterminded by a single man. It also helped assuage the fears of whites worried that Nat Turner represented a movement of slaves intent on ending their captivity through violence, if necessary.

Ironically, Turner's characterization by his interviewer, Thomas Gray, also solidified Turner's reputation as a highly intelligent individual—a fact that undermined the slaveholding elite's conceptualization of slaves as practically inhuman and thus incapable of rational and intelligent thought, let alone rebellion against slavery. Turner was hanged for his crimes on November 11, 1831.

Nat Turner lives on in historical memory as a hero, a villain, a murderer, a liberator, and as a rebellious mastermind. He also, in many ways, serves as a prism through which our own interpretations of historical events can be filtered and as a reminder that the business of historical interpretation is shaped as much by our present circumstances as by the circumstances of the past.

—Dave Powell

Further Reading

French, Scot. *The Rebellious Slave: Nat Turner in American Memory*. Boston: Houghton Mifflin, 2004.

Greenberg, Kenneth S. ed. *Nat Turner: A Slave Rebellion in History and Memory*. New York: Oxford University Press, 2003.

Wilmore, Gayraud S. *Black Religion and Black Radicalism: An Interpretation of the Religious History of Afro-American People*. 2nd ed. Maryknoll, NY: Orbis Books, 1983.

A Contemporary Account of Nat Turner's Revolt (1831)

Nat Turner (1800–1831) was the leader of a bloody slave rebellion that erupted in Southampton County, Virginia, on August 21, 1831. A slave of Samuel Turner, Nat was a literate and religious man who came to believe that God had chosen him to carry out some great task. In August 1831, Nat Turner viewed a solar eclipse as the signal for him and his band of followers to rise up against the whites who enslaved them. Moving from plantation to plantation, the rebels freed all slaves and killed all whites whom they encountered. The 55 deaths caused by Turner and his followers was the largest number of fatalities in any antebellum slave insurrection. The rebellion was quickly suppressed, but Turner remained at large for two months. After his capture, he was swiftly convicted of murder and executed. Reproduced her is an account of the uprising that appeared in the (Richmond) Enquirer *in late August 1831.*

The Banditti

A fanatic preacher by the name of Nat Turner (Gen. Nat Turner) who had been taught to read and write, and permitted to go about preaching in the country, was at the bottom of this infernal brigandage. He was artful, impudent and vindictive, without any cause or provocation, that could be assigned. He was the slave of Mr. Travis. He and another slave of Mr. T. a young fellow, by the name of Moore, were two of the leaders. Three or four others were first concerned and most active.

They had 15 others to join them. And by importunity or threats they prevailed upon about 20 others to cooperate in the scheme of massacre. We cannot say how long they were organizing themselves—but they turned out on last Monday early (the 22d) upon their nefarious expedition. . . . They were mounted to the number of 40 or 50; and with knives and axes—knocking on the head, or cutting the throats of their victims. They had few firearms among them—and scarcely one, if one, was fit for use. . . . But as they went from house to house, they drank ardent spirits—and it is supposed, that in consequence of their being intoxicated, or from mere fatigue, they paused in their murderous career about 12 o'clock on Monday.

A fact or two, before we continue our narrative. These wretches are now estimated to have committed sixty-one murders! Not a white person escaped at all the houses they visited except two. One was a little child at Mrs. Waller's, about 7 or 8 years of age, who had sagacity enough to Creep up a chimney; and the other was Mrs. Barrow, whose husband was murdered in his cotton patch, though he had received some notice in the course of the morning of the murderous deeds that were going on; but placed no confidence in the story and fell victim to his incredulity. His wife bid herself between weather-boarding, and the unplastered lathing, and escaped, the wretches not taking time to hunt her out. It was believed that one of the brigands had taken up a spit against Mr. Barrow, because he had refused him one of his female slaves for a wife.

Early on Tuesday morning, they attempted to renew their bloody work. They made an attack upon Mr. Blunt, a gentleman who was very unwell with the gout, and who instead of flying determined to brave them out. He had several pieces of firearms, perhaps seven or eight, and he put them into the hands of his own slaves, who nobly and gallantly stood by him. They repelled the brigands—killed one, wounded and took prisoner (Gen. Moore), and we believe took a third who was not wounded at all. . . .

The militia of Southampton had been most active in ferreting out the fugitives from their hiding places. . . . But it deserves to be said to the credit of many of the slaves whom gratitude had bound to their masters, that they had manifested the greatest alacrity in detecting and apprehending many of the brigands. They had brought in several and a fine spirit had been shown in many of the plantations of confidence on the part of the masters, and gratitude on that of the slaves. It is said that from 40 to 50 blacks were in jail—some of whom were known to be concerned with the murders, and others suspected. The courts will discriminate the innocent from the guilty.

It is believed that all the brigands were slaves—and most, if not all these, the property of kind and indulgent masters. It is not known that any of them had been the runaways of the swamps and only one of them was a free man of color. He had afterwards returned to his own house, and a party sent there to apprehend him. He was accidently seen concealed in his yard and shot. . . .

Nat, the ringleader, who calls himself General, pretends to be a Baptist preacher's great enthusiast—declares to his comrades that he is commissioned by Jesus Christ, and proceeds under his inspired directions—that the late singular appearance of the sun was the sign for him, &c., &c., is among the number not yet taken. The story of his having been killed at the bridge, and of two engagements there, is ungrounded. It is believed he cannot escape.

The General is convinced, from various sources of information, that there existed no general concert among the slaves. Circumstances impossible to have been feigned, demonstrate the entire ignorance on the subject of all the slaves in the counties around Southampton, among whom he has never known more perfect order and quiet to prevail.

Source: *Enquirer* (Richmond, VA), August 30, 1831.

Texas Revolt (1835–1836)

In August 1821, a revolutionary entered San Antonio de Bexar, the capital of Spanish, now Mexican Tejas. Although in the dying days of Spanish rule, insurgents had been nothing new to the frontier province, this rebel was different. He came armed, not with guns, but with surveying tools. His goals lay not in establishing a new political order, but rather, an economic one. His promise of prosperity was the standard raised. To his potential audience, American's dealing with the horrific economic crisis of the Panic of 1819 was desperate for hope. So much so that Stephen F. Austin's contract for settling 300 families was complete in just one year, with 297 families established.

Austin ceaselessly worked to insure the success and prosperity of his colonists. He expanded his colonial contracts and assured many beneficial items for his colonists: Tax-free status for six years, legalization of slavery, and duty-free ports (James E. B. Austin to J. H. Bell, Austin Papers, 589; and Stephen Austin to Luciano Garcia, Austin Papers, 703). Crucial to Austin's success was that his colonists stay out of politics. Mexico, distracted by its own nation building, was too preoccupied with establishing its government and order to pay attention to distant Texas. Left in this status of salutary neglect, Texas prospered.

By 1828, however, events in Mexico City had calmed down enough that once again attention could be paid to Texas. General Manuel Mier y Terán was dispatched to Texas, and his observations horrified him. Mexican sovereignty was almost nonexistent. He fearfully stated that "these colonies, whose industriousness and economy receive such praise, will be the cause for the Mexican federation to lose *Tejas* unless measures are taken soon" (Terán to President Guadalupe Victoria, March 28, 1828, as seen in Terán 2000, 32).

When Terán sent his report to Mexico, the Mexican congress responded by issuing the Decree of April 6, 1830. This decree called for the establishment of a military presence in Texas and a limit on immigration, and it directly affected the region's prosperity by removing the tax-exempt status and collection of tariffs. Many histories argue that a myriad of points about the decree ignited frustrations. The bans on immigration, and even slavery, are listed as flashpoints of the Texas rebellion. A critical insight sees these points as secondary. The true threat that compelled the Texians to action was the threat to prosperity. As historian Crane Brinton argued, revolutions begin when there "is the existence among a group . . .

of a feeling that prevailing conditions limit or hinder their economic activity" (Brinton 1965, 33). In other words, the prosperity that had visited the colonies was threatened.

With the presence of Mexican troops off the Texas coast, the period of salutary neglect was over. In the Department of Nacogdoches, Juan Davis Bradburn arrived with troops and erected a brick and stockade fort garrisoned; it was an obvious show of force (Henson 1982, 50), and the colonists saw it as such. Much of the garrison consisted of convict-soldiers (Henson 1982, 52). Bradburn began to impress their slaves for further construction of his fortress, and told them that they should be free. Although many aggravating secondary items were present, the main threat to the agrarian economy was the flashpoint of outright revolt: maritime commercial enforcement.

Bradburn's first attempt to collect customs was thwarted by colonial petitions. When legal restrictions were removed, Bradburn was ready. In November 1831, all ports were closed save the one at Anahuac—the fort supplied with a garrison. At Brazoria, some captains, chafing at the limitation, simply defied the order and began to float downstream. Including one vessel, the *Nelson* that was fired upon, and in response, an enraged crewman, Spencer H. Jack fired his own rifle, wounding one of the guards (Henson 1982, 83). This outraged Bradburn, who declared martial law.

Bradburn not only continued tariff collections, but enlarged his threat to prosperity by taking "property from the colonists, disclaimed their land titles, and declared that all of their slaves were freed" (Lewis 1969, 5). Some questioning colonists, including lawyer William Barrett Travis and Spencer Jack's brother Patrick C. Jack, were thrown into jail. When yet another Jack, William, arrived to free his brother, Bradburn responded by telling him he had 15 minutes to leave, or he too would be arrested.

William left and spread the word of this injustice. Volunteers arrived to take up arms against this threat to prosperity. By June 4, the rebel numbers had reached 130 and although still outnumbered by the Mexican force of 162, the rebels were determined. Fort Velasco was put under siege.

A group was formed to travel to Brazoria to retrieve three cannons (Rowe 1903, 282–283). A merchant schooner, *Brazoria*, was requisitioned. By the time Velasco was reached, the rebel numbers included from 150 to 190. Ugartecha would not allow them to pass, and a battle ensued lasting more than 10 hours (Henson 1982, 107–108). Continual fire from the Texians on the shore, and cannonade from the *Brazoia*, silenced the Mexican cannon. While rainfall limited the effectiveness of the rifle troops, the cannon on the *Brazoria* continued to fire. At 10:00 a.m. with his powder ruined, Ugartecha was forced to raise the white flag (John Austin to Francisco M. Duclor, Lamar 1968, vol. 1, 100–101).

Casualties of the battle depended on which side was believed. The Mexican report stated 7 Mexican dead and 19 wounded, while 7 Texians were killed and 15 wounded (Hill 1962, 16). The Texian observer of the battle, however, claimed only 6 Texian dead, none wounded and 34 Mexican dead and wounding, "I think about 40" ("Alexander Thompson to William Thompson" 1904, 326–327). The casualties on both sides of the battle, however, were insignificant compared to its consequences.

Then, an event in Mexico City occurred assisted the Texians. A young general, Santa Anna, had carried out his Plan of Vera Cruz, attempting to return Mexico to the Liberal Constitution of 1824. In the battle of federalism, the Texians claimed a federalist victory of state rights (J. Austin to F. Duclor, Lamar 1968, vol. 1, 101). At Anahuac, the commander of the garrison at Nacogdoches, Colonel Jose de la Piedras, seemed to reinforce this notion when he found Bradburn had extended his authority and dismissed him. As the revolutionaries had "thus obtained their object" of "shewing [*sic*] the Military that the constitution should be adhered to and the civil power rule"—in other words, with the threat to prosperity gone—the militants simply "return'd home peaceably" (Alexander Thompson to William Thompson, Lamar 1968).

General Jose Antonio Mexica and 400 soldiers arrived to ensure all was well, and remained at this location to observe the Texians for one week. He found the colonists "placid, loyal, and exulted" over Santa Anna's victories. Pleased at his discovery, Mexica sailed away on July 24, giving the Texas *santanistas* his blessing.

The Texians—bloodied by the lessons learned—believed they had learned how to make changes in the Mexican political system. Now that they had cast their lot with the federalists, the Texians continued in pursuit of a goal that would grant them the political voice that they sought, and the prosperity they craved—separate Mexican statehood.

Flush with victory, the Texians called a series of political meetings known as the Consultation of 1832 and 1833. Their main object was to ensure prosperity. This could be achieved by tariff reduction and separation from their sister state Coahuila. Stephen Austin, with Erasmo Seguin and Dr. James Miller, were chosen to present the petition to Mexico City on April 13, 1833.

The Texians apparently seemed to believe that now that their petitions had been filed, they could let down their vigilance. All points seemed to display the victory of their rights. Tariff enforcement had not returned. The "Decree of April 6" had been repealed. Texas would receive additional representation in the legislature. English could be used in legal documents (Barker 1928, 113–114; Report of Ugartechea to Teran, Lamar 1968, vol. 1, 100–101; Henson 1976, 39). Prosperity had returned to the coasts. It is not surprising, then, that news of Austin's arrest in Saltillo on January 3, 1834, was lost in the other victories the Texians had gained.

Unbeknownst to the Texians were the conditions of Austin's arrest. His incarceration was harsh. He remained incarcerated for almost a year, without any charges being pressed. He was released on December 25, 1834, but without his passports he would remain in Mexico City until July 11, 1835.

During Austin's absence, the Texians followed Austin's rule of staying out of politics, and Texas prospered. A Mexican general, sent to spy on the Texians, not only found all placid, but also was certain "that Texas is soon destined to be the most flourishing section of its republic"(Almonte 1925, 178).

The peace in Texas was inspired not by federalist promises, but rather, distance from the capital, Mexico City. Specifically, Santa Anna had grown more centralistic. To continue his consolidation of power, he ordered all state militia reduced (Henson 1976, 69–70). Many provinces revolted, but as Texas did not, it was ignored. Texas's sister state of Coahuila rebelled, and although they cried to Texas for support, few assisted. Prosperity lived in Texas, and few were willing to rock the boat.

Then on January 1, 1835, Colonel Ugartechea, still in military command, dispatched various garrisons to differing locations in Texas. Customs collections were to begin at Anahuac, and it would be enforced by soldiers and a new revenue cutter (Barker 1928, 137, 152). With salutary neglect ending, a threat to the prosperity in the region appeared (Andrew Briscoe to J.D. Allen, McDonald 1995, 110). The owners of a stopped vessel, the *Ohio*, went to their attorney, William Barrett Travis, to file a protest.

Travis responded through what he had done in the past: he led a popular revolt. Specifically, he led 30 rebels to expel the threat at Anahuac (Barker 1901, 200). They were successful, but rather than receiving accolades, Travis was berated for his threat to the peace and told he would have to make a public apology (Travis to Henry Smith, Lamar 1968, vol. 5, 81). The moneyed interests believed that activity might bring repression. The action, however, was too much, Martin Perfcto de Cós, the military commander in Texas, found the Texians show wanting and called for the arrest of those who had taken part in the expulsion. Sensing a threat to prosperity, Columbia put out the call for another political meeting, the Consultation ("W. H. Wharton and Others Call for a Public Meeting," Lamar 1968, vol. 1, 219).

The catalyst that shook the Texians from inactivity was arrival of the same man who warned them to remain politically inactive. Stephen F. Austin arrived back in Texas on September 2, 1835. That prior day, some Texians at Anahuac became enraged at the capture of a brig, the *Tremont*, by the Mexican schooner of war, the *Correo de Mejico*. The Texians recaptured the *Tremont*. As Austin's boat, the *San Felipe*, arrived, the Mexican captain, Thomas Thompson, was preparing to retake the *Tremont*. The Texians disembarked Austin and used the *Laura* to tow the *San Felipe* to capture the *Correo*. Upon boarding the *Correo*, Thompson, unable to find his papers, was arrested. Austin responded by preparing his people to resist. With Austin back in Texas, activity began. Committees of correspondence maintained information on Mexican troop movements. A call was issued for another political consultation to prepare ("W. H. Wharton and Others Call for a Convention," Lamar 1968).

Two weeks before the political meeting, however, fighting erupted. In a threat surpassing prosperity and striking survival, Mexican general Martin Perfecto de Cós dispatched more than 100 dragoons to retrieve a cannon from Gonzales. In its short history, Gonzales had been destroyed twice by Native American attacks. All this changed once they were given a fieldpiece by the Mexican government. The "cannon" was nothing more than a spiked armament captured from Spanish rebels. While its firing was inaccurate, it was able to make a loud noise, which was enough of a threat to persuade Native Americans against attack.

Now however, Mexican forces were arriving to take the town's guardian. When the Mexican forces arrived on September 29, a meager 18 Texians stood in determined opposition on the opposite bank of the swollen Guadalupe River. The Texians were determined to hold on to the cannon as it was seen as necessary for survival—discouraging Native American attacks (Smithwick 1983, 76). Although Lieutenant Francisco Castañeda was prevented from crossing, he waited for the stream recede.

During Castañeda's delay, messengers rode to the countryside crying for reinforcements. By October 1, the Texians' numbers swelled to over 180, and preparations were being made to fight the next day. On October 2, 1835, after parley failed, the rebel flag declaring "Come and Take it" was unfurled by the cannon now mounted on a wagon. In what is known as the "Lexington of Texas," shots were fired, and one, possibly two Mexicans were killed. As the Texians held the woods, Castañeda retreated with his troops. The Texians faced no losses, and they were emboldened for a fight (T. J. Rusk, "Account of the fight at Gonzales," Lamar 1968). The only problem is, they did not agree on what they were fighting for. Indeed, one observer, Noah Smithwick, attempted to explain: "Some were for independence, some were for the Constitution of 1824; and some were for anything, just so long as it was a row" (Smithwick 1983, 76).

Enraptured by the relatively easy victory at Gonzales, George M. Collinsworth led a contingent of 49 men to remove the threat of troops by capturing the Presidio at Goliad (La Bahia), and hopefully capture General Cós. (Anonymous, Lamar 1968) As they marched, their numbers increased to probably about 120 men. On October 10, the Texian force was able to catch the Mexican guards by surprise. The Presidio was captured after about 30 minutes of resistance by the guards. Although the Texians were bloodied, none were killed, while Mexican forces faced 3 dead, 7 wounded, and more than 21 taken prisoner (R. R. Royal to Stephen Austin, *Austin Papers*, III, 179).

By October 12, Stephen F. Austin, now commander in chief, decided that the forces mustering at Gonzales should capture San Antonio. They took the battle to Cós, rather than allow him to attack the settlements piecemeal. In dealing with the rebel Texians, Cós was shocked by their aggression. In his reply to Austin's request to vacate, he points that he, if anything, was too nice to the colonists: "I might be accused of weakness, for having taken too much into consideration, [for] the local interests of those new settlers, who wish to prosper by going beyond the bounds set by nature herself" (Martin Perfecto de Cós to Stephen Austin, Lamar 1968, vol. 5, 86) Cós then implied to Austin that if his army does not desist, a violent reprisal will follow (Martin Perfecto de Cós to Stephen Austin, Lamar 1968, vol. 5, 87). The Texian numbers grew and included residents of San Antonio like Plácido Benavides and around 30 other *Bexareños* on October 15. On October 22, Juan Sequin joined the fight, notifying Austin that many others in San Antonio were in support of the federalist cause (Hardin 1994, 28).

Rather than diminishing the will to fight, the unified Texians continued their march. The first engagement occurred on October 28. Ninety rebels, led by James Bowie, took on the approximately 400 Mexican soldiers at Mission Nuestra Señora de la Purísima Concepción. The Texians had one inarguable strength: their weapons. The Kentucky long rifles of the Texians were superior in distance and accuracy to the Mexican Brown Bess muskets. Utilizing this strength to the fullest, the Mexican force was forced to retreat at the loss of 27 Mexican casualties. The Texians meanwhile, had only one death.

With this victory, however, the Texians decided to lay siege to Bexar. This form of wisdom over valor may have been smart, but this warfare was extremely stagnant to troops ready for action. Its effectiveness was displayed November 26 by a skirmish known as the "Grass Fight." A group of Texians attacked an incoming mule train that was believed to hold gold. According to participant Henry Dance, a force of 350 Mexican solders was engaged. The results of the battle were simple. The Mexican army was "defeated and left the field 15 men left Dead [*sic*] on the ground and many borne upon horses while our loss was one man wounded in the shin [*sic*]" (Henry C. Dance to the Editors, Lamar 1968, vol. 5, 95). The Texians were disappointed at only finding grass in the mule parcels. The fact that feed for the animals had to be brought in displayed the siege's effectiveness. The Texians also captured letters with the troubling news that reinforcements were on the way.

Stephen Austin was called away to the consultation and William H. Wharton was placed in charge. The Texians, however, soon grew anxious. On December 5, Ben Milam was ready. The cry of "Who will go to San Antonio with old Ben

Milam" was answered by more than 300 Texians. In grueling house-to-house fighting, the Texians were able to slowly push the enemy back. Despite the fact Milam "fell Dead [,] Shot through the Brains with a Rifle while walking about encouraging his men," the advance continued (Henry C. Dance to the Editors, Lamar 1968, vol. 5, 97). By December 10, Cós dispatched a soldier carrying the flag of surrender. In the peace agreement, Cós promised that he would not interfere with the Texians and their battle for the Liberal Constitution of 1824.

With the battle for freedom being fought in the forefront, in the background, 48 delegates of the Consultation set about the work of explaining what the fight was for, and how best prosperity could be maintained. One faction, the War Party, wanted an immediate declaration of independence. The other group, the Peace Party, believed the best interests of Texas would lie in staying in Mexico (Notes Concerning the Consultation and Convention, Lamar 1968, vol. 2, 394–395). They had been able to prosper and could prosper again. To do so, however, both a return to the Liberal Constitution of 1824 and separate Mexican statehood would be needed (J. Kerr, "Address against Independence," Lamar 1968, vol. 1, 287–292). Indeed, it was believed that the remaining Mexican federalists would rise to the side of the Texians. On November 6, a vote was called for. Only 15 of the delegates wanted independence, whereas 33 voted for separate Mexican statehood ("Notes Concerning the Consultation and Convention," Lamar 1968, vol. 2, 395–396).

With reason for fighting decided, on November 7, 1835, a new provisional government was formed. With its birth, the all the unity that had bound the delegates disappeared. Henry Smith of the War Party was chosen provisional governor while members of the General Council were of the Peace Party. In the dying moments of unity, Stephen Austin was dispatched to the United States for aid, while Sam Houston was chosen to be commander in chief of the army.

Even the slightest semblance of unity disappeared over disagreement on a proposed expedition to capture Matamoras. To those who gave support, it seemed like the smart thing to do. By taking the war to Mexico, specifically Matamoras would provide many benefits to Texas. Besides removing pressure on Texas, it would provide a clarion call for Mexican federalists. Economically, Texas could use the money from the customs collected at Matamoras; with the war distant, the economy would face less damage. To the opposition, Texas could barely afford the army it had, much less afford the waste on an expedition that may fail (James W. Fannin to J. W. Robinson, Lamar 1968, vol. 1, 333). Overriding the governor's veto, Dr. James Grant was dispatched with 300 troops to take Matamoros. (Colonel W. G. Cook, Lamar 1968, vol. 4, part I, 42). Governor Smith responded, by disbanding the council. The council responded by removing the governor. Both sides left vowing to hold another meeting at Washington-on-the-Brazos on

March 1, 1836 (Notes Concerning the Consultation and Convention, Lamar 1968, vol. 2, 395). During this time of need for solidarity and preparation, the government was absent.

This lack of cohesion by the government was reflected in most of the military matters. Units, hesitant to listen to an unknown Sam Houston, either disobeyed or acted without orders. Even groups such as the Matamoros expedition, once dispatched soon turned piecemeal as rival groups went in pursuit of specific interests (Reuben R. Brown, Account of His Part in the Texas Revolution, Lamar 1968, vol. 5, 366–372). Some simply returned home. Although Colonel James C. Neill, knowing he would have needed 1,000 more men to protect San Antonio, he decided with his meager force to reinforce fortifications at the Alamo. As the months passed into February, the urgency, and therefore speed diminished. Neill's requests for additional reinforcements also went unanswered (Winders 2004, 89).

Infighting and disunity caused a waste of the Texians' most precious resource—time; Santa Anna was beset by no such difficulty. When the capture of Bexar and the humiliation of General Cós became known, Santa Anna planned to crush the rebel Texians. Utilizing the two main roads into Texas, the *El Camino Real* and the Atascosito road, his troops could quickly eradicate the problems. The *El Camino Real* wound through the center, while the Atascosito skirted the coast. Through these two routes, the rebels would be crushed. As speed was paramount, Santa Anna quickly amassed and dispatched his forces. He rushed to the *El Camino Real* to capture San Antonio; meanwhile, General José Urrea would take 500 infantry and cavalry up the Atascosito road to capture Goliad. By February 16, 1836, Santa Anna had crossed the Rio Grande.

The effects of this rushed march should have reaped huge benefits. Indeed by February 21, Santa Anna was on the outskirts of San Antonio de Bexar catching the Texian rebels by surprise. The unseasonable weather, however, prevented the crossing of a flooded steam. He had to wait two days for the waters to subside. This allowed his presence to be known, and the alarm to be raised, while the garrison prepared for battle.

As the rebels and their families rushed to sanctuary at their garrison at the Alamo, the Mexican army prepared itself for a siege. Both sides were confident of victory. The rebels, numbering a little more than 200, were confident of reinforcement. The Mexican army, numbering around 2,000, believed a siege would starve the rebels into submission while artillery pummeled the defenses. By February 24, the siege began. Although the Texian rifles prevented the enemy from getting within 200 yards of the fort, Travis began to use what he felt was his most powerful weapon—a pen. Risking their lives, couriers rushed from the defenses carrying dispatches. At first, the letters were full of confidence and bravado. For example, in his letter of February 24, Travis, still sure of reinforcement, proudly boasts of how the enemy's cannonade killed none, and his defiance to demands of surrender (Wallace et al. 2002, 96). Travis pled to both the government, which had not even officially met yet, as well as the commander at Goliad to send a relief column. As time passed, only 32 men from Gonzales fought their way in to reinforce the garrison.

By the 10th day of the siege, its effectiveness was evident. As Travis found his letters unanswered, his pen became sardonic. In his letter of March 3, Travis, prophetically exclaimed he would "fight the enemy on its terms and his bones would rebuke the lethargy of his countrymen."

Travis would not have to wait long. On the evening of March 5, the Mexican cannon stopped firing. The majority of the 189 Texians succumbed to exhaustion and slept. The Mexican army of 1,800 soldiers advanced under the cover of darkness. They would have caught the Texians unaware had not a nervous *soldado* began to cry out "Viva Santa Anna." Awakened, the Texian defenders quickly rallied. Initial waves were repulsed; Santa Anna was eventually able to take the citadel. The clearing fog of war revealed 600 Mexican dead, compared to 189 defenders. The surviving family members, such as the Dickersons, were allowed to leave so they could tell the colonials what might be in store for them. The news, spread like wildfire across the Texas prairie, had a mixture of effects. Many families immediately began evacuation in the "Runaway Scrape," taking only provisions they could carry. Some however, facing the seriousness of the calamity, formed volunteer units to fight against the centralist threat.

Meanwhile, the new government found itself in a desperate situation. The 44 delegates met in a freezing Hall in Washington-on-the-Brazos. News from Stephen F. Austin was not good, as many investors had supported a previous Mexican federalist revolutionary, General José Antonio Mexía, whose expedition met with disastrous failure in November 1835. Mexía's political connection with Texas soured many responses to Austin's pleas of support for a federalist revolution as he arrived in the city in January 1836. Letters were sent home telling the Texians that if they wanted financial support, independence should be declared. (Miller 2004, 105.) In the litany of aggressions committed causing the separation, the document states that although the colonists who "colonize[d] the wilderness" were rewarded by suffering "military commandants, stationed among us, to exercise arbitrary acts of oppression and tyranny," and making "Piratical attacks upon our commerce, by commissioning foreign desperadoes, and authorizing them to seize our vessels, and convey the property of our citizens to far distant parts for confiscation."

Only for the cause of "self-preservation" were the Texians in favor of splitting (Texas Declaration of Independence, in Wallace 2002, 98–99). So on March 2, 1836, the collected delegates approved the declaration and Texas was to be free, although those who died at the Alamo would never know.

While Santa Anna was busy engaging the garrison on the *El Camino Real*, General José Urrea was preparing to decimate resistance along the Atascosito road. Arriving at Matamoros on January 31, Urrea found the town safe. The threat of Texian attack had apparently become victim of sloth. The Matamoros expedition had stalled at San Patricio, close to the Nueces River, in search of more horses. Urrea crossed the Rio Grande with a diminutive force of 320 infantry, 230 dragoons, and a small field gun and rushed to meet the enemy (Hardin 2004, 61). This gamble would pay huge dividends as by February 27, Urrea was able to catch a smaller army both unaware and divided. At 3:00 a.m., Urrea pounced upon Johnson's group of 60 men.

By dawn, fighting had ceased. Fort Lipantitlán and 32 rebels were captured. Twenty Texians dead with the loss of only one soldier and four wounded to the Mexican force. Indeed, only eight men, including Colonel Johnson were able to escape. Questioning the citizenry, Urrea discovered that Grant would soon be returning from his horse foray. Near the banks of Agua Dulce Creek, Urrea prepared an ambush. On March 2, the Texians unknowingly walked into the trap. Dr. Grant and about 40 soldiers were slaughtered in the resulting battle.

Meanwhile, at Goliad, Commander James Walker Fannin found himself a victim of Texas's inaction. Many of the benefits that seemingly assisted his garrison, proximity to Copano provided fresh recruits from the United States, provision of supply, and the walls of his defense strong, seemingly made him strong. Appearances however, were deceiving. Demands were thrust upon him. The Matamoros expedition had drawn off needed supply and soldiers. As events accelerated, desperate petitions began to flow. Pleas for reinforcement, evacuation protection, and consolidation of his units all demanded action. Meanwhile, the Mexican army was advancing. Fannin dispatched Captain Amon B. King to help evacuate the families at Refugio. Supremely confident, King harassed the local ranchers. To his surprise, he ran into the advance guard of Urrea's army. Rather than leaving the field after the short battle, King sent word for reinforcement (Samuel Brown, Battle of the Mission [Refugio], Lamar 1968, vol. 2, 8–10) Fannin agreed and dispatched William Ward and his Georgia Battalion to the rescue. Upon arrival, on March 13, they found that King and his men fortified in Refugio Mission. The group of 60 Mexican soldiers retreated and used their time to harass local Tejanos. This waste played directly into Urrea's hand. On March 14, he arrived with his main force to find the rebels once again inside the mission. Although King and Ward defended the mission, they ran out of gunpowder. At nightfall, they attempted escape. As their harassment of local ranchers had won them few friends, King and his men were soon rounded up and taken prisoner. Ward's men were captured piecemeal and also taken prisoner. With the countryside pacified, Urrea began to march on his objective, Goliad (Samuel Brown, Battle of the Mission [Refugio], Lamar 1968, vol. 2, 8–10).

At Goliad, Fannin did nothing with the myriad of calls placed before him. On February 26, he did try to take 320 of his men and four cannon to relieve the Alamo however a wheel came off one of his wagons. As problems continued until sunset and into the next day, it was decided to stay at the fort.

By March 13, Fannin finally received orders from his superior, General Samuel Houston. Fannin was ordered to abandon Fort Defiance (Goliad) and retreat to Victoria. Fannin was ready, but he wanted to wait on King and Ward's return. So he wasted four days only to discover they had been captured. On March 18, he prepared for withdrawal, and on March 19, the troops began the move finally towards Victoria. Fannin remained assured the Mexican army would not attack his more than 400 Texians (Hardin 2004, 61).

Urrea's army, which had been reinforced to more than 1,600 soldiers, was on the outskirts of Goliad, at the same time that Fannin began his retreat. Fannin unknowingly aided the enemy by stopping his troops after only an hour's march for a rest in the middle of an open field. Urrea discovered the vulnerable Texians and quickly used his cavalry to deprive them of cover. Although the Texians fought ferociously, they soon ran out of water to swab their guns. By nightfall, the tally of 9 Texians dead and 51 wounded was small compared to their predicament. With water and food nonexistent and gunpowder running low, morale plummeted.

Sunrise intensified the grimness of the Texians situation. Overnight, the remainder of Urrea's troops and artillery had arrived. Now facing a vastly superior foe, the Texians sallied forth under a flag of truce (Joseph E. Field, "Fannin's Surrender," *Lamar Papers*, vol. 5, 120–121). Although only an unconditional surrender would be granted, it was believed that they would be treated as prisoners of war. They were marched back to Goliad, the prisoners were confident. So on March 27, Palm Sunday, the prisoners were led out of the fort, believing they would be sent to the United States. None questioned the fact that 83 of the prisoners, including a 14-year-old boy, were kept inside the fort. No resistance was offered. Santa Anna, however, saw the Texians as nothing more than pirates, and as such, they could be killed. After being lined up in three separate groups, their guards received the order to fire. Although 28 Texians were able to escape, 342 Texians fell dead in what was known as the "Goliad Massacre" (S. T. Brown, "Account of his Escape from Goliad," *Lamar Papers*, vol. 2, 8–10).

News of the martyrs for freedom spread among a backdrop of chaos. On March 11, Houston, who had been away negotiating peace with the Cherokee, had returned to Gonzales to find that his army had been reduced to only 347 men. Although believing he would be joined by Fannin's men, the general knew he could not waste time. He began a series of retreats, and with each step, he incorporated more volunteers and training. With Santa Anna close behind, many believed that Houston was trying to get as close to the American border as possible to try to draw in American units. Then, on April 18, scout Erastus "Deaf" Smith captured a Mexican courier whose dispatches showed Santa Anna had lightened his forces in the race to catch the rebel government on the run. For the first time in more than a month of retreat, Houston turned south. By the next day, knowing that Santa Anna would be arriving at Buffalo Bayou, the Texians took up camp in the woods. Hearing the Texians were in the area, Santa Anna showed up at the bayou and made camp only three-fourths of a mile away from the Texian camp.

On the afternoon of April 21, 1836, just 18 minutes would forever change America. Although a minor cavalry skirmish had broken out the day before, all had remained placid. The Mexican forces had received 540 reinforcements earlier that afternoon bringing their numbers up to around 1,200 *soldados*, outnumbering the 910 Texians. At noon, Houston held a council of war. With excitement building, between 3:00 and 4:00 in the afternoon, the Texian army began their advance. A hill rising 15 feet had kept the Texian movements from enemy view, and after being at station for more than 33 hours, the Mexican soldiers were exhausted. At 4:30, the Texians crested the hill and, filled with rage and shouting "Remember the Alamo—Remember La Bahía," attacked, catching the enemy totally off guard. Although the battle lasted only 18 minutes, the slaughter continued until the Texians became exhausted. Six hundred fifty Mexicans were killed, and more than 700 were taken prisoner, including Santa Anna. Only 9 Texians were killed, and 30 wounded. Houston took Santa Anna prisoner, where he was forced to recognize the independence of Texas.

In its mad pursuit of self-governance for the sake of prosperity, Texas had won independence. Texas would last almost 10 years as an independent nation, surrounded by both danger and opportunity. The fact that Texas was a slave state status slowed attempts at annexation. Mexico's reluctance to recognize Texas's independence, and later its borders, also impeded talks. The eventual annexation of Texas by the United States would lead to the Mexican-American War over conflict about the border. The lands acquired from that war, in turn, laid the groundwork for the Civil War.

—*Andrew Galloway*

See also all entries under Bear Flag Revolt (1846).

Further Reading

"Alexander Thompson to William Thompson." August 5, 1832. *Texas State Historical Association* 7, no. 4 (April 1904): 326–328.

Almonte, Juan N. "Statistical Report on Texas, 1835." Translated by C. E. Castañdea. *Southwestern Historical Quarterly* 28, no. 3 (January 1925): 177–222.

Annual Report of the American Historical Association for 1919. *The Austin Papers*. Edited by Eugene Barker. Vol. 2. Part I, Vol. 3. Washington, DC: Government Printing Office, 1924.

Barker, Eugene C. "Difficulties of a Mexican Revenue Officer in Texas." *Texas Historical Association Quarterly* 4, no. 3 (January 1901): 190–202.

Barker, Eugene C. *Mexico and Texas 1821–1835*. Dallas, TX: P. L. Turner Company, 1928.

Brinton, Crane. *The Anatomy of Revolution*. New York, Prentice-Hall, 1938. Revised ed., New York: Vintage Books, 1965.

Hardin, Stephen L. *The Alamo 1836: Santa Anna's Texas Campaign*. Westport, CT: Osprey Publishing, 2004.

Hardin, Stephen L. *Texian Iliad: A Military History of the Texas Revolution*. Austin: University of Texas Press, 1994.

Henson, Margaret Swett. *Juan Davis Bradburn: A Reprisal of the Mexican Commander of Anahuac*. College Station: Texas A&M University Press, 1982.

Henson, Margaret Swett. *Samuel May Williams: Early Texas Entrepreneur*. College Station: Texas A&M University Press, 1976.

Hill, Jim Dan. *The Texas Navy*. Reprint ed. New York: Perpetua Book, 1962.

Lamar, Mirabeau Buonaparte. *The Papers of Mirabeau Buonaparte Lamar*. Vols. 1, 2, 4, and 5. Edited by Gulick, et al. Austin, TX: Pemberton Press, 1968.

Lewis, Carroll A., Jr. "Fort Anahuac: The Birthplace of the Texas Revolution." *Texana* 1 (Spring 1969): 1–11.

Miller, Edward L. *New Orleans and the Texas Revolution*. College Station: Texas A&M University Press, 2004.

McDonald, Archie P. *William Barret Travis: A Biography*. Austin, TX: Eakin Press, 1995.

Rowe, Edna. "The Disturbances at Anahuac in 1832." *Texas State Historical Association* 6, no. 4 (April 1903): 265–299.

Smithwick, Noah. *The Evolution of a State or Recollections of Old Texas Days*. Austin: University of Texas Press, 1983.

Teran, Manuel de Mier, *Texas by Teran*: *The Diary Kept by General Manuel de Mier y Teran on His 1828 Exploration of Texas*. Edited by Jack Jackson. Translated by John Wheat. Austin: University of Texas Press, 2000.

Wallace, Ernest. David M. Vigness, and George B. Ward, eds. *Documents of Texas History*. Austin: Texas State Historical Association, 2002.

Weber, David J. *The Mexican Frontier 1821–1846: The American Southwest Under Mexico*. Albuquerque: University of New Mexico Press, 1982.

Winders, Richard Bruce. *Sacrificed at the Alamo: Tragedy and Triumph in the Texas Revolution*. Abilene, TX: State House Press, 2004.

Battle of the Alamo (1836)

After initial victories in their war for independence, the Texians were supremely confident. Indeed, 111 of the 189 defenders had routed the Mexican army from San Antonio during the siege of Bexar. San Antonio was valuable real estate as it lay on the major land route into Tejas, the *camino real*. The provisional government remanded Commander Samuel Houston's recommendation for the Alamo's destruction, as it was considered "the key to Texas."

This seemed a monumental task. The garrison was underprovisioned, undermanned and unprepared. Although six of the defenders were native-born Tejanos, 27 had been born in Europe, the remainder were born in the United States. Only 40 had lived in the Mexican province for more than two years. Their ages ranged

As depicted in a painting of the Battle of the Alamo by Percy Moran, Mexican soldiers under Gen. Antonio López de Santa Anna besiege Texans barricaded inside the Alamo during the Texas Revolution Numbering approximately 189 men, the Texans fought off the Mexicans, who numbered around 3,000 to 4,000 troops, for 13 days until the Mexican Army finally overran the Alamo on March 6, 1836. (Library of Congress)

from 15 to 56. Although a trickle of volunteers from the United States, like the New Orleans Greys and others led by David Crockett, emboldened the commanders, they were still desperately shorthanded. However, they believed that reinforcement would surely come.

Santa Anna shocked the Texians by arriving in San Antonio on February 23. As Texian co-commander William B. Travis knew that the garrison could not last long against Santa Anna's forces, he confidently dispatched messages to both Gonzales and the General Council for reinforcement.

On February 24, the Mexican army laid siege. As the other commander, James Bowie, was sick, Travis took full command. It was during this siege that Travis issued "never surrender or retreat" letters for reinforcements "to come to our aid, with all dispatch." Although "the immortal 32," a group from Gonzales, fought their way through the enemy to reach the Alamo, they were the lone reinforcements.

By March 3, the effectiveness of the siege was evident. Mexican cannons had severely weakened the walls. Travis wrote a letter of defiant rebuke: "I shall have to fight the enemy on his own terms; yet I am ready to do it, if my countrymen do not rally to my relief, I am determined to perish in defense of this place, and my bones shall reproach my country for her neglect."

Before nightfall on March 5, the Mexican guns fell silent. In the silence, many Texians collapsed into exhausted sleep. By 3:00 a.m., Santa Anna assembled some 1,800 assault troops for the attack. With tension building, by 5:00 a.m., one nervous soldier shouted "Viva Santa Anna." Other Mexican *soldados* responded with shouts of their own that alerted the slumbering Texians into action.

Travis ran to his position, where he was shot in the forehead and killed. With the defenses deprived of a commander, the first wave of attack was repulsed. On the second wave, the defensive line collapsed. Some retreated to the Long Barracks, where combat became hand to hand. Others were cut down by light cavalry. By dawn, the 90-minute battle had concluded. At the cost of 600 lives, Santa Anna had killed 189 known rebels. All were burned on a funeral pyre, save José Enrique Esparza, whose body was identified by his brother and given a Christian burial.

So why do Americans, and Texans in particular, so cherish a battle that ended in defeat? Militarily, little was gained. Houston, in treaty with the Cherokee, was not with his army. Santa Anna had wasted supply, forcing his maneuver to San Jacinto. However, both politically, and morally, this sacrifice was indispensable to the rebels. When Susannah Dickenson and Travis's slave Joe relayed the news of what had happened, Travis's death reproached the Texians. With danger made actual, a rallying point was created. Combined with the news of the Goliad Massacre, where 342 rebels who were promised clemency were cut down, the threat of tyranny was made real. Civilians began the "runaway scrape" to America, while the Texian soldiers prepared to meet Santa Anna. Burning in righteous outrage, it should come as no surprise that as the Texians crested the hill at San Jacinto, "Remember Goliad, Remember the Alamo!" was their clarion call.

—Andrew Galloway

Further Reading

Groneman, Bill. *Alamo Defenders: A Genealogy, the People and Their Words*. Austin, TX: Eakin Press, 1990.

Winders, Richard Bruce. *Sacrificed at the Alamo: Tragedy and Triumph in the Texas Revolution*. Abilene, TX: State House Press, 2004.

Austin, Stephen F. (1793–1836)

In the wake of the Panic of 1819, Stephen F. Austin was down on his luck. His family's fortune was wiped out, and its privilege gone. The young Austin, once a business, civic, and community leader, found himself unemployed, and he found the knowledge gained at school and at Transylvania University to be useless. Drifting from Missouri to New Orleans, Austin searched unsuccessfully for employment. Cap in hand, he accepted financing from a lawyer, Joseph H. Hawkins, in the hopes that his father might get another break in Spanish territory. His father was granted an empresario (land agent) contract in Texas, but then he died, and left his grant to Austin.

Utilizing his political acumen, business savvy, and a long-suffering persistence; Austin worked out a colonization plan so grand and successful he would become known as the Father of Texas. Austin's empresario contract survived numerous governments. Austin maneuvered to ensure prosperity for his settlers. He chose rich alluvial soil between the Brazos and Colorado rivers for settlement. His land allotments grew from 640 acres per head of household, to a Spanish league (4,428 acres). Austin's surveying allowed for the easy transfer of title. Austin enabled the landing of foreign registered vessels at Galveston by 1825. The maritime prosperity encouraged officials to turn a blind eye to other illegitimate landing points. Austin worked for other empresarios, and this generosity placed others on the periphery of his colonies, limiting Native American attacks and thereby increasing the desirability of his lands.

Austin worked out other compacts. Austin's colonials did not have to pay the total amount for their land until after a year. Texas was free of tariffs for seven years, and debt collection cases could not be heard in Texas courts for 12 years. Austin was even able to get the prohibition on slavery lifted for Texas to encourage colonization.

Austin's endeavors flourished. By 1829, General Mier y Terán was shocked to find Tejanos outnumbered by "ten to one." The Decree of April 6, passed in 1830, attempted to stymie foreign influence. Austin, as well as many Texans, was infuriated at these impediments. He traveled to Texas's sister state, Coahuila, to argue for Texas. In his absence, the threats to prosperity prompted the Texans to rebel. The Mexican commanders at Fort Anahuac and Velasco were forced to surrender. To avoid trouble, the Texans proclaimed loyalty to the new leader of Mexico—Antonio Lopez de Santa Anna.

Austin returned to find Texans excited about the possibility of separate Mexican statehood. While he found the desire to push ahead politically unwise, Austin took leadership positions in political conventions of 1832 and 1833. Austin was chosen to represent Texas before the Mexican Congress.

Austin won many concessions for Texas. Overjoyed, he wrote that preparations for separate statehood should begin. This letter was intercepted and found dangerously insubordinate by Santa Anna, who ordered Austin's arrest. In Saltillo, Austin was taken into custody and escorted back. Although not charged, he remained incarcerated until December 1834 and was not allowed to leave Mexico City until July 1835.

Austin returned to Texas a changed man. His conciliatory approach was gone. As Mexico was ready to exert authority over Texas, another political meeting, the Consultation, was called for. Before that could happen, the opening shots of the Texas revolution occurred at Gonzales, October 2.

Austin was elected to command the Texian volunteers at the siege of Bexar (San Antonio). By November, the provisional government sent Austin and two others as commissioners to the United States. Austin labored in New Orleans to gain men, money, supplies, and recognition for Texas. He was fairly successful and returned after the victory at San Jacinto. In September 1836, Austin bid for the first president of the Republic, but was defeated by Samuel Houston. He accepted an offer to be the Republic's secretary of state. This final service did not last long. At Columbia, Austin's exhausted body could not take the cold of the winter. He contracted an ailment that soon progressed to pneumonia. Stephen Austin died on December 27, 1836, leaving the nation that became a state forever in his debt.

—*Andrew Galloway*

Further Reading

Barker, Eugene C., ed. *The Austin Papers*. Washington, DC: Government Printing Office, 1928.

Cantrell, Gregg. *Stephen F. Austin: Empresario of Texas*. New Haven, CT: Yale University Press, 1999.

Houston, Samuel (1793–1863)

Samuel Houston, the fifth of nine children, was born in Virginia on March 2, 1793. His father died shortly after completing the sale of the old estate and acquisition of new lands in eastern Tennessee. Young Samuel preferred his father's books to either schoolwork or labor. When his family tried to force him to be a clerk at their store, Houston ran away. He headed west, albeit only eight miles, to live as a Cherokee.

With the Cherokee, Houston gained valuable lessons. Chief Oo-loo-te-ka ("He who puts away the drum") was known for his willingness to search for conciliation rather than war. This deeply affected the young Houston. He found favor, was adopted into the chief's own family, and given the name of "Colonneh," which translates to "The Raven," a sign of good luck.

Shortly after the six-foot, two-inch Houston returned to American society, the War of 1812 began. While Houston's charisma propelled him to sergeant, it was his bravery and military skill that caught the eye of General Andrew Jackson. So impressed was Jackson that Houston was cared for by Jackson's own doctor and granted convalescences in Jackson's home. Though he did receive three near-fatal wounds during his service, he was a first lieutenant when he left the army in 1818.

After passing the bar, Houston turned to politics. In a meteoric rise, by 1823 and 1825, Houston was elected to Congress, and in 1827, he became governor of Tennessee. By 1829, Houston took Eliza Allen as his bride. But as quickly as his star rose, it fell twice as fast. As he was preparing for reelection, his three-month marriage fell apart. Historians still have no idea why Eliza packed her bags and went home. Houston responded by resigning, escaping west to "Indian territory," (today known as Oklahoma). There he met both the Cherokee and a whiskey bottle.

By 1832, Houston moved west once again, to Texas. Quickly he became embroiled in politics. He represented Nacogdoches at the Convention of 1833. By 1835 he was appointed general of the military district east of the Trinity, and he was elected a representative to the Consultation of 1835. By 1836, independence from Mexico was decided and Sam Houston was elected commander in chief of the armies of the new Republic of Texas.

Although at first, only some respected his title, the defeats of the Alamo and Goliad solidified loyalty. Houston conducted a masterful retreat. His soldiers thirst for battle culminated on April 21, 1836, at the Battle of San Jacinto. In a battle that officially lasted only 18 minutes, Santa Anna was defeated, and independence was won.

Houston served the new republic from the start. He was elected as Texas's first president in 1837. And after tenure as a congressman, he ran and won the presidency again in 1841. In his terms, he carried a pacific policy towards relations with Mexico and a balanced budget. Wanting always what was best for Texas, Houston worked for annexation to the United States, and although it remained out of his grasp, Texas eventually was annexed under his hand-picked successor, Anson Jones.

After Texas joined the United States, Houston still worked for Texas as senator. This was done until 1859, when Houston left national office to serve as governor of Texas, making him the first and only American to serve as governor of two different states. He did this in the hopes that he could keep Texas in the Union, but by 1861, this was impossible. As he preferred to whittle in the basement of the capital rather than take an oath of allegiance to the Confederacy, Houston was removed from office in March of that year.

Though demonized by some of the populace, his love for Texas never died. On July 26, 1863, he lay in his bed in Huntsville, fading from pneumonia. As his wife Margaret read from the Bible, the 70-year-old Houston spoke. A fading whisper carried his last words "Texas . . . Texas . . . Margaret."

—*Andrew Galloway*

Further Reading
Campbell, Randolph B. *Sam Houston and the American Southwest*. 2nd ed. New York: Longman Publishers, 2002.

Santa Anna, Antonio Lopez de (1794–1876)

Antonio Lopez de Santa Anna was a leader who personified ambition, and who possessed the skills to thrive in most of the political chaos of his life. Born February 21, 1794, to a middle-class family in Jalpa, Vera Cruz, he refused limitations. By 1810, at age 16, he entered the Spanish Vera Cruz battalion as a cadet. Under the leadership of Joaquín de Arredondo, he displayed his martial talent. By 1813, Lieutenant Santa Anna was in Tejas. At the battle of Medina, Arredondo put to the sword 1,300 of the 1,400 rebels; Spain, meanwhile, lost only 55 men. Arrendondo proceeded to disdainfully pacify and depopulate Tejas through a campaign of terror and mass executions. Besides a citation for bravery, Santa Anna learned strong lessons on dealing with insurgents.

A controversial figure in Mexican history, Antonio López de Santa Anna became Mexico's president in 1833. Though he won some battles, notably at the Alamo, he was forced into retirement following his defeat in the Texas Revolution in 1836. Ten years later, Santa Anna led Mexico through the disastrous Mexican-American War that resulted in a massive loss of Mexican territory and a humiliating defeat for Santa Anna's forces. (North Wind Picture Archives)

Feeling change in the political winds, and despite his promotion to brevet lieutenant colonel, Santa Anna threw his support to rebel Agustin de Iturbide in 1821. Although he received the rank of general and helped Mexico win independence, he remained unsatisfied. By 1823, he overthrew the increasingly despotic Emperor Iturbide. Seen as a champion of liberalism, he was promptly elected military governor of Yucatan in 1824. As an expedition to Cuba floundered, he grew tired of his position and resigned. Moving to Vera Cruz, he married, and was made governor.

Spain's attempt to re-conquer Mexico in 1829, brought Santa Anna a needed diversion. Winning fame through repulsion of the Spanish, he announced his retirement. Three years later, however he was back. Santa Anna, feeling the change of political winds, overthrew the centralist government. By 1833, his victorious army brought a return to federalism. Under his presidency, Mexico was given back to her people—at least for six months. By 1834, Santa Anna demanded the states disband their militias, causing 11 states to rebel. Mercilessly, the rebellions were put down. When Santa Anna defeated the state militia of Zacatecas, he allowed the "rape of Zacatecas," where his soldiers looted for 48 hours.

At the end of this campaign, Texas began her fight for independence at Gonzales, October 2, 1835, and Santa Anna rushed to Texas. Ordering no quarter to the Texians at the battle of the Alamo, followed by the slaughter of 350 Texians at Goliad, Santa Anna followed the formula of halting rebellion. His failure to post guards San Jacinto, on April 6, 1836, was a supreme miscalculation, and Samuel

Houston used this opportunity to attack. The surprised Santa Anna was defeated in less than 18 minutes. After capture, he signed the Treaty of Velasco, recognizing the independence of Texas.

After a trip to the United States, the disgraced Santa Anna retired to his estates in Mexico, where opportunity arose again. Over Mexico's debt, the French invaded beginning the "Pastry-War." Though the French were forced to retreat, Santa Anna lost a leg to shrapnel. Riding the fame, he served as president in 1839 and liked it so much that he overthrew the presidency of Bustamante in 1841 and became dictator. His greed and excesses led to an empty treasury. By 1845, he was exiled to Cuba.

Events brought Santa Anna home, namely the Mexican-American War. Santa Anna convinced the American president, James K. Polk, that he could negotiate peace. Allowed to return to Mexico, he raised an army of 18,000 to fight the invaders. After a draw against Zachary Taylor at Buena Vista, he retreated to Mexico City. He then had to face Winfield Scott's army. An oversight at Cerro Gordo led to his retreat and the capture of Mexico City. Following the surrender to the United States, Santa Anna was again exiled.

By 1853, Mexico was wrought with difficulties and called Santa Anna back. To help fill the empty treasury, Santa Anna sold more than 20 million acres to the United States of America in the Gadsden Purchase. By 1855, Santa Anna was overthrown and banished. Over more than 11 years, Santa Anna plotted his return. Upon landing in Mexico however, he was again arrested and banished. In exile, he wandered throughout the Caribbean. He was finally allowed back to Mexico in 1874. His pleas for a pension for his service to Mexico fell on deaf ears. Living on the grace of his son-in-law, Santa Anna slowly faded for three years. On June 21, 1876, he died in obscurity.

—*Andrew Galloway*

Further Reading

Hardin, Stephen. *The Alamo 1836: Santa Anna's Texas Campaign*. Westport, CT: Praeger, 2004.

Meyer, Michael C., and William L. Sherman. *The Course of Mexican History*. 4th ed. New York: Oxford University Press, 1991.

Dorr Rebellion (1841–1842)

The 1842 constitutional crisis that briefly resulted in the state of Rhode Island having two competing popularly elected governments and the threat of an armed civil war is sometimes referred to as "Dorr Rebellion" or "Dorr's War." The persistence of the terms of the original 1663 colonial charter that was wholly inadequate for the society brought forth by the American Revolution was, more than 50 years later, the source of active resentment. As the rest of the United States moved toward a more expansive and inclusive definition of who had suffrage, Rhode Island remained trapped under a system that defined the electorate narrowly and whose original provisions had no method of amendment. Before, during, and after the rebellion, both political parties used the "Dorr War" to advantage with followers. For Democrats, popular sovereignty found its hero in Thomas Dorr and his followers. Whigs saw a cautionary tale about insurrections and mobbing driven by Jacksonian politics.

The charter system favored rural free-hold farmers, and in a state where the American industrial revolution was born and the percentage of men in the commercial sector was high, the practical effect was the disenfranchisement of between 40 and 60 percent of the adult white male population by 1840. Only "freemen" who were defined as native-born adult white male land holders and their eldest sons had access to the ballot, the right to serve on juries, and the ability to sue in court. Increasingly, the majority of the state's population was concentrated in towns and cities and was at a political disadvantage in the General Assembly. Democrats and Whigs claimed to be bound by the provisions of the original charter's terms, which allowed alterations by the London government, but the system suited them both. Democrats who wanted suffrage expanded to foreign-born white men who immigrated for work in the textile mills wanted native-born black men excluded. At a stalemate in terms of the parameters of reform, both parties concentrated on gaining power in the state, while the disenfranchised grew restive as they watched the rest of the nation continue to expand the franchise state by state.

Popular reform efforts in the decades prior to the 1842 rebellion failed—most notably that of the Rhode Island Constitutional Party of the 1830s. The Rhode Island Suffrage Association founded in 1840 was more determined. Their position was that the majority had earned the right with the Revolution to determine the nature of their government. The Suffragists had widespread support, and former Whig assemblyman Thomas Wilson Dorr quickly became the leader of the party. Dorr, a Harvard-educated attorney, was himself a beneficiary of the existing system as the son of a prosperous man whose holdings included extensive real estate and textile mills. His father, Sullivan Dorr, was in fact active in the Charterite opposition during the crisis.

In October 1841, the Suffrage Association held a statewide constitutional convention to force the issue of reform. The resulting "People's Constitution" included a widely expanded definition of suffrage, modified the legislative apportionment for the state, established an independent judicial system, and included a state bill of rights. The Suffragists ran an extralegal statewide referendum, which drew up to 60 percent of the white male population of the state. The vote, the organizers claimed, was nearly 14,000 (or more than half the total male population of the state) for the People's Constitution and fewer than 100 against. The figure, whether correct or incorrect, was significant not only for its claims about a true popular sovereignty on the question but because the turnout percentage would have had to include a clear majority of already enfranchised freeholders. The response from the state government and Charterites was to offer a competing constitution with many of the same reforms. The "Law and Order Constitution" was opposed by the Dorrites. The opposition from the Suffragists was primarily located in the constitution's failure to include the large population of foreign-born white men who made up a significant percentage of their party. Thomas Dorr and the Suffragists boycotted the referendum and, ironically, had an active ally at the polls in the form of hard-line Charterites who opposed any amendment to the original charter that served them so well. The Charterite Law and Order Constitution was put to a public referendum in March 1842, and it too passed, giving the state two popularly approved new constitutions. Despite the clear message that a majority of voting Rhode Island men found reform adequate, Dorr and the Suffragists pressed on calling for an election of a new governor and legislature under the terms of its constitution of October 1841.

The Rhode Island General Assembly and Governor Samuel Ward King responded by passing legislation (popularly called the "Algerine Law") that criminalized the activities of the Suffrage Association and its supporters. It was now treason against the state of Rhode Island to run for office in the upcoming April 1842 election called by the Suffrage Association or to attempt to assume any office. Knowing that the Suffrage Association was strongest in the northern half of the state, the law provided for trial of violators by the state Supreme Judicial Council, who openly supported the existing government and whose authority allowed it to try defendants in such cases in areas where reliably loyal jury pools could be found.

On April 18, 1842, the supporters of the People's Constitution elected 35-year-old attorney Thomas Wilson Dorr as governor and a full slate of legislative candidates who called themselves the "People's Government" and the legitimate government of the majority of Rhode Islanders. Two days later, on April 20, 1842, the official election was held, and Samuel Ward King was reelected. As both the factions under Dorr and King claimed legitimacy, the state had two complete rival governments. King immediately appealed to President John Tyler for assistance in putting down what was moving quickly in the divided state in the direction of civil war. Tyler reaffirmed the King administration's legal rights but urged compromise rather than military intervention. King's government began arrests of known Dorrites, while Thomas Dorr and 200 of the Suffragists headed to the capital at Providence in May 1842 with the intention of seizing the state arsenal. The Suffragists found a large contingent of men guarding the arsenal (including Dorr's own father and uncle) and dispersed without incident. Governor King declared martial law in the state and called out the militia. Thomas Dorr, along with many of the Suffragists, fled the state. Dorr was indicted in absentia in August 1842.

Although the Suffragists' 1842 coup failed, King and his charter government still faced widespread dissatisfaction with the constitutional situation. To ameliorate this dissent, a new constitution was adopted in April 1843. The vote was extended to all native-born adult males (including free blacks) who had been in the state for at least two years. Thomas Dorr, still in exile, believed that the time was right to return and press for more reforms by raising the additional reform issues in a trial for treason. Dorr returned to Rhode Island in October 1843 and was, as he planned, arrested.

Dorr was jailed at Providence for six months before his trial. Authorities moved him to the center of the conservative Charterite region of Newport for a trial that began on April 2, 1844. Dorr based his defense on the idea that treason could only be committed against the nation, not an individual state, and that during the statewide crisis of 1842 when the Algerine Law was passed, he and the People's Constitution government were the legitimate government because the voters had overwhelmingly approved the constitution they had created. The judges rejected this line of defense and did not allow the jury to rule upon it. They asserted that since allegiance is due to a state, treason could be committed against it. Further, they declared that the legislature elected in 1843 was legitimate and that no judge or jury could rule on the legitimacy of that in 1842. The jury's authority in the trial, according to the court, was circumscribed by law to considering the facts of the case under the existing law. Since Dorr did not refute the facts surrounding his actions in 1842, he was found guilty of treason against the state on May 6, 1844, and sentence to life in solitary confinement at hard labor. By all reports, Dorr did suffer the harshest terms of the sentence for at least one year. He was denied visitation by family, exercise beyond work, and any reading materials. In 1845, the state offered him amnesty in return for an oath of allegiance to the 1843 constitution. Dorr, in poor health due to conditions at the state prison and his treatment, refused.

Dorr's situation and the large number of supporters for the original rebellion returned the issue to the political arena in the gubernatorial race in 1845. Sympathy for the harsh penalty Dorr received and his firmness on rejecting amnesty for principle won him widespread sympathy from a faction known as "liberationists." When a sympathetic government was elected in 1845, they passed a bill on June 27 of that year, releasing him from prison. His civil rights were restored only in 1851. Dorr had appeals in the system while in prison, abandoning the effort only in 1849. In 1854, the state legislature passed a bill that annulled the original conviction, but the state Supreme Court ruled it unconstitutional. Thomas Dorr died on December 27, 1854, still convinced that he was right in 1842 and refusing to back down. The U.S. Supreme Court, deciding on the one case that reached it rising out of Dorr's War, *Luther v. Borden* (1849), determined that the people had no such rights to rebel without the consent of their government. With that decision written by Justice Roger B. Taney, Abraham Lincoln would, in 1861, challenge the secession of the southern states and justify martial law. But the decision reached in relation to the Dorr Rebellion of 1842 had more profound implications as it called into doubt the legitimacy of the Revolution that created the nation itself as Thomas Dorr would have recognized.

—*Gretchen A. Adams*

See also all entries under Whiskey Rebellion (1794); Molly Maguires (1870s); Brooks-Baxter War (1874); Black Patch War (1909); Bonus Army (1932); Battle of Athens (1946); Sagebrush Rebellion (1979–1981); World Trade Organization Protests (1999).

Further Reading

Dennison, George M. *The Dorr War: Republicanism on Trial, 1831–1861*. Lexington: University Press of Kentucky, 1976.

Gettleman, Marvin E. *The Dorr Rebellion: A Study in American Radicalism, 1833–1849*. New York: Random House, 1973.

Howe, Daniel Walker. *What Hath God Wrought*: *The Transformation of America, 1815–1848*. New York: Oxford University Press, 2007.

Wilentz, Sean. *The Rise of American Democracy: From Jefferson to Lincoln*. New York: W. W. Norton, 2005.

Charterites

By the early 1840s, most states had regularlized their suffrage qualifications to reflect contemporary ideas about democratic participation. Rhode Island, unlike most of the rest of the United States, had nothing approaching universal white male suffrage even 50 years after the American Revolution. The royal charter issued by Charles II in 1663 that created the original colony still marked the parameters of suffrage and even some access to the courts. Although the original charter was a model of enlightened political liberalism in the 17th century, it was woefully inadequate not only for a republic, but for a state whose economy was shifting quickly from agrarian freehold farms to a commercial and industrial base. The constitutional crisis that arose in 1842 called "Dorr Rebellion" (or "Dorr's War") pitted traditionalists called "Charterites" against the "Dorrites" or "Suffragists" of the Rhode Island Suffrage Party lead by Thomas Wilson Dorr. The conflict featured a short period during which the state had two elected governments claiming legitimacy, which nearly erupted into an armed civil war.

The original charter privileged the landowning farmers and their eldest sons by restricting not only voting rights, but jury service and the right to file lawsuits to this class of men. As the northern half of Rhode Island led the industrializing and urbanizing efforts of the post–War of 1812 United States, political power in the state was concentrated into ever-decreasing circles. The southern portion of the state, with its flatter terrain, retained much more of its agricultural base and became the stronghold for the "Charterites" when the Rhode Island Suffrage Association rose in 1840 as a party-based challenger to the state's electoral status quo. The Suffragists' party attracted not only the large number of foreign-born men in the state who had immigrated to work in the textile mills in the northern cities and towns, but those native-born men whose future was tied not to farming but to wage labor.

The Suffragists organized a referendum on their "People's Constitution" that allegedly received 14,000 approving votes and fewer than 100 in favor of the existing charter. The supporters of the charter in state government understood the mood of the people and organized their own counter-reforms in the form of the "Freeholder's Constitution." That, too, passed by a wide margin and contained most of the critical reforms the Dorrites wanted. The Dorrites, however, rejected the constitution because it excluded foreign-born residents of the state from voting. In response, in April 1842, they elected a new legislature and Thomas Dorr as governor, declaring it the will of the people. Governor Samuel Ward King responded by appealing to the federal government, without much success. With two factions claiming to be the legally elected government, the Dorrites attempted to seize the state arsenal at Providence on May 19, 1842.

Charterites came out in full force to defend the arsenal, and the group included Thomas Dorr's own father, Sullivan, and his uncle Crawford Allen. The show of force dissipated the crowd, and the Charterites, fearing an attack in Woonsocket, fortified a building there as well. Despite the strength of the Suffragist movement in that mill city, no attack materialized. But most practical Charterites either favored some modification to the old colonial charter or saw the political expediency in setting the terms of reform themselves. Toward that end, they held their own convention in the Charterite stronghold of Newport and offered their "Law and Order Constitution" to the electorate for a referendum. In November 1842, despite a Dorrite boycott, it passed by a landslide margin. Most of the elements of the People's Constitution were present, with the notable exception that black men who were otherwise eligible were granted suffrage and the foreign-born men who filled the mills of Rhode Island were excluded. The Charterite constitution took effect in May 1843 and brought Rhode Island into the mainstream of the movement toward universal male suffrage in the United States.

—*Gretchen A. Adams*

Further Reading

Dennison, George M. *The Dorr War: Republicanism on Trial, 1831–1861*. Lexington: University Press of Kentucky, 1976.

Gettleman, Marvin E. *The Dorr Rebellion: A Study in American Radicalism, 1833–1849*. New York: Random House, 1973.

Howe, Daniel Walker. *What Hath God Wrought: The Transformation of America, 1815–1848*. New York: Oxford University Press, 2007.

Dorr, Thomas Wilson (1805–1854)

Thomas Wilson Dorr, the leader of a rebellious faction who precipitated a constitutional crisis in Rhode Island in 1842, was born in Providence, Rhode Island, on November 5, 1805, to a Sullivan Dorr, a wealthy textile manufacturer, and his wife. Educated at the exclusive Philips Exeter Academy in Massachusetts and a graduate of Harvard College in 1823, Dorr went on to study law in New York and returned to Providence to practice law and begin a career in state politics in 1827. Elected to the Rhode Island General Assembly in 1834 as a Whig, Thomas Dorr benefitted from the state's restrictive constitution and, by any measure, seems an unlikely organizer of an armed rebellion that briefly made him governor, but that ended with him convicted of treason and imprisoned. But the actions of the "Dorrites" established universal male suffrage in line with the rest of the United States in Rhode Island by 1845.

More than 50 years after the American Revolution, Rhode Island still operated under the terms of the 1663 royal charter granted by King Charles II of England. By 1841, the state was unique in its antiquated methods of determining legislative representation, its failure to adopt some form of universal suffrage for adult white men, and its failure to have a written bill of rights. The original charter that privileged freehold farmers and their eldest sons increasingly not only restricted the expansion of the electorate in the rapidly urbanizing and industrializing state and effectively disenfranchised those whose economic fortunes began to rely on commercial activities and wage labor, but concentrated the state's political power in the shrinking rural population. In 1840, Thomas Dorr joined the Rhode Island Suffrage Association to address the grievances against the state government. Dorr quickly rose to the leadership of the Suffragists, who called a popular convention in 1842. There, they created a "People's Constitution" whose primary feature was general suffrage for white adult men in the state. The government and its supporters, known as "Charterites," responded to the overwhelming support for the Dorrite movement by offering their own "Freeholder's Constitution" that included virtually all the reforms advocated by Dorr and his followers. The Suffragists, having attracted a significant following from the foreign-born mill workers, opposed the Freeholder's Constitution because of its failure to extend the franchise to that group. The Freeholder's Constitution also passed a public referendum, and each group claimed, after statewide elections in April 1842, to be the legally elected government of Rhode Island.

The Charterites, led by Governor Samuel Ward King, appealed to President John Tyler for federal assistance in putting down the Dorr Rebellion. Tyler was reluctant to enter into the fray and urged King to find a compromise. The attack on the state arsenal by Dorrites in May was quickly routed by the state militia, and martial law was imposed. Dorr and many of his followers fled Rhode Island when the Charterite legislature and Governor King proved determined to prosecute them under the quickly passed "Algerine Law" that labeled their actions treason against the state of Rhode Island, placing a $5,000 bounty on Dorr's head.

Dorr remained in exile until October 1843, when he hoped that the recent constitutional reforms that were finally approved by the legislature would protect him. King, however, had him arrested and tried in the Charterite stronghold of Newport. Dorr was found guilty and sentenced to solitary confinement for life at hard labor. He was offered an amnesty after one year's imprisonment, largely as a political move by Governor King because of the widespread public sympathy for his situation. Dorr refused the terms and was released only when the legislature passed an unconditional amnesty bill on his behalf in 1845. The election of his uncle Phillip Allen to the governorship in 1851 resulted in the restoration of his civil rights, but an attempt by the General Assembly to nullify the original verdict in 1854 was a short-lived victory as the state Supreme Court deemed the move unconstitutional. Dorr died shortly thereafter at the age of 49, having given his health and much of his life to the cause of fighting for universal male suffrage.

—Gretchen A. Adams

Further Reading

Dennison, George M. *The Dorr War: Republicanism on Trial, 1831–1861*. Lexington: University Press of Kentucky, 1976.

Gettleman, Marvin E. *The Dorr Rebellion: A Study in American Radicalism, 1833–1849*. New York: Random House, 1973.

Howe, Daniel Walker. *What Hath God Wrought: The Transformation of America, 1815–1848*. New York: Oxford University Press, 2007.

Universal White Male Suffrage

The Revolutionary generation placed a premium on the "independence" of an individual when considering voting capabilities. Only when a man (or, in some states, white women and free black men and women) had sufficient economic independence could he be relied upon to act in the interests of the commonweal rather than himself. Individual states determined the terms by which citizens qualified to vote, but virtually all states through the first decades of independence used some formula of property ownership or personal worth. The decades after the War of 1812 saw rapid expansion in all areas of national life, and each combined to increase the pressure on states to widen the electorate. As states moved toward a universal white male suffrage, though, they regularized the status of a voter by both race and gender by disenfranchising all women and black men.

The improvements in transportation and communication increased the dissemination of ideas. Campaign biographies, religious tracts that stressed individualism and were in tune with natural-rights ideology in politics, the partisan nature of newspaper publishing, and the overtly political nature of commemorations and oratory created a political culture that was pervasive. The rise of industry concentrated wage laborers, craftsmen, and commercial men away from the countryside and effectively disenfranchised many. In addition, the patchwork quality of suffrage qualifications and the increasingly democratic nature of not only American society in general, but in the newly settled areas in particular where suffrage was often automatically granted on arrival, put pressure on all of the states to liberalize their requirements. The Democratic Party capitalized on the movement to recruit white working-class men, and most states had reduced any economic thresholds to voting to virtually none for white men by the early 1820s.

Rhode Island was the most noticeable holdout from this trend toward universal white male suffrage, even as it was in the forefront of the industrialization that reduced the opportunities for individual access to voting rights. The state had failed to create a constitution in the post-Revolutionary years, but relied instead on the 1663 charter granted by King Charles II to create the colony. Unusually progressive for its day in its granting of religious freedom, by 1842, it was stunningly anachronistic. All voting rights, the ability to bring suit in court, or to serve on a jury were tied to freehold rights. A landed farmer and his eldest son had rights, while the large number of wage laborers and small business owners without real estate holdings did not. The state had a constitutional crisis in 1842 with Dorr's Rebellion, which threatened civil war and briefly saw two governments with popular support each claiming authority in the state before order was restored. Ultimately, the conservative Charterists prevailed, but practical considerations forced them to make the necessary reforms to extend suffrage not only to nearly all white adult men in the state, but, against the trend nationwide, Rhode Island included black men as well. With the inclusion of Rhode Island in the democratizing trend of the antebellum decades, nearly universal white male suffrage was achieved by 1845.

—*Gretchen A. Adams*

Further Reading

Dennison, George M. *The Dorr War: Republicanism on Trial, 1831–1861*. Lexington: University Press of Kentucky, 1976.

Gettleman, Marvin E. *The Dorr Rebellion: A Study in American Radicalism, 1833–1849*. New York: Random House, 1973.

Howe, Daniel Walker. *What Hath God Wrought: The Transformation of America, 1815–1848*. New York: Oxford University Press, 2007.

Wilentz, Sean. *The Rise of American Democracy: From Jefferson to Lincoln*. New York: W. W. Norton, 2005.

Luther v. Borden: The Judicial Aftermath of Rhode Island's Dorr Rebellion (1849)

In 1841, the Rhode Island People's Party, a group organized by Thomas Dorr, drafted a new state constitution, which was then ratified by a statewide vote. The new constitution was meant to replace the state's original constitution, which was based on a charter issued by Charles II in 1663, and which enfranchised only a tiny proportion of the state's population. Dorr was elected governor by the newly enfranchised voters, but the charter government refused to accept the new constitution as valid and declared a state of insurrection. In the ensuing military struggle, Dorr's forces were defeated and he fled the state. When he returned, he was tried and convicted for treason and sentenced to life imprisonment, though the legislature soon after ordered his release.

Reproduced here are excerpts of the 1849 Supreme Court decision in Luther v. Borden, *which arose out of a suit filed by Martin Luther, a supporter of Dorr, who was seized in his house by officers of the charter government during the insurrection. Luther argued that the charter government was not the legal government and its officers thus had no right to act as they did. In his opinion for the majority, Chief Justice Roger B. Taney, a longtime supporter of Andrew Jackson, refused to rule on the question of the charter government's legitimacy, saying that such a question was political and beyond the power of the Court to decide. This decision, in effect, upheld the charter government as the legal government of Rhode Island at the time of the Dorr incident.*

Mr. Justice Taney delivered the opinion of the court:

... The charter government ... passed resolutions declaring that all acts done for the purpose of imposing [Dorr's] constitution upon the State to be assumption of the powers of government, in violation of the rights of the existing government and of the people at large; and that it would maintain its authority and defend the legal and constitutional rights of the people.

But notwithstanding the determination of the charter government, and those who adhered to it, to maintain its authority, Thomas W. Dorr, who had been elected governor under the new constitution, prepared to assert the authority of that government by force, and many citizens assembled in arms to support him. The charter government thereupon passed an act declaring the State under martial law, and at the same time proceeded to call out the militia, to repel the threatened attack and to subdue those who were engaged in it. In this state of the contest, the house of the plaintiff, who was engaged in supporting the authority of the new government, was broken and entered in order to arrest him. The defendants were, at the time, in the military service of the old government, and in arms to support its authority.

The Circuit Court ... instructed the jury that the charter government and laws under which the defendants acted were, at the time, the trespass is alleged to have been committed, in full force and effect as the form of government and paramount law of the State, and constituted a justification of the acts of the defendants as set forth in their pleas.

It is the opnion of the Circuit Court that we are now called upon to review.

Certainly, the question which the plaintiff proposed to raise by testimony he offered has not hereto fore been recognized as a judicial one in any of the State courts. ...

In Rhode Island, the question has been directly decided. Prosecutions were there initiated against some of the persons who had been active in the forcible opposition to the old government. And in more than one of the cases evidence was offered on the part of the defense similar to the testimony offered in the Circuit Court, and for the same purpose; that is, for the purpose of showing that the proposed constitution had been adopted by the people of Rhode Island, and had, therefore, become the established government, and consequently that the parties accused were doing nothing more than their duty in endeavoring to support it.

But the courts uniformly held that the inquiry proposed to be made belonged to the political power and not to the judicial; that it rested with the political power to decide whether the charter government had been displaced or not; and when that decision was made, the Judicial Department would be bound to take notice of it as the paramount law of the State, without the aid of oral evidence or the examination of witnesses; that, according to the laws and institutions of Rhode Island, no such change had been recognized by the political power; and that the charter government was the lawful and established government of the State during the period in contest, and that those who were in arms against it were insurgents, and liable to punishment. This doctrine is clearly and forcibly stated in the opinion of the Supreme Court of the State in the trial of Thomas W. Dorr, who was the governor elected under the opposing constitution, and headed the armed force which endeavored to maintain its authority.

It is worthy of remark . . . when we are referring to the authority of State decisions, that the trial of Thomas W. Dorr took place after the constitution of 1843 went into operation. The judges who decided that case held their authority under that constitution; and it is admitted on all hands that it was adopted by the people of the State, and is the lawful and established government. . . .

The point, then raised here has been already decided by the courts of Rhode Island. The question relates, altogether, to the constitution and the laws of that State; and the well settled rule in this court is, that the courts of the United States adopt and follow the decisions of the State courts in questions which concern merely the constitution and laws of the State.

Upon what ground could the Circuit Court of the United States which tried this case have departed from this rule, and disregarded and overruled the decisions of the courts of Rhode Island? . . . [T]he power of determining that a State government has been lawfully established, which the courts of the State disown and repudiate, is not one of them. Upon such a question the courts of the United States are bound to follow the decisions of the State tribunals, and must therefore regard the charter government as the lawful and established government during the time of this contest.

Moreover, the Constitution of the United States, as far as it has provided for an emergency of this kind, and authorized the general government to interfere in the domestic concerns of a State, has treated the subject as political in its nature, and placed power in the hands of that department.

Under . . . the Constitution it rests with Congress to decide what government is the established one in a State. For as the United States guarantee to each State a republican government, Congress must necessarily decide what government is established in the State before it can determine whether it is republican or not. And when the senators and representatives of a State are admitted into the councils of the Union, the authority of the government under which they are appointed, as well as its republican character, is recognized by the proper constitutional authority. And its decision is binding on every other department of the government, and could not be questioned in a judicial tribunal. . . .

So, too, as relates to the clause in the above mentioned article of the Constitution.... Congress... provided that, "in case of an insurrection in any State against the government thereof, it shall be lawful for the President of the United States, on application of the Legislature of such State or of the executive (when the Legislature cannot be convened), to call forth such number of the militia of any other State or States, as may be applied for, as he may judge sufficient to suppress such insurrection."

By this act, the power of deciding whether the exigency had arisen upon which the government of the United States is bound to interfere, is given to the President.... [H]e must determine what body of men constitute the Legislature, and who is the government, before he can act.... If there is an armed conflict, like the one of which we are speaking, it is a case of domestic violence, and one of the parties must be in insurrection against the lawful government. And the President must, of necessity, decide which is the government, and which party is unlawfully arrayed against it, before he can perform the duty imposed upon him by the act of Congress.

After the President has acted and called out the militia, is a circuit court of the United States authorized to inquire whether his decision was right? Could the court, while the parties were actually contending in arms for the possession of the government, call witnesses before it and inquire which party represented a majority of the people?... If the judicial power extends so far, the guarantee contained in the Constitution of the United States is a guarantee of anarchy, and not of order. Yet if this right does not reside in the courts when the conflict is raging, if the judicial power is at that time bound to follow the decision of the political, it must be equally bound when the contest is over. It cannot, when peace is restored, punish as offenses and crimes the acts which it before recognized, and was bound to recognize, as lawful.

It is true that in this case the militia were not called out by the President. But upon the application of the governor under the charter government, the President recognized him as the executive power of the State, and took measures to call out the militia to support his authority if it should be found necessary for the general government to interfere; and it is admitted in the argument, that it was the knowledge of this decision that put an end to the armed opposition to the charter government, and prevented any further efforts to establish by force the proposed constitution. The interference of the President, therefore, by announcing his determination, was as effectual as if the militia had been assembled under his orders. And it should be equally authoritative. For certainly no court of the United States, with a knowledge of this decision, would have been justified in recognizing the opposing party as the lawful government; or in treating as wrongdoers or insurgents the officers of the government which the President had recognized, and was prepared to support by an armed force. In the case of foreign nations, the government acknowledged by the President is always recognized in the courts of justice. And this principle has been applied by the act of Congress to the sovereign States of the Union.

The remaining question is whether the defendants, acting under military orders issued under the authority of the government, were justified in breaking and entering the plaintiff's house.... Unquestionably a military government, established as the permanent government of the State, would not be a republican government and it would be the duty of Congress to overthrow it. But the law of Rhode Island evidently contemplated no such government. It was intended merely for the crisis, and to meet the peril in which the existing government was placed by the armed resistance to its authority. . . . And if the government of Rhode Island deemed armed opposition so formidable, and so ramified throughout the State, as to require the use of its military force and the declaration of martial law, we see no ground upon which this court can questions its authority. It was a state of war; and the established government resorted to the rights and usages of war to maintain itself, and to overcome the unlawful opposition. And in that state of things the officers engaged in its military service might lawfully arrest anyone, who, from the information before them, they had reasonable grounds to believe was engaged in the insurrection; and might order a house to be forcibly entered and searched, when there were reasonable grounds for supposing he might be there concealed. . . . No more force, however, can be used than is necessary to accomplish this object. And if the power is exercised for the purposes of oppression, or any injury willfully done to person or property, the party by whom, or by whose order, it is committed would undoubtedly be answerable.

Upon the whole, we see no reason for disturbing the judgment of the Circuit court. The admission of evidence to prove that the charter government was the established government of the State was an irregularity, but is not material to the judgment. . . .

Much of the argument on the part of the plaintiff turned upon political rights and political questions, upon which the court has been urged to express an opinion. We decline doing so. The high power has been conferred on this court of passing judgment upon the acts of the State sovereignties, and of the legislative and executive branches of the federal government, and of determining whether they are beyond the limits of power marked out for them respectively by the Constitution of the United States. This tribunal, therefore, should be the last to overstep the boundaries which limit its own jurisdiction. And while it should always be ready to meet any question confided to it by the Constitution, it is equally its duty not to pass beyond its appropriate sphere of action, and to take care not to involve itself in discussions which properly belong to other forums. No one, we believe, has ever doubted the proposition, that, according to the institutions of this country, the sovereignty in every State resides in the people of the State, and that they may alter and change their form of government at their own pleasure. But whether they have changed it or not by abolishing an old government, and establishing a new one in its place, is a question to be settled by the political power. And when that power has decided, the courts are bound to take notice of its decision, and to follow it.

The judgment of the Circuit Court must therefore be affirmed.

Source: 48 U.S. (7 How.) 1 (1849).

Philadelphia Nativist Riots (1844)

Riots took place on May 6–8, and July 6–7, 1844, in Philadelphia, Pennsylvania, where there had been a rise in anti–Roman Catholic sentiment with many people worried about the increasing Irish Catholic population, so many Irish people having immigrated to the United States with the increase in the severity of the Irish potato famine.

Following the outbreak of the potato famine in Ireland, many Irish started to immigrate to the United States and elsewhere, and many of these immigrants headed for the major cities in the United States, where the start of the Industrial Revolution had led to the demand for a large unskilled labor force. Many poor immigrants headed for Philadelphia, amongst other places. This led to some tensions as the existing population was largely Protestant, and most of the new immigrants were Roman Catholic. In the early 1840s, anti-Catholic leaflets were distributed around Philadelphia, and matters came to a head on November 10, 1842. All students in government schools in Philadelphia started the day by reading the Protestant King James version of the Bible. This had been accepted since the Anglicans took over the reins of the government of the city from the Quakers in the 1740s. However on that day, the Roman Catholic bishop of Philadelphia, Francis Kenrick, wrote to the Board of Controllers of Public Schools asking that Roman Catholic children should be allowed to read the Douai version of the Bible. He also asked that Roman Catholic students be excused from Protestant religious education classes. The board agreed with this and ordered that no child should be forced to take part in religious teaching, and that parents could nominate the version of the Bible from which they wished to read.

In late 1843, rumors started circulating that a school director from Kensington, Hugh Clark, who was Catholic, had visited a girls' school and asked the principal to stop reading the Bible. The principal then complained that she would rather lose her job than obey that command, to which Clark reported that he found students had stopped reading the Bible to use a different version. He felt that this was confusing and suggested that perhaps the Bible reading should stop. This was soon interpreted as a Roman Catholic interfering in the religious observances of Protestants and that the Catholics were trying to stop the reading of the Bible.

As a result, on May 3, 1844, the primary supporters of the Protestant nativist movement, the American Republican Party, held a meeting in Kensington denouncing the situation. As the talk took part in a largely Roman Catholic Irish area, there were many hecklers, and people hissed the speakers off the stage as well as throwing missiles at them. Three days later, the nativists returned in large numbers and started urging for action. As it started raining soon afterwards, the crowd moved into a local market where inflamed rhetoric led to scuffles between protesters and counterprotesters. People from the nearby buildings then started opening fire, and one or two nativists were shot dead. Soon a large crowd of nativists went on the rampage, and they attacked the nearby Seminary of the Sisters of Charity and the house of some well-known Catholics. Two more nativists were killed, but the riot was eventually controlled as constables from nearby areas were brought into Philadelphia.

On May 7, nativists urged for Protestants to rise up and stop attempts by the Roman Catholics to control the city. Marching to Kensington, there were nativists who shot at passersby and vice versa. It was during these riots that nativists burned down the Hibernia fire station, the original market used in the street dispute on the previous day, and about 30 homes. General George Cadwalader had to call out the local militia to try to calm down the situation, and Bishop Kenrick issued a statement asking for all Catholics to avoid confrontations.

The matter calmed down slightly, but on May 8, rioting started again with nativists marching on Kensington and burning down St. Michael's Roman Catholic Church and its rectory, and also attacking the Seminary of the Sisters of Charity, the target of the earlier riot. It was largely contained in Kensington, but another nativist crowd gathered and marched on St. Augustine's Roman Catholic Church, on Fourth Street in central Philadelphia. Mayor John Morin Scott pleaded with the crowd and deployed troops nearby, but they were unable to stop people from setting fire to the church and cheering when the steeple fell. During these riots, some 14 people were killed, 50 badly injured, 200 forced to flee, and property worth some $150,000 was damaged or destroyed.

It was clear that the rioting was directed against the Irish Catholics, not the German Catholics, and Mayor Scott had the militia standing guard on Catholic properties. Bishop Kenrick also tried to diffuse the situation by ordering that all Catholic churches close on the following Sunday (May 12) to avoid any provocation. On June 18, the grand jury blamed the Irish Catholics for starting the trouble, and on the authorities for not reacting fast enough to the escalating situation. Nativists argued that they were victims of the Catholics and that Mayor Scott was in a large part responsible for the problems.

Gradually, the situation calmed down, but on July 4, a large demonstration by the Native American Party took place to coincide with Independence Day. Father John Patrick Dunn of the Church of St. Philip Neri was worried that his church might bear the brunt of any rioting, and asked for a company of soldiers to help guard it. Twenty-five muskets were made available to the church. Five of these were later found to be defective, but the demonstration passed off peacefully. However, on the following day, several thousand nativists started demonstrating in front of the church, and Father Dunn deployed his armed volunteers to protect the place. At that point, the sheriff intervened, disarming those guarding the church and urging the mob to disperse. However, a man who had been injured in the May riots called on the crowd to search the church in case there were any other weapons there. Another search by the militia unearthed a keg of gunpowder, and also 53 muskets and 10 pistols. The search party remained to guard the church, and the crowd gradually dwindled away.

At noon on July 6, another crowd appeared outside the church, and after a show of force by the militia—numbering 150—they dispersed. Three cannons were then deployed, and when the crowd started throwing rocks at the militia, General Cadwalader ordered the firing of one of the cannons. After protests, he countermanded the order and, on the following day, released a man called Charles Naylor, who had been involved in begging Cadwalader not to open fire. It was not long before the demonstrators themselves laid their hands on a cannon and started firing it at the church. A second cannon was then found at the wharfs and used to fire at the church. Massive rioting then took place, and with soldiers firing on the crowd, seven were killed and nine seriously wounded. By the early morning, the militia had seized control of both cannons, and there were 15 to 20 dead, including some soldiers. Governor David R. Porter continued to move soldiers into the city, and by July 7, there were about 5,000 militia. Gradually, the numbers were scaled down, but tension remained, especially after the grand jury again blamed the Catholics for the rioting, but this time supported the actions of authorities.

There were worries that there might be rioting in other cities, especially in New York City, but these did not eventuate. The Nativist Riots were to become an election issue that the Whig Party used to garner support from the nativists, an action condemned by the Democratic Party. The presidential elections saw a victory for the Democrat, James Polk (who won Pennsylvania), over the Whig, Henry Clay.

—*Justin Corfield*

See also all entries under Pueblo Revolt (1680); Philadelphia Election Riot (1742); Pima Revolt (1751); Know-Nothing Riots (1855–1856).

Further Reading

Clark, Dennis. *The Irish in Philadelphia: Ten Generations of Urban Experience*. Philadelphia: Temple University Press, 1973.

Weigley, R. F., et al., eds. *Philadelphia: A 300-Year History*. New York: W. W. Norton & Company, 1982.

Catholicism

With the exception of the French in parts of Canada, most of the settlers in North America during the 18th century were from Britain or the Netherlands, and the vast majority of these were Protestant. Some, such as the Pilgrim Fathers who had arrived in the 17th century, were Puritans. As such, there was widespread distrust of the Roman Catholics in many parts of North America, and in the United States after it gained its independence. Some of this was clearly doctrinal, but many Protestants were nervous about a large group that took their spiritual leadership from the Papacy. These two reasons for anti-Catholic hatred in Philadelphia—especially the latter—helped the Protestant protagonists during the Nativist Riots in 1844.

There had been Roman Catholics among some of the early settlers in what became the United States. Lord Baltimore had hoped that Catholics might settle in Maryland, although they were never more than a small minority of the state's inhabitants. There were also the French in areas such as New Orleans, and the Spanish to the west. However, not until the early 19th century were there large influxes of Irish Catholics into Pennsylvania. This came with the Irish potato famine, and hundreds of thousands of Irish leaving Ireland each year in the hope of a new life in the United States, Australia, or elsewhere. As this coincided with industrialization in the United States, this led to many flocking to Philadelphia, where they found work in the newly enlarged iron and steel foundries, or in the factories nearby.

As most of these newly arrived Irish Catholics were poor, it was not unnatural that many sent their children to the local government schools, which in turn led to friction over the readings from the Bible. This was the reason that was easily exploited by the nativists, who claimed that the Catholic children would prevent Protestants from using their own Bibles, thereby forcing Protestant children to study religion as Catholics.

The Roman Catholic bishop, Francis Kenrick, was soon drawn into the dispute. He had been born in Dublin, Ireland, had been trained at Rome, where he was ordained, and then appointed to a chair of theology at a seminary at Bardstown, Kentucky, in 1821. During his time in Kentucky, he was involved in what is now termed "interfaith dialogue," whereby he worked with local Protestants. It was precisely because of this that, in 1830, he was appointed to take over the diocese of Philadelphia, which had been badly managed. He proved active in working with a cholera epidemic that broke out in 1832.

The rioting in 1844 came as a shock to many of the Catholics in Philadelphia, and Kenrick immediately decided to play down the situation, entrusting the defense of churches to the civil authorities and temporarily stopping church services to prevent anything said from inflaming the situation. It resulted in some Catholic property being lost in the riots, two churches being set on fire, and antagonism with some of the more aggressive members of the congregation. However, it did win praise from many in Philadelphia, and a number of prominent people from the city subsequently converted to Catholicism. However, in 1848, Pope Pius IX opposed the liberal revolutions in Europe, and this would once again lead to antagonism between Catholics and nativists.

—*Justin Corfield*

Further Reading

Clark, Dennis. *The Irish in Philadelphia: Ten Generations of Urban Experience*. Philadelphia: Temple University Press, 1973.

Purcell, Richard J. "Francis Patrick Kenrick." *Dictionary of American Biography*. Vol. 5, 339–340. New York: Charles Scribner's Sons, 1960.

German Americans

The first Germans known to have settled in the United States were some artisans who lived in Jamestown in 1608, but the first place to have a significant German community was Germantown, Pennsylvania, which was established in 1683 near Philadelphia. Initially, most of the Germans moving to North America were Protestants, including many members of small religious sects who faced persecution in Europe. Some of the Hessian soldiers who came over to fight for the British in the American War of Independence also settled in the Americas, and indeed in the 1790 census, the first taken since independence, it appeared that some 9 percent of the white population of the new nation were Germans or of German descent. The major focus of these was in Pennsylvania, where they made up about a third of the entire population of the state, but until the 1810s, the overwhelming majority of these were Protestants.

Following the end of the War of 1812, increasing numbers of Catholic Germans were moving to North America. The Germans in Philadelphia, especially the Catholics and the members of the small sects such as the Mennonites, Anabaptists, and Moravians, saw the Quakers in Pennsylvania as natural allies against the Anglican ascendancy. Some were artisans working in cities such as Philadelphia, but many were farmers who brought with them intensive agricultural practices which proved successful in the fertile soils of Pennsylvania. It may seem odd that the Germans who were Lutherans and those who were Catholic should make common cause. These were collectively known as the Pennsylvania "Dutch," a corruption of "Deutsch," but also because many of the Germans in Pennsylvania at the time came from the Rhineland, the Palatine, and other areas near the Netherlands.

Many of the early German Americans in the United States were politically aware, having left Europe for religious or political reasons. Indeed, large numbers of Catholics who moved to Philadelphia after 1815 did so to escape the settling of scores that took place in the former Confederation of the Rhine, the pro-French "state" established by Napoleon between 1806 and 1813. Many more politically conscious Germans were to migrate to the United States after the failure of the Revolutions of 1848.

Because many of the German businessmen tended to favor members of their community, it was not unnatural that antagonisms arose, and it was not long before Germans became targets of hatred in the 1844 Nativist Revolts. Although many of the Nativists focused their hatred on Roman Catholics, for Germans, they did not seem to discriminate, as many of the Germans attacked were Protestants.

—*Justin Corfield*

Further Reading

Barry, Colman J. *The Catholic Church and German Americans*. Washington, DC: Bruce Publishing Co., 1953.

Luebke, Frederick C. *Germans in the New World*. Urbana: University of Illinois Press, 1990.

Wood, Ralph, ed. *The Pennsylvania Germans*. Princeton, NJ: Princeton University Press, 1942.

Index

Abel, I. W., 996
Abernathy, Ralph, 910
Abolitionists
   and Harpers Ferry raid, 415, 420
   and John Brown, 257–258,
   as moral reformers, 416, 425–426
   and Nat Turner, 269
   overview, 279–280
   and slave system, 252
   and women's movement, 474
Abortion
   and *Roe v. Wade*, 1055–1056
Abourezk, James, 1076
Acadians, 118
"Account of the Boston Tea Party" (Hewes) (1772), 204–206
"Account of the Course of the [Homestead] Strike," 637–640
"Account of the Destruction of Lt. Governor Hutchinson's House by the Stamp Act Rioters in Boston, An" (1765), 148–150
"Account of the Killings at the Mining Encampment in Ludlow, Colorado," 718–719
"Account of Violence between Strikers and Company Security Guards," 634–637
Acequia (ditch), 39
Acoma Pueblo nation, 39
Act for the Better Ordering and Governing Negroes and Other Slaves in This Province, An (1740), 73–74
Adams, Abigail
   and the Boston Tea Party, 195
   and women's movement, 473
Adams, Henry, 1067, 1069
Adams, John
   ambassadorship, 157
   biography, 157–158
   on Boston Massacre crowd, 158
   and Boston Massacre defense, 154, 155, 159
   and the Boston Tea Party, 196
   First Continental Congress, 200
   and Jonathan Mayhew, 146
   and the protest movement, 143
   reaction to repeal of Stamp Act, 136
   and Thomas Preston, 161–162
Adams, John Quincy
   and antiwar activism, 927
   and John Adams, 158
Adams, Samuel
   biography, 139–140
   and the Boston Tea Party, 194, 195, 196
   First Continental Congress, 200
   Granary Burying Ground, 159
   and John Adams, 157
   on Shays' Rebellion, 215
   and Stamp Act Congress, 145
   and Stamp Act protests, 130, 132, 141
Addams, Jane
   antiwar activism, 928
   and women's movement, 480
"Address to Judiciary Committee of House of Representatives of the House of Representatives by Victoria C. Woodhull," 494–496
"Address to the People" (Brooks-Baxter War), 546
"Address to the People of Hampshire County, Massachusetts, Setting Forth the Causes of Shays' Rebellion, An" (1786), 223–224
Adelantado (economic power), 39
Admiralty Act, 130–131
Admiralty Courts
   colonial, 130–131, 143
   protests against, 134, 141
   and Stamp Act Congress, 144
   trial by jury, 147
Advocate of Peace journal, 927
African Americans
   and the civil rights movement (1953–1968), 891–901

African Americans (continued)
  collective action, xxiii–xxiv
  and Detroit Riots (1967), 987–992, 993–994
  disenfranchisement of, 318
  and Great Migration, 757, 773–775
  and Homestead Strike, 625
  and Jewish Americans, 693–694
  and Ku Klux Klan, 542
  and Louisiana 1870 population, 537
  lynching of, 775, 776
  and New Orleans Riot (1866), 449–452
  New York Draft Riots, 435, 438–439
  and northern migration, 766
  and police brutality, 880–881
  and racism, 445–446
  and Radical Republicans, 552
  and Red Summer Riots, 765, 767–771
  right to vote, 456
  and Tulsa Race Riot (1921), 771, 801–804
  and Watts Riots (1965), 965–971
  and Zoot Suit Riot, 869, 874, 875
African American soldiers
  and Houston Riot, 749
  overview, 753–754
Agua Dulce Creek, 298
Ahmann, Mathew, 905
Aiken Massacre, 384–385
Akeley (Ekley), Francis, 196
Akerman, Amos Tappan (attorney general), 537–538
A. L. A. Schecter Poultry Corp v. United States, 855
Alabama
  and civil rights movement, 895, 896, 897–898, 899
  and First Missouri Compromise, 356
  and SCLC, 910
Alamance, Battle of, 172, 177–178, 181, 182
Alamo, Battle of (1836), 296, 300, 303, 309
Alarm, The, 578, 585
"Albion Hall," 857
Alcatraz Island Occupation (1969–1970)
  collective action, xxii, 1031–1034
  and Indians of All Tribes, 1035–1036
  and John Trudell, 1039–1040
  and Red Power, 1074

  and Richard Oakes, 1037, 1039
  and the termination policy, 1038–1039
"Alcatraz Proclamation to the Great White Father," 1035, 1040–1042
Alema, Octabiana, 730
"Algerine Law," 312, 313, 317
Algiers Motel Incident, The (Hersey), 990
Algonquian nation, 17
Allegheny Arsenal, 566, 569–570
Allen, Crawford, 316
Allen, Levi, 538
Allen, Phillip, 318
Allen, William, 91–93
Allentown (PA), 93
Allerton, Isaac, 2, 5
Almanza Dragoons, 105
Alpha Kappa Alpha (AKA), 1047, 1048
Altgeld, John Peter
  Haymarket Riot, 582
  on Pullman Strike, 648
Altimira, José, 343
Amalgamated Association of Iron and Steel Workers (AA)
  "Account of the Course of the Strike," 637–640
  "Account of Violence between Strikers and Company Security Guards," 634–637
  and Homestead Strike, 619–627
  lockout, 631
  overview, 629–630
American Academia of Arts and Science, 218
American Anti-Slavery Society (AASS)
  Declaration of Sentiments, 415
  established, 279
  and Susan B. Anthony, 484
  and women's movement, 474
American Association of University Women (AAUW), 1047, 1048
American Civil Liberties Union, 929
American Civil War
  and antiwar activism, 927–928
  and Bleeding Kansas, 347, 351
  causes of, 425–427, 441–442
  and conscription, 442
  and Copperheads, 443
  Elisha Baxter, 549
  guerilla warfare, 353
  and Harpers Ferry Raid, 420–421

Joseph Brooks, 550
Nauvoo Legion, 392
and Neal S. Dow, 366–367
and New York Draft Riots, 435
American Colonization Society, 445
American Crisis (Paine), 141
American Equal Rights Association (AERA)
and Nineteenth Amendment, 490
and NWSA, 487–488
and Susan B. Anthony, 484–485
and women's movement, 477, 483
American Federation of Labor (AFL)
and auto industry, 847–849, 852–853
and Boston Police Strike, 758, 761, 762
and IWW, 744
and John L. Lewis, 667
and Knights of Labor, 599
overview, 851–852
and socialism, 746
unionization, 762–763
American Federation of State, County and Municipal Workers, 763
American Football League, 898–899
American Friends Service Committee, 932
American Independence, 181
American Independent Party, 1009, 1023
American Indian Movement (AIM)
Broken Treaties protest, 1067–1070, 1074
and Dick Wilson, 1079, 1082, 1083
and FBI, 1080–1081
and John Trudell, 1040
overview, 1071–1072
and Pine Ridge Reservation, 1082
Red Power, 1073–1074
and Wounded Knee occupation, 1075–1077
American Indian Studies Program, 1036–1037
American Indians. *See* Native Americans
American Legion, 802
American Nurses Association (ANA), 1047, 1048
American Olympic Committee, 840
American Party. *See* Know-Nothing Party
American Peace Society, 927
American Railway Union (ARU)
overview, 651–652
Pullman Strike, 643–650, 651–652
and socialism, 746

American Republican Party
formation, 373, 378
and Philadelphia Nativist Riots, 326
American Revenue Act (1733), 127
American Revolution
and Boston Massacre, 151
and nativism, 378
and Pine Tree Riot, 183
Polish soldiers, 665
and Regulator Movement, 173–174
and suspicious fires, 83
and war bonds, 228–229
William Tryon, 182
and women's movement, 473
American Tobacco Company (ATC)
and Black Patch War, 697, 698
and DTDPPA, 702–703
overview, 701–702
American War of Independence. *See* American Revolution
American Woman Suffrage Association (AWSA)
overview, 483–484
and women's movement, 478, 488 479–480
American Workers Party (AWP), 848, 852–853
"Americanization," 869, 877
Americans Against Escalation in Iraq, 933
Amherst College, 761
Amherst, Jeffrey
biography, 117–118
French and Indian War, 118
Ohio River Valley, 121
and Pontiac's Rebellion, 109, 112, 113–114, 117, 118
smallpox epidemic, 124
Ammon, Robert, 569
Amoskeag River, 188
Amoss, David, 699
"Article by James McPartland Describing His Infiltration of the Molly Maguires, An" 467–471
An Impartial Relation of the First Rise and Cause of the Recent Differences in Publick Affairs (Husband), 180
Anacostia Flats
Battle of, 835–836
and BEF, 831, 833

Anacostia Flats (continued)
  and Douglas MacArthur, 840
  and Walter Waters, 844
Anarchism
  and Alexander Berkman, 626
  bombings, 575, 586–587
  and the Haymarket Riot, 575, 577, 585
  overview, 585–586
Anarchist circular (Spies), 591–592
Ancient Order of the Hibernians (AOH), 459, 461
Anderson, William ("Bloody Bill"), 353
Andreas McKenna Polling and Research, 1133
Andros, Sir Edmund
  Dominion of New England, 59
  Leisler's Rebellion, 53
Andry, Manuel, 262
"Angel of the Coal Camp," 709
Anglican Church
  and Arthur Dobbs, 179
  and Philadelphia Election Riot, 91–93
  and William Tryon, 181, 182
Anglican Communion, 95
Anglo-Powhatan War, 12
Angola, 70, 71
Anthony, Susan B.
  biography, 484–486
  and ERA, 1053
  illegal voting, 497–499
  and Nineteenth Amendment, 490
  and NWSA, 487–489, 490
  "Social Purity" Speech, 501–504
  and women's movement, 477–478, 480, 483
Anthracite Board of Trade, 461
Anthracite Coal Region, 661–662
Anti-Catholicism
  in Colonial New York, 61, 62
  and Irish immigrants, 445
  and Know-Nothing Party, 373–374, 377
  Leisler's Rebellion, 53, 54, 60
  and nativism, 378
  Philadelphia Nativist Riots, 325
  and Stamp Act protests, 132
Antietam, Battle of, 428
Anti-Imperialist League, 928–929, 933
Anti-Imperialist periodical, 929

Antiquities Act (1906), 1091
Anti-Semitism
  Bloody Monday, 377
  Springfield Race Riot, 689, 691
Antiwar activism
  A Father's Disgust, 960–961
  and Chicago Riots (1968), xxiv, 1009–1017
  collective action, xxiv, 925–935
  and counterculture, 937–938
  Green Corn Rebellion (1917), xxiv, 739–742, 743–744, 950–951
  and the Moratorium, 941–942
  SDS leaflet, 950–951
  United States v. Spock, 957–960
Apaches
  in New Mexico, 29, 30, 34–35
  Pima Revolt, 100
  and Tohono O'odham, 106, 107
Appalachia, 797
Appeal to Reason, 746
Appomattox, Battle of, 428
Appomattox Court House, 441
Aquash, Anna Mae, 1081
Arapaho, 613
Arau, Sergio, 1131
Arbeiter-Zeitung. See Die Arbeiter-Zeitung
Arbitration, 644, 647
Arce, Francisco, 335
Ariovistus D. Pardee and Company, 661
Arizona
  "Day without an Immigrant" protests, 1129, 1131
  Franciscan missionaries, 37
  Plan de San Diego, 727
  Pima Revolt, 99, 100, 101
Arkansas
  American Civil War, 551
  Brooks-Baxter War, 545–547
  and civil rights movement, 894, 895
  WCU, 739
Arkansas Central Railroad, 546
Arkansas National Guard, 895
Arkansas Territory, 476
Army of Northern Virginia, 428
Army Topographical Engineers, 333, 337, 341
Arnold, F. W., 651
Arredondo, Joaquín, 308

Arson
  in colonial New York, 83
  and Detroit Riots, 989
  and Watts Riot, 967, 973–974
Articles of Confederation
  call for reworking, 237
  and Shays' Rebellion, 214
Assembly Bill 413, 1085
Atascosito road, 296, 298
Atchison (KS), 348
Atchison, David
  as proslavery activist, 348, 349
  Topeka Constitution, 362
Athens, Battle of (1946), xxii, 883–885
Athens Water Company, 884
"Athletic clubs," 768
Atkinson, Edward, 928
Atkinson, Theodore, 185
Atkinson, Ti-Grace, 1047
Atlanta (GA)
  "Day without an Immigrant" protests, 1129, 1130
  Great Migration, 773
  1906 race riots, 778
Atlanta Constitution
  and Atlanta Race Riot (1906), 681
Atlanta Race Riot (1906)
  collective action, xxiv, 681–687
  and economic competition, 685
  and white supremacy, 686–687
Atlantic Journal, 681
Attica Prison Riot
  collective action, xxiii–xxiv, 1059–1061
  cruel and unusual punishment, 1063–1064
Attucks, Crispus
  biography, 158–159
  and Boston Massacre, 153, 154
Atwood, Caleb, 185
Auboyneau, John, 80, 89
Auchmuty, Robert, 154, 157
Austin, Stephen F.
  biography, 305–306
  and Texas Revolt, 289, 291–295, 297
Australia, 189
Austro-Hungarian Empire
  and Eastern European immigrants, 665
  and Lattimer Massacre, 663

Authorized Bible, 95
Auto Workers Union
  and labor movement, 847
Autobiography of Malcolm X, 908
Automobile industry
  and Detroit Riots, 988
  and labor movement, 847
Avondale Mine disaster
  and Molly Maguires, 460
  and unionism, 466
Ayeta, Father, 33, 42
Aztlán, 731

Babbitt, Bruce, 1086
Baboquivari Mountains, 100, 104
Backcountry farmers
  American Revolution, 174
  Regulator Movement, 169
  and Shays' Rebellion, 207
Bacon, Nathaniel
  and Bacon's Rebellion, 3–7, 12–13, 20
  biography, 3–4, 9–10
  "Declaration of the People of Virginia," 6, 22–26
  "Manifesto," 21–24
  significance, 1, 7
  and Susquehannock Indians, 4, 18
Bacon's Rebellion (1676)
  collective action, xxii, 1–7
  and Sir William Berkeley, 3
"Badlands," 689, 693–694
Baird, General, 450–451
Baird, Eva-Lee, 933
Baker, Ella, 912
Baker, Newton
  military segregation, 753
  and Red Summer Riots, 768
Bakke case, 899
Baldwin, James, 277
Baldwin-Felts Detective Agency
  and Blair Mountain Battle, 793
  and industrial violence, 715
  and Matewan Massacre, 799–800
  Paint-Creek/Cabin-Creek Strike, 797
  and Sid Hatfield, 798, 799
  and UMWA, 717
Baldwin, Roger, 929

Bale, Edward Turner, 339–340
Baltimore (MD)
   and Great Railroad Strikes, 563, 566, 569
   Know-Nothing Party, 373, 374
   Know-Nothing Riots, 374
   and Plug Uglies, 373, 374, 379–380
   and Rip Raps, 380–381
Baltimore and Ohio Railroad
   and Great Railroad Strikes, 563, 570
   and Harpers Ferry raid, 419
Baltimore, Lord (Cecilius Calvert), 329
Bandholtz, Harry, 794
Bankruptcy law, 214
Banks, Dennis
   AIM leadership, 1067, 1068
   and Wounded Knee Occupation, 1075
Banks, Nathan B., 449
Bannan, Benjamin, 460
Bapst, John, 370
Barbados assemble, 54
Barbee, John, 377
Barnett, Ross, 896
Barnett, Terri, 1101
Barre, Isaac, 129–130
Barrett, Edward, 579
Barry, Marion, 912
Bates, Daisy, 895
Bathurst, Robert, 70, 77
"Battle of Seattle," 1121, 1123
Battle of Toledo, 847, 852–853
Baxter, Elisha
   biography, 549–550
   Brooks-Baxter War, 545–547, 551–552
   and Joseph Brooks, 550, 551
Bayard, Nicholas, 54, 55
Bear Flag, 336, 341
Bear Flag Republic, 336, 337, 342, 344
Bear Flag Revolt (1946), xxiv, 333–338
Bear Flaggers, 339–341, 344
Beard, Dewey, 607
Beard, William, 134–135
Beauregard, Pierre G. T., 382
Beaver, 195
Beaver Falls strike, 626
Beaver-hunting grounds, 17–18
Beckwith, George, 927

Beecher, Catherine
   and Nineteenth Amendment, 490
   and women's movement, 474
Beecher, Henry Ward
   and AWSA, 483–484
   and Nineteenth Amendment, 490
Beekman, David, 239
Beekman, Henry, Jr., 85
Bellecourt, Clyde, 1067
"Benefit of clergy," 253
Benevolence organizations, 473, 474, 479
Bennett, Henry, 699
Bennett, Ned, 265
Bennett, Rolla, 265
Benton, Benjamin, 374, 379–380
Benton, Thomas Hart, 341, 342
Berger, Victor, 653–654, 746
Berkeley, William
   Bacon's Rebellion, 2–7, 9–10
   biography, 11–13
Berkman, Alexander
   antiwar activism, 929
   and Homestead Strike, 626
Bernard, Francis, 130
Bernhisel, John Milton, 394
Berrigan, Fathers Philip and Daniel, 931
Bethune, Mary McLeod, 677–678
Bexar. *See* San Antonio de Bexar
Bible, Douai version, 326
Bidwell, John, 333
Big Foot
   and Pine Ridge Reservation, 1081, 1082
   Wounded Knee Massacre, 605, 606, 607
"Big Four," 987, 993
Big Hole, Battle of, 554
Bill of Rights (1689)
   Constitutional ratification, 238
   and Lattimer Massacre, 663
   and Stamp Act protests, 129
Bills of exchange, 229
Biracialism, 415
Birmingham (AL), 773
Birth of a Nation (film), 542, 805
Bishop, Joseph, 629
Bituminous coal, 707
Black, William Perkins, 581–582

"Black belt," 347
Black codes
 after Nat Turner's Rebellion, 275
 and New Orleans Race Riot (1900), 671
 during Reconstruction, 450, 454, 456
Black Coyote, 607
Black feminism, 1044–1045
Black Hawk War (1865–1868), 392
Black Panthers
 and Democratic National Convention (1968), 1010, 1012
 and SCLC, 911
 and Stokely Carmichael, 904,
 as symbol, 903
"Black Patch," 697, 702
Black Patch War (1909), xxii, 697–699, 703
Black Power (Carmichael/Hamilton), 903
Black Power movement
 Detroit Riot (1967), 899
 and Malcolm X, 908
 Newark Riot (1967), 899
 and Riots, 899
 and SNCC, 913
 and Stokely Carmichael, 903
Black Thursday, 459
"Black Wall Street," 801
"Blackballed," 861
Blacklists
 Haymarket Riot, 575
 Ludlow Massacre, 709
 Pullman Strike, 545, 652
Blackmun, Harry, 1055–1056
Blackstone, William, 129, 141, 143
Blackwell, Antoinette Brown, 476, 477, 478
Blackwell, Elizabeth, 476, 478
Blackwell, Emily, 476, 478
Blackwell, Henry
 and AWSA, 483, 488, 490
 and Nineteenth Amendment, 490
 and women's movement, 476, 478
Blair Mountain Battle (1921), xxii–xxiii, 793–795, 797–798
Bland, Giles, 4
Blatch, Harriott Stanton, 480–481, 490
Bleeding Kansas (1854), xxiv, 347–352
"Blind pig" raid, 989
Blodgett, Samuel, 184

"Bloody Act," 172
"Bloody Monday," 377–378
"Bloody Thursday," 858, 861–862, 865
Bloomer, Amelia, 475
Bloomer, Dexter, 476
"Blue book" unions, 857, 862, 867. *See also* Waterfront Employers Union (WEU)
Blue Cloud, Peter, 1035
Blue Lake, 1034, 1067, 1071
Blue Ridge Mountains, 3
Bock, Irwin, 1015–1016
"Body of the People," 194
"Bo-hunk," 665–666
Bolshevik Revolution, 757. *See also* Russian Revolution
Bolt, Robert, 103
Bombing, 578, 586–587
Bonfield, John, 578
Bonus Army protests (1932)
 collective action, xxii, 829–834
 "Maintaining Order in the District of Columbia, President Hoover's Letter and Press Conference," 844–846
Bonus Expeditionary Force (BEF), 829–834, 843
Book of Common Prayer, 95
Book of Mormon, 390, 394
Border ruffians
 Bleeding Kansas, 347, 349, 350, 351
 jayhawkers, 354–355
 and Pottawatomie Massacre, 360
 Topeka Constitution, 361
Bordoise (Bordois), Nicholas, 858, 861
Boss (Royko), 1022
Boston Gazette
 Boston Massacre engraving, 160, 163
 Crispus Attucks, 158
 John Adams' articles, 157
 Thomas Preston's letters, 161
Boston Latin School
 James Bowdoin, 217
 Samuel Adams, 139
Boston Massacre (1770)
 atmosphere following, 139
 collective action, xxii

Boston Massacre (1770) (continued)
   "George R. T. Hewes' Account," 164–166
   overview, 151–156
   Revere's engraving, 151, 152, 154, 155, 160, 164
   "Richard Palmes's Account," 166–167
   trials, 154–155
Boston Police Strike (1919), collective action, xxii–xxiii, 757–759, 761
Boston Port Act, 197, 199
Boston Tea Party (1773)
   collective action, xxii, 191–198
   George R. T.'s account of, 204–206
   opposition policies, 143
   and Pine Tree Riot, 187
   and Samuel Adams, 140
   taxation of tea, 147, 193
Boston University, 904
Boudinot, Elias, 239
Boudouin, Pierre, 217
Bouquet, Henry
   Ohio River Valley, 114
   Pontiac's Rebellion, 113
   smallpox epidemic, 124
Bowdoin, James
   and Alexander Hamilton, 239–240
   biography, 217–218
   election defeat, 213
   and Massachusetts General Court, 219
   and Shays' Rebellion, 210, 211, 212–213, 217, 221
Bowdoin College, 218
Bower Hill, 231, 232, 233
Bowie, James
   Battle of the Alamo, 304
   Texas Revolt, 294
Boxley, George, attempted uprising, (1815), xxiii, 254, 255, 261–262
"Boxley's Plot," 161
Brackenridge, Hugh Henry, 230, 232, 244
Bradburn, Juan Davis, 290, 291
Braddock, Edward, 118
Bradford, Gamaliel, 928
Bradley, Tom, 1098–1099
Bradstreet, John, 114
Bradwell v. Illinois, 499–500
Brandeis University, 1026

Branding, 155, 157
Brando, Marlon
   and Alcatraz Island occupation, 1033
   and Red Power, 1074
Brands, H. W., 608
Brantley, Etheldred T., 271
Brantley, Green, 538
Brazoria, 290
Breslin, Jimmy, 1057
Bridges, Alfred Renton "Harry"
   biography, 862–863
   and Bloody Thursday, 861
   West Coast Longshoremen's Strike, 857, 859, 865, 867
Brimm, Benjamin, 539
Brindletail Republicans, 545–546, 550
Briseno, Theodore, 1096, 1097
Britain
   and Boston Tea Party, 196–197
   martial law, 241
   and Ohio River Valley, 121
   Pine Tree Riot, 183
   Seven Years' War, 118–119
   Stamp Act protests, 127–137
   and temperance, 371
   women's suffrage, 480–481
British Imperial, 697
Briton, Crane, 289–290
Broadsides
   Boston Massacre, 160, 163
   colonial media, 159–160
Brock, Clarence, 750
Broken Treaties protest. *See* Trail of Broken Treaties protest
Brooke, Edward W.
   and civil rights movement, 899
   and Kerner Commission, 996
Brooks, Joseph
   biography, 550–551
   Brooks-Baxter War, 545–547, 552
   and Elisha Baxter, 549
Brooks, Preston, 351, 360
Brooks-Baxter War (1874), xxii, 545–548
Brooks v. Baxter, 546, 549
Brotherhood of Locomotive Engineers, 570
Brotherhood of Locomotive Firemen, 570, 651, 652

Brotherhood of Railway Conductors, 570
Brotherhood of Sleeping Car Porters, 909
Brown Bess muskets, 294
Brown, Edmund G., 976–985
Brown, John
   antebellum slave revolts, 257–258
   biography, 423–425
   and Bleeding Kansas, 348–350, 351, 416
   Harpers Ferry Raid, xxiii, 257–258, 415–421, 424–425
   "Last Speech to the Court and Last Statement before Execution," 430–432
   Pottawatomie Massacre, 359–361, 423–424, 426
   "Southern Editorial Response to the Raid on Harper's Ferry, Virginia," 432–434
   trial of, 420
Brown, Oliver, 417, 419
Brown, Owen (father), 423
Brown, Owen (son), 417
Brown, Sam, 941, 942
Brown, William, 158
Brown v. Board of Education of Topeka, Kansas
   and civil rights movement, 893
   and segregation, 678, 679, 807
Bruce, Louis R., 1069
Bryan, William Jennings
   nomination of, 653
   antiwar activism, 928
Bryant, Roy, 894
Buchanan, James
   biography, 389–390
   and Bear Flag Revolt, 334
   and Brigham Young, 395–396
   and Dorothea Dix, 486–487
   and First Missouri Compromise, 357
   and Harpers Ferry Raid, 419
   opposition to polygamy, 393
   Utah War, 383, 386
"Bucket law," 83
Buckshots society, 466
Buda, Mario, 587
Budenz, Louis, 843
Bull, William, 70, 77
Bull Head, 605
Bull Run, First Battle of, 382

Bullion, Reverend Father, 622
Bureau of Indian Affairs (BIA)
   Broken Treaties protest, 1068, 1069
   Dakota Uprising, 611–612
   and Dick Wilson, 1083
   and FBI, 1080
   overview, 1079–1080
   and Red Power, 1074
   sit-ins, 1032
   and Sitting Bull, 615
   Wounded Knee Massacre, 601, 604, 608–609
   Wounded Knee Occupation, 1075
Bureau of Land Management (BLM)
   "Organic Act," 1089
   and public lands, 1090, 1091
   and Sagebrush Rebellion, 1086
Burford, Anne Gorsuch, 1093
Burgan, Michael, 162
Burger, Warren, 1056
Burke, John, 136
Burnett, Robert, 1067
Burns, Anthony, 429
Burr, Aaron, 241–242
Burroughs, William, 1012
Burton, Mary, 80, 81, 85–86, 89
Burton, Scott, 689
Buses, integration, 895
Bush, George H. W., 1106–1120
Bush, George W.
   and Direct Action Network, 1125
   and Gale Norton, 1094
   and immigration reform, 1129, 1131
"Bushwackers," 353, 354
Bushy Run, Battle of, 113
Butler, William, 171
Byles, Reverend Mather, 153
Byrd, Harry Flood Byrd, 894

Cadwalader, George, 326, 327
Caesar, 80, 87–88, 89, 90
Caldwell, James, 153
Calhoun, Meredith Smith, 537
Calhoun, William, 541
California
   admission to Union, 394
   Bear Flag Revolt, 333–338
   Chinese immigrants, 593, 597

California (continued)
  and Franciscan missionaries, 37, 38
  Governor's Commission Report on the Watts Riots, 976–985
  J. C. Frémont's expeditions, 341–342
  Plan de San Diego, 727
  "Proclamation Declaring California an Independent Republic," 345–346
  and women's suffrage, 480
  Zoot Suit Riot, 869–875
California Gold Rush, 391
California Highway Patrol (CHIP), 965
California National Guard
  and Los Angeles Uprising, 1098
  and Watts Riot, 966–967
  and West Coast Longshoremen's Strike, 858
Calvin, John, 57
Calvinism, 57–58
Camino Real de Tierra Adentro (Royal road), 27, 33, 39
Camp Floyd, 387
Camp Furlong, 751, 753
Camp Logan, 749, 750, 753, 754
Campaign for Economic Democracy, 1025
Campanella, Roy, 897
Campbell Act, 662
Canada
  French and Indian War, 118
  and Jeffrey Amherst, 117
  and Nez Percé's flight, 554, 559
  Sitting Bull, 615
  women's suffrage, 481
Canales, J. T., 737
Cannibals All! (Fitzhugh), 275
Cannon, George Q., 393
Cantrell, Paul
  Battle of Athens, 883–885
  and Pat Mansfield, 887, 888–889
Capdeville, Paul, 672
Cape Breton Island, 117
Cape Fear River Port, 133
Capone, Al, 371
Caraway, Hattie, 481
Carey, Hugh, 1060
Carleton, J. H., 396–414
Carmichael, Stokely (Kwame Ture)
  and *Bakke* case, 899
  biography, 903–904
  and Black Power, 903, 904
  and SNCC, 903, 913
Carnegie, Andrew
  antiwar activism, 928
  and Carnegie Steel Company, 630
  and Henry Clay Frick, 630
  and Homestead Strike, 620, 621
  as "robber barons," 571
  and unionism, 634
Carnegie Institute of Technology, 631
Carnegie Steel Company
  "Account of the Course of the Strike," 637–640
  and Amalgamated Association of Iron and Steel Workers (AA), 629
  and Homestead Strike, 619–627
  overview, 630–631
Carpetbaggers
  and Brooks-Baxter War, 545
  and freedmen, 541
  and Ku Klux Klan, 542
  overview, 453–454
Carr, Patrick, 153
Carrillo, José A., 336
Carroll, Charles, 926
Carroll, John, 153
Carson, Kit, 336, 337
Carson, Moses, 336
Carter, Rosalynn, 1054
Carwardine, William, 644
Cass, Lewis
  and First Missouri Compromise, 357
  popular sovereignty, 358
Castañeda, Francisco, 293
Castro, José
  and Bear Flag Revolt, 333–337
  and Ezekiel Merritt, 340
  and J. C. Frémont, 342
Castro, Manuel, 333, 336
Cathedral of the Assumption, 377
Catholicism
  colonial New York, 61–62
  early settlers, 329
  in industrial Philadelphia, 325–327
  and Jesuit order, 103–104
  Maine Irish, 370,
  in Mexico, 733

in New Amsterdam, 61
and Know-Nothing Party, 373, 374
"Cato's Rebellion," 71
Catt, Carrie Chapman
   and Nineteenth Amendment, 490
   and women's movement, 480, 481
Cavanaugh, Jerome, 988, 989
Cayuga Indians, 111
Cazabat, Alphonse, 538
Central Christian Advocate, 550
Central European immigrants
   and Homestead Strike, 620
   and Lattimer Massacre, 662, 665–666
   and Ludlow Massacre, 707
Central Labor Council (CLC), 848
Central Labor Union, 576
Chaffin, Tom, 335, 342
Chafin, Don, 793, 794
Chambers, Ed
   and Blair Mountain Battle, 793
   murder of, 799, 800
Chancellorsville, Battle of, 428
Channing, William Ellery, 486–487
"Charcoal Alley," 966, 967
Charles I (king of England)
   execution, 59, 187
   and Sir William Berkeley, 1
Charles II (king of England)
   Bacon's Rebellion, 7
   beheading of, 121
   colonial administration, 53
   and colonial Pennsylvania, 91, 96
   and Navigation Act, 142
   and Rhode Island charter, 315, 317
Charles, Jaspar, 675
Charles, Robert
   biography, 675–676
   New Orleans Race Riot, 671–673
Charleston (SC)
   Red Summer Riots, 765, 767–768
   slave economy, 75
   Stamp Act protests, 133
   Stono Rebellion, 70
   Vesey's uprising, 265–266
Charter of Liberty and Privileges (NY), 53
Charterites, 312, 315–316, 317, 319
Cherokee Indians, 307

Cherry Creek (SD), 605
Chertoff, Michael, 1129
Cheslak, Mike, 661
Cheyenne, 613
Cheyenne River Reservation, 602
Chicago (IL)
   "Cook County Coroner's Report Regarding the 1919 Chicago Race Riot" 778–782
   Commission on Race Relations, 771
   "Day without an Immigrant" protests, 1129–1130, 1131
   Great Migration, 773–774
   Haymarket Riot, 575–583
   and Ku Klux Klan, 542
   McCormick Harvesting Machine Company, 590
   Red Summer Riots, 768–769, 778
   WPUS, 565, 573
Chicago and Great Western Railroad, Egan, 646
Chicago Daily News, 647
Chicago Eight, 1015, 1019
Chicago Evening Post, 647
Chicago Herald, 647, 648
Chicago Journal, 647
Chicago Race Riot
   "Cook County Coroner's Report," 778–782
   collective action, xxiv, 1009–1017
Chicago Seven
   overview, 1019–1020
   trial, 1015–1016, 1019–1020, 1024–1025, 1028
Chicago Tribune, 647
Chicano Movement
   and African Americans, xxiii
   and Texas Rangers, 737
Chichimeca Indians, 27
Chief Eusebio, 334
Chief Joseph
   biography, 558–559
   and Nez Percé's flight, 553–555
   "relocation," 560
   Surrender Speech, 561
Chief Joseph the Elder, 553, 558
Chief Kayashuta, 111
Chief Looking Glass, 554
Chief Ol-loo-te-ka, 307

Chief Solano
  Bear Flag Revolt, 336
  and Vallejo, 344
Chief White Bird, 554
Child custody, 473, 475–476
China, 594
Chinese Exclusion Act
  in New York, 369
  and racism, 445, 597, 599
  repeal of, 269
  in Seattle, 593
Chinese immigrants
  overview, 597–598
  in Seattle, 593
Church of England
  creation of, 95–96
  restoration of, 91
Church of Jesus Christ of Latter-day Saints
  and Brigham Young, 395
  and Nauvoo Legion, 391
  overview, 390–391
  and polygamy, 390, 391, 392–394, 395
Church of the Brethren, 925
Church Women United (CWU), 1047, 1048
Cincinnati (OH)
  Great Migration, 773–774
  and race riots, 777
Circuit Court Act (1769), 173
Circular letters
  and Samuel Adams, 139, 140
  Stamp Act protests, 131, 141, 143, 144
  and Townshend Act, 204
Citizenship
  Bradwell v. Illinois, 499–500
  Chinese immigrants, 593
  and civil rights movement, 892
Civil Federation of Chicago, 646–647
Civil Rights Act (1875), 891
Civil Rights Act (1964)
  excerpts from, 915–924
  and Feminist Movement, 1049
  and March on Washington, 909
  and Martin Luther King Jr., 906
  passage of, 898–899
  and segregation, 807

and SNCC, 912
Civil Rights Act (1968)
  and March on Washington, 910
  and Martin Luther King Jr., 906
Civil rights activities
  Attica Prison Riot, xxiii–xxiv, 1059–1061
  "Day without an Immigrant" protests (2006), xxiii–xxiv, 1129–1132
  Detroit Riots (1967), xxiii–xxiv, 987–992
  Los Angeles Uprising (1992), xxiii–xxiv, 1095–1099
  Plan de San Diego (1915), xxiii, 727–732, 734
  Watts Riots (1965), xxiii–xxiv, 965–971
  women, xxiii, 473–482, 1043–1050
  Zoot Suit Riot (1942), xxiii, 869–875, 879–880
Civil Rights Bill (1991), 900
Civil rights movement (1953–1968)
  history of, 891–901
  as model movement, xxiii
Civilian Conservation Corps, 833
Claiborne, William C. C.
  and Charles Deslondes's Uprising, 262–263
  martial law, 241–242
Clansman, The (Dixon), 805
Clark, Ramsey, 1015
Clark, George A., 550
Clark, Hugh, 325
Clark, Kenneth Bancroft, 893
Clark, Mamie Phipps, 893
Clarke (Clark), Fred, 672, 673
Clarke, George, 79
Clarke, Septima, 896
Clay, Henry, 327
Clayton, Powell, 545, 546, 550, 551–552
Clayton Antitrust Act
  and AFL, 851
  and unionizing, 763
Cleage, Albert, 988
Clearwater, Frank, 1077
Clemente, Esteban, 30, 43
Cleveland, Grover
  on Pullman Strike, 647, 648, 652
  Seattle Riot, 594
Cleveland (OH), 773–774
Clifford, Nathan, 366

Clinton, Bill, 1123
Coahuila, Diego Ortiz Parilla, 106
Coahuila, 291, 292
Coal and Iron Police, 661
Coal mining
   in Appalachia, 797
   and Blair Mountain Battle, 793–794
   and Ludlow Massacre, 707–711
   and Molly Maguires, 459, 460–461
   in Pennsylvania, 465–466
   and UMWA, 716–717
   and unionism, 466–467
Coastal planters, 169
Cochran, Jacob, 392
Cochran, William, 244
Code Pink, 932–933
Cody, William F. "Buffalo Bill," 604, 615
Coercive Acts (Intolerable Acts), 197, 199–200
Coffin, William Sloan, 957–960
Colfax, Schuyler, 537
Colfax Massacre (1873), xxiv, 537–539
Collective bargaining, 854
College, the Market, and the Court, The (Dall), 476
Collins, Judy, 1016
Collinsworth, George M., 293
Colonial tradition
   American Revolution, 83, 173–174, 192, 228–229
   Bacon's Rebellion (1676), 1–7
   Boston Massacre (1770), xxii, 151–156
   Boston Tea Party (1773), 140, 143, 147, 187, 191–198
   collective action, xxii
   Pine Tree Riot (1772), 183–185, 187
   Regulator Movement (1771), 169–175
   Stamp Act Protests (1765), 127–137
Colonial Virginia
   House of Burgesses, 13–15
   indentured servants, 15–16
   tobacco, 19–20
Colonization Laws (1573), 39
Colorado
   coal production, 713
   "Day without an Immigrant" protests, 1129, 1131
   Ludlow Massacre, 707–710
   Plan de San Diego, 727
   women's suffrage, 479
Colorado Fuel and Iron Company (CF&I)
   Ludlow Massacre, 707, 708–710
   overview, 713–714
   and UMWA, 717
Colorado National Guard, 707, 710
Columbia (SC), 174
Columbus (OH), 773–774
Colville Indian Reservation, 559
Comanches, 34
Combahee River Collective, 1046
Commission on Law Enforcement and Administration, 994
Commission on the Status of Women (CSW), 1048
Committee for a SANE Nuclear Policy, 930–931
Committee for Non Violent Action, 930–931
Committee of Industrial Organizations (CIO)
   and UMWA, 715, 717. *See also* Congress of Industrial Organizations (CIO)
"Commune," 565
Communism
   and BEF, 832, 833
   and West Coast Longshoremen's Strike, 864
Communist Party of the United States (CPUSA), 857, 867
Commutation fees
   and conscription, 442
   and New York Draft Riots, 435, 440
Compromise of 1850
   and civil rights, 891
   and Nat Turner's Rebellion, 275
   and popular sovereignty, 358
   and State of Deseret, 394
Compromise of 1876, 677
Compromise of 1877, 479
Comstock Law, 496
"Concentration camps," 730
"Conductors," 283
Confederate States of America (Confederacy)
   and American Civil War, 441
   and conscription, 442
   establishment of, 426
   and guerilla warfare, 353
   and Robert E. Lee, 428

Confederation Army, 228, 233
Confederation on the Rhine, 331
Conference of Concerned Democrats, 942
Confessions of Nat Turner, The (Styron), 276–277, 280–281
Congregationalism, 58
Congregationalist Church, 474, 475, 476
Congress of Industrial Organizations (CIO)
   and AFL, 763, 851
   and auto industry, 849
   and Harry Bridges, 859, 863
   and John L. Lewis, 667
Congress of Racial Equality (CORE)
   and civil rights movement, 896
   and Jim Crow Laws, 678
   and March on Washington, 909
   and SNCC, 912
   and Stokely Carmichael, 903
"Congressional Debate on Women's Suffrage," 491–493
Congressional Party, 480
Conkey's Tavern, 210, 221
Conley, Arthur, 578, 579
Connecticut
   and Coercive Acts, 197
   Dominion of New England, 59
   earliest intergovernmental assemble, 54
   and Shays' Rebellion, 213
Conners, T. J., Homestead Strike, 625
Connor, Eugene "Bull," 898, 911
"Conscience Whigs," 927
Conscientious objectors, 929
Conscription
   and American Civil War, 441, 442–443
   and New York Draft Riots, 435, 440, 443
Conscription Act (1917)
   Green Corn Rebellion, 739, 740
   overview, 743–744
Constitution of 1843 (RI), 313
Constitutional Convention (1787)
   and Shays' Rebellion, 214
   and slavery issue, 279
Consultation
   divided approach, 295
   and Sam Houston, 307
   and Stephen Austin, 306
   and Texas Revolt, 291, 292, 293

"Contemporary Account of Nat Turners Revolt, A" 286–288
Continental Army
   and Alexander Hamilton, 239
   Daniel Shays service in, 207, 210, 211, 220–221
   and Pine Tree Rioters, 185
Continental Congress
   and Coercive Acts, 197
   overview, 200–201
   and Regulator Movement, 174
   Robert Morris, 229
   and Samuel Adams, 140
Continuation of the Impartial Relation, A (Husband), 180
Contraception, 533–536
Conway, Henry, 135
Conyers, Congressman John, 989
Cook, George William, 785–789
"Cook County Coroner's Report Regarding the 1919 Chicago Race Riot" (1920), 778–782
Cooke, Jay, 563
Cooke, Philip St. George, 386
Coolidge, Calvin
   and BEF, 830
   biography, 761–762
   and Boston Police Strike, 757, 758, 759, 761
   and veterans' rights, 841–842
"Coolie" population, 593
Copley, John Singleton
   and the Boston Tea Party, 195
   painter, 154
Copperheads
   and American Civil War, 441
   and antiwar activism, 927
   and New York Draft Riots, 436
   opposition to emancipation, 443, 445
   overview, 443–444
Corman, James C., 996
Coronado, Francisco Vasquez de, 27, 37, 39
Correo de Mejico, 292–293
Corruption, 169, 170
Cortina, Juan, 736
Cós, Martin Perfecto de, 292, 293, 294, 295, 296
"Cotton Curtain," 969

Cotton gin, 425
Couche's Fort, 233
Counter Reformation, 103
Counterculture, 937
Cowie, Thomas, 336
Coxey's Army, 740
Crazy Hawk, 607
Creedence Clearwater Revival, 1033, 1039
Crisis, The, 695–696
Crockett, David, 303–304
Croghan, George, 109
Cromwell, Oliver
   Navigation Act 142
   and the Quakers, 91
Cromwell, Richard, 12
Cronin, Daniel, 593–594
Crook, George "Three Stars," 604
Crooked Creek Gap, 794
Crosby, Judge Ernest, 928
Crow, 613
Cruger, John, Jr., 85
Cruger, Nicholas, 239
Cruikshank, William J. "Bill," 539
Crump, E. H. "Boss," 883, 887, 888
Cruzate, Domingo Jironza Petris de, 34, 35, 42
Cuba, 928
Cuffee, 80, 88
Culberson, Jack, 1121
"Cult" of domesticity, 1043–1044
Cumming, Alfred
   and Brigham Young, 395
   Civil War, 387
   Utah War, 383, 385
Cummings, P. M., 461
Cummings v. Richmond County Board of Education, 893
Cunningham, William, 741
Cuny Table, 604
Currency Act, 127
Curtis, Edwin, 758
Curtis, Jennie, 644
Custer, George, 553, 602, 614, 615
Cygon, Steve, 853
Czech immigrants, 665

Daily News, 436
Dakota Nation
   and Dakota Uprising, 611–613
   Indian treaties, 1073
Dakota Uprising (1862), 611–613
Daley, Richard J.
   and Abbie Hoffman, 1026
   biography, 1021–1022
   and Chicago Seven, 1019
   and Democratic National Convention (1968), 1009, 1011, 1013, 1014–1015, 1017
   and Tom Hayden, 1024
Dall, Caroline, 476
Dame, William Horne, 392
Dana, John W., 365
Dance, Henry, 294
Dark Tobacco District Planters' Protective Association (DTDPPA)
   and ATC, 701
   overview, 702–703
Dartmouth, 194, 195
Davis, Jefferson, 444
Davis, John W., 761
Davis, Paula Wright, 475
Davis, Rennie
   Chicago Eight, 1015, 1019
   and Chicago Seven, 1019, 1020
   and the Mobe, 1010, 1012, 1013, 1019, 1027, 1028
Davis Island Dam, 623
Day, John T.
   New Orleans Race Riot (1900), 671–672
   and Robert Charles, 676
Day Book, The, 346
"Day without a Mexican, A" 1131
"Day without an Immigrant" protests (2006), xxiii–xxiv, 1129–1132
Days, Luke, 210, 211, 212
De facto segregation, 806–807
De jure segregation, 807
De La Beckwith, Byron, 897, 900
De la Rosa, Luis, 729, 731
De Peyster, Isaac, 85
De Revoire, Apollos, 163
"Deadwork," 708, 709
Death in a Promised Land (Ellsworth), 803

Debs, Eugene V.
    antiwar activism, 929
    and ARU, 651
    biography, 652–654
    and Brotherhood of Locomotive
        Firemen, 570
    and IWW, 744, 745
    opposition to World War I, 747
    and Pullman Strike, 644, 645, 649, 657
Debt collection
    Depression (1783–1788), 209
    Shays' Rebellion, 207, 210, 211, 214
Debtor imprisonment, 169
Declaration of Independence
    and John Adams, 157
    and Samuel Adams, 140
"Declaration of Pedro Naranjo" (1681), 49–51
"Declaration of Rights and Grievances"
        (Jefferson), 201
"Declaration of Rights and Grievances, The"
        (Stamp Act Congress), 144
    Stamp Act protests, 134
Declaration of Rights of Women, 504–508
"Declaration of Sentiments," 489
"Declaration of the People of Virginia" (1676),
        6, 24–26
Declaratory Acts
    passage of, 140–141, 146
    Stamp Act protests, 131, 135–136
Decree of April 6, 1830, 289, 291
Degan, Mathias J., 578
DeKlyne, Theodore W., 539
Delaware Indians
    Ohio River Valley, 121
    Pontiac's Rebellion, 111, 112, 113, 120
"Delaware Prophet," 109, 119–120
Deleon, Daniel, 745
Dellinger, David
    Chicago Eight, 1015, 1019
    and Chicago Seven, 1019, 1020
    and the Mobe, 1010, 1012, 1027, 1028
Deloria, Vine, Jr., 1036, 1067
Deluge Engine Company, 365
"Demagoguery," 130
Democratic National Convention (1968),
        1022–1023
Democratic National Convention (2000), 1125

Democratic Party
    and Atlanta Race Riot (1906), 681
    Battle of Athens, 883, 888
    Bloody Monday, 377
    Brooks-Baxter War, 545–547, 549
    and Chicago Riots, 1009–1013
    and Chicago Seven, 1019
    and Copperheads, 443
    the Moratorium, 941–942
    and New Orleans Riot (1866), 450
    and Know-Nothing Party, 373
    and popular sovereignty, 358
    Rhode Island suffrage, 311
    Rip Rap attacks, 380–381
    slavery split, 426
    and Utah War, 386–387
    and white working-class men, 319
Dempsey, Hugh, 626
Denny, Reginald
    and Damien Monroe Williams, 1105, 1106
    Los Angeles Uprising, 1097, 1101–1102
    on Phil Donahue show, 1101
Denver (CO), 1129, 1130
Denver, James, 351
Department of Justice, 537, 539
Department of Labor, 1048
DePaul Law School, 1021
"Depiction of Events at the Ludlow Camp,"
        719–726
Depression of 1783–1788, 207–208, 209, 222
"Description of Denmark Vesey (1822),"
        266–267
"Description of Stono Rebellion" (1739),
        76–78
Desegregation, 896–897
Deseret, 394
Deslondes, Charles
    antebellum slave revolts, 252, 255–256, 257
    German Coast uprising (1811), xxiii, 262–263
Detroit
    Great Migration, 773–774
    and Ku Klux Klan, 542
Detroit Free Press, 987–988, 993, 994–995
Detroit Riot (1943), 892
Detroit Riot (1967)
    Black Power movement, 899
    collective action, xxiii–xxiv, 987–992

Detroit River, 112–113
DeVoto, Bernard, 1085
Dia Sin Immigrantes, 1129
Diaz del Carpio, José, 100–101
Diaz, Jose, 872
Díaz, Porfirio, 733–734
Dickenson, Susannah, 304
Dickinson, John
    "Letters from a Farmer in Pennsylvania," 204
    Stamp Act protests, 134
Dickinson, Martin, 872
Die Arbeiter-Zeitung, 577, 581, 585
Dillard University, 673
Dinwiddie, Robert, 118
Direct Action Network, 1121–1122, 1125–1126
Discourse Concerning Unlimited Submission (Mayhew), 146
"Displaced homemaker," 1046
Disqualifying Act (1787)
    Massachusetts General Court, 219
    Shays' Rebellion, 212–213, 217
District of Columbia. *See* Washington, D.C.
Divorce reform, 473, 474, 477, 478
Dix, Dorothea, 486–487
Dixon, Thomas, 805
Dobbs, Arthur, 178–179, 181
"Doll test," 893
Domestic violence, 1044
Dominion of New England
    colonial conglomeration, 58–59
    Leisler's Rebellion, 53
Dongan, Thomas 61–62
Donnegan, William, 689, 690
Dorr, Sullivan, 312, 316
Dorr, Thomas Wilson
    biography, 316–318
    and Charterites, 315
    and Dorr's Rebellion, 311, 312, 313–314, 319
"Dorrites," 315, 317
Dorr's Rebellion (1841), collective action, xxii, 311–314
"Dorr's War," 311
Dorsey, Stephen F., 546
Dostie, Anthony Paul, 450, 451, 453

Douglas, Stephen A.
    Bleeding Kansas, 347
    and First Missouri Compromise, 357
    popular sovereignty, 358–359
Douglass, Frederick
    abolitionist, 279, 425
    and Harpers Ferry raid, 415, 417
    and John Brown, 258, 423
    and Susan B. Anthony, 484
    and women's movement, 475
Dow, Neal S.
    and Irish immigrants, 369, 370
    Portland Rum Riot, 365–366
    and the temperance movement, 366, 367, 371
Doyle, Arthur Conan, 459–460
Doyle, James P., 360
Doyle, John E., 578
"Draft Rioter's letter to *New York Times* and *Time*'s response," 447–448
Dred Scott decision
    and Buchanan administration, 389
    and civil rights, 891
    and First Missouri Compromise, 357–358
Dresel, Emil, 344
Dry, William, 133
Du, Soon Ja, 1099
Du Bois, W. E. B.
    anti-lynching campaigns, 776
    and civil rights, 771
    on black soldiers, 753
    and Houston Riot, 751
    and Jim Crow Laws, 677–678
    and NAACP, 695
    and National Afro-American League, 695
    "Talented Ten," 683
Duffy, Thomas, 461
Duke, James B., 701
Duke of York. *See* James II
Duncan, Bob, 740
Duncan, J. K., 382
Duncan, Thomas, 85
Dunmore, Lord, 241
Dunn, John Patrick, 326–327
Dunn, Susan, 257
Dunn, William F., 604
Durán, Fray Andrés, 31

Durrell, E. H., 450
Dustin, William, 185
Dutch fur trade, 18
Dutch immigrants, 84
Dutch Reformed Church, 61–62
Dyer, Leonidas, 782
Dyer Anti-Lynching bill, 782–789
Dynamite bombs, 586–587
Dysentery, Bacon's death from, 7, 9

Eagler, John, 661
Earth First! 1125
East India Company
   and the Boston Tea Party, 193, 195, 196
   and Coercive Acts (Intolerable Acts), 197
   importation of tea, 147
East Louisiana Railroad Company, 679
Eastern European immigrants
   Lattimer Massacre, 662
   Ludlow Massacre, 707
   overview, 665–666
Economic justice, 1126–1127
"Economic Plan," Alexander Hamilton, 240
Economic/political protests
   Athens, Battle of (1946), 883–885
   Black Patch War (1909), 697–699, 703
   Bonus Army protests (1932), 829–834
   Brooks-Baxter War (1874), 545–548
   collective action, xxii
   Dorr's Rebellion (1841), 311–314, 319
   Molly Maguires (1870s), 459–462
   Sagebrush Rebellion (1979), 1085–1087
   Shays' Rebellion (1787), 207–216
   Whiskey Rebellion (1794), 227–235, 238
   World Trade Organization protests (1999), 1121–1124
Ecorse River meeting, 109
Ecuyer, Simeon
   and Pontiac's Rebellion, 112
   and smallpox epidemic, 124
Edict of Nantes, 58, 217
Edisto River, 70
"Editorial Response to John Brown's Raid on Harper's Ferry, Virginia," 432–434
Edlund, John (Attica Prison Riot), 1060
Edlund, John (Haymarket Riot), 579
Edmonds, Kelton, 913

Edmunds Act, 393
Edmunds-Tucker Act, 479
Education
   and Freedmen's Bureau, 541
   and women's rights, 1044
   women's movement (1870), 473–474, 478
Edward VI (king of England), 95
Edwards, George, 993–994
Egan, John M., 646, 647
Ehrlichman, John, 1069
Eight-hour work day
   and Haymarket Riot, 582
   union demand, 575–576, 587–588
Eighth Amendment, 1063
Eisenhower, Dwight David
   Anacostia Flats Battle, 835
   and BEF, 833
   and civil rights movement, 894
   and Nelson Rockefeller, 1064
Ekirch, A. Roger, 174
El Camino Real, 296, 298
Elaine (AK), 765, 769–770
Elaine Massacre, 770
Eleanor, 195
Electric Auto-Lite Company, 847, 848, 852
Elizabeth I (queen of England), 188
   and Anglican Church, 95
Ellsworth, Scott, 803
Ely, Samuel, 210
Emancipation Proclamation (1863)
   abolition of slavery, 280
   as military necessity, 441, 445
   and New York Draft Riots, 435–436
Emerson, Ralph Waldo
   and antiwar activism, 927
   and George Luther Stearns, 429
   on John Brown, 420
Employee Representative Plan (ERP), 713–714
Encomiendas (tribute), 28, 30, 39
Enforcement Act (1870), 537, 538, 539
Engerman, Stanley, 253
Engle, George, 580, 581, 582
English Civil War
   religious conflict, 61
   and royal authority, 187
Enlightenment philosophy, 279
Enrollment Act, 442

Environmentalists, 1085, 1086
Episcopalian church, 95
Equal Employment Opportunity Commission
    and feminist movement, 1045
    and March on Washington, 909
Equal Pay Act, 1049
Equal Rights Amendment (ERA)
    and feminist movement, 1043, 1046, 1048, 1049
    overview, 1053–1055
    and women's movement, 481–482
Equality League of Self-Supporting Women, 480
Erie Indians
    Ohio River Valley, 121
    and Susquehannock Indians, 17
Esparza, José Enrique, 304
Espionage Act
    and American socialists, 746
    and IWW, 741, 744, 745
Essex Junto, 926
Evans, Jodie, 932–933
Evansville (IN), race riots, 778
Evers, Medger
    and civil rights movement, 897
    and Jim Crow Laws, 677–678
    and Ku Klux Klan, 805
Ex parte Bollman and Swartwout, 242
Ex parte Milligan, 242–243
"Excepts from a *New York Times* Account of the New York City Draft Riots," 446–447
"Excerpts from an Article by James McPartland Describing His Infiltration of the Molly Maguires," 467–471
Excise tax, 227, 229–230, 231–232
"Executive Committee," WPUS, 565, 573
Executive Order 9981, 892
Express, 346
"Eyewitness Account of the Massacre at Wounded Knee," 616–617

Fabian socialists, 746
Factories, 575
Fair Employment Practices Committee, 891–892
Fair Labor Standards Act (1938)
    and eight-hour day, 588
    and NIRA, 855

Fair trade movement, 1126–1127
Fallon, William, 339
"False Pretenses," 932
Fannin, Commander James Walker, 298–299
Fanning, Edward, 171
Farmers' Alliance, 697
Father of Texas, 305
"Father's Disgust with Antiwar Demonstrations, A" 960–961
Faubus, Orval, 895
Faulkner, William, 231–232
Fayetteville Democrat, 545
Federal Bureau of Investigation (FBI)
    and AIM leaders, 1069–1070
    and Alcatraz Island occupation, 1033
    and Chicago Seven trial, 1016, 1020
    and Dick Wilson, 1079
    Wounded Knee Occupation, 1075, 1076, 1077, 1080–1081
Federal labor unions (FLUs), 847–848
Federal Land Policy and Management Act (FLPM, 1976)
    overview, 1089–1090
    public lands, 1091
    and Sagebrush Rebellion, 1085
Federal Republican, 926
Federal supremacy, 237–238
Federalism, 227
Federation for American Immigration Reform, 1130
Federation of Organized Trade and Labor Unions, 588, 589
Fellowship for Reconciliation
    antiwar activism, 930–931
    and SNCC, 912
Felts, Albert
    and Matewan Massacre, 800
    and Sid Hatfield, 798, 799
Felts, Lee
    and Matewan Massacre, 800
    and Sid Hatfield, 798, 799
Felts, Tom
    and Matewan Massacre, 800
    and Sid Hatfield, 799
Feminine Mystique, The (Friedan), 1045

Feminist movement, 1043–1052. *See also* Women's movement (1870)
Ferguson, John, 679
Fessenden, William P., 366
Festival of Life, 1010, 1012, 1026
Few, James, 177
Fielden, Samuel J., 578, 580, 581, 582
Fifteenth Amendment
   and Reconstruction, 455, 456
   and women's movement, 477, 478, 483, 488
Figueroa, José, 343
Fillmore, Millard
   and Know-Nothing Party, 374–375
   and Rip Raps, 381
"Final Report of the Grand Jury on the Tulsa Race Riot," 808
Findlay, William, 230
Fink, Walter, 719–726
Fire Ordinance, 83
Fires
   colonial New York, 83–84
   New York Slave Insurrection, 79–81. *See also* Arson
First Great Awakening, 170
First Great Migration (1910–1930), 773, 907
First Infantry Armory, 577
Fischer, Adolph, 580, 581, 582
Fishman's Pawn Shop, 689, 693
Fitch, Henry D.
   Bear Flag Revolt, 336
   and Sonoma, 344
Fite, H. C., 741
Fitzhugh, George, 251, 275
Flanigan, Harris, 545
Flavin, Timothy, 579
Flint Sit-Down Strike, 849, 853
Florida
   and civil rights movement, 895
      racial segregation, 677
      Treaty of Paris (1763), 119. *See also* Spanish Florida
Flowers, Eli H., 538
Floyd, John, 274
Focus
   Hope, 991

Fogel, Robert, 253
"Fomenters of disturbances," 604, 605, 615
Fonda, Jane
   and Alcatraz Island occupation, 1033
   and Tom Hayden, 1025
Foot Hood Three Statement, 951–957
Foran, Thomas, 1015, 1019
Forbes, John, 118
Ford, Betty, 1054
Ford, Gerald, 1065
Ford, Henry, 832
Ford, Henry L., 336, 337, 339
"Foreign slaves," 262
"Forks, the," 227, 229, 231, 234
Forrest, Nathan Bedford, 805
Forstall, Lewis, 673
Forsyth, James W., 606, 607–608
Fort Anahuac
   and Stephen Austin, 306
   Texas Revolt, 290, 292
Fort Bedford, 111, 113
Fort Bridget, 385
Fort Burd, 111
Fort, Charles H.
   and DTDPPA, 703
   Statement, 703–706
Fort Detroit
   Pontiac's Rebellion, 109, 111, 112–113, 114, 120
   Pontiac's role, 123
Fort Duquesne
   French and Indian War, 118
   Pontiac's role, 122
Fort Edward Augustus, 111
Fort Fayette, 234
"Fort Frick," 621
Fort Jackson Treaty, 1072–1073
Fort James, 53, 60
Fort Laramie Treaty, 1073
Fort Le Boeuf, 111
Fort Ligonier, 111, 113
Fort Limhi, 385
Fort Lipantilán, 298
Fort Louisbourg, 117, 118
Fort MacArthur, 871, 881

Fort Miamis, 110
Fort Michilimackinac, 110–111
Fort Necessity, 118
Fort Niagara, 114
Fort Oswego, 114, 123
Fort Ouiatenon, 111
Fort Pitt
   Pontiac's Rebellion, 111–114, 117
   smallpox epidemic, 124
Fort Presque Isle 111
Fort Ridgley, 612
Fort Sandusky, 110
Fort Scott, 350, 351
Fort St. Joseph, 111
Fort Sumter
   and American Civil War, 441
   fall of, 426
   and Beauregard, 382
Fort Vancouver, 594
Fort Velasco
   and Stephen Austin, 306
   Texas Revolt, 290
Fort Venango, 111
Fort William Henry, 122
Fort Yates, 604
Fortune, T. Thomas, 695
Fourteenth Amendment
   and *Plessy v. Ferguson*, 679
   and Reconstruction, 454, 456
   and women's movement, 477, 478, 483, 488
Fowler, George, 336
Fox, George, 97
Fox, Vincente, 1131
Fox News coverage, 1129
Foy, William, 623
France
   and Calvinist religion, 58
   expulsion of Jesuits, 103–104
   Leisler's Rebellion, 54
   and Ohio River Valley, 121
   and Santa Anna, 310
   Seven Years' War, 118–119
Franchise Amendment, 546
Franciscan missionaries
   and Pueblo Indians, 28, 29, 41
   religious order, 37–38
   and Tohono O'odham, 107

Frank Leslie's Illustrated Weekly, 620
Franklin, Benjamin
   Boston Tea Party, 194, 196
   Stamp Act protests, 130
Frappolly, William, 1015–1016
Free Blacks
   Charterites, 316
   Dorr's Rebellion, 311, 313
   Rhode Island extended suffrage, 319
Free Soilers
   Bleeding Kansas, 348, 349, 351
   and Jayhawkers, 355
   and Pottawatomie Massacre, 360
Freed, Barrt. *See* Hoffman, Abbott "Abbie"
Freedmen's Bureau, 541
Freedom Now Suite, 897
Freedom Riders
   and civil rights movement, 896
   and SNCC, 912
   and Stokely Carmichael, 903
Freedom Schools, 912
Freedom Summer, 903
"Freeholder's Constitution," 315, 317
Freeman's Journal, 346
Freemasons, 389
Frelinghuysen, Frederick T., 491, 492–493
Frémont, John Charles
   Bear Flag Revolt, 333–337
   biography, 341–343
   and Brigham Young, 395–396
   Republican presidential candidate, 375, 389, 426, 551
   Salt Lake City surveyor, 393
French and Indian War (1754–1763)
   British victory, 127, 140, 142, 146
   and colonial debt, 139
   and Jeffrey Amherst, 117
   overview, 118–119
French Revolution, 181, 234
French, Scot, 273
Freneau, Philip, 230
Frick, Henry Clay
   and Homestead Strike, 620–621, 624, 626, 629
   lockout tactic, 631–632
Friedan, Betty, 1045
Fries' Rebellion (1790s), 238, 240

Froines, John, 1015, 1019
Frye, Marquette, 965, 968
Fugitive Slave Act
  and Harpers Ferry Raid, 415
  and Nat Turner's Rebellion, 275
  opposition to, 429
Fuller, Margaret, 476
Funston, Frederick, 728
Fusionists, 541

Gadsden, Christopher, 135
Gadsden Purchase, 310
Gage, Thomas
  Boston Massacre 151–152
  and Coercive Acts, 197
  martial law, 241
  and Pontiac's Rebellion, 113, 114
  and royal authority, 187
  and Thomas Preston, 161
Gale, Henry, 211
Gallatin, Albert, 230
Galloway, Joseph, 201
Galveston Bay, 106
Gambrill, Henry, 374, 379, 380
Gangs
  and nativism, 373, 374, 378–381
  Zoot Suit Riot, 870
Gangs of New York, The (film), 379
Garland, Augustus H., 549
Garnet, Henry Highland, 415
Garrick (Gerrish), Edward, 152–153, 154
Garrison, William Lloyd
  abolitionist, 279, 425
  and women's movement, 475
Garry, Charles, 1015, 1019
Garvey, Marcus
  Jim Crow Laws, 677–678
  Universal Negro Improvement Association, 907
Gary, Joseph C., 581
Gates, Daryl, 1097
Gazette (Little Rock, AR), 545, 546
Gell, Monday, 265
General Allotment Act (1887), 1072, 1073
General Assembly of Deseret, 394–395
General Land Office (GLO), 1089, 1091

General Land Reform Act (1891), 1089
General Managers Association (GMA), 645, 646, 647, 648
General Order Number 11, 353–354
Genet, Edmund, 234
Geneva, 57
Geneva Club, 80
Genocide, 5, 6
Genovese, Eugene, 252–253
George I (king of England), 187
George II, (king of England), 187
George III, (king of England)
  celebration of, 136
  reconciliatory efforts, 141, 143
  and Stamp Act protests, 131
"George R. T. Hewes' Account of the Boston Massacre," 164–166
Georgia
  and civil rights movement, 896
  and SCLC, 911
  slave codes, 73
German Americans, 776
German Coast, 252, 255–256, 262–263
German immigrants
  and anarchism, 585
  in colonial Pennsylvania, 91, 92
  as early settlers, 330
  Fries' Rebellion (1790s), 238
  and Know-Nothing Party, 373–374, 377
  and nativism, 378
  in New York City, 84
  and New York Draft Riots, 437
  and Regulator Movement, 169
Gettysburg, 436
  Battle of, 428, 437
Ghost Dance
  and Pine Ridge Reservation, 1081
  and Sitting Bull, 615
  and Wounded Knee Massacre, 601, 602, 603, 604–607, 608
Ghost Shirts, 601, 606–607
GI Bill, 833–834, 842
GI Nonpartisan Ticket
  Battle of Athens, 883–885
  and Pat Mansfield, 887
Gibbon, John, 554
Gilbert, Abigail, 220

Gillespie, Archibald
  Bear Flag Revolt, 334, 335, 340
  and J. C. Frémont, 342
Ginsberg, Allen
  and Chicago Seven trial, 1016
  Democratic National Convention (1968), 1011–1012
"Girls local," 643
Gladwin, Henry, 109–110
"Glass City," 848
Glassford, Superintendent Pelham
  and BEF, 831, 832, 835
  and Douglas MacArthur, 840
  and Walter Waters, 843–844
Glenn Pool oil field, 801
Globalization
  overview, 1127
  WTO protests, 1121
Glorious Revolution
  Dominion of New England, 59
  Leisler's Rebellion, 55, 61
"Go Down Moses (Let My People Go)," 282
Gold Star Mothers, 931–932
"Golden Mountain," 593
Goldfinch, John, 152–153
Goldman, Emma
  antiwar activism, 929
  excerpts, 522–528
Goliad. See Presidio (Goliad/La Bahia)
"Goliad Massacre," 299
Gompers, Samuel, AFL, 746, 762–763
  antiwar activism, 928
  and Boston Police Strike, 759, 761
"Good-Bye, My Lover," 546
Goodhue, Grace Ann, 761
Gookin, Charles, 97
Gordon, Francis, 111
Gould, Jay
  as "robber barons," 571
  and Southwestern Railroad, 599
Gowen, Franklin B., 460–461, 462, 715
"Gradualists," 695
Graham, Henry, 397
Granary Burying Ground, 159
"Grand Jury's Final Report on Tulsa Race Riot," 808
Grandfather clause, 456

Grandmothers against the War, 933
Grangers, 697
Grant, James, 295, 298
Grant, Ulysses S.
  and American Civil War, 441
  and Brooks-Baxter War, 547, 549, 550, 551
  and Colfax Massacre, 537
  and Native American relocations, 557
"Grass Fight," 294
Gray, Joseph E., 599
Gray, Samuel, 153
Gray, Thomas Ruffin
  and Nat Turner, 270–271, 273–274, 286
  and Nat Turner's "Confessions," 276–277, 280–281
Grazing Service, 1089
Great Alamance Creek, 172, 177
Great Depression
  and AFL, 763
  and American socialists, 746
  and Anacostia Flats Battle, 835
  and BEF, 830
  and Mexican Americans, 869, 870, 877
  and Nativism, 869, 870
  overview, 836–837, 838
  and veterans' rights, 842
  and women's rights, 1043
Great Dragon Swamp, 6
"Great Emancipator," 445
Great Lakes region, 112, 117, 120
Great Migration
  African Americans, 773–775
  and civil rights movement, 891
  post–World War I, 757
  and Red Summer Riots, 765–766
Great Northern Railroad
  and ARU, 643, 651
  and Eugene Debs, 652
  and Sitting Bull, 604
Great Railroad Strike (1877), 563–568, 572–573
Great Sioux Reservation, 1081
Great Uprising (1877), 715
"Great War," 743, 829
Greek War of Independence, 429
Greeley, Horace
  and Liberal Republicans, 545
  and Women's Movement, 477

Green, Bobbie, 1101
Green Corn Rebellion
 antiwar activism, 929
 collective action, 739–742, 743–744
Green Corn Rebellion, The (Cunningham), 741
Green, Shields, 417
Green, William, 848
Greenleaf, Stephen, 155
Greenville, George, 127, 129, 130, 135, 143
Grew, Mary, 927
Griffith, D. W., 542, 805
Grigsby, John
 Bear Flag Revolt, 335–336, 337, 339
 and Sonoma, 344
Grimké, Angelina, 474
Grimké, Sarah, 474
Grimm, Marshal Lloyd, 1077
Grivot, M., 383
Grosscup, Peter S., 648, 649
"Group System," UMWA, 708
"Guardians of the Oglala Nation" (GOON), 1076, 1079–1080, 1083
Guemes, Juan Francisco de, Conde de Revillagigedo, 105
Guerilla war
 Bleeding Kansas, 349, 350, 351
 John Brown, 416
 Kansas and Missouri, 353–354
Guerrero, Francisco, 334
Guest worker program, 1129
Guinn v. United States, 456
Gullah community, 265
Gullah Jack, 265
Gundlach, Jacob, 344
Guthrie, Arlo, 1016
Guzmán, Nuño de, 27
Gwyther, Thomas, 460

Hadley, Ozra A., 551–552
Hadnot, James West, 539
Hager, Talmadge, 908
Hahn, George Michael, 450, 453
Haight, Isaac, 392
Haight-Ashbury, 937
Haines, Matthew, 1098
Haiti. *See* Saint Domingue
Haley, Alex, 908

Hall, Dominick, 242
Halle, Mabel, 690
Hallgren, Mauritz A., 843
Hamer, Fannie Lou, 898
Hamilton, Alexander
 and Albert Gallatin, 230
 on Articles of Confederation, 237
 biography, 239–241
 and strong central government, 237
 Whiskey Rebellion, 228–232, 234, 238, 241
 whiskey tax, 243
Hamilton, Charles V., 903
Hamlin, Hannibal, 370
Hampshire Herald, "Letter Listing the Grievances of the Rebels" (1786), 224–225
Hampton, Wade, 262
Hancock, John
 and the Boston Tea Party, 196
 and Daniel Shays, 215, 221
 Granary Burying Ground, 159
 Massachusetts General Court, 219
 Shays' Rebellion, 213
 tax reduction, 223
Hansen, Jacob, 579
Hansford, Thomas, 7
Hanson, Alexander, 926
Haraszthy, Agoston, 344
"Hard coal," 661–662
Harding, Warren
 and Blair Mountain Battle, 793
 and Calvin Coolidge, 757, 759, 761
Harjo, Suzan Shown, 1069
Harlem Riot (1943), 892
Harlins, Latasha, 1099
Harmer, John L., 1092
Harney, William S., 383–384
Harper, Ida Husted, 486
Harpers Ferry
 armory raid on, 416, 417–420, 424–425
 and John Brown uprising, 257–258, 415–421, 424–425
 "Southern Editorial Responses," 432–434
Harper's Weekly
 on Chinese immigrants, 597
 on Pullman Strike, 647
Harriman, E. H., 571
Harriman, W. Averell, 1064

Harrington, Michael, 943
Harris, B. H., 927
Harris, Fred, 995
Harris, Matthew L., 159
Harris, Sidney, 539
Harrison, Benjamin, 626
Harrison, Carter H., 580
Hartford Convention, 925
Hartford Female Seminary, 474
Hartigan, James, 153
Hartranft, John F., 566
Harvard College/University
   and Boston Police Strike, 758
   and James Bowdoin, 217
   and John Adams, 157
   and John Wentworth, 183, 184
   and Sam Brown, 941
   and Samuel Adams, 139
   and Thomas Wilson Dorr, 312, 316
Hastings, Daniel H., 662
Hatch, Orrin, 1085–1086
Hate That Hate Produced, The, 907
Hatfield, Albert Sidney "Sid"
   biography, 793–799
   and Blair Mountain Battle, 793
   and Matewan Massacre, 800
Hatfield-McCoy feud, 798
Hawaii, 928
Hawk, David, 941, 942
Hawkins, Coleman, 897
Hawkins, Joseph H., 305
Hayden, Tom
   biography, 1024
   Chicago Eight, 1015, 1019
   and Chicago Seven, 1019, 1020, 1024–1025
   and the Mobe, 1010, 1012, 1019, 1027, 1028
   Port Huron Statement, 943
Hayes, Rutherford B.
   and Chief Joseph, 559
   and Compromise of 1876, 677
   and Great Railroad Strikes, 564, 566, 569
   Native American reservations, 557
Haymarket Massacre, 715
Haymarket Riot (1886), 575–583, 585–586, 588
   and Knights of Labor, 599
   and Mayday, 589
   and unionization, 762
Haywood, William D. "Big Bill"
   antiwar activism, 929
   and Eugene Debs, 654
   and IWW, 667, 744, 745
Heard, William H., 672
Hearsey, Henry J., 671
Hearst, William Randolph, 864
Heaters and Rollers National Association, 629
Heathcote, Thomas, 643–644
Heinde, Frederick, 623
Henderson, John, 451, 453
Henderson, Judge Richard, 171
Hennessy, Chief David, 671
Henrico County plantation, 4
Henry, Knox
   and Battle of Athens, 884
   and Pat Mansfield, 887
Henry, Patrick
   address to House of Burgesses, 14, 15
   and Articles of Confederation, 237
   First Continental Congress, 200, 201
   Stamp Act Congress, 145
   Stamp Act protests, 130, 141
   Stamp Act Resolution (1765), 147–148
Henry VIII (king of England) 95, 188
Hermanos Penitentes, 38
Hersey, John, 990
Hett, Rene, 85
Hewes, George R. T
   "Account of the Boston Massacre" (1770), 164–166
   "Account of the Boston Tea Party" (1772), 204–206
Higginson, Thomas Wentworth, 417, 429, 430
Highland Folk School, 900
Híjar, José Maria, 343–344
Hill, James J., 571
Hill, James P., 651
Hill, Joe, 745
Hillbillies, 698
Hillquit, Morris, 653–654
Hillsborough Superior Court, 171
Hinds, James M., 550
Hinks, Samuel, 374
"Hippies," 937
Hispanics, 877

History of Woman Suffrage (Anthony/Stanton), 486
History of Women in Industry in the United States (excerpts), 516–522
HMS Glasgow, 161
HMS Huron, 113
HMS Michigan, 113
Hoar, George H., 928
Hoffman, Abbott "Abbie"
  biography, 1025–1027
  Chicago Eight, 1015, 1016, 1019
  and Chicago Seven, 1019, 1020, 1025–1027
  counterculture, 937
  and the Mobe, 1028
  and Tom Hayden, 1024–1025
  and the Yippies, 1010, 1011, 1012, 1019
Hoffman, Julius
  and Abbie Hoffman, 1025–1026
  and Chicago Seven trial, 1015, 1016, 1019–1020
Hogarth, William, 370
Holcroft, John, 244
Hollowell, Mary Lou, 698, 699
Hollowell, Robert, 699
Holmes, John, 274
Holmes, Robert, 110
Home Guard volunteers, 594
"Home remedy," 230
Homestead Act (1862), 1091
Homestead Strike
  "Account of the Course of the Strike," 637–640
  "Account of Violence between Strikers and Company Security Guards," 634–637
  collective action, 619–627
  and industrial violence, 715
Hood, James, 897
Hood, Zachariah, 132
Hoover, Herbert
  and BEF, 832–833
  and Great Depression, 836
  "Letter to the District Commissioner and from his Press Conference," 844–846
Hoover, J. Edgar
  and BEF, 832
  and civil rights movement, 898
  and Watts Riot, 968
Hoovervilles
  and Great Depression, 837, 839
  overview, 837–839
Hopi Pueblo, 45
Hopkins, John P., 647
Horcasitas Jail, 105
Horsmanden, Daniel, 80, 81, 85
Horton, Rev. Dr., 451
Horton, Silphia, 900
Horton, Willie, 989
Hose (Holt), Sam, 675–676
Hotchkiss guns, 606
House, Anthony, 546
House of Burgesses
  and Bacon's supporters, 14–15
  and curtailment of rights, 13–14
  establishment, 13
  and Stamp Act protests, 130
  Stamp Act Resolution (1765), 147–148
  and Virginia elites, 15
House of Representatives
  and Know-Nothing members, 373
  and polygamy, 393
  Victoria C. Woodhull Address, 494–496
Houston, Samuel
  Battle of the Alamo, 303, 304
  biography, 307–308
  and Santa Anna, 309–310
  and Stephen Austin, 306
  Texas Revolt, 295, 296, 299–300
Houston immigration protests, 1130, 1131
Houston Riot (1917), 749–752, 753–754
Howard, George
  and ARU, 651
  Pullman Strike, 645, 649
Howard, Oliver Otis, 554, 559
Howard, T. R. M., 893
Howard University, 903
Howe, Julia Ward
  and AWSA, 483, 488, 490
  and Nineteenth Amendment, 490
  and Women's Movement, 478
Howe, Samuel Gridley
  and Dorothea Dix, 486–487
  secret six, 417, 429, 430

Howell, Clark, 681
Howell, Rednap, 171
Howell, R. K., 450
Hubay, Frank, 853
Hubbard, John, 365
Hubbard, Leverett, 185
Huckabee, Mick, 552
Hudson Motor Car Company, 847, 848
Hudson v. McMillan, 1063
Hughes, John, 439
Hughson, John, 30, 81, 87–88
Huguenots, 58, 60
Humphrey, Hubert
   and Democratic National Convention (1968), 1022, 1023
   and 1968 election, 1009, 1012, 1013, 1017
   and Richard J. Daley, 1021
Hundred Years' War, 188
Hungarian immigrants, 665
Hunt, Vita, 750
Hunter, James
   Battle of Alamance, 177
   Regulator Movement, 171
Hurley, Patrick, 832
Huron Indians
   Pontiac's Rebellion, 109, 110, 111, 113
   and Susquehannock Indians, 17, 18
Hurtado, Al, 335
Husband, Herman
   and American Revolution, 174
   biography, 179–181
   Regulator Movement, 170, 171, 172
Hussein, Saddam, 932
Hutchinson, Thomas
   and the Boston Tea Party, 193–194, 195, 196, 197
   "Destruction of His House" 148–150
   removal of, 197
   and royal authority, 187
   and Stamp Act protests, 132

"I Have a Dream" speech (King), 897, 905, 909
Idaho, 479
Ide, William B.
   Bear Flag Revolt, 335, 336
   as Bear Flagger, 339

   and "Proclamation Declaring California an Independent Republic," 345–346
   and Sonoma, 344
Illinois Central rail cars, 649
Illinois Confederation, 123
Illinois National Guard
   and Democratic National Convention (1968), 1011
   and Red Summer Riots, 769
Immigrant white men
   Charterites, 316
   Dorr's Rebellion, 311, 313
Immigration and Customs Enforcement (ICE), 1129
Imperial Custom Service, 127
In Search of Our Mother's Gardens (Walker), 1044–1045
Indentured servants
   Bacon's Rebellion, 1, 7
   Colonial Virginia, 15–16
   and tobacco crops, 20
Independence movements
   Bear Flag Revolt (1946), 333–338
   collective action, xxiv
   Texas Revolt (1835–1836), 297, 289–301
Independent Oglala Nation, 1076
Indian Appropriation Act (1851), 557
Indian Appropriation Act (1871), 1068
Indian land
   Bacon's Rebellion, 3
   and House of Burgesses, 14
   and tobacco crop, 20
Indian Reorganization Act (1934), 557
Indian Self-Determination and Education Act, 1034
Indiana Asbury University (DePauw University), 550
Indiana Volunteers, 439
"Indians," slave classification, 73–74
Indians of All Tribes
   and Alcatraz Island occupation, 1032
   overview, 1035–1036
Indigo
   colonial South Carolina, 75
   and Stono Rebellion, 69
Individualism, 318
Industrial violence, 714–716

Industrial Workers of the World (IWW)
  antiwar activism, 929
  and Eugene Debs, 653–654
  and Knights of Labor, 599
  and mining, 667
  overview, 744–745
  suppression, 741, 744–745
  and the WCU, 740
Industrialism, 311, 315
  History of Women in Industry in the United States, 516–522
"Infamous documents," 633
Inflation, 208, 209
Ingoldesby, Richard, 55
Inter-University Committee for Debate on Foreign Policy, 1028
"Interfaith dialog," 329
Internal improvements, 441
International Harvester Company, 591
International Ladies' Garment Workers Union, 1047–1048
International Longshoreman and Warehouseman's Union (ILWU), 859, 863
International Longshoreman's Association (ILA)
  and Bloody Thursday, 861–862
  and communism, 864
  and Harry Bridges, 862–863, 865
  lynchings of, 776
  overview, 865–866
  and West Coast Longshoremen's Strike, 857, 858, 859, 864, 867
International Woman Suffrage Association, 480
International Workers' Day, 589
International Working People's Association (IWPA)
  and anarchism, 585, 586
  and eight-hour day, 588
International Workingmen's Association (IWA), 593–594
Internet
  and antiwar activism, 933–934
  and Direct Action Network, 1125
Interposition, 894
Interstate Commerce Commission (ICC), 895, 896
Intolerable Acts, 143, 146. *See also* Coercive Acts.

Invalid Corps, 437
"Investigation into a New York Slave Conspiracy" (1741), 85–90
Iraq War, 925, 932–934
Ireland
  and Molly Maguires, 459, 460
  and potato famine, 325, 329, 369
Irish immigrants
  and Arthur Dobbs, 178
  discrimination against, 445
  immigration patterns, 325–329, 463–464
  and Know-Nothing Party, 373, 377
  in Maine, 366, 369–370
  and Molly Maguires, 460–461
  and nativism, 378–379
  and New York Draft Riots, 437, 438
  and Philadelphia Nativist Riots, 326
  and Portland Rum Riot, 366
  and Regulator Movement, 169
"Iron-clad documents," 633
Iroquois Confederacy
  in the Ohio River Valley, 121
  and Pennsylvania native tribes, 464
  and Pontiac's Rebellion, 114
Iroquois Indians
  Leisler's Rebellion, 54
  Ohio River Valley, 121
  and Pontiac's Rebellion, 111, 113
  and Susquehannock Indians, 17
Irwin, Godfrey, "Account of the Killings at the Mining Encampment in Ludlow, Colorado," 718–719
Isla de Tiburón, Diego Ortiz Parilla, 105–106
Isleta Pueblo, 32, 33
Italian immigrants, 708
Italian Regie Tobacco Company
  and ATC, 702
  Black Patch War, 697
Iturbide, Augustin de, 309

Jack, Patrick C., 290
Jack, Spencer H., 290
Jack, William, 290
Jackson, Andrew
  Indian treaties, 1072–1073
  martial law, 242
  and Samuel Houston, 307

Jackson, Barbara, 993
Jackson, Harry, 864
Jackson, Jesse, 911
Jackson, Mahalia, 897
Jackson, Maynard, 899
Jacksonboro (Jacksonborough), 70
Jacquette, Tommy, 965
James, Frank, 354
James, Jessie, 354
James, Joe, 689
James, William, 928
James I (king of England), 19
James II (king of England)
  Calvinist opposition, 58
  Dominion of New England, 58–59
  and Leisler's Rebellion, 53
Jamestown
  Bacon imprisoned, 5
  burning of, 6, 9, 10
  recapture of, 7
Japan, 841
Japanese immigrants, 708
Jarrett, John, 629
Jay, John, 231
Jayhawkers
  Bleeding Kansas, 350, 351
  and guerilla warfare, 353
  overview, 354–355
Jefferson, Thomas
  election of, 238
  First Continental Congress, 200, 201
  House of Burgesses, 15
  on Shays' Rebellion, 215
  on slavery, 256–257, 274
  "tree of liberty" quote, xxi
Jenkins, Charles, 437
Jenkins, Esau, 895
Jenkins, Herbert, 996
Jenks, Amelia, 476
Jennings, Ranger N. A., 737
Jennison, Charles
  Bleeding Kansas, 350
  Jayhawkers, 345, 355
Jesuits
  Catholic order, 103–104
  and Diego Ortiz Parilla, 106
  Pima Revolt, 100, 103, 104
  and Tohono O'odham, 107
Jewish Americans
  and African Americans, 693–694
  in New Amsterdam, 61
Jim Crow laws
  and Atlanta Race Riot, 682, 685
  and civil rights movement, 891
  and Houston Riot, 749, 750, 753
  New Orleans Race Riot, 671
  overview, 676–678
  Plessy v. Ferguson, 679
  in Texas, 754
"John Brown's Last Speech to the Court and
      Last Statement before Execution," 430–432
Johnson, Abraham, 185
Johnson, Absalom, 253
Johnson, Andrew
  and New Orleans Riot (1866), 450–451
  and Reconstruction, 454
Johnson, Dean, 1013–1014
Johnson, Hinton, 907
Johnson, Hugh S., 854
Johnson, James, 951–953, 956–957
Johnson, Lyndon B.
  and antiwar activism, 931
  and civil rights legislation, 898, 900, 909,
      910, 912
  and Commission on Law Enforcement and
      Administration, 994
  and Democratic National Convention (1968),
      1009, 1022, 1023
  and Detroit Riots, 989
  and the Kerner Commission, 973, 995, 996
  and Martin Luther King Jr., 906
Johnson, Robert, 230
Johnson, William, 109, 111, 113, 114
Johnston, Albert Sidney
  Civil War, 387
  Utah War, 384, 385, 386, 387
Johnston Riot Act (1771)
  and Battle of Alamance, 177
  provisions, 171–172
Jones, Anson, 308
Jones, Mary Harris "Mother"
  and Baldwin Felts Detective Agency, 717
  and IWW, 744
  and Ludlow Massacre, 708, 709

Jones, Samuel (Bleeding Kansas), 349
Jones, Samuel "Golden Rule" (antiwar movement), 928
Jordan, David Starr, 928
Jornada del Muerto (Journey of the Dead Man), 27, 33
Josephson, Matthew, 571
Journal of Occurrences (Samuel Adams), 139
Juet, Robert, 84
Jumonville Affair, 143
Jurich, Steve, 661
Jury trial
  Admiralty Courts, 147
  colonial protests, 131, 134
  and slave contradictions, 256
  Stamp Act Congress, 144
Justice Act, 197, 199

Kagi, John, 419
Kane, Thomas L., 385
Kanner, Isadore, 689, 693–694
Kansas Territory
  "Bleeding Kansas," 347–351
  guerilla warfare, 353–354
  and Jayhawkers, 354
  and John Brown, 423–424
  statehood, 363
  Topeka Constitution, 361–363
Kansas-Nebraska Act (1854)
  Bleeding Kansas, 347
  and Jayhawkers, 354
  and popular sovereignty, 358–359
Karlin, Judge Joyce Ann, 1099
Kars, Marjoleine, 174
Kavanagh, Edward, 370
Kearney, Stephen Watts, 48, 342
Kehoe, John, 459, 461
Keliher, Sylvester
  and ARU, 651
  on Pullman Strike, 649
Keller, A. C., 579
Kelley, Florence, 480
Kellogg, William Pitt, 538, 539
Kellogg-Briand Pact (1928), 761–762
Kelsey, Andrew, 339–340, 344
Kelsey, Ben, 339–340, 344
Kelsey, Sam, 335, 339–340, 344

Kennedy, John A., 437
Kennedy, John F.
  and civil rights movement, 896, 897, 908–909
  and CSW, 1048
  Proclamation and Executive Order against State Resistance to Desegregation in Mississippi, 913–915
  and SCLC, 911
Kennedy, Robert F.
  assassination of, 1009, 1023
  and civil rights movement, 896
  and Democratic National Convention (1968), 1022, 1023
Kenny, Kevin, 461
Kenrick, Francis, 325, 326, 329–330
Kensington (PA), 325, 326
Kent State, 938–940
Kentucky
  Black Patch War, 697–699, 702
  Bloody Monday, 377
  and Whiskey Rebellion, 230
Kentucky long rifles, 294
Kerner, Otto, 973–997, 995–996
Kesey, Ken, 937
Kessell, John L., 29
Keteltass, Abraham, 85
Khaki Shirts, 844
"Kick back," 857, 862
Kicking Bear, 602, 603, 608
Killingsworth, Tyrone David, 1106
Kilroy, Matthew
  Boston Massacre, 153
  manslaughter conviction, 155, 157
King, Amon B., 298
King, Howard, 993
King, John H., 578
King, Martin Luther, Jr.
  antiwar activism, 931
  assassination, 899, 903–904, 906, 1009
  biography, 904–906
  and civil rights movement, 895, 897, 898
  and Jim Crow Laws, 677–678
  and Malcolm X, 907
  March on Washington, 905, 909
  and the Mobe, 1028
  Nobel Prize, 898, 931
  and Richard Daley, 1011, 1021

and SCLC, 910
and Stokely Carmichael, 903
King, Rodney Glen
   biography, 1102–1103
   and Los Angeles Uprising, 1095, 1096
King, Samuel Ward
   and Charterites, 315–316
   and Dorr's Rebellion, 312, 313
   and Thomas Wilson Dorr, 317–318
King, W. H., 736
King, William Mckenzie, 710
King James Bible, 95
"King of the Mollies," 459
King Philip's War, 1, 2
Kino, Eusebio, 107
Kirkpatrick, James, 233
Kiva, 29, 30
Klamath Lake, 334
Knight, William T., 335, 340
Knights of Labor
   and AFL, 851
   and Chinese exclusion, 598, 599
   and Homestead Strike, 626
   and industrial violence, 715
   overview, 598–600
   and Seattle Riot, 593–594
   and UMWA, 716
   and unionization, 762
Knights of the Golden Circle, 927
Know-Nothing Party
   Bloody Monday, 377
   and Maine, 370
   and Neal S. Dow, 366
   nativism, 378
   and Plug Uglies, 379
   and Rip Raps, 380–381
   and vigilance committees, 381–382
   and Wompanoag gang, 380
Know-Nothing Riot (1866), 373–375
Knox, Henry, 215
Knox, Hugh, 239
Knox, Philander C., 22, 623
Koon, Stacey, 1095, 1096, 1097
Korean immigrants, 970
Krause, Allison, 939

Ku Klux Klan
   and Atlanta Race Riot (1906), 684, 685
   and Brooks-Baxter War, 545
   and early guerilla warfare, 354
   and Jim Crow Laws, 677
   and Joseph Brooks, 550
   and lynching, 775
   in "New South," 541
   overview, 542–543, 805–806
   post–World War I, 757
   in rural Oklahoma, 741
Ku Klux Klan Act, 538, 539, 805
Kucher, Joseph, 579
Kuklos ("circle"), 805
Kunstler, William, 1015, 1019

L'Ouverture, Toussaint, 255
La Bufa silver mine, 27
La Nueva México, 27
La Salineta, 42
Labor unions
   Blair Mountain, Battle of, 793–795, 797–798
   and Boston Police Strike, 757–759, 761
   Great Railroad Strikes, 563–568, 572–573
   growth of, 762–763
   and Haymarket Riot, 575–583, 585–586, 588
   and Homestead Strike, 619–27 and Ludlow Massacre, 707–711
   martial law, 243
   and New Deal, 715–716
   and Pullman Strike, 643–650
   Toledo Auto-Lite Strike, 847–850
   West Coast Longshoremen's Strike, 847, 857–859, 861–865
Lacrosse, 110–111
LaFollette. Robert, 761
Lake Erie, 112–113
Lakota (Sioux) Indians
   overview, 613–614
   Wounded Knee Massacre, 601, 602, 604, 605, 606, 607–608
Lally, John F., 672
Lamb, Peter, 671–672, 676
Lamm, Richard, 1086
Lamont, Daniel S., on Pullman Strike, 647
Land Ordinance survey, 1090–1091

Lane, James H.
  Bleeding Kansas, 348–349, 350, 351
  "Redlegs," 353, 355
Laney v. United States, 789–791
Langdon, Frank W., 460, 461
Larkin, Consul Thomas, 334, 342
Lassalle, Ferdinand, 746
Lassen, Peter, 334
"Last Speech to the Court and Last Statement before Execution" (John Brown), 430–432
Laton School, 673
Lattimer Massacre (1897)
  collective action, 661–664
  "Strikers Resolutions and Editorials," 668–669
Laura (Texas Revolt), 292–293
Laurens, Henry, 133
"Law and Order Constitution"
  Charterites, 316
  Dorr's Rebellion, 312
"Law for the Better Preventing of Fire, A" 83
Lawrence (KS), 348, 349
Lawrence raid
  guerilla warfare, 353–354
  and Jayhawkers, 355
  and Pottawatomie Massacre, 360
Lawson, John, 709, 710
League for the Advancement of States' Equal Rights (LASER)
  and Ronald Reagan, 1092
  and Sagebrush Rebellion, 1086
League of Nations, 757
League of United Latin American Citizens (LULAC), 731
League of Women Voters, 481
Leary, Timothy, 1016
Leavenworth (KS), 348
Lecompton Constitution, 350, 362–363
Lee, "Light Horse" Harry, 427, 926
Lee, John D., 387
Lee, Robert E.
  biography, 427–429
  and Harpers Ferry Raid, 419, 428
Lee, Spike, 908
Lee, William Henry Fitzhugh, 366–367
Leese, Alcalde (Major) Jacob, 335, 344
Lehigh Coal Mining Company, 466

Leisler, Jacob
  biography, 60–61
  Calvinist faith, 58, 60, 62
  colonial regime, 53, 54
  execution of, 55, 61
  "Letter to the Governor and Committee of Safety of Boston" (1689), 62–63
  "A Modest and Impartial Narrative," (1690), 63–67
  opposition to, 54
Leisler's Rebellion (1689), 53–56, 58
Lenox, David, 232, 233
Lerman, Steven, 1095–1096
Lester, Julius, 253
"Letter from a Birmingham Jail" (King), 898
"Letters from a Farmer in Pennsylvania" (Dickinson), 204
"Letter to the Governor and Committee of Safety of Boston" (Leisler, 1689), 62–63
Lewis, John
  and SNCC, 912, 913
Lewis, John L.
  and CIO, 763
  and UMWA, 667, 717
Lewis and Clark Expedition, 553
"Lexington of Texas," 293
Ley, Peter, 579
Liberal Constitution of 1824 (Mexico), 291, 295
Liberal feminism, 1044, 1046–1047
Liberal League, 594
Liberal Republicans
  and Brooks-Baxter War, 545, 550–551
  and Radical Republicans, 552
"Liberationists," 314
Liberator, The, 279, 475
Liberia, 274–275
Liberty Party, 429
Liberty Tree
  Andrew Oliver effigy, 159
  Boston Massacre, 153
  Stamp Act protests, 131–132
Life and Work of Susan B. Anthony (Anthony/Harper), 486
Ligonier, Sir John, 117
Lily, 475, 477
Lincoln, Abbey, 897

Lincoln, Abraham
   and Bleeding Kansas, 351
   and conscription, 441
   and Copperheads, 443, 444
   election of, 238, 389, 420–421
   and Emancipation Proclamation, 280
   martial law, 242, 314
   and New York Draft Riots, 435, 440
   and Pinkertons, 632
   and Reconstruction, 454
   slave repatriation, 445
   and Southern voters, 426
   "Ten Percent Plan," 449
Lincoln, Benjamin
   on Disqualifying Act, 213
   Shays' Rebellion, 211, 212
Lincoln, Mary Todd, 340
Lindsay, John V, 996
Lingg, Louis
   bomb making, 587
   Haymarket Riot, 580, 581, 582
Lithuanian immigrants, 661
Little Big Horn
   Battle of, 553, 602, 614
   and Sitting Bull, 615
Little Bill (steamer), 624
Little Crow, 612
Little, Malcolm. *See* Malcolm X
"Little Rock Nine," 895
Lively, C. E., 799
Livingston, Robert, 134, 144
Livingston, William, 239
Lloyd, Thomas, 97
Locke, Gary, 1123
Locke, John, 139
Lockouts
   Homestead Strike, 621, 622, 632
   overview, 631–632
Lockwood, Belva Ann, 478
Logan, James, 97
Logan, Rayford, 891
London Chronicle, 157
Long, Alexander, 927
Long, Richard, 761
Long Island, 197
Long Strike (1875), 716
Longest Walk demonstration, 1073–1074

Longfellow, Henry Wadsworth
   and antiwar activism, 927
   Paul Revere's Ride, 162
Longshoremen
   defined, 857
   and scrap metal, 859, 863
Longstreet, James, 538
Longview (TX), 765, 768
Looting
   Detroit Riots, 989
   Los Angeles Uprising, 1098
   Watts Riot, 967, 973, 974–975
Los Angeles (CA)
   "Day without an Immigrant" protests, 1129, 1130
   Governor's Commission Report on the Watts Riots, 976–985
   and Mexican Americans, 877
   "Progress Report of the Presidential Task Force on Recovery," 1106–1120
   Zoot Suit Riot, 869–875, 879–881
Los Angeles Police Department (LAPD)
   police brutality, 879
   and Rodney King, 1103–1105
   and Watts Riot, 965–971
   and Zoot Suit Riot, 873, 874
Los Angeles Times, 759
Los Angeles Uprising (1992), 1095–1099
Loudoun, Lord, 118
Louiaillier, Louis, 242
Louis XIV (king of France), 58
Louisiana
   Charles Deslondes's German Coast Uprising, 252, 255–256, 262–263
   and civil rights movement, 894
   and Colfax Massacre, 537–539
   Freedmen, 541
   and New Orleans Riot, 449–452
   racial segregation, 677, 678
Louisiana Purchase
   and Bleeding Kansas, 347
   and First Missouri Compromise, 356
   and Indian treaties, 1073
Louisville (KY), 377
Louisville, New Orleans
   and Texas Railroad (LNO&T), 675
Lowell, John, 926

Lowell, Lawrence, 758
Lowery, Joseph, 911
Loyalists, Boston Massacre, 152
   and the Boston Tea Party, 193
   defined, 151
Loyola, Ignatius, 103
Lucas County Unemployed League (LCUL), 848, 852–853
Lucy (slave), 254
Ludlow Massacre (1914)
   collective action, 707–711
   "Godfrey Irwin's Account of the Killings at the Mining Encampment in Ludlow, Colorado," 718–719
   "Walter Finks Depiction of Events at the Ludlow Camp," 719–726
Ludlow tent colony, 707, 709, 710, 713
Luis of Pitic, 105
Luther v. Borden (1849)
   Dorr's Rebellion, 314
   Supreme Court decision, 319–323
Lutherans, 61
Lutwyche, Edward Goldstone, 184
Lyford Courant, 729
Lyman, Stanley D., 1079
Lynchings
   and Jim Crow Laws, 677
   and NAACP, 695
   and New York Draft Riots, 436, 439
   overview, 775–776
   and Plan de San Diego, 729, 730
   Red Summer Riots, 765, 767
   and segregation, 807
   Springfield Race Riot, 689

MacArthur, Douglas
   Anacostia Flats Battle, 835–836
   and BEF, 829, 831, 832, 833
   biography, 840–845
Madison, James
   and antiwar activism, 926, 933
   on Articles of Confederation, 237
   martial law, 242
   on Shays' Rebellion, 213, 215
   on strong central government, 237
Magna Carta
   English rights, 146
   and salutary neglect, 142
   and Stamp Act, 129, 131, 141, 144
Maguire, Connor, 466
Mailer, Norman, 1016
Maine
   and First Missouri Compromise, 356
   Irish immigrants, 369–370
   Portland Rum Riot, 365–367
"Maine Law," 365, 366, 370, 371
Maine Temperance Union, 365, 366
"Maintaining Order in the District of Columbia, President Hoover's Letter and Press Conference," 844–846
"Major J. H. Carleton's "Special Report on the Mountain Meadows Massacre," 396–414
Malcolm X
   biography of, 907
   murder of, 899, 969
Malcolm X (film), 908
Malone, Vivian, 897
Mamaltee, 112, 124
Manassas, Second Battle of, 428
Mancusi, Warden Vincent, 1064–1065
Manhattan Island, 84–85
"Manifesto" (N. Bacon), 21–24
Mann, Horace, 486–487
Mann, Tess, 160, 163
Mansfield, Pat
   Battle of Athens, 883–885, 888, 889
   biography, 887–888
March Against Fear, 899, 903
"March Island" campaign, 859
March on Washington for Jobs and Freedom
   and civil rights movement, 891–892, 897
   and Martin Luther King Jr., overview, 908–910, 905
   and SCLC, 911
   and SNCC, 912
March on Washington for Peace in Vietnam, 931
Maritime Workers Industrial Union (MWIU)
   and communism, 864
   and ILA, 865
Markham, William, 97
Marriage, 476, 1044
Marriage and Love (Goldman), 526–528
Marshal, Thomas, 154

Marshall, John, 1072
Marshall, Thurgood
  appointment to Supreme Court, 899
  and *Brown v. Board of Education*, 893
Martial law
  Arkansas, 546, 547, 551
  and Blair Mountain Battle, 793
  Dorr's Rebellion, 313
  and New Orleans, 451
  overview, 241–243
Martin, James, 661, 663
Martin Luther King federal holiday, 900, 906
Marx, Karl, 746
Marxism, 564, 567, 572
Mary (queen of England), 53–54
Maryland
  antiwar activism, 926
  and Bacon's Rebellion, 1, 2, 3, 5, 10
  Catholic settlers, 329
  and civil rights movement, 897
  and Great Railroad Strikes, 563
  intergovernmental assemble, 54
  Know-Nothing Party, 373
  and Plug Uglies, 373, 374, 379–380
  and Rip Raps, 380–381
  and Shays' Rebellion, 214
  and Susquehannock Indians, 17, 18
  and vigilance committees, 382–383
Masculinity, 871, 872, 875, 880–881
Mason, George
  Bacon's Rebellion, 1–2
  House of Burgesses, 15
Massachusetts
  and Calvin Coolidge, 761
  Dominion of New England, 59
  intergovernmental assemble, 54
  Shays' Rebellion, 207–215
  Stamp Act Congress, 139, 144
  Stamp Act protests, 130, 131, 134–135
  Townshend Act, 204
  women's property rights, 476–477
Massachusetts General Court
  overview, 218–219
  taxation, 222–223
Massachusetts Government Act, 197, 199
Massachusetts House of Representatives, 217
Massachusetts Humane Society, 218

Massachusetts Institute of Technology, 941
Matamoras, 295, 296, 298
Matewan Massacre
  and Blair Mountain Battle, 793, 797–798
  overview, 799–800
  and Sid Hatfield, 798–799
Matheson, Scott, 1086
Matson Navigation Company, 863
Matthew, Thomas, 1
Maverick, Samuel, 153
May Day, 589
Mayflower replica seizure, 1067, 1071
Mayhew, Jonathan, 145, 146
Mayos Indians, 100
Mays, Terry M., 71, 74, 78
McCallum, 369
McCarthy, Eugene
  antiwar candidate, 1009, 1010, 1013
  and Democratic National Convention (1968), 1022–1023
  and Sam Brown, 941
McCarthyism
  and AFL, 851
  and antiwar activism, 930
McCaulay, William, 153
McCleary, William H., 622, 624, 625
McClellan, George B., 444
McClure, John "Poker Jack," 546, 551
McCone Commission (Watts Riot), 968
McConnell, Ward, 1101–1102
McCord, Jim Nance, 887
McCormick, Cyrus, 590
McCormick, Leander, 590
McCormick Harvesting Machine Company
  and Haymarket Riot, 576–577
  and Knights of Labor strike, 599
  structure/policies, 590–591
McCormick Reaper Works. See McCormick Harvesting Machine Company
McCorvey, Norma, 1055
McCrady, Edward, Jr., 456
McCulloch, William M., 996
McEnery, John O., 538
McEntire, Carl, 1068
McFarlane, James, 233
McGillicuddy, Valentine, 603

McGovern, George
  and David Mixner, 942
  and Democratic National Convention (1968), 1013, 1023
  and Wounded Knee occupation, 1076
McKenna's Corner, 661
McKinley, William
  and antiwar activism, 933
  and Atlanta Race Riot, 681–682
McKinney, Jesse, 538
McLaughlin, James "White Hair"
  and Sitting Bull, 615
  Wounded Knee Massacre, 603, 604
McLean, Evalyn, 831
McLuckie, John, 624
McMahon, John K., 579
McMinn County War, or Battle of Athens, 883–885, 887–889
McNary-Haugen farm bill, 761
McNelly, Leander, 737
McParlan (McPartland), James
  "An Article Describing His Infiltration of the Molly Maguires," 467–471
  and Molly Maguires, 459, 461
Means, Russell
  AIM leadership, 1067, 1069
  and Dick Wilson, 1083
  and Wounded Knee occupation, 1075
Mechanics' Institute, 450, 451
Medina, Battle of, 308
Memorial to the Massachusetts Legislature (Dix), 487
"Men of Worth," 194
Mennonites
  antiwar activism, 925
  in New Amsterdam, 61
Mental health reform, 486–487
Meredith, James, 896, 899, 903
Merriam, Frank
  and Bloody Thursday, 861
  and West Coast Longshoremen's Strike, 858
Merritt, Ezekiel "Stuttering Zeke," 335, 340
Merritt, John, 85
Merritt Conspiracy Act (1887), 592
Methodism, 370
Methodist Episcopal Church, 550
Metzel, Katherine, 652

Mexía (Mexica), Jose Antonio, 291, 297
Mexican-American War
  annexation of Texas, 300
  antiwar activism, 925, 927, 933
  and Indian treaties, 1073
  and Robert E. Lee, 427–428
  and Santa Anna, 309, 310
Mexican Americans
  overview, 877–878
  and police brutality, 878–880
  in Watts, 969
  and Zoot Suit Riot, 869–875
Mexican immigrants
  "Day without an Immigrant" protests, 1129–1131
  Ludlow Massacre, 707, 708
Mexican Revolution
  and Plan de San Diego, 727, 728
  and United States, 733–734
Mexico
  and acquisition of Utah, 383
  and Bear Flag Revolt, 333–338
  Plan de San Diego, 727–732
  and Santa Anna, 309–310
  and Texas Revolt, 289–301
  and United States, 733–734
Micheltorena, Manuel, 333
  campaign against, 339, 340
Michigan Civil Rights Commission, 994
Michigan Daily, 1024
Michigan National Guard, 989–990
Michigan State Police, 990
Michigan Volunteers, 439
"Middle class," 132
Milam, Ben, 294–295
Milam, J. W., 894
Milchrist, Thomas E., 647, 648, 649
Miles, Nelson A.
  and antiwar activism, 928
  Nez Percé's flight, 554, 558
  and Sitting Bull, 615
  and Wounded Knee Massacre, 603, 604, 605, 607–608
Military Order of Santiago, 39, 41
Militia Act (1862), 435
Millenarianism, 181
Miller, Antoine, 1105

Miller, James, 291
Miller, Jeffrey, 939
Miller, Oliver, 233
Miller, William, 232, 233
Milligan, L. B., 927
Milligan, Lambdin P., 242–243
Mine Safety Act (1869), 466
Mine War of 1920–1921, 794, 797–798, 799
Miners
   Chinese immigrants, 597–598
   defined, 666
   historical overview, 666–667
   Pima Revolt, 99
Miners Journal, 460
"Miners March," 793
Mingo Creek Association
   Tom the Tinker warnings, 244
   Whiskey Rebellion, 231
Mingo Creek militia, 232–233
Mingo Indians
   Ohio River Valley, 121
   Pontiac's Rebellion, 113. *See also* Iroquois
Miniger, Clem, 848
Minikus, Lee, 965
Minneapolis General Strike, 847
Minnesota Uprising (1864), 611–612
Minor (VA), 478
Minor v. Happersett, 478
Minstrel Republicans, 545–546, 550–551
Minuit, Peter, 84
Missemer, W. S., 651
Mission, The (film), 103
Mission Nuestra Señora de la Purísima Concepción, 294
Mission San Francisco Solano, 343
Mission San Xavier del Bac, 107
"Missionary Era," 29
Missionary work, 103
Mississauga Indians, 111
Mississippi
   and civil rights movement, 894, 897, 898, 903
   "Proclamation and Executive Order against State Resistance to Desegregation," 913–915
   women's property rights, 476
Mississippi Flood (1916), 766

Mississippi Freedom Democratic Party (MFDP)
   and civil rights movement, 898
   and Malcolm X, 908
   and SNCC, 912
"Mississippi Plan," 675
Mississippi Poor People's Corporation, 1026
Mississippi River, 227
Mississippi Summer Project, 912
Missouri
   and Bleeding Kansas, 347, 348
   guerilla warfare, 353–354
   and Jayhawkers, 354
   and Missouri, slavery, 274
Missouri Compromise (1820–1821)
   Bleeding Kansas, 347, 348
   Maine statehood, 365
   overview, 356–358
   and Stephen Douglas, 359
Mitchell, Ann Lytton, 239
Mitchell, John, 716–717
Mixner, David, 942
Model 1803 Rifle, 392
"Modest and Impartial Narrative, A" (Leisler) (1690), 63–67
Mohawk Indians
   Leisler's Rebellion, 54
   Pontiac's Rebellion, 111
Molly Maguires (1870s)
   collective action, 459–462
   "Excerpts from An Article by James McPartland Describing His Infiltration," 467–471
   and industrial violence, 715
   and unionism, 466–467
Molly Maguires, The (film), 462
Monongahela River, 619, 622
Monopolies, 697
Monroe, James
   Gabriel Prosser uprising, 253, 264
   on slave resettlement, 274–275, 279
Monroe, John T., 450
Montagu, Admiral, 195
Montcalm, Louis Joseph, Marquis de, 118
Montgomery, Hugh
   Boston Massacre, 153, 161
   manslaughter conviction, 155, 157

Montgomery, James, 350, 351, 355
Montgomery, John B., 337
Montgomery Improvement Association (MIA), 895, 910
Montreal (Canada), 109
Moore, Gregory, 940
Moore, Putnam, 272
Moore, Thomas, 272
Moore v. Dempsey, 771
Mora, August T., 671, 676
Mora, Dennis, 951–954
Moran, Percy, 303, 304
Morehouse College, 904
Morgan, Ephraim, 793
Morgan, Michael, 1037
"Mormon fundamentalists," 393
Mormon Nauvoo Militia, 385
"Mormon War," 383
Mormons. *See* Church of Jesus Christ of Latter-day Saints
Morrill Anti-Bigamy Act, 393
Morris, Gouverneur, 926
Morris, Robert
   and Alexander Hamilton, 239–240
   strong central government, 237
   and Whiskey Rebellion, 228–229
Moses, Bob, 912
"Moses of Her People, The" 283
Moses story, 282–283, 284
Most, Johann, 585, 586–587
Mother Jones magazine, 743–744
Motherhood, 1044
Mott, Lucretia
   and ERA, 1053
   and Nineteenth Amendment, 489
   and women's movement, 474
Moulin, Michael, 1097
Mount Holyoke College
   and Lucy Stone, 475
   and women's movement, 474
Mount Vernon Hook-and-Ladder Company, 379
Mountain Meadows Massacre
   and Brigham Young, 396
      "Major J. H. Carleton's Special Report," 396–414

   and Nauvoo Legion, 392
   and Utah War, 384, 386, 387
Mountain States Legal Foundation, 1093
MoveOn.org, 933
Ms. magazine, 1957
Muckrakers, 571, 572
Mudgett, Ebenezer, 184, 185
Muhammad, Elijah, 907–908
"Mulattoes" classification, 73–74
Muller v. Oregon, 515–516
Munson, "Rube," 740
Murietta, Joaquin, 336
Murphy, L. J., 578, 579
Murphy, T. J., 1101
Muskie, Edmund, 1012, 1023
Muste, A. J.
   antiwar activism, 931
   and the Mobe, 1028
"Mustizoes" classification, 73–74
"My Day" column, 885

Nafaratte, Emiliano, 728–729
Nakota Sioux, 613
"Napoleon of Temperance," 365
Naranjo, Pedro, 49–51
Nash, Christopher Columbus, 537, 538–539
Nash, Diane, 912
Nation of Islam, 907, 908
National Advisory Commission on Civil Disorders Report, on Watts, 973–997
National Afro-American League, 695
National American Woman Suffrage Association (NAWSA), 1053
   and Nineteenth Amendment, 490
   and Susan B. Anthony, 486, 489
   and women's movement, 479–480, 481, 484
National Association for the Advancement of Colored People (NAACP)
   and black soldiers, 753
   and civil rights movement, 891, 892, 895, 897
   and Elaine Massacre, 770, 771
   established, 776
   and Houston Riot, 751, 755
   and Jim Crow Laws, 678
   and March on Washington, 909
   overview, 694–695

and Roy Wilkins, 905
and Springfield Race Riot, 691, 694
National Black Feminist Organization (NBFO), 1046
National Catholic Conference for Interracial Justice, 905
National Citizen and Ballot Box, 489
National Commission on the Causes and Prevention of Violence. See *Rights in Conflict*
National Council of Churches, 1076
National Council of Jewish Women, 1047–1048
National Council of Negro Women, 1047–1048
National Federation of Business and Professional Women's Clubs, 1047–1048
National Female Anti-Slavery Society, 474
National Grange, 697, 702
National Guard, 896–897
National Historic Landmark, 626
National Indian Youth Council (NIYC), 1035, 1073–1074
National Industrial Recovery Act (NIRA, 1933)
 and auto industry, 847
 and labor unions, 715, 865
 overview, 854–855
 and UMWA, 717
National Labor Relations Act (1935)
 and New Deal, 715
 and NIRA, 855
 and West Coast Strike, 859
National Liberation Front, 930
National Mobilization to End the War in Vietnam (Mobe)
 and Democratic National Convention (1968), 1010, 1011, 1012, 1019
 overview, 1027–1029
 and Tom Hayden, 1024
National Negro Committee. See National Association for the Advancement of Colored People (NAACP)
National Organization for Women (NOW), 1045
National Park Service, 1091
National Peace Action Coalition, 1028
National Progressive Union of Miners and Mine Laborers, 716

National Prosecuting Committee on Lattimer Victims (NPCCLV), 663
National Recovery Administration, 854
National Soldiers' Bonus League of America, 844
National Student Association (NSA)
 and David Hawk, 941
 and SNCC, 912
National Student Christian Federation, 912
National Temperance Convention (1851), 365
National Tribal Chairman's Association, 1071
National Urban League (NUL)
 and March on Washington, 909
 and Whitney Young, 905
 on Watts, 969
National Woman Suffrage Association (NWSA)
 and AWSA, 483
 and Nineteenth Amendment, 490
 overview, 487–489
 and Susan B. Anthony, 484, 488–489
 and women's movement, 477–478, 479–480
National Woman's Party (NWP)
 and ERA, 1053
 and feminist movement, 1043, 1046, 1049
 and women's suffrage, 480, 481
National Women's Conference, 1054
National Women's Political Caucus (NWPC)
 and feminist movement, 1046
 and Gloria Steinem, 1057
National Women's Rights Convention, 475
Native American Party
 and nativism, 378
 and Philadelphia Nativist Riots, 326
Native Americans
 Alcatraz Island occupation, 1031–1034, 1037, 1038–1039
 "Alcatraz Proclamation to the Great White Father," 1035, 1040–1042
 Bacon's Rebellion, 1–7, 10
 and Bear Flag Revolt, 334, 336
 Dakota Uprising, 611–613
 and Jeffrey Amherst, 117, 118
 and John Charles Frémont, 334, 335
 and Mormons, 391–392
 Nez Percé's Flight, 553–555
 and Papago Revolt, 107
 and Pima Revolt, 99–103

Native Americans (continued)
    and Plan de San Diego, 727
    and plantation economies, 69
    and Pontiac's Rebellion 109–115
    Pueblo Revolt, 27–35
    reservations, 557
    Seris Revolt, 100
    Trail of Broken Treaties protest, 1067–1070
    and "termination" policy, 1031, 1038–1039
    and Texas Rangers, 736
    treaties, 1072–1073
    Wounded Knee Massacre, 601–609
    and Wounded Knee occupation, 609, 1075–1077
Nativism
    and Germans, 331
    and Know-Nothing Party, 373
    and Mexican Americans, 869, 877
    overview, 378–379
    Philadelphia, 325–327
"Natural rights of mankind," 134
Nauvoo Legion
    overview, 391–392
    Utah War, 384, 387, 392
Navajos, 34–35
Naval Reserve Armory, 871–873
Navigation Acts
    Dominion of New England, 59
    and salutary neglect, 142
Naylor, Charles, 327
Neal, Samuel, 337, 340
"Necessary evil," 257
Neeb, Oscar (Haymarket Riot), 580, 581, 582
"Negroes" classification, 73–74
Neill, James C., 296
Nelson (Texas Revolt), 290
Nentvig, Juan, 100
Neolin (Delaware Prophet)
    biography, 119–120
    and Pontiac, 123
    Pontiac's Rebellion, 109
Netherlands
    Calvinist religion, 58
    John Adams's ambassadorship, 157
    religious freedom, 61

Nevada
    and Frémont's expedition, 341
    and Sagebrush Rebellion, 1085
Neville, John, 231–233
New Deal
    and AFL, 851
    and labor unions, 715
    and NIRA, 854
    and UMWA, 717
    and unions, 710
"New Departure," 478
New Detroit Committee, 991
New England
    and antiwar activism, 925–926, 927
    backcountry-coastal conflict, 169
    Know-Nothing Party, 374
New England Emigrant Aid Company, 348
New England Regulation
    Massachusetts General Court, 219
    Shays' Rebellion, 207, 210–211, 212, 214, 221
New France, 119, 121
New Hampshire
    Dominion of New England, 59
    Pine Tree Riot, 183
    and Shays' Rebellion, 213
    shipbuilding, 188
    state constitution, 185
New Hampshire Gazette (Pine Tree Riot), 184
New Helvetia, 333, 334
New Immigrants
    industrial violence, 714
    Ludlow Massacre, 708
New Jersey, 196
New Left, 943
New Market Fire Company, 380
New Mexico
    Cruzate governorship, 34, 42
    "Day without an Immigrant" protests, 1129, 1130
    "Missionary Era," 29, 47
    Otermín governorship, 31, 32–34, 41–43
    Plan de San Diego, 727
    Spanish division, 32
    Spanish settlement, 27–29, 37
    Treviño governorship, 30–31
    Vargas governorship, 35, 43, 47
New Mobilization, 941, 942

New Netherland, 61
New Orleans (LA)
　Battle of, 242
　Catholic settlers, 329
　and Charles Deslondes, 262–263
　Colfax Massacre, 537–539
　"Day without an Immigrant" protests, 1129, 1130
　martial law, 241–242
　and Neal S. Dow, 366–367
　Treaty of Paris (1763), 119
　and vigilance committees, 382
New Orleans Citizens' Committee, 678, 679
New Orleans Race Riot (1900), 671–673
New Orleans Riot (1866), 449–452, 453
New Right, 1049
"New South," 541, 681, 682
New Spain, 99
New Ulm, 612
"New Urban Black," 968
New York (city)
　and Boston Tea Party, 196
　Chinese immigrants, 369
　Draft riot, 446–447, 927–928
　and Great Migration, 773–774
　Hoovervilles, 838
　Know-Nothing Party, 373
　Know-Nothing Riots, 374–375
New York (state)
　colonial, 55, 61–62, 79–80, 83, 84
　"Day without an Immigrant" protests, 1129, 1130
　intergovernmental assembly, 54
　Leisler's Rebellion, 53–56
　and Shays' Rebellion, 213
　and Stamp Act Congress, 134, 144–145
　women's property rights, 476
New York Committee of Vigilance, 382
New York Conspiracy, 79–81, 85–90
New York Daily Tribune, 451
New York Draft Riots (1863), 435–440
New York Fire Brigade (establishment), 83
New York Harbor cadets, 439
New York Infirmary for Indigent Women and Children, 476
New York Militia, 439
New York National Guard, 1060

New York Post, 273
New York Radical Feminists, 1047
New York Slave Insurrection, 79–81, 85–90
New York State Militia, 437
New York State Vigilance Committees, 382
New York Times
　on ARU, 646
　on Boston Police Strike, 758
　"Excepts from an Account of the New York City Draft Riots," 446–447
　Haymarket Riot, 579
　and New York Draft Riots, 438
　on Pinkertons', 623
　on polygamy, 393
　on Pullman Strike, 647
　robber barons, 571
　on Watts Riot, 969
New York Volunteer Fire Department, 83
New York Volunteers, 439
Newark Community Union Project, 1024
Newark Riot (1967), 899
Newburyport (NH), 188
Newby, Dangerfield, 417, 419
Newman, William, 749
Newport (RI), 133
Newton, Robert C., 546
Neylan, John Francis, 864
Nez Percé
　"Chief Joseph's Surrender Speech," 561
　flight, 553–555
　relocation, 560
Niagara Movement, 695
Nicholson, Francis
　Dominion of New England, 59
　Leisler's Rebellion, 53, 54
Nickels, Greg, 1123
"Nig Five," 701
Night Riders
　and Black Patch War, 697, 698–699, 703
　and DTDPPA, 701
Nineteenth Amendment
　overview, 489–491
　women's movement (1870s), 473, 481, 1053
Nixon, Richard M.
　and antiwar activism, 942
　and Broken Treaties protest, 1069, 1071–1072
　Cambodian invasion, 938

Nixon, Richard M. (continued)
  election of 1968, 1009, 1014, 1017, 1022, 1023
  and the Mobe, 1028
  and Native Americans, 1031, 1033, 1034, 1067
  resignation, 1065
  and Vietnam War, 941
Niza, Fray Marcos de, 37
"No Justice, No Peace," 1097
"No taxation without representation"
  English origin, 145–147
  protest slogan, 129, 131, 141, 143
Noble and Holy Order of the Knights of Labor. *See* Knights of Labor
Noiret, Charles A., 672, 676
Nonconformist movements, 96
"Nonresistance," 415
Norfolk (VA), 773
Norris-LaGuardia Act, 633
North Carolina Agricultural and Technical College 895, 903, 912
North Carolina
  and Arthur Dobbs, 178–179
  Battle of Alamance, 177–178
  and civil rights movement, 895, 896
  Johnston Riot Act, 171–172
  and Nat Turner, 273
  Regulator Movement, 170
  Stamp Act protests, 132
  and U.S. Constitution, 174
  Whiskey Rebellion, 230, 231
North Carolina Gazette, 133
North Carolina Regulator Movement, 169–172, 173–175
North Elba, 416, 423
North End Caucus, 163
North, Lord, 197, 199
Northampton (MA), 761, 762
Northern Pacific Railroad, 563, 593, 615
Northwest Passage expeditions, 178
Northwest Territory, 210
Norton, Gale, 1094
Nuevo Reyno de Andalucia, Parilla, 105
Nugent, Robert, 437
Nursing profession, 476

O'Donnell, Hugh, 624
O'Hare, Kate Richards, 747

Oacpicagigua, Luis
  biography, 104–105
  Pima Revolt, 100, 101, 103, 104–105
Oakes, James, 255, 256
Oakes, Louis, 1104
Oakes, Richard
  and Alcatraz Island occupation, 1032, 1033, 1037, 1039
  biography, 1036–1037
  and Broken Treaties protest, 1067
  and Indians of All Tribes, 1035, 1036
  and termination policy, 1038
Oates, Steven, 420
Obama, Barack, 933
Oberlin College, 474, 475
Obrajes (sweatshops), 38
Obscene literature, 496
"Obstructive demonstration," 944
Occoneechees, 4
Occupational Safety and Health Administration, 717
Ochs, Phil, 1012, 1016
Office of Federal Indian Relations and Community Construction, 1068
Oglala Sioux Civil Rights Organization (OSCRO), 1075, 1079
Oglethorpe, James
  "Description of Stono Rebellion" (1739), 76–78
  Stono Rebellion, 70, 71
Ohio, 563
Ohio Company, 178
Ohio National Guard
  Kent State, 939, 940
  and Toledo Auto-Lite Strike, 849, 852, 853
Ohio River Valley
  British penetration, 112, 114, 117, 118, 120
  colonial era, 121–122
Ohkay Owingeh Pueblo, 28, 31–32, 39, 47
Ojeda, Bartolomé de, 34–35
Ojibwas
  Nakota Sioux, 613
  Pontiac's Rebellion, 109, 110, 111, 120
Oklahoma
  Green Corn Rebellion, 739
  and Ku Klux Klan, 741
  Tulsa Race Riot, 771, 801–804

"Oklahoma Commission to Study Tulsa Race Riot of 1921 Reports," 809–828
Oklahoma National Guard, 802, 803
Olatunji, 897
Old South Church (ME), 370
"Old Sow," 392
Older Women's League (OWL), 1046–1047
"Olive Branch,' 143
Oliver, Andrew
   Liberty Tree effigy, 159, 202
   Stamp Act protests, 132
Olney, Richard, 647, 648, 649
Omaha, 765, 769
On the Waterfront (film), 862
One Flew over the Cuckoo's Nest (Kesey), 937
Oneida Indians, 111
Onondaga Indians, 111
Oñate, Juan de
   biography, 39, 41
   and Franciscans, 37
   governorship of New Mexico, 27, 28, 29, 33, 47
   picture, 40
Opdyke, George, 438
Operation Dewey Canyon III, 931–932
Opponents of War, (Peterson/Fite) 1917–1918, 741
Order in Council, 54
Order of Good Templars, 371
"Order of the American Knights, The," 242
Order of the Star-Spangled Banner, 373
Oregon, 341, 480
Oregon Territory, 385
Organization of African Unity, 908
Organization of Afro-American Unity, 908
Orphan Asylum for Colored Children, 438
Osawatomie militia
   and Bleeding Kansas, 349–350
   and John Brown, 416, 424
   and Pottawatomie Massacre, 360–361
Osgood, Charles, 709, 713
Oswald, Russell, 1060
Otermín, Antonio de
   biography, 41–43
   New Mexico, 31, 32–34
Other American, The (Harrington), 943
Otis, Harrison Gray, 926

Otis, James, 130, 141, 146
Ottawa Indians, 109, 110, 111, 120
Ottoman Empire, 665
Overseers, 253
Owens, Richard, 337
Oxford Union Debate, 908

Pace, John T.
   and BEF, 832
   and Walter Waters, 843, 844
Pachucos, 871, 875
Padilla, Juan
   and Bear Flag Revolt, 336
Padrés, José Maria, 343–344
Pagago Revolt, 107
Page, Sarah
   and Tulsa Race Riot, 801, 802
Paine, Robert Treat
   and Boston Massacre prosecution, 154
Paine, Thomas
   and Stamp Act protests, 130, 141, 143
Paint Creek–Cabin Creek Strike (1913–1914), 797, 799
Palmer, A. Mitchell
   government raids, 757
   and Red Scare, 741
Palmer, Bertha
   and Pullman Strike, 646–647
Palmer, John M.
   and Homestead Strike, 625
Palmes, Richard
   and "Account of the Boston Massacre" (1770), 166–167
Pamunkey Indians
   Bacon's Rebellion, 6
   and "Pamunkey and Chickahominy march," 11
Pan Handle Railroad
   and Pennsylvania Railroad strikes, 569
Pan-Slavic sentiment, Eastern European, 665
Panic of 1819
   Stephen Austin, 305
   and Texas Revolt, 289
Panic of 1837
   and Susan B. Anthony, 484
   and women's property rights, 476
Panic of 1873
   and Chinese immigrants, 593

Panic of 1873 (continued)
    and Great Railroad Strike (1877), 563, 564
    and Pullman Palace Car Company, 655, 656
    Pullman Strike, 643–644
Paper currency
    and American Revolution, 208–209, 213
Parilla, Diego Ortiz
    biography, 105–106
    and Oacpicagigua, 104, 105
Parker, Isaac
    and antiwar activism, 926
Parker, Theodore
    and antiwar activism, 927
    Harpers Ferry Raid, 415
    secret six, 417, 429, 430
Parker, Timothy
    and antiwar activism, 926
Park, Maud Wood
    and women's movement, 481
Parker, William
    and Pine Tree Riot, 185
Parks, Rosa
    and civil rights movement, 895
    and Martin Luther King Jr., 904
    and SCLC, 910
Parma
    and expulsion of Jesuits, 103–104
Parsons, Albert
    anarchism, 585
    eight-hour day, 588
    and Haymarket Riot, 578, 580, 581, 582
Parsons, Elsie Clews, 46
Partido Liberal Mexicano
    and Plan de San Diego, 728
Pasadena City College
    and Rodney King, 1102
"Pastry-War," 310
Patawomeck Indians
    and Bacon's Rebellion, 1
Patman, Wright
    and BEF, 830, 831, 832, 835
    and veterans' rights, 842
    and Walter Waters, 843, 844
Patronato Real, 37
Patterson, Bradley H., 1034
Patterson, Daniel T.
    and martial law, 242

Patterson, Robert "Tut," and civil rights movement, 893
Pattison, Robert, Homestead Strike, 624, 625
Patton, George
    Anacostia Flats Battle, 835
    and BEF, 829
    and Douglas MacArthur, 840
Paul, Alice
    and ERA, 1053
    and feminist movement, 1043
    and Nineteenth Amendment, 490
    and women's suffrage, 480–481
Paul Potter Speech of Students for a Democratic Society Delivered at the Washington Monument (1965), 945–950
Paul Revere's Ride (Longfellow), 162
Pawnee
    and Lakota Sioux, 613
Payment in lieu of taxes (PILT), 1090
Peace Democrats
    and antiwar activism, 927
Peace Movement
    and antiwar activism, 925
Peace Party, Texas Revolt, 295
Pearson, Drew
    on Anacostia Flats Battle, 835–836
    and Douglas MacArthur, 840–841
Pecan State Prison, 1106
Peck, George R.
    and Pullman Strike, 646
"Peculiar institution," 251
Peden, Katherine Graham
    and Kerner Commission, 996
Pelham, Henry
    and Boston Massacre picture, 154, 163
Peltier, Leonard
    and Pine Ridge Reservation, 1082
Pence, George
    and Baldwin-Felts, 799
Penn, William, 93
    colonial Pennsylvania, 91
    and Pennsylvania, 464
    Quaker faith, 96, 97
Pennsylvania
    backcountry-coastal conflict, 169
    colonial settlement, 91
    Fries' Rebellion (1790s), 238

German immigrants, 330–331
George Thomas, 93
Herman Husband, 181
Homestead Strike, 619–627
Irish immigrants, 325, 329
Lattimer Massacre, 661–664, 668–669
and Molly Maguires, 460
natural resources, 464–465
religious freedom, 97
settlement of, 464
Stamp Act protests, 134–135
Whiskey Rebellion, 227–228, 231
Pennsylvania Charter (1682), 92
Pennsylvania "Dutch," 330–331
Pennsylvania Freeman
and antiwar activism, 927
Pennsylvania National Guard
and Homestead Strike, 625
Pennsylvania Railroad
and Andrew Carnegie, 630
and Great Railroad Strikes, 563, 569, 570
Pennsylvania Supreme Court, Philadelphia Election Riot, 93
Pentagon, attack on, 932
People's Coalition for Peace and Justice
and the Mobe, 1028
"People's Constitution"
and Charterites, 315
Dorr's Rebellion, 312, 313, 317
People's Council of America for Democracy and Peace
and antiwar activism, 930
"People's Government" (RI), 313
Peoria Indians
and Illinois Confederacy, 123
Peralta, Pedro de, New Mexico, 29, 47
Perez, Judge Leander
and civil rights movement, 894
Perkins, Frances, 481
and West Coast Longshoremen's Strike, 864
Pernicious system of religion," 604
Perry, David
and Nez Percé flight, 554
Peter Zenger Case
and Stamp Act protests, 131
Peters, Andrew Jones
and Boston Police Strike, 758

Peterson, Esther, 1048–1049
Peterson, Gilbert, 741
Petion, Henri, 263
Pettigrew, Richard
and Wounded Knee Massacre, 603
Philadelphia
Constitutional Convention (1787), 214, 215
Continental Congress (1774), 200
Great Migration, 773–774
and Ku Klux Klan, 542
race riots (1834), 777
Philadelphia and Reading Coal Company, 460–461
Philadelphia and Reading Railroad
and Molly Maguires, 716
wage cuts, 715
Philadelphia Election Riot (1742), xxiv, 91–93
Philadelphia Female Anti-Slavery Society
and Women's Movement, 474
Philadelphia National Guard
and Pennsylvania Railroad strikes, 569
Philadelphia Nativist Riots (1844), collective action, xxiv, 325–327
Philippine-American War, antiwar activism, 925, 928
Philippines
and Douglas MacArthur, 840, 841
Spanish-American War, 928, 933
Philips Exeter Academy
and Thomas Wilson Dorr, 316
Philipse, Adolph, 80
Philipse, Frederick, 85
Philo, Baptiste, New Orleans Race Riot (1900), 672
Picket lines
Homestead Strike, 622
Toledo Auto-Lite Strike, 848–849
Pico, Pío
Bear Flag Revolt, 333, 335
and J. C. Frémont, 342
Picurís Pueblo, 34
Piedras, Jose de la
and Texas Revolt, 291
Pierce, Franklin
Bleeding Kansas, 348, 350, 357
and Dorothea Dix, 486–487

Pierce, Franklin (continued)
  Kansas-Nebraska Act, 359
  Topeka Constitution, 361
Pierce, Lenard
  New Orleans Race Riot (1900), 672
  and Robert Charles, 675
Pierson, Robert, 1015
Pike, Zebulon, 1073
Pima Revolt (1751)
  collective action, xxi–xxii, 99–103
  and Jesuit Order, 103
  and Parilla, 105–106
  and Tohono O'odham, 107
Pine Ridge Reservation
  AIM, 609
  and BIA, 1079
  and Dick Wilson, 1082–1083
  FBI infiltration, 1080–1081
  overview, 1081–1082
  Wounded Knee Massacre, 602, 603, 605, 607, 608
  Wounded Knee occupation, 1075
Pine Tree Riot (1772)
  and collective action, xxii, 183–185
Pine Tree Tavern
  and Pine Tree Riot, 184
Pinkerton, Allan, agency founder, 621, 632
Pinkerton, Robert A., 621–622
Pinkerton agents
  and Homestead Strike, 621–622
  and Molly Maguires, 461
Pinkerton National Detective Agency
  "Account of Violence between Strikers and Company Security Guards," 634–637
  and Homestead Strike, 619, 621, 623–625
  and industrial violence, 715
  overview, 632–633
Pío, Padre Juan, 32
Pitcairn, Robert
  and Pennsylvania Railroad strike, 569
Pits Bessemer Steel Works
  and AA, 619
Pitt, William (the Elder)
  and Jeffrey Amherst, 117
  replacement of, 203
  Stamp Act protests, 131, 135, 136
  western defense, 143

Pittsburgh (PA)
  and Great Migration, 773–774
  and Great Railroad Strikes, 566, 569–570
Pittsburgh Gazette
  Benjamin Well's resignation, 232
  warning to tax collectors, 230, 244
Pius IX (pope)
  and Dorothea Dix, 487
  opposition to liberalism, 330, 374
Pizaña, Aniceto, Plan de San Diego, 728, 729, 731
"Placemen," 237
Plan de San Diego (1915)
  collective action, xxiii, 727–732, 734
  and Tejanos, 735–736
  and Texas Rangers, 737
  translations of, 732
Plan of Vera Cruz, Santa Anna, 291
Plantations
  colonial South Carolina, 75
  Stono Rebellion, 69
Planter elites/class
  and slavery, 251, 253
Planters' Protective Association (PPA)
  and Black Patch War, 697–699
Plasters and Laborers Union,
  Rodney King, 1102
Platte County Self-Defense Association,
  Bleeding Kansas, 349
Plessy, Homer, 678, 679
Plessy v. Ferguson
  and Atlanta Race Riot (1906), 682
  and civil rights, 891, 893
  de jure segregation, 807
  and Jim Crow Laws, 677
  overview, 678–679
Plug Uglies
  and Know-Nothing Party, 373, 374
  overview, 379–380
  and Rip Raps, 380
  and vigilance committees, 381–382
Plumsted, Clement, 92
Plunkett, James
  and Haymarket Riot, 579
Plural marriage. *See* Polygamy
Plymouth, Dominion of New England, 59

Plymouth, earliest intergovernmental assembly, 54
Pohé-yemo. *See* Popé
Police brutality
  defined, 878
  extent of, 878–880
  Houston Riot 751
Police harassment
  and Detroit Riots, 987, 993
Police Protective League, 1104
Polish immigrants
  and Eastern European immigrants, 665, 666
  Lattimer Massacre, 661, 665
Political corruption
  and Battle of Athens, 883–885, 888–889
Polk, James K.
  and antiwar activism, 927, 933
  election victory, 327
  and Mexican War, 733
  and Santa Anna, 310
Poll tax
  and Atlanta Race Riot (1906), 681
  and political machines, 888
  Shays' Rebellion, 209–210
Polygamy (Mormons), 390, 391, 392–394
Pontiac, biography, 122–123
Pontiac's Rebellion (1763), collective action, xxi–xxii, 109–115
Pony Express, origin, 387
Poor Law, Anglican Church, 95
Poor People's Campaign
  and Martin Luther King Jr., 906
  and SCLC, 911
Popé
  biography, 43, 45
  picture, 44
  Pueblo Revolt, 31–32, 34–35, 42
Pope, Gabriel
  and Watts Riot, 965
Pope's Day, Stamp Act protests, 131–132
Popular sovereignty
  and Bleeding Kansas, 347
  and Jayhawkers, 354
  Rhode Island suffrage, 311
  and slavery, 358–359
Populist Party
  and Knights of Labor, 599
  and tobacco farmers, 697, 702
Port Huron Statement
  and counterculture, 937
  and Tom Hayden, 1012, 1024
  SDS, 943
Porteous, Gabriel
  and New Orleans Race Riot (1900), 672
Porter, David R.
  and Philadelphia Nativist Riots, 327
Portland Rum Riot (1855)
  and collective action, xxiv, 365–367
Portugal
  and expulsion of Jesuits, 103–104
Possum Hunters
  and Black Patch War, 697
Potato famine
  and Irish immigration, 325, 369
Potawatomi Indians
  and Pontiac's Rebellion, 109, 120
Pottawatomic Rifles
  and Bleeding Kansas, 349
Pottawatomie Massacre
  Bleeding Kansas, 349
  and John Brown, 423–424, 426
  overview, 359–361
Potter, Paul, speech delivered at the Washington Monument (1965), 945–950
Powderly, Terence V., 462
  Knights of Labor, 598, 599
  on Pinkertons, 533
Powell, Colin, 900
Powell, Dave
  antebellum slave rebellions, 258, 262, 263
  Nat Turner section, 277, 280, 281, 283, 284, 286
Powell, Laurence
  and Los Angeles Uprising, 1095, 1096, 1097
Powhatan Chiefdom
  Bacon's Rebellion, 3
  Sir William Berkeley, 11–12
  and Susquehannock Indians, 17
  tobacco wars, 19–20
Poyas, Peter
  and Vesey's uprising, 265, 266
Pratt, R. H.
  and Wounded Knee massacre, 603
"Prayed clergy," 155

Prayer Pilgrimage for Freedom
   and civil rights movement, 897
   and SCLC, 910–911
"Preliminary and Final Reports of the
      Oklahoma Commission to Study the Tulsa
      Race Riot of 1921," 809–828
Prentice, George D., incendiary writings, 377
Presbyterian organization model,
   Calvinism, 58
Presidio
   Bear Flag Revolt, 337
   and Mariano Vallejo, 343
Presidio (Goliad/La Bahia), Texas Revolt,
   293–294, 296, 298–299
Presidio del Pitic, Diego Ortiz Parilla, 105
Preston, Thomas
   biography, 161–162
   Boston Massacre, 153
   Boston Massacre trial, 154–155, 157
Price, John G.
   and Brooks-Baxter War, 545, 550
Price, Rena
   and Watts Riot, 965, 970
Prichett, Laurie
   and civil rights movement, 898
Primus Plot (1720), slave rebellion, 76
Prince (slave)
   and New York Slave Insurrection, 80,
      87–88, 89, 90
Prioleau, J. C.
   and Vesey's uprising, 266
Prioleau, Peter
   and Vesey's uprising, 265
"Proclamation and Executive Order against
      State Resistance to Desegregation in
      Mississippi," 913–915
"Proclamation Declaring California an
      Independent Republic," 345–346
"Proclamation to the Great White Father,"
   1035, 1040–1042
Professions
   and Women's Movement, 476, 478
"Progress Report of the Presidential Task Force
      on Los Angeles Recovery," 1106–1120
Progressive Era
   journalists, and "robber barons," 571, 572
   race riots, 777

Progressive Labor Party
   and Haymarket Riot, 583
Progressive movement
   and Nineteenth Amendment, 490
Prohibition
   and temperance movement, 371
Prohibition Party, electoral showing, 371
   and Neal S. Dow, 367
"Project C," 897–898
Promised land," 252
"Proned," 1104
Property rights
   Chinese immigrants, 593, 597
   women's movement (1870), 473, 474,
      475–477, 478
Property taxes, Fries' Rebellion (1790s), 238
Proposition 14
   and Watts Riot, 968, 969
Proposition F, 1097
Proprietary Party, Philadelphia Election Riot,
   91, 92
Prosser, Gabriel
   and antebellum slave revolts, 252, 253, 254,
      255, 256, 257
   Virginia uprising (1799), xxiii, 263–265
Prosser, Thomas
   and Gabriel, 256, 263–264
Protestant Reformation
   and Jesuit Order, 103
Protestants, early settlers, 329
Province of New York, 84
"Provisional Constitution" (John Brown), 417
Provoost, Davide, 85
Prudon, Victor
   and Bear Flag Revolt, 335
   and Sonoma, 344
Public Advertiser, The (Samuel Adams), 139
Public domain, overview, 1090–1091
   and Sagebrush Rebellion, 1085
Public housing projects
   and Detroit Riots, 995
Public Land Law Review Study, FLPMA, 1089
Public lands
   BLM, 1089
   FLPMA, 1089–1090
   overview, 1090–1091
   Sagebrush Rebellion, 1085

Public Ledger, "Strikers Resolutions and Editorials" 668–669
Public schools, Philadelphia Nativist Riots, 325
Pueblo de los Angelos
  and Diego Ortiz Parilla, 105
Pueblo people
  arrival of Spaniards, 27–28
  Indian attacks, 34
  reciprocal sharing, 28
  religious traditions, 29, 45–46
  revolt of, 32–35, 38, 41–42
  Spanish demands, 28, 29–30
Pueblo Religion (Clews), 46
Pueblo Revolt (1680), xxi, 31–35, 41–42
  "Declaration of Pedro Naranjo" (1681), 49–51
Puerto Rico, Spanish-American War, 928
Pulaski Circuit Court, Brooks-Baxter War, 546
Pullman, George
  and Pullman Palace Car Company, 654, 655, 657
Pullman Loan and Savings Bank, 656
Pullman Palace Car Company, 654
  ARU strike, 643–650
  overview, 654–655
  Report on the Railway Strikes of 1894, 657–659
  wage cuts, 655–657
Pullman Strike (1894)
  and AFL, 851
  collective action, xxii–xxiii, 643–650
Puritanism, 57
Puritans, Calvinism, 58
  Dominion of New England, 59
  and Quakers, 95, 96
Putnam, Rufus, Shays' Rebellion, 212

Quakers, antiwar activism, 925
  in colonial Pennsylvania, 96–97
  New Amsterdam, 61
  Philadelphia Election Riot, 91–93
  and women's movement, 475
Quantrill, William Clark
  and Bushwackers, 353
Quartering Act (1765)
  Coercive Acts, 197, 199
  passage of, 128
  and provisions, 203–204
Quartering and Mutiny Acts, protests against, 141
Quebec Act, Canadian rights, 199
Quebec, colonial attack, 54
  French and Indian War/Seven Years' War, 118, 191, 192
Quigly, John
  and Pine Tree Riot, 184
Quimbly, William
  and Pine Tree Riot, 185
Quimby, Aaron
  and Pine Tree Riot, 184
Quincy, Josiah II
  and Boston Massacre defense, 154, 157
Quincy, Samuel
  and Boston Massacre prosecution, 154
Quipo (knotted cord), 31

Raboteau, Albert J., 284
Race
  Pullman Strike, 645–646
  and Pullman Palace Car Company, 655
Race riots
  Atlanta Race Riot (1906), xxiv, 681–687
  Bleeding Kansas (1854), xxiv, 347–352
  Colfax Massacre (1873), xxiv, 537–539
  collective action, xxiv
  Houston Riot (1917), xxiv, 749–752, 753–754
  after King's death, 906
  Know-Nothing Riot (1866), xxiv, 373–375
  Lattimer Massacre (1897), xxiv, 661–664
  New Orleans Race Riot (1900), xxiv, 671–673
  New Orleans Riot (1866), xxiv, 449–452, 453
  New York Draft Riots (1863), xxiv, 435–440, 777
  overview, 777–778
  Philadelphia Nativist Riots (1844), xxiv, 325–327
  Portland Rum Riot (1855), xxiv, 365–367
  Red Summer (1919), xxiv, 765–772
  Seattle Riot (1886), xxiv, 593–595
  Springfield Race Riot (1908), xxiv, 689–692, 778
  Tulsa Race Riot (1921), xxiv, 771, 801–804
"Race to the bottom," 1121, 1126, 1128

Racism
   and Atlanta Race Riot (1906), 681
   and New York Draft Riots, 436, 439, 777
   overview, 444–446
   Springfield Race Riot, 689, 690, 691, 778
Radical feminism
   and women's rights, 1044, 1047
Radical Republicans
   and Reconstruction Act, 552
"Radio Free Alcatraz," 1039–1040
Railroad strike (1877)
   and Molly Maguires, 461–462
Railroad workers, 570–571
Railroads
   ARA, 651–652
   Chinese immigrants, 593
   East Louisiana Railroad Company, 679
   industrial violence, 715
   LNO&T, 675
   Pullman Strike, 643–650
   and racial segregation, 677, 679
   Report on the Railway Strikes of 1894, 657–659
   state bond aid, 546
Railway Times
   and ARU, 651
Rainach, William
   and civil rights movement, 894
Raleigh (NC), 174
Ramos, Bailio, Plan de San Diego, 727
Ranchería Indians, 38
Randolph, A. Philip
   and civil rights movement, 891–892, 897
   March on Washington, 909
Randolph, Edmund, Whiskey Rebellion, 230, 231
Rankin, Janet, 481
"Rape of Zacatecas," 309
Rathbun, William, on King beating, 1099
Rather, Dan
   and Democratic National Convention (1968), 1013
Ray, James Earl, 899, 906
Reagan, Ronald
   Martin Luther King holiday, 906
   public lands policy, 1091–1092
   and Sagebrush Rebellion, 1086

Realities of Irish Life, The (Trench), 459
Rebellion in Newark (Hayden), 1024
Reckless Decade, The (Brands), 608
Reconstruction (1863–1877)
   Brooks-Baxter War, 545–547
   and Compromise of 1876, 677
   overview, 454–455
   and woman's suffrage, 488
Reconstruction Act (1867)
   and Brooks-Baxter War, 545
   and New Orleans Riot (1866), 451
   Radical Republicans, 552
Red Cloud
   and Black Hills, 614
   Red Cloud, Wounded Knee Massacre, 602, 605
"Red Napoleon," 555
"Red necks," 793
"Red Power" movement
   and Alcatraz occupation 1035, 1037, 1039, 1040
   and civil rights movement, xxiii
   overview, 1073–1074
Red Scare
   and American socialists, 746
   and Boston Police Strike, 759
   and Red Summer Riots, 765
   and socialism, 741
"Red Special," 653
Red Summer (1919)
   and collective action, xxiv, 765–772
Red Tomahawk, Wounded Knee Massacre, 605
"Redeemers," 238
"Redlegs," 353, 355
Redpath, James
   and John Brown, 424
Redstockings
   and Feminist Movement, 1047
Ree, Richard, Los Angeles Uprising, 1098
Reeder, Andrew, Bleeding Kansas, 348
Refugio Mission, Texas Revolt, 298
Regional Council of Negro Leadership, civil rights movement, 893
Register, Robert C.
   and Colfax Massacre, 538

"Regulation, The"
  North Carolina, 169
  South Carolina, 169, 172
Regulation Association, 170
Regulation Movement, Shays' Rebellion, 210–212, 214
Regulator Movement (1771)
  and collective action, xxii, 169–175
Regulator revolt
  and William Tryon, 132, 171–172
Reid, Whitelaw
  and Homestead Strike, 625–626
"Reign of the Rabble," 446
Reimer (Raymer), Abraham
  and Springfield Race Riot, 690–691, 693
Religion
  Broken Treaties protest, 1068
  Calvinism, 57–58
  collective action, xxiv
  Colonial New York, 61–62
  Colonial Pennsylvania, 95, 96–97
  early settlers, 329
  Indian Shakers, 602
  Leisler's Rebellion (1689), xxiv, 53–56
  Nat Turner, 270, 271
  Philadelphia Election Riot (1742), xxiv, 91–93
  and Regulator Movement, 170, 179–180
  slave preachers, 254, 283–284
  and the Temperance movement, 371
  Utah War (1857–1858), xxiv, 383–387
Religious Society of Friends. *See* Quakers
Relocation, Native American policy, 560
Remick, Christian, Boston Massacre picture, 154
Rental property
  and Pullman Palace Car Company, 656–657
Repartimientos (labor), 28
Report on the Railway Strikes of 1894, 657–659
"Report on the Riots in Detroit, Vance Report," 997–1008
Representative government
  and Leisler's Rebellion, 53, 55–56
"Reproductive freedom," 1058
Republic of Texas
  established, 733
  and Tejanos, 735

Republican National Convention (2000)
  and Direct Action Network, 1125
Republican Party
  and Bleeding Kansas, 351
  Brooks-Baxter War, 545, 549
  and Calvin Coolidge, 761
  and Know-Nothing Party, 373, 374–375
  and Neal S. Dow, 366
  and Nelson Rockefeller, 1064–1065
  Maine, 370
  New Orleans Riot (1866), 449–451
  opposition to polygamy, 393
  opposition to slavery, 426
  overview, 551–552
  and Reconstruction, 454–455
  "termination policy," 1031
"Republican womanhood," 473–474
Reservations, Native Americans, 557, 1031
Reserve Officers Training Corps
  and SDS, 944
Revere, Paul
  biography, 162–164
  Boston Massacre area plan, 155
  Boston Massacre engraving, 151, 152, 154, 155, 160, 163
  and the Boston Tea Party, 196
Revolution, The (Anthony), 485–486
Revolutionary War Science (Most), 586–587
Revolutions of 1848, 331
Reyes Berryessa, José de los
  and Bear Flag Revolt, 337
Reynolds, David, 416
Rhode Island
  colonial charter, 311
  Dominion of New England, 59
  Stamp Act protests, 133
  universal white male suffrage, 318–319
Rhode Island Constitutional Party
  and Dorr's Rebellion, 311
Rhode Island General Assembly
  and Dorr's Rebellion, 312
Rhode Island Suffrage Association
  and Charterites, 315
  Dorr's Rebellion, 311–312, 313
  and Thomas Wilson Dorr, 317
Rhode Island Suffrage Party
  and Charterites, 315

Rhodes, James A.
   and Kent State, 939
Ribbonmen
   Molly Maguires, 459
   secret society, 466
Ribicoff, Abraham
   and Democratic National Convention (1968), 1013, 1023
   and Richard J. Daley, 1021
Rice
   in colonial South Carolina, 75
   Stono Rebellion, 69
"Rich man's war, poor man's fight," 436
Richard Palmes's Account of the Boston Massacre" (1770), 166–167
Richardson, Ebenezer, Boston Massacre, 152
Richardson, George, Springfield Race Riot, 689
Richardson, Gloria
   and civil rights movement, 897
Richardson, Bill, 1130
Right to bear arms
   and Battle of Athens, 885
Rights in Conflict, 1014–1015, 1016–1017
Río Abajo (NM), 32, 33
Río Arriba (NM), 32
"Rioter's Letter to the *New York Times* and the Newspaper's Response (1863), A," 447–448
Rip Raps
   Know-Nothing Party, 373, 374
   overview, 380–381
   and Plug Uglies, 379
   and vigilance committees, 382–383
Roach, Max, and civil rights movement, 897
Roarity, James
   and Molly Maguires, 461
"Robber barons"
   and Great Railroad Strikes, 565–566
   overview, 571–572
Robertson, Curtis, alias of Robert Charles, 675
Robinson, Bernice
   and civil rights movement, 896
Robinson, Charles
   Bleeding Kansas, 348, 349
   Topeka Constitution, 362
Robinson, Jackie, 892, 897
Robledo, Francisco Gomez, 41, 42

Rockefeller, John D.
   and CF&I, 713
   Ludlow Massacre, 707, 708–710
   "robber barons," 571
Rockefeller, Nelson A.
   and Attica Prison Riot, 1060, 1064–1065
   biography, 1064–1065
Rockefeller Plan, CF&I, 710, 713
Rockefeller, Winthrop, 552
Rockingham, second marquis of
   and Stamp Act protests, 135
Rocky Mountain News, on Ludlow Massacre, 709
Rocky Mountain region
   heavy industry, 707, 713, 714
   Sagebrush Rebellion, 1086
Roe v. Wade, 1055–1056
Rolfe, John, 19
Romney, George
   and Detroit Riots, 989
Roosevelt, Eleanor, on Battle of Athens, 885
Roosevelt, Franklin
   African Americans voting rights, 456
   on Anacostia Flats Battle, 836
   and BEF, 833
   and civil rights movement, 891–892
   and Douglas MacArthur, 840
   and Great Depression, 837
   and Toledo Auto-Lite Strike, 848, 849
   and union movement, 861, 862, 864, 865
   and veterans' rights, 842
Roosevelt, Theodore
   and antiwar activism, 933
   and Atlanta Race Riot (1906), 681–682
Rose, Ernestine, women's property rights, 477
Rose, Thomas, Stono Rebellion, 70, 77
Rosebud Reservation, Wounded Knee Massacre, 602, 603
Rossi, Angelo
   and Bloody Thursday, 861
Rotch, Francis
   and the Boston Tea Party, 195–196
"Rough music," 229
Rouzan, Joe
   and Watts Riot, 965, 967
Rowland, Dick
   and Tulsa Race Riot, 801, 802

Royal authority
  and Pine Tree Riot, 187–188
Royal Navy (Britain)
  Pine Tree Riot, 183
  shipbuilding, 188
Royer, Daniel
  and Wounded Knee Massacre, 603
Royko, Mike, on Richard J. Daley, 1022
Rubin, Jerry
  and Abbie Hoffman, 1026
  antiwar activism, 937
  Chicago Eight, 1015, 1019
  and Chicago Seven, 1019, 1020
  Yippies, 1010, 1011
Ruffin, Josephine
  and AWSA, 483, 488, 490
Ruger, Thomas H.
  and Wounded Knee Massacre, 604
Rumford Fair Housing Act
  and Watts Riot, 968, 969
"Runaway Scrape," 297, 304
Rural regions, Green Corn
    Rebellion, 739
Rushmore, Mount, 1033–1034
Russ, Cliff, 1104–1105
Russian Jews
  and Eastern European immigrants, 665
Russian Revolution
  and American socialists, 746
Russo-Japanese War
  and Douglas MacArthur, 840
Rustin, Bayard
  and civil rights movement, 897
  and March on Washington, 909
  and SCLC, 910
Rutland, William R.
  and Colfax Massacre, 538
Ryan, Joseph
  and ILA, 858, 865

Sacco, Nicola, 586, 587
Sachaman, John
  and Haymarket Riot, 579
Sacramento (CA)
  and Bear Flag Revolt, 333
Saenz, Florencio
  and Plan de San Diego, 729

Sagebrush Rebellion (1979)
  and collective action, xxii, 1085–1087
Sagebrush Rebels, 1092, 1093
"Sagebrush Solution," 1092
Saint Domingue (Haiti)
  and Charles Deslondes, 262, 263
  and Denmark Vesey, 265
  slave uprising, 255–256
Salinas Pueblo, 30, 43
Salter, Bill
  and Baldwin-Felts, 799
Salutary neglect
  Stamp Act Protests, 127, 142–143
  Texas Revolt, 289, 290, 292
Salvation Army
  and BEF, 831
Samas, David, "Statement of the Fort Hood
    Three," 951–953, 954–956
San Antonio de Bexar,
  Battle of the Alamo, 303
  and Stephen Austin, 306
  Texas Revolt, 289, 294, 296
San Carlos de Buenavista, Pima Revolt, 101
San Felipe Pueblo, 49
San Felipe, Texas Revolt, 292–293
San Francisco (CA)
  Bear Flag Revolt, 334, 337
  counterculture, 937
  "Day without an Immigrant" protests, 1129,
      1130
  and Great Railroad Strikes, 563–564, 566
  and Seattle General Strike, 867
  West Coast Longshoremen's Strike,
      857–859, 866–867
San Francisco General Strike Committee,
    West Coast Longshoremen's Strike, 859
San Francisco Indian Center, 1031, 1035,
    1037, 1038
San Francisco Industrial Association
  and West Coast Longshoremen's Strike, 858,
      861, 866–867
San Francisco Police Department
  and West Coast Longshoremen's Strike, 858,
      861–862, 864
San Francisco State University
  and Alcatraz Island occupation, 1031–1032
  and Richard Oakes, 1036–1037

San Gabriel de Yungue, 28, 47
San Ignacio de Tubac, Pima Revolt, 101
San Jacinto
　and Santa Anna, 309–310
San Jacinto, Battle of, 306, 307
San Juan (NM), 28, 31
San Juan Pueblo, 43, 45, 47
San Miguel Mission, Santa Fé, 47
Sanborn, Franklin
　and Secret Six, 417, 429, 430
Sand Creek Massacre (1864)
　and Dakota Nation, 612–613
Sandía Pueblo, 33
Sando, Joe, 45
Sandy Creek Association
　Herman Husband, 180
　Regulator Movement, 169–170
Sanger, Margaret, on *Sex Education and Contraception*, 533–536
Sangre de Cristos, 47
Santa Anna, Antonio López de
　Battle of the Alamo, 303
　biography, 308–310
　and Stephen Austin, 306
　Texas Revolt, 291, 292, 296, 297, 298, 299–300
Santa Clara, Bear Flag Revolt, 335, 337
Santa Fé (NM)
　"city different," 47–48
　Pueblo Revolt, 32, 35, 42, 47
Santa Gertrudis de Altar, Pima Revolt, 101
Santanistas, 291
Santee Sioux Reservation
　and John Trudell, 1039
Santo Domingo Pueblo, 39
Sash, Moses, Shays' Rebellion, 211
Satrom, Leroy, Kent State, 939
Sauk Indians, Pontiac's Rebellion, 110
"Scabs"
　and Haymarket Riot, 576
　Pullman Strike, 645, 646
　West Coast Longshoremen's Strike, 858, 861
Scalawags
　and Ku Klux Klan, 542
　Radical Republicans, 552
Schafly, Phyllis, 1049

Schell, Paul, WTO protests, 1123
Schenectady, Leisler's Rebellion, 54, 60
Scheuer, Sandra, Kent State, 939
Schmidt, Ethan, Bacon's Rebellion, 7, 10, 13, 15, 16, 18, 20
Schmidt, Fritz
　and Haymarket Riot, 576
Schnaubelt, Rudolph
　and Haymarket Riot, 580–581
Schofield, John M., on Pullman Strike, 647
"School trusts," land, 1090
Schroeder, William, Kent State, 939
Schultz, Richard, Chicago Seven trial, 1015, 1019
Schurz, Carl, antiwar activism, 928
Schuyler, Adoniah, 85
Schuyler, Elizabeth, and Alexander Hamilton, 239
Schuyler, Philip
　and Alexander Hamilton, 239
Schwab, Michael, Haymarket Riot, 580, 581, 582
"Scientific racism," 682
Scorsese, Martin, 378–379
Scotland
　and Calvinist religion, 58
Scott, John Morin
　and Philadelphia Nativist Riots, 326
Scott, Shirley, 993
Scott, Thomas A.
　and Great Railroad Strikes, 566, 569
Scott, Winfield
　and Robert E. Lee, 427–428
　and Santa Anna, 310
Scottish immigrants, Regulator Movement, 169
Sea Island Citizenship Schools
　and civil rights movement, 896
Seale, Bobbie
　Black Panthers, 1012, 1019
　Chicago Eight, 1015
Seattle (WA)
　Battle of, 1121–1123
　Hooverville, 839
Seattle General Strike (1919)
　and post–World War I, 757
　support for, 867
Seattle Riot (1886)
　and collective action, xxiv, 593–595
Secession, and American Civil War, 441

"Second American Revolution," 1086
Second Great Migration (1940–1970)
 African Americans, 773
 and segregation, 807
Second Reconstruction
 and civil rights movement, 892
Secret ballot, Regulator Movement, 170
Secret Six
 and Harpers Ferry raid, 417
 overview, 429–430
Sectionalism
 and American Civil War, 441
Sedelmayr, Jacobo, Pima Revolt, 100
Sedition Act
 and American socialists, 746
Sedition Act
 and IWW, 741, 744, 745
Seeger, Pete, 900
 and Chicago Seven trial, 1016
Segregation
 and Atlanta Race Riot (1906), 682, 684
 Jim Crow Laws, 671, 677
 overview, 806–807
 Plessy v. Ferguson, 678–679
 Tulsa Race Riot, 801
 U.S. military, 753
Seguin, Erasmo, Texas Revolt, 291
Seider, Christopher
 and Boston Massacre, 152
Selective Service Bill (1917)
 military segregation, 753
 overview, 743–744
Self Leadership for all Nationalities Today (SLANT), Watts, 969
Seminary of the Sisters of Charity
 and Philadelphia Nativist Riots, 326
Semple, Robert Baylor "Bob"
 Bear Flag Revolt, 335
 Bear Flagger, 340
Seneca Falls Convention
 and ERA, 1053
 and Feminist Movement, 1043
 and Nineteenth Amendment, 489, 490
 and NWSA, 488
 women's movement (1870), 473, 474, 475
Seneca Falls Declaration
 and women's movement, 474, 475, 481

Seneca Indians
 and Pontiac's Rebellion, 109, 111, 113–114
"Separate but equal," 678, 679, 682, 807
"Separate Car Act," 678, 679
Sequin, Juan
 and Texas Revolt, 294
Serbian immigrants
 and Ludlow Massacre, 708
Sergeant York (film), 740, 743
Seris Revolt (1749)
 Diego Ortiz Parilla, 105
 and Pima Revolt, 100
Servicemen
 defined, 880
 and Zoot Suit Riot, 871–875, 879–881
Settlement house movement
 and Women's Movement, 480
Settlers, Bleeding Kansas, 348
"Sevastopol Policy," 385
Seven Days Battles
 and Robert E. Lee, 428
Seven Years War, 103–104
 and Arthur Dobbs, 179
 and the Boston Tea Party, 191, 198
 British success, 151
 end of, 109
 and French and Indian War, 118–119
 Ohio River Valley, 121
 Pine Tree Riot, 183
 and Pontiac, 122
Seventh Kansas Cavalry
 and Jayhawkers, 355
71 Hustlers, 1105
Sex Education, Margaret Sanger, 533–536
Seymour, Horatio
 and New York Draft Riots, 437, 439–440
Shakers, Indian religious tradition, 602
Shangreau, John
 and Wounded Knee Massacre, 606
Shannon, Thomas
 and Haymarket Riot, 579
"Shape up," 857, 862
Shapp, Milton
 and Molly Maguires, 461
Shattuck, Job
 and Shays' Rebellion, 211

Shaw, Anna Howard
  and Women's Movement, 480
Shaw, Daniel
  and Colfax Massacre, 538
Shaw University
  and civil rights movement, 896
  SNCC, 912
Shawnee Indians
  Ohio River Valley, 121
  Pennsylvania native tribe, 464
  Pontiac's Rebellion, 111, 113, 120
  and Susquehannock Indians, 17
Shawnee Mission, Bleeding Kansas, 348, 349
"Shawnee Prophet," 120
Shays, Daniel
  biography, 220–221
  and Lafayette, 211, 220
  Massachusetts General Court, 219
  Shays' Rebellion, 207, 208, 210, 212, 213, 215, 237
Shays' Rebellion (1787)
  "An Address to the People of Hampshire County, Massachusetts, Setting Forth the Causes of Shays' Rebellion" (1786), 223–224
  collective action, xxii, 207–216
  "Letter to the *Hampshire Herald* Listing the Grievances of the Rebels" (1786), 224–225
  and Massachusetts General Court, 318
  and Regulator Movement, 174, 207, 210–211, 212, 214, 219
Shelly v. Kraemer
  and segregation, 807
Shepard, William
  and Shays' Rebellion, 207, 211
Sherbrooke, Sir John S.
  and antiwar activism, 926
Sherburn John
  and Pine Tree Riot, 183–184
Sherman Antitrust Act
  and on Pullman Strike, 648
Sherman, Henry "Dutch Henry"
  and Pottawatomie Massacre, 360
Sherman, William Tecumseh
  and Nez Percé flight, 554
Shiloh, Battle of
  and Albert Sidney Johnston, 387

Shipbuilding
  deforestation, 188
  employment, 188–189
Shippen, Edward, 97
Shoemaker, Charles
  and Haymarket Riot, 579
Short Bull
  and Wounded Knee Massacre, 602, 603, 608
Shoshone
  and Lakota Sioux, 613
Shults, Robert
  and Haymarket Riot, 579
Shuttlesworth, Fred
  and SCLC, 910
Siegenthaler, John
  and civil rights movement, 896
Sierra Club
  and James Watt, 1093
  and Sagebrush Rebellion, 1086
Sign of the Green Tree
  and Whiskey Rebellion, 230
Silent Brigade
  and Black Patch War, 697
Simi Valley (CA)
  and Rodney King trial, 1096–1097
Simmons, William Joseph
  and Ku Klux Klan, 542, 805
Simons, J.
  and Haymarket Riot, 579
Siney, John, 466
Singer, Melanie
  and Los Angeles Uprising, 1095
Sioux Indians
  overview, 613–614
  return of Mount Rushmore, 1033–1034
  Wounded Knee Massacre, 601, 602, 604, 605, 606, 607–608
Sit-ins
  antiwar activism, 931
  BIA, 1033
  and civil rights movement, 895
  SNCC, 912
  Stokely Carmichael, 903
Sitting Bull (Tatanka Yotanka)
  biography, 614–615
  and Pine Ridge Reservation, 1081

Wounded Knee Massacre, 602–603, 604–605, 614
"Skimmington," 229
Sklencar, Marge, 942
Slave Codes, South Carolina, 71, 73–74, 76
Slave education, after Nat Turner's Rebellion, 270, 274
Slave owners
   dilemma, 252
   "slave problem," 256–257
"Slave power," 351
Slave preachers, 254, 283–285
Slave rebellions, Charles Deslondes's German Coast Uprising (1811), xxiii, 252, 255–256, 262–263
   collective actions, xxiii, 251–259
   Denmark Vesey's uprising (1822), xxiii, 252, 255, 256, 257, 265–266
   Gabriel Prosser's Virginia Uprising (1799), xxiii, 252, 253, 254, 255–256, 263–265
   George Boxley (1815), xxiii, 254, 255
   John Brown at Harpers Ferry (1859), xxiii, 257–258, 415–421
   legacy, 257–258
   Nat Turner's Rebellion (1831), xxiii, 252, 254, 255, 269–278
   New York Slave Insurrection (1741), xxiii, 79–81
   Stono Rebellion (1739), xxiii, 69–72, 76
Slave trade, end of, 891
Slave violence, Nat Turner's Rebellion, 272–273
Slavery
   abolition of, 449
   and American Civil War, 425–426
   American contradictions, 256
   Bacon's Rebellion, 1, 6, 7
   Bleeding Kansas, 347–352
   Buchanan administration, 389
   Colonial New York, 84
   common misconception, 253
   Emancipation Proclamation, 441
   and federalism, 238
   and First Missouri Compromise, 356–358
   and indentured servants, 16
   justifications, 251
   Massachusetts ban on (1783), 891
   after Nat Turner's Rebellion, 270, 274–275
   and New York Draft Riots, 435–436
   and popular sovereignty, 358–359
   in South Carolina, 75–76, 84
   and Texas Revolt, 289
   tobacco crop, 19
   Topeka Constitution, 361–363
Slaves
   antebellum population, 253
   armed rebellion, 255–257
   bondage culture, 253–255, 282–283
   classification of persons, 73–74
   patterns of resistance, 252–255
   Pima Revolt, 99
   price of rebellion, 252
   resettlement of, 274, 279–280
Sleepers, secret society, 466
Sleepy Lagoon
   and Zoot Suit Riots, 872, 879
Sloat, John Drake
   Bear Flag Revolt, 337
   and J. C. Frémont, 342
Sloughter, Henry, 55
   and Jacob Leisler, 60–61
Slovak immigrants
   and Eastern European immigrants, 665
   Lattimer Massacre, 661, 665
Smallpox
   Jeffrey Amherst, 117
   Pontiac's Rebellion, 111, 112, 123, 124–125
Smith, Charles Ferguson, Utah War, 386
Smith, Erastus "Deaf"
   and Texas Revolt, 300
Smith, Frank
   and Attica Prison Riot, 1060–1061
Smith, George Venable
   and Seattle Riot, 594
Smith, Gerrit
   and John Brown, 423, 429–430
   Harpers Ferry Raid, 415
   Secret Six, 417, 429
Smith, Gloria Steinem, 1056
Smith, H. T.
   and Haymarket Riot, 579
Smith, Henry
   and Texas Revolt, 295–296
Smith, Hoke
   and Atlanta Race Riot (1906), 681, 685

Smith, Howard, 1049
Smith, John, on Susquehannock Indians, 17
Smith, Joseph, 390
    and Brigham Young, 395
    and Nauvoo Legion, 391
    polygamy, 393
    visit of John the Baptist, 389
Smith, Lot, Utah War, 385, 387
Smith College
    and Betty Friedan, 1045
Smithfield Quarters
    Colfax Massacre, 537, 538–539
Smithwick, Noah
    and Texas Revolt, 293
Snow, Kneeland S.
    and Houston Riot, 749–750
Snowden, George R., Pinkertons, 633
Snyder, Jacob Rin, Sonoma vineyards, 344
Social culture, women's share, 529–533
Social Darwinists
    and American industrialists, 572
"Social Purity" speech (Susan B. Anthony), 501–504
Socialism
    American, 746–747
    and Green Corn Rebellion, 739–740
    Haymarket Riot, 575, 576, 577
Socialist anarchism, ideology, 585
Socialist Labor Party
    and anarchism, 585
    bomb use, 586
    and WPUS, 573
Socialist Party of America, 746
    antiwar activism, 930
    and Eugene Debs, 653
    suppression, 741
"Society within society," 255
Sociological Department, CF&I, 709, 713
Sociology for the South (Fitzhugh), 275
Socorro (assistance) village, 27–28
"Soft coal," 661–662
"Solitude of Self" Address, 510–512
Solomon (slave), 253, 254
Sommers, Tish, and OWL, 1046
Sonoma (CA), Bear Flag Revolt, 333, 335, 336, 337, 340
    Bear Flaggers, 339

    overview, 343–345
    vineyards, 344
Sons of Liberty
    and the Boston Tea Party, 193, 194, 195
    overview, 202–203
    Paul Revere, 163
    response to Coercive Acts, 197
    Samuel Adams, 140
    Stamp Act protests, 132, 133–134, 141, 143, 202
    Townshend Act, 204
    Townshend Act protest, 202–203
Sorcery, Pueblo Indians, 31, 43
Sorubiero, Peggy (Margaret), New York Slave Insurrection, 80, 88, 89
Souls of Black Folk (Du Bois), 683
South Carolina
    and civil rights movement, 896
    colonial, 75–76
    Denmark Vesey's uprising, 265–266
    Regulator Movement, 169, 172–175
    secession of, 390
    and Shays' Rebellion, 214
    Slave codes, 73–74, 76
    Stamp Act protests, 133
    state capital, 174
    Stono Rebellion, 69–72
South Carolina Assembly
    Regulator Movement, 173
    slave code, 73, 74
    Stono Rebellion, 69–70, 71
South Dakota
    and Lakota Sioux, 614
    and Pine Ridge Reservation, 1081
    Wounded Knee Massacre, 604
"South Texas," Tejanos, 735
Southampton County Rebellion (1831), 257, 273, 274–275, 280, 285
Southern Christian Leadership Conference (SCLC)
    and civil rights movement, 895, 897–899
    and Jim Crow Laws, 678
    and March on Washington, 909
    and Martin Luther King Jr., 904, 905
    overview, 910–911
"Southern Editorial Response to John Brown's Raid on Harper's Ferry, Virginia," 432–434

Southern European immigrants
  Lattimer Massacre, 662
  Ludlow Massacre, 707
"Southern Freedom Movement," 893
Southern Manifesto, and civil rights
    movement, 894
Southwest Strike (1886)
  and Texas Rangers, 736
Southwestern Railroad
  and Knights of Labor strike, 599
Spain
  contract with Oñate, 28, 39
  expulsion of Jesuits, 100, 103–104
  and Santa Anna, 309
  Stono Rebellion, 69, 71
  Treaty of Paris (1763), 119
Spalding, Martin
  and Bloody Monday, 377
Spanish Decree (1733)
  and slave emancipation, 69
Spanish Florida
  and Stono Rebellion, 69–70, 71
Spanish-American War
  antiwar activism, 925, 928
  and Theodore Roosevelt, 681
Sparks, Lee
  and Houston Riot, 750
Spears, John
  and Green Corn Rebellion, 740
"Special Rangers," 729, 737
Speed, James S.
  and Bloody Monday, 377
Spence, Homer
  and Green Corn Rebellion, 740
Spencer, Anna Carlin
  and *Woman's Share in Social Culture*,
    529–533
Spencer, George, 85
Sperry, Howard, West Coast Longshoremen's
    Strike, 858, 861
Spicer Manufacturing Company, 851
Spies, August
  anarchism, 585
  Anarchist circular, 591–592
  and eight-hour day, 588
  and Haymarket Riot, 576, 577–578,
    580–581, 582
  and McCormick Harvesting Machine
    Company, 590–591
"Splendid isolation," 128, 134
Spock, Benjamin
  and the Mobe, 1028
  United States v. Spock, 957–960
Sports, and women's rights, 1044
Spring Mobilization Committee to End the War
    in Vietnam, 1028
Springarn Medal, Daisy Bates, 895
Springfield (IL) Race Riot (1908), collective
    action, xxiv, 689–692, 778
Springfield (OH) Race Riots
    (1904–1906), 778
Springfield armory, Shays' Rebellion,
    207, 212
Stamp Act (1765)
  British responses, 135
  colonial responses, 128, 129, 131–134
  fiscal solvency, 127
  passage of, 127–128, 129, 146
  repeal of, 131, 135, 139, 141, 145, 146
  and Sons of Liberty, 202
Stamp Act Congress
  attendees, 134, 144
  overview, 144–145
  Samuel Adams, 139
  and Stamp Act protests, 130, 131, 141, 146
Stamp Act Protests (1765)
  and collective action, xxii, 127–137
Stamp Act Resolution (1765), 147–148
Stamper, Norm
  and WTO protests, 1123
"Standing army"
  and Whiskey Rebellion, 227
Standing Rock Reservation
  and Sitting Bull, 615
  Wounded Knee Massacre, 602, 603, 604–605
Stanford, Leland
  and "robber barons," 571
Stanton, Edwin M.
  and New Orleans Riot (1866), 450
Stanton, Elizabeth Cade
  Introduction to The Woman's Bible,
    512–514
  and Nineteenth Amendment, 489–490
  and NWSA, 487–488, 490

Stanton, Elizabeth Cade (continued)
   on "Solitude of Self," 510–512
   and Susan B. Anthony, 484, 485–486
   and women's movement, 474, 477–478, 480, 483
Stanton, James, Haymarket Riot, 578–579
Starr, Paddy
   and Wounded Knee Massacre, 607
State governments, martial law, 243
State of Deseret (proposed Mormon state), 394–395
"Statement of the Fort Hood Three," 951–957
States' rights
   and American Civil War, 441
Stauffer, John, 423
St. Augustine (FL), and Stono Rebellion, 69
St. Augustine's Roman Catholic Church, Philadelphia Nativist Riots, 326
Stearns, George Luther
   and Secret Six, 417, 429, 430
Steel Workers Organizing Committee, 629
Stein, Dan, 1130
Steinem, Gloria, 1056–1058
Stephens, Uriah
   and Knights of Labor, 598
Stevedores
   and West Coast Longshoremen's Strike, 857
Steward, Ira
   and the eight-hour day, 587–588
Stewart, Charles
   and Bleeding Kansas, 351
Stith, Gerald
   and vigilance committees, 382
St. Louis (MO)
   and Great Railroad Strikes, 565
   WPUS, 573
St. Louis *Times*, WPUS, 573
St. Martin of Tours church
   and Bloody Monday, 377
St. Mary Magdalen Church
   and Homestead Strike, 622
St. Michael's Roman Catholic Church
   and Philadelphia Nativist Riots, 326
Stockton, Robert F.
   and J. C. Frémont, 342

Stokely Speaks
   Black Power to Pan-Africanism (Carmichael), 904
Stoll, Joost, Leisler's Rebellion, 54
Stone, Lucy
   and AWSA, 483, 484, 488, 490
   and Nineteenth Amendment, 490
   and women's movement, 475, 476, 477, 478, 479
Stone Mountain Coal Corporation
   and Matewan Massacre, 799
   and Sid Hatfield, 798
Stono Rebellion (1739), xxiii, 69–72, 73, 76
   impact of, 79
Stony Point
   and Shays' commendation, 211, 220
Stop ERA, 1049
Storrow, James Jackson
   and Boston Police Strike, 758
Stotesbury, Edward T.
   and Douglas MacArthur, 840–841
Stowe, Harriet Beecher, 279
Stowell, David O., 564, 571
St. Patrick's Church, Maine, 369
St. Paul Chamber of Commerce, and ARU, 651
St. Regis Mohawk Reservation, Richard Oakes, 1032, 1036, 1038
Stricker, John, and antiwar activism, 926
Strikebreakers
   Homestead Strike, 621, 622, 625
   Pinkertons, 633
   and Toledo Auto-Lite Strike, 849
"Strikers Resolutions and Editorials," Lattimer Mine, 668–669
Strong, Caleb
   and antiwar activism, 926
Stronghold
   and Wounded Knee Massacre, 603–604, 605
Stuart, Charles Edward (Bonnie Prince Charlie), 187
Stuart, J. E. B.
   and Harpers Ferry Raid, 419
   and Robert E. Lee, 428
Stuart, John, Lord Bute, 132, 160
Student Nonviolent Coordinating Committee (SNCC)
   antiwar activism, 931

and civil rights movement, 896
and Malcolm X, 908
and March on Washington, 909
overview, 912–913
and SCLC, 911
and Stokely Carmichael, 903, 913
Students for a Democratic Society
antiwar activism, 930–931, 937, 944
antiwar leaflet, 950–951
and Democratic National Convention (1968), 1010
and Tom Hayden, 1024
overview, 943–945
Paul Potter speech, 945–950
and SNCC, 912
Stump, Henry
and Know-Nothing Party, 374
Stuyvesant, Peter
and religious conflict, 61
Styron, William
and *The Confessions of Nat Turner*, 277, 281
Subterranean Pass Way," 423
Succession
and federalism, 238
Suffrage
Bacon's Rebellion 5
colonial Rhode Island, 311
House of Burgesses, 14, 15
Suffragists, Charterites, 315
Sugar Act (1733), fiscal solvency, 127
Sugar Mound
and Bleeding Kansas, 350
Sullivan, Tom
and Los Angeles Uprising, 1099
Sumner, Charles
attack by Brocks, 351, 360
and Dorothea Dix, 486–487
Sumner, Edwin V., Wounded Knee Massacre, 605
Sumner, William Graham, antiwar activism, 923
Supreme Court cases
A.L.A. Schechter Poultry Corp v. United States, 855
Bakke case, 899
Brooks v. Baxter, 546, 549

Bradwell v. Illinois, 499–500
Brown v. Board of Education, 678, 679, 807, 893
Cummings v. Richmond County Board of Education, 893
Guinn v. United States, 456
Hudson v. McMillan, 1063
Laney v. United States, 789–791
Luther v. Borden (1849), 314, 319–323
Minor v. Happersett, 478
Moore v. Dempsey, 771
Muller v. Oregon, 515–516
Native American treaty rights, 1038–1039
Plessy v. Ferguson, 677, 678–679, 891, 893
Roe v. Wade, 1055–1056
Shelly v. Kraemer, 807
United States v. Cruikshank, 538
Williams v. Mississippi, 675
Wolff v. McConnell, 1063
Supreme Judicial Council, Dorr's Rebellion, 312
"Surrender Speech of Chief Joseph of the Nez Percé," 561
Surveyor of the King's Woods, Pine Tree Riot, 184
Susan B. Anthony
amendment, 488–489, 490
letter to, 508–510
Susquehannock Indians
Bacon's Rebellion, 1–5, 10, 17, 18
geographic penetration, 17
Pennsylvania native tribe, 464
trade, 17–18
Sutter, John
Bear Flag Revolt, 333, 334
and Bear Flaggers, 339, 340
and J. C. Frémont, 342
Sutter's Fort
and Bear Flag Revolt, 333, 334, 335, 336, 337, 340
Swann, Thomas
Know-Nothing Party, 374
and Plug Uglies, 379, 380
and Rip Raps, 380, 381
Swift, Granville
and Bear Flag Revolt, 337
Bear Flagger, 340

Swisshelm, Jane
  and divorce law reform, 477
Synod of Dort, Calvinism, 57

"Tac Squad," 987, 993
Taft, Charles
  and Toledo Auto-Lite Strike, 849
Taft, William Howard
  and NAACP, 695
Taft-Hartley Act (1947)
  and AFL, 851
Take Back the Night Marches, 1050
Tallmadge, James
  and First Missouri Compromise, 356
Taney, Roger B., and *Luther v. Borden*
  (1849), 314
Taos Pueblo Indians, return of Blue Lake, 1034,
  1067, 1071
Tappan, Arthur, 279
Tariff collection
  and Texas Revolt, 290
Tariffs
  and American Civil War, 441
Tax collectors
  Tom the Tinker warnings, 244
  Whiskey Rebellion, 228–229, 230
Taxation
  Alexander Hamilton, 239, 240
  Bacon's Rebellion, 3, 5
  Boston Massacre, 151
  British-colonial conflict, 191–192
  House of Burgesses, 14
  Regulator Movement, 169, 170
  Samuel Adams' opposition, 139
  Shays' Rebellion, 207, 210, 211, 214,
    222–223, 237
  and salutary neglect, 142–143
  Stamp Act Congress, 144
  Stamp Act protests, 127–129, 131, 136
  and Texas Revolt, 289
  Townshend Act, 203
  Whiskey Rebellion, 227, 229,
    243–244
Taylor, Dwight (Fishman), Los Angeles
  Uprising, 1098
Taylor, Stewart
  and Harpers Ferry Raid, 419

Taylor, Zachary
  and Santa Anna, 310
Tea Act
  and the Boston Tea Party, 193,
    194, 195
Tea Party (2010), collective action, xxiv
Tea tax, consequences, 192–193
Teaching American History in South Carolina
  (website), 74
Teaching profession
  and women's movement, 476
Teamsters Union
  and West Coast Longshoremen's
    Strike, 858, 865
Teapot Dome Scandal
  and Warren Harding, 761
Tear gas
  Attica Prison Riot, 1060
  and BEF, 829
  and Blair Mountain Battle, 794
  Kent State, 939
  and Toledo Auto-Lite Strike, 849
Tejanos
  overview, 735–736
  and Plan de San Diego, 729–730
  and Texas Rangers, 737
Telemaque. *See* Vesey, Denmark
Temperance
  and Quakers, 270
  and religion, 371
  and women's movement, 475, 479, 484
"Ten Days War," 710
"Ten Percent Plan," 449, 454
Tennessee
  Battle of Athens, 883–885
  Black Patch War, 697–699, 702
  Ku Klux Klan, 805
  racial segregation, 677
  Regulator settlers, 178
  and Sam Houston, 307
Tenskwatawa, "Shawnee Prophet," 120
Terán, Manuel Mier
  and Stephen Austin, 306
  Texas Revolt, 289
Termination
  and Broken Treaties protest, 1068
  and Red Power, 1074

"Termination 'policy
  overview, 1038–1039
  Republican Party, 1031
Terrell, Joseph M.
  and Atlanta Race Riot (1906), 686
Testerman, C. C.
  and Sid Hatfield, 798, 800
Tet Offensive
  and Chicago Riot, 1009
  and Democratic National Convention (1968), 1022
Teton Sioux
  and Sitting Bull, 614
  tribes of, 613
Texas
  Franciscan missionaries, 37, 38
  Plan de San Diego, 727–732
  racial segregation, 677
  and Sam Houston, 307–308
  and Santa Anna, 309–310
  and Stephen Austin, 305–306
  Texas Revolution, 733
"Texas Fever," 739
Texas Gulf Coast
  and Diego Ortiz Parilla, 106
Texas National Guard
  and Houston Riot, 750
Texas Rangers
  overview, 735–737
  and Plan de San Diego, 729, 730
Texas Revolt (1835–1836)
  and collective action, xxiv, 289–301
Thirteen Amendment
  abolition of slavery, 280, 456
  abolitionist victory, 499
  and Susan B. Anthony, 484
38th Street Gang
  and Zoot Suit Riots, 872
Thirty Year's War, religious conflict, 60, 61
Thomas, George, Pennsylvania governor, 93
Thomas, Neval H., Anti-Lynching bill, 783–785
Thompson, Thomas, Texas Revolt, 292, 293
Thomspon, Robert, execution of, 177
Thoreau, Henry David
  and antiwar activism, 927
  on John Brown, 420
Thorton, Charles, Kerner Commission, 996

Tikas, Louis
  and Ludlow Massacre, 708, 709
Till, Emmet, murder of, 894
Tilton, Theodore
  and John Brown, 420
Tinner, Grover, 1106
To Be a Slave (Lester), 253
Tobacco
  Bacon's Rebellion, 1
  Black Patch War, 697–699
  Colonial Virginia, 19–20
  indentured servants, 15–16
Tobias, J. N.
  and Joseph Brooks, 550
Todd, William
  and Bear Flag Revolt, 334, 336, 340–341
Tohono O'odham ("People of the Desert"), 106–107
Toledo Auto-Lite Strike (1934)
  and collective action, xxii–xxiii, 847–850, 852–853
Tolpuddle Martyrs, 633
Tom the Tinker, 243–244
"Tombstone Bonus," 830, 842
Tompiro Pueblo, 43
Topeka (KS)
  Bleeding Kansas, 348
  Topeka Constitution, 361–363
Topeka Constitution
  Bleeding Kansas, 348, 350
  overview, 361–363
Torre, Joaquin de la, Bear Flag Revolt, 336, 337
Tourgee, Albion
  and *Plessy v. Ferguson*, 679
Townshend, Charles, 151, 203–204
Townshend Act (1767)
  and Boston Massacre, 151, 192, 193
  overview, 203–204
  Samuel Adams' opposition, 139
  and Sons of Liberty, 202–203, 204
Trade
  Bacon's Rebellion, 3, 10
  House of Burgesses, 14
  Susquehannock Indians, 17–18
Trade unions
  and Great Railroad Strikes, 564
  and Homestead Strike, 619–627

"Traditional rights of Englishmen," 146
Traffic in Women (Goldman), excerpts, 523–526
Trail of Broken Treaties protest (1972)
  and collective action, xxii, 1067–1070, 1074
Trans-Continental Railroad, Chinese immigrants, 593, 597
Transcendentalism
  and antislavery militancy, 417, 420
Transylvania University
  and Stephen Austin, 305
Traverse des Sioux Treaty (1851), 611
  and Indian treaties, 1073
Travis, Joseph, 272
Travis, William Barrett
  Battle of the Alamo, 304
  Texas Revolt, 290, 292, 296–297
Treaty of Fort Laramie
  and Pine Ridge Reservation, 1081
Treaty of Paris (1763), 119
"Tree of liberty," xxi, xxiv
Tremont (Texas Revolt), 292
Trench, W. Steuart, 459
Treviño, Juan Francisco, New Mexico, 30–31
Troy Female Seminary
  and Elizabeth Cady Stanton, 475
  and women's movement, 474
Trudell, John
  and Alcatraz Island occupation, 1033
  biography, 1039–1040
Truman, Harry S.
  and civil rights movement, 892
  and desegregation, 807
  and Douglas MacArthur, 841
Truth, Sojourner
  and Nineteenth Amendment, 490
  "Urges Fight for Equal Rights for All Women," 493–494
  and women's movement, 475
Tryon, William
  and Arthur Dobbs, 179
  Battle of Alamance, 177–178
  biography, 181–182
  Regulator Movement, 171–172
  Stamp Act protests, 132–133, 182

Tubman, Harriet, 283
Tubutama mission, Pima Revolt, 100
Tudor, John, "Destruction of Lt. Governor Hutchinson's House by the Stamp Act Rioters in Boston," 148–150
Tuke, William, 486
Tulsa Race Riot (1921)
  collective action, xxiv, 801–804
  "Final Report of the Grand Jury," 808
  interwar race riots, 771
  "Oklahoma Commission to Study Tulsa Race Riot of 1921," 809–828
Tulsa Race Riot Commission, 804
Tulsa Tribune, on Tulsa Race Riot, 802
Tupatú, Luis, 34–35
Tur, Bob and Marika, Los Angeles Uprising, 1097–1098
Ture, Kwame. *See* Carmichael, Stokely
Turkey
  and Eastern European immigrants, 665
Turner, Frederick Jackson
  and frontier thesis, 261
  and Nineteenth Amendment, 490
Turner, Henry M.
  and Robert Charles, 676
Turner, Nat
  antebellum slave revolts, 252, 254, 255, 256, 257
  biography, 269–272, 285–286
  and civil rights, 891
  "confession," 274, 276–277
  Confessions of Nat Turner, The, 276, 280–281
  "A Contemporary Account of Nat Turner's Revolt," 286–288
  rebellion (1831), xxiii, 270, 271–273
  retribution, 273–274
  significance, 274–277
Turtle's Heart, Pontiac's Rebellion, 112, 124
Tuscarora Indians, Pontiac's Rebellion, 111
Tuttle, Jotham, Pine Tree Riot, 185
"20 Point Position Paper"
  AIM, 1071–1072
  Broken Treaties protest, 1067–1068, 1069–1070
Two Sicilies (Naples), expulsion of Jesuits, 103–104
Two Treatises of Government (Locke), 139

Tyler, John
    and Dorr's Rebellion, 313, 317

Ugartecha, Texas Revolt, 290, 292
Ukrainians
    and Eastern European immigrants, 665
Una, and Women's Movement, 475, 477
Underground Railroad, 283
    and John Brown, 416, 423
Undocumented immigrants, 1133–1134
Union Army
    African American soldiers, 445
    and Copperheads, 444
Union Conscription Act (1863)
    and New York Draft Riots, 436
Union Mills
    and Homestead Strike, 626
Union of Soviet Socialist Republics, 665
Union Pacific Railroad
    and ARU, 651
    Chinese immigrants, 598
    Knights of Labor strike, 599
    and Red Cloud, 614
Unionism, 466–467
    and Molly Maguires, 466–467
Unitarians
    and Women's Movement, 475
United Auto Workers, formation, 849, 852
United for Peace and Justice, antiwar
    activism, 933
United Mine Workers Association (UMWA)
    and AFL, 851
    in Appalachia, 797
    and Blair Mountain Battle, 793, 794
    and Lattimer Massacre, 663–664
    and Ludlow Massacre, 707, 708–710, 713
    and Matewan Massacre, 799, 800
    modern leadership, 667
    overview, 716–717
    and Sid Hatfield, 798
United Order of Railway Employees
    and Eugene Debs, 652
United Sons of Vulcan, 629
United States
    annexation of Texas, 300, 733
    Bear Flag Revolt, 333–338
    and Native American treaties, 1072–1073

Plan de San Diego, 727–732
    and Santa Anna, 309, 310
    temperance movement, 371
    women's suffrage achieved, 481
    World War I, 743
United States v. Cruikshank, 538
United States v. Spock, excerpts from, 957–960
United Steelworkers, 629
Universal Negro Improvement Association,
    and Earl Little, 907
Universal white male suffrage
    Charterites, 316
    overview, 318–319
    Thomas Wilson Dorr, 317, 318
University of Alabama
    and civil rights movement, 897
University of California at Berkeley
    and Alcatraz Island occupation,
        1031–1032, 1037
University of Mississippi
    and civil rights movement, 896
University of Southern Mississippi
    and civil rights movement, 896
Up from Slavery (B. T. Washington), 683
"Uppity," 682, 685
Uptown KKK, 894
Urban ghettos
    and New York Draft Riots, 438–439
Urrea, José, Texas Revolt, 296, 298
Ury, John, New York Slave Insurrection, 81
U.S. Army Nurses
    and Dorothea Dix, 486, 487
U.S. Chamber of Commerce
    and BEF, 829–830
U.S. Coast Guard
    and Alcatraz Island occupation, 1032, 1033
U.S. Commission on Industrial Relations,
    Ludlow Massacre, 710
U.S. Conference of Catholic Bishops, "Day
    without an Immigrant" protests, 1131
U.S. Constitution
    Eighth Amendment, 1063
    federal supremacy, 237–238
    Fifteenth Amendment, 455, 456, 477–478,
        483, 488, 677
    Fourteenth Amendment, 454, 456, 477, 478,
        483, 488, 679

U.S. Constitution (continued)
  Herman Husband, 181
  James Bowdoin, 218
  Massachusetts General Court, 219
  nativism, 378
  Nineteenth Amendment, 473, 481, 489–491, 1053
  North Carolina's ratification, 174
  and Shays' Rebellion, 207
  Thirteen Amendment, 280, 456, 485
U.S. Forest Service (USFS), public lands, 1090, 1091
U.S. Mail, Pullman Strike, 646
U.S. Military Academy (West Point)
  and Douglas MacArthur, 840
  and New York Draft Riots, 439
  and Robert E. Lee, 427, 428
U.S. Portsmouth, Bear Flag Revolt, 334, 337
U.S. Steel Corporation, 631
U.S. Strike Commission
  and Pullman Palace Car Company, 656, 657
  and Pullman Strike, 646
  Report on the Railway Strikes of 1894, 657–659
USS Cyane, Bear Flag Revolt, 334
Utah
  creation of, 394
  Mormon settlement, 390–391
  women's suffrage, 479
Utah War, collective action, xxiv, 383–387
Ute Indians, New Mexico, 34
Utopian socialists, 746

Vaarck, John, 80
Vallandingham, Clement L.
  and antiwar activism, 927
  and Copperheads, 443–444
Vallejo, Mariano
  Bear Flag Revolt, 334, 335, 336, 337
  and J. C. Frémont, 342
  and Sonoma, 343–344
Valley of Fear (A.C. Doyle), 459–460
Van Cortlandt, Stephanus
  and Leisler's Rebellion, 54, 55
Van deer Veen, Elsie Tymens, 60
Van den Bosch, Laurentius, 62
Van Horne, David, 85

Van Vliet, Stewart
  and Utah War, 384
Van Zant, Winant, 85
Vance, Cyrus
  and Detroit Riots, 989, 990
  "Report on the Riots in Detroit," 997–1008
Vandalia Railroad
  and Eugene Debs, 652
Vanderbilt, Cornelius, as "robber baron," 571
Vanzetti, Bartolomeo, 586, 587
Vargas, Don Diego de, New Mexico, 35, 43, 47
Versailles Treaty, 757
Vesey, Denmark
  and antebellum slave revolts, 252, 255, 256, 257
  "Description," 266–267
  uprising (1822), xxiii, 265–266
Vesey, Joseph, 265
Veterans
  Battle of Athens, 883–885
  and BEF, 829–834
Veterans' rights, 841–843
Vice-admiralty courts
  colonial, 130, 131
  Pine Tree Riot, 184
  Townshend Act, 203
Victoria (queen of England)
  and Dorothea Dix, 486–487
Vietnam Moratorium Committee, 941
Vietnam protests
  and Stokely Carmichael, 903
Vietnam Summer experiment, 941
Vietnam Veterans Against the War (VVAW)
  and antiwar activism, 931
Vietnam War
  and Abbie Hoffman, 1026
  antiwar activism, 925, 930–932
  and Martin Luther King Jr., 906
  and Tom Hayden, 1024
Vigilance Committees
  and Know-Nothing Party, 381–382
Vigilantism
  and Battle of Athens, 885
  Black Patch War, 698–699, 703
  and Plan de San Diego, 729
  and segregation, 807

West Coast Longshoremen's Strike, 858–859, 864
Villa, Pancho, 731
Vindication of the British Colonies in 1765, A (Otis), Stamp Act protests, 130
Violence
   abolitionists, 425–426
   and Atlanta Race Riot (1906), 683, 686–687
   "Bleeding Kansas," 347–351, 359, 362
   Black Patch War, 698–699
   civil rights movement, 968
   coal mines, 460
   Great Railroad Strikes, 566, 567, 569
   Harpers Ferry Raid, 415, 416
   industrial, 714–716
   Molly Maguires, 461–462
   "New South," 541
   and Plan de San Diego, 730
   Red Summer Riots, 765, 767–770
   Seattle Riot, 594
   slave rebellions, 252, 253
   slave system, 251, 253, 256, 257
Virginia
   Boxley attempted uprising, 254, 255, 261–262
   and civil rights movement, 894
   Dinwiddie, 118
   and formation of Confederacy, 426
   Nat Turner's Rebellion (1831), 269–278, 280
   and Robert E. Lee, 427
   and Shays' Rebellion, 214
   slave population, 264
   Whiskey Rebellion, 230
Virginia Colony
   Bacon's Rebellion, 1–7
   Berkeley governorship, 11–13
   and Susquehannock Indians, 17
Virginia Company
   and revocation of charter, 23
Virginia General Assembly, response to Nat Turner's Rebellion, 274–275
"Virtual representation," doctrine of, 129, 135, 141, 143, 144, 146
"Visible saints," 57
"Voice of Alcatraz," 1039
Voice of Missions, 676

Vollmer, August, 1104
Volstead Act, Prohibition, 371
Voorhies, Albert
   and New Orleans Riot (1866), 450
Voter Education Project
   and SNCC, 912
Voter registration
   and civil rights movement, 896
Voting rights
   Confederate States of America (Confederacy), 456
   and New Orleans Riot (1866), 449, 450, 451
Voting Rights Act (1964), renewal of, 899
Voting Rights Act (1965)
   and March on Washington, 909–910
   and Martin Luther King Jr., 906
   and SCLC, 911
   and SNCC, 912

Waddell, Hugh, Battle of Alamance, 177
   and Regulator Movement, 172
"Wage slaves," 251
Wages
   and black migration, 766
   cuts in industrial, 715
   Homestead Strike, 621, 634
   Pullman Palace Car Company, 656–657
Waggonner, Joe D., Jr.
   and civil rights movement, 894
Wagner, Robert
   and antilynching campaigns, 776
Wagner Labor Relations Act
   and labor unions, 715
"Wakarusa War," 349
Walker, Alice
   and black feminism, 1044–1045
Walker, Daniel
   and *Rights in Conflict*, 1014–1015, 1016–1017, 1021–1022
Walker, Edwin, on Pullman Strike, 648, 649
Walker, Quok, 425
Walker, Wyatt T., and SCLC, 911
Walker Commission, on "police riot," 1009, 1014–1015, 1016–1017, 1021–1022, 1026
"Walker War," 392
Wall Street, established, 84

Wallace, George
    and civil rights movement, 897
    1968 election, 1009, 1013, 1023
Wallace's Tavern, 70, 77
Wallowa Valley
    and Nez Percé flight, 553, 554, 558, 559
Walpole, Sir Robert
    financial class, 239
    and royal authority, 187
    and salutary neglect, 142
War bonds, American Revolution, 228–229
    debt repayment, 238
War of Austrian Succession, 79, 91
    Jeffrey Amherst as aide-de-camp, 117
War of 1812
    antiwar activism, 925–926, 933
    and electorate, 318
    German Catholic immigrants, 330
    martial law, 242
    and Sam Houston, 307
War of Jenkins' Ear, 79, 91
    and Pine Tree Riot, 183
War of Religions (France), 61
War Party, Texas Revolt, 295
War Powers Act (1973), antiwar activism, 933
War Resister's League, antiwar activism, 930–931
Ward, William, Haymarket Riot, 578
Ward, William, Colfax Massacre, 537, 538
Ward, William, Texas Revolt, 298
Warmoth, Henry Clay, Colfax Massacre, 537
Warren Court
    and civil rights movement, 893
Warren, Mercy Otis, 195
Warren, William, Boston Massacre, 153
Washington, Booker T.
    accommodation policies, 683
    antiwar activism, 928
    and civil rights movement, 891
    impact of Atlanta Race Riot (1906), 685
    and Jim Crow Laws, 677–678
Washington, D.C.
    "Day without an Immigrant" protests, 1129, 1130
    Describing Events during Race Riot (1919), 789–791
    Know-Nothing Riots, 375, 379
    "President Herbert Hoover's Letter to the District Commissioner and from his Press Conference," 844–846
    Red Summer Riots, 768
Washington, George
    and Alexander Hamilton, 239
    on democratic-republican societies, 234
    First Continental Congress, 200
    French and Indian War, 118
    House of Burgesses, 15
    and John Adams, 157–158
    Jumonville Affair, 142
    and "Mad Anthony" Wayne, 232
    Proclamation against the Whiskey Rebellion (1794), 245–248
    "Second Proclamation against the Whiskey Rebellion" (1794), 248–249
    on Shays' Rebellion, 215
    Whiskey Rebellion, 228, 230–231, 232
Washington, John
    and Bacon's Rebellion, 2, 5
Washington, Lewis
    and Harpers Ferry Raid, 418
Washington and Lee University
    and Robert E. Lee, 428
Washington National Guard, WTO protests, 1123
Washington Post, on Anacostia Flats Battle, 835–836
Washington State Convention and Trade Center, WTO protests, 1121, 1122–1123
Washington Territory, Chinese immigrants, 593
Washington-on-the-Brazos
    and Texas Revolt, 295–296, 297
Wasicun, and Wounded Knee Massacre, 601, 602, 604, 608
Wasumaza, and Wounded Knee Massacre, 607
Waterfront Employers Union (WEU),
    and West Coast Longshoremen's Strike, 865
Waterfront Worker, The, 857
Waterman, Charles M., and vigilance committees, 382
"Watermelon Army," 234
Waters, Walter W.
    and BEF, 830–831
    biography, 843–844
Watkins, Arthur V., and termination policy, 1038

Watson, Henry Keith, 1101, 1105
Watson, Thomas E., and Atlanta Race Riot (1906), 681
Watt, James
  and Ronald Reagan, 1093, 1094
  Sagebrush Rebellion, 1086, 1087
Watts, Robert, 85, 89
Watts Labor Community Action Center, Los Angeles Uprising, 1098
Watts Riots (1965)
  collective action, xxiii–xxiv, 965–971
  Governor's Commission Report on the Riots, 976–985
Watts Riot (1992), 970
Wayne, "Mad Anthony," and Washington, 232
"We Shall Overcome," 900
Weare, Judge Meshech, Pine Tree Riot, 185
Weather Underground, 1017
  counterculture, 937–938
"Wedding Protest," 476
Weihe, William, and Homestead Strike, 624
Weiner, Lee, and Chicago Eight, 1015
Weinglass, Leonard, and Chicago Seven trial, 1015, 1019
Welborn, J. F., and Ludlow Massacre, 709
Wells, Benjamin, Whiskey Rebellion, 232
Wells, James, and Plan de San Diego, 730
Wells, James M.
  and New Orleans Riot (1866), 450
Wells, Philip, "Eyewitness Account of the Massacre at Wounded Knee," 616–617
Wells-Barnett, Ida B.
  anti-lynching campaigns, 776
  black civil rights, 771
  and Jim Crow Laws, 677–678
  and Nineteenth Amendment, 490
Welsh miners, and Molly Maguires, 460
Wemms, William, Boston Massacre, 153
Wentworth, Benning, 183, 187
Wentworth, John, and Pine Tree Riot, 183, 187
Wesley, John, 370
West Africa, slaves from, 69, 75
West Coast Longshoremen's Strike (1934), xxii–xxiii, 347, 857–859, 861–865
  and Bloody Thursday, 861
West Point. See U.S. Military Academy (West Point)

West Virginia
  and Blair Mountain Battle, 793, 794
  and Great Railroad Strikes, 563, 564, 569
  and Sid Hatfield, 798
  and UMWA, 797
West Virginia Mine Wars, and UMWA, 717
Western Federation of Miners, and industrial violence, 715
Western Reserve Antislavery Society, John Brown, 423
Western Union, Knights of Labor strike, 599
Whally, Frank, and Green Corn Rebellion, 740
"Wharf rats," 857, 861
Wharton, William H., Texas Revolt, 294
Whatley, Thomas, and Thomas Hutchinson, 193–194
Whig Party
  death of, 426
  and Nativists, 327
  and Republican Party, 551
Whigs, Rhode Island suffrage, 311
"Whipping Post Club," 139
Whiskey Rebellion (1794)
  and Alexander Hamilton, 240
  collective action, xxii, 227–235, 238, 243–244
  and Herman Husband, 181
  "President George Washington's Proclamation Against the Whiskey Rebellion" (1794), 245–248
  "President George Washington's Second Proclamation Against the Whiskey Rebellion" (1794), 248–249
  and Regulator Movement, 174
White Bird Canyon, Nez Percé's flight, 554
White Citizens Councils (WCC), and civil rights movement, 893–894
White Clay Valley, Wounded Knee Massacre, 608
"White Indians," 172
White, Byron, 1056
White, Private Hugh, Boston Massacre, 152, 153
White, Walter, and Elaine Massacre, 770
White Lance, Wounded Knee Massacre, 605
White supremacy, 686–687
Whiteblade, Margaret, 272–273
Whiteboys, 459

Whitefield, George, and Herman Husband, 179–180
Whiting, Benjamin, Pine Tree Riot, 184–185
Whiting, William, and Shays' Rebellion, 211
Whitney, C., and Haymarket Riot, 578
Whitside, Samuel, Wounded Knee Massacre, 605, 606
Whittier, John Greenleaf, 279
Whytock, John, and Brooks-Baxter War, 546
Wickes, Thomas, and Pullman Strike, 644–645
"Wildcat" strikes, and Great Railroad Strikes, 564, 570
Wilder, L. Douglas, 900
Wilderness Act (1964), and public lands, 1091
Wilderness Society, and Sagebrush Rebellion, 1086
Wilkins, Elbert, and Los Angeles Uprising, 1098
Wilkins, Roy
  Kerner Commission, 996
  and March on Washington, 909
  and Martin Luther King Jr., 905
Wilkinson, James, and martial law, 241–242
Wilkinson, James, Pottawatomie Massacre, 360
Willard, Emma, and Women's Movement, 474
Willard, Francis, and Women's Movement, 479
William III (king of England), and Leisler's Rebellion, 53–54, 55, 60
William and Mary, and Leisler's Rebellion, 53–54
William of Normandy, and shipbuilding, 188
William of Orange, and invasion of England, 53
William Styron's Nat Turner Ten Black Writers Respond, 277
Williams, Damien Monroe, 1101, 1105–1106
Williams, George Henry
  debate on women's suffrage, 491–492
  and Brooks-Baxter War, 547
Williams, William, 272
Williams v. Mississippi, disenfranchisement, 675
Willys-Overland Motor Company, auto industry, 848
Wilmington (NC), Great Migration, 773
Wilmore, Gayraud, 265

Wilson, Dick (Richard)
  and BIA, 1079
  biography, 1082–1083
  and Pine Ridge Reservation, 1082
  Wounded Knee Massacre, 602
  Wounded Knee Occupation, 1075, 1076
Wilson, Jack. *See* Wovoka
Wilson, Wayne, and Watts Riot, 965
Wilson, Woodrow
  and antiwar activism, 929, 930
  and Boston Police Strike, 757, 758
  and Green Corn Rebellion, 740
  and Houston Riot, 751
  and Jim Crow Laws, 677
  and Ludlow Massacre, 710
  military segregation, 753
  preparedness campaign, 766
  and Samuel Gompers, 763
  and veterans' rights, 841–842
  and women's suffrage, 481, 490, 491
Wind, Timothy, Los Angeles Uprising, 1096, 1097
"Winning Plan," 490
"Winter intermission," 385
Winters, Jonathan, and Alcatraz Island occupation, 1033
Winthrop, Fitz-John, Leisler's Rebellion, 54
WITCH, and feminist movement, 1047
Witchcraft trails, presumption of guilt, 127
"Wobblies," 744, 745
Wolfe, James, French and Indian War, 118
Wolfe, Tom, 1057
Wolff v. McConnell, Attica Prison Riot, 1063
Woman in the Nineteenth Century (Fuller), 476
Woman's Bible, Elizabeth Cady Stanton's *Introduction*, 512–514
Woman's Journal, AWSA, 483
Woman's Share in Social Culture (A. G. Spencer), 529–533
Woman's Tribune, NWSA, 489
"Womanism," 1044–1045
Women
  collective action, xxiii, 473–482
  disenfranchisement of, 318
  History of Women in Industry in United States, 516–522

Shays' Rebellion, 213
and the temperance movement, 371
Women's Action Alliance, and Gloria
    Steinem, 1057
Women's Bureau, 1048–1049
Women's Christian Temperance Union
    (WCTU)
  established, 371
  and Susan B. Anthony, 486
  and women's movement, 479
Women's Division of the United Methodist
    Church,
  and feminist movement, 1047–1048
Women's Equity Action League (WEAL),
  and feminist movement, 1046
Women's International League for Peace and
    Freedom, antiwar activism, 930–931
Women's Loyal National League,
  and women's movement, 477
Women's movement (1870),
  and collective action, xxiii, 473–482
Women's New York State Temperance Society,
    and Susan B. Anthony, 484
Women's Political Union, and women's
    movement, 480, 490
Women's Social and Political Union, 481
Women's Strike for Peace, antiwar
    activism, 931
Women's suffrage
  antebellum women's movement, 473,
    475–476
  congressional debate, 491–493
  post–Civil War, 477–479, 485–486, 487–489
Wompanoag gang
  Know-Nothing Party, 374
  and Plug Uglies, 379
  and Rip Raps, 380
Wood, Fernando, and antiwar activism, 927
Wood, Leonard, and Douglas MacArthur, 840
Woodhull, Victoria C.
  Address to Judiciary Committee of House of
    Representatives, 494–496
  and women's movement, 478
Woods, George, and Battle of Athens, 884
Woods, William A.
  and Eugene Debs, 652
  on Pullman Strike, 648

Woodstock Festival, and counterculture, 937
Woodward, James G., and Atlanta Race Riot
    (1906), 683
Working Class Union (WCU), and Green Corn
    Rebellion, 739, 740
Workingmen's Benevolent Association (WBA)
  and Molly Maguires, 460
  and unionism, 466
Workingmen's Party of the United States
    (WPUS)
  and Great Railroad Strikes, 564–565, 567
  overview, 572–573
World Anti-Slavery Convention, and Women's
    Movement, 474
World Economic Forum, Direct Action
    Network, 1125–1126
World Trade Center, attack on, 932
World Trade Organization (WTO)
  and Direct Action Network, 1121–1122,
    1125–1126
  protests (1999), xxii, 1121–1124
World War I
  and American socialism, 746–747
  antiwar activism, 925, 929–930
  and BEF, 829
  Conscription Act, 743
  and Eastern European immigrants, 665
  and Eugene Debs, 653
  and Great Migration, 773
  and labor movement, 763
World War II
  and women's rights, 1043
Worthley, Jonathan
  and Pine Tree Riot, 185
Worthley, Timothy
  and Pine Tree Riot, 185
Worton, William, 1104
Wounded Knee Massacre (1890)
  collective action, xxi–xxii, 601–609,
    614, 1070
  "Philip Wells's Eyewitness Account," 616–617
Wounded Knee occupation (1973)
  and BIA, 1079–1080
  collective action, xxii, 609, 1075–1077
  and the FBI, 1080–1081
Wovoka
  and Wounded Knee Massacre, 601, 602

Wright, William
   and Colfax Massacre, 539
Writ of Assistance, defined, 130
Wrovsch, Frank
   and Haymarket Riot, 579
Wyandot Indians
   and Pontiac's Rebellion, 109, 113, 120
Wyandotte Constitution, Kansas, 363
Wyat, William
   and Boston Massacre trial, 154–155
Wyoming
   Chinese immigrants, 598
   J. C. Frémont's expedition, 341
   women's suffrage, 473, 479

Yakama nation
   and return of Mount Adams, 1034
Yapuis Indians, Pima Revolt, 100
Yellow Bird, Wounded Knee massacre, 606–607
"Yellow-dog contracts"
   examples of, 640–641
   overview, 633–634
   Pits Bessemer Steel Works, 619
Yellowstone National Park, 1089
"Yippies," 937
   and Abbie Hoffman, 1026
   and Democratic National Convention (1968), 1010, 1011, 1014, 1019
Yonley, T. D. W.
   and Brooks-Baxter War, 546
York, Alvin, 743

Yost, Benjamin
   and Molly Maguires, 460, 461
Young andrew J.
   and SCLC, 911
Young, Brigham
   biography, 395–396
   Great Salt Lake, 341–342
   and James Buchanan, 389
   Mormon settlement in Utah, 390–391
   Nauvoo Legion, 391
   on polygamy, 393
   State of Deseret, 394
   Utah War, 383, 384, 385–386
Young, Coleman, election of, 991
Young, Whitney
   and March on Washington, 909
   and Martin Luther King Jr., 905
Younger, Cole, "Bushwackers," 354
Youth International Party (Yippies)
   and Abbie Hoffman, 1026
   and Democratic Party Convention, 1010, 1011, 1014, 1019
Yuille, Lei, 1101

Zacatecas mine, 27, 39
Zenger, Peter, Stamp Act protests, 131
Zía Pueblo, 34
Zinn, Howard, on slave whippings, 253
Zoot suit, symbolic dress, 869, 878
Zoot Suit Riot (1942), xxiii, 869–875
   and police brutality, 878–880
   and servicemen, 880–881
Zuñi Trail (New Mexico), 29